DARK AND CRUEL WAR

DARK AND CRUEL WAR

The Decisive Months of the Civil War
September–December 1864

Don Lowry

HIPPOCRENE BOOKS
New York

For information, address:
HIPPOCRENE BOOKS, INC.
171 Madison Avenue
New York, NY 10016

Library of Congress Cataloging-in-Publication Data

Lowry, Don.
    Dark and cruel war : the decisive months of the Civil War,
September–December 1864 / Don Lowry.
        p.   cm.
    Includes bibliographical references (p.   ) and index.
    ISBN 0-7818-0168-0
    1. United States—History—Civil War, 1861–1865—Campaigns.
I. Title.
E470.L875   1993
973.7′37—dc20   93-23035
                                                                CIP

Printed in the United States of America.

"In the name of common sense, I ask you not to appeal to a just God in such a sacrilegious manner. You who, in the midst of peace and prosperity, have plunged a nation into war—dark and cruel war—who dared and badgered us to battle, insulted our flag, seized our arsenals and forts that were left in the honorable custody of peaceful ordnance-sergeants, seized and made 'prisoners of war' the very garrisons sent to protect your people against negroes and Indians, long before any overt act was committed by the (to you) hated Lincoln Government; tried to force Kentucky and Missouri into rebellion, spite of themselves; falsified the vote of Louisiana; turned loose your privateers to plunder unarmed ships; expelled Union families by the thousands, burned their houses, and declared, by an act of your Congress, the confiscation of all debts due Northern men for goods had and received! Talk thus to the marines, but not to me . . ."

—Major General William Tecumseh Sherman, USA
to General John Bell Hood, CSA

CONTENTS

PART TWO—RICHMOND AND PETERSBURG

PART THREE—COUNTER-OFFENSIVES

PART FOUR—GEORGIA AND TENNESSEE

MAPS

PROLOGUE

This book is the third volume in a series of four which, when completed, will tell the story of the final year of the American Civil War. The first book, *No Turning Back*, begins with the appointment of Ulysses S. Grant as general-in-chief of the Union armies and covers his coordinated campaign by all Federal forces up to the crossing of the Army of the Potomac to the south side of the James River. The second book, *Fate of the Country*, begins with the first attacks on Petersburg and carries the narrative through the fall of Atlanta.

There should be no reason, however, why this volume could not be read alone as a chronological narrative of a three-month period that saw a radical improvement in the fortunes of the Union cause. During the summer of 1864 Northern backing for the war to save the Union had reached its all-time low. When Grant had been put in overall command back in March hopes had been high, but since then one Federal force after another had either been defeated or had seemingly bogged down without gaining anything tangible, while the casualty lists had grown ever longer. It was an election year, and Confederate agents were conspiring with Northern Democrats to defeat Lincoln's bid for a second term on a promise of putting an end to the war, even if it meant recognizing Confederate independence. But when General William Tecumseh Sherman captured Atlanta in early September, Northern hopes began to revive.

The present volume begins at that point and carries the narrative through Sheridan's victories in the Shenandoah Valley, which gave further evidence that the Confederacy could be beaten: through several moves by Grant to extend his hold on the supply lines leading into Petersburg, Virginia, and the Confederate capital, Richmond; and on through Sherman's march to the sea and the Rebels' simultaneous attempt to reconquer Tennessee.

As in the previous two volumes, it has not been my objective to dig up new facts but rather to gain understanding by arranging them in chronological order across the entire spectrum of events related to the progress of the war. For this reason, notes are provided only to indicate the sources of quotations. All quotes in the text are presented with the same spelling and punctuation as found in the sources noted.

Again I would like to thank my wife, Julie, and my son, James, for their continued assistance, encouragement, faith, and forbearance through this third volume.

PART ONE

THE SHENANDOAH

"Go in!"

—Lieutenant General Ulysses S. Grant

to Major General Philip H. Sheridan

CHAPTER ONE

Amid Great Rejoicing

2–4 September 1864

"Atlanta is gone," Southern belle Mary Chesnut wrote in her diary on 2 September 1864. "Well that agony is over. Like David, when the child was dead, I will get up from my knees, will wash my face and comb my hair. There is no hope, but we will try to have no fear."[1]

On the third day of September 1864 Abraham Lincoln, 16th president of the United States, issued a proclamation of thanksgiving and prayer: "The signal success that Divine Providence has recently vouch-safed to the operations of the United States fleet and army in the harbor of Mobile and the reduction of Fort-Powell, Fort-Gaines, and Fort-Morgan, and the glorious achievements of the Army under Major General Sherman in the State of Georgia, resulting in the capture of the City of Atlanta, call for devout acknowledgment to the Supreme Being in whose hands are the destinies of nations. It is therefore requested that on next Sunday, in all places of public worship in the United States, thanksgiving be offered to Him for His mercy in preserving our national existence against the insurgent rebels who so long have been waging a cruel war against the Government of the United States, for its overthrow; and also that prayer be made for the Divine protection to our brave soldiers and their leaders in the field, who have so often and so gallantly perilled their lives in battling with the enemy; and for blessing and comfort from the Father of Mercies to the sick, wounded, and prisoners, and to the orphans and widows of those who have fallen in the service of their country, and that he will continue to uphold the Government of the United-States against all the efforts of public enemies and secret foes."[2]

The American Civil War was well into its fourth year, and the victories for which Lincoln desired the nation to give thanks had finally brought to an end a summer of discontent for the North. After a string of victories in the trans-Allegheny West, Ulysses S. Grant had been promoted to the three-star rank of lieutenant general—he was the first to hold it since George Washington—and put in command of the entire Federal war effort. He had made his headquarters with the Union's largest army, the Army of the Potomac, with the object of defeating the South's main force, commanded by Robert E. Lee, or at least tying it down so that it could not interfere with other Union operations. In early May the Army of the Potomac had crossed the Rapidan River and entered the Wilderness of Virginia, an area of dense thickets and limited visibility, where it had collided violently with Lee's Army of Northern Virginia. Meanwhile another Federal force, the Army of the James, had steamed up its namesake river and landed on a peninsula between Richmond, the Confederate capital, and Petersburg, a key hub of the railroad supply lines running into Richmond from the south. But after a few feeble probes toward both cities this force had been driven back to its peninsula, known as Bermuda Hundred, by Southern reinforcements hurried up from the Carolinas.

Throughout the spring Grant and Lee had repeatedly collided in a series of bloody battles as the Northern commander sidled his way from the Rapidan to the James River. Then on the 15th of June Grant had slipped away from Lee and crossed to the south side of the James for an attack on Petersburg. The outer defenses had been captured, but new inner defenses held, and the armies of the Potomac and the James had settled into a siege of Petersburg.

A small Union force had advanced up the Shenandoah Valley that spring only to be defeated at New Market. But while the victorious Confederates went off to reinforce Lee's main army, the Northern force, under a new commander, advanced up the Valley again, picking up reinforcements coming over from West Virginia. This time the Federals got as far as Lynchburg. But Lee detached first the victors of New Market and then the entire 2nd Corps of his army to save that vital supply center. The Union army, under Major General David Hunter, had not had enough supplies left to engage in battle with a force of that size and had retreated over the mountains into West Virginia. The commander of the Confederate forces, Lieutenant General Jubal A. Early, had then advanced down the Shenandoah Valley and reached the outskirts of Washington, but Northern reinforcements sent up from Petersburg had arrived in time to save the capital. After that a stalemate had ensued in this theater of operations also, with various poorly coordinated Federal forces unable to drive Early farther than the northern end of the Valley, where he was a constant threat to Maryland, Pennsylvania and Washington. Grant had finally sent his most promising young general, Philip H. Sheridan, to take command of all the Union forces in that area.

While all of this had been going on, Major General William T. Sherman, commander of all Union forces between the Appalachians and the Mississippi, had led a force consisting of three armies of varying sizes from Chattanooga, Tennessee, into Georgia. He had maneuvered the South's only other large force, the Army of Tennessee, all the way to the outskirts of the important rail and munitions center of Atlanta. Confederate president Jefferson Davis had then fired that army's commander, Joseph E. Johnston, and replaced him with the younger, less skilled, but more pugnacious General John B. Hood, who had attacked Sherman three times without accomplishing anything other than increasing the casualty lists. Then this campaign had also bogged down into siege operations.

Northern confidence in the war effort hit its all-time low that summer as everything seemed to grind to a halt. It was an election year, and the prospects of Lincoln's reelection had dropped along with public support for the war. Various secret pro-Southern societies in the Northern states, known collectively as Copperheads, increased in strength and plotted various acts of violence and rebellion of their own. The Democrats had wound up their national convention by naming Major General George B. McClellan their candidate for president. McClellan, who had once been general-in-chief and the first commander of the Army of the Potomac, had been chosen partly in hope of appealing to the soldiers and the pro-war Democrats. But the party's platform contained a plank that declared that the war was a failure and that peace with the South should be negotiated immediately.

However, in early August the tide had begun to turn when Admiral David G. Farragut had blasted his way into Mobile Bay, closing the South's last major port on the Gulf of Mexico. Then Sherman had worked his way around Atlanta, cutting all of its railroad supply lines and forcing Hood to evacuate the city. It was this pair of victories that had led Lincoln to call for national prayers of thanksgiving.

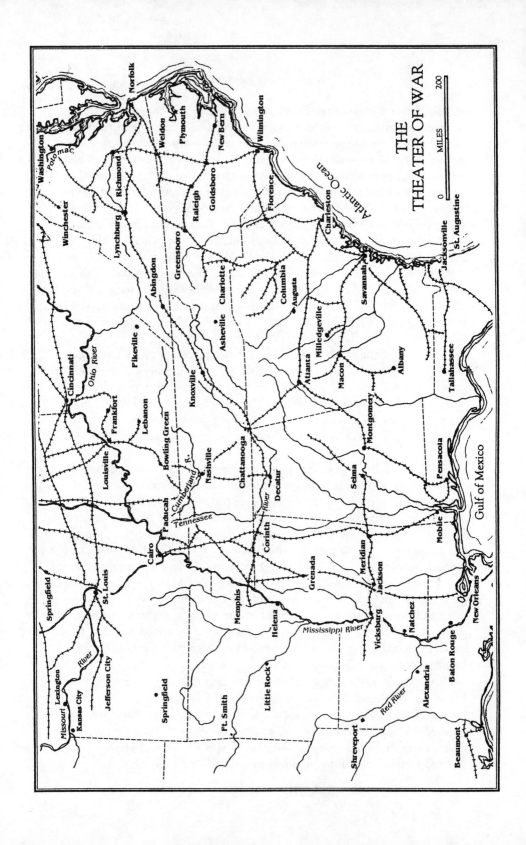

THE
THEATER OF WAR

MILES
0   200

In the Shenandoah Valley, Lieutenant General Jubal Early's Confederate Army of the Valley was camped in the general neighborhood of
Winchester, while Major General Philip Sheridan's Union Army of the
Shenandoah had just advanced from Harper's Ferry and Halltown to
take up positions about 10 miles east of Winchester at Clifton and
Berryville. Between these armies lay Opequon Creek, which followed
the general course of the valley from southwest to northeast to empty
into the Potomac River. "The whole country is very open," Early wrote,
"being a limestone country which is thickly settled and well cleared, and
affords great facilities for the movement of troops and the operations
of cavalry."[3]

"In studying this campaign of the lower Valley," an early historian of
it wrote, "nothing is more noticeable than the singularly different purposes on which the minds of the two opposing leaders were bent. Early's
attention was much absorbed in breaking and keeping broken the Union
line of railroad, not only as a material damage to the Northern cause,
but on account of the moral effect of this step as an evidence of Confederate strength in laying hold and keeping control of the chief military line
between Washington and the West. For this reason the daily skirmishes
and reconnaissances on the Halltown front, even when favorable to his
troops . . . evidently seemed to him of minor consequence, and caused
him little elation; whereas the occupation of Martinsburg, on the railroad, even by a handful of Union cavalry, was always enough to affect
the movements of his whole army, if necessary, to dislodge it. Sheridan,
on the contrary, was wholly intent on the problem of how to make sure
of a victory over the enemy in his immediate front, and hence paid
comparatively little attention to what was going on along the railroad.
The probable issue of this diversity of aims was that sooner or later
Sheridan, by persistency and vigilance, would, unobserved, or at least
unmolested, move into a position dangerous to Early, while the Confederate general, too regardless of his immediate opponent's projects, in his
warfare against the North as a whole, would sacrifice his own safety."[4]

The month before, Lee had detached another force from his army
about Richmond and Petersburg. It consisted of Joseph B. Kershaw's
division of infantry plus a battalion of artillery from his 1st Corps as
well a division of cavalry commanded by his nephew, Fitzhugh Lee.
This combined arms team was led by the commander of the 1st Corps,
Lieutenant General Richard H. Anderson, and had at first been sent to
the area around Culpeper Court House to threaten Washington while
most of the Federals from the area were off in the Shenandoah Valley.
But a move by Sheridan up the Valley had led to Anderson being sent
to reinforce Early. This had led Grant, fearing that the odds were unfa-

vorable, to order Sheridan to stay on the defensive until his pressure on Lee would force the latter to recall some of the forces in the Shenandoah to the main army at Petersburg and Richmond.

That day had come, for Lee had ordered Anderson to return, and on 3 September he started marching east toward Berryville, unaware that Sheridan was also advancing toward the same town. About an hour before sunset Anderson stumbled upon the smallest of Sheridan's three infantry corps, the 8th, commanded by Sheridan's old friend, Major General George Crook. Crook's two small divisions, more properly known as the Army of West Virginia, were composed of the troops who had fought at New Market and who had retreated from before Lynchburg. An indecisive battle followed, which darkness soon ended.

Far up the valley to the southwest, famous Confederate cavalry general John Hunt Morgan reached Greeneville, Tennessee, on 3 September. Officially he had been suspended from command of the Department of Southwest Virginia and East Tennessee pending a court of inquiry into his conduct of an unauthorized raid into Kentucky that he had made back in June. Among other things, it was charged that Morgan had authorized the robbing of a bank at Mount Sterling, Kentucky. Whether he had authorized it or not, the bank certainly had been robbed by some of his men, who also indulged in many other acts of plundering in a state that the Richmond government considered part of the Confederacy. "The conduct of our command was such as to cause a man to blush at the name of Confederate soldiers," one of Morgan's officers wrote.[5] But Morgan's successor had not yet arrived at his headquarters in Abingdon, Virginia, when word reached Morgan that a Federal force was approaching Bull Gap, Tennessee, from Union-held territory farther south. He had quickly resumed command and led his mobile force of about 2,000 men to Greeneville, where he deployed them to cover the roads leading from Bull's Gap.

Greeneville was a town of mixed loyalties, but Morgan and his staff were welcome at the finest house in town, the home of Mrs. Catherine Williams, where he had stayed before. Mrs. Williams had two sons in the Confederate army and another in the Union army. The wife of the latter, Lucy Williams, was living there with her mother-in-law. It was a hot, humid night, with a thunderstorm brewing, and, while the Confederate officers sat in the parlor chatting and sipping wine with the elder Mrs. Williams, Lucy offered to take a buggy to a nearby farm and bring back some watermelons for their guests. She left, but she did not return.

The storm came, and Morgan and his staff officers retired to their upstairs rooms, but the general was restless. He kept pacing the floor and peering out the window to make sure his pickets were still around the house in spite of the rain. The storm finally ended, and at dawn Morgan sent an officer to his men's nearby bivouac to alert them for an early match. Suddenly rifle fire was heard, first from one direction, then another. Hastily the general pulled on trousers and boots over his night-shirt and rushed to a window. Through a mist he could see that the streets below were filled with the blue uniforms of Union soldiers. Some of his officers suggested that they should surrender. "It's no use for me," replied Morgan, who had escaped from a Federal prison less than a year before. "They've sworn never to take me prisoner again."[6]

Morgan told one of his officers to cover him with his revolver while he dashed to the stable to get their horses. As Federal soldiers began pounding on the front door he slipped out the back and raced across the yard. However, he found that he was cut off from the stable and turned back, taking temporary shelter in an arbor that screened the house. His white nightshirt betrayed him, however, and he was spotted. "That' him!" a woman called out to the Union soldiers from across the street. "That's Morgan, over there among the grape vines!"

"Don't shoot; I surrender," Morgan yelled.

"Surrender and be God damned—I know you," one Federal answered and fired his carbine, followed immediately by several others.

"My God," Morgan groaned and fell into some bushes.

"I've killed the damned horse thief," the Union soldier said.[7]

Morgan's men heard the shooting and charged the town but were bloodily repulsed by the Union cavalrymen, who were commanded by Brigadier General Alvan C. Gillem. The Confederates retreated 14 miles before sending back a patrol to find out what had happened to their commander. Meanwhile, Morgan's body was stripped to its drawers, thrown across a horse and paraded through the town, then thrown into a muddy ditch beside the road. Later two of his captured staff officers were allowed to take the body back to Mrs. Williams' house, clean it and dress it, and lay it out in her parlor. There it was left for his men to find when the patrol returned later that day.

His men were greatly affected by their commander's death. "Any one of us—all of us—would gladly have died in his defense," a lieutenant wrote, "and each one would have envied the man who lost his life defending him. So much was he trusted that his men never dreamed of failing him in anything he attempted. In all engagements he was our guiding star and hero."[8]

Up in the Shenandoah, the encounter between Anderson and Crook the night before had alerted Early to Sheridan's advance to Berryville, and at dawn on the fourth he moved with three divisions to Anderson's support, leaving his fourth division to hold Winchester. Fearing for the safety of Anderson's supply wagons, Early placed one division to support Kershaw's left and took the other two farther north in an attempt to divert Sheridan's attention by threatening his right. This move brought Early to high ground, and for the first time he got a full view of the new Union position, which he could see was already being strengthened by troops digging entrenchments. It was decided that Anderson would have to return to Winchester and take a more southerly route to rejoin Lee. That night Early withdrew his entire force to the west side of the Opequon.

Down in Georgia on that fourth day of September, the Confederate commander who had evacuated Atlanta, General John Bell Hood, reported by telegraph to General Braxton Bragg, nominal general-in-chief of the Confederate Army—nominal because President Jefferson Davis made all the real decisions himself. "I think the officers and men of this army feel that every effort was made to hold Atlanta to the last," Hood wrote. "I do not think the army is discouraged." Many men in the ranks of his Army of Tennessee would not have agreed with him. "Well old Sherman flanked us out of Atlanta most beautifully and scientifically," one Rebel soldier wrote. "I don't know what is to blame but the counter movement on our side was very bunglingly executed."[9]

Sherman's soldiers would have seconded that evaluation. Most of them were writing home that day, for they had just received their first mail since setting off to sever Atlanta's supply lines. "We have whoop the rebs and got Atlanta," was how one of them put it.[10] Another wrote that Sherman "was a great military genius who depends upon his brains to win his victories instead of the lives of his men."[11] A third Federal wrote that "it was a very cute trick that Billy Sherman played on Hood, whose whole army is completely demoralized and routed. So much for being a damn traitor." A fourth claimed that "Sherman has Hood under his thumb nail as completely as ever one man had another."[12] Yet another said, "Our confidence in Sherman has been fulfilled to the uttermost. Gen. Sherman is loved by all."[13]

"A little before nine o'clock on the evening of September 4," recorded one of Grant's staff officers, Lieutenant Colonel Horace Porter, "while the general was having a quiet smoke in front of his tent, and discussing the campaign in Georgia, a despatch came from Sherman announcing the capture of Atlanta, which had occurred on September 2. It was immediately read aloud to the staff, and after discussing the news for a few minutes, and uttering many words in praise of Sherman, the general wrote the following reply: 'I have just received your despatch announcing the capture of Atlanta. In honor of your great victory I have ordered a salute to be fired with shotted guns from every battery bearing upon the enemy. The salute will be fired within an hour, amid great rejoicing.'"[14]

Sherman was also writing that day, to Major General Henry W. Halleck, who had been general-in-chief of the U.S. Army before Grant's promotion and who had been retained by that general at the Washington headquarters with the new title of chief of staff. Although he had not yet even reached Atlanta personally, Sherman had, he said, decided to evacuate the entire civilian population of the city. "I was resolved to make Atlanta a pure military garrison or depot," he wrote in his memoirs, "with no civil population to influence military measures. I had seen Memphis, Vicksburg, Natchez, and New Orleans, all captured from the enemy, and each at once was garrisoned by a full division of troops, if not more; so that success was actually crippling our armies in the field by detachments to guard and protect the interests of a hostile population." To Halleck he said, "If the people raise a howl against my barbarity and cruelty, I will answer that war is war, and not popularity-seeking. If they want peace, they and their relatives must stop the war."[15]

---

1. Mary Boykin Chesnut, *A Diary From Dixie* (New York, 1905), 434.

2. Roy P. Basler, editor, *The Collected Works of Abraham Lincoln* (New Brunswick, N.J., 1953), vol. 7, 533–534.

3. Jubal Anderson Early, *War Memoirs* (Bloomington, Ind., 1960), 414.

4. George E. Pond, *The Shenandoah Valley in 1864* (New York, 1883), 143–144.

5. Samuel Carter III, *The Last Cavaliers: Confederate and Union Cavalry in the Civil War* (New York, 1979), 284.

6. Ibid., 285.

7. Shelby Foote, *The Civil War: a Narrative* (New York, 1974), vol. 3, 596.

8. Carter, *The Last Cavaliers*, 286.

9. James Lee McDonough and James Picket Jones, *War So Terrible: Sherman and Atlanta* (New York, 1987), 312.

10. Ibid., 310.

11. Ibid., 311.

12. Ibid., 310.

13. Ibid., 311.

14. Horace Porter, *Campaigning With Grant* (New York, 1897), 285.

15. W. T. Sherman, *Memoirs of General William T. Sherman* (New York, 1886), Vol. 2, 111.

CHAPTER TWO

Appeal Against the Thunderstorm

5–14 September 1864

Up in the Shenandoah Valley the next day, the fifth, the Confederates returned to their positions west of the Opequon and discovered that a cavalry division of Sheridan's army was on their side of the creek and moving toward Winchester from Martinsburg, driving the Rebel cavalry before it. As had become routine, Early had to use his infantry to help his overmatched horsemen handle the Union troopers. Major General Robert E. Rodes' division was sent to drive them back again. It was but one in a long series of such skirmishes, but once again Early's attention was drawn northward toward Martinsburg and the railroad and away from Sheridan's main army to the east of him. Meanwhile, as Sheridan later reported, "In these skirmishes the cavalry was becoming educated to attack infantry lines."[1] On the sixth day of September, rain storms broke over the Shenandoah Valley, and they continued for several days, putting an end to further movements by both Early's and Sheridan's armies.

Much farther south that same day, at Meridian, Mississippi, Lieutenant General Richard Taylor assumed command of the Confederate Department of Alabama, Mississippi and East Louisiana. Both the North and the South continued to follow the U.S. Army's prewar policy of dividing the country into geographical departments. Most of the armies on both sides were actually just the mobile forces of one or more of these departments, or of portions of departments, called districts.

Taylor, who was the son of the late president Zachary Taylor and brother of Confederate president Jefferson Davis' first wife, was a native of Louisiana and had been the commander of the District of West Louisiana in the Trans-Mississippi Department. He had defeated the Union expedition up the Red River, and as a reward he had been promoted. Now, partly to get him away from the commander of the department, with whom he had been quarreling, he was transferred to the east side of the Mississippi. It had been hoped that he could bring his troops with him, but after several weeks of trying, the effort had been abandoned. The Federal gunboats were patroling the Mississippi so closely that, as a Rebel scout declared, "A bird, if dressed in Confederate gray, would find it difficult to fly across the river."[2] Taylor did manage to get across, but without his troops, and so he was assigned to replace Lieutenant General S. D. Lee, who had recently been sent to take over the 2nd Corps of the Army of Tennessee after Hood had been promoted to command of that entire army.

Taylor's new command included the area described by its name: Alabama, Mississippi, and that part of Louisiana east of the Mississippi River. Many of its forces had gone to reinforce the Army of Tennessee in May when Sherman had begun his advance on Atlanta. Most of what forces were left were scattered around northern Mississippi under the very formidable Major General Nathan Bedford Forrest, and around the city of Mobile, Alabama, where the Union army and navy had recently captured the forts guarding the entrance to the bay. Forrest, aided by unseasonal heavy rains, had recently turned back a Federal expedition into northern Mississippi in a campaign that included a spectacular, if not particularly fruitful, raid on Union-occupied Memphis. But the most important parts of Taylor's department, New Orleans and the banks of the Mississippi River, had been in Union hands for a long time. In fact, only the day before, Louisiana voters who had taken an oath of allegiance to the Union had ratified a new state constitution, one which abolished slavery.

Forrest had been in the process of transferring some of his troops to bolster the defenses of Mobile, but on the fifth, before Taylor's arrival, he had telegraphed directly to President Davis: "If permitted to do so with 4,000 picked men and six pieces of artillery of my present command, I believe I can proceed to Middle and West Tennessee, destroy enemy's communication or cripple it, and add 2,000 men to my command."[3] Davis promptly wired his brother-in-law, Taylor, suggesting that perhaps he should send Forrest on such an expedition. Taylor replied that "five minutes after my arrival at Meridian, I issued the orders contemplated in your dispatch; the movement is now in process of execution."[4] In a report to General Bragg, the nominal general in chief, he showed a rare selfless regard for the grand strategic situation at the expense of his own department: "Regarding the campaign in Georgia of paramount importance, I have ordered Major-General Forrest to proceed at once into Tennessee with his command for the purpose of breaking the lines of communication of General Sherman . . . This will be productive of more benefit than the detachment of a portion of it for the defense of Mobile. The former is of general, the latter of local, interest, and it is better to risk the fall of Mobile than to leave any reasonable efforts and means untried to defeat Sherman."[5]

In his memoirs, written well after the war, Taylor described how "a train from the north, bringing Forrest in advance of his troops, reached Meridian, and was stopped; and the General, whom I had never seen, came to report. He was a tall, stalwart man, with grayish hair, mild countenance, and slow and homely of speech. In a few words he was informed that I considered Mobile safe for the present, and that all of our energies must be directed to the relief of Hood's army, then west of Atlanta. The only way to accomplish this was to worry Sherman's communications north of the Tennessee River, and he must move his cavalry in that direction at the earliest moment.

"To my surprise, Forrest suggested many difficulties and asked numerous questions: how he was to get over the Tennessee; how he was to get back if pressed by the enemy; how he was to be supplied; what should be his line of retreat in certain contingencies; what he was to do with prisoners if any were taken, etc. I began to think he had no stomach for the work; but at last, having isolated the chances of success from causes of failure with the care of a chemist experimenting in his laboratory, he rose and asked for Fleming, the superintendent of the railway, who was on the train by which he had come. Fleming appeared—a little man on crutches (he had recently broken a leg), but with the energy of a giant—and at once stated what he could do in the way of moving supplies on his line, which had been repaired up to the Tennessee boundary. Forrest's whole manner now changed. In a dozen sharp sentences he told his wants, said he would leave a staff officer to bring up his supplies, asked for an engine to take him back north twenty miles to meet his troops,

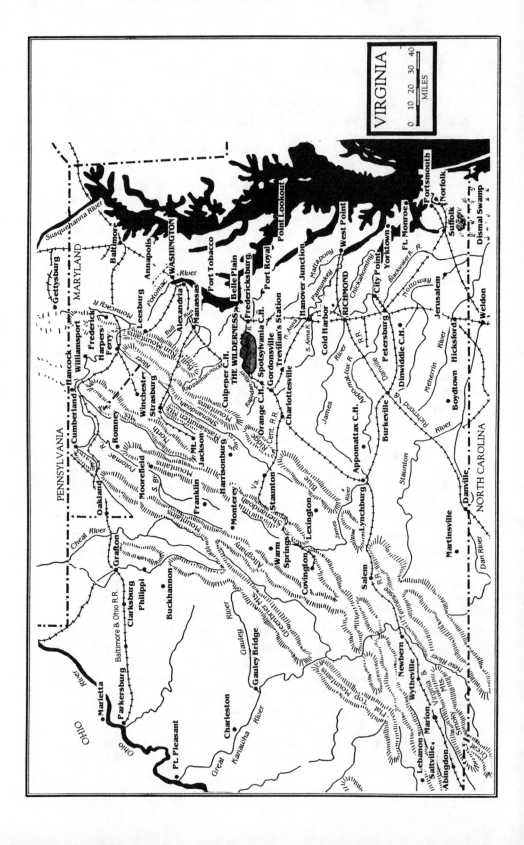

informed me that he would march with the dawn, and hoped to give an account of himself in Tennessee."[6]

The *Charleston Courier* published a lead story that day, 7 September, lamenting the fall of Atlanta because it would weaken the peace movement in the North: "All of us perceive the intimate connection existing between the armies of the Confederacy and the peace men in the United States. These constitute two immense forces that are working together for the procurement of peace. . . . Our success in battle insures the success of McClellan. Our failure will inevitably lead to his defeat."[7]

Sherman issued orders that day for the complete evacuation of all civilians from Atlanta, and he notified Hood, the Confederate commander, of this order: "I have deemed it to the interest of the United States that the citizens now residing in Atlanta should remove, those who prefer it to go south, the rest north. For the latter I can provide food and transportation to points of their election in Tennessee, Kentucky or farther north. For the former I can provide transportation by [railroad] cars as far as Rough and Ready, and also wagons; but . . . it will be necessary for you to help the families from Rough and Ready to the cars at Lovejoy's." As for their slaves, he said that "no force shall be used toward the blacks, one way or the other. If they want to go with their masters or mistresses, they may do so; otherwise they will be sent away, unless they be men, when they may be employed by our quartermaster. Atlanta is no place for families or non-combatants, and I have no desire to send them north if you will assist in conveying them south."[6]

"I knew, of course, that such a measure would be strongly criticised," Sherman later wrote, "but made up my mind to do it with the absolute certainty of its justness, and that time would sanction its wisdom. I knew that the people of the South would read in this measure two important conclusions: one, that we were in earnest; and the other, if they were sincere in there common and popular clamor 'to die in the last ditch,' that the opportunity would soon come."[7]

The next day, the eighth, Sherman finally reached Atlanta for the first time himself. He set up his headquarters in the home of a Judge Lyons, opposite one corner of the courthouse square. From there he commanded what was known as the Military Division of the Mississippi. This consisted of three departments, each of which contributed to his field force in Georgia as well as administering and garrisoning their own territories. The largest of these was the Department and Army of the Cumberland, commanded by Sherman's friend and West Point classmate, Major General George H. Thomas. Besides numerous garrisons in Tennessee, it consisted of three corps of infantry, the 4th, 14th, and 20th, now stationed at Atlanta, and three divisions of cavalry in the area. The smallest of Sherman's three forces was the Department and Army of the Ohio, commanded by Major General John M. Schofield, and other than garrisons in Kentucky and east Tennessee, it consisted of one corps of infantry, the 23rd, stationed at Decatur, east of Atlanta, and one division of cavalry. The third force was the Department and Army of the Tennessee, commanded by Major General Oliver O. Howard. Other than sizable garrisons in Mississippi and west Tennessee, it consisted of three corps of infantry, the 15th, 16th, and 17th, stationed southwest of Atlanta at the village of East Point. Actually only half of the 16th Corps was with Sherman. The other half had been fighting in northern Mississippi and was now on its way to St. Louis to help guard against a large force of Rebels known to be heading for Missouri from Arkansas under a former governor of Missouri, Major General Sterling Price.

General George McClellan, one of Grant's predecessors as general-in-chief of the army, presented his acceptance of the Democratic party's nomination for president that day. In it he rejected the peace-at-any-price plank in the party's platform: "I could not look in the face of my gallant comrades of the Army and Navy, who have survived so many bloody battles, and tell them that their labors, and the sacrifice of so many of our slain and wounded brethren had been in vain." But whereas Lincoln insisted that the South give up both its independence and slavery, McClellan said that "the Union is the one condition of peace. We ask no more."[10] Neither slavery, nor, for that matter, war, were even mentioned in his carefully worded letter. McClellan was still very popular, "almost worshiped," as one soldier put it, in the Army of the Potomac, the North's largest army, which he had forged out of the wreckage left from the first battle of Bull Run. But that did not necessarily mean that the soldiers would vote for him. "On one side is war," one of them wrote, "and stubborn, patient effort to restore the old Union and national honor; on the other side is inglorious peace and shame, the old truckling subserviency to Southern domination, and a base alacrity in embracing some vague, deceptive political subterfuge instead of honorable and clearly defined principles."[11]

The next day, 9 September, Major General Wade Hampton, the commander of the cavalry corps of Lee's Army of Northern Virginia, paid a visit to his commander. Robert Edward Lee was 57 years old that year, but the stress of command had already turned his hair and beard white. For over two years—since he had begun his string of spectacular victories by driving McClellan away from the outskirts of Richmond—he had been the idol of the South. Hampton was 46 that year. He was not a professional soldier, but had been one of the wealthiest men in the South before the war. He had raised a regiment-sized unit at his own expense when the war came, and had been first a brigade and then a division commander of cavalry before succeeding to command of the entire corps about a month before. Now he dismounted in front of Lee's headquarters, a tent erected in the shade of the ancient trees before a pleasant Petersburg home called Violet Bank, not far from the Appomattox River. Hampton carried with him a ham that his scouts had brought him from the area east of Petersburg. He presented it to Lee, who in turn sent it to a nearby hospital to be served to the wounded soldiers there. Like all his soldiers, they were very short on rations. But Hampton had a plan that would help to feed the men and strike a blow at the enemy at the same time.

A few days before, Lee had asked him to look into the possibility of a raid on the rear of the Union position. Since the Army of the Potomac had crossed to the south bank of the James River in the middle of June and linked up with the Army of the James, the Federal forces had constructed powerful defenses east of Petersburg and had gradually extended them around to the south until they had severed the railroad running south to Weldon, North Carolina. Grant made his headquarters, and a huge supply base had been built up, at the little port town of City Point. "A sudden blow in that quarter might be deterimental to him," Lee had recently told Hampton.[12]

Hampton's best scout, Sergeant George D. Shadburne, had brought him a detailed description of the points of interest in the Federals' rear: hospital, wagons, pontoon train, wharves, and warehouses, and the types and numbers of troops at all these locations. The attention of the sergeant and both generals had lighted especially upon the fact that a herd of approximately 3,000 beef cattle—rations on the hoof for the Union army—was being grazed at Coggins Point, about five miles east of City Point, and was guarded only by about 120 soldiers and 20 unarmed civilian drovers. Three miles farther south, at Sycamore Church, were the 250 men of the 1st District of Columbia Cavalry Regiment. If a large body of Confederate cavalry could make its way unnoticed around the southern flank of the Union defenses it could capture this herd of cattle, not only striking a physical and psychological blow against the enemy, but making a truly sizable addition to Southern rations. The danger, as both generals well knew, would be the return trip. Nevertheless, it was worth the gamble. But they would wait a little while to see if they could catch the Federals at a vulnerable moment.

Down in Georgia that day, the ninth, General Hood sent an answer to Sherman's notification of his order for the evacuation of Atlanta: "I do not consider that I have any alternative in this matter. I therefore accept your proposition to declare a truce of two days, or such time as may be necessary to accomplish the purpose mentioned, and shall render all assistance in my power to expedite the transportation of citizens in this direction . . . Permit me to say that the unprecedented measure you propose transcends, in studied and ingenious cruelty, all acts ever before brought to my attention in the dark history of war. In the name of God and humanity, I protest, believing that you will find that you are expelling from their homes and firesides the wives and children of a brave people."[13]

Sherman was not the kind of man to let such accusations go unanswered, so the next day, the tenth, he wrote back: "You style the measures proposed 'unprecedented,' and appeal to the dark history of war for a parallel, as an act of 'studied and ingenious cruelty.' It is not unprecedented; for General Johnston himself very wisely and properly removed the families all the way from Dalton down, and I see no reason why Atlanta should be excepted. Nor is it necessary to appeal to the dark history of war, when recent and modern examples are so handy. You yourself burned dwelling-houses along your parapet, and I have seen to-day fifty houses that you have rendered uninhabitable because they stood in the way of your forts and men. You defended Atlanta on a line so close to town that every cannon-shot and many musket-shots from our line of investment, that overshot their mark, went into the habitations of women and children. General Hardee did the same at Jonesboro', and General Johnston did the same, last summer, at Jackson, Mississippi. I have not accused you of heartless cruelty, but merely instance these cases of very recent occurence, and could go on and enumerate hundreds of others, and challenge any fair man to judge which of us has the heart of pity for the families of a 'brave people.'

"I say that it is kindness to these families of Atlanta to remove them now, at once, from scenes that women and children should not be exposed to, and the 'brave people' should scorn to commit their wives and children to the rude barbarians who thus, as you say, violate the rules of war, as illustrated in the pages of its dark history.

"In the name of common sense, I ask you not to appeal to a just God in such a sacrilegious manner. You who, in the midst of peace and prosperity, have plunged a nation into war—dark and cruel war—who dared and badgered us to battle, insulted our flag, seized our arsenals and forts that were left in the honorable custody of peaceful ordnance-sergeants, seized and made 'prisoners of war' the very garrisons sent to protect your people against negroes and Indians, long before any overt act was committed by the (to you) hated Lincoln Government; tried to force Kentucky and Missouri into rebellion, spite of themselves; falsified the vote of Louisiana; turned loose your privateers to plunder unarmed ships; expelled Union families by the thousands, burned their houses, and declared, by an act of your Congress, the confiscation of all debts due Northern men for goods had and received! Talk thus to the marines, but not to me, who have seen these things, and who will this day make as much sacrifice for the peace and honor of the South as the best-born Southerner among you! If we must be enemies, let us be men, and fight it out as we propose to do, and not deal in such hypocritical appeals to God and humanity. God will judge us in due time, and he will pronounce whether it be more humane to fight with a town full of women and the families of a brave people at our back, or to remove them in time to places of safety among their own friends and people."[14]

That same day, the governor of Georgia released the members of the state militia who had been called out to help defend Atlanta to go home for the fall harvest.

The next day, the eleventh, the mayor and two members of the city council of Atlanta, "for the time being the only legal organ of the people of said city," as they put it, wrote a touching letter to Sherman asking him to reconsider his order for the evacuation of civilians and giving instances of the kinds of hardships it would impose: "Many poor women are in advanced state of pregnancy, others now having young children, and whose husbands for the greater part are either in the army, prisoners, or dead. Some say: 'I have such a one sick at my house; who will wait on them when I am gone?' Others say: 'What are we to do? We have no house to go to, and no means to buy, build, or rent any; no parents, relatives, or friends, to go to.' Another says: 'I will try and take this or that article of property, but such and such things I must leave behind, though I need them much.' We reply to them: 'General Sherman will carry your property to Rough and Ready, and General Hood will take it thence on.' And they will reply to that: 'But I want to leave the railroad at such a place, and cannot get conveyance from there on.'

"We only refer to a few facts, to try to illustrate in part how this measure will operate in practice. As you advanced, the people north of this fell back; and before your arrival here, a large portion of the people had retired south, so that the country south of this is already crowded, and without houses enough to accommodate the people, and we are informed that many are now staying in churches and other out-buildings.

"This being so, how is it possible for the people still here (mostly women and children) to find any shelter? And how can they live through the winter in the woods—no shelter or subsistence, in the midst of strangers who know them not, and without the power to assist them much, if they were willing to do so?

"This is but a feeble picture of the consequences of this measure. You know the woe, the horrors, and the suffering, cannot be described by words; imagination can only conceive of it, and we ask you to take these things into consideration.

"We know your mind and time are constantly occupied with the duties of your command, which almost deters us from asking your attention to this matter, but thought it might be that you had not considered this subject in all of its awful consequences, and that on more reflection you, we hope, would not make this people an exception to all mankind, for we know of no such instance ever having occurred—surely never in the United States—and what has this *helpless* people done, that they should be driven from their homes, to wander strangers and outcasts, and exiles, and to subsist on charity?"[15]

Sherman answered this appeal the next day, the twelfth: "I have read it carefully, and give full credit to your statements of the distress that will be occasioned, and yet shall not revoke my orders, because they were not designed to meet the humanities of the case, but to prepare for the future struggles in which millions of good people outside of Atlanta have a deep interest. We must have peace, not only at Atlanta, but in all America. To secure this, we must stop the war that now desolates our once happy and favored country. To stop war, we must defeat the rebel armies which are arrayed against the laws and Constitution that all must respect and obey. To defeat those armies, we must prepare the way to reach them in their recesses, provided with the arms and instruments which enable us to accomplish our purpose. Now, I know the vindictive nature of our enemy, that we may have many years of military operations from this quarter; and, therefore, deem it wise and prudent to prepare in time. The use of Atlanta for warlike purposes is inconsistent with its character as a home for families. There will be no manufactures, commerce, or agriculture here, for the maintenance of families, and sooner or later want will compel the inhabitants to go. Why not go now, when all the arrangements are completed for the transfer, instead of waiting till the plunging shot of contending armies will renew the scenes of the past month? Of course, I do not apprehend any such thing at this moment, but you do not suppose this army will be here until the war is over. I cannot discuss this subject with you fairly, because I cannot impart to you what we propose to do, but I assert that our military plans make it necessary for the inhabitants to go away, and I can only renew my offer of services to make their exodus in any direction as easy and comfortable as possible.

"You cannot qualify war in harsher terms than I will. War is cruelty, and you cannot refine it; and those who brought war into our country deserve all the curses and maledictions a people can pour out. I know I had no hand in making this war, and I know I will make more sacrifices today than any of you to secure peace. But you cannot have peace and a division of our country. If the United States submits to a division now, it will not stop, but will go on until we reap the fate of Mexico, which is eternal war. The United States does and must assert its authority, wherever it once had power; for, if it relaxes one bit to pressure, it is gone, and I believe that such is the national feeling. This feeling assumes various shapes, but always comes back to that of Union. Once admit the Union, once more acknowledge the authority of the national Government, and, instead of devoting your houses and streets and roads to the dread uses of war, I and this army become at once your protectors and supporters, shielding you from danger, let it come from what quarter it may. I know that a few individuals cannot resist a torrent of error and passion, such as swept the South into rebellion, but you can point out, so that we may know those who desire a government, and those who insist on war and its desolation.

"You might as well appeal against the thunder-storm as against these terrible hardships of war. They are inevitable, and the only way the people of Atlanta can hope once more to live in peace and quiet at home, is to stop the war, which can only be done by admitting that it began in error and is perpetuated in pride.

"We don't want your negroes, or your horses, or your lands, or any thing you have, but we do want and will have a just obedience to the laws of the United States. That we will have, and if it involves the destruction of your improvements, we cannot help it.

"You have heretofore read public sentiment in your newspapers, that live by falsehood and excitement; and the quicker you seek for truth in other quarters, the better. I repeat then that, by the original compact of Government, the United States had certain rights in Georgia, which have never been relinquished and never will be; that the South began war by seizing forts, arsenals, mints, custom-houses, etc., etc., long before Mr. Lincoln was installed, and before the South had one jot or title of provocation. I myself have seen in Missouri, Kentucky, Tennessee, and Mississippi, hundreds and thousands of women and children fleeing from your armies and desperadoes, hungry and with bleeding feet. In Memphis, Vicksburg, and Mississippi, we fed thousands upon thousands of the families of rebel soldiers left on our hands, and whom we could not see starve. Now that war comes home to you, you feel very different. You deprecate its horrors, but did not feel them when you sent car-loads of soldiers and ammunition, and moulded shells and shot, to carry war into Kentucky and Tennessee, to desolate the homes of hundreds and thousands of good people who only asked to live in peace at their old homes, and under the Government of their inheritance. But these comparisons are idle. I want peace, and believe it can only be reached through union and war, and I will ever conduct war with a view to perfect and early success.

"But, my dear sirs, when peace does come, you may call on me for any thing. Then will I share with you the last cracker, and watch with you to shield your homes and families against danger from every quarter.

"Now you must go, and take with you the old and feeble, feed and nurse them, and build for them, in more quiet places, proper habitations to shield them against the weather until the mad passions of men cool down, and allow the Union and peace once more to settle over your old homes at Atlanta."[16]

That same day, Hood was answering Sherman's last letter to him, saying "you have chosen to indulge in statements which I feel compelled to notice, at least so far as to signify my dissent, and not allow silence in regard to them to be construed as acquiescence. I see nothing in your communication which induces me to modify the language of condemnation with which I characterized your order." He disputed Sherman's claims that General Johnston had set a precedent for evacuating Atlanta. "He depopulated no villages, nor towns, nor cities, either friendly or hostile. He offered and extended friendly aid to his unfortunate fellow-citizens who desired to flee from your fraternal embraces." He also disputed that either Hardee or himself had set a precedent. "General Hardee defended his position in front of Jonesboro' at the expense of injury to the houses; an ordinary, proper, and justifiable act of war. I defended Atlanta at the same risk and cost. If there was any fault in either case, it was your own, in not giving notice, especially in the case of Atlanta, of your purpose to shell the town, which is usual in war among civilized nations. No inhabitant was expelled from his home and fireside by the orders of General Hardee or myself, and therefore your recent order can find no support from the conduct of either of us . . . I made no complaint of your firing into Atlanta in any way you thought proper. I make none now, but there are a hundred thousand witnesses that you fired into the habitations of women and children for weeks, firing far above and miles beyond my line of defense. I have too good an opinion, founded both upon observation and experience, of the skill of your artillerists, to credit the insinuation that they for several weeks unintentionally fired too high for my modest field works, and slaughtered women and children by accident and want of skill.

"The residue of your letter is rather discussion," he wrote. "It opens a wide field for the discussion of questions which I do not feel are committed to me." He nevertheless went on to discuss them one by one. "You charge my country with 'daring and badgering you to battle.' The truth is, we sent commissioners to you, respectfully offering a peaceful separation, before the first gun was fired on either side. You say we insulted your flag. The truth is, we fired upon it, and those who fought under it, when you came to our doors upon the mission of subjugation. You say we seized upon your forts and arsenals, and made prisoners of the garrisons sent to protect us against negroes and Indians. The truth is, we, by force of arms, drove out insolent intruders and took possession of our own forts and arsenals, to resist your claims to dominion over masters, slaves, and Indians, all of whom are to this day, with a unanimity unexampled in the history of the world, warring against your attempts to become their masters. You say that we tried to force Missouri and Kentucky into rebellion in spite of themselves. The truth is, my Government, from the beginning of this struggle to this hour, has again and again offered, before the whole world, to leave it to the unbiased will of these States, and all others, to determine for themselves whether they will cast their destiny with your Government or ours; and your Government has resisted this fundamental principle of free institutions with the bayonet, and labors daily, by force and fraud, to fasten its hateful tyranny upon the unfortunate freemen of these States. You say we falsified the vote of Louisiana. The truth is, Louisiana not only separated herself from your Government by nearly a unanimous vote of her people, but has vindicated the act upon every battle-field from Gettysburg to the Sabine, and has exhibited an heroic devotion to her decision which challenges the admiration and respect of every man capable of feeling sympathy for the oppressed or admiration for heroic valor. You say that we turned loose pirates to plunder your unarmed ships. The truth is, when you robbed us of our part of the navy, we built and bought a few vessels, hoisted the flag of our country, and swept the seas, in defiance of your navy, around the whole circumference of the globe. You say we have expelled Union families by thousands. The truth is, not a single family has been expelled from the Confederate States, that I am aware of; but, on the contrary, the moderation of our Government toward traitors has been a fruitful theme of denunciation by its enemies and well-meaning friends of our cause. You say my Government, by act of Congress, has confiscated 'all debts due Northern men for goods sold and delivered.' The truth is, our Congress gave due and ample time to your merchants and traders to depart from our shores with their ships, goods, and effects, and only sequestered the property of our enemies in retaliation for their acts—declaring us traitors, and confiscating our property wherever their power extended, either in their country or our own.

". . . You issue a sweeping edict, covering all the inhabitants of a city, and add insult to the injury heaped upon the defenseless by assuming that you have done them a kindness . . . And because I characterize what you call a kindness as being real cruelty, you presume to sit in judgment between me and my God; and you decide that my earnest prayer to the Almighty Father to save our women and children from what you call kindness, is a 'sacrilegious, hypocritical appeal.'

"You came into our country with your army, avowedly for the purpose of subjugating free white men, women, and children, and not only intend to rule over them, but you make negroes your allies, and desire to place over us an inferior race, which we have raised from barbarism to its present position, which is the highest ever attained by that race, in any country, in all time . . . You say, 'Let us fight it out like men.' To this my reply is—for myself, and I believe for all the true men, ay, and women and children, in my country—we will fight you to the death! Better die a thousand deaths than submit to live under you or your Government and your negro allies!"[17]

Sherman's boss, as well as his opponent, was writing to him that day. "On September 12 General Grant called me into his tent," wrote Horace Porter, Grant's aide, "turned his chair around from the table at which he had been sitting, lighted a fresh cigar, and began a conversation by saying: 'Sherman and I have exchanged ideas regarding his next movement about as far as we can by correspondence, and I have been thinking that it would be well for you to start for Atlanta to-morrow, and talk over with him the whole subject of his next campaign. We have debated it so much here that you know my views thoroughly, and can answer any of Sherman's questions as to what I think in reference to the contemplated movement, and the action which should be taken in the various contingencies which may arise. Sherman's suggestions are excellent, and no one is better fitted for carrying them out. I can comply with his views in regard to meeting him with ample supplies at any point on the seacoast which it may be decided to have him strike for. You can tell him that I am going to send an expedition against Wilmington, North Carolina, landing the troops on the coast north of Fort Fisher; and with the efficient cooperation of the navy we shall no doubt get control of Wilmington harbor by the time he reaches and captures other points on the sea-coast. Sherman has made a splendid campaign, and the more I reflect upon it the more merit I see in it. I do not want to hamper him any more in the future than in the past with detailed instructions. I want him to carry out his ideas freely in the coming movement, and to have all the credit of its success. Of this success I have no doubt. I will write Sherman a letter, which you can take to him.' The general then turned to his writing-table, and retaining between his lips the cigar which he had been smoking, wrote the communication. After reading it over aloud, he handed it to me to take to Atlanta."[18]

The letter said: "I send Lieutenant-Colonel Horace Porter, of my staff, with this. Colonel Porter will explain to you the exact condition of affairs here, better than I can do in the limits of a letter. Although I feel myself strong enough now for offensive operations, I am holding on quietly, to get advantage of recruits and convalescents, who are coming forward very rapidly. My lines are necessarily very strong, extending from Deep Bottom, north of the James, across the peninsula formed by the Appomattox and the James, and south of the Appomattox to the Weldon road. This line is very strongly fortified, and can be held with comparatively few men; but, from its great length, necessarily takes many in the aggregate. I propose, when I do move, to extend my left so as to control what is known as the Southside, or Lynchburg & Petersburg road; then, if possible, to keep the Danville road cut. At the same time this move is made, I want to send a force of from six to ten thousand men against Wilmington . . . What you are to do with the forces at your command, I do not exactly see. The difficulties of supplying your army, except when they are constantly moving beyond where you are, I plainly see. If it had not been for Price's movement, Canby could have sent twelve thousand more men to Mobile. From your command on the Mississippi, an equal number could have been taken. With these forces, my idea would have been to divide them, sending one-half to Mobile, and the other half to Savannah. You could then move . . . so as to threaten Macon and Augusta equally. Whichever one should be abandoned by the enemy, you could take and open up a new base of supplies. My object now in sending a staff-officer to you is not so much to suggest operations for you as to get your views, and to have plans matured by the time every thing can be got ready. It would probably be the 5th of October before any of the plans here indicated will be executed . . .

"In conclusion, it is hardly necessary for me to say that I feel you have accomplished the most gigantic undertaking given to any general in this war, and with a skill and ability that will be acknowledged in history as unsurpassed, if not unequalled. It gives me as much pleasure to record this in your favor as it would in favor of any living man, myself included."[19] Porter departed for Atlanta the next day, the thirteenth.

On that thirteenth day of September, Price's Confederate force for an invasion of Missouri was completed, as it was joined at Pocahontas, Arkansas, by Brigadier General Jo Shelby's forces and a large number of mostly unarmed recruits that the latter had conscripted in his recent activities in northern Arkansas. This brought Price's forces up to 14 cannon and 12,000 cavalry, although only about 8,000 of the latter were armed and about 1,000 lacked horses. It was hoped that weapons and mounts could be picked up for the rest by capturing small Union garrisons and that the force would soon be augmented by Missouri recruits. It had originally been planned to send the three divisions of Rebel infantry in Arkansas as part of an even larger invasion of Missouri, but then the Confederate government had ordered the transfer of the infantry to the east side of the Mississippi with Richard Taylor. They had not been able to get past the Union navy. Meanwhile the cavalry had set out alone from southern Arkansas, crossing the Arkansas River west of Little Rock. It was hoped that the secret society of Copperheads, still commonly referred to in Missouri as the Order of American Knights, would provide valuable support to the Rebels.

St. Louis was the first objective of Price's advance, "which if rapidly made, will put you in possession of that place, its supplies, and military stores," he was told by his boss, General Edmund Kirby Smith, "and which will do more toward rallying Missourians to your standard than the possession of any other point." And the recruiting, or conscription, of more soldiers was another objective of the expedition. Price also hoped to control enough of Missouri, for a while at least, to hold an election for a new governor and legislature. The legal term of the legislature elected in 1860 had expired and the governor had died. The lieutenant governor, Thomas C. Reynolds, was riding with Price's army, ready to assume civil authority in whatever part of the state Price's forces could control. It was important to Confederate Missourians to hold as much of the state as possible, otherwise the Confederacy might have to concede Missouri to the United States in any negotiated peace. Another objective was to divert Union forces from Atlanta and Mobile. As Grant's letter shows, it was already succeeding in that regard. It remained to be seen whether Missouri could be conquered. If Price was compelled to retreat, he was to follow the Missouri River westward to Kansas and the Indian Territory—now Oklahoma—"sweeping that country of its mules, horses, cattle, and military supplies of all kinds," as well as recruits.[20]

The next day, the fourteenth, Sherman sent a short answer to Hood's recent long letter: "I agree with you that this discussion by two soldiers is out of place, and profitless; but you must admit that you began the controversy by characterizing an official act of mine in unfair and improper terms. I reiterate my former answer, and to the only new matter contained in your rejoinder add: We have no 'negro allies' in this army; not a single negro soldier left Chattanooga with this army, or is with it now. There are a few guarding Chattanooga, which General Steedman sent at one time to drive Wheeler out of Dalton.

"I was not bound by the laws of war to give notice of the shelling of Atlanta, a 'fortified town, with magazines, arsenals, founderies, and public stores;' you were bound to take notice. See the books."[21]

To a visiting clergyman Sherman complained of the Confederate general's charges: "To be sure I have made war vindictively; war is war, and you can make nothing else of it; but Hood knows as well as anyone I am not brutal or inhuman."[22]

---

1. U.S. War Department, *The War of the Rebellion: a Compilation of the Official Records of the Union and Confederate Armies* (Washington, 1893), Series I, Vol. 43, part I, 46.

2. Foote, *The Civil War.* 3:575.

3. *Official Records,* 52:II:731.

4. Ibid., 39:II:819.

5. Ibid., 52:II:732.

6. Robert Selph Henry, *"First With the Most" Forrest* (New York, 1991), 349.

7. John G. Nicolay and John Hay, *Abraham Lincoln: A History,* Vol. 9 (New York, 1904), 352–353.

8. Sherman, *Memoirs,* 592.

9. Ibid., 585.

10. Stephen W. Sears, *George B. McClellan: The Young Napoleon* (New York, 1988), 376.

11. Bruce Catton, *A Stillness at Appomattox* (Garden City, N.Y., 1957), 323.

12. *Official Records,* 42:II:1233.

13. Sherman, *Memoirs,* 592–593.

14. Ibid., 594–595.

15. Ibid., 599.

16. Ibid., 600–602.

17. Ibid., 596–598.

18. Porter, *Campaigning With Grant,* 288.

19. Sherman, *Memoirs*, 586–587.

20. Albert Castel, *General Sterling Price and the Civil War in the West* (Baton Rouge, 1968), 202.

21. Sherman, *Memoirs*, 602.

22. McDonough and Jones, *War So Terrible*, 317.

CHAPTER THREE

I Hate to See That Old Cuss Around

14–16 September 1864

On the fourteenth of September General Halleck, the Union chief of staff at Washington, wired Grant at City Point about the situation in the Shenandoah Valley: "It is represented to me by reliable business men that the long and continued interruption of the Ohio and Chesapeake and Baltimore and Ohio Railroads is very seriously affecting the supply of provisions and fuel for public and private use in Baltimore, Washington, Georgetown, and Alexandria. Unless the canal can be opened very soon a sufficient supply of winter's coal cannot be procured before the close of navigation. The gas companies are already thinking of stopping their works for want of coal. The canal and railroad have been several times repaired and as often destroyed. They, therefore, urge the great importance of driving Early far enough south to secure these lines of communication from rebel raids, and that if Sheridan is not strong enough to do this he should be reinforced."[1]

The same morning, Grant telegraphed Halleck: "I will leave here to-

morrow morning for the Shenandoah Valley to see Sheridan. Will not
pass through Washington either coming or going unless it is the wish of
the President or Secretary of War that I should do so. Everything is quiet
here and indications are that it will remain so until I take the offensive."[2]
Grant explained the purpose of this visit in his memoirs: "I knew it was
impossible for me to get orders through Washington to Sheridan to make
a move, because they would be stopped there and such orders as Halleck's caution (and that of the Secretary of War) would suggest would
be given instead, and would, no doubt, be contradictory to mine."[3]
Seven hours later he informed Major General George G. Meade, commander of the Army of the Potomac, by the telegraph that connected
their two headquarters: "I shall leave here tomorrow morning for General Sheridan's headquarters. Will be gone for five days. General Butler
also leaves here to-day to be absent a few days. You will, therefore,
assume command of all the forces operating in this field if you find it
necessary." Later he added: "I think it would be well to push reconnaissances, both west and south from our extreme left, to ascertain if any
movements are in contemplation." Meade replied that night with the
assurance that "our cavalry is out so far to the south that any advance
meets the enemy at once. I do not think the enemy will be likely to
attack our immediate left or the rear of it, but may, perhaps, endeavor
to threaten still farther round in the direction of Prince George Court-
House so as to try and draw us away from our intrenched lines. This
would be running a great risk on their part unless they have a very large
force." He closed with the assurance that "I will be vigilant and keep a
sharp lookout."[4]

The Rebel scout, Sergeant George Shadburne, had informed Wade
Hampton on the twelfth that Grant would be leaving for the Valley on
the fifteenth. How he had obtained this information is not known. But
this was the break the Confederates had been hoping for. With Grant
gone, the Union command structure might be slow to react to a raid on
the Federal cattle herd. Five hours before Grant wired Halleck of his
intention to visit Sheridan, Hampton's troopers were already on the
road. Only his generals and their adjutants knew their destination. "So
little do soldiers know of the intentions of their officers," one Rebel
remembered, "that some said we were going to surprise and capture a
brigade of negro troops, and we began in a spirit of humor to tell what
we were going to do with our shares of the negroes. We had no idea that
beeves had any place in the picture at all."[5] The sun was going down by
the time they crossed the Weldon Railroad well south of the Union positions. After pushing on for a mile or so to the crossing of Rowanty
Creek they went into camp for the night.

But the Southerners were not the only ones with scouts and spies. "While occupying the ground between Clifton and Berryville," Sheridan wrote in his memoirs, ". . . I felt the need of an efficient body of scouts to collect information regarding the enemy, for the defective intelligence-establishment with which I started out from Harper's Ferry early in August had not proved satisfactory. I therefore began to organize my scouts on a system which I hoped would give better results than had the method hitherto pursued in the department, which was to employ on this service doubtful citizens and Confederate deserters. If these should turn out untrustworthy, the mischief they might do us gave me grave apprehension, and I finally concluded that those of our own soldiers who should volunteer for the delicate and hazardous duty would be the most valuable material, and decided that they should have a battalion organization and be commanded by an officer, Major H. K. Young, of the First Rhode Island Infantry. These men were disguised in Confederate uniforms whenever necessary, were paid from the Secret-Service Fund in proportion to the value of the intelligence they furnished, which often stood us in good stead in checking the forays of Gilmore, Mosby, and other irregulars. Beneficial results came from the plan in many other ways too, and particularly so when in a few days two of my scouts put me in the way of getting news conveyed from Winchester. They had learned that just outside of my lines, near Millwood, there was living an old colored man, who had a permit from the Confederate commander to go into Winchester and return three times a week, for the purpose of selling vegetables to the inhabitants. The scouts had sounded this man, and finding him both loyal and shrewd, suggested that he might be made useful to us within the enemy's lines; and the proposal struck me as feasible, provided there could be found in Winchester some reliable person who would be willing to cooperate and correspond with me. I asked General Crook, who was acquainted with many of the Union people of Winchester, if he knew of such a person, and he recommended a Miss Rebecca Wright, a young lady whom he had met there before the battle of Kernstown, who, he said, was a member of the Society of Friends and the teacher of a small private school. He knew she was faithful and loyal to the Government, and thought she might be willing to render us assistance, but he could not be certain of this, for on account of her well-known loyalty she was under constant surveillance. I hestiated at first, but finally deciding to try it, despatched the two scouts to the old negro's cabin, and they brought him to my headquarters late that night. I was soon convinced of the negro's fidelity, and asking him if he was acquainted with Miss Rebecca Wright, of Winchester, he replied that he knew her well. Thereupon I told him what I wished to do, and after a

THE SHENANDOAH VALLEY

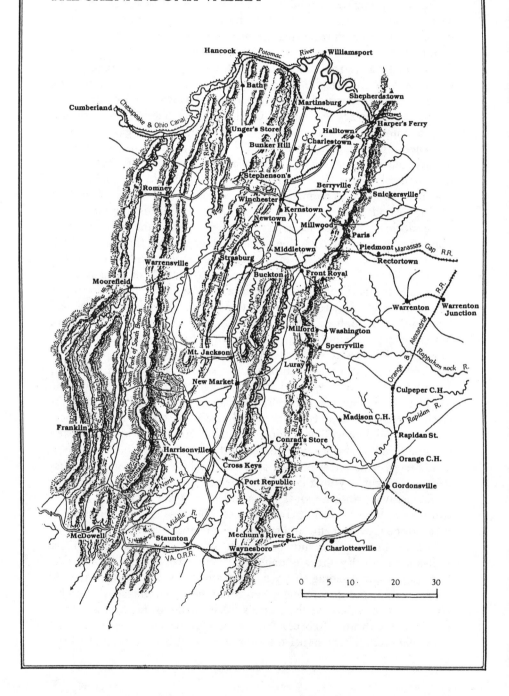

little persuasion he agreed to carry a letter to her on his next marketing trip. My message was prepared by writing it on tissue paper, which was then compressed into a small pellet, and protected by wrapping it in tinfoil so that it could be safely carried in the man's mouth. The probability of his being searched when he came to the Confederate picket-line was not remote, and in such event he was to swallow the pellet."[6]

The letter said: "I learn from Major-General Crook that you are a loyal lady and still love the old flag. Can you inform me of the position of Early's forces, the number of divisions in his army, and the strength of any or all of them, and his probable or reported intentions? Have any more troops arrived from Richmond, or are any more coming, or reported to be coming?"[7]

The timing of this move was extremely fortunate, for not only was Grant on his way to confer with Sheridan about the latter taking the offensive, but the very Confederate move for which both had been waiting had finally taken place. At dawn on 15 September, Anderson, with Kershaw's Division of infantry and Cutshaw's battalion of artillery, marched out of Winchester, heading for Richmond. That evening a convalescent Confederate officer visited the home of Rebecca Wright's mother and, in the course of a conversation about the war, happened to mention that Kershaw's infantry and Cutshaw's artillery had started on their way to rejoin Lee.

On 15 September General Sherman, down in Georgia, sent a telegram to Halleck, in Washington. After saying that his report on his campaign against Atlanta was completed and would soon be forwarded, and mentioning that he was waiting for a courier from Grant, he reported that the governor of Georgia "has disbanded his militia, to gather the corn and sorghum of the State. I have reason to believe that he and [Confederate vice president] Stephens want to visit me, and I have sent them a hearty invitation."[8]

He also said that he would exchange 2,000 prisoners with Hood. The general exchange of prisoners between the North and South had broken down some months back, partly over the question of the treatment of black soldiers in the Federal army. But Hood had suggested an exchange for Union prisoners being held at the vast camp at Andersonville, south of Macon, Ga. "Some of these prisoners had already escaped and got in," Sherman wrote in his memoirs, "had described the pitiable condition of the remainder, and, although I felt a sympathy for their hardships and sufferings as deeply as any man could, yet as nearly all the prisoners who had been captured by us during the campaign had been sent, as fast as taken, to the usual depots North, they were then beyond my control.

There were still about two thousand, mostly captured at Jonesboro', who had been sent back by cars, but had not passed Chattanooga. These I ordered back, and offered General Hood to exchange them for [General] Stoneman, [Colonel] Buell, and such of my own army as would make up the equivalent; but I would not exchange for his prisoners *generally*, because I knew these would have to be sent to their own regiments, away from my army, whereas all we could give him could at once be put to duty in his immediate army."⁹

In southeastern Virginia on the fifteenth, as Grant steamed down the James River and up Chesapeake Bay, Hampton's troopers spent the morning riding eastward. Before noon the head of the column crossed the Norfolk & Petersburg Railroad, or what was left of it. The rails had long since been taken up by one army or the other. Near Ebenezer Church local resident Captain John Belsches joined the raiders as a guide, and a little farther on they came to Crook's Bridge over the Blackwater River. However, there was no bridge there anymore, only charred pilings and a hundred-foot-wide stream of water. Hampton's engineer officer and his pioneers spent the afternoon rebuilding the bridge while the cavalrymen rested. Then about dark the span was complete and the advance guard was sent across. But the main force stayed in camp for supper and more rest. The meager meal was greatly enhanced when Hampton broke the news to the men in the ranks of what they were going to do. While they dined on cornpone and raw sweet potatoes, found growing nearby, they dreamed of beef steak, roast beef, beef stew—two million pounds of beef! Only with difficulty could their enthusiasm be restrained sufficiently to keep them from raising a ruccous that the Yankees would be sure to hear, even though none had yet been seen.

While the men rested, or celebrated their coming feast, Hampton gave his orders to his generals. Major General W. H. F. ("Rooney") Lee, son of the Confederate commanding general, would take his division and two pieces of artillery northwestward up Lawyer's Road until it intersected the Powhatan Stage Road just east of Prince George Court House and about five miles south of City Point. There he would establish a roadblock to protect against Federals that might be sent back from their main line. Then he would move eastward on the Stage Road toward Coggins Point and the cattle herd. Brigadier General James Dearing and his brigade from the Department of North Carolina and Southern Virginia would follow Lee to the Hines Road, where they would turn to the northeast and proceed to Cocke's Mill on the Stage Road east of Coggins Point, to cut off escape in that direction. Hampton would stay with Brigadier General Tom Rosser's brigade of Brigadier General Matthew Butler's division, the only other force brought along. It would follow Dearing but turn off onto Walls Road, which led north to Sycamore Church. There it would overwhelm the small 1st District of Columbia Cavalry and push on to Coggins Point and round up the cattle. Dearing was to move west along the Stage Road as soon as he heard the firing at Sycamore Church. The whole force would break camp at midnight and attack just before dawn.

Up in the Shenadoah Valley early the next day, 16 September, Tom Laws, the black man whom Sheridan's new scouts had found, took a load of vegetables into Winchester, with the general's note hidden in his mouth. He was not stopped, and he delivered the little ball of tinfoil to Rebecca Wright that morning, telling her that an important message was hidden inside, and that he would return for a reply before leaving town. "At first Miss Wright began to open the pellet nervously," Sheridan wrote, "but when told to be careful, and to preserve the foil as a wrapping for her answer, she proceeded slowly and carefully, and when the note appeared intact the messenger retired, remarking again that in the evening he would come for an answer.

"On reading my communication Miss Wright was much startled by the perils it involved, and hesitatingly consulted her mother, but her devoted loyalty soon silenced every other consideration, and the brave girl resolved to comply with my request, notwithstanding it might jeopardize her life."[10] She wrote an answer based on what the visiting Confederate officer had let slip the night before: "I have no communication whatever with the rebels, but will tell you what I know. The division of General Kershaw, and Cutshaw's artillery, twelve guns and men, General Anderson commanding, have been sent away, and no more are expected, as they cannot be spared from Richmond. I do not know how the troops are situated, but the force is much smaller than represented. I will take pleasure hereafter in learning all I can of their strength and position, and the bearer may call again."[11]

Her reply reached Sheridan that evening. "Miss Wright's answer proved of more value to me than she anticipated," he wrote, "for it not only quieted the conflicting reports concerning Anderson's corps, but was most important in showing positively that Kershaw was gone, and this circumstance led, three days later, to the battle of the Opequon, or Winchester as it has been officially called. Word to the effect that some of Early's troops were under orders to return to Petersburg, and would start back at the first favorable opportunity, had been communicated to me already from many sources, but we had not been able to ascertain the date for their departure. Now that they had actually started, I decided to wait before offering battle until Kershaw had gone so far as to preclude his return, feeling confident that my prudence would be justified by the improved chances of victory; and then, besides Mr. Stanton kept reminding me that positive success was necessary to counteract the political dissatisfaction existing in some of the Northern States. This course was advised and approved by General Grant, but even with his powerful backing it was difficult to resist the persistent pressure of those whose judgment, warped by their interests in the Baltimore and Ohio railroad, was often confused and misled by stories of scouts (sent out from Washington), averring that Kershaw and Fitzhugh Lee had returned to Petersburg, Breckinridge to southwestern Virginia, and at one time even maintaining that Early's whole army was east of the Blue Ridge and its commander himself at Gordonsville."[12]

Not long after receiving Rebecca Wright's reply, Sheridan received word to meet General Grant at Charlestown, and he immediately rode there from his headquarters at Clifton. Grant was already there when he rode up. "When Sheridan arrived," Grant wrote in his memoirs, "I asked him if he had a map showing the positions of his army and that of the enemy. He at once drew one out of his side pocket, showing all roads and streams, and the camps of the two armies. He said that if he had permission he would move so and so (pointing out how) against the Confederates, and that he could 'whip them.' Before starting I had drawn up a plan of campaign for Sheridan, which I had brought with me; but, seeing that he was so clear and so positive in his views and so confident of success, I said nothing about this and did not take it out of my pocket."[13]

"He pointed out so distinctly how each army lay; what he could do the moment he was authorized, and expressed such confidence of success," Grant wrote in his official report, "that I saw there were but two words of instructions necessary—Go in! For the conveniences of forage, the teams for supplying the army were kept at Harper's Ferry. I asked him if he could get out his teams and supplies in time to make an attack on the ensuing Tuesday morning [20 September]. His reply was, that he could before daylight on Monday. He was off promptly to time, and I may here add, that the result was such that I never since deemed it necessary to visit General Sheridan before giving him orders."[14]

While the two generals conferred under a giant oak at Charlestown they were being watched by men of Sheridan's army. A sergeant in the Vermont Brigade of the 6th Corps, which had been part of the Army of the Potomac until a couple of months before, recognized the visitor. "That's Grant," he told a companion. "I hate to see that old cuss around. When that old cuss is around there's sure to be a big fight on hand."[15]

1. *Official Records,* 43:II:83–84.

2. Ibid., 43:II:83.

3. Ulysses S. Grant, *Personal Memoirs of U. S. Grant* (New York, 1886), Vol. 2, 327.

4. *Official Records,* 42:II:816.

5. Edward Boykin, *Beefsteak Raid,* (New York, 1960), 212.

6. Philip H. Sheridan, *Personal Memoirs of P. H. Sheridan* (New York, 1888), Vol. 2, 1–4.

7. Jeffry D. Wert, *From Winchester to Cedar Creek: The Shenandoah Campaign of 1864* (Carlisle, Pa., 1987), 42.

8. Basler, ed., *The Collected Works of Abraham Lincoln,* 8:9, n. 1.

9. Sherman, *Memoirs,* 585.

10. Sheridan, *Memoirs,* 2:4–5.

11. Wert, *From Winchester to Cedar Creek,* 42.

12. Sheridan, *Memoirs,* 2:5.

13. Grant, *Memoirs,* 2:327–328.

14. Ibid., 2:583.

15. Bruce Catton, *Grant Takes Command* (Boston, 1968–1969), 363.

CHAPTER FOUR

I Gave the Order to Whip Him

16–19 September 1864

In the pre-dawn darkness of 16 September, Hampton's troopers groped forward toward Sycamore Church. Scouts found that the gap in the Union defenses where the road passed through on the way to Coggins Point had been blocked with felled trees. "The moon had set and, although the sky was cloudless, the night in the woods was very dark," wrote Rosser, commander of the center column. "My men were ordered to march in silence, but the road was hard and in the profound stillness of the night the tramp of the horses could be heard a long distance, and I knew it would be impossible to surprise the enemy so I made my arrangements to fight. I knew I would find a regiment of cavalry at Sycamore Church and I knew that every man of them would be in position and ready for me on my arrival. I brought up the 12th Virginia and gave orders to the commander, Colonel Massie, a very galant officer, to charge just as soon as he was challenged by the enemy." But no challenge came, no sign and countersign, in fact, no sound at all from the Federal defenses. "I was riding by the side of Colonel Massie," Rosser wrote, "telling him how to proceed in the event of his being able to dislodge the enemy, when as if by the flash of lightning, the front was all ablaze with musketry."[1] It was 4 a.m.

Two squadrons of the 12th Virginia charged down the road, but the 1st District of Columbia Cavalry was the best-armed regiment in either army, being equipped with the Henry repeating rifle, a forerunner of the Winchester. This weapon held fifteen bullets and could be fired as fast as the user could work a lever and pull the trigger. Only the darkness prevented the Union troopers from annihilating the two Rebel squadrons. The entire 12th Virginia then charged, using their revolvers to return the Federal fire, but again the Confederates were driven back. Then Rosser sent in the 7th Virginia in a dismounted skirmish line. Some of these Virginians worked around the flanks of the Union defenses while others dragged the felled trees out of the road, and still others returned the Yankee fire as best they could. While this was going on, Rosser formed the rest of his brigade, the 11th and 12th Virginia regiments and the 35th Virginia Battalion, for another charge. They pounded down the road with a Rebel yell, through the gap the 7th Virginia had cleared, and into the Federal camp. The Union commander, Major J. Stannard Baker, was struck on the head by a Confederate saber while trying to rally his men, and resistance soon disintegrated in the face of overwhelming numbers. The entire fight lasted only a half-hour. Very few Federals escaped. Many of those who did fled to the north to warn the guards of the cattle herd.

"The enemy had a strong position," Hampton wrote, "and the approaches to it being barricaded he had time to rally in the road around his camp where for some time he fought as stubbornly as I have ever seen him do. But the gallantry and determination of Rosser's men proved too much for him and he was completely routed, leaving his dead and wounded on the field and his camp in our hands."[2]

Rosser's men looted the camp, including a couple of sutlers' wagons stuffed with cigars, cakes, cheese, pickles, and other luxuries that were as rare to the Confederates as beef itself. Several hundred horses and mules were captured, as well as plenty of blankets and most of the Federals. So were a couple of hundred Henry rifles, but these were of limited use to the Rebels, since the Confederacy lacked the copper needed to manufacture the brass cartridges they used. Off to the west could be heard the sound of firing from Rooney Lee's division and his two guns. From the east came the sound of more firing, indicating that Dearing was in action.

The cattle guards at Coggins Point had heard the firing a few miles to

the south, around Sycamore Church, but did not know what to make
of it, nor of the more distant firing to the east and west. Something was
up, but so far it did not seem to involve them. Their commander, Captain
Henry H. Gregg of the 13th Pennsylvania Cavalry, had just completed
his morning rounds of his picket posts and dismounted for breakfast
when he heard a sudden burst of nearby gunfire and saw a large group
of men and horses running toward him from the south. He immediately
sent an orderly to alert Captain Nathaniel Richardson, who was the
commissary of subsistence of the armies operating against Richmond.

"At twenty minutes before 5 o'clock Friday morning I was awake,"
Richardson wrote. "Light was just beginning to glimmer in the east,
when an orderly reported to me from Captain Gregg, saying that the
picket-line had been attacked at three points. He further stated that Captain Gregg would again report to me, if it was necessary to move off the
cattle. I arose and instantly called upon the chief herder to get up, informing him that the picket-line had been attacked. I then went through
a large portion of the camp ordering the men to get up and saddle their
horses. I then gave orders to saddle my horse, and in ten minutes from
the time of receiving word from Captain Gregg, was at the corral. I
ordered the watch to leave the corral, and saddle their horses. I came
back to the camp, distant thirty rods, and heard shouting and sharp
firing. I forthwith ordered the fence pulled down and the cattle driven
out. I then turned to go to the corral again when I heard the yell of a
charge, looked around and saw many hundred mounted men charging
up to my camp and upon the men who were just leaving it."[3]

These were Rosser's men. But as they came within carbine range
Rosser called a halt and sent forward one man with a handkerchief tied
to his saber to demand a surrender. Sergeant Albert Kenyon, in charge of
the Union picket line, refused. Rosser ordered the 35th Virginia Cavalry
Battalion, better known as White's Comanches, to charge, which they
did, scattering the pickets in wild flight. Sergeant Kenyon was shot
through the neck, and Captain Gregg, who had just ridden up, was
captured after having his revolver knocked out of his hand by a Rebel
saber.

Then the Confederates caught sight of the cattle. "When I came in
sight of the beeves they were running rapidly in the direction of the
James River," Rosser wrote. "The herders had thrown down the fence
of the corral and firing pistols and yelling, Indian fashion, had stampeded
the cattle and they were running like mad. I ordered the 7th Virginia,
which had just overtaken me, to run their horses until they got in front
of the herd, then to turn up it and stop it. This order was not easily
obeyed for the young steers ran like buffalo, and it was requiring too

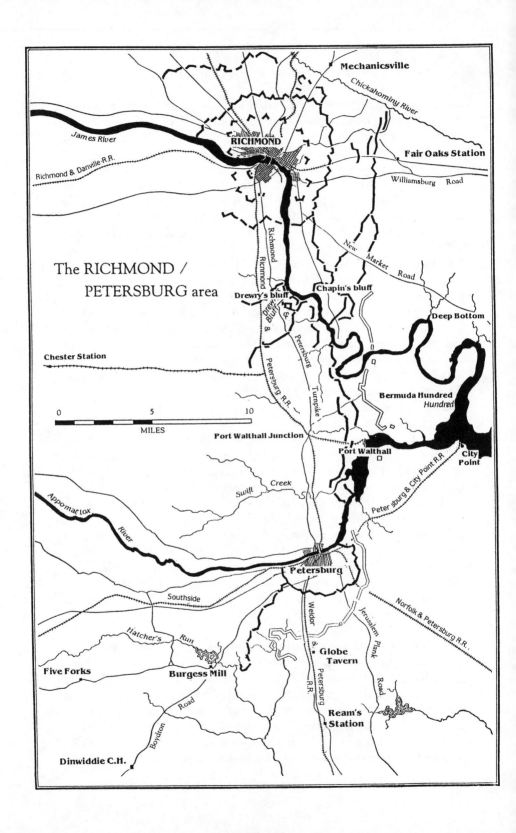

The RICHMOND /
PETERSBURG area

Mechanicsville

Chickahominy River

James River

RICHMOND

Richmond & Danville R.R.

Fair Oaks Station

Williamsburg Road

New Market Road

Richmond & Petersburg R.R.

Drewry's bluff

Chapin's bluff

Deep Bottom

Drew. Bluff &

Petersburg Turnpike

Petersburg R.R.

Chester Station

Bermuda Hundred
Hundred

0   5   10

MILES

Port Walthall Junction

Port Walthall

City
Point

Swift   Creek

Petersburg & City Point R.R.

Appomattox   River

Petersburg

Southside

Norfolk & Petersburg R.R.

Weldon

Jerusalem Plank Road

Hatcher's   Run

Five Forks

Burgess Mill

Globe
Tavern

Petersburg R.R.

Road

Ream's
Station

Boydton   Road

Dinwiddie C.H.

much of jaded cavalry to force it into a race like this, but after running a mile or so the steers slackened their pace and the cavalry was thus able to get in front of them, and then to round them up and quiet them, turn them about and start them to the pens of their new masters on the Dixie side of the line."[4]

The Federal cattle guards were routed. Captain Richardson, the commissary, recorded the scene: "The enemy came up shooting and firing with great vehemence, and driving before them numbers of the First District of Columbia Cavalry and the Thirteenth Pennsylvania Cavalry. By the time the fence was pulled down and twenty cattle out, mules and dismounted horses, mingled with retreating cavalrymen and herders, were fleeing from the enemy. The enemy were nearly around the whole herd. I saw that all was lost. With the chief herder and several remaining men I now joined in the retreat, the enemy firing at us and following closely. In half a mile we struck the middle Prince George Court-House road; I then started for General Meade's headquarters. By going to the left I had passed most of the retreating force who followed close in my rear, a few in advance. Within a mile we met another strong force of the enemy charging up to us and firing upon us. I wheeled my horse and came back a quarter of a mile; the enemy pressing up, I turned into the woods . . . Not over fifteen minutes [elapsed] from the time I received word that the lines had been attacked, until my camp, with the cattle, were in possession of the enemy. Some of my men had not time to saddle their horses before they were prisoners. The enemy charged in wide and deep column upon the camp and herd, surrounding them on all sides. Outside of and independent of this line of attack, it held the telegraph road running to Fort Powhatan by the James River. The middle road running from the telegraph road to the stage road and the stage road leading back to the telegraph road."[5]

By 6 a.m., with the help of a few captured drovers and some herd dogs that Sergeant Shadburne had provided, the Rebels turned the cattle down Walls Road toward Sycamore Church, prodding them into position with their sabers like picadors at a bullfight. All together there was enough beef in that herd to feed Lee's entire army for forty days. As the Rebels and the steers disappeared down the road, Federal gunboats on the James, finally made aware of what was happening ashore, began to lob giant exploding shells at them. But that only served to hasten their exit.

Other Federals were beginning to get word that a large Confederate force was loose in the army's rear. At 5 a.m. a courier from the commander of the 11th Pennsylvania Cavalry brought word of Rooney Lee's approach to Brigadier General August Kautz, commander of the Cavalry Division of the Army of the James, who was in charge of the defenses and pickets of the Union rear. The telegraph line to City Point was cut, but he sent word to Meade's headquarters, as well as to Brigadier General Henry Davies, in temporary command of the 2nd Cavalry Division of the Army of the Potomac, the only cavalry left to Meade when the rest had been transferred with Sheridan to the Shenadoah Valley. But Kautz did not yet suspect the size of the Rebel force or their true objective. Kautz got out of bed, dressed, and rode to the sound of firing to find out just what was going on. Finding the Confederates to be in greater force than the 11th Pennsylvania could handle, he sent the 3rd New York Cavalry to block the Rebel advance. At 7 a.m. he sent off a dispatch to Davies' adjutant. "I am fearful that the First District of Columbia may be entrapped," he said, but still did not mention the cattle herd. To Major General Andrew A. Humphreys, the capable chief of staff of the Army of the Potomac, Kautz sent a message saying, "I believe the enemy to have planned the capture of the First District of Columbia Cavalry, which I think was their object, and I fear they have succeeded."[6]

Humphreys, however, was sure that the Rebel cavalry, reported to be anywhere from 6,000 to 25,000 strong, would make a dash on City Point. That sleepy little town had, since the arrival of Grant and his two armies, turned into a great port. It had more than a mile of wharves to accommodate the daily average of 40 steamboats, 75 sailing vessels, and 100 barges. There were huge warehouses for the quartermaster, ordnance, and commissary departments, bakeries, blacksmith shops, and on the bluff overlooking the waterfront was a hospital, which could handle 10,000 patients and covered 200 acres. All of this was bound to be a tempting target for the Rebels and something that the Federals could not afford to let them seize, even temporarily. The commander of the Union post at City Point received a warning from Brigadier General Marsena Patrick, Provost Marshal General of the Army of the Potomac: "The enemy has broken through our line near Sycamore Church and may dash into City Point. Place all the troops under your control in the best possible position to defend the depot."[7]

Batteries of light artillery were sent galloping for City Point from the front lines farther west, and signals were made to the gunboats in the James River to come to the defense of the army's base. Stevedores from the wharves, prisoners from the stockade, walking wounded from the hospital, all were alerted for possible duty in the defenses, and anxious messages shot back and forth from one Union headquarters to another as something like panic swept over the rear areas of the Federal army. Humphreys sent for a brigade of infantry and a battery of light artillery to move to Prince George Court House and block the road to Meade's headquarters, but, he said, "at the rate they moved we should have had no assistance from them if [Rooney] Lee had tried his hand at picking us up."[8]

In fact, Rooney Lee had run into the 3rd New York Cavalry, which put up a stout defense until the Confederate horse artillery was brought into action. Then, according to plan, the Rebels had turned to the east down the Stage Road, scattering a squadron of the 11th Pennsylvania Cavalry before them. When they reached Walls Road they turned to the south and formed a rear guard for Rosser and his plunder of cattle, prisoners, and captured wagons. Among the prisoners was Major Baker, commander of the 1st District of Columbia, with a saber wound that had almost split his skull. He was tended by a captured Union surgeon.

Dearing's Brigade had run into a small battalion of the 1st District of Columbia Cavalry at Cocke's Mill. These Federals, unaware of what had befallen the rest of their regiment, retreated toward Sycamore Church. "But in the meantime," the chaplain of the Union regiment wrote, "the enemy, having secured their prisoners and plundered the camp, had formed a semicircle across the road, and dressed in our uniform, and were mistaken for our own men. Successful resistance was now impossible and having done all that brave men could do, like men [the Federals] yielded to their fate."[9] Rosser's and Rooney Lee's forces, with the cattle and prisoners, hurried down Walls Road while Dearing's Brigade turned around and headed back down the Hines Road, the way it had come, to take over the lead of the column where the two roads converged. Sergeant Shadburne counted the captured cattle and reported that there were 2,485 steers and one cow. Hampton divided them into four small herds with short intervals in between to make them easier to control—and to defend, once the Federals got organized for a counterattack.

At 8:30 a.m. Kautz sent off another message to Davies' adjutant, saying that "the attack has developed itself as a foray on the cattle herd and the First District of Columbia Cavalry, although nothing definite has been heard from that direction." He added that he "did not know that the cattle were there until this morning." Twenty minutes later he told Humphreys, "I cannot tell how much force the enemy have, but I suspect they must have two or three regiments . . . I suspect the whole movement to be the capture of the cattle and the 1st District Cavalry."[10] But at 11:30 a.m. he reported to Humphreys a rumor that the Confederate raiders numbered 14,000, while he had only about 500 men and two pieces of artillery with him. Nevertheless, he moved on down the

Powhatan Road toward Sycamore Church, while Meade directed Davies to move south from the main Union line down the Jerusalem Plank Road to head the Rebels off.

At 10 a.m. Hampton's column crossed the Blackwater at the reconstructed Cook's Bridge. From there he sent Rosser's Brigade and the horse artillery back the way they had come the day before, to old Captain Belches' Mill on the Jerusalem Plank Road, for he had anticipated that Davies would come that way in an attempt to block his path. Rosser was to keep the Federals at bay while Rooney Lee's troopers took charge of the cattle, protected by Dearing's Brigade as advance guard, and turned south at a fork five miles beyond the Blackwater to follow a more southerly route back to their lines. When the last of his troopers crossed Cook's Bridge, Rooney Lee ordered the engineers to blow it up, but they had not brought any demolitions with them. They tried to burn it, but the wood was too green or too wet. So they had to dismantle the bridge, throwing the pieces into the stream, and they were barely finished when the head of Kautz's pursuit reached the far bank. The two forces exchanged shots across the river until the tail of the Rebel column disappeared from sight.

Rosser sent White's Comanches ahead with the horse artillery. They were to hold Belches' Mill until the rest of his brigade could get there at a less wearing pace. "White moved off with his usual promptness," Rosser remembered, "and reached the point indicated just as the enemy got there; but White was able to secure the desired position, which by nature was a strong one, and by dismounting his men he was able to hold it against a force much larger than his own. There was a large millpond on his left and a swamp on his right and the plank road was the only avenue by which the enemy could attack him."[11] Davies had brought about 2,100 cavalrymen and six pieces of horse artillery down the Jerusalem Plank Road, followed by a brigade of infantry, and dismounted Federal troopers were working their way through the swamp on White's right flank when Rosser arrived with the rest of his Laurel Brigade.

A few miles to the southeast, Hampton and the main Confederate column were just reaching a small stream at Neblitt's Mill when they heard the sound of firing at Belches'. Hampton sent a detachment under Colonel Miller ahead two miles to Hawkinsville, where it was to turn to the northwest up the Jerusalem Plank Road to reinforce Rosser, and Dearing was to follow with his entire brigade. Just after Miller's and Dearing's men rode off, the cattle, who had not had a bite or a drink since being captured, stampeded for Neblitt's mill stream and pond.

Rounding them up delayed Hampton's departure with Rooney's Lee's troopers, but about the time the troopers and dogs had the herd back on the road, a courier from Rosser rode up to Hampton to report that he could not hold on much longer, for the Yankees had gotten around his right flank and were plastering his line with artillery. Hampton sent back word that Miller and Dearing were already on the way, then, turning the herd and plunder over to Major Reid Venable of his staff, protected by one regiment, he led the rest of Rooney Lee's division to join the fight.

The Federals, meanwhile, kept threatening Rosser's right, and their artillery was superior to the Confederate guns. Rosser's men were barely holding on when Miller's and Dearing's reinforcements arrived. These stiffened the Southern resistance, and when Hampton arrived about sunset he ordered Rooney Lee to charge. "Hampton rode down in front of the line," one Virginia trooper remembered, "making inquiries, giving words of cheer, 'Keep cool, boys! We're going in fast! Ride 'em down! Cut 'em down!' His moving figure could be seen against the crimson sky from which the sun had just disappeared. The guns were flashing in front of him, and behind him, and the meteor-like shells were passing over his head. Such was the scene on which fell the curtain of night. It was a scene typical of the picturesque Hampton who moved securely amidst the fire of battle."[12] With a Rebel yell and the blare of bugles, Rooney's troopers charged forward and drove Davies' Federals back, ending the battle. Hampton followed only far enough to get his men back onto the road on which they had moved east the day before, and, leaving a rear guard near Ebenezer Church, he put his men into camp at Wilkinson's Bridge over Rowanty Creek.

Kautz finally got his men across the Blackwater River, but at about 9 p.m. they ran into a Confederate outpost just east of Hawkinsville. Unable to see what he was up against, and fearing that it was Hampton's main column, Kautz fell back a couple of miles and called a halt until morning. That night Major Venable got the cattle across the upper reaches of the Nottoway River at Freeman's Ford and on westward to bed down in a meadow near Stony Creek. The next morning, Venable, with the cattle, was reunited with Hampton and the main force and they made their way up the Flat Foot Road to the Boydton Plank Road and back to the Confederate lines.

On that same seventeenth day of September, Grant, returning from his visit to Sheridan, met with John W. Garrett, the president of the Baltimore & Ohio Railroad. Garrett wanted to know when Sheridan was going to drive Early away so that he could safely operate his line again. Grant told him it should be safe within four days. Again Grant bypassed Washington, and that night he stepped off the train at Burlington, N.J., where his wife had recently settled with their four children. "They say I live here," he remarked to two men on the platform, "but I don't know where." The local policeman escorted him to his new home, pestering him with questions about the army along the way. It was well after midnight when he knocked on the door. His wife, Julia, came out on the upstairs porch and asked softly, "Is that you, Ulyss?"[13]

Grant was very close to his family, and his enforced absences from them were not easy for him to bear. Julia and the children had recently visited the general at City Point, staying on a steamboat in the river. "The morning after their arrival," Horace Porter wrote, "when I stopped into the general's tent, I found him in his shirt-sleeves engaged in a rough-and-tumble wrestling-match with the two older boys. He had become red in the face, and seemed nearly out of breath from the exertion. The lads had just tripped him up, and he was on his knees on the floor grappling with the youngsters, and joining in their merry laughter, as if he were a boy again himself. I had several despatches in my hand, and when he saw that I had come on business, he disentangled himself after some difficulty from the young combatants, rose to his feet, brushed the dust off his knees with his hand, and said in a sort of apologetic manner: 'Ah, you know my weaknesses—my children and my horses.'"[14]

That same day, Captain Thomas N. Conrad, chaplain of the 3rd Virginia Cavalry, led a small team of secret agents out of Richmond heading for Washington to explore the possibilities of capturing President Abraham Lincoln and spiriting him across the Potomac. Conrad carried a letter from Confederate secretary of war James Seddon directing Lieutenant Colonel John S. Mosby, commanding a battalion of partisans in northern Virginia, to "aid and facilitate the movements of Captain Conrad."[15] Lieutenant Charles H. Cawood, commanding a secret Signal Corps base in northern Virginia, was also directed to cooperate.

Lincoln, that day, was answering Sherman's report that the governor of Georgia might pay him a visit. "I feel great interest in the subjects of your despatch mentioning corn and Sorghum & a contemplated visit to you," he said.[16] That evening, Sherman replied: "I will keep the Department fully advised of all developments as connected with the subject in which you feel so interested. A Mr. Wright, former member of Congress from Rome Ga. and a Mr. King of Marietta are now going between Gov Brown and myself. I have said that some of the people of Georgia are now engaged in rebellion begun in error and perpetuated in pride; but that Georgia can now save herself from the devastation of war preparing for her, only by withdrawing her quota out of the confederate army, and aiding me to repel Hood from the border of the State; in which event instead of desolating the land, as we progress I will keep our men to the high roads and commons, and pay for the corn and meat we need and take. I am fully conscious of the delicate nature of such assertions, but it would be a magnificent stroke of policy, if I could without wasting a foot of ground or of principle arouse the latent enmity to Jeff Davis, of Georgia. The people do not hestitate to say, that Mr. Stevens [Confederate vice president and a Georgian] was, and is, a Union man at heart, and they feel that Jeff Davis will not trust him or let him have a share in his government."[17]

As the summer of 1864 had worn on without obvious successes by Federal arms, important Republicans had grown fearful that Lincoln could not be reelected. One group, the radical wing of the party, had even gone so far as to nominate its own candidate for president. This had been Major General John Charles Fremont, who had been the Republican party's first presidential candidate back in 1856. But after the victories at Mobile Bay and Atlanta, and now that the Democrats had adopted a platform so blatantly favoring peace at any price, the various Republican factions began to return to the fold. Fremont announced, that seventeenth day of September, that he was withdrawing his name from the list of candidates, although he still considered that Lincoln's administration "has been politically, militarily, and financially a failure, and that its necessary continuance is a cause of regret for the country."[18] He preferred it, however, to the alternative of seeing McClellan elected and the Union dissolved.

Then Lincoln wrote a note to his postmaster general, Montgomery Blair: "You have generously said to me more than once that whenever your resignation could be a relief to me it was at my disposal. The time has come. You very well know that this proceeds from no dissatisfaction of mine with you personally or officially."[19] Blair, along with his father, an influential politician since Andrew Jackson's day, and his brother, Frank, Jr., who was simultaneously a member of Congress and a corps commander in Sherman's armies, had become bitter political enemies of Fremont and his radical backers. While Fremont always denied that there was any deal involved, the dismissal of Montgomery Blair from his cabinet was obviously Lincoln's answer to Fremont's withdrawal and an effort to heal the divisions in his party. "In the beginning of this quarrel," Lincoln's secretaries later wrote, "the Blairs were unquestionably right; but being unjustly assailed by the Radicals, the natural pugnacity of their dispositions would not permit them to rest firmly planted on their own ground. They entered upon a course of hostility that was at first confined to their factious enemies, but which gradually broadened and extended till it landed them both in the Democratic party. Montgomery Blair was doubtless unconscious of his progress in that direction. He thought himself the most zealous of Republicans until the moment that he declared himself the most zealous of Democrats."[20] But for the time being, Blair accepted his dismissal with good grace and went home to Maryland to campaign for Lincoln's reelection. "The President has, I think, given himself, and me too, an unnecessary mortification in this matter," he told his wife, "but then I am not the best judge and I am sure he acts from the best motives."[21]

Grant found it difficult to get any rest at his new home in New Jersey on the eighteenth. Word had quickly spread throughout the town that he was there. By the time he had finished his breakfast and had lit his first cigar, a crowd had formed around his house. So Julia invited her neighbors in to meet her husband. The general, who less that four years before had been an unknown ex-captain working in his family's leather goods store in Galena, Illinois, did not like being a celebrity. "The scene at the house on Sunday morning," he wrote to Julia after returning to City Point, "was what I had to go through the whole way. It is but little pleasure now for me to travel."[22]

Brief showers of rain fell in the Shenadoah Valley that day, where Sheridan was busy preparing his forces and his orders for the offensive he had promised Grant. He planned to move toward Newtown, on the Valley Turnpike south of Winchester, to cut Early's communications to Richmond and force him into a fight. Early was aware of his vulnerability in that direction but felt it was a risk he had to take. "The relative positions which we occupied rendered my communications to the rear very much exposed," he wrote, "but I could not avoid it without giving up the lower Valley. The object of my presence there was to keep up a threatening attitude towards Maryland and Pennsylvania, and prevent the use of the Baltimore & Ohio Railroad, and the Chesapeake and Ohio Canal, as well as to keep as large a force as possible from Grant's army to defend the Federal Capital. Had Sheridan, by a prompt movement, thrown his whole force on the line of my communications, I would have been compelled to attempt to cut my way through, as there was no escape for me to the right or left, and my force was too weak to cross the Potomac while he was in my rear. I knew my danger, but I could occupy no other position that would have enabled me to accomplish the desired object.

"If I had moved up the Valley at all, I could not have stopped short of New Market, for between that place and the country, in which I was, there was no forage for my horses; and this would have enabled the enemy to resume the use of the railroad and canal, and return all the troops from Grant's army to him. Being compelled to occupy the position where I was, and being aware of its danger as well as apprised of the fact that very great odds were opposed to me, my only resource was to use my forces so as to display them at different points with great rapidity, and thereby keep up the impression that they were much larger than they really were. The events of the last month had satisfied me that the commander opposed to me was without enterprise, and possessed an excessive caution which amounted to timidity. If it was his policy to produce the impression that his force was too weak to fight me, he did not succeed, but if it was to convince me that he was not an energetic commander, his strategy was a complete success, and subsequent events have not changed my opinion."[23]

Supplies of rations and ammunition arrived at Sheridan's camp from Harper's Ferry during the day and were distributed to the men. Orders were issued for excess baggage to be sent to the rear, and all units were to be ready to march by 3 p.m. But after the men had taken down their dog-house tents and filled their knapsacks and cartridge boxes new orders were announced. The army would not march until 2 a.m. the next day. Grumbling, no doubt, about indecision in high places, the men pitched their tents again and cooked their suppers.

The cause of this sudden change of plan was a message Sheridan received that afternoon from Brigadier General William Woods Averell, commander of his 2nd Cavalry Division. While the rest of Sheridan's army was in camp around Berryville, east of Opequon Creek, Averell's division was farther north, attempting to guard the Baltimore & Ohio from Martinsburg. His message to Sheridan indicated that Early, with a brigade of cavalry and two divisions of infantry, was heading his way. Early had heard that Averell's men were at work repairing the Baltimore & Ohio, and, not considering his cavalry to be strong enough to push them back and drive them away, he moved with half of his infantry, leaving the rest with Fitz Lee's cavalry to watch Sheridan. Major Henry Kyd Douglas, on Ramseur's staff said, "Such rashness seemed to invite disaster; it was simply bravado, and I have never seen any satisfactory defense of it. I remember well the anxiety felt at our Headquarters when we knew of this movement, and it would have been greater had we known that General Grant was then at Harper's Ferry in consultation with General Sheridan and giving him his orders. The air seemed to have a sulphurous smell . . . Genl Early, in these movements seems to rely too much upon the caution and timidity of Sheridan."[24]

"This considerably altered the state of affairs," Sheridan wrote, "and I now decided to change my plan and attack at once the two divisions remaining about Winchester and Stephenson's depot, and later, the two sent to Martinsburg; the disjointed state of the enemy giving me an opportunity to take him in detail, unless the Martinsburg column should be returned by forced marches."[25]

However, forced marches were just what Early ordered. At the telegraph office in Martinsburg, from which he had driven Averell and the repair crews, he found evidence that Grant had paid a visit to Sheridan "and I expected an early move."[26] The Confederates were just as aware as the Federals of what Grant's presence meant. "This made us, private soldiers, feel very bad," wrote a Georgia infantryman, "for we knew if it were true, we would soon have trouble."[27] By the time the Rebels went into bivouac that night, Rodes' Division had reached Stephenson's Depot and Major General John Gordon's, Bunker Hill. Nevertheless, fourteen miles separated Gordon's position from Major General Dodson Ramseur's division, camped east of Winchester on the road to Berryville. The Southern cavalry was even further separated. Meanwhile, Sheridan employed one of Grant's favorite tricks by using his regimental bands to disguise the noise of his preparations for movement. "The enemy are having lots of music in their camp," a Virginia trooper recorded in his diary that day. "I never heard so many bands playing at one time."[28]

Major General John M. Schofield had graduated from West Point the same year as Sheridan, 1853. He was the commander of the Department of the Ohio, one of the three departments that constituted Sherman's Military Division of the Mississippi. Although his contribution to Sherman's field army consisted of only two divisions of the 23rd Corps plus a cavalry division, he was also responsible for all Union forces in Kentucky and east Tennessee. With the pause in active operations after the capture of Atlanta, Sherman had allowed him to return to these areas to look after their administration. On the eighteenth he met in Louisville with Brevet Major General Stephen G. Burbridge, commander of the District of Kentucky.

There Burbridge gained Schofield's permission for a mounted raid on Saltville, in southwestern Virginia. This place was the South's main source of salt, which was vital to the war effort as a preservative for meat. Without that salt the Confederate troops would be even more poorly fed than they were. Burbridge had started out on just such a raid back in June but he had turned back when he had learned that Confederate brigadier general John Hunt Morgan had beaten him to the punch by launching his last raid into Kentucky. Burbridge had caught up with Morgan and defeated him badly, driving him back over the mountains, but the salt works had been spared Union attention for three months. This time Burbridge and his subordinate, Brigadier General Nathaniel McLean, were to take a division of 5,000 cavalry and mounted infantry from Mount Sterling, Kentucky. Also, Brigadier General Alvan C. Gillem would lead his brigade of cavalry from the Army of the Cumberland—the troops who had killed Morgan—toward the same objective from eastern Tennessee. Gillem would be joined by a small division of dismounted cavalry and heavy artillerymen serving as infantry who were drawn from Schofield's garrisons in Tennessee.

Major General Sterling Price's three newly reorganized divisions of Confederate cavalry crossed from Arkansas into Price's home state of Missouri the next day, 19 September. It was the day before the former governor's 55th birthday. Brigadier General Joseph O. "Jo" Shelby commanded the left, three brigades moving through the Ozark Mountains. Major General John S. Marmaduke commanded two brigades on the right, near the Mississippi River. Major General James S. Fagan commanded the three brigades in the center column, escorting the rickety train of supply wagons, a thousand head of beef cattle, and acting-governor Reynolds, who had been in exile in Texas. Major General William S. Rosecrans, the commander of the Union army's Department of Missouri, later wrote of this time that "Rebel agents, amnesty oath-takers, recruits, sympathizers, O.A.K.'s, and traitors of every hue and stripe had warmed into life at the approach of the great invasion."[29]

The attention of the Federal commanders west of the Mississippi was temporarily diverted from Price's invasion, however, by an attack at Cabin Creek in Indian Territory—now Oklahoma—that same day by a brigade of 800 Confederate Cherokees, Creeks, and Seminoles and a brigade of 1,200 Texans upon a Union train of 300 government and sutlers' wagons out of Fort Scott, Kansas. The train's 600 defenders were scattered by a pre-dawn attack, and the Confederates captured the wagons, along with 740 mules and $1,500,000 worth of guns, ammunition, medicine, clothing, boots, shoes, and food that had been intended for the soldiers and refugee Indians at Fort Gibson.

President Lincoln was writing to General Sherman again that day: "The State election of Indiana occurs on the 11th. of Ocotber, and the loss of it to the friends of the Government would go far towards losing the whole Union cause. The bad effect upon the November election, and especially the giving the State Government to those who will oppose the war in every possible way, are too much to risk, if it can possibly be avoided. The draft proceeds, notwithstanding its strong tendency to lose us the State. Indiana is the only important State, voting in October, whose soldiers cannot vote in the field. Any thing you can safely do to let her soldiers, or any part of them, go home and vote at the State election, will be greatly in point. They need not remain for the Presidential election, but may return to you at once. This is, in no sense, an order, but is merely intended to impress you with the importance, to the army itself, of your doing all you safely can, yourself being the judge of what you can safely do."[30]

It was on that same nineteenth day of September that the herd of captured cattle was paraded through Petersburg to the delight of sidewalks full of civilian spectators waving handkerchiefs and flags. That evening Grant returned to City Point. He was not happy when he heard what had occurred in his absence. The theft of the cattle herd remained a sore subject with him for quite a while. Some days later a visiting politician asked him when he expected to starve Lee out and capture Richmond. "Never," he replied, "if our armies continue to supply him with beef-cattle."[31] But on the results of his trip he was far more sanguine. "I ordered Sheridan to move out and whip Early," he told his staff. "I presume the actual form of the order was to move out and attack him," one of the officers replied. "No," Grant said, "I mean just what I say: I gave the order to whip him."[32]

---

1. Boykin, *Beefsteak Raid*, 227.
2. *Official Records*, 42:I:945.
3. Ibid., 42:I:28.
4. Boykin, *Beefsteak Raid*, 237.
5. *Official Records*, 42:I:28–29.
6. Ibid., 42:II:873–874.
7. Ibid., 42:II:853–854.
8. Boykin, *Beefsteak Raid*, 250.
10. *Official Records*, 42:II:875–877.
11. Boykin, *Beefsteak Raid*, 259.
12. Ibid., 267.

13. Ishbell Ross, *The General's Wife: The Life of Mrs. Ulysses S. Grant* (New York, 1959), 173. This source indicates that this visit occurred "soon after the reelection of Lincoln," meaning, no doubt, the trip that began on 17 November (see chapter 32). However, Catton's narrative in *Grant Takes Command* places Grant's first visit to his Burlington residence after his September visit to Sheridan, and this is confirmed in Grant's memoirs (2:328–329), and by a telegram from Grant to Halleck in the *Official Records*, 43:II:96.

14. Porter, *Campaigning With Grant*, 283.

15. William A. Tidwell, with James O. Hall and David Winfred Gaddy, *Come Retribution: The Confederate Secret Service and the Assassination of Lincoln* (Jackson, Miss., 1988), 258.

16. Basler, ed., *The Collected Works of Abraham Lincoln*, 8:9.

17. Ibid., 8:9–10, n. 1.

18. Nicolay and Hay, *Abraham Lincoln*, 9:43–44.

19. Ibid., 9:340–341.

20. Ibid., 9:335.

21. Foote, *The Civil War*, 3:559–560.

22. Catton, *Grant Takes Command*, 363.

23. Jubal Anderson Early, *War Memoirs* (Bloomington, Ind., 1960), 415.

24. Henry Kyd Douglas, *I Rode With Stonewall* (Chapel Hill, 1940), 295–296.

25. Sheridan, *Memoirs*, 2:10.

26. Early, *War Memoirs*, 419.

27. Wert, *From Winchester to Cedar Creek*, 45.

28. Ibid.

29. Castell, *General Sterling Price*, 208.

30. Basler, ed., *The Collected Works of Abraham Lincoln*, 8:11.

31. Porter, *Campaigning With Grant*, 299.

32. Ibid., 298.

CHAPTER FIVE

We Did Not Know Phil Sheridan

19 September 1864

Sheridan's Union soldiers were roused at 1 a.m. on 19 September 1864. An hour later Brigadier General James Harrison Wilson's 3rd Division of cavalry led the way westward toward the crossings of Opequon Creek and Early's position around Winchester. Wilson was only 27 and just four years out of West Point, but he was one of the bright young men who had been selected to bring aggressive leadership to the Federal cavalry. Before that he had been an engineer officer on the staffs of several high-ranking generals, including Grant.

Behind Wilson's horsemen came Sheridan's infantry, artillery and wagons. There were three corps of them, of disparate sizes and experience. The 6th Corps contained around 12,000 men. It had always been a part of the Army of the Potomac, from McClellan's first campaign, until it had been detached to defend Washington from Early's raid a few weeks before. Hard campaigning, expired enlistments, and heavy casualties from the Wilderness to Petersburg had worn it down to little

73

more than half the strength it had had in May. Its discipline had fallen off and its men were weary, but they were battle-hardened veterans—among the best in the Union army. They had been commanded since Spotsylvania by Major General Horatio G. Wright, then 44 years old and an 1841 graduate of West Point. Sheridan's confidence in them is indicated by the fact that they were at the head of the infantry column.

The 19th Corps also contained around 12,000 men, but this included a brigade that had been left behind to guard Harper's Ferry. This corps had spent most of the war garrisoning Louisiana, where it had recently been part of Major General Nathaniel Banks' unsuccessful expedition up the Red River. Its soldiers were not used to the large field battles of the Virginia campaigns, but they were used to success over their Confederate counterparts, despite the recent debacle on the Red. They were commanded now by Brevet Major General William H. Emory, who had been a division commander in the corps until it had been transferred to Virginia just in time to help chase Early from Washington back to the Valley.

The remaining force of infantry in Sheridan's Army of the Shenandoah was properly known as the Army of West Virginia, but was now commonly called the 8th Corps, although its two divisions had not actually been part of that corps since the summer before, when the Department of West Virginia had been split off from the Middle Department. This small force numbered perhaps 7,000 men, counting one of its five brigades that was left behind to guard the wagons, and was made up of units that had spent most of the war garrisoning various parts of the Shenandoah Valley and West Virginia. They had been defeated more often than not by their Confederate counterparts, due more to inadequate leadership than to any failings on their own part. Their abilities and morale were suspect, and they brought up the rear this day. Since Sheridan's arrival they had come under the command of Brevet Major General George Crook, 35, who had been their most successful division commander, and who had been a friend of Sheridan's since they had been at West Point together.

By 4:30 a.m. Wilson's troopers reached the ford across the Opequon. On the other side of the creek the road led through a narrow, two-mile-long canyon, and Wilson's orders were to clear that canyon and gain a foothold on the high ground beyond. The commander of his leading brigade, Brigadier General John B. McIntosh, sent the 2nd New York Cavalry into the gorge, partially mounted and partially dismounted, where it surprised and routed the pickets of the 23rd North Carolina Infantry, wounding and capturing their colonel. The rest of the Confederate regiment regrouped and fell back slowly, and McIntosh added the

5th New York Cavalry to the attack, pushing the North Carolinians beyond the canyon, where they joined the rest of their brigade, Brigadier General R. D. Johnston's, behind breastworks made of fence rails on a slight elevation. Johnston sent off a courier to inform his division commander, Major General Stephen Dodson Ramseur, of this Union advance.

Ramseur was a young man for an infantry division commander, only 27. He had graduated from West Point in the same class with Wilson and had succeeded to divisional command at Spotsylvania in May. As commander of the only Confederate division remaining between the Federals and Winchester, he had seriously blundered by not blocking the canyon along the road from Berryville with a larger force than the 23rd North Carolina. His small cork had been easily popped by Wilson's troopers, and now most of Sheridan's army was about to funnel through that narrow canyon and fall upon his lone division. However, Sheridan had also erred in not sending his infantry along more than that one road. By the time they all got to the front Early had reunited his army.

Ramseur notified Early of the Union attack and sent Brigadier General John Pegram's brigade of Virginians to reinforce Johnston's North Carolinians, but they were too little too late. The sun was above the horizon when, about 6 a.m., McIntosh's two New York cavalry regiments advanced against Johnston's defenses. The North Carolinians staggered the troopers with a volley, and artillery fire from a nearby Southern battery drove the Federals back. While they regrouped, McIntosh sent the 18th Pennsylvania forward in a mounted charge, supported by the fire of a battery of horse artillery. The Pennsylvanians were also driven back, losing their commander, but they reformed and came on again with the two New York regiments and caught Pegram's Brigade only partially deployed.

The Virginians broke and ran, and then so did the North Carolinians, back across an open field under a withering fire from the Union horse artillery and the repeating carbines of the Union cavalry. "It is a mistery to me how we got out," one Tarheel wrote, and Ramseur admitted that his men "did some tall running."[1] Ramseur sent the 57th North Carolina forward from his remaining brigade and then rode among his retreating men swinging a borrowed rifle at any who refused to stop. He and his staff and brigade officers managed to halt the rout in some woods near the Valley Turnpike, about 500 yards behind their starting point. Then they repulsed the pursuing Federals and drove them back to their starting point near the canyon.

Just then, about 7 a.m., Sheridan arrived at the front. He stopped to tell McIntosh, who had been wounded in the charge of the 18th Pennsylvania and would lose his leg, "You have done nobly."[2] Then he established his headquarters on some high ground and began examining the area ahead. It was near 8 a.m. when the head of Wright's 6th Corps emerged from the canyon and began to form line of battle on the high ground beyond. Meanwhile Emory was fuming because his 19th Corps had to wait, not only for Wright's men to file by, but for his seemingly endless train of guns and wagons as well. Finally the 6th Corps wagons were parked so that the 19th Corps troops could pass them, but by then it was 9 a.m.

As the 19th Corps troops filed through the canyon they found that "the shaded grass for some distance flanking the pike was covered with wounded men, the results of the cavalry fight of the early morning," one of them recorded. "A field hospital had been established and the surgeon's knife was in full play." The infantry, on their way to their first big battle in Virginia, asked a wounded cavalryman, "Are there many Johnnies ahead?" To the Northern soldiers their Southern counterparts were always Johnny Reb' or just Johnny. "Oh, yes," replied the troopers, "plenty of them, and they are gritty this morning. They mean to fight to-day." "Have you had much of a fight?" the infantryman asked. "Yea, we've had a close twist," the cavalryman confirmed, "but we couldn't budge 'em, and we had to wait for you fellows to come up."[3]

By then, or soon after, Rodes' Confederate division was arriving on the field. It had already been prepared to march from Stephenson's Depot, five miles north of Winchester, when Early's order arrived for it to hurry to Ramseur's aid. And Gordon's Division soon arrived at Stephenson's Depot from Bunker Hill and continued on toward Winchester. The sound of firing from up ahead hastened the men's steps. "We decided that it was a general attack by Sheridan," one of them rememberd, "but we knew we could whip Sheridan easily, notwithstanding the large odds we believed he had against us."[4] Meanwhile, Early rode to join Ramseur.

Sheridan formed the 6th Corps with Ricketts' 3rd Division on the right of the Berryville Pike in two lines, Getty's 2nd Division on the left in a single line, and Russell's 1st Division in reserve. Wilson's cavalry moved to the far left, beyond Abraham's Creek. At the same time Rodes deployed his Confederate division a few hundred yards north and west of Ramseur's position, in open fields and a patch of woods. Grimes' Brigade of North Carolinians held Rodes' right, Cox's North Carolinians the center behind a stone wall, and Cook's Georgians the left. Battle's Brigade of Alabamans formed in echelon behind and to the left of Cook. Batteries of light artillery deployed on both flanks of Rodes' line, while the division's sharpshooters were sent out as skirmishers.

By 10 a.m. Gordon's Division had arrived and filed into position to Rodes' left. Terry's Brigade of Virginians formed on Gordon's right, nearest to Rodes. York's Louisiana Brigade held the center, and Evans' Brigade of Georgians, under Colonel Edmund Atkinson, the left. Two batteries of artillery extended the Rebel line to an east-west stream called Red Bud Run. North of the stream were six guns of the horse artillery, posted where they could enfilade the flank of any Federals attacking Gordon's front. They were backed up by both brigades of Fitzhugh Lee's cavalry division.

While the artillery dueled and the new arrivals of both sides deployed, Ramseur's Division fell back to a position straddling the Berryville Pike near the farm of Enos Dinkle, Sr. This was, however, still somewhat in advance of Rodes' and Gordon's divisions. The Confederate cavalry brigade of Brigadier General Bradley Johnson extended Ramseur's line to Abraham's Creek. Even farther south another brigade of Rebel horsemen, under Brigadier General William L. "Mudwall" Jackson, faced off against Wilson's troopers where the Senseney Road crossed a north-south stretch of Abraham's Creek.

At about 10 a.m., as Gordon's Confederates were filing into place and Ramseur's were falling back to Dinkle's farm, Emory's Union 19th Corps finally reached the front. Brigadier General Cuvier Grover's large 2nd Division filed into position to the right of the 6th Corps, while Brigadier General William Dwight's smaller, 1st Division, down to two brigades because one was guarding Harper's Ferry, formed to protect Grover's right and rear.

The early arrivals on both sides had to wait in place all morning while the others filed into position and the artillery dueled. "Awaiting orders!" one Union soldier complained. "That is the time that tries the courage of the bravest. Once in the heat and hurry and inspiration of the battle, the average soldier forgets fear in the excitement of the hour; but to stand at a safe distance, though within easy sight and hearing of the conflict, ready, expectant, every nerve strung, awaiting the word of command to march into a hailstorm of death, that is the crucial test. It is at such a time that all the mental struggle involved in a soldier's death is undergone, leaving nothing but the mere physical pang of sudden dying to complete the sacrifice."[5]

Another Federal remembered that "it was one of the most beautiful of early-autumn days: the air was cool and mellow, the sun shed a tempered warmth and the whole face of nature smiled in the harvest-time." He added that, "there was little premonition of the impending carnage, for nothing more than desultory firing was heard along our front, and that

was the preliminary death-play of the skirmishers."[6] Then, at 11:40 a.m.
a single gun was fired to signal a general Union advance.

On the Federal right, the front line of Grover's 2nd Division of the
19th Corps, Birge's 1st and Sharpe's 3rd brigades, emerged from some
trees and attacked across a 600-yard-wide open field toward a second
woods. Musketry came from the tree line ahead but it did not phase the
slow, deliberate advance of the well ordered Union ranks. However, the
oblique fire of the Confederate horse artillery from north of Red Bud
Run "made lanes in the advance of the enemy," as a Southern cavalry
officer observed.[7] Sheridan had intended for these two brigades to merely
advance part of the way across the field and then lie down, but as they
neared the designated point a drunken staff officer rode out in front of
Birge's brigade and yelled, "Charge bayonets! Forward! Double-quick!"[8]
The Federals surged forward toward the second wood. More Confederate volleys came from the trees ahead, but the Rebels were firing high
and the bullets whistled menacingly but harmlessly overhead.

Birge's men drove the Southern skirmishers through the woods, out-
distancing Sharpe's brigade. Atkinson's brigade of Gordon's Division,
on the Confederate left, was deployed in a ravine at the west end of
these woods. "What's the matter? What's the matter?" these Georgians
called out as their skirmishers came running back. "You'll soon see,"
they were told.[9] When Birge's Yankees could be seen advancing through
the trees the Rebels staggered them with a volley. The Federals replied
in kind. "The roar of battle," a Union lieutenant wrote, "as the two lines
fairly met, sounding in a thunderous burst of volleys, pealed up from
that woods; and smoke and flame streamed out in a long line, as though
the whole forest had been suddenly ignited. The conflict was as fierce as
the fiercest battle fought by Grant, from the Rapidan to Petersburg."[10]

Shells from the Confederate horse artillery burst among the trees,
showering branches and splinters down on the combatants. Then
Sharpe's brigade came up on Birge's left, and the Georgians could not
stand. For the first time in their long career they broke and ran from the
Yankees. Grover tried to stop his men from pursuing, but they were so
excited by the sight of their enemies in full retreat that they could not
be restrained. However, they were soon struck by the fire of seven Confederate guns that were to the left and rear of Atkinson's position, and
counterattacked by Gordon with his other two brigades, along with the
recovered Georgians.

Gordon was "a superb, magnetic leader," as one of his men described
him, "the most glorious and inspiring thing I ever looked upon." Another of his soldiers said he was "the most prettiest thing you ever did

see on a field of fight. It 'ud put fight into a whipped chicken just to look at him."[11] His division overlapped the flanks of the two Union brigades. Colonel Sharpe went down with a bullet in the groin and, with a Rebel yell, Gordon's men drove the Federals back through the woods, where they ran into another of Grover's brigades, Molineux's 2nd, which had followed Sharpe's and Birge's. These Yankees tried to stem the Rebel tide, but they too were overlapped by Gordon's larger force. Their flank regiments melted away until the 13th Connecticut and the 159th New York, in the center, were surrounded and captured. Grover's other brigade, Shunk's 4th, positioned to Molineux's right rear, was struck next. First it was plastered by the Rebel artillery and then the Confederate infantry closed in on three sides. The Federals turned and ran back across the open field toward their starting place, and the Rebels "raised one of the awflest yells that ever met my ears," an Iowa soldier remembered. "Our battery," said an officer in the Southern horse artillery, "if possible, excelled itself, and a more murderous fire I never witnessed than was plunged into this heterogeneous mass as they rushed back. We could see the track of the shot and shell as they would scatter the men, but the lanes closed up for another to follow."[12]

Every regimental commander in Grover's division had been killed or wounded, along with 1,500 men. Red-headed corps commander William Emory rode forward to rally what was left, telling the disordered mass of troops not to waste time sorting themselves out. "Never mind your own regiment!" he yelled. "Never mind if you belong to fifty regiments! Make a regiment here!"[13] And the two brigades of Dwight's 1st Division advanced to the edge of the first woods, where they were immediately struck by the fire of the Rebel guns to their right front. The 114th New York charged forward about 500 yards and then went to earth, firing and loading while lying down, not an easy operation with muzzleloading rifles. For twenty minutes the New Yorkers withstood the deadly fire of Gordon's veterans before they were ordered to fall back into the first woods. There they were joined by two more New York regiments of Beal's 1st Brigade and with them they charged into the open field again, their heads bowed as if advancing into a hail storm. They were met by a murderous volley from Gordon's men in the edge of the second woods, but they advanced to a fence line within 200 yards of the Confederates, from which they fired off all their ammunition and retreated back to the first woods.

As they withdrew, Emory led the 12th Connecticut and the 8th Vermont of McMillan's 2nd Brigade forward to a knoll near the woods, while a pair of howitzers were brought up to reply to the Rebel guns. Emory ordered the two regiments to charge, but the colonel of the 12th

Connecticut was struck by a shell, as were many of his men, and the two regiments clung to their knoll. The 12th's senior captain finally got it moving and it advanced to an undulation of ground about 200 yards from the Confederates. The 8th Vermont came up on its left, and for the next two hours the two regiments engaged Gordon's entire division in a fire fight. One of the Vermonters remarked upon the democracy of danger and death. "There is absolute equality for the time being," he said. "All are on the same plane, so to speak, the rich and the poor, the high and low, the learned and unlearned. The minnie ball and the screeching shell make no distinction, but plough their cruel furrows until exhausted, or pass on like invisible fiends."[14] Meanwhile, Emory patched together a new line in the woods behind them from the rest of Dwight's division and the survivors of Grover's.

Getty's and Ricketts' 2nd and 3rd divisions of the 6th Corps also advanced upon hearing the signal gun at 11:40 a.m. Bidwell's 3rd Brigade of Getty's division was on the left, with one regiment beyond Abraham's Creek. The rest of the brigade charged up a hill, slowed by very severe Confederate artillery fire, and pushed back the forward pickets of Godwin's Brigade of Ramseur's Division. Wheaton's 1st Brigade, in the center of Getty's division, drove back the skirmishers of Pegram's Brigade and, despite losing its formation while advancing through woods, captured 10 officers and 171 men and forced the withdrawal of a Rebel battery. Meanwhile Bidwell brought up a battery of Union guns to support the infantry. Warner's Vermont Brigade, on Getty's right, ran up against Rebel sharpshooters posted on the far side of a ravine. The Vermonters plunged into this swampy depression and took what cover they could behind six-foot-tall trees while waiting for Ricketts' division to catch up.

Emerson's 1st Brigade, on the left of Ricketts' 3rd Division, had the key role of following the Berryville Pike. Everybody else was supposed to guide on it. However, 600 yards beyond the Union starting point the road turned sharply to the left, or south. Emerson dutifully followed the road and, under heavy artillery fire, got only as far as the Confederate skirmish line, lost two of his regimental commanders, and wound up in the same ravine with Warner's Vermonters. Ricketts' other brigade, Colonel Joseph Keifer's 2nd, conformed with Emerson's turn, advanced through the rough terrain of Ash Hollow, and lost contact with the 19th Corps on its right. Then both of Ricketts' brigades began a charge up the hill that was taken up by Warner, then Wheaton, then Bidwell. They drove Ramseur's three brigades back and chased off two more Rebel batteries. Emerson's brigade broke through the Confederate center at Dinkle's farm and both Union brigades drove past Dinkle's barn toward

Winchester as more Southern artillery opened fire on them, including some that had been supporting Gordon. Keifer saw that the 19th Corps was in trouble and that his right flank was therefore exposed. So he sent three of his seven small regiments toward those guns. They stopped 200 yards from them, dropped to the ground, and opened fire. Soon the gunners began to fall and then the rest abandoned their pieces to save themselves.

But there was a gaping empty space several hundred yards wide between Keifer's right and the 19th Corps, and into this space Major General Robert Rodes thrust his favorite brigade. While Gordon's counterattack drove Grover's division back to its starting point, Rodes shifted Battle's Brigade of Alabamans to his right and led it toward Keifer's flank. This had been his own brigade before he had been promoted to division commander after Chancellorsville. "Charge them, boys!" he told them now. "Charge them." Then a Union artillery shell exploded above him, shattering his skull, and he fell. Early himself was on hand to see this key attack go in. "I lifted my hat to the old hero as we ran forward . . .," an Alabama captain remembered, "and noticed how proudly he watched our impetuous advance." Battle's brigade charged the three regiments on Keifer's right. "The brave Alabamans rushed at the enemy like tigers," one Confederate said, "and for a time the two lines were so near each other that the paper of their cartridges flew into our faces."[15] Then Keifer's men broke and ran. Battle pressed on, and the rest of Ricketts' division retreated before this threat to its flank in a disorganized mass. Another witness said the Federals were "all mixed up and running for dear life. I have never seen such a deadly volley fired as those noble Alabamans fired at the retreating enemy. It was so terrible that it really looked sickening. It seemed that the first volley cut down half of their line."[16] Getty's division also had to fall back, although in better order. The 156th New York from the 19th Corps blundered into Battle's path and lost over a hundred men in a matter of minutes before beating a hasty retreat into some nearby woods.

"After the repulse of our 3rd Division," wrote Captain Elisha Hunt Rhodes, 22-year-old commander of the 2nd Rhode Island, "it was generally thought that we would wait until dark and then retire to our fortified camps at Clifton. But we did not know Phil Sheridan."[17] The defeat of Grover's division was beyond Sheridan's view, but he saw the disaster that befell Ricketts division and ordered the remaining division of Wright's 6th Corps, Russell's 1st, to counterattack. Wright said that "the fate of the day depended on the employment of this force."[18]

This division had been waiting all morning, taking a pounding from Southern artillery but unable to hit back. One shot stuck the horse of

Captain Kempf, commander of the 5th Wisconsin, then bounded down the line of his regiment, wounding several men. "The horse, a large white animal, had a part of his flank shot off and started on a run with his tail hanging by a piece of flesh," Elisha Rhodes told his diary. "The Captain jumped to his feet and shouted: 'There goes my . . . horse, my . . . haversack, my . . . blankets, my . . . canteen' and he also named over all of his traps that went off on his horse. (The blank spaces above may be supplied with adjectives.) Notwithstanding the fact that shot and shell were plunging into our Brigade, the group of officers including myself who witnessed this scene rolled in the sand convulsed with laughter."[19]

Two batteries of Union artillery slowed up the Confederate advance while Russell brought up two of his brigades. Campbell's 1st Brigade was deployed behind the guns across the Berryville Pike with Colonel Oliver Edwards' 3rd Brigade on its right. Then, at about noon, they advanced into the ravine that had foiled Russell's division and scrambled up the other side. On the right flank was the 37th Massachusetts, armed with Spencer repeating rifles. These Bay Staters drove a number of Confederates before them until they came to a cornfield. On the other side, in a strip of woods, was Rodes' entire division, now commanded by Brigadier General Bryan Grimes.

"The 2nd R.I. reached a little knoll near a house," Captain Rhodes recorded, "and finding a heavy stone wall in my front I formed behind it and opened fire. While in this position the 37th Mass, one of the best Regiments I ever saw, and armed with Spencer Seven Shooting Rifles, had advanced well to the front and could be seen about a mile to my right, laying upon the ground exposed to the fire of the Rebel guns in a redoubt. Colonel Edwards rode up to me and pointing to the 37th Mass. said: "For God's sake, Rhodes, take the 2nd R.I. and go and help Montague." (The Lt. Col. commanding the 37th Mass. is George L. Montague.) I withdrew my Regiment from the hill and moving at a run along the rear of where the 37th was located. The Rebels seeing my movement shelled us unmercifully, but we kept on and were soon in the woods. Behind this grove I saw the ammunition train and on one wagon in large letters "37th MASS." As they use a copper cartridge, a special wagon is provided for them. Suspecting that the 37th was out of ammunition I hastily caused several boxes to be opened and then had our boys fill their pockets with cartridges. I then deployed the Regiment as a skirmish line and instructed the officers and men to move to the front at a double quick, form on the right of the 37th, have their men lay down and then close intervals to the left by creeping on the ground. The plan worked well, and we reached our position with the loss of only two or three men. I reported to Colonel Montague who was the only man on his feet, and he said: "You can do no good, for I have no ammunition." I told my story, and the cartridges were distributed to his men. The Rebel guns in the earthwork were about four hundred yards off, and a white guidon showed above the parapets. I had my Regiment rise, fire a volley, and then lay down and load again. We did this until the Rebel guns were silenced. We remained here until the main line advanced to our position."[20]

For thirty minutes Brigadier General David Russell's two brigades then slugged it out with Grimes' four. Russell himself was killed early on, when a piece of shell pierced his heart. Wright described Russell as "an officer whose merits were not measured by his rank, whose zeal never outran his discretion, whose abilities were never unequal to the occasion."[21] Sheridan was particularly saddened by Russell's death: "In the early days of my army life he was my captain and friend and I was deeply indebted to him, not only for sound advice and good example, but for the inestimable service he had just performed, and sealed with his life."[22] Russell was temporarily replaced by Colonel Oliver Edwards of the 3rd Brigade.

Grimes' four brigades began to gain the advantage over Edwards' two, not only because of numbers but because of their superior skill, as well. "They aimed better than our men," a Federal officer admitted, "they covered themselves (in case of need) more carefully and effectively; they could move in a swarm, without much care for alignment and touch of elbows. In short, they fought more like redskins, or like hunters, than we."[23] But they were about to meet another master of tactics. As the Confederates advanced they were taken in flank by the final brigade of Russell's division, Upton's 2nd.

Brigadier General Emory Upton was a grim, ambitious, talented officer of only 25 years of age, an 1861 graduate of West Point. He had wanted to be a general since he was a boy, and he was a serious student of the art of war who would go on to become the leading tactical theorist of the post-war regular army. One of his officers said that Upton had "the appearance of a man who was deeply impressed with the seriousness of warfare and has mastered its science." Wilson, the cavalry division commander, considered Upton "incontestably the best tactician of either army." He had won his star at Spotsylvania, where he had planned and led a brigade-sized attack that had penetrated the formidable Rebel entrenchments held by Rodes' Division. Two days later Grant had copied Upton's tactics with an entire corps, had broken the Confederate line, and had captured most of a division. But there was more to Upton than innovative tactics and a scholarly understanding of his profession.

Another of his officers believed that "of all the men that I have ever met, no one was more thoroughly in earnest than . . . Upton."[24]

Now Upton led his three small regiments (two even smaller ones were guarding wagons in the rear) into the concealing rocks and trees of Ash Hollow, where they would face the advancing Grimes' left flank at an oblique angle. He ordered his men to fix bayonets and not to fire until he gave the order. Then he waited until the oncoming Rebels were within 200 yards before he yelled, "Ready, aim, fire." After the volley he shouted, "Forward, charge!" A watching Federal soldier wrote that "the charge of his brigade was the finest spectacle in the infantry battle of the day. Gen. Upton himself rode at the advance of his lines, and drawing his sword sat his horse like a centaur, calling his men forward."[25] The colonel and many of the men of the 14th North Carolina surrendered, and when Edwards' and Campbell's brigades joined the attack the rest of Grimes' men retreated to their starting place. But there they reformed and stood off the attacking Northerners, and the battle on this part of the field settled into a temporary standoff.

---

1. Wert, *From Winchester to Cedar Creek*, 49.
2. Ibid.
3. Ibid., 50.
4. Ibid., 53.
5. Ibid., 56.
6. Ibid.
7. Ibid.
8. Ibid., 57.
9. Ibid.
10. Ibid.
11. Ibid., 58.
12. Ibid., 60.
13. Albert Hemingway, "Whirling Through Winchester," *America's Civil War*, May 1991, 42.
14. Wert, *From Winchester to Cedar Creek*, 62.
15. Ibid., 66.
16. Ibid., 67.
17. Robert Hunt Rhodes, ed., *All For the Union: The Civil War Diary and Letters of Elisha Hunt Rhodes* (New York, 1985), 183.
18. Wert, *From Winchester to Cedar Creek*, 67.

19. Rhodes, *All For the Union*, 183.

20. Ibid., 183–184.

21. Wert, *From Winchester to Cedar Creek*, 68.

22. Sheridan, *Memoirs*, 2:23–24.

23. Wert, *From Winchester to Cedar Creek*, 68.

24. Ibid., 69.

25. Ibid., 69–70.

CHAPTER SIX

Like a Thunderclap Out of a Clear Sky

19 September 1864

While Wilson's 3rd Division of cavalry had led the 6th and 19th corps through the narrow canyon on the Berryville Pike, Merritt's 1st Division had moved toward two lower fords on the Opequon north of the canyon. Brigadier General Wesley Merritt was another of those talented young cavalry officers. Like Wilson, he had also graduated from West Point in 1860. And he looked even younger than his 30 years, partly because, unlike most men of that era, he wore neither beard nor mustache. A staff officer said he was "tall, slender, and intellectual looking. He had a constitution of iron, and underneath a rather passive demeanor concealed a fiery ambition." Merritt was accompanied by Sheridan's chief of cavalry, Brigadier General A. T. A. Torbert, himself only 31 but from the West Point class of 1855. His orders from Sheridan were, "if opposed only by the enemy's cavalry, you will cross the creek at daylight and follow them up."[1] Once across the Opequon, Merritt was to link up with Averell's 2nd Division, coming south along the Valley Turnpike.

It was still dark when Colonel Charles Russell Lowell's Reserve Brigade of Merritt's division reached Seiver's Ford. Lowell, 29, a Harvard man from a prominent Massachusetts family, was another of the cavalry's talented young men. One of Sheridan's aides said there was "no cooler head or better brain in all the army, no one to be more absolutely relied upon," than Lowell. The 2nd U.S. Cavalry was dismounted and deployed on high ground overlooking the crossing, and an officer called out to the Confederate pickets on the other side, "We don't want to kill you fellows, and you had better get away; we are coming after you."[2] The Rebels did not take this advice, and when the regulars splashed across the ford they fired at them. But the Federals soon overran the small force of pickets, and as the sun rose behind them the rest of Lowell's brigade began to cross the creek.

About three quarters of a mile farther north, Custer's 1st Brigade crossed at Locke's Ford. George Armstrong Custer, then 24, was the quintessential bright young cavalry general of the Federal army. Two years after graduating at the bottom of the West Point class of 1861 he was promoted from captain to brigadier general of volunteers just in time for the Gettysburg campaign. He had soon proved the promotion to be well merited. During his raid toward Richmond back in May, Sheridan had called Custer "the ablest man in the Cavalry Corps."[3] An officer on Torbert's staff left this description of Custer: "He was scarcely more than a boy in years, but was a man of tremendous energy and immense power. His great height and striking countenance made him a very imposing figure. His blue eyes, blond moustach and great mass of blond curling hair falling almost to his waist gave him the appearance of one of the Vikings of old, and his fancy for startling effects was still farther indicated by his dress which I remember about this time to have consisted of an immensely broad 'slouch' hat, a black velvet jacket heavily trimmed with gold lace, riding breeches of the same, and immensely long cavalry boots . . . One thing I have forgotten and that perhaps the most conspicuous article of his apparel—around his neck, loosely knotted, he generally wore a long flowing ribbon or cravat of brilliant red cashmere or silk. This streamed behind him as he rode, and made him a marked man a mile away."[4]

Custer found the ford well defended and sent the 6th Michigan Cavalry forward dismounted to some fences and buildings overlooking the crossing to provide covering fire. Then he ordered the 7th Michigan to charge across the creek, but the major in command of the 25th New York, which had just been assigned to Custer's brigade, requested the honor of leading the way. Custer assented, sending the 7th Michigan in behind them. However, when they charged, the Confederate fire threw the New Yorkers into confusion and they veered into the 7th Michigan, so that both regiments had to retreat. With that, Custer called upon his favorite saber regiment, the 1st Michigan. And he told his brigade band, "Follow that regiment and when you see me wave my sword give 'em some music."[5]

The colonel of the 1st sent a couple of squadrons ahead to divert the Rebels' attention while the rest of the regiment moved forward carefully toward the creek. Meanwhile, Major Thomas Howrigan of the 1st rode over to the commander of the 6th Michigan to ask for more covering fire. "They are shooting my men off their horses," he complained, and just then a bullet struck the saddlebag right behind his leg. He opened the flap and pulled out the top of a shattered bottle, still corked. "God damn their damn souls," Howrigan cursed, "they have broken my whiskey bottle." And with that he turned and galloped back to his men at the ford.[6] There the band had become a bit overeager and gotten itself sandwiched between the 1st Michigan's two advanced squadrons and the main body. An officer was just starting to chide the musicians for getting in the way when a loud cheer drowned him out. Custer waved his sword, the band started to play, and the 1st Michigan splashed across Opequon Creek, riding right over the Confederate rifle pits and driving the defenders away. From prisoners, Custer learned that he had been fighting troops from Breckinridge's infantry division.

Major General John C. Breckinridge had been vice president of the United States in the Buchanan administration and the 1860 presidential candidate of the Southern wing of the Democratic party. He had been a division commander in the Confederacy's western army until the spring of 1864. He had then been assigned to command the Department of Southwestern Virginia. From there, Lee had called upon him to move north to defend the Shenandoah Valley, which he had done admirably by defeating part of the Union Army of West Virginia at New Market. Then he had taken his two small infantry brigades to reinforce Lee, but in his absence the Federals had marched up the Shenandoah Valley. So Breckinridge had been sent to head them off and had soon been joined by Early with the 2nd Corps of Lee's army. Early had given Breckinridge command of an unofficial corps consisting of his own division, now under Brigadier General Gabriel C. Wharton, and Gordon's Division. However, Early's recent move against Martinsburg had broken up this corps, and Breckinridge was left with only Wharton's division, now consisting of three small brigades.

Today he had been given the assignment, with the aid of a battalion of artillery, of protecting Early's northern flank while the three divisions of the old 2nd Corps dealt with Sheridan's main thrust. When Rodes and Gordon had marched for Winchester, Breckinridge had moved Wharton's three brigades from Stephenson's Depot toward the Opequon. Wharton's own brigade, under Colonel Augustus Forsberg, was sent toward Locke's Ford, and it was some of his skirmishers that Custer encountered, along with the pickets of the 22nd Virginia Cavalry of Bradley Johnson's brigade. The rest of Forsberg's brigade was placed in some earthworks about a mile back from the ford with Colonel Thomas Smith's brigade deployed to Forsberg's right rear. The other brigade, commanded by Colonel George S. Patton, grandfather of the World War II general, was sent toward Seiver's Ford and put into some defenses on high ground about a mile and a half from the creek.

The advance of the Union horsemen was repeatedly delayed by encounters with Rebel cavalry and infantry skirmishers who took advantage of every ditch, fence, wall, and clump of trees, all of which were plentiful. Neither side was inclined to fight all out since each had been assigned the primary job of keeping the other out of the main fight. When Custer encountered Forsberg's main defenses, he stopped to wait for the rest of Merritt's division to come up, while using skirmishers and an attached battery of horse artillery to keep the Rebels busy. Merritt did not seem to be in any hurry.

Averell's 2nd Division of the Union cavalry crossed the Opequon near Darkesville about 5 a.m. and almost immediately ran into the 23rd Virginia Cavalry of Imboden's Brigade, which doggedly opposed and slowed the Federal advance for three hours. At Bunker Hill the 23rd was joined by the 62nd Virginia Mounted Infantry and the brigade's temporary commander, Colonel George Smith, and soon thereafter the brigade's other unit, the 18th Virginia Cavalry, also came in. Smith deployed his three regiments in line across the Valley Pike, and Averell did the same with his seven regiments. Just before 10 a.m. the Federals charged, and, although the Rebels fought stubbornly, the larger Union force overlapped both of the Virginians' flanks, and they eventually had to turn and flee. They were able, however, to regroup and again form line farther south.

At around 10 a.m. Breckinridge pulled Forsberg's brigade back to join Smith's, along with two batteries of artillery, in fieldworks on a ridge about two miles east of Stephenson's Depot. When Custer reported that the Confederates seemed to be withdrawing and that he intended to follow them, Merritt sent Lowell's Reserve Brigade to link up with Custer at last. When Lowell's men came up on his left just before 11 a.m., Custer decided to attack "to test the strength and numbers of the enemy."[7] The 1st and 7th Michigan and 25th New York were launched in a mounted charge across fields of buckwheat, supported by the 2nd U.S. Cavalry of Lowell's brigade. The 1st Michigan, in the lead, penetrated the Southern defenses and headed for a battery of Rebel guns, but the artillery fire from their front and infantry fire from both flanks broke the Wolverines' formation and momentum and they turned back, as did the rest of the column. All the Federals had to show for their courage was the information that Breckinridge's infantry was still present in force.

But at 11:40 a.m., when Sheridan sent the 6th and 19th Corps forward, Early ordered Breckinridge to bring his infantry and artillery to a position on the Valley Turnpike a mile north of Winchester. "To the withdrawal of this division," an officer in Rodes' Division wrote, "though necessary perhaps, may be attributed the loss of the day, for now our disasters commenced."[8] When the three brigades of infantry pulled out, all that remained between Merritt's Federals and Winchester was Brigadier General John McCausland's small brigade of cavalry. At the same time, Early ordered Wickham's Brigade of Fitz Lee's cavalry division, under its senior colonel, Thomas Munford, to reinforce Smith and McCausland, and he ordered Fitz Lee to take overall command of the cavalry north of Red Bud Run.

At about 1:30 p.m. Merritt finally ordered his division to advance westward toward the Valley Turnpike. Colonel Thomas Devin's 2nd Brigade was finally brought across the Opequon and sent along the road to Stephenson's Depot, while Lowell and Custer rode across country on his right. About a mile east of the turnpike Devin came upon McCausland's Confederate cavalry, and he sent the 18th Pennsylvania forward in a mounted charge, supported by horse artillery. McCausland's Virginians turned and fled "over the cleared fields like so many sheep," as one Union trooper put it.[9] Colonel George Smith, who had his three regiments on McCausland's left, facing north, wheeled two of them to the right and struck the pursuing Federals in the flank. But as the Pennsylvanians fell back, Devin sent in the 19th New York Cavalry against Smith's front and the 9th New York against their flank, and Smith's brigade followed McCausland's in retreat to the south. The two Southern units regrouped in a pine forest about a mile up the road, where they were met by Fitz Lee.

Major General Fitzhugh Lee was the nephew of Robert E. Lee, and thus the cousin of Rooney Lee. He was 29 years old and had graduated from West Point in 1856, where he and Averell had been good friends. He was stocky and jovial but a very competent cavalry commander. Some, possibly including himself, had expected that he would succeed Jeb Stuart in command of the Cavalry Corps. Instead, his uncle had given the job to Hampton and had sent Fitz, under Anderson, to northern Virginia. When Anderson had taken Kershaw's infantry division back to Lee, Fitz's cavalry had been left with Early. Now, as he joined Smith and McCausland, he had with him what had been Lomax's Brigade, before that officer had been transfered to command Early's cavalry. The brigade was now commanded by Colonel William H. Payne. Fitz Lee's other brigade had been sent to the south of Abraham's Creek, where Wilson's Union cavalry was threatening the Confederate right flank.

Averell's division now connected with Merritt's and, under Torbert, they both headed south. Custer's official report describes what happened next: "At this time five brigades of cavalry were moving on parallel lines; most, if not all, of the brigades moved by brigade front, regiments being in parallel columns of squadrons. One continuous and heavy fire of skirmishers covered the advance, using only the carbine, while the line of brigades as they advanced across the open country, the bands playing the national airs, presented in the sunlight one moving mass of glittering sabers. This, combined with the various and bright-colored banners and battle-flags, intermingled here and there with the plain blue uniforms of the troops, furnished one of the most inspiring as well as imposing scenes of martial grandeur ever witnessed upon a battle-field. No encouragement was required to inspirit either man or horse. On the contrary, it was necessary to check the ardor of both until the time for action should arrive."[10]

Soon this awesome force came upon Fitz Lee's three brigades deployed in open pine woods. Custer's report continued: "No obstacles to the successful maneuvering of large bodies of cavalry were encountered; even the forests were so open as to offer little or no hinderance to a charging column. Upon our left and in plain view could be seen the struggle now raging between the infantry lines of each army, while at various points columns of light-colored smoke showed that the artillery of neither side was idle. At that moment it seemed as if no perceptible advantage could be claimed by either, but that the fortunes of the day might be decided by one of those incidents or accidents of the battlefield which, though insignificant in themselves, often go far toward deciding the fate of nations. Such must have been the impression of the officers and men composing the five brigades advancing to the attack. The enemy wisely chose not to receive our attack at a halt, but advanced from the wood and charged our line of skirmishers."[11]

The Confederate countercharge drove back the Union skirmishers and part of Custer's brigade, in the center of the line, breaking up the massive five-brigade formation, but could accomplish little else against such odds. Custer's report continued: "The enemy relied wholly upon the carbine and pistol; my men preferred the saber. A short but closely contested struggle ensued, which resulted in the repulse of the enemy. Many prisoners were taken, and quite a number on both sides left on the field."[12] Fitz Lee was badly wounded in the leg while trying to rally his men.

The Federals drove the Rebels back through the woods behind them, and beyond. "The country for a mile," one of Custer's regimental commanders remembered, "was full of charging columns—regiments, troops, squads—the pursuit taking them in every direction where a mounted enemy could be seen."[13] Custer continued: "The division of General Averell moved on the right of the pike and gave its attention to the small force of the enemy which was directing its retreat toward the commanding heights west of the town. My command, by agreement with General Averell, took charge of all forces of the enemy on the pike and those in the immediate vicinity of the ground to its left. Other portions of the First Division made a detour still further to my left, so that which had lately been one unbroken line was now formed into several columns of pursuit, each with a special and select object in view. Within three-quarters of a mile from the point where the enemy had made his last stand he rallied a portion of his forces. His line was formed beyond a small ditch, which he no doubt supposed would break if not wholly oppose an attacking column. Under most circumstances such might have been the case, but with men inspired with a foretaste of victory greater obstacles must be interposed. Without designating any particular regiment the charge was sounded, and portions of all the regiments composing my brigade joined in the attack. The volleys delivered by the enemy were not sufficient to check the attacking column, and again was the enemy driven before us, this time seeking safety in rear of his line of infantry."[14]

Early had sent Breckinridge's three brigades and the three batteries of King's artillery battalion to his right when he got word that the cavalry guarding his left was retreating. Quickly he ordered King's guns and Breckinridge's infantry back to his left, and Patton's brigade plus the artillery arrived just in time to save his cavalry from the pursuing Union troopers. The advance of Averell's two brigades caused King's Rebel batteries to also take shelter behind Patton's infantry.

Custer scraped together as many of his men as he could easily find and, not seeing Patton's men behind a stone wall, charged a retiring Confederate battery. The Rebel infantry rose up from behind their wall and fired into the flank of Custer's troopers, driving most of them back.

Custer, who had been well out in front of his troops, suddenly found himself all alone except for the sergeant who always followed him with his personal guidon to mark his location on the field. Just as Custer turned back, the sergeant was hit by a bullet and fell off his horse, although still alive. There were Rebels all around the general and the sergeant, but Custer jumped down, hoisted the wounded man by the seat of his pants and his jacket collar, slung him over the back of his own horse, and swatted the animal on the rump with the flat of his sword. As the horse carried the wounded man to safety, the general turned to face on foot the Confederates who were closing in on him. With his saber and the staff of the guidon he parried their bayonet thrusts for about 30 seconds. Then a squadron of the 6th Michigan came to his rescue. The major commanding the squadron called Custer's act of heroism "as brave a thing as I ever saw Custer do."[15] Carrying his own guidon now, the general fell back behind a sheltering ridge to reassemble his command.

Crook, in deploying his two small divisions on Emory's right, had placed Colonel Joseph Thoburn's 1st Division between the 19th Corps' right and Red Bud Run. Then he had led Colonel Isaac H. Duval's 2nd Division across that stream and turned westward. By then Fitz Lee's two cavalry brigades had been sent elsewhere, as we have seen, and Crook encountered no opposition. Soon he discovered that he was beyond the left flank of Early's main line. He deployed Duvall's infantry for an attack, with the 1st Brigade, under Colonel Rutherford B. Hayes (the future president) on the left and Colonel Daniel D. Johnson's 2nd Brigade on the right. His three batteries, under Captain Henry du Pont, of the Delaware chemical family, also deployed, ready to support the advance of the infantry.

Meanwhile, Crook sent Captain William McKinley of his staff (another future president) back across the Red Bud to inform first Thoburn and then Sheridan of his intention to attack the Confederate left. In his official report, written after the war, and his much later memoirs, Sheridan took credit for ordering this flank attack. The claim cost him the friendship of Crook, who maintained that "so far as I know the idea of turning the enemy's flank never occurred to him, but I took the responsibility on my own shoulders."[16] And du Pont backed up Crook's claim.

It was precisely 3 p.m. on du Pont's watch when "with a tremendous shout which resounded along the lines of the Nineteenth Corps, our Second Division rushed forward to the charge." Du Pont's guns opened a covering fire and Duval's infantry, under heavy fire from Southern infantry and artillery, ran through a cornfield and a meadow down the slope to Red Bud Run. Colonel Johnson was wounded, and Duval was hit in the thigh but kept on going. The Federals were temporarily stopped by the stream, which was really a slough some thirty or forty yards wide with a moss-covered surface and a soft mud bottom. "No one probably knew of it until its banks were reached," Rutherford Hayes said. As he wrote his wife a couple of days later, "To stop was death. To go on was probably the same; but on we started again." Hayes' horse was soon mired in the mud, and when it fell on its side Hayes crawled to the south bank, one of the first to get across. All of the Federals were bogged down to some extent. "Some were almost under the water," one witness noted, "some waist deep & some knee deep & were pulling each other through. They all had hold of each other & those on the bank were pulling those in the slough out."[17]

Finally they got across, all organization lost, all order gone, in what Crook called "one great throng." And on they charged, although the Rebel rifle fire was "an uninterrupted explosion, without break or tremor." One of Hayes' aides said, "I never saw the killed and wounded lying thicker on the ground than here."[18] Meanwhile, Thoburn's 1st Division charged across the 600 yards of open field that Grover's division had crossed that morning. Gordon's Rebels waited until they were half-way across and then hit them with a volley, but the Federals came on with deafening yells and cheers, and Gordon's men, caught between the two forces, one closing in from the north and the other from the east, decided it was time to retreat. They fell back in good order, while the rapid advance through the woods they had occupied turned Thoburn's ranks into a disordered mob. "Had we moved in such a manner as to preserve our lines," Thoburn explained, "the enemy would have escaped unhurt, or else driven us back."[19]

The 8th Vermont and 12th Connecticut of the 19th Corps had dueled with Gordon's entire division for two hours before the 8th Corps' attack had chased Gordon away. When Thoburn's division swept past them the commander of the 8th Vermont led his regiment forward against the enemy also, telling his men, "we'll drive them to hell." The commander of the 12th Connecticut told his men, "The Eighth Vermont is going to the d——l, but they shan't go ahead of us!" The two regiments followed Thoburn's advance through the woods, helping to chase Gordon's Division out. Their brigade commander, Brigadier General James McMillan, rode up and ordered them to stop, but they ignored him, advancing on into the open beyond the woods. However, they were met by "a most murderous volley" and fell back to the edge of the woods.[20] By then they had fired off most of their ammunition.

As Crook's two divisions came together, Gordon reformed his men behind Grimes' division and at right angles to it, facing north. On their left, also facing north, was Wharton's division, now reunited, with Breckinridge again commanding both divisions. These Confederates, and a number of guns, pounded the advancing Federals, but, without re-forming, they "rushed on heedless of the destructive fire of shot, shell, canister and musketry," Crook reported. However, they now had about 800 yards of uphill, open ground to cross against Gordon's and Breckin-ridge's infantry, who were protected by stone walls and modest en-trenchments, plus those guns and enfilading fire from Grimes' men. "The rebels had the advantage in numbers, position, and cover," one Federal reported, "and their fire seemed to increase in intensity every minute." A member of the 34th Massachusetts, which approached some Confeder-ates behind a stone wall, said, "A vivid sheet of fire, like the burning, blinding lightning's glare, ran along the front, and a deadly storm of grape and bullets tore through our ranks. It seemed as if half the regiment went down before that single volley."[21] The 8th Corps' attack ground to a halt and its men went to ground, seeking what cover they could find but keeping up their return fire. Crook rode off looking for help.

To Thoburn's left were two regiments of Emory Upton's brigade of the 6th Corps who had advanced to help drive Gordon's Division back, but they too were stalled. Like Crook, Upton, who was now in com-mand of what had been Russell's division, went in search of help. He found the 8th Vermont and the 12th Connecticut of the 19th Corps. He wanted the Vermonters to fire on some artillery about 150 yards away, but the guns were partially obscured by smoke, and the colonel of the Vermont regiment thought they belonged to a Union battery and refused to fire. The colonel and the general engaged in a heated argument until the smoke blew away, revealing a Confederate battle flag. "Fire on that battery!" the colonel ordered.[22] The Rebel cannon soon fell silent, but most of the Vermonters had used up what little had been left of their ammunition. Meanwhile, General McMillan had brought up the 160th New York to replace the 12th Connecticut, and about then, shortly before 4 p.m., Crook rode up in search of help for his stalled attack.

In the strongest of terms, Crook urged McMillan to advance his men to the aid of Thoburn's division, but McMillan was under orders from Emory to go no farther so he refused. Upton then sided with Crook, but McMillan would still not relent without new orders from Emory. Crook said Upton was "nearly crying" with anger.[23] Then Crook ap-pealed directly to the colonel of the 8th Vermont, but his men were out of ammunition and he too refused to advance. Crook angrily rode back to his corps, as Upton did to his division. The battle would have to be concluded without the help of the 19th Corps.

However, at 4 p.m. the entire 6th Corps advanced in a line 1,500 yards wide, with Getty's 2nd Division still on the left, Rickett's 3rd Division in the center and the 1st Division, now under Upton, on the right. Three Union batteries followed the infantry to provide supporting fire. A thousand yards west of them were the Confederate divisions of Ramseur and Grimes, backed up by several guns, which were already firing on the advancing Northern troops. "There is a strange fascination in a scene like this," a Union officer wrote, "which almost tempts one to suspend duty, and look around him. On your right and left men go down, while you are commending their good fighting, and urging them to keep up the work. They fall in front of you,—some lapsing heavily to the ground, stricken with instant death; while others settle slowly down, and limp or crawl back as best they may. It is a scene replete with horrors, and ringing with unearthly cries and noises."[24]

The Federals came on steadily and deliberately in what one witness called "those living lines of men like foaming waves of ocean."[25] Getty's men again crossed Dinkle's farm and drove in Ramseur's skirmishers. The Rebel main line held its ground for a while then began to fall back to the west, still in good order, still fighting back. Gordon's and Breckinridge's divisions, now under renewed attack by Crook, fell back to the southwest. Before 5 p.m. the Confederates had formed an L-shaped line behind stone walls and old earthworks on high ground just east of Winchester. The angle in this line rested on a redoubt containing Rebel artillery. But still the Federals advanced. The Confederate fire was destructive, but the Northerners knew they were winning and that knowledge was a powerful stimulant to courage and determination. "I certainly never enjoyed anything more than the last three hours" of that battle, Rutherford Hayes told his wife.[26] Another Union officer noticed an Irishman in the ranks: "While loading and reciting some prayers in a jumbling sort of way . . . he would shout, 'Now Jeff Davis, you son of a bitch, take that.'" One Federal who saw Sheridan said he "looked as happy as a schoolboy."[27]

It had been a hard day for Sheridan. His plans had gone awry and Early had countered every move he had made, but if strategy would not work surely power and determination would. Now he played his strong suit, inspiring and leading his men in person. No one was better at it than he was. "His influence on his men was like an electric shock," one Union officer wrote of Sheridan's charisma, "and he was the only commander I have ever met whose personal appearance in the field was an immediate and positive stimulus to battle—a stimulus strong enough to turn beaten and disorganized masses into a victorious army. Many of our generals were more warmly loved by the soldiers . . . but none, to the best of my belief, carried such a convincing air of success to the minds of his men, or could get the last drop of strength out of their bodies, when an effort was demanded, in the style of Philip H. Sheridan. They simply believed he was going to win, and every man apparently was determined to be on hand and see him do it."[28]

"About 5 p.m. General Sheridan rode down the line hat in hand, and the whole Army cheered and shouted itself hoarse," Captain Rhodes of the 2nd Rhode Island remembered.[29] Sheridan rode up and down the line of troops on his big black horse, Rienzi, stopping to give little pep talks from time to time. To one regiment he said, "Boys the only way we have to Do is to Kill Every Son of a Bitch." This was answered by "Such a cheering I never heard Before," one soldier wrote home. A Confederate shell exploded under Sheridan's horse but harmed neither animal nor rider. "Damn close," he told the nearest troops, "but we'll lick h—l out of them yet." Such heroics and exhortations had a very strong effect upon his soldiers. "The enthusiasm of the men became unbounded," one Union officer recorded. Then Sheridan rode up to Getty, on the left end of the line, and told him that he had sent orders for Torbert's cavalry and Crook's infantry to attack again. "Press them, General, they'll run," Sheridan said. "Press them, general, I know they'll run."[30]

Custer received an order to attack and for him "not to spare one damned ounce of horse-flesh." But he could see that there was still too large a force of Southern infantry in the defenses to his front for such an attack to be successful. He reasoned that the pressure of the Union infantry would soon cause this force to be weakened and that his chances would then be much improved. He requested "that I might be allowed to select my own time for making the charge," and this was granted. Soon Custer saw Confederate infantry being withdrawn from the lines opposite him and he rode to Torbert to get permission to make the attack. Torbert, however, refused, saying the Rebels were still too strong. Custer tried every means of persuasion, in which he was aided by Colonel Lowell, but Torbert would still not agree. Finally Custer declared, "I will charge anyway." Torbert muttered, "All right; make the charge and break them up."[31]

Cavalry charges in the Napoleonic tradition had been almost universally unsuccessful against unbroken infantry in the American Civil War, due in part to the superiority of that era's rifled muskets over older smoothbore models, but mostly to the fact that the wooded country of eastern Virginia and most of the trans-Allegheny West made the deployment of sufficiently large mounted formations almost impossible. In the Shenandoah Valley, however, the country was cleared, and the area around Winchester was ideal for the employment of cavalry en masse. Wesley Merritt said, "The field was open for cavalry operations such as the war had not seen."[32] Confederate staff officer Henry Kyd Douglas said that "it was evident our troops had more dread of Sheridan's cavalry than of his infantry and our cavalry was unequal to them."[33]

Soon Custer's troopers started forward at a walk, heading straight for the Rebel left. Behind them came the rest of Merritt's division, as well as Averell's. Then the pace was increased to a trot and finally to a gallop. "No man ever saw a more thrilling sight," one Northerner wrote. "Every man's saber was waving above his head," a New Yorker remembered, "and with a savage yell, we swept down upon the trembling wretches like a besom of destruction." It was, an onlooking Union infantry officer said, "the most gallent & exciting cavalry charge I ever saw." Another Federal said, "It was like a thunder-clap out of a clear sky, and the bolt struck home."[34]

"The enemy upon our approach turned and delivered a well-directed volley of musketry," Custer reported, "but before a second discharge could be given my command was in their midst, sabering right and left, capturing prisoners more rapidly than they could be disposed of."[35] Custer's brigade struck Wharton's front and "the enemy's line broke into a thousand fragments under the shock," Merritt reported. Lowell's Reserve Brigade then hit Gordon's Division and Devin's brigade "burst like a storm of case-shot" upon the angle in the Confederate line, where Gordon's right joined Grimes' left. There followed a wild melee, which one Federal trooper called a "carnival of death." Gordon's and Wharton's men ran southward for their lives. "I never seen any men Run faster then the Rebels Run last Munday after we got them drivin out in the open plaine," one Northerner wrote home, "it was fun To see them Running."[36]

Many of the Rebels surrendered. Colonel Patton went down with a mortal wound while trying to stop the rout. Breckinridge also exposed himself to danger trying to rally his men. "His Apollo-like face was begrimed with sweat and smoke," Gordon remembered. "He was desperately reckless—the impersonation of despair. He literally seemed to court death." Gordon appealed to his commander not to take such chances. "Well, general," the former vice president replied, "there is little left for me if our cause is to fail."[37] But Gordon led him to the rear.

In the midst of the melee, Commissary Sergeant Andrew J. Lorish of the 19th New York Cavalry in Devin's brigade snatched a Confederate battleflag from its color bearer. "Shoot that d——d Yankee!" a Rebel shouted. "He's got our flag!" A dozen men raised their rifles to fire, but Lorish brandished his saber and said, "Ground your arms, or I'll send every soul of you to hell in a minute."[38] The Southerners obeyed and Lorish escaped with his trophy. A corporal in the same regiment also captured a Rebel flag and both men were awarded the Congressional Medal of Honor.

The Confederate gunners tried their best to stop the Union pursuit. Colonel Thomas Carter, Early's chief of artillery, was wounded by a shell fragment. Captain George Chapman's Monroe Battery lost one gun, and a shell became lodged in the barrel of another due to the crew's haste. The artillerymen worked hard to clear the gun while infantrymen streamed past them. General Early himself rode up and shouted, "Stop that, you damned fools! You'll kill yourself and anybody about you." One of the gunners, not recognizing their plainly dressed commander, told the general to "go to hell, you damned old clodhopper and tend to your own business."[39] Early just grinned and rode on, perhaps glad to see that somebody in his army still had some fight in him, while the crew also headed south, taking their clogged gun with them.

Averell's two brigades, west of the Valley Turnpike, advanced against the high ground west of Winchester where there were some old earthworks built by a Union garrison earlier in the war. Fitz Lee's two brigades of Southern cavalry arrived just in time to defend these forts from Averell's attack. But the Federals regrouped and charged again and this time the Rebels retreated. Wilson had been ordered to move around the Rebels' southern flank and cut off their escape, but he did not seem to try very hard to get past Lomax's two cavalry brigades guarding that area.

The collapse of Breckinridge's two northward-facing divisions exposed the flank and rear of Grimes' and Ramseur's divisions. Early sent word for Grimes to refuse—or pull back—his left flank to face this new danger. Grimes rushed to the critical point. "Upon coming into the open field," he later wrote his wife, "I perceived everything to be in the most inextricable confusion—horses dashing over the field, cannon being run to the rear at the top of the horses' speed, men leaving their command, and scattering in confusion." Many of Grimes' men saw the same sight, and groups of them began to join the retreat before they could be cut off. Grimes threatened "to blow the brains out" of those who ran, but, as he told his wife, "Our troops did not behave with their usual valor."[40]

Somehow he managed to get his flank turned to face north despite his horse being shot out from under him and three of his staff officers being wounded. Then he moved his division to the southern portion of Winchester, where he saw women standing in the streets pleading with the retreating soldiers to stand and fight. One of these women was General Gordon's wife. She was so persistent in staying near her husband during this campaign that Early had once said, "If my men would keep up as she does, I'd never issue another order against straggling."[41]

Ramseur's Division was the farthest from the point of the Union breakthrough and had more time to retire in good order. His three brigades withdrew slowly, stopping to fire occasional volleys at the pursuing Federals. The 20th North Carolina and perhaps other Southern regiments formed a hollow square. This was the traditional Napoleonic defense against cavalry attack, seldom needed or used in the Civil War. One of Ramseur's brigade commanders, Brigadier General Archibald C. Godwin, was killed instantly by a shell fragment that struck him in the head. South of Winchester these Rebels formed a rear guard that saved the supply wagons and artillery.

"I thout we could whipe the world we was so well fortifide," one of Ramseur's men wrote to a relative in a poorly spelled but accurate summary of the afternoon's events, "but I was badly deceived the enemy flanke our cavelery on our left and came up in rearer of us. This was one of the awfull times for us I ever saw and I hope to never to see another such a time with our army. It was a perfect skidaddle every man fore him self I say to you cousin it was god blessing to us it was neare nite or the most of our army the would have ben taken prisoner . . . they was maney tears shed in giting out from that place."[42]

"Down through the streets of Winchester fled the Rebels," Captain Rhodes of the 2nd Rhode Island wrote, "and our Cavalry pursued, and firing up and down the streets took place. Darkness came on and put an end to the fight. Around one house, surrounded by a picket fence, I counted 16 dead Cavalrymen shot off their horses by Rebels in the yard. The Rebels left their dead and wounded on the field as well as one piece of Artillery and several caissons. After the fight the men were wild with joy. I could have knelt and kissed the folds of the old flag that waved in triumph. We captured several Rebel flags which were displayed along the front of our line. I cried and shouted in my excitement and never felt so good before in my life. I have been in a good many battles but never in such a victory as this."[43]

"Night found Sheridan's hosts in full and exultant possession of much-abused, beloved Winchester," wrote a wounded, captured Southern officer. "The hotel hospital was pretty full of desperately wounded and dying Confederates. The entire building was shrouded in darkness during the dreadful night. Sleep was impossible, as the groans, sighs, shrieks, prayers, and oaths of the wretched sufferers, combined with my own severe pain, banished all thought of rest . . . Our scattered troops, closely followed by the large army of pursuers, retreated rapidly and in disorder through the city. It was a sad, humiliating sight."[44] But the

Union pursuit was not vigorous, for the Federals were almost as worn out and disorganized by victory as were the Confederates by defeat. However, the retreat continued into the night, not stopping until the Rebels had reached Newtown. The Federals made camp in the fields around Winchester.

Sheridan and Crook rode into the town not long after the Confederates left it and went to the home of Rebecca Wright to thank her for her help. Sheridan sat down at one of the desks in her school and wrote a dispatch to Grant: "I have the honor to report that I attacked the forces of General Early on the Berryville pike at the crossing of Opequon Creek, and after a most stubborn and sanguinary engagement, which lasted from early in the morning until 5 o'clock in the evening, completely defeated him, and, driving him through Winchester, captured about 2,500 prisoners, 5 pieces of artillery, 9 army flags, and most of their wounded . . . The conduct of the officers and men was most superb. They charged and carried every position taken up by the rebels from Opequon Creek to Winchester. The enemy were strong in number and very obstinate in their fighting."[45] Then he issued orders for the army to take the road south at 5 a.m.

A report by Sheridan's chief of staff was soon being quoted in all the Northern newspapers: "We have just sent them whirling through Winchester, and we are after them tomorrow. This army behaved splendidly."[46] Thus ended what Custer called "the bulliest day since Christ was born."[47]

On the retreat south, Early, who had voted against secession but had nevertheless followed his state when it had seceded, turned to Breckinridge, who had been the champion of the South's right to take slavery into the new western territories—the issue that had led to the election of Lincoln, to secession, and to war. "What do you think of the 'rights of the South in the Territories,' now?" he asked.[48]

---

1. Wert, *From Winchester to Cedar Creek*, 71.

2. Ibid., 72.

3. Gregory J. W. Urwin, *Custer Victorious: The Civil War Battles of General George Armstrong Custer* (East Brunswick, N.J., 1983), 147.

4. Wert, *From Winchester to Cedar Creek*, 73.

5. Urwin, *Custer Victorious*, 179.

6. Ibid., 180.

7. Wert, *From Winchester to Cedar Creek*, 76.

8. Ibid., 78.

9. Ibid.

10. *Official Records*, 43:I:456.

11. Ibid.

12. Ibid.

13. Stephen Z. Starr, *The Union Cavalry in the Civil War*, vol. 2 (Baton Rouge, 1981), 276.

14. *Official Records*, 43:1:456–457.

15. Urwin, *Custer Victorious*, 184.

16. Wert, *From Winchester to Cedar Creek*, 82.

17. Ibid., 84–85.

18. Ibid., 85.

19. Pond, *The Shenandoah Valley In 1864*, 166.

20. Wert, *From Winchester to Cedar Creek*, 89.

21. Ibid., 86.

22. Ibid., 89.

23. Ibid., 90.

24. Ibid.

25. Ibid., 91.

26. Ibid., 92.

27. Ibid., 93.

28. Ibid., 93–94.

29. Rhodes, *All For the Union*, 184.

30. Wert, *From Winchester to Cedar Creek*, 94.

31. Urwin, *Custer Victorious*, 185.

32. Wert, *From Winchester to Cedar Creek*, 94.

33. Douglas, *I Rode With Stonewall*, 297.

34. Wert, *From Winchester to Cedar Creek*, 95.

35. *Official Records*, 43:I:458.

36. Wert, *From Winchester to Cedar Creek*, 95.

37. Ibid., 96.

38. Ibid.

39. Ibid., 95–96.

40. Ibid., 96–97.

41. Douglas Southall Freeman, *Lee's Lieutenants: A Study in Command*, vol. 3 (New York, 1944), 581, n. 127.

42. Wert, From *Winchester to Cedar Creek*, 97.

43. Pond, *The Shenandoah Valley in 1864*, 166–167.

44. Rhodes, *All for the Union*, 185.
45. *Official Records*, 43:1:24–25.
46. Foote, *The Civil War*, 3:554.
47. Urwin, *Custer Victorious*, 188.
48. Wert, *From Winchester to Cedar Creek*, 109.

CHAPTER SEVEN

The Famous Soldier of the West

19–21 September 1864

At 9 a.m. on the same day as the battle of the Opequon, 19 September 1864, the steamer *Philo Parsons* made its regular stop at Amherstburg on Lake Erie where several men came on board carrying an old trunk. They joined two men who had boarded at Detroit the night before. At 4 that afternoon one of these men entered the ship's wheelhouse, drew a Colt navy model revolver and announced, "This is a prize ship of the Confederacy."

The first mate was stunned. "Are you men Rebels?" he asked.

"We are, sir," he was told, "and you are our prisoner."

At gunpoint, one of the Confederate agents took the wheel. "Sit there in that chair," the leader told the first mate. "And in a while you'll soon see fireworks."[1]

The Rebel leader was John Yates Beall, 28, acting master of privateers in the Confederate Navy. The year before, he had played havoc with Union shipping on Chesapeake Bay until he had been captured. He and his men had been charged with piracy by their captors, but when the Confederate government had threatened to retaliate against Federal prisoners they had been exchanged. He had then slipped through Union lines, made his way to Detroit, and crossed into Canada to join the Southern agents working out of there. He had a plan for opening a whole new theater of war on the great lakes. The United States had only one gunboat on the lakes, the USS *Michigan,* and if he could capture it he could free the Confederate prisoners of war at Johnson's Island and use them and the gunboat to threaten every Northern city on or near the lakes.

At a meeting in Toronto the Rebel agents worked out the details. Captain Charles Cole, who had ridden with Confederate cavalry raiders John Hunt Morgan and Nathan Bedford Forrest before coming to Canada, was sent to Sandusky, Ohio, where he posed as a wealthy young Philadelphia banker. He contacted members of a new Copperhead group in Ohio calling itself the Order of the Star but, what was more important, he managed to wangle an introduction to the captain of the *Michigan,* and soon he was hosting lavish parties for him and his officers, "sumptuous dinners, dispensed with the choicest wines."[2] This led to invitations to visit the gunboat, and then to an introduction to the commandant of the prison on Johnson's Island, where he also became a frequent visitor. Messages were passed to the Rebel prisoners on tiny slips of paper inserted in cigars the spendthrift banker passed out to the Confederate officers, alerting them to the agents' plan right under the noses of the Union guards.

Cole was going to put the *Michigan* temporarily out of action by drugging the champagne at one of his dinner parties for her officers. Meanwhile, Beall and twenty men would seize the *Philo Parsons.* When Cole signaled his success by firing off a signal rocket, the *Parsons* would sail in, the gunboat would be seized, and the prisoners, armed with weapons smuggled past bribed guards and backed by the guns of the *Michigan,* would break out. They would then capture the arsenal at Sandusky and, as Confederate commissioner to Canada Jacob Thompson put it, "form a nucleus of an army, which could be used for greater things."[3]

After seizing the *Philo Parsons,* Beale and his men threw all of its freight overboard and held its passengers, mostly women, at gunpoint. The ship's first mate claimed they also robbed the cash box of eighty dollars. When the large steamer *Island Queen* came by they ran her down and boarded her. "This ship is a prize of the Confederate States of America," Beall announced. "I want you not to resist."[4] Among the passengers were 35 officers and men of the 130th Ohio Infantry Regiment, but they were all unarmed and were easily captured. After giving their paroles not to fight again until properly exchanged, they were set ashore on the American side. The *Queen* was then scuttled in the middle of the lake, and the Rebels continued on their way in the *Philo Parsons*.

At 11 p.m. they reached Middle Bass Island, and half a mile off they could see the lights of the *Michigan*, anchored off Johnson's Island. There they waited until midnight for Cole's signal rocket, but when none was seen the men approached Beall in the wheelhouse.

"Get back to your posts," Beall told them.

"We can't, sir," one of them answered. "It's too late."

"What do you mean?" Beall demanded.

"There won't be any rockets. We've been betrayed," came the answer. "To go on means suicide."

Beall was not inclined to give up so easily. "Signal the engine room, John," he told his second in command. "We'll attack the *Michigan*." But the men refused to participate in such a risky venture. Beall finally gave up, but first he made the men sign what he called "a memoir of your treachery and cowardice." He said later that he never thought they would sign it, but they did. Then they steamed across to the Canadian side, abandoned the ship, and set it on fire. All Beall's plans and work also went up in smoke. "Bitter, bitter defeat," he called it.[5]

On board the *Michigan*, servants from the Sandusky Hotel were preparing another of Cole's sumptious dinners for the captain and his officers at about the same time that the *Parsons* steamed up to Middle Bass Island. Cole was in his hotel room dressing for the party, where he planned to spike the champagne, when a servant reported that he had successfully delivered his message to "his friend on West Street," the leader of the local Copperheads. "The gentleman said he would see you this evening," the servant added. But then came a knock on the door and, before he could answer, it was kicked in. The hotel clerk, a Union lieutenant, and five armed soldiers walked in.

"Are you Captain Cole?" the officer asked.

"Yes, I am," he admitted.

"You are under arrest. You must come with me," he was told.

"On what charge, sir?" Cole demanded.

"Treason," came the answer.[6]

Cole was eventually tried by court martial, convicted, and sentenced to hang. But when he signed a confession and took the amnesty oath he was released. Meanwhile, news of the Confederate plot soon threw the Northern cities bordering the lakes into a panic, while the *Michigan* was laid up with an engine that had been wrecked by an engineer Cole had bribed. And Beall returned to Toronto to hatch new plots for bringing war to the great lakes.

Out in Missouri, early on the morning of 20 September, two bands of Confederate guerrillas, led by George Todd and John Thrailkill, rode into Keytesville and surrounded the courthouse. Todd was a half-crazy murderer who had taken over most of the infamous William Quantrill's band by the simple means of threatening Quantrill with a gun to his head. Inside the courthouse was a garrison of 35 Union militiamen commanded by Lieutenant Anthony Pleyer. Thrailkill rode forward with a white flag and announced that he had 250 men and that if the Federals did not surrender in fifteen minutes he would burn the entire town and kill the entire garrison. Pleyer, on the advice of the sheriff of the county, surrendered. Seven of his men joined the bushwhackers, as the guerrillas were generally known, and the rest were paroled by Thrailkill, who signed himself as a Confederate major. He complimented Pleyer on his decision to surrender, saying that if the Federals had fired a single shot he could not have prevented his men from "burning the last house in town and killing every man at the same time."[7] Thrailkill made a speech extolling the Confederacy, then the guerrillas robbed the civilians of their horses and guns, burned the courthouse, and marched the sheriff and another prominent Union man out of town and shot them.

Confederate President Jefferson Davis left his capital of Richmond on 20 September to try to repair some of the damage recently done to his cause in Georgia. And another traveler reached his destination in Georgia that day. Lieutenant Colonel Horace Porter of Grant's staff arrived in Atlanta to confer with Sherman.

"My mind was naturally wrought up to a high pitch of curiousity to see the famous soldier of the West, whom I had never met," Porter remembered. "He had taken up his quarters in a comfortable brick house belonging to Judge Lyons, opposite the Court-house Square. As I approached I saw the captor of Atlanta on the porch, sitting tilted back in a large arm-chair, reading a newspaper. His coat was unbuttoned, his black felt hat slouched over his brow, and on his feet were a pair of slippers very much down at the heels. He was in the prime of life and in the perfection of physical health. He was just forty-four years of age, and almost at the summit of his military fame. With his large frame, tall, gaunt form, restless hazel eyes, aquiline nose, bronzed face, and crisp beard, he looked the picture of 'grim-visaged war.' My coming had been announced to him by telegraph, and he was expecting my arrival at this time. I approached him, introduced myself, and handed him General

Grant's letter. He tilted forward in his chair, crumpled the newspaper in his left hand while with his right he shook hands cordially, then pushed a chair forward and invited me to sit down. His reception was exceedingly cordial, and his manner exhibited all the personal peculiarities which General Grant, in speaking of him, had so often described.

"After reading General Grant's letter, he entered at once upon an animated discussion of the military situation East and West, and as he waxed more intense in his manner the nervous energy of his nature soon began to manifest itself. He twice rose from his chair, and sat down again, twisted the newspaper into every conceivable shape, and from time to time drew first one foot and then the other out of its slipper, and followed up the movement by shoving out his leg so that the foot could recapture the slipper and thrust itself into it again. He exhibited a strong individuality in every movement, and there was a peculiar energy of manner in uttering the crisp words and epigrammatic phrases which fell from his lips as rapidly as shots from a magazine-gun. I soon realized that he was one of the most dramatic and picturesque characters of the war. He asked a great deal about the armies of the East, and spoke of the avidity with which he read all accounts of the desperate campaigns they were waging. He said: 'I knew Grant would make the fur fly when he started down through Virginia. Wherever he is the enemy will never find any trouble about getting up a fight. He has all the tenacity of a Scotch terrier. That he will accomplish his whole purpose I have never had a doubt. I know well the immense advantage which the enemy has in acting on the defensive in a peculiarly defensive country, falling back on his supplies when we are moving away from ours, taking advantage of every river, hill, forest, and swamp to hold us at bay, and intrenching every night behind fortified lines to make himself safe from attack. Grant ought to have an army more than twice the size of that of the enemy in order to make matters at all equal in Virginia. When Grant cried "Forward!" after the battle of the Wilderness, I said: "This is the grandest act of his life; now I feel that the rebellion will be crushed." I wrote him, saying it was a bold order to give, and full of significance; that it showed the mettle of which he was made, and if Wellington could have heard it he would have jumped out of his boots. The terms of Grant's despatch in reply to the announcement of the capture of Atlanta gave us great satisfaction here. I took that and the noble letter written by President Lincoln, and published them in general orders; and they did much to encourage the troops and make them feel that their hard work was appreciated by those highest in command.'

"After a while lunch was announced, and the general invited me to his mess, consisting of himself and his personal staff. Among the latter

I met some of my old army friends, whom I was much gratified to see again. The general's mess was established in the dining-room of the house he occupied, and was about as democratic as Grant's. The officers came and went as their duties required, and meals were eaten without the slightest ceremony. After we were seated at the table the general said: 'I don't suppose we have anything half as good to eat out here as you fellows in the East have. You have big rivers upon which you can bring up shell-fish, and lots of things we don't have here, where everything has to come over a single-track railroad more than three hundred miles long, and you bet we don't spare any cars for luxuries. It is all we can do to get the necessaries down this far. However, here is some pretty fair beef, and there are plenty of potatoes,' pointing to the dishes; 'and they are good enough for anybody. We did get a little short of rations at times on the march down here, and one of my staff told me a good story of what one of the men had to say about it. An officer found him eating a persimmon that he had picked up, and cried out to him, "Don't eat that; it's not good for you." "I'm not eatin' it because it's good," was the reply; "I'm tryin' to pucker up my stomach so as to fit the size of the rations Uncle Billy Sherman's a-givin' us."'

"After lunch we repaired to a room in the house which the general used for his office, and there went into an elaborate discussion of the purpose of my visit. He said: 'I am more than ever of the opinion that there ought to be some definite objective point or points decided upon before I move farther into this country; sweeping around generally through Georgia for the purpose of inflicting damage would not be good generalship; I want to strike out for the sea. Now that our people have secured Mobile Bay, they might be able to send a force up to Columbus. That would be of great assistance to me in penetrating farther into this State; but unless Canby is largely reinforced, he will probably have as much as he can do at present in taking care of the rebels west of the Mississippi. If after Grant takes Wilmington he could, with the cooperation of the navy, get hold of Savannah, and open the Savannah River up to the neighborhood of Augusta, I would feel pretty safe in picking up the bulk of this army and moving east, subsisting off the country. I could move to Milledgeville, and threaten both Macon and Augusta, and by making feints I could manoeuver the enemy out of Augusta. I can subsist my army upon the country as long as I can keep moving; but if I should have to stop and fight battles the difficulty would be greatly increased. There is no telling what Hood will do, whether he will follow me and contest my march eastward, or whether he will start north with his whole army, thinking there will not be any adequate force to oppose him, and that he can carry the war as far north as Kentucky. I don't care much which he does. I would rather have him start north, though; and I would be willing to give him a free ticket and pay his expenses if he would decide to take that horn of the dilemma. I could send enough of this army to delay his progress until our troops scattered through the West could be concentrated in sufficient force to destroy him; then with the bulk of my army I could cut a swath through to the sea, divide the Confederacy in two, and be able to move up in the rear of Lee, or do almost anything else Grant might require of me. Both Jeff Davis, according to the tone of his recent speeches, and Hood want me to fall back. That is just the reason why I want to go forward.'

"The general then went into a long discussion of the details which would have to be carried out under the several contingencies which might occur. He said: 'In any emergency I should probably want to designate a couple of points on the coast where I could reach the sea as compelled by circumstances; and a fleet of provisions ought to be sent to each one of the points, so that I would be sure of having supplies awaiting me.' I told him this had been discussed by General Grant, and it was his intention to make ample provisions of that nature. The general said further: 'You know when I cut loose from my communications you will not hear anything from me direct, and Grant will have to learn of my whereabouts, and the points where I reach the coast, by means of scouts, if we can get any through the country, and possibly depend largely upon the news obtained from rebel newspapers. I suppose you get these papers through the lines just as we do here.' I said: 'Yes; and I think more readily. The enemy is always eager to get the New York papers, and as we receive them daily, we exchange them for Richmond and Petersburg papers, and obtain in that way much news that is valuable. There will be no difficulty in hearing of your movements almost daily.' At the close of the conversation I told the general I was anxious to get back to headquarters as soon as it would suit his convenience. He asked me to stay a couple of days, saying he would talk matters over further, and would write some communications for General Grant, a report, and also a list of the names of officers whom he wished to have promoted, if it could be prepared in time."[8]

That day Sherman wrote one letter to Grant and one to Halleck. To Grant he said: "As to the future, I am pleased to know that your army is being steadily reenforced by a good class of men, and I hope it will go on until you have a force that is numerically double that of your antagonist, so that with one part you can watch him, and with the other push out boldly from your left flank, occupy the Southside Railroad, compel him to attack you in position, or accept battle on your own terms.

"We ought to ask our country for the largest possible armies that can be raised, as so important a thing as the self-existence of a great nation should not be left to the fickle chances of war." He then discussed the desirability and possibilities of Grant capturing Wilmington from the sea. He thought that should be followed by sending the fleet against Savannah. "It once in our possession, and the river open to us, I would not hesitate to cross the State of Georgia with sixty thousand men, hauling some stores, and depending on the country for the balance. Where a million of people find subsistence, my army won't starve; but, as you know, in a country like Georgia, with few roads and innumerable streams, an inferior force can so delay an army and harass it, that it would not be a formidable object; but if the enemy knew that we had our boats in the Savannah River I could rapidly move to Milledgeville, where there is abundance of corn and meat, and could so threaten Macon and Augusta that the enemy would doubtless give up Macon for Augusta; then I would move so as to interpose between Augusta and Savannah, and force him to give us Augusta, with the only powder-mills and factories remaining in the South, or let us have the use of the Savannah River. Either horn of the dilemma will be worth a battle. I would prefer his holding Augusta (as the probabilities are); for then, with the Savannah River in our possession, the taking of Augusta would be a mere matter of time. This campaign can be made in the winter.

"But the more I study the game, the more am I convinced that it would be wrong for us to penetrate farther into Georgia without an objective beyond. It would not be productive of much good. I can start east and make a circuit south and back, doing vast damage to the State, but resulting in no permanent good; and by mere threatening to do so, I hold a rod over the Georgians, who are not over-loyal to the South. I will therefore give it as my opinion that your army and Canby's should be reenforced to the maximum; that, after you get Wilmington, you should strike for Savannah and its river; that General Canby should hold the Mississippi River, and send a force to take Columbus, Georgia, either by way of the Alabama or Appalachicola River; that I should keep Hood employed and put my army in fine order for a march on Augusta, Columbia, and Charleston; and start as soon as Wilmington is sealed to commerce, and the city of Savannah is in our possession.

"I think it will be found that the movements of Price and Shelby, west of the Mississippi, are mere diversions. They cannot hope to enter Missouri except as raiders; and the truth is that General Rosecrans should be ashamed to take my troops for such a purpose. If you will secure Wilmington and the city of Savannah from your centre, and let General Canby have command over the Mississippi River and country west of it, I will send a force to the Alabama and Appalachicola, provided you give me one hundred thousand of the drafted men to fill up my old regiments; and if you will fix a day to be in Savannah, I will insure our possession of Macon and a point on the river below Augusta. The possession of the Savannah River is more than fatal to the possibility of Southern independence. They may stand the fall of Richmond, but not of all Georgia.

"I will have a long talk with Colonel Porter, and tell him every thing that may occur to me of interest to you.

"In the mean time, know that I admire your dogged perserverance and pluck more than ever. If you can whip Lee and I can march to the Atlantic, I think Uncle Abe will give us a twenty days' leave of absence to see the young folks."⁹

Sherman's note to Halleck served mainly as a cover letter for copies of the correspondence he and Hood had exchanged over the evacuation of the citizens of Atlanta. "In explanation of the tone which marks some of these letters," he wrote, "I will only call your attention to the fact that, after I had announced my determination, General Hood took upon himself to question my motives. I could not tamely submit to such impertinence; and I have also seen that, in violation of all official usage, he has published in the Macon newspapers such parts of the correspondence as suited his purpose. This could have had no other object than to create a feeling on the part of the people; but if he expects to resort to such artifices, I think I can meet him there too.

"It is sufficient for my Government to know that the removal of the inhabitants has been made with liberality and fairness, that it has been attended with no force, and that no women or children have suffered, unless for want of provisions by their natural protectors and friends.

"My real reasons for this step were:

"We want all the houses of Atlanta for military storage occupation.

"We want to contract the lines of defense, so as to diminish the garrison to the limit necessary to defend its narrow and vital parts, instead of embracing, as the lines now do, the vast suburbs. This contraction of the lines, with the necessary citadels and redoubts, will make it necessary to destroy the very houses used by families as residences.

"Atlanta is a fortified town, was stubbornly defended, and fairly captured. As captors, we have a right to it.

"The residence here of a poor population would compel us, sooner or later, to feed them or to see them starve under our eyes.

"The residence here of the families of our enemies would be a temptation and a means to keep up a correspondence dangerous and hurtful to our cause; a civil population calls for provost-guards, and absorbs the attention of officers in listening to everlasting complaints and special grievances that are not military.

"These are my reasons; and, if satisfactory to the Government of the United States, it makes no difference whether it pleases General Hood and *his* people or not."[10]

Hood was not pleased, nor was he content to sit and wait for Sherman's next move. "On the 21st," Sherman wrote, "Hood shifted his army across from the Macon road, at Lovejoy's, to the West Point road, at Palmetto Station, and his cavalry appeared on the west side of the Chattahoochee, toward Powder Springs; thus, as it were, stepping aside, and opening wide the door for us to enter Central Georgia. I inferred, however, that his real purpose was to assume the offensive against our railroads."[11] Mary Chesnut, the Southern diarist, saw the danger in this move. "The end has come," she wrote, "no doubt of the fact. Our Army has so moved as to uncover Macon and Augusta. We are going to be wiped off the face of the earth. Now what is there to prevent Sherman taking General Lee in the rear. We have but two armies, and Sherman is between them now."[12]

Before Sherman had taken Atlanta he had sent most of his cavalry on a raid to cut the railroad supply lines into that city and, if possible, to liberate Union prisoners of war being held at Macon and Andersonville. The raid had failed miserably, due mostly to the highly effective counter-measures taken by Hood's chief of cavalry, Major General Joseph "Fighting Joe" Wheeler. But it had led Hood into making a serious mistake. Knowing that Sherman's cavalry was greatly reduced in numbers and efficiency, he sent Wheeler with better than half of his cavalry to raid Sherman's railroad supply line in northern Georgia and Tennessee. It was a mistake, because while Wheeler was a highly effective fighter he and his men were overly fond of plundering and not at all inclined to the kind of hard work involved in destroying railroads. As one Georgia politician put it, "I cannot say he has done no good, for he has relieved the poor people here of his plundering, marauding bands of cowardly robbers . . . I hope to God he will never get back to Georgia." Wheeler had made a few half-hearted attacks on the railroad in northern Georgia and then ridden on into east Tennessee, where he did his cause absolutely no good at all. As the same politician observed, he had "avoided all depots where there was as much as an armed sutler."[13] By the time Wheeler had finally hit Sherman's main line from Nashville, the Northern general had taken advantage of his absence to march undetected around to the south of Atlanta and cut its rail lines with almost his entire army, forcing Hood to abandon the city.

Now, on the 21st of September, Wheeler returned to Confederate territory by crossing to the south side of the Tennessee river at Tuscumbia, Alabama. There he met the much more effective Major General Nathan Bedford Forrest, who was headed in the other direction with three of his own brigades. Wheeler wrote to Hood: "General Forrest thinks that the aid of my force for ten or twelve days would be of great service to him and materially affect the success of his expedition . . . However, unless I hear from you, will start [back to Georgia] as directed as soon as possible. General Williams being absent with half my command, I will only be able to bring back 2,000 men."[14]

However, a letter from Forrest indicates that he was not really so eager to have Wheeler's help: "I met Major-General Wheeler to-day at Tuscumbia . . . He claims to have about 2,000 men with him; his adjutant-general says, however, that he will not be able to raise and carry back with him exceeding 1,000, and in all probability not over 500.

"One of his brigades left him and he does not know whether they are captured or have returned, or are still in Middle Tennessee.

"His whole command is demoralized to such an extent that he expresses himself as disheartened, and that, having lost influence with the troops, and being unable to secure the aid and co-operation of his officers, he believes it to the interest of the service that he should be relieved of command."[15]

One reason Wheeler's force was so diminished was that many of his men had fallen behind due to broken down horses, or perhaps had just felt like taking a break from the war. Wheeler did give Forrest two regiments which had been part of the latter's own brigade when he had been in the Army of Tennessee, but they totalled only about sixty men. "When I left the brigade with him last November it then numbered over 2,300 men," Forrest wrote to his boss, Richard Taylor. "I hope to be instrumental in gathering them up."[16] Taylor, knowing that Wheeler was senior to Forrest on the list of major generals, replied that he relied greatly upon Forrest's "skill and energy in accomplishing the object of the present movement, and to this end desire and authorize you to be guided in your operations by your own good judgment, reporting directly to me and acting independently of any officer, regardless of rank, with whom you may come in contact."[17]

---

1. James D. Horan, *Confederate Agent: A Discovery in History* (New York, 1954), 159–160.
2. Ibid., 158.

3. Ibid.
4. Ibid., 160.
5. Ibid., 161–162.
6. Ibid., 164.
7. Albert Castel, *William Clarke Quantrill: His Life and Times* (New York, 1962).
8. Porter, *Campaigning With Grant*, 289–295.
9. Sherman, *Memoirs*, 587–589.
10. Ibid., 591–592.
11. Ibid., 615.
12. Chesnut, *A Diary From Dixie*, 435–436.
13. Carter, *The Last Cavaliers*, 258.
14. Ibid., 259.
15. Ibid.
16. Henry, *"First With the Most" Forrest*, 351.
17. Ibid., 352.

CHAPTER EIGHT

We Have Whipped the Flower of the Rebel Army

22 September 1864

On 21 September, two days after the battle of the Opequon, as the Federals called it, or the third battle of Winchester according to the Confederates, Sheridan put his troops in motion for another attack on Early's Army of the Valley. The Confederate commander had ended his retreat at Fisher's Hill, a formidable position southwest of Strasburg which he had occupied the month before. "This was the only position in the whole Valley," Early later wrote, "where a defensive line could be taken against an enemy moving up the Valley, and it had several weak points. To have retired beyond this point would have rendered it necessary for me to fall back to some of the gaps of the Blue Ridge, at the upper part of the Valley, and I determined therefore to make a show of a stand here, with the hopes that the enemy would be deterred from attacking me in this position, as had been the case in August."[1]

But things had changed since August. On the earlier occasion Sheridan had been new to his job, unfamiliar with the area, and had received orders from Grant to assume the defensive. Now he was leading a victorious army in pursuit of a defeated foe. He had received promotion to brigadier general in the regular army, word from Grant that the general-in-chief had ordered another 100-gun salute fired with shotted guns, and the personal congratulations of President Lincoln. He intended to attack as soon as possible despite the strength of the position.

And it was strong. A member of Upton's brigade said Fisher's Hill was "one of the strongest positions I have ever seen." Another Federal said, "It was evident that a direct assault must fail. Bravery alone could never gain us the upper Valley."[2] Near Strasburg, about 20 miles southwest of Winchester, the Shenandoah Valley is split in two by the Massanutten Mountains. The Shenandoah River also splits, with the North Fork on one side of the Massanutten chain and the South Fork on the other. Fisher's Hill is just northwest of the North Fork, not far from where it turns to the southeast to round the last of the Massanuttens, known as Three Top Mountain, and joins the South Fork. About four miles northwest of the Massanuttens was Little North Mountain, forming the other side of the main valley. Fisher's Hill "is so formed," one of Sheridan's men wrote, "that it appears a huge, high-fronted billow of earth and rocks, which had some time been rolling down the Valley, and became strangled between these two mountains and held still, with its frowning crest looking northward, where it now sternly faced our advance."[3] Aptly named Tumbling Run coursed to the southeast along the base of the hill to join the North Fork of the Shenandoah, forming a moat the Federals would have to cross just to get at the hill, on top of which were breastworks the Rebels had built the month before.

On the Confederate right, next to the river, which was the strongest part of the position, Early placed what had been Breckinridge's Division, now again under Wharton, for that day orders were received for Breckinridge to return to his own Department of Southwestern Virginia, which was being invaded from both Kentucky and Tennessee. On Wharton's left, extending across the Valley Turnpike, was Gordon's Division. Next was the division that had been commanded by Ramseur, but was now under Brigadier General John Pegram, because Early had transferred Ramseur to the command of what had been Rodes' Division. That was the biggest and best division in the Army of the Valley and it needed an experienced commander. Nor was Ramseur a stranger to that division for he had once commanded one of its brigades. Ramseur's new division was on Pegram's left on a wooded section of the hill, but it did not reach all the way to Little North Mountain. To make that connection, most of Lunsford Lomax's cavalry division was dismounted and placed on a wooded hog-back ridge between the main hill and the mountain. However, McCausland's Brigade of Lomax's cavalry was placed at the other end of the line, between the North Fork and Three Top Mountain. Meanwhile, Fitz Lee's cavalry division, now under its senior brigade commander, William Wickham, had been sent to block the smaller valley of the South Fork, known as the Luray Valley, which lies between the Massanutten range and the Blue Ridge.

Sheridan's army had covered the 20 miles from Winchester to Strasburg on the twentieth, and that night he had met with his corps commanders in his tent pitched beside the turnpike south of Cedar Creek. They agreed that Early's position was too strong for a frontal assault. Crook suggested a turning movement around the Confederate left, and Sheridan agreed. But he saw surprise as the essential element in his plan. The 6th and 19th Corps were already close enough to the Rebels for any move they made to be observed from the Southern signal station up on Three Top Mountain. But Crook's 8th Corps had been kept well back behind Cedar Creek, with the wagons. That night Crook brought his two divisions closer and placed them in the concealment of some woods. Meanwhile, Sheridan sent Torbert with Merritt's cavalry division southeast to join Wilson's division at Front Royal, at the entrance to the Luray Valley. From there they were to sweep up the smaller valley and cross the Massanutten range at its only gap, which led to New Market. There they would block the Confederates' retreat route.

At dawn on the 21st, Wilson's two brigades charged through the fog with a terrific yell and blaring bugles against Munford's brigade of Fitz Lee's division, which was stationed between the South Fork and Front Royal. Munford's Virginians held their own at first until two of Wilson's regiments came in on their flank. Then they broke, with the 2nd Virginia having to fight its way out. South of the town Munford's men reformed behind Wickham's other brigade, Payne's, and both retreated up the Luray Valley. When Torbert arrived with Merritt's division he found Wilson's pursuit stalled at Gooney Run, six miles south of Front Royal. When Wickham learned of Merritt's arrival he waited until dark and then fell back another six miles to Milford.

A little before noon on the 21st, officers in the 6th and 19th corps read the men the congratulatory telegrams from President Lincoln, General Grant, and Secretary of War Stanton for the victory at Winchester. They responded with three cheers. Then they moved forward around

Strasburg behind the cover of their skirmishers and took up positions opposite Fisher's Hill. Some 6th Corps units had a small battle with some of Pegram's men before the latter gave up a knoll called Flint Hill, which gave the Federals a good view of the Confederate position. By then the sun had set. After dark the Northerners extended to the left and dug in along a convex line north of Early's. Emory's two divisions held the left, next to the North Fork, with Wright's three divisions extending beyond them. Averell's cavalry division covered the Union right along the Back Road. Crook's two divisions moved shortly after dark to another woods about a mile from Strasburg. There they rested again until morning, when they began a slow, circuitous march through ravines and trees toward the wooded slopes of Little North Mountain.

Throughout the morning of the 22nd the 6th Corps and the 19th Corps skirmished with the Rebels to their front, and the artillery of both sides occasionally threw a shot or shell at each other. Then at about 11:30 a.m. Sheridan ordered Emory to put some pressure on the Confederates in order to keep them too busy to worry about where Crook's 8th Corps was or what it might be up to. So about 45 minutes later Emory sent some of his infantry to drive the Rebels out of some rifle pits they called "bull pens" on the north side of Tumbling Run. This they did, even though the defenses were, as Emory described them, "strongly barricaded and strongly manned."[4] Between 1 and 2 p.m. Brigadier General James Ricketts' 3rd Division of the 6th Corps extended the Union line farther to the west and drove more Southern skirmishers south of Tumbling Run. In its new position, Ricketts' infantry division connected with Averell's cavalry division.

These movements by the 19th and 6th corps convinced Early that Sheridan would not be deterred from attacking the Fisher's Hill defenses this time. He issued orders for a withdrawal to the south to begin at midnight "as I knew my force was not strong enough to resist a determined assault."[5]

By the time Ricketts had moved into position and Early had issued his orders, Crook's 8th Corps was approaching the base of Little North Mountain. "I led the way in person," Crook wrote, "following my way up a succession of ravines, keeping my eyes on the signal station on top of the mountain, so as to keep out of their sight, making the color bearers trail their flags so they could not be seen."[6] Crook conferred with Averell and requested that one of his two brigades of cavalry support the attack of the infantry while the other protect their rear. When the infantry reached the Back Road, which ran along the foot of the mountain, Crook brought Thoburn's 1st Division from the rear of the column up alongside the 2nd Division, which was now commanded by Rutherford Hayes since Duval had been wounded late on the afternoon of the nineteenth. There the men discarded their knapsacks and arranged their other equipment in such a way that no clink of metal would reveal their presence. Then the march was resumed.

Despite all their efforts, the Federals were spotted. General Grimes saw both divisions moving along the mountainside about 3 p.m. and reported this fact to his new superior, Dodson Ramseur, urging him to shift at least one brigade to the support of Lomax's cavalry. Ramseur replied that he would have to confer with General Early first. "During that hour I suffered more than I've ever done in my life," Grimes told his wife. "My anxiety for the fate of the army was intolerable." A diarist in the Confederate artillery noted, "We can see them plainly climbing up the side of North Mountain. Gen. Early knows this," he added, without saying what made him think so, "and has troops there to meet them, and unless he has, we will have to get from this position, and very quickly."[7] Lomax was also aware of Crook's presence and turned his three small brigades to face to the west while dispatching a request to Ramseur that the latter send some infantry to occupy his former defenses. However, Averell's Union cavalry got there first, interposing between Lomax and Ramseur and threatening the former's rear.

Crook's advance encountered a few Rebel cavalry videttes, who fired at the Federal infantry and then vanished among the trees. And some Confederate guns fired a few shells in their direction. Then the Union advance ran into the Rebel picket reserve, which also fired a few shots and fled into the forest. This brief outburst caused the Confederate artillery to lob a few more shells in that direction, but did little harm and soon stopped. Meanwhile, Crook formed his two divisions facing to the east. Thoburn's division was on the left and Hayes' on the right, each with one brigade in front and the other about 15 or 20 yards behind it. Then at about 4 p.m., as the Rebel guns resumed their fire, the Federals started down the side of the mountain with a tremendous shout. "And unless you heard my fellows yell once," Crook wrote, "you can form no conception of it. It beggars all description."[8]

Down the steep slope they ran, "like a western cyclone," through "almost impenetrable cedar thickets," which broke up all their formations. When they reached the bottom of the slope, "the men rushed on," Hayes wrote, "no line, no order, all yelling like madmen." As they came out of the forest they spotted the main position of Lomax's cavalry. "The sight of this," a Union colonel wrote, "instead of checking the men, seemed to inspire them with new ardor. Every man yelled, if possible, louder than before, and each regiment strove to be the first in with its colors." When they struck the dismounted troopers of Bradley John-son's, William Jackson's, and George Smith's brigades the Rebels scat-tered, some running for their horses, others sprinting into the woods to the south. "Our cavalry," one Southern infantryman wrote, "rushed down like the swine with an overdose of devils."[9] The 1st Maryland Cavalry Battalion counterattacked in an effort to stem the Union on-slaught but its captain was seriously wounded and it was easily driven off.

Ramseur quickly moved his left brigade, Battle's, from its earthworks to a prominent ridge across the Federals' path. There the Alabamans knelt behind stone walls to fire a volley. And a battery of Virginia artil-lery turned its guns to fire double cannister, like giant shotguns, into the attackers. This slowed the Union advance, particularly that of Thoburn's men, nearest the Rebel guns, and some of the Federals turned and ran. But they were met by General Crook, who pelted them with rocks and drove them back to their duty. Cullen Battle, meanwhile, kept his Alabamans in their place by clubbing any who tried to run with a cedar stick. Another battery of Confederate guns was wheeled into position behind Battle's infantry and added its fire to the defense. But with Tho-burn's men within 60 yards of the Confederates and Hayes' division overlapping Battle's flank, the Rebels abandoned their stone walls and fell back, leaving one of the Virginia battery's guns behind.

Ramseur pulled Brigadier General William R. Cox's brigade of North Carolinians out of the main line and sent it toward Battle's left flank. But Cox got lost in the woods and wandered off to the southwest, and without his brigade to block Hayes' progress the future president's Union division enfiladed the flank of Battle's retreating Alabamans, and they scattered just as Lomax's dismounted cavalry had, many of them throwing away their weapons and anything else that would slow up their flight. Next Crook's men encountered half of Grimes' Brigade posted on another wooded ridge across their line of advance. The fire of the Confederates slowed what Grimes called "an avalanche" of Federals, but the return fire was deadly and the other half of the brigade, still facing north, suddenly began retreating.[10]

When the sound of Crook's attack reached him, Sheridan exclaimed, "By God, Crook is driving them!"[11] And he sent orders to Wright to advance his 6th Corps. Within minutes, Ricketts' 3rd Division began advancing, its skirmishers out front with orders to concentrate their fire on the Confederate artillery. As the Southern defenders opened fire, the Federals obliqued to their right and four batteries of the 6th Corps plas-tered the Rebel position with shot and shell, while Wright's other two divisions joined the advance. Under the cover of woods, Ricketts' men reached the base of Fisher's Hill and began to climb its steep face. Then "with wild and victorious shouts" they swarmed over Ramseur's defenses, while his one remaining brigade, Crook's, joined the retreat heading south.[12] Then the part of Grimes' Brigade that was facing north also ran, followed by the part that had been facing west. Grimes himself, having lost his mount and sprained an ankle, escaped on an artillery horse, along with the colonel of one of his regiments.

The Federals captured four cannon on this part of the field, although whether they were captured by Crook's men or Ricketts' was a matter of dispute. Early arrived at this part of his line in time to see the North Carolinians running. He urged the 13th Virginia on the left end of Pegram's line to fire into them but they refused, joining the retreat instead. Early sent a staff officer to bring Wharton's Division to the left, but before it could arrive Getty's division of the 6th Corps attacked Pegram's front. One of Getty's brigades lagged behind and another retreated under the Confederate rifle and cannon fire, but while it reformed the other brigade, Colonel James M. Warner's 2nd, splashed across Tumbling Run. Pegram's defenders "poured in one tremendous volley as the troops were struggling across the defile," Getty reported, "then broke and fled in the wildest disorder."[13] Sheridan, who was riding with these troops, yelled, "Run boys, run! Don't wait to form! Don't let 'em stop!" One exhausted soldier replied that he was too tired to run. "If you can't run, then holler," Sheridan told him.[14] The Federals pulled themselves up the slope of Fisher's Hill by grabbing hold of bushes and rocks and scrambled over Pegram's defenses "in a confused delirious mass."[15] More cannon were captured, including an entire battery, and a couple of them were turned against their former owners.

The 1st Division of the 6th Corps, now under Brigadier General Frank Wheaton since the death of Russell and the wounding of Upton, had left its 3rd Brigade behind to garrison Winchester. But the other two charged Gordon's position, east of Pegram's. Lieutenant Colonel Edward L. Campbell's three New Jersey regiments led the way up the slope. "So rapidly did the men dash up the hill," Campbell reported, "that the enemy had no time to reload their pieces, after the first discharge, before our men were upon them, and receiving a heavy fire they broke and fled in utter confusion, leaving their artillery."[16] Scores of Gordon's men were captured as well as the guns. Wharton's Division, coming over from the right, was caught up in the rout of Gordon's and Pegram's men and they all retreated to the south. Meanwhile Grover's 2nd Division of the 19th Corps swept over Wharton's abandoned defenses, capturing a cannon that had been left behind.

Cox's Brigade of Ramseur's Division, the one that had lost its way when sent to reinforce Battle's Brigade, reached the Valley Turnpike in time to act as rear guard for the retreat of Early's demoralized army. Hundreds of the Confederates ran up the side of Massanutten Mountain. A few others surrendered, saying they had had enough of short rations and lost battles, but most followed the turnpike south as far and as fast as they could well into the night. "All the army was nearly exhausted," one Rebel said. "I was so fatigued till I spit blood," he added. "The rout of wagons, caissons, limbers, artillery, and flying men was fearful as the stream swept down the pike toward Woodstock," wrote one Southerner, "as many thought the enemy's cavalry was aiming to get there by the Middle Road and cut us off."[17]

But this time the Union cavalry played no major part in the battle. Averell seemed more interested in gathering up spoils than in chasing the Rebels. After pursuing for a few miles and capturing a number of guns, wagons and prisoners he stopped for the night in the absence of orders from Sheridan "or anyone else."[18] Why he should need additional orders to continue to pursue a routed foe he never explained. When the Northern infantry officers got their intermingled commands reorganized, Emory's 19th Corps, which had done the least fighting, led the pursuit, followed by Wright's 6th Corps. Crook's 8th Corps was left behind to rest and to guard the prisoners. Sheridan ordered Devin's brigade of cavalry, which had been guarding the army's rear, to the front, but it would be hours before it overtook the lead. Meanwhile the Federal infantry pressed on after the retreating Rebels.

Sheridan sent off a telegram to Grant that night: "I have the honor to report that I achieved a most signal victory over the army of General Early at Fisher's Hill today . . . Only darkness has saved the whole of Early's army from total destruction. The First and Third Cavalry Divisions went down the Luray Valley to-day, and if they push on vigorously to the main valley, the result of this day's engagement will be more signal."[19]

Torbert, with most of Merritt's division and all of Wilson's, was still off in the Luray Valley. Shortly after midnight Torbert sent Custer's brigade across the South Fork of the Shenandoah to flank Wickham's cavalry that was defending Gooney Run. When he was in position, Wilson's division advanced, only to find that the Confederates had spotted Custer's move and had withdrawn during the night.

Pushing on to the south, at about 7 a.m. the Federals found the Rebel horsemen defending Overall's Run at Milford. The Southerners had built breastworks of logs, stumps, fence rails, and rocks on a bluff overlooking the stream. Their right was protected by a spur of the Blue Ridge and their left by the South Fork of the Shenandoah and Massanutten Mountain. "Johnnys in a strong position," one of Custer's men noted in his diary.[20] Torbert feinted against Colonel William Payne's brigade on the Confederate left and tried to turn the Rebel right. But Colonel Thomas Munford, who was in temporary command of the division while Wickham was off conferring with Early, sent a squadron to reinforce that flank, as well as three buglers spaced at the distance they would be if riding with three regiments. When they sounded the charge and the Rebels fired, the Union envelopment was called off.

Torbert decided that the Confederate position could neither be turned nor taken. "Their line was very short," he reported, "and the banks of the creek so precipitous it was impossible for the men to get across in order to make a direct attack. In addition to their naturally strong position they were posted behind loophole breastworks, which extended clear across the valley. Not knowing that the army had made an attack at Fisher's Hill, and thinking that the sacrifice would be too great to attack without that knowledge, I concluded to withdraw."[21] A colonel in Custer's brigade wrote: "Torbert made a fiasco of it. He allowed Wickham . . . with at most two small brigades, to hold him at bay and withdrew without making any fight to speak of . . . If Custer or Merritt had been in command it would have been different."[22]

The battle at Fisher's Hill had been so one-sided, the Confederate tendency to retreat rather than fight so strong, that casualties were remarkably light on both sides. The Federals lost 36 killed, 414 wounded and 6 missing. The Rebels, 30 killed, 210 wounded, and 885 missing. Union troops captured 14 Southern guns. To the ecstatic Federals, it was Bull Run in reverse. "We have whipped the flower of the Rebel army," Rutherford Hayes wrote; "they are scattered in all directions."[23]

1. Early, *War Memoirs*, 429.

2. Wert, *From Winchester to Cedar Creek*, 111.

3. Ibid., 109.

4. *Official Records*, 43:I:283.

5. Early, *War Memoirs*, 430.

6. Wert, *From Winchester to Cedar Creek*, 119.

7. Ibid., 120.

8. Ibid., 121.

9. Ibid.

10. Ibid., 123.
11. Ibid., 129.
12. Ibid., 123.
13. *Official Records*, 43:I:192.
14. Wert, *From Winchester to Cedar Creek*, 129.
15. Ibid., 126.
16. *Official Records*, 43:I:170.
17. Wert, *From Winchester to Cedar Creek*, 127.
18. Starr, *The Union Cavalry in the Civil War*, 2:281.
19. Wert, *From Winchester to Cedar Creek*, 129.
20. Ibid., 131.
21. *Official Records*, 43:I:428.
22. Starr, *The Union Cavalry in the Civil War*, 2:289, n. 63.
23. Wert, *From Winchester to Cedar Creek*, 129.

CHAPTER NINE

Close with the Enemy

22–25 September 1864

On that same 22nd day of September, Gillem's Union cavalry brigade, moving from east Tennessee toward Saltville, ran into opposition in the form of three extremely small brigades of Confederate cavalry. These were commanded by brigadier generals Basil Duke, George Cosby, and John Vaughn. Duke commanded what was left of John Hunt Morgan's old division, now consolidated into one brigade of two battalions totaling a mere 322 men. The other two brigades were not much larger. Vaughn was the senior commander, and despite the small size of his force he did his best to stall the Federal advance, striking at Gillem's column at Bull's Gap. Satisfied that he had attracted the attention of all the Rebels that were left in the area, Gillem sent word to Burbridge, up in Kentucky, that the latter's way was clear to Saltville, and suggested that after it was taken Burbridge should move down and take Vaughn in the rear while Gillem hit him from the front.

A military commission convened in Indianapolis that day to try several leading Copperheads who had been arrested for treason. Among the defendants was Harrison H. Dodd, Grand Commander of the Order of the Sons of Liberty for Indiana. Soldiers had found boxes in his office marked "Sunday school books" that were full of weapons and ammunition. Others being tried included Deputy Grand Commander Horace Heffren, Grand Secretary William H. Harrison, Dr. William Bowles, the order's military commander for Indiana, and three of his subordinate "generals," Andrew Humphreys, Stephen Horsey, and J. J. Bingham, editor of the *Indiana State Sentinel* and chairman of the Democratic State Committee. As soon as the preliminaries were out of the way, Dodd was arraigned and his lawyer immediately challenged the right of a military commission to try him or any other civilian. The state was not under martial law, he said, and the civil courts were functioning. Major H. L. Burnett, the judge advocate, however, claimed that the president's proclamation of 25 September 1862 had put all who aided and abetted the South's insurrection under martial law. The commission, headed by Brevet Brigadier General John T. Wilder, withdrew to consider the question and then returned to overrule the lawyer's objection. He was, however, granted a recess to prepare his defense.[1]

Wilder was a combat veteran. He had led the famous Lightning Brigade of mounted infantry regiments in the Army of the Cumberland, which was now part of Sherman's forces down in Georgia. Neither he nor his officers were likely to show any mercy to Northern civilians who aided and abetted the Southern rebellion or plotted one of their own while their fellow citizens were risking life and limb in the army.

Meanwhile, some of Sherman's officers who were also politicians from the states of the old Northwest, where the Copperhead conspiracy was strongest, were being sent home to drum up support for the war effort. Major General John A. Logan departed for home that very day. He was commander of the 15th Corps in the Army of the Tennessee, one of Sherman's three armies, but before the war he had been an influential Democratic congressman from Illinois. Despite the fact that he had been passed over by Sherman for the command of the Army of the Tennessee when its previous commander had been killed in July, he now returned to Illinois and stumped the state in support of the Lincoln administration and the war effort. Another Illinois congressman, Elihu B. Washburne, who had been Grant's political sponsor throughout the war, had written to Logan: "We want your clarion voice to echo over our state and arouse the Union and patriotic people to the salvation of the country."[2]

Logan's help was very valuable to the Republicans and the Union cause, but in the North the news of the two victories in the Shenandoah Valley was an even better support for the reelection of Lincoln. "Phil Sheridan has made a speech in the Shenandoah Valley," wrote congressman and former general James A. Garfield, "more powerful and valuable to the Union cause than all the stumpers in the Republic can make—our prospects are everywhere heightening." As for McClellan, the Democratic candidate and another former general, as one of Sheridan's men put it in a letter to his home town newspaper, "The 'hero of the seven days retreat' is fast becoming unpopular in the army."[3]

Even as Logan was taking leave of his 15th Corps it was being enlarged. It received a division that day that was transferred from the 16th Corps. The latter was a strange organization. During most of its existence its units had been scattered. The start of the 1864 campaign had found part of it garrisoning in southwest Tennessee, part, called the Right Wing, loaned to the Department of the Gulf for the campaign up the Red River, and another part, called the Left Wing, campaigning in Georgia with Sherman. However, not long before Atlanta fell, the commander of the Left Wing, Grenville Dodge, later chief engineer of the Union Pacific Railroad, had been wounded. Now his Left Wing was broken up. One of its divisions was given to the 17th Corps and the other to Logan's 15th. Meanwhile, the former commander of the entire 16th Corps, Major General Stephen A. Hurlbut, took on a new job that day. He assumed command of the Department of the Gulf, which was now part of Canby's Military Division of West Mississippi.

At 4 a.m. on the 23rd Jubal Early broke the news to Lee of his second defeat in the Valley: "Late yesterday the enemy attacked my position at Fisher's Hill and succeeded in driving back the left of my line, which was defended by the cavalry, and throwing a force into the rear of the left of my infantry line, when the whole of the troops gave way in a panic and could not be rallied. This resulted in a loss of twelve pieces of artillery, though my loss in men is not large. I am falling back to New Market, and shall endeavor to check the enemy if he advances. Kershaw's division had better be sent to my aid, through Swift Run Gap, at once."[4] Early thus blamed his men for his misfortune. But Gordon wrote, after the war, that "it is not just to blame the troops. There are conditions in war when courage, firmness, steadiness of nerve, and self-reliance are of small avail. Such were the conditions at Fisher's Hill."[5] A Federal chaplain who inspected the Confederate position the day after it was captured might have disagreed. "I was surprised to see how much Nature had done to fortify the place; my wonder and amazement are that we ever took the place. *But we did.*"[6]

Early on the morning of the 23rd Captain Samuel Chapman, with a squadron of about 120 men from Mosby's Confederate ranger battalion, learned that an ambulance train with an escort of about 200 Federals was nearing Front Royal. He sent Captain Walter E. Frankland with about

45 men to attack the train guard from the front while he took the rest of his command to hit it from the rear. But before he could launch his attack he spied Lowell's brigade of Merritt's Union cavalry approaching on its way back from Milford. He sent his own men back toward Chester Gap in the Blue Ridge and went personally to stop Frankland. However, by the time he arrived the charge had already been made and Frankland was driving the Federal guards back on the ambulances. "Call off your men; you are attacking a brigade!" Chapman told him. "Why, Sam, we've whipped them," Frankland replied, but, reluctantly, he obeyed the order.[7] The retreating Rebels were chased by the Northerners, who "came up like a flock of birds when a stone is cast into it," as one Confederate wrote.[8] And a small party of the 2nd U.S. Cavalry under Lieutenant Charles McMasters tried to cut off their retreat. However, the Confederates made good their escape, killing McMasters in the process, and to the pursuing Federals it looked as though McMasters had been shot while trying to surrender. The main body of the Rebels got away, but six of them were captured.

Mosby's guerrilla tactics and his habit of taking refuge among the sympathetic civilians of the area were considered unfair by most Federal soldiers, and the rangers were known to often wear captured blue Union overcoats to hide their gray uniforms. Now the apparent murder of a surrendering Federal officer threw many of the Northerners into a rage. Merritt ordered the six prisoners to be executed in revenge. Two of them were shot in a yard behind the Front Royal Methodist church. Another was led to a nearby farm, where he was also shot. A fourth was not actually a member of the rangers but a 17-year-old boy from Front Royal who had gone along in hopes of joining the band. His widowed mother ran to the Yankees and pleaded for her son's life, but one soldier threatened to behead her as well as her son with his saber. Then men from Custer's brigade led the youth into a nearby field where one trooper emptied his revolver into the boy. The other two prisoners were offered their lives if they would divulge information about Mosby's headquarters, but they refused to talk. Some of McMaster's men then led them to a large walnut tree where they were hung while a band played "Love Not, The One You Love May Die." First, however, one of them told the Yankees, "Mosby'll hang ten of you for every one of us." The Federals left the bodies hanging with a sign attached to one of them that said, "Such is the fate of all of Mosby's men." As one of Custer's troopers observed, it was a "hard war."[9]

The van of the pursuing Union infantry reached Woodstock at about 3:30 a.m. on the 23rd, marched on through the town, and finally went into bivouac on the far side. As so often happened after a battle, it was raining. Devin's cavalry brigade took over the pursuit and chased the Rebels as far as the town of Mount Jackson. The rest of the 19th and 6th corps arrived at Woodstock throughout the morning, as did Sheridan. Before noon he learned that his hopes for trapping Early's Confederates between Torbert's two cavalry divisions and the rest of the army were not going to be realized and he railed against his friend Torbert's ineptitude.

As is often the case in such matters, however, it was a second person to offend who caught the full force of the general's anger. When Averell's division finally reached the head of the column Sheridan and Averell exchanged "some hot words" about the cavalry division's part in the pursuit so far. "It would seem he sought some object upon which to vent his spleen," one witness said; "and instead of removing the really incompetent Torbert, that splendid fighter, the gallant Averell, became the victim of his pent-up wrath." The same witness wrote that "it can be stated from positive knowledge that while Averell maintained a calm and civil demeanor, Sheridan manifested unreasonable anger, refusing to listen to any explanations."[10]

Averell said: "I replied that I had received no information or instructions from him. He stated that he could not find me. I asked him if he had tried, to which he made no reply, but stated that the rebel army was a perfect mob, which would run away upon the firing of a single gun, and that he desired me to go and put in my cavalry. I assured him that I never hesitated to put in where there was any chance of success. The tone, manner, and words of the major general commanding indicated and implied dissatisfaction." But Averell disputed the claim that the Confederate army had been reduced to a mob. "The loss of his guns at Fisher's Hill had been inconsiderable, and his troops had been too well handled and his stragglers too few to justify in my mind an opinion that he was totally demoralized."[11] At any rate, Sheridan told him to "proceed to the front at once, and in conjunction with Devin, close with the enemy."[12]

At about 3 p.m. Averell finally caught up with Devin and took command of all the pursuing cavalry. They pushed the Rebels beyond Mount Jackson, but on the heights south of the town they could see Early's entire army. "The position, naturally strong, had been strengthened by artificial defenses," Averell reported. "The enemy was fully on the alert and perfectly able to hold the position against five times my force, and a signal officer reported to me that the enemy was moving a brigade or division around my right."[13] Averell notified Sheridan of this development and that after dark he intended to withdraw across a creek and go into camp. When he received this Sheridan replied: "I do not want you to let the enemy bluff you or your command, and I want you to distinctly understand this note. I do not advise rashness, but I do desire resolution and actual fighting, with necessary casualties, before you retire. There must now be no backing or filling by you, without a superior force of the enemy actually engaging you."[14] When he learned that Averell had already gone into camp without waiting for this answer, Sheridan sent another dispatch directing that he turn over command of his division to Colonel William H. Powell and proceed to Wheeling, W. Va., to await orders that never came.

Just after dawn on the next day, the 24th, Kershaw's Division of Confederate infantry and Cutshaw's Battalion of artillery left Orange Court House in a driving rain, marching back to the Shenandoah Valley. General Anderson, however, went on to Richmond to resume command of the rest of his 1st Corps in Lee's army.

The Union 6th and 19th corps were back on the road again on the 24th, joined now by Crook's 8th Corps. At about 10 a.m. the Federals caught up with Early's forces deployed on Rude's Hill, north of New Market, where Breckinridge had defeated Sigel back in May to begin the current round of battles in the Valley. While his artillery probed the Rebel position and infantry skirmishers crossed the North Fork of the Shenandoah, Sheridan sent what was now Powell's division to try to turn the Confederates' left flank and Devin's brigade to get around their right. When Early saw this, he ordered his army to withdraw, a half of each division falling back about a mile and stopping to cover the withdrawal of the other half. South of New Market, at a place called Tenth Legion Church, Early formed his entire command in line of battle in the open. "It was a grand sight," one Southerner wrote, "and I never expect to see its like again." A Northern officer agreed: "From the top of the hills we could see the enemy's long lines of battle stretching across the valley, and moving away from us. Passing over cleared fields or plowed fields, their lines could hardly be distinguished from the ground, save by the flashing of their musket-barrels in the sun. Before their lines of battle were their skirmish lines, which were continually attacked by a line of our cavalry skirmishers. Behind the cavalry skirmish line was an infantry line of skirmishers, and when the first line was checked, the second immediately came up, and the enemy moved on."[15]

At around 5 p.m. the Federals made camp south of New Market. Throughout the day Torbert's cavalry, again moving south at Sheridan's order, pushed Wickham's Rebel troopers southward up the Luray Valley. That evening the Northern horsemen bivouacked at the foot of the pass that led across the Massanuttens to New Market, while Wickham withdrew farther south. Early's infantry also marched on during the night.

Out in Missouri on the 24th, George Todd's and John Thrailkill's bushwhackers were joined by three more bands, led by Dave Poole, "Bloody Bill" Anderson, and William Clarke Quantrill himself. These groups and leaders had had their differences in the past, but they agreed to put them aside and to cooperate. It was not long, however, before they were engaged in what one witness called "an animated and heated argument." Anderson and Todd wanted to attack the nearby town of Fayette, while Quantrill, their old commander, was opposed on the grounds that the place was too well defended. Anderson and Todd controlled most of the men, however, and they told Quantrill, "We are going into Fayette no matter what! If you want to come along, all right. If not then you can go back into the woods with the rest of the cowards!"[16] Anderson was in a fighting mood. The day before, after ambushing some Union supply wagons, killing twelve soldiers and three black teamsters, he had lost six men to pursuing Federals, who had scalped the corpses, a practice Anderson's men were fond of themselves. Now Anderson said that the town would be so easy to take that he and his men would go in first and take care of the garrison, and then all Todd would have to do was sack the place.

Anderson's men rode into Fayette at 10:30 a.m. wearing Union uniforms, and the people of the town, taking them for Federal troops, paid little attention to them, evidently not noticing the scalps dangling from many of their bridles, until one overly eager guerrilla started shooting at a black man wearing a Union uniform who was standing on the sidewalk. The civilians then ran for cover and the Federal garrison, about thirty men, took up position in the brick court house and a blockhouse on a hill outside of town, determined to fight rather than take their chances on surrendering to these bushwhackers.

Anderson's gang galloped on through town, killing two Federal soldiers, but otherwise doing little damage, and when Todd's gang rode in it was greeted by a volley of rifle fire from the court house. The guerrillas returned fire with their revolvers, but succeeded only in breaking a number of windows. Then they too rode on through town, and soon received a call from Anderson to come help him take the blockhouse. Todd arrived to find that Anderson had already charged the blockhouse once and lost several men killed and wounded. The enraged Todd ordered his own band to charge, but the defenders, protected by the thick log walls and firing through narrow loopholes shot down several of his men also. He reformed them and led them forward again, but with the same result.

After that, Todd and Anderson decided to call off the attack, and they loaded their thirty wounded men into commandeered wagons and carriages and rode away, leaving thirteen dead guerrillas. Quantrill took one of the wounded men and rode off. Todd, who was raving like a madman, blamed Quantrill for their losses for some reason and wanted to go after him and kill him, but his men eventually talked him out of it.

On the 24th Hood consented to Sherman's request that he be allowed to send clothes and other items to the Union prisoners at Andersonville. Sherman telegraphed to a friend who was president of the Sanitary Commission in St. Louis for all the underwear and soap he could spare as well as 1,200 fine-tooth combs and 400 pairs of shears for cutting hair. "These articles indicate," he said, "the plague that most afflicted our prisoners at Andersonville."[17]

Sherman's three Union armies occupying the Atlanta area dangled at the end of a railroad supply line that stretched back through Chattanooga to Nashville and on up to Louisville and Cincinnati. There were actually two rail lines on the stretch between Nashville and Chattanooga. The Nashville & Chattanooga Railroad was the more direct route, running northwest-southeast between the two cities. The other was the Tennessee and Alabama Railroad, which ran due south from Nashville to Decatur, Alabama, where it connected with the Memphis & Charleston running east to converge with the Nashville & Chattanooga at Stevenson, Alabama and on into Chattanooga. Athens, Alabama, was a town on the Tennessee & Decatur not far north of its junction with the Memphis & Charleston. It was protected by a nearby earthen fort, which was garrisoned by 600 Union infantrymen.

Early on the morning of 24 September eight pieces of Confederate horse artillery opened fire on the fort, "casting almost every shell inside the works," as the garrison's commander reported. Forrest's cavalry had surrounded the town and fort the night before, and that morning, after his artillery had made its presence felt, he sent in a note under a flag of truce demanding the garrison's "immediate and unconditional surrender."[18] The Northern commander declined at first but then agreed to a parley, during which Forrest used the old trick of showing his men and guns in various places to make it look as though there were three times as many of them as there really were. The Federals surrendered in time for Forrest to give his full attention to a relief force of some 700 men sent up from Decatur, which, after three hours of heavy fighting, also surrendered.

Two blockhouses protecting the railroad were also captured, bringing the total captures to 1300 men, 300 horses, two cannon, two locomotives with cars, 38 wagons, and numerous other items of supply and equipment. The prisoners were sent south, the horses were distributed among Forrest's men, the trains were also destroyed, and all supplies that could not be used or carried were also destroyed. Then the Confederates marched northward along the railroad, destroying track as they went.

The next day the Rebels came to the railroad trestle over Sulphur Branch. It was 300 feet long and 72 feet high with a blockhouse at each end and a fort nearby. The Union commander refused to surrender until Forrest's guns hammered the fort for two hours, leaving its interior "perforated with shell, and the dead lying thick along the works," as Forrest reported.[19] A second demand for surrender was accepted, yielding 973 prisoners, 300 horses, 2 guns, and more supplies. These prisoners were also sent south, along with the captured guns and four others, for the bombardment had reduced the ammunition supply to the point that they were no longer useful. Then the Confederates rode north again, leaving the buildings in the fort, the two blockhouses, and the trestle burning behind them.

Sherman sent a telegram to Halleck on the 25th: "Hood seems to be moving, as it were, to the Alabama line, leaving open the road to Macon, and also to Augusta; but his cavalry is busy on all our roads. A force, number estimated as high as eight thousand, are reported to have captured Athens, Alabama; and a regiment of three hundred and fifty men sent to its relief. I have sent Newton's division [2nd of the 4th Corps from Thomas' Army of the Cumberland] up to Chattanooga in cars, will send another [Corse's 4th Division of the 15th Corps of Howard's Army of the Tennessee] to Rome [Georgia]. If I were sure that Savannah would soon be in our possession, I should be tempted to march for Milledgeville and Augusta; but I must first secure what I have. Jeff. Davis is at Macon."[20]

It was true that Confederate president Jefferson Davis had been in Macon. But he reached Hood's headquarters at Palmetto that day, the 25th. An honor guard of Tennessee troops was standing in the rain to meet him at the station. Davis promptly launched into a speech meant to raise their hopes and their spirits by intimating that Hood would soon be launching a counteroffensive that would carry them northward. "Be of good cheer," he told them, among other things, "for within a short while your faces will be turned homeward and your feet pressing the soil of Tennessee." This was answered with cheers and Rebel yells, but there were also some cries from the ranks asking for the return of Hood's predecessor: "Johnston! Give us Johnston!"[21]

A Union spy was among the crowd and soon passed on to Sherman the substance of Davis' speech. "It was a repetition of those he had made at Columbia, South Carolina, and Macon, Georgia, on his way out, which I had seen," Sherman wrote. "Davis seemed to be perfectly upset by the fall of Atlanta, and to have lost all sense and reason. He denounced General Jos. Johnston and Governor Brown as little better than traitors; attributed to them personally the many misfortunes which had befallen their cause, and informed the soldiers that now the tables were to be turned; that General Forrest was already on our roads in Middle Tennessee; and that Hood's army would soon be there. He asserted that the Yankee army would have to retreat or starve, and that the retreat would prove more disastrous than was that of Napoleon from Moscow. He promised his Tennessee and Kentucky soldiers that their feet should soon tread their 'native soil,' etc., etc. He made no concealment of these vainglorious boasts, and thus gave us the full key to his future designs. To be forewarned was to be forearmed, and I think we took full advantage of the occasion."[22] When Grant heard about Davis' predictions of a disastrous Federal retreat, he dryly remarked: "Mr. Davis has not made it quite plain who is to furnish the snow for this Moscow retreat through Georgia and Tennessee."[23]

Confederate spy Captain Thomas Conrad reached Washington about 25 September and began watching for a chance to kidnap President Lincoln. "I had to ascertain Mr. Lincoln's customary movements first. . . ," he wrote. "LaFayette Square only a stone's throw north of the White House entrance was the very place I needed as vantage ground. Partially concealed by the large trees of the park, I found no difficulty in observing the official's ingress and egress, noting about what hours of the day he might venture forth, size of the accompanying escort, if any: and all other details . . . Hours and days of watching were necessary before I learned that he usually left the President's quarters in the cool of the evening on pleasant days, driving and accompanied in his private carriage, straight out Fourteenth Street to Columbia Road then across to the high elevation . . . We had to determine at what point it would be most expedient to capture the carriage and take possession of Mr. Lincoln; and then whether to move with him through Maryland to the lower Potomac and cross or to the upper Potomac and deliver the prisoner to Mosby's Confederacy for transportation to Richmond. To secure the points necessary for reaching a proper conclusion about all these things, required days of careful work and observation . . . Having scouted the country pretty thoroughly . . . we finally concluded to take the lower Potomac route."[24]

On that 25th day of September, Grant wired Sheridan to send either Torbert or Wilson to Sherman to take command of all of the latter's cavalry. Grant's chief of staff, Brigadier General John A. Rawlins, who was on medical leave, wrote to another member of Grant's staff that day about another of Grant's recent personnel changes: "One of the best military moves Grant has made since his appointment to the command of all the armies, is that of putting Sheridan in command of Washington, Baltimore and the Maryland and Penn borders. The fruits of it are our recent brilliant victories in the Shenandoah. But for the Generals persistency in having all the country contiguous to Washington put under one man Early today would have been raiding in force in both Md. & Pa., and I will venture an opinion still further, that had General Grant attempted to communicate his recent order to Sheridan to move, through Halleck, instead of going himself, he would have failed and Early would still have held his old position near Winchester. I may be mistaken in this, but I dont think I am. The fact is, Grant and Halleck have never looked through the same military glasses."[25] A colonel in the Army of the Potomac, whose diary indicates that he had been pessimistic ever since McClellan had been fired almost two years before, recorded that day that "at times I cannot help thinking that these victories are the beginning of the end, the death-blows to the rebellion. I have never seen the time when the army thought the war so near its close. The men are in good spirits, and I think will behave well should anything be attempted."[26]

---

1. George Fort Milton, *Abraham Lincoln and the Fifth Column* (New York, 1942), 308–311.
2. McDonough and Jones, *War So Terrible*, 320.
3. Wert, *From Winchester to Cedar Creek*, 141.
4. *Official Records*, 43:II:878.
5. Wert, *From Winchester to Cedar Creek*, 128.
6. Ibid., 129.
7. James J. Williamson, *Mosby's Rangers* (New York, 1896), 239–240.
8. Wert, *From Winchester to Cedar Creek*, 152.
9. Ibid., 153.
10. Starr, *The Union Cavalry in the Civil War*, 2:282 and n. 43.
11. *Official Records*, 43:I:500.
12. Sheridan, *Memoirs*, 2:43.
13. *Official Records*, 43:I:500.

14. Ibid., 43:1:505.
15. Wert, *From Winchester to Cedar Creek*, 134.
16. Castel, *William Clarke Quantrill*, 185.
17. Sherman, *Memoirs*, 618.
18. Henry, *"First With the Most" Forrest*, 354.
19. Ibid., 356.
20. Sherman, *Memoirs*, 2:140–141.
21. Steven E. Woodworth, *Jefferson Davis and His Generals: The Failure of Command in the West* (Lawrence, 1990), 291.
22. Sherman, *Memoirs*, 2:141.
23. Porter, *Campaigning With Grant*, 313.
24. Tidwell, Hall and Gaddy, *Come Retribution*, 291.
25. Wert, *From Winchester to Cedar Creek*, 141.
26. Catton, *Grant Takes Command*, 365.

CHAPTER TEN

The Severe Rules of War

25–28 September 1864

By sunset on 25 September Early's infantry divisions had reached Brown's Gap in the Blue Ridge Mountains, where they went into camp, while Lomax's cavalry picketed the South Fork of the Shenandoah. To reach this position the Army of the Valley had rounded the south end of Massanutten Mountain, where the Luray Valley rejoined the main Valley, and spread eastward. By this move Early stepped aside and allowed Sheridan an open path should he want to proceed farther up the Valley, but his position in the gap would threaten the supply line of any Union force that did so, while allowing him to receive the reinforcement of Kershaw's Division returning from east of the mountains. The Confederate commander greatly felt the need for Kershaw's return and for any more help he could get, especially cavalry. He wrote to Lee that day:

"In the fight at Winchester I drove back the enemy's infantry, and would have defeated that, but his cavalry broke mine on the left flank, the latter making no stand, and I had to take a division to stop the progress of the former and save my trains, and during the fighting in the rear the enemy again advanced, and my troops fell back, thinking they were flanked. The enemy's immense superiority in cavalry and the inefficiency of the greater part of mine has been the cause of all my disasters.

In the affair at Fisher's Hill the cavalry gave way, but it was flanked. This could have been remedied if the troops had remained steady, but a panic seized them at the idea of being flanked, and without being defeated they broke, many of them fleeing shamefully. The artillery was not captured by the enemy, but abandoned by the infantry.

"My troops are very much shattered, the men very much exhausted, and many of them without shoes.

"When Kershaw arrives I shall do the best I can, and hope I may be able to check the enemy, but I cannot but be apprehensive of the result. I am informed that all the reserves have [been] called from the Valley. I think Sheridan means to try Hunter's campaign again, and his superiority in cavalry gives him immense advantage. If you could possibly spare Hampton's division it ought to be sent here at once.

"I deeply regret the present state of things, and I assure [you] everything in my power has been done to avert it. The enemy's force is very much larger than mine, being three or four to one."[1]

Wickham brought Fitz Lee's division in from the Luray Valley that night, and Kershaw's infantry arrived the next morning. That same day, Anderson and his 1st Corps staff reached Richmond.

In what had become the backwash of the Valley campaign, Captain Elisha Hunt Rhodes and his 2nd Rhode Island Infantry were returning to Winchester on the 26th after escorting a wagon train of supplies as far as Strasburg. "At Newtown," Rhodes recorded in his diary, "a Negro told me that Mosby and some of his men were in town and would attack us as we passed through. I caught a citizen and sent him to Colonel Mosby with my compliments and told him to get out of the town or I would burn it. The citizen asked me if I had orders to burn the town. I told him we would have the fire and get the order afterwards." This seemed to produce the desired result, for the Confederates left the town. The Federals could see them up in the hills, out of range. "I did not propose to have them attack me from the houses," Rhodes explained. He sent skirmishers into the village and, finding that the Rebels had indeed left, followed with the rest of his small regiment. He posted pickets around the town and his men cooked their dinners in the streets. The citizens of the town had mixed reactions to the presence of these Federals in their midst. "We found plenty of milk, peaches and grapes which the people gladly sold to us," he said. "One lady invited me into her house and gave me a good lunch. Two young ladies present turned their chairs and sat facing the wall, but this did not take my appetite away."[2]

Sheridan's Army of the Shenandoah did not follow Early beyond Har-

risonburg, near the south end of the Massanutten ridge, but on the 26th
his wide-ranging cavalry began destroying the crops and livestock of the
area to ensure that it would not support Early's army again, let alone
Lee's main force at Petersburg and Richmond. Factories, mills, barns,
and the track of the Virginia Central Railroad all went up in flames
during a week in which, as one Union soldier wrote, "the fire demon
reigned supreme."[3] Torbert, with Wilson's division and Lowell's brigade
of Merritt's division proceeded to Staunton on the 26th. That same day
Sheridan assigned Custer to the command of what had been Averell's
2nd Cavalry Division of the Department of West Virginia. Grant wired
Sheridan that day about the effect of Early's defeats upon the Confederate high command and about what Sheridan should do next. "Your victories have created the greatest consternation," he said. "If you can
possibly subsist your army to the front for a few days more, do it, and
make a great effort to destroy the roads about Charlottesville and the
[James River & Kanawha] canal wherever your cavalry can reach it."[4]

Grant was also thinking about what Sherman should do next. "It will
be better to drive Forrest out of Middle Tennessee as a first step," he
said in a dispatch sent that day, "and do any thing else you may feel
your force sufficient for. When a movement is made on any part of the
sea-coast, I will advise you. If Hood goes to the Alabama line, will it
not be impossible for him to subsist his army?" Sherman replied that
same day: "I have already sent one division (Newton's) to Chattanooga,
and another (Corse's) to Rome. Our armies are much reduced, and if I
send back any more, I will not be able to threaten Georgia much. There
are men enough to the rear to whip Forrest, but they are necessarily
scattered to defend the roads. Can you expedite the sending to Nashville
of the recruits that are in Indiana and Ohio? They could occupy the
forts. Hood is now on the West Point road, twenty-four miles south of
this, and draws his supplies by that road. Jefferson Davis is there to-day,
and superhuman efforts will be made to break my road."[5]

In addition to thinking up new projects for Sherman's and Sheridan's
armies, Grant has ideas for his more immediate commands: Meade's
Army of the Potomac and Butler's Army of the James. He had been
planning to send part of the latter to capture Fort Fisher in North Carolina. This was to have sealed off Wilmington, the most important of the
South's remaining ports, and to have opened it as a supply source for
Sherman to march to. In conjunction with such a move Grant had also
planned for Meade to make another attempt to cut the last railroad leading into Petersburg. He had originally set 5 October for the initiation of
these moves, but Sheridan's victories and advance had caused Grant to
worry that Lee might send reenforcements to Early in an attempt to

redress the situation in the Valley. He decided therefore to move up the date for this offensive by a week in order to either prevent or take advantage of any detachment of Lee's forces.

Also, he put off the amphibious move against Fort Fisher in favor of a move by Butler's army to the north side of the James River against the outer defenses of Richmond itself. Major General Benjamin F. Butler, commander of the Army of the James, had suggested this. He and Grant made a reconnaissance by steamboat up the James on the 26th to take a personal look at the situation. Butler owed his high rank to his political influence rather than any military competence but he was an able administrator and planner. Moreover, he ran a sophisticated intelligence apparatus that told him that the Rebels were extremely weak on the north side of the James at that time. Although the Confederate capital was protected by several lines of ingeniously designed earthworks, there were relatively few men stationed in them. The Federals also had very few men on the north side of the James, namely a small garrison of a bridgehead on a northward loop of the river, known as Deep Bottom, and another small force that was digging a canal across the peninsula within a westward loop called Dutch Gap. But Butler proposed to shift a major part of his army to the north side in a secret and rapid move for an attack that he thought might well take the Rebel capital and propel him on a wave of popularity into the White House itself.

Grant was not so sanguine about taking Richmond, but he expected that the threat of doing just that would draw Confederate forces from Petersburg and make it easier for Meade's Army of the Potomac to slip around the Rebel defenses south of Petersburg to cut its two remaining supply lines: a wagon road that led around the Union works at Globe Tavern to reach the railroad running south to Weldon, North Carolina, and the Southside Railroad, which ran along the south bank of the Appomattox River to Lynchburg. At the very least, this two-pronged attack should certainly dissuade Lee from sending any sizable reinforcements to Early.

Out in southern Missouri on that 26th day of September, Sterling Price's invading Confederates turned aside from their advance on St. Louis to deal with a Union force at Pilot Knob. While Shelby's Division was sent farther north to isolate the garrison by cutting the railroad to St. Louis, the rest of Price's raiders rode westward toward these Federals. A few miles southeast of Pilot Knob Fagan's Division ran into resistance from Union pickets at Shut-In Gap and were even driven back by Federal reinforcements. Darkness and rain put an end to the fighting, but it was renewed on the morning of the 27th, and by 10 a.m. the Union forces had been driven back through Arcadia and Ironton to an earthwork known as Fort Davidson, just west of the town of Pilot Knob.

Fort Davidson was an enclosed earthwork of seven sides, each of which was nine feet tall and ten feet thick, and the whole was surrounded by a dry moat that was as deep as the sloping walls were high. Inside were four 32-pounder siege guns, three 24-pounder howitzers, six lighter guns and three 12-inch mortars, not to mention 200 veteran infantrymen from A. J. Smith's force whom Ewing had brought with him from St. Louis and about 700 other Union soldiers. It would not be easily stormed. In command was Brigadier General Thomas Ewing, commander of the District of St. Louis, sent down by Rosecrans to find out what Price was up to. Ewing, who was Sherman's foster brother and also his brother-in-law (Sherman had married his foster father's daughter), had authored, the summer before, the infamous Order No. 11, which had driven all civilians from four western counties of Missouri in an attempt to put a stop to the depredations of Southern guerrillas in that area. He was unlikely to survive capture by the Confederates, and he knew it. His second-in-command, Colonel Thomas C. Fletcher, was the Republican candidate for governor of Missouri and equally anxious to avoid falling into Confederate hands. So when Price sent a delegation under a flag of truce to demand the surrender of the fort, Ewing sent it back with a defiant challenge. When the demand was repeated, Ewing not only repeated his challenge but threatened to fire on the next delegation sent to him, white flag or no white flag.

Although the Union fort commanded an excellent field of fire in all directions over a level plain, which was broken only by a dry creek bed about 150 yards to the south and east, there were high hills on three sides within rifle range, including Shepherd's Mountain and Pilot Knob, which gave the town its name. Captain T. J. Mackey, Price's chief engineer, advised planting guns on these hills to bombard the Federals out of the fort, but just as Price was about to give the order, some local civilians came and begged him not to shell the fort because the Union garrison was holding Southern sympathizers as hostages, who might be killed by the shelling. This was not true, but Price believed it. However, Fagan claimed that his division alone could take the fort in twenty minutes, and Marmaduke said that, with the support of two guns on Shepherd's Mountain, he could capture it in even less time. Price decided to send both divisions, with the support of the two guns on the mountain.

Marmaduke formed his 3,000 men, dismounted, on the north slope of Shepherd's Mountain, southwest of the fort, and Fagan formed his 4,000 at the base of Pilot Knob, southeast of the fort. Both divisions had to cross about 900 yards of open space to reach the Union position. While the two divisions were being put in place, Dobbin's Brigade of Fagan's Division, with 1,500 men, was sent to the north side of the fort to cut off the garrison's only line of retreat, the road to Potosi, and two cannon were manhandled up the side of Shepherd's Mountain. At a little after 2 p.m. they opened fire. However, it was difficult to depress their muzzles sufficiently to hit the fort, whose big guns, on the other hand, returned fire with deadly accuracy and soon silenced the Rebel artillery.

Price had warned his two division commanders that they must advance simultaneously and keep their forces even with each other, but their ranks were soon broken by rocks and timber in their paths and Marmaduke's men fell behind while Fagan's forged ahead. The Union guns concentrated on the latter division, and its entire right wing broke and ran back to Pilot Knob, leaving Brigadier General William L. Cabell's veteran brigade on the left to carry on alone. It advanced at the double quick, stopping occasionally to fire and reload, losing men at every step, drove the Federals from some outer trenches, and reached the moat. But there it stopped, and then it too broke and fled in disorder for the rear. The Union artillery commander, Lieutenant David Murphy, leapt up on the parapet in full view of both sides, cursed the Confederates, and urged the Federals to redouble their fire. Marmaduke's men, meanwhile, had made it to the dry creek bed, but, when Cabell's Brigade broke, the Federals concentrated their fire on them, inflicting heavy losses. Only Clark's Brigade advanced beyond the creek. It too made it to the ditch just outside the fort, and it also broke, running back to the dry creek bed. There Marmaduke's Division remained until darkness made it safe to withdraw. Fagan begged Price for permission to try again, but the latter said he would not make another attack that day. Cabell called this "a damned wise decision."[6] The Rebels fell back after dark with nothing to show for their efforts except 1,500 casualties. The Union garrison had lost 73.

Under the cover of darkness both sides turned from fighting to building. The Confederates set to work constructing ladders for scaling the fort's earthen walls when they renewed the attack the next day, while a courier galloped off to the north to bring Shelby's Division back to help out. The Federals, after spiking their heavy guns, built a drawbridge across their moat, which they covered with canvas to muffle the sound of their movements, and at 3 a.m. slipped out of the fort and marched up the Potosi road undetected, despite the nearness of Dobbin's Brigade. Colonel Fletcher said that these Rebels may have mistaken the Union column for other Confederates changing position.

Ewing and his survivors were an hour on their way when the slow fuse they had left sputtering behind them finally set off the powder magazine in the fort. Even then the Rebels did not catch on but thought the explosion indicated some accident in the fort and hoped that it meant that the surviving Yankees would surrender in the morning. It was not until 8 a.m. that Price, staying at a house in Arcadia, learned that Ewing had slipped away, and it was almost noon before Marmaduke's men had mounted up and started after him. By then, Ewing's column was entering Caledonia, ten miles north of Pilot Knob, where it met and routed the van of Shelby's Division, heading south to rejoin Price. Then Ewing turned to the west, heading for Rolla. It was several hours later when Marmaduke joined Shelby at Caledonia and led the combined force in pursuit. But by the time they caught up with Ewing's rear guard the Federals were on a stretch of road with steep cliffs on both sides, making it impossible to attack their flank, and A. J. Smith's veterans and a battery of artillery beat off every attempt to charge up the road.

A hundred fifty miles northwest of Pilot Knob, Bloody Bill Anderson's bushwhackers rode into the town of Centralia, Missouri, on the morning of the 27th and proceeded to pillage the stores and houses and forced the terrified inhabitants to fix breakfast for them. At the railroad depot they found a barrel of whiskey and several cases of new boots, and helped themselves to both. At 11 a.m. the stagecoach from Columbia rolled into town and the guerrillas met it with drawn revolvers. The passengers were robbed of their watches and their cash.

A half-hour later a train pulled in from the east and was stopped by a volley from the bushwhackers. Anderson, who was wearing a blue uniform coat, ordered the passengers off and discovered that they included 24 unarmed Union soldiers on furlough or recently discharged. Some of them hesitated when they saw the guerrillas, but Anderson shot two of them and the rest stepped down, along with the other passengers. Anderson had the soldiers line up on one side of the station platform and the civilians on the other. "You Federal soldiers have just killed six of my soldiers, scalped them and left them on the prairie," Anderson said, referring to the running fight he had had after capturing Union wagons several days before. "From this time forward I ask no quarter and give none. Every Federal soldier on whom I put my finger shall die like a dog. If I get into your clutches I expect death. You are all to be killed and sent to hell. That is the way every damn soldier shall be served who falls into my hands."[7] The soldiers protested that they had had nothing to do with the killing of his men. They were from Sherman's army in far-off Georgia. One waved a crutch to show that he was crippled. But Anderson ordered them to take off their uniforms so that his men could have them for disguises, then, after setting aside one Sergeant Thomas

Goodman, whom he said he had special plans for, he turned and gave the order to fire. All the Federals were killed except one, who, although wounded, ran toward the guerrillas, broke through their ranks, slid under the train, and then under the station platform. The guerrillas set fire to the station and waited with drawn guns. When the lone soldier emerged from the smoke he managed to level two of them with a club before they riddled him with twenty bullets.

Anderson turned next to the civilian passengers, who were terrified at what they had just witnessed, and he relieved them of their watches, jewelry and cash. A young man who tried to hide some money in his boot was killed, as was a German who hid his watch. Collecting $3,000 from the express car, the guerrillas set fire to the train and sent it rolling down the track, passing over and mangling some of the bodies on its way. Soon a freight train rolled in, and the bushwhackers killed its crew and plundered its cars. Then they mounted up and rode back to their camp three miles away, taking Sergeant Goodman with them, to tell the other gangs about all the fun they had had.

Not long afterwards, three companies of Union militia rode into Centralia, led by Major A. V. E. Johnson. When he saw what the bushwhackers had done, Johnson vowed to get them, but the townspeople warned him that the guerrillas were numerous and well armed and pleaded with him to wait for reenforcements. "I will fight them anyhow," the angered major said, and leaving 36 men to guard the town, he took the other 111 to follow the raiders.[8] Their approach was spotted, however, and the guerrillas all mounted up and formed a long curved line on a hill.

The Federals, being mounted infantry, not true cavalry, dismounted, left every fourth man to hold their horses, loaded their muskets, fixed bayonets, and started up the hill. "My God," one bushwhacker exclaimed, "the Lord have mercy on them, they're dismounting to fight!"[9] The guerrillas then charged down on them with a savage yell. The Federals fired one volley, but most of their shots were too high and only three Rebels were killed and ten wounded. The rest galloped on, and the militiamen turned and ran. Each bushwhacker was armed with three or four revolvers, and they shot down every Union soldier in the main line, including those who tried to surrender. The Union horseholders fled toward Centralia, but most of them were caught and killed before they reached it. The militiamen who had been left in the town also fled and many of them were also overtaken and killed before they reached the safety of a blockhouse at the nearby town of Sturgeon. Only 23 militiamen survived out of the 147 who had ridden into town with Major Johnson. Johnson himself was among the dead, shot, it was said, by 17-

year-old Jesse James. The bushwhackers then returned to pillage Centralia once more and to mutilate the bodies of many of their enemies.

In northern Virginia, Lieutenant Walter Bowie departed Fauquier County that day with 25 men from Mosby's partisan battalion on a very unusual mission. Bowie was a 25-year-old Marylander who had apparently spent most of 1862 setting up and running a clandestine courier route through Maryland to deliver Northern newspapers and other publications to Richmond. He had spent a month in a Federal prison after being charged with spying, but had escaped. A few months later he had narrowly escaped recapture by posing as a black woman. Now he was being sent to Annapolis for the purpose of capturing Governor Augustus Bradford of Maryland.

In southern Tennessee that day, the 27th, Forrest and his raiding Confederate cavalry advanced northward along the Nashville & Decatur Railroad, which they had been tearing up—enough to put it out of operation for six weeks—pushing toward the town of Pulaski against increasing Union resistance. The Federal garrison of the town had been reinforced both by cavalry falling back from in front of Forrest and by troops of all three combat arms hurried down from Nashville by train. By the time the Rebels came up against the fortifications of Pulaski there were more Federals on hand than Confederates. Forrest waited until dark, then had campfires built along his positions to make it look as though his men were going into bivouac, then marched them away, heading for the Nashville & Chattanooga Railroad, which was two days' hard march to the east.

President Lincoln sent a telegram to Sherman on the 27th: "You say Jeff. Davis is on a visit to Hood. I judge that Brown and Stephens are the objects of his visit."[10] Grant was also writing Sherman that day: "It is evident, from the tone of the Richmond press and from other sources of information, that the enemy intend making a desperate effort to drive you from where you are. I have directed all new troops from the West, and from the East too, if necessary, in case none are ready in the West, to be sent to you. If General Burbridge is not too far on his way to Abingdon, I think he had better be recalled and his surplus troops sent into Tennessee."[11] That same day Gillem advanced from Bull's Gap, still heading toward Saltville, despite the best efforts of Vaughn's three small brigades of Rebel horsemen.

Grant wrote to Halleck in Washington that day to have railroad repair crews ready to put the Orange & Alexandria Railroad back in operation, as he expected Sheridan to advance on Charlottesville. He also wrote to Secretary of War Stanton about procedures for allowing the soldiers to vote in the upcoming election: "The exercise of the right of suffrage by the officers and soldiers of armies in the field is a novel thing. It has, I believe, generally been considered dangerous to constitutional liberty and subversive of military discipline. But our circumstances are novel and exceptional. A very large proportion of legal voters of the United States are now either under arms in the field, or in hospitals, or otherwise engaged in the military service of the United States.

"Most of these men are not regular soldiers in the strict sense of that term; still less are they mercenaries, who give their services to the Government simply for its pay, having little understanding of the political questions or feeling little or no interest in them. On the contrary they are American citizens, having still their homes and social and political ties binding them to the States and districts from which they come and to which they expect to return.

"They have left their homes temporarily to sustain the cause of their country in the hour of its trial. In performing this sacred duty they should not be deprived of a most precious privilege. They have as much right to demand that their votes shall be counted in the choice of their rulers as those citizens who remain at home. Nay, more, for they have sacrificed more for their country.

"I state these reasons in full, for the unusual thing of allowing armies in the field to vote, that I may urge on the other hand that nothing more than the fullest exercise of this right should be allowed, for anything not absolutely necessary to this exercise cannot but be dangerous to the liberties of the country. The officers and soldiers have every means of understanding the questions before the country. The newspapers are freely circulated, and so, I believe, are the documents prepared by both parties to set forth the merits and claims of their candidates.

"Beyond this nothing whatever should be allowed. No political meetings, no harangues from soldiers or citizens, and no canvassing of camps or regiments for votes. I see not why a single individual not belonging to the armies should be admitted into their lines to deliver tickets. In my opinion the tickets should be furnished by the chief provost-marshal of each army, by them to the provost-marshal (or some other appointed officer) of each brigade or regiment, who shall on the day of election deliver tickets irrespective of party to whoever may call for them. . .

"In the case of those States whose soldiers vote by proxy, proper State authority could be given to officers belonging to regiments so voting to receive and forward votes. As it is intended that all soldiers entitled to vote shall exercise that privilege according to their own convictions of right, unmolested and unrestricted, there will be no objection to each party sending to armies, easy of access, a number of respectable gentlemen to see that these views are fully carried out."[12]

Grant also issued orders for the planned moves against Richmond and Petersburg. Lee seemed to have no inkling of Grant's plans to attack him. Instead, his mind, as Grant suspected, was on the Valley. He had little that he could send to Early, but he sent what he could. In response to Early's complaints about the inferiority of his cavalry, Lee could not spare all of Hampton's Division, but he did send him Rosser's Brigade, which departed that day. And he also sent some fatherly advice:

"I very much regret the reverses that have occurred to the army in the Valley, but trust they can be remedied. The arrival of Kershaw will add greatly to your strength, and I have such confidence in the men and officers that I am sure all will unite in the defense of the country. It will require that every one should exert all his energies and strength to meet the emergency. One victory will put all things right. You must do all in your power to invigorate your army. Get back all absentees; maneuver so, if you can, as to keep the enemy in check until you can strike him with all your strength. As far as I can judge, at this distance, you have operated more with divisions than with your concentrated strength. Circumstances may have rendered it necessary, but such a course is to be avoided if possible. It will require the greatest watchfulness, the greatest promptness, and the most untiring energy on your part to arrest the progress of the enemy in his present tide of success. All the reserves in the Valley have been ordered to you. Breckinridge will join you or co-operate, as circumstances will permit, with all his force. Rosser left this morning for Burkeville (intersection of Danville and South Side Railroads), whence he will shape his course as you direct. I have given you all I can; you must use the resources you have so as to gain success. The enemy must be defeated, and I rely upon you to do it . . . The enemy's force cannot be so greatly superior to yours. His effective infantry, I do not think, exceeds 12,000 men. We are obliged to fight against great odds. A kind Providence will yet overrule everything for our good."[13]

In the Shenandoah on the 27th, Torbert, with Wilson's division and Lowell's brigade of Union cavalry, moved through Staunton to Waynesboro. This town was near Rockfish Gap, where the Virginia Central Railroad, on its way from Charlottesville to Staunton, penetrated the Blue Ridge Mountains about 15 miles southwest of Early's position at Brown's Gap. Torbert's objective was the destruction of the railroad bridge over the South River, a tributary of the South Fork of the Shenandoah.

Early, however, was also on the move that day. He drove Merritt's two brigades of Union cavalry across the South Fork at Port Republic. Learning then of Torbert's advance to Waynesboro, he marched the next morning, the 28th, to that town with most of his army, while Wickham took his brigade of Fitz Lee's cavalry up the South River near the mountains in order to block Rockfish Gap. Torbert had already found the gap protected by two companies of Virginia reserves with two pieces of artillery, but they were no match for his three brigades. His men had already burned the railroad station and a nearby tannery and were busily tearing up the iron railroad bridge and throwing the pieces into the river when Wickham appeared and opened fire from a neighboring ridge with his horse artillery. Pegram's Confederate infantry division soon approached and the rest of Early's army was not far behind. Wilson wanted to stay and fight, but Torbert decided to fall back after dark to rejoin Sheridan's main army.

In Tennessee on the 28th Forrest's raiders were still marching along muddy, unpaved byroads from Pulaski to strike the Nashville & Chattanooga Railroad. Pushing his men along, the general came upon some artillerymen with a captured caisson that was stuck in the mud beyond their ability to move it. "Who has charge here?" he demanded. "I have, sir," a captain answered. "Then why in hell don't you do something?" Forrest demanded, throwing in a few insulting profanities. "I'll not be cursed out by anyone, even a superior officer," the frustrated captain shot back, and with that he grabbed up a lighted torch and thrust it into an ammunition chest. Forrest spurred his horse to get out of range of the explosion that was bound to follow this suicidal act, but no explosion came. "What infernal lunatic is that just out of the asylum down there?" he asked his staff. "He came near blowing himself and me up with a whole caisson full of powder." The staff officers just laughed and explained that the ammunition had already been unloaded from the caisson to make it lighter and that the captain had bluffed him. Forrest joined in the laughter, but he never cursed that particular captain again.[14]

Lieutenant General Richard H. Anderson, recently returned to Richmond from the Valley with his 1st Corps staff, was assigned on the 28th to command the Confederate defenses east of Richmond, manned by two brigades from his corps plus a number of artillery and reserve infantry units and one cavalry brigade from the Department of Richmond. Another Confederate command change was also made that day. President

Davis, still in Georgia, transferred Lieutenant General William J. Hardee from command of the 1st Corps of Hood's Army of Tennessee to command of the Department of South Carolina, Georgia and Florida. Major General Benjamin F. Cheatham succeeded to command of the corps.

Hardee had been wanting a transfer ever since Davis had passed over him to promote Hood, then his junior, to succeed Joseph E. Johnston as commander of the Army of Tennessee. Hood and Hardee, at least partly due to the latter's attitude, had not been able to work well together. At first Davis had tried to talk Hardee into a more cooperative attitude, but finally it was clear that either Hood or Hardee would have to go. Although Hood had his faults, it would be much harder to find a general to replace him as army commander than one to replace Hardee in corps command. In fact, Hardee had suggested that Johnston be given another chance at command of the army, but Davis would have none of that. He and Johnston had not gotten along since early in the war and, after the general's retreat to the gates of Atlanta without a fight or even a promise of one, Davis was not ready to trust him again. Hardee had then suggested General P. G. T. Beauregard, who had commanded that army briefly in 1862, as a replacement for Hood. Beauregard was then commanding the Department of Southern Virginia and North Carolina, but since Lee had been drawn into his department, south of the James River, by Grant's moves against Petersburg, Beauregard had been reduced to little better than a corps commander under Lee. And Beauregard was jealous that Early had been given a semi-independent command in the Valley that he thought should have been his. In short, he wanted to be out from under Lee's immediate command.

Davis did not get along with Beauregard much better than with Johnston, but although he would not give him Hood's job—or Early's—he did have a new assignment for him. Beauregard would be given command of a new military division to correspond with Sherman's Union command and to consist of Hood's Army and Department of Tennessee and Richard Taylor's Department of Alabama, Mississippi and East Louisiana. This would silence some of the critics who wanted Beauregard given a more important command, increase cooperation between the two departments involved, and provide both Taylor and Hood with the benefit of Beauregard's greater experience, all without having to trust the latter with direct command of either department. So Hood would stay, and Hardee would have to go.

Hood's opponent, Sherman, replied to Lincoln on the 28th: "I have positive knowledge that Mr. Davis made a speech at Macon, on the 22nd, which I mailed to General Halleck yesterday. It was bitter against

General Jos. Johnston and Governor Brown. The militia are on furlough. Brown is at Milledgeville, trying to get a Legislature to meet next month, but he is afraid to act unless in concert with other Governors. Judge Wright, of Rome, has been here, and Messrs. Hill and Nelson, former members of Congress, are here now, and will go to meet Wright at Rome, and then go back to Madison and Milledgeville. Great efforts are being made to reinforce Hood's army, and to break up my railroads, and I should have at once a good reserve force at Nashville. It would have a bad effect, if I were forced to send back any considerable part of my army to guard roads, so as to weaken me to an extent that I could not act offensively if the occasion calls for it."[15]

That same day, Halleck responded to Sherman's report on his evacuation of civilians from Atlanta and his correspondence with Hood and with the mayor of Atlanta. "The course which you have pursued in removing rebel families from Atlanta, and in the exchange of prisoners, is fully approved by the War Department. Not only are you justified by the laws and usages of war in removing these people, but I think it was your duty to your own army to do so. Moreover, I am fully of opinion that the nature of your position, the character of the war, the conduct of the enemy (and especially of non-combatants and women of the territory which we have heretofore conquered and occupied), will justify you in gathering up all the forage and provisions which your army may require, both for a siege of Atlanta and for your supply in your march farther into the enemy's country. Let the disloyal families of the country, thus stripped, go to their husbands, fathers, and natural protectors, in the rebel ranks; we have tried three years of conciliation and kindness without any reciprocation; on the contrary, those thus treated have acted as spies and guerrillas in our rear and within our lines. The safety of our armies, and proper regard for the lives of our soldiers, require that we apply to our inexorable foes the severe rules of war. We certainly are not requirred to treat the so-called non-combatant rebels better than they themselves treat each other. Even here in Virginia, within fifty miles of Washington, they strip their own families of provisions, leaving them, as our army advances, to be fed by us, or to starve within our lines. We have fed this class of people long enough . . . I would destroy every mill and factory within reach which I did not want for my own use. This the rebels have done, not only in Maryland and Pennsylvania, but also in Virginia and other rebel States, when compelled to fall back before our armies. In many sections of the country they have not left a mill to grind grain for their own suffering families, lest we might use them to supply our armies. We must do the same.

"I have endeavored to impress these views upon our commanders for the last two years. You are almost the only one who has properly applied them. I do not approve of General Hunter's course in burning private houses or uselessly destroying private property. That is barbarous. But I approve of taking or destroying whatever may serve as supplies to us or to the enemy's army."[16]

1. *Official Records*, 43:I:557–558.
2. Rhodes, *All For the Union*, 187.
3. Wert, *From Winchester to Cedar Creek*, 144.
4. *Official Records*, 43:II:177.
5. Sherman, *Memoirs*, 2:141–142.
6. Castel, *General Sterling Price*, 215.
7. Jay Monaghan, *Civil War on the Western Border 1854–1865* (New York, 1955), 318.
8. Castel, *William Clarke Quantrill*, 191.
9. Ibid.
10. Basler, ed., *The Collected Works of Abraham Lincoln*, 7:27.
11. Sherman, *Memoirs*, 2:143–144.
12. *Official Records*, 42:II:1045–1046.
13. Ibid., 43:I:558–559.
14. Henry, *"First With the Most" Forrest*, 358.
15. Sherman, *Memoirs*, 2:142.
16. Ibid., 2:128–129.

PART TWO

RICHMOND AND PETERSBURG

"It seems to me the enemy must be weak enough at one or the other place to let us in."

—Lieutenant General Ulysses S. Grant

to Major General George G. Meade

CHAPTER ELEVEN

We Must Capture That Fort

28–29 September 1864

The city of Petersburg lay on the south, or right, bank of the Appomattox River, which emptied into the James River a bit to the northeast, near City Point. Petersburg was important because through it ran all but one of the supply lines coming into Richmond from the south. The Confederate defenses of Petersburg ran in a semicircle from the Appomattox east of the city to the same river west of town. The Federals had originally attacked the city on the east side, back in June, and although the original entrenchments on that side of the city had been captured, new lines had been dug just as fast. So the Union forces had also dug themselves in, and now two lines of defenses lay within a few hundred yards of each other there.

Over the course of the summer, the Union lines had been extended to the southwest, at increasing range from the Rebel defenses. For if the city could not be taken by assault, still those lines of supply could be cut outside of the city. In August, the 5th Corps and 9th Corps of the

Army of the Potomac had made another move to the west that, after beating off Southern counterattacks, had extended the Federal lines across the Petersburg & Weldon Railroad, which led due south to North Carolina. The Union defenses turned to the south just west of the tracks near Globe Tavern, then soon turned back to the east to protect the rear of the main line. Between these two lines, the Federals had built the U.S. Military Railroad, which connected Globe Tavern with the wharves at City Point, making it easier to bring supplies to the frontline troops.

Of course, this toehold on the Weldon Railroad prevented the Confederates from using that line to bring supplies directly into Petersburg. But they still brought them to Stony Creek Depot a few miles farther south, where they were transferred to wagons and hauled around this Union salient. To protect the nearer end of this wagon route and the only other railroad supply line, the Southside Railroad which roughly paralleled the Appomattox River and entered the city from the west, Lee had recently begun the construction of another line of entrenchments which extended on a southwesterly tangent from the southwest sector of the main semi-circle of defenses. This line roughly paralleled a highway called the Squirrel Level Road.

Grant's plans for the Petersburg front were aimed at breaking those last supply lines into the city. First he had Meade make an obvious move to strengthen the left of his line around Globe Tavern with the object of attracting attention away from Butler's move across the James until it could get well under way. That move, in turn, was expected to draw Confederate reserves to the defense of Richmond, which would allow Meade to move out to the west and cut one or both of those remaining two supply lines. If both were cut, Petersburg would soon have to be abandoned, and Richmond would fall soon thereafter.

The general-in-chief did not dictate how his two army commanders were to achieve their objectives, but left it to them to plan their own moves, subject to his approval. Meade outlined his plans to his chief subordinates at 7:30 p.m. on the 28th. Two divisions of Major General John G. Parke's 9th Corps and two more from Major General Gouverneur K. Warren's 5th Corps would form his strike force, along with most of Brigadier General David M. Gregg's 2nd Cavalry Division, which was all that was left of his army's Cavalry Corps since the rest of it had been sent to the Shenandoah Valley the month before. If necessary he would call on other units to reinforce these, or if Butler's move should cause the Confederates to abandon Petersburg or weaken it to the point of making its defenses vulnerable, the entire army might advance. He therefore ordered all units to be under arms and ready to move at 4 a.m. on the 29th. Engineers were to have pontoon trains ready to move at a

moment's notice, in case they should be needed for crossing the Appomattox. Throughout the night supply wagons and hospital units packed
up and moved to City Point in order to be out of the way for whatever
followed. Between 3 and 4 a.m. Brigadier General Robert B. Potter's
2nd Division of the 9th Corps and four batteries of artillery moved west
with a good deal of fanfare from its reserve position into the Globe
Tavern salient.

Major General Benjamin Franklin Butler, commander of the Union
Department of Virginia and North Carolina, and of its field force, the
Army of the James, brought his senior subordinates together at his head-
quarters at Point of Rocks on the Bermuda Hundred peninsula on that
night of 28 September. These subordinates were Major General David
B. Birney, commander of the 10th Corps, Major General Edward O. C.
Ord, commander of the 18th Corps, and Brigadier General August V.
Kautz, commander of the Cavalry Division of the Army of the James.

Birney, like Butler, was a political general. While Butler had been an
influential Massachusetts Democrat before the war, Birney had been a
Philadelphia lawyer and was the son of abolitionist James G. Birney,
who had been the Liberty party's presidential candidate in 1840 and
1844. Birney had been a division commander, and a pretty good one, in
the 2nd Corps in the Army of the Potomac until Grant had recently
given him the 10th Corps.

Ord was a regular army officer who had graduated from West Point
in 1839. He and Meade had been fellow division commanders in the 1st
Corps back in 1862. Then Ord had been transferred to Grant's Army of
the Tennessee, where he had commanded first a division and then the
13th Corps, going with the latter to the Department of the Gulf after
Vicksburg. But he had seen relatively little combat due to being out with
wounds and illness much of the time. Lately he had held temporary jobs
in the Department of West Virginia and the Middle Department, and he
was one of Grant's favorite generals because of his aggressive leadership.

Kautz was also a regular, but much younger than Ord, having graduated from West Point in 1852, the year before Sheridan. He had been
born in Baden, Germany, but had been raised in the same southern Ohio
town where Grant had grown up some 10 years ahead of him. He had
been Butler's chief of cavalry since before the opening of the 1864 campaign in May. He had shown some talent at raiding Rebel railroads,
but had not had much chance to show what he could do in a large-
scale battle.

Butler, the amateur general for whom military service was merely a
stepping stone on what he hoped was the road to the White House, had

proven himself to be an able, if heavy-handed, administrator and was developing some considerable talents as a military planner. Now he presented his three subordinates with a written plan for their coming operations north of the James River. No less than Richmond itself, which had been the goal of Union operations for three long years, was their objective. Drawing troops away from Petersburg, as far as Butler was concerned, was a secondary consideration. Butler's 16-page document included a good assessment of the location and strength of Confederate units north of the James, which it numbered at a mere 3,000 men, not counting the numerous artillery units. And Butler's plan would hit those few defenders with 26,600 men in a surprise attack that was to begin at 4:30 the next morning.

Ord was to lay a pontoon bridge and cross the James at Aiken's Landing, southwest of Deep Bottom, take two of the three divisions of his 18th Corps up the Varina Road, capture an entrenched camp, take the Confederate bridges around Chaffin's Bluff, and then proceed up the Osborne Turnpike to Richmond. Birney, with most of his own 10th Corps plus the division of black troops from the 18th Corps, would cross at Deep Bottom and advance along the New Market Road toward the capital. And, as soon as Birney cleared the Rebels off New Market Heights, Kautz's cavalry would cross at Deep Bottom and move farther north to the Darbytown Road before turning to the west toward Richmond. No artillery would encumber the columns, and wagons were forbidden to even cross the river without Butler's permission.

Preparations for these moves had been going on for a couple of days. Nevertheless, no word of it had reached the Confederates. "In all my experience," a reporter for the New York *Times* wrote, "I never before knew a plan to be kept so profoundly secret."[1] Many of the units involved had to be quietly withdrawn from the line of defenses across the neck of the Bermuda Hundred peninsula, leaving most of the artillery behind. The infantry were replaced with various odds and ends, including five big new Pennsylvania regiments who had less than a month's experience at the front. Some of these new recruits were said to have received $1,500 in bounties for enlisting, which was a very sizable sum in those days. This, of course, was resented by the veteran soldiers who had enlisted out of patriotism. One of these green Pennsylvanians seeing the experienced troops marching by asked them if they were going to a battle. "Oh, yes," one of the old soldiers replied; "we never move without going into a battle." The neophyte then asked if the new regiments would also be ordered into the fight. "No, indeed," the veteran replied. "They won't put you in—you cost too much to be risked in a battle; we didn't cost anything—so they stick us in everywhere."[2]

After dark the men of Ord's two divisions were brought quietly to the south bank of the James opposite Aiken's Landing, where they were allowed to rest, boil coffee, and prepare themselves for the next day. Engineers started laying a pontoon bridge to the north shore at 7:30 p.m., but work was delayed when it was found that a lower-than-expected tide had exposed a section of muddy river bottom. Dragging the pontoon boats over the sticky mud was not easy. Nevertheless, the bridge was completed by 2 a.m. It consisted of a plank roadway laid over 67 boats with a total span of 1,320 feet. Dirt and hay were spread over the bridge to muffle the noise of marching feet, and by 3 a.m. the 1st Division of the 18th Corps began crossing in a dense fog, led by the 118th New York and the 10th New Hampshire. Both regiments had just been issued Spencer repeating rifles. They encountered no resistance, and they spread out in a skirmish line on the north bank to cover the crossing of the rest of the division. The 2nd Division followed, and then the engineers, and still no shots had been fired and no Rebels seen. The most dangerous part of the operation had gone off without a hitch.

Things did not go so smoothly at Deep Bottom. Brigadier General Charles J. Paine, commander of the 3rd Division of the 18th Corps, had assembled nine of his regiments of United States Colored Troops—former slaves and a few freed men under white officers. But then seven of them had been there already, guarding the bridgehead. However, Paine had also recalled men to the ranks from extra-duty details, provost guards, and even some prisoners and raw recruits to fill up the ranks. However, midnight came and still the 10th Corps had not arrived from Petersburg.

Butler had originally ordered Birney to move his men to Bermuda Hundred on the 27th, but to maintain the secrecy of his plan he had told the corps commander that this was in preparation for embarking on the 29th for transport to another front. Birney either misunderstood or disobeyed this order, keeping his men in reserve east of Petersburg until late on the 28th. His men were already moving by the time he learned, at the conference at Butler's headquarters, that instead of taking ship for new fields his men were supposed to storm New Market Heights. His artillery and engineers had begun to march at noon, but his infantry had not moved until 3 p.m.

The troops had believed the rumor that they were going to be sent to North Carolina and had been looking forward to getting away from the trench warfare around Petersburg. But when the column bypassed all the docks and marched into Jones's Neck, the peninsula that led to Deep Bottom, they knew that they were instead going to make another attack on the Confederate defenses on New Market Heights. Their spirits slumped just as darkness brought its usual empediments to marching columns: sudden stops, long waits, hurrying to catch up. Soon the men were tired and the ammunition wagons caused further delays. And this corps, especially its 2nd Division, was already notorious for straggling.

Birney had at least seen to it that they were not encumbered by excess clothing or other possessions in their packs, and he had limited the wagons accompanying the troops to those carrying ammunition. The main wagon train did not follow until 9 p.m. But thousands of men fell behind, strewn in the wake of the dwindling column. One Federal said, "Many who never fell out before dropped exhausted by the wayside." A brigade commander said, "My surgeons reported that they never saw so many men break down from sheer exhaustion as that night."[3] The 2nd Division had lost about one third of its strength by the time it had reached the bridgehead. Some of these men revived after a rest and eventually caught up with their units, but not in time to participate in the initial attack. The head of the column reached the bridgehead at 2 a.m. and the rear, not counting the stragglers, got there at about 3:30. This gave the men almost no time to rest before they were ordered to stand to arms and be ready to attack at 4 a.m.

Neither Union force had crossed the James undetected. Ord's crossing had been reported to Colonel John M. Hughs at the nearby Signal Hill defenses. He commanded the only veteran infantry brigade in all of the Department of Richmond. It consisted of five Tennessee regiments who had been badly understrength when they had been brought from east Tennessee under Brigadier General Bushrod Johnson back in May. Now, after fighting in the early battles around Bermuda Hundred and Petersburg, the entire brigade numbered fewer than 400 rifles. Johnson had, meanwhile, been given command of a division in Beauregard's Department of Southern Virginia and North Carolina, and discipline in the brigade had suffered under Hughs. It would not have counted as a first-rate unit in Lee's Army of Northern Virginia, but it was the best unit available to Lieutenant General Richard Ewell, commander of the Department of Richmond. It was therefore manning the outermost line of defense for the capital.

However, the Confederate units holding the New Market Line were first class units indeed. They were Benning's Brigade of Georgians and Gregg's Texas Brigade, both from Field's Division of Anderson's 1st Corps. Both were well known, highly respected units. In fact, the Texas Brigade was considered Lee's Old Guard. It was actually composed of three regiments from Texas and one from Arkansas, and it had originally been commanded by John Bell Hood, by then commanding the Army of Tennessee down in Georgia. However, both brigades were much reduced in size and, like Hughs' brigade, not under their official commanders. Benning's Brigade was under the temporary command of Colonel Dudley DuBose of the 15th Georgia and Gregg's was under Lieutenant Colonel Frederick Bass of the 1st Texas.

Two battalions of reserves from the Department of Richmond also helped to man the New Market Line. All of these were the units Anderson was to take charge of now that he had returned from the Shenandoah, but he had not yet assumed command on the morning of 29 September. Brigadier General John Gregg, of the Texas Brigade, was the senior officer present and in charge of the entire line until Anderson took over, which was why his brigade was being commanded by Bass. Gregg's two brigades were part of Lee's Army of Northern Virginia, so he was therefore independent of Ewell.

Upon hearing that the Yankees had crossed the James at Aiken's Landing, Hughs sent all his baggage to the rear and ordered his little brigade to man the defenses on Signal Hill. Gregg's men were already awake and eating their breakfasts when word came that Federals were advancing toward their position on New Market Heights from Deep Bottom. Gregg sent the news to both Ewell and Lee. The army commander received this information at 6:30 a.m. and immediately did just what Grant hoped he would do: he ordered his mobile reserve, Field's other three brigades, to move from the Squirrel Level Line southwest of Petersburg to the outer defenses of Richmond. But it would take all day for them to move that far, even with the help of the railroad between the two cities. When Ewell got the word, he called for the mobilization of all reserves and local defense forces, which were composed of old men, boys, and men whose occupations exempted them from conscription into the regular forces. But turning them out would also take hours.

Ewell had been planning to attack, in the near future, the Federals who were digging a canal at nearby Dutch Gap. So he assumed that the Union objective was to forestall this with a preemptive attack on Signal Hill. He therefore concentrated on defending that position and the entrenched camp on Chaffin's farm, where he had his headquarters. Meanwhile, Gregg concentrated his forces on New Market Heights, reinforced by the three regiments of Brigadier General Martin W. Gary's cavalry brigade from the Department of Richmond, who left their horses and manned the defenses alongside the Texas, Arkansas, and Georgia infantry. "Our line running down the river was so long, and our troops so few in number," wrote a soldier who doubled as a correspondent for the *Columbia Daily South Carolinian*, "that it was impossible to man it along its whole length at the same time, and we were obliged to trust to watching the enemy closely, and hurrying troops to the points threatened."[4] But with nobody to coordinate the commands of Gregg and Ewell, the Rebels were unaware that the Varina Road leading from Aiken's Landing had been left undefended.

By 4 a.m. Birney had his leading troops formed for the attack on New Market Heights. On the right, Brevet Major General Alfred H. Terry's 1st Division of the 10th Corps marched up the main road from Deep Bottom. On the left, Paine's black troops, the 3rd Division of the 18th Corps, marched up the Grover House Road. The 1st Brigade of the 3rd Division of the 10th Corps, also composed of black troops and commanded by Birney's brother, Brigadier General William Birney, at first followed a central lane, but it soon turned back into the main road, placing it behind Terry's division. Brigadier General Robert S. Foster's 2nd Division of the 10th Corps followed Paine's division. The 10th Corps artillery, Paine's recruits, another new regiment from Pennsylvania that belonged to Foster's division, and Kautz's cavalry were all left behind until the more seasoned infantry cleared the way.

New Market Heights was a hill forty or fifty feet higher than the surrounding area. It ran east to west for about a mile before turning to the north where Bailey's Creek ran southward along its eastern flank to empty into the James at Deep Bottom. The southeastern corner of the hill was the steepest part, and therefore the hardest to assault. Previous Union attacks north of the James had bypassed it to the east and had tried to outflank the hill by moving west along the Darbytown Road. But such a move took time and gave the Rebels a chance to react. This time Butler's plan called for a feint against the eastern part of the heights while the real assault was made farther west where the hill was not so steep. If successful, such an attack might cut the Southern defenders off from Richmond. This plan, however, forced the Federals to cross Four Mile Creek, which ran roughly west to east just south of the heights and met Bailey's Creek at Deep Bottom. Between swampy Four Mile Creek and the heights ran east-west New Market Road. Between the road and the heights were two lines of abatis and the entrenchments for the Rebel infantry. On the crest were the guns of the Confederate artillery. However, counting Gary's dismounted cavalry, the Texas Brigade, and one battalion of reserves, there were only about 1,800 Rebel infantrymen in the defenses.

Farther south was the east-west Kingsland Road, which swung to the north to connect with the New Market Road right under the guns of a Confederate redoubt on the steep southeast corner of the heights. Upon reaching the Kingsland Road, Terry formed his three brigades in line of battle, and William Birney's brigade formed in column of battalions behind them. When Paine's leading brigade, Colonel Samuel Duncan's 3rd, reached the Kingsland Road, Paine sent his two regiments to connect with Terry's right. Then, under the cover of his skirmishers, he massed Colonel Alonzo Draper's 2nd Brigade in column of companies just north of the road, where the men lay down, waiting for further orders. Colonel John Holman's 1st Brigade was placed in reserve behind Duncan. Foster's entire division massed in column of battalions on the Grover House Road. It fell, however, to Duncan's two regiments, 1,100 men supported on their right by the dismounted troopers of the 2nd United States Colored Cavalry deployed as skirmishers, to make the attack alone. At 5:30 a.m., as the sun was rising, Duncan's two regiments, the 4th and 6th United States Colored Troops, splashed across Four Mile Creek in the morning mist and formed ranks on the other side.

Butler had deliberately arranged to give the black soldiers the key role in this operation. Unlike most Federal generals, he was willing to give the blacks a chance to prove themselves in a major attack. "In the Army of the Potomac," he once said, "negro troops were thought of no value." He said that "negro troops had had no chance to show their value or staying qualities in action." He had told Grant, when planning this attack, "I want to convince myself whether, under my own eye, the negro troops will fight; and if I can take with the negroes, a redoubt that turned Hancock's corps on a former occasion, that will settle the question."[5]

The Texans, who manned the section of the defenses Duncan's two regiments approached, held their fire until the Federals, who advanced with loaded but uncapped muskets, reached the first line of abatis. This was composed of cut-down trees. When the attackers were thoroughly entangled in this obstruction, both the Rebel infantry and the guns on the heights opened fire, while one regiment of Gary's Southern cavalry advanced to a position from which it could enfilade Duncan's right flank. Most of the blacks who got through the slashing were cut down before they could reach the second line of abatis. Some of those who did reach and get through this second obstruction—composed of long rows of X-shaped, sharpened sticks attached to logs and called *chevaux-de-frise*—actually crossed the parapet of the Southern defenses, but they were soon surrounded and either killed or captured. Such was the hatred of the Rebels for black soldiers that some were murdered after surrendering.

The rest of the attackers withdrew to the safety of the ravine through which Four Mile Creek flowed. "It was a perfectly terrible encounter," one of them wrote, "we were all cut to pieces."[6] Duncan himself was wounded four times, and command of the brigade devolved upon Colonel John Ames of the 6th USCT. General Paine had made little effort to support Duncan's attack. He had advanced Draper's 2nd Brigade too late and Holman's 1st Brigade not at all. Now Birney told him to attack again.

And again Paine sent in only part of his division. This time he sent Draper's 2nd Brigade, whose three regiments were placed side by side, each deployed in a column two companies wide and five deep. Holman did send one regiment, the 22nd USCT, as skirmishers to protect Draper's left, but the rest of his brigade and Ames' survivors did not participate. When all was ready, Draper's men crossed Four Mile Creek and advanced through the field across which Duncan had attacked. The morning fog was gone by then, and the Confederate artillery lashed out at the advancing columns as they advanced, but the blacks charged up the slope, floundered through a marshy tributary to the creek, and into the first line of abatis. Here they lost their formation and were stopped by the fire of the Texas Brigade. A reporter from the *Philadelphia Inquirer* noted that the "ground was difficult to advance over . . . and the fire from the Rebel rifle-pits was rapid and deliberate, the charging column suffered terribly."[7] Disregarding Draper's futile attempts to get them to continue their advance, the men began to return the Rebel fire. Troops in the open cannot expect to win a fire fight with men protected by earthworks, but these stood their losses for what Draper called "half an hour of terrible suspense."[8] "It was a wonderful, a sublime sight," wrote the correspondent for the *Times*, "to see those black men stand up to the mark."[9]

But Gregg, who was then farther west, near the Varina Road, saw that another Union column was attacking the weak Confederate center. He realized that his troops were in danger of being cut off if he stayed on New Market Heights. So he sent orders for his men to abandon that position and to hurry west. When the Rebel fire began to slacken, Draper's men finally responded to their officers' urgings to resume their advance. A few men ran forward, yelling, and others joined the rush until the entire brigade was surging forward again. They passed through the outer abatis, crossed the chevaux de frise, climbed the sloping parapet of the Rebel defenses, and drove off the few Southerners who had not already retreated, then followed the Rebels up the hill and captured the summit itself.

"Who dare say, after this," wrote the reporter for the *Times*, "that negroes will not fight?" The question was settled, as far as Ben Butler was concerned. He wrote later that as he rode among his jubilant troops he felt in his "inmost heart that the capacity of the negro race for soldiers had then and there been fully settled forever."[10] There were over 800 casualties in Paine's division to back up that statement.

Holman's 22nd USCT reformed from skirmish line to line of battle and swept over the Confederate parapet to the west of Draper's men, then pushed westward down the trenches, driving off a Southern artillery unit and its two guns. At the other end of the Rebel line the artillery in the redoubt also retreated, as Terry's skirmishers captured the Confederate trenches east of Draper's attack. The Rebel gunners got away just before two of Terry's regiments clambered up the steep slope and into the redoubt. The artillery, Gregg's infantry, and Gary's cavalry fell back and left the Federals in undisputed possession of New Market Heights. Soon thereafter, Kautz's Union cavalry passed through the 10th Corps and headed north toward the Darbytown Road.

Just before daylight Ord's column began advancing up the Varina Road. The 188th New York and the 10th New Hampshire, with their repeating rifles, led the way, along with the divisional sharpshooter battalion. About a mile from Aiken's Landing they encountered pickets from the combined 17–23rd Tennessee of Hughs' brigade but easily drove them back. "Heave after them—double quick!" the commander of the leading brigade, Brigadier General Hiram Burnham, ordered, and the Federals chased the Tennesseans, capturing the picket camp.[11] Except for a few men who fell out to drink the coffee they found still steaming over the campfires, they advanced up the road a total of two miles, bypassing Hughs' position on Signal Hill, until they came to the edge of a clear field and within sight of the outer wall of Ewell's entrenched camp.

All that prevented the United States Navy and a fleet of transports from steaming up the James River and capturing Richmond was a pair of forts on high ground overlooking a north-south stretch of the river. Drewry's Bluff was on the west, or right, bank; Chaffin's Bluff was on the east, or left, bank. Ewell's entrenched camp was merely the landward defense for the water batteries at Chaffin's Bluff. When they learned that Federals had crossed the river in strength, the Confederates' first concern was naturally for the protection of Chaffin's Bluff. And it was assumed that the enemy would advance up the Osborne Turnpike, which ran close to the river and headed straight for the water batteries on the bluff.

One battalion of artillerymen under the temporary command of Major Richard Cornelius Taylor was all that was available for the immediate defense of the camp. Fearing that the camp's outer earthen wall, which had a right-angle corner at its southernmost point, could not be held by such a small force, Ewell had it spread out along shorter inner defenses, known as the Diagonal Line, which ran northeast from the river about

430 yards to a hill covered with a complex of earthworks called Fort Harrison. Just north of Fort Harrison the camp wall, which there curved to the northwest, connected with another line of earthworks running northeast that was known as the Exterior Line of the defenses of Richmond. Major Taylor's 200 artillerymen were at first told to take up muskets and man the line from Jones's Salient, near the bluff, along the diagonal line to Fort Harrison and beyond it into a couple of batteries on the nearest part of the Exterior Line as far as the point where the Varina Road passed through on its way to Richmond. However, when Taylor saw that the Union force was approaching by the Varina Road and not the Osborne Turnpike, he realized that the southern half of his small command was out of position for opposing it.

As the fleeing pickets from Hughs' brigade crossed the open field in front of the defenses and entered the sally port, Taylor ordered his gunners to set aside their muskets and man the guns. Many of the heavy guns that had been in these defenses had been shifted to Petersburg over the preceding months and replaced with puny 6-pounders, discarded by the field artillery of Lee's army as obsolete and too small. There were seven heavy guns of a wide variety of calibers in Fort Harrison and Battery 8, which was just in front of it on the same hill, along with two of the little 6-pounders. But only four of those guns were found to be in working order. Of the four guns in the small manned stretch of the Exterior Line northeast of the fort, the ammunition on hand would fit only two.

Gregg was near this western end of the Exterior Line, and it was then that he sent word for his troops to abandon the New Market Line and act to stop this more dangerous move up the Varina Road. Meanwhile he deployed the 1st Virginia Reserve Battalion along the defenses from Fort Harrison to Battery No. 11, which was just east of where the Varina Road entered the Exterior Line. This was reinforced by Hughs' skirmishers and the small 63rd Tennessee from the same brigade. Half of the 17th Georgia of DuBose's brigade had been in the camp that morning to escort a detail of slave and convict laborers, and these five companies helped to man Fort Harrison. But, until further reinforcements could arrive, there were only about 800 Confederates to man the line from Jones's Salient to Battery No. 11 against approximately 8,000 Federals in Ord's column.

Ord's skirmishers finished driving Hughs into the entrenched camp and Brigadier General George J. Stannard's 1st Division of the 18th Corps deployed for attack while Ord, Stannard, and the latter's three brigade commanders spent ten or fifteen minutes reconnoitering across the open field that their troops would have to cross to reach the Rebel defenses. It was obvious to them that Fort Harrison was the primary obstacle to their progress. Ord at first sent orders for the 1st New York Engineers to entrench a position that would mask the fort and allow his force to bypass it. But that would take a lot of time and the engineers would have to be brought up from the tail of the column before they could even start. So that plan was quickly scrapped. Instead, Ord decided that he would attack as soon as his 2nd Division could be deployed beside Stannard's 1st. But even that would take time, and Stannard soon convinced Ord that it would be better to attack immediately with his single division than to give the Confederates any more time to get organized and bring up reinforcements. If they could take Fort Harrison, he reasoned, they would hold the dominant position on the field and could force the evacuation of all the adjacent lines.

Most of the 21st Connecticut plus single companies from two other regiments had now joined the 118th New York and the 10th New Hampshire on the skirmish line. Behind them came that part of Brigadier General Hiram Burnham's 2nd Brigade that was not on the skirmish line: namely the 96th New York in line of battle straddling the Varina road and the 8th Connecticut in column of divisions—that is, two companies wide by five deep—on the road. Colonel Samuel H. Roberts' entire 3rd Brigade was deployed in column of divisions behind Burnham on the right of the road, while Colonel Aaron F. Stevens' 1st Brigade was formed in similar fashion on the left of the road. Ord ordered Brigadier General Charles A. Heckman's 2nd Division to attack on Stannard's right, but Stannard was to advance without waiting for it.

Just after 6 a.m. the Union skirmishers moved to the left to protect that flank while the rest of the 1st Division advanced along the Varina Road with bayonets fixed and rifles carried at right shoulder shift. A huge shell from an 8-inch gun in the fort screamed harmlessly over the heads of the Federals, and then so did another. The attackers laughed at such poor shooting, but a third shell cut through the 3rd Brigade, taking out thirteen men. Other Confederate guns now found the range, but the Federals came on with grim determination. Ord, Stannard, and Burnham, all watching from the woods that the column had just left, sent staff officers to urge Stevens and Roberts to hurry before the Rebel fire cut the attackers to pieces or the Confederates rushed reinforcements to the fort. But the colonels refused to step up the pace, for to cross the mile of open field to the fort at the double-quick would leave the men too exhausted to assault it.

As the Varina Road approached Fort Harrison from the southeast it crossed a small tributary of Three Mile Creek and then curved to the north to enter the Exterior Line near Battery No. 11. When the Federals left the road to continue straight on toward the fort, Major Taylor ordered his gunners to change from shells to double charges of grapeshot. Stannard's men were nearing the bottom of the hill on which Fort Harrison stood when the 8-inch gun fired its 160 pounds of iron balls. However, the recoil dismounted the barrel from its carriage, ending the big gun's contribution to the battle, and the Federals kept coming.

The heavy Rebel fire had caused the attackers to edge to their right, and this in turn exposed their left flank to fire coming in from the Diagonal Line, throwing the 1st Brigade into confusion. Colonel Stevens went down with a hip wound that ended his career, but Lieutenant Colonel John B. Raulston succeeded him and got his men moving again. The entire division ran for the foot of the hill, where they would be safe from the guns in the fort, which could not be depressed enough to bear on them. There Colonel Roberts let them catch their breath.

Ord, Stannard, and Burnham, from the rear, could see Gregg's infantry hurrying from New Market Heights down the Exterior Line to reinforce the Confederate defenses, and they sent staff officers urging Roberts to hurry. But by the time the messages arrived the colonel had already decided that the men had rested long enough. Roberts, who had risen from a sick bed to lead his brigade that day, gave the order "in a slow, drawling, and an even, monotonous voice: 'Come, boys, we must capture that fort—now get up and start!'" He, too, knew that time was on the side of the Rebels. "Now, men," he said, "just two minutes to take that fort! Just two minutes, men!"[12]

They had lost all formation in their dash for the foot of the hill, so the Federals swarmed up the slope in a disorganized mess. As they came into view, the Confederates opened fire with rifles and cannon, and another big Southern gun was dismounted by its own recoil, this time a 32-pounder. The attackers returned one volley and charged into the dry moat at the foot of the earthen walls of the fort. From there they began to clamber up the sloping walls, some on ladders they had brought with them and some on bayonets stuck into the dirt. The men of the 1st Virginia Reserves were the first to break and run, but they were soon followed by the Tennesseans, who were low on ammunition, and then the artillerymen. Just then Major Taylor met Lieutenant Colonel John M. Maury, his battalion's regular commander, returning to duty. He was too late. "The jig is up," Taylor told him, "we are surrounded."[13] Maury had arrived just in time to be captured. The Federals first swept over the ramparts of the northern part of the fort and then around and over the traverse that divided it and also captured the southern part. Taylor was badly wounded in this action and captured. It was then only 7 a.m. and the 18th Corps had already taken the key to the fortified camp, to

Chaffin's Bluff, and to the Exterior Line of the defenses of Richmond. Five hundred casualties were the price for this success.

---

1. Noah Andre Trudeau, *The Last Citadel: Petersburg, Virginia June 1864– April 1865* (Boston, 1991), 208.
2. Richard J. Sommers, *Richmond Redeemed: The Siege of Petersburg* (Garden City, N.Y., 1981), 23.
3. Ibid., 27.
4. Trudeau, *The Last Citadel*, 210.
5. Dudley Cornish Taylor, *The Sable Arm: Black Troops in the Union Army, 1861–1865* (Lawrence, KS, 1956), 278–279.
6. Sommers, *Richmond Redeemed*, 35.
7. Trudeau, *The Last Citadel*, 209.
8. Sommers, *Richmond Redeemed*, 37.
9. Trudeau, *The Last Citadel*, 209.
10. Taylor, *The Sable Arm*, 280.
11. Sommers, *Richmond Redeemed*, 38.
12. Ibid., 47.
13. Ibid., 48.

CHAPTER TWELVE

The Ground Was Covered With Our Slain

29 September 1864

Sometime between 5 and 5:30 that morning the other half of Grant's two-pronged offensive got under way as Brigadier General David Gregg's 2nd Cavalry Division of the Army of the Potomac formed column near the western end of the Union lines. His two brigades of cavalry plus a battery of horse artillery contained a total of about 4,350 men. One regiment, a handful of pickets, and those men and horses not up to hard marching were all the cavalry that was left to guard the army's rear beyond the eastern end of its south-facing line of defenses. But the best defense is always a good offense. With Gregg's large division moving to threaten Petersburg's communications the Rebels would not be able to spare anything larger than small guerrilla bands for raiding the Union rear areas. And Gregg made no effort to hide his move from the Confederates. In fact his men rode out of camp accompanied by martial airs played by the mounted band of the 1st Maine Cavalry. At about 6:30 a.m. the column passed through the Union defenses, heading south down the Halifax Road, which roughly paralleled the Petersburg & Weldon Railroad.

Wade Hampton had planned a formal review of Rooney Lee's 3rd Division of his Cavalry Corps for that morning. That division's two brigades were in general reserve near Dinwiddie Court House, well to the southwest of Petersburg and near the wagon road from Stony Creek Depot. The 2nd Division, under Rooney's cousin, Fitzhugh Lee, was, of course, up in the Shenandoah Valley with Early, as was Rosser's Laurel Brigade, just detached from the 1st Division two days before. The other two brigades of the 1st Division, which had been Hampton's own but was now commanded by his old friend Brigadier General Matthew Butler, plus the attached cavalry brigade of the Department of North Carolina and Southern Virginia, were in local reserve farther east, backing up a line of cavalry pickets which stretched due south from the Squirrel Level Line and then turned southeast to Reams's Station. The troopers of Rooney Lee's division had formed ranks in a large field, but before Hampton could inspect them orders arrived from army headquarters for the division to move to the north side of the James to help meet the Union offensive there. The Southern troopers set off for Petersburg along the Boydton Plank Road, but before they reached the city Hampton received word that the Union cavalry was driving in the pickets of Matthew Butler's division. He ordered Lee's division to stop just west of town and wait there until the situation developed.

David Gregg's Federals marched about halfway to Reams's Station, and then, at about 7 a.m., Gregg led his 2nd Brigade due west. Meanwhile his 1st Brigade, under Brigadier General Henry E. Davies, continued down the Halifax Road. From a junction about a mile north of Reams's Station one battalion of the 1st New Jersey Cavalry dashed on to the station, and routed an outpost of the 7th Georgia Cavalry, while another battalion of the 1st New Jersey chased other Rebel horsemen southwest toward Monk's Neck Bridge over Rowanty Creek. Southern resistance soon stiffened along that road and Davies, having completed his mission, contented himself with holding what he had gained, and for the rest of the daylight skirmishing was the only fighting he did.

Meanwhile, most of Gregg's other brigade pushed on to the west into unknown territory. It soon ran into Confederate outposts, who fought a delaying action which slowed, but could not stop, the Union advance. By 9:30 a.m. the Federals had crossed the Squirrel Level Road to the southwest of the end of the defensive line of the same name, and pushed on westward to Hatcher's Run, a tributary of Rowanty Creek, and found it guarded by a force that seemed ready to stand and fight. Unknown to them, Hampton, Matt Butler, and most of the latter's division, now barred their path to the southwest. The Federals, however, were not looking for a fight. Their mission was to reconnoiter the area and to threaten the Confederate supply lines enough to keep Lee from sending as many reinforcements north of the James as he would otherwise like to do. Specifically they hoped to reach the Boydton Plank Road.

A regiment was left to guard the crossing of Hatcher's Run and the rest of the Union brigade pushed on to the west along a little country road. At 11 a.m. the Federals cut the telegraph line along another north-south road and captured a civilian wagon belonging to a blockade runner. Again the Northern troopers found the way south blocked by Hampton's men, so they left another force to defend this crossing of Hatcher's Run also and turned to the north. Soon they came to an intersection marked erroneously on Union maps as "Miss Pegram's." There they were told by civilians that Confederate infantry was not far down the road. Realizing that they could go little farther without a fight and that they risked being surrounded and cut off, they turned back, rejoining the troops guarding the north bank of Hatcher's Run at about 1 p.m. There Gregg left a picket line of his own and then withdrew the rest of the brigade to Wyatt's plantation, west of the Halifax Road, where high ground overlooked a tributary of Hatcher's Run called Arthur's Swamp, along which the Rebel picket line had been posted that morning. From there he sent the 1st Maine Cavalry up another road to the northwest toward Poplar Spring Church, but it too soon found its way barred by strong Rebel cavalry forces and turned back. At 1:45 p.m. Gregg sent off a dispatch to Humphreys, Meade's chief of staff, saying, "The road leading from Wyatt's to Poplar Spring Church is heavily barricaded and picketed. I have withdrawn my force to the vicinity of Wyatt's, and do not think any further results can be produced in this direction."[1]

On the north side of the James, the 1st Division of the 18th Corps was too disorganized by its charge and subsequent fight to advance any farther for a while. Almost immediately it came under fire from a battery of light artillery which had just taken position in Fort Johnson, at the northeastern corner of the entrenched camp, where it joined the intermediate Line of the Richmond defenses. Rifle fire was also coming in from some Rebels who had rallied around the wooden barracks north and west of the fort. Experienced gunners among the Federals manned a few cannon in the fort to reply to this Confederate fire. Ord, Stannard and Burnham had ridden to the fort by then. In fact, Burnham himself helped to turn one of the guns, but he was killed by a bullet in the stomach. At about the same time, Colonel Roberts, who had led the charge despite being sick, now collapsed and had to pass command of the 3rd Brigade to Colonel Edgar M. Cullen of the 96th New York. Colonel Michael T. Donohoe, who had commanded the divisional skirmish line, succeeded Burnham in command of the 2nd Brigade.

It was about 8 a.m. before Ord, Stannard, and Lieutenant Colonel Cyrus Comstock of Grant's staff got the 1st Division moving again, although it was still an unwieldy, disorganized mob of soldiers. They drove off what was left of the 1st Virginia Reserve Battalion and captured the wooden barracks. The 2nd Virginia Reserve Battalion soon arrived on the scene, however, and was followed shortly by Colonel DuBose's Georgia brigade of John Gregg's force. Gregg ordered these troops to counterattack and retake Fort Harrison, but this was far beyond their capabilities. Stannard's renewed advance soon caused the inexperienced reserves to panic and flee in disorder to the Intermediate Line. Only the 20th Georgia of DuBose's small brigade actually advanced toward Fort Harrison. It was surprised by a large force of Federals, which attacked it from around a bend in the entrenchments, and lost heavily in prisoners before beating a hasty retreat. DuBose, meanwhile, took the rest of his regiments to Fort Johnson and counterattacked from there down the northeast face of the entrenched camp. But his leading regiment, the 2nd Georgia, was easily repulsed, and DuBose decided to content himself for the moment with defending Fort Johnson.

One factor in DuBose's decision might have been the sight of another large body of Federals approaching. Brigadier General Charles A. Heckman's 2nd Division of the 18th Corps had followed Stannard's 1st up the Varina Road and had taken a few casualties from Confederate fire that had overshot the leading division. One of these shots disabled a gun in a battery that had, despite Butler's orders, inserted itself between the two divisions in the line of march. Another shell had knocked Colonel Edward H. Ripley, commander of Heckman's lead brigade, from his horse and stunned him. He recovered in a few minutes, however, by which time the disabled gun had been cleared from the road, and the 2nd Division resumed its march.

While Stannard's division had been making its attack, Ord had sent Heckman's through the woods along Three Mile Creek to attack the Rebel defenses on Stannard's right. However, the woods turned out to be swampy and full of impenetrable thickets and brambles, and the 2nd Division had still been floundering about, losing all formation, when the 1st Division had attacked and captured Fort Harrison. Ripley, with one regiment, the 9th Vermont, managed to avoid the worst of the woods.

This unit followed the Varina Road toward Battery No. 11, where the road penetrated the Exterior Line, and the Virginia artillerists there, already shaken by the capture of Fort Harrison and the retreat of the reserves, fled upon the approach of this lone regiment without firing a shot.

The 158th New York, of the 1st Brigade, emerged from the woods just after Ripley's Vermonters crossed, the road behind them, and attacked Battery No. 10, between Battery No. 11 and Fort Harrison. After dropping to the ground to avoid a blast of grapeshot, the New Yorkers stormed the battery and captured its two guns. Both the Vermonters and the New Yorkers then contented themselves with holding what they had captured until the rest of their division caught up. But their presence forced Gregg to place some of his forces in the Intermediate Line north of Fort Johnson, facing east, to block any further advance by the Federals from the Exterior Line.

John Gregg was also worried about the rest of his small force, which had not yet arrived from New Market Heights. It might yet be cut off. So he rode eastward and soon found his Texans and Arkansans and the 25th Virginia Battalion strung out in a long column moving westward along the New Market Line and suffering from the effects of their forced march. He let them take a fifteen-minute rest then led them west again. But when he emerged from the woods along Three Mile Creek, Gregg discovered that most of Heckman's 2nd Division had now joined the two advanced regiments in the Exterior Line. Realizing that his men were in no shape to attack such a large force, Gregg led them back into the woods, then north and around the Federals to the Intermediate Line. From there he was planning to launch a counterattack to retake Fort Harrison, but the pressure on the Georgians forced him to abandon that idea and to use his Texans and Virginians on the defensive.

Ord's attention, however, was not on these events on his right. He was personally leading a small force of junior officers and skirmishers in the opposite direction down the Diagonal Line in the hope of cutting off the Confederate bridges over the James. Stannard followed with as much as could be organized of his 2nd and 3rd brigades. The Confederate artillerymen manning the Diagonal Line fell back before these Federals to the last three batteries on the line. From there some manned the guns while others took up muskets, and soon their combined fire stopped this unorganized Union advance. The Federals were therefore stymied, at least temporarily, on both flanks, and heavy woods in the center of the entrenched camp concealed the Confederate weakness there. In those woods Ewell was putting together a scratch force from Hughs' men, some artillerymen, and the 25th Virginia Battalion.

Lieutenant General Richard S. Ewell had been a division commander under Stonewall Jackson and had succeeded him in command of the 2nd Corps of Lee's Army of Northern Virginia. He had lost a leg in the Second Bull Run campaign, and had fallen from his horse at Spotsylvania, and illness had forced him to relinquish the corps to Early, who had taken it first to Lynchburg, then to Washington, and then to defeat in the Valley. Meanwhile, Ewell, partially recovered, had been given command of the Department of Richmond. He was still not a well man, but he was determined to lead his troops on the field in the crucial hour. "I remember very distinctly how he looked," one of his men wrote, "mounted on an old gray horse, as mad as he could be, shouting to his men and seeming to be everywhere at once . . . His cool courage and presence wherever the fight was hottest contributed as much . . . as any one man could have done."[2] As a corps commander he had not shown much talent for strategic thinking or subtle maneuvers, but when it came to the rough and tumble of a straight up fight there were few commanders who could do any better than Dick Ewell.

Ord had also shown more talent, during his career, for leading by example on the field of battle than for controlling or maneuvering large forces. And on this day he chose to personally take charge of the small force that spearheaded the drive down the Diagonal Line instead of directing the overall movements of his two divisions. And before he could revert to his status as corps commander he was put out of action for the rest of the battle by a bullet wound in the right thigh. The bone was not broken, so he applied a tourniquet to stop the bleeding and went on, but a surgeon soon examined the wound and insisted that it required immediate treatment, so Ord relinquished his command to Heckman and started to the rear. Before leaving he told his successor that "my orders were to occupy such works as we took, and with any spare forces we had to push on, attacking the works toward Richmond in succession."[3] Unfortunately for the Union cause, he did not specify a route for the latter effort, and instead of attacking the Intermediate Line from the rear via Fort Harrison, Heckman moved straight ahead, attacking it frontally from the Exterior Line.

There was nothing in Heckman's background that suited him for the responsibility thus thrust upon him. He had been a sergeant in the Mexican War and a railroad conductor between the wars, and his Civil War experience had been mostly garnered in garrison duties in North Carolina and eastern Virginia. In the operations of the Army of the James earlier in 1864 he had proven himself brave but unskillful as a brigade commander and had been captured. He had then been returned in one of several special exchanges of officers just in time to take over command of the 2nd Division a few days before the current operation began. Now he had suddenly succeeded to command of one of the two corps of the Army of the James at a critical moment in that operation. In over his head, he thrashed about in a frenzy of ill-considered activity. First, he ordered Ripley to advance from Battery No. 11 with his 2nd Brigade of the 2nd Division and to attack forts Gregg and Gilmer on the Intermediate Line north of Fort Johnson.

There were only two regiments in that brigade to start with, and most of the men of the 8th Maine had still not caught up since being entangled in the woods. Ripley used those who had rejoined to form a skirmish line to protect the 9th Vermont as it began to advance in line of battle. Almost immediately his little force came under fire from Rebel artillery in both forts. Ripley soon sent a staff officer to ask Heckman to come and see the situation for himself and decide whether it was worthwhile for his brigade to brave such fire. He ordered his men to fall back and lie down in the shelter of the Varina Road, which was somewhat lower than the surrounding terrain, while he awaited the general's reply—which never came.

Next, Heckman sent the 3rd Brigade of his 2nd Division to attack Fort Johnson. This was the only organized brigade left in Heckman's entire force. It had been at the tail of the column as it marched from Aiken's Landing and had not been sent through the woods that had disrupted the rest of the division. But Ord and Heckman had been too busy with problems at the front to give it any directions until now. Meanwhile it had marched up the Varina Road to Battery No. 11, where it had stopped to await orders. Like Ripley's brigade, it had only two regiments. However, one of them was one those large heavy artillery regiments serving as infantry, the 2nd Pennsylvania. Like most of these big units, it consisted of three battalions of four companies each. The brigade commander, Colonel Harrison Fairchild, placed its 1st Battalion in his first line, and backed it up with a second line that consisted of the other two battalions. His other regiment, the 89th New York, brought up the rear. When these arrangements were made, the brigade advanced at the double quick.

Colonel DuBose of the Georgia brigade was in personal charge of the defense of Fort Johnson, with about 200 men in the fort itself and two regiments and a battery in the entrenchments to the north. The fire of their artillery did little damage to the advancing Federals but the latter's own inexperience did. The 3rd Battalion of the 2nd Pennsylvania Heavy

Artillery was very short on officers and soon it drifted off to the north and out of the fight, and the 89th New York fell behind when the brigade crossed a small branch of Cornelius Creek. That left only two battalions in formation as they entered a cornfield on the other side of the stream. The men were becoming exhausted from double-quicking so far, and shells from the Confederate artillery were starting to take their toll. Now the Rebel gunners switched to cannister and the veteran Georgia riflemen opened fire.

The Pennsylvanians began to fall, and their commander was decapitated. His successor ordered the 2nd Battalion to provide covering fire and he took his 1st Battalion on alone for the final assault on the fort. It got as far as the dry moat in front of the defenses, but the few men who tried to scale the ramparts were shot or captured and the rest were trapped there between the lines. The 89th New York had caught up by then and made a half-hearted attack, but soon it joined the 2nd Battalion of heavies behind whatever cover could be found in the cornfield and returned the Rebels' fire as best it could. The 3rd Battalion, meanwhile, moved toward Fort Gregg but was easily stopped by artillery fire and, like Ripley's small brigade, fell back to the cover of the sunken road. A detachment of Georgia infantry, supported by fire from Fort Johnson, was soon sent out to attack these Federals on their left flank, and the latter retreated all the way to Battery No. 11. This move cut off the 150 men of the 1st Battalion who were still in the moat and they surrendered.

Gregg soon learned from these prisoners that it was the 18th Corps that had been attacking him, and he sent this information on to Lee. If that much of Butler's army was north of the James, not much of it could be left on the Bermuda Hundred peninsula between Petersburg and Richmond. So the commanding general sent orders to Major General George E. Pickett, whose division held that part of the line, to withdraw one brigade from the front ready to move north of the James. Pickett actually withdrew one regiment from each of his four brigades and formed them into a provisional brigade under Colonel Edgar Montague, and soon they received orders to move north. Long before they arrived, the Rebels defending the southwestern end of the Diagonal Line from Stannard's advance were reinforced by the rest of Hughs' Tennessee brigade from Signal Hill, along with more artillerymen from the same place. That was at around 10 a.m.

Ord, who had remained nearby after yielding command to Heckman, was dismayed at his corps' lack of progress since taking Fort Harrison. He had sent messages to both Butler and Grant asking for more artillery, more ammunition, and a new commander for his corps, but without receiving a reply. So at about 10 a.m. he proceeded by ambulance to

Deep Bottom in search of Grant. However, failing to find him, he eventually crossed the James River to get his leg taken care of. Even there he continued to send off dispatches to headquarters about the needs at the front.

Ord had failed to find Grant because the general-in-chief had gone forward to confer with Butler. He had received word from the latter that both New Market Heights and Fort Harrison had been captured, and he went to have a first-hand look at the situation. As he rode from Deep Bottom to New Market Heights he passed the black soldiers of the 1st Brigade of the 3rd Division of the 10th Corps, commanded by Brigadier General William Birney, brother of David Birney. "As soon as Grant was known to be approaching," wrote a white officer in the brigade, "every man was on his feet & quiet, breathless quiet, prevailed. A cheer could never express what we felt."[4] Farther along he came to the white troops of the 10th Corps, who cheered him loudly.

While David Birney's men were reformed and sent marching to the northwest on the New Market Road, Butler reported the results of the morning's action to Grant in glowing terms. Foster's 2nd Division of the 10th Corps, which had so far taken no part in the action, led Birney's column, strewing more exhausted stragglers in its wake. A detachment from Gary's Rebel cavalry manned the Exterior Line where the New Market Road passed through it, and Foster deployed his leading brigade, Colonel Rufus Daggett's 1st, to support his skirmishers. Grant overtook Foster's column during this pause and calmly watched the fight despite bullets, as Horace Porter of his staff put it, "stirring up the dust in every direction."[5] Only then did the lieutenant general notice that his six-year-old son Jesse, who had been permitted to ride the boat with his father to Deep Bottom, had tagged along with him and his staff on his Shetland pony. Grant's habitual calm was temporarily disrupted until a staff officer took hold of the pony's bridle and led the reluctant youngster to safety. Daggett's men soon drove off the Confederate cavalrymen and captured that part of the Exterior Line. The men of the 2nd Division, feeling that they were on the road to Richmond and victory at last, gave the credit to Grant. One of them remembered that they "cheered till they fairly raised the old fellow, cigar and all, from his saddle."[6]

Grant then cut across country to see how the 18th Corps was doing and arrived at Fort Harrison only a few minutes too late to see Ord before he left. Without the benefit of a briefing from the corps commander, the general-in-chief did not realize that the 18th Corps attack had already ground to a halt. Heckman had put in motion the two brigades that were to attack the intermediate line but their fate was not yet known. In fact, the new corps commander spoke mostly about his intention of filling Fort Harrison with the light guns of the corps' artillery brigade. From that work, Grant got the closest look at Richmond that he had yet had in the war, an indistinct view of the church spires of the distant city.

At around 10:20 a.m. the Confederate Navy joined the fray. Two wooden gunboats and two ironclads from the James River Squadron opened fire and soon found the range. They were joined later by a fifth boat. The rather inaccurate fire of their heavy guns did relatively little damage, but provided additional deterence to any further Union moves toward the James River bridges.

About 10 minutes later Grant sat down on the ground in Fort Harrison with his back to the parapet and his legs tucked under him to write an order for Birney to push on along the New Market Road. "When the general had reached the middle of the despatch," Horace Porter wrote, "a shell burst directly over him. Those standing about instinctively ducked their heads, but he paid no attention to the occurence, and did not pause in his writing, or even look up. The handwriting of the despatch when finished did not bear the slightest evidence of the uncomfortable circumstances under which it was indited."[7] After sending off a brief report to Washington of the morning's successes he returned to Deep Bottom, where he could keep in touch with both Butler and Meade.

At about 10 a.m. Kautz's 2,200 Union cavalrymen approached the Intermediate Line along the Darbytown Road, well to the north of where the 10th Corps had penetrated the Exterior Line along the New Market Road. Rebel artillerymen were manning the defenses, and they greeted the approaching Federals with fire from several guns. Kautz put his men in the shelter of a nearby ravine while he made a personal reconnaissance. But there was little to see except strong earthworks and frowning guns. There was no way to tell how many—or how few—defenders might be waiting in the trenches. So he led his small division farther north in search of a better way into Richmond.

At around 11 a.m., Richard Anderson, commander of the Confederate 1st Corps, arrived at the front, where he was briefed by Ewell and evidently put in charge of a section of the defenses. By then Heckman had stopped attacking and was content to hold what had been captured and engage the Rebels in a fire fight. For the latter he now had the able assistance of the artillery brigade of the 18th Corps, which had recently arrived. Most of its guns were placed in and around Battery No. 11 and Fort Harrison and were used to shell Fort Johnson.

Foster's division, meanwhile, after a brief rest in the Exterior Line defenses it had captured, pushed on up the New Market Road. About a mile farther on, however, Daggett's brigade, still in the lead, ran into more of Gary's Confederate cavalry, backed up this time by a battery of light artillery. Some woods had screened the Rebels from the view of the advancing Federals until the guns suddenly blasted their front while more distant artillery in Fort Gilmer on the Intermediate Line enfiladed their flank. Daggett tried to put his brigade into an attack formation but it proved an impossible task under the crossfire of the Southern guns, and the brigade soon ran for the shelter of the woods it had just traversed. Foster then formed all three of his brigades into attack columns within the woods, but the trees and uneven ground made it impossible for the regiments to keep their proper alignment. When Foster finally got them moving forward, Gary's troopers fell back and avoided contact, having accomplished their assignment of delaying the Union advance. Gary left his artillery where the road entered the Intermediate Line and led his cavalry north to oppose the advance of Kautz's Federal horsemen. Foster did not follow.

It was 1 p.m. or a little after when Kautz's troopers approached the Intermediate Line again, this time along the Charles City Road, about a mile north of the Darbytown Road. They were met again by Confederate artillery, commanded there by Lieutenant Colonel John C. Pemberton. The year before, Pemberton had been a lieutenant general, but that was before he had surrendered Vicksburg, Mississippi, to Grant. This time the gunners were backed up by infantry from Brigadier General Patrick T. Moore's Local Defense Brigade, and out in front were the pickets of the 7th South Carolina Cavalry of Gary's Brigade. These were easily driven in by the Federals, but the Rebels' heavy guns dissuaded Kautz from attacking the defenses. Instead he sheltered his men in some nearby woods and brought up a battery of horse artillery, which dueled with the Confederate gunners for about an hour without accomplishing anything. Finally the guns were also pulled back into the woods and Kautz waited—perhaps for the Rebels to get bored and go away.

Meanwhile, Birney decided that it would be too dangerous to bypass Fort Gilmer. But to attack it he needed the rest of his force, so he deployed Foster's division and waited. This would provide a chance for a few of the division's hundreds of stragglers to catch up. Nevertheless Foster's division would go into combat that day with only a bit more than a third of its 3,600 men still in the ranks. Birney, in the meantime, conducted a personal reconnaissance of the Confederate position in the Intermediate Line. Paine's division of black troops and William Birney's brigade of the same had followed along the New Market Road, with

Terry's 1st Division of the 10th Corps bringing up the rear. However, the head of the column reached the empty Exterior Line around noon and Paine, not knowing that Birney was waiting, brought the march to a halt with his own division just beyond those defenses and the others in the field east of it. This gave the men some badly needed rest and a chance for them to finally eat something for the first time that day.

At 12:50 p.m. Butler, also unaware that Birney was waiting for the rest of his force to come up, informed Grant that "Birney is at this moment making his attack."[8] It was, however, 45 minutes later before the attack finally went in. Then Foster's 2nd Division of the 10th Corps moved due south in line of battle against Fort Gilmer. William Birney's brigade was to attack from the east but was not yet ready. Paine's division was to remain near the New Market Road as a reserve for Foster, while one brigade of Terry's division would play the same role for Birney's brigade. Terry's other two brigades had been left back at the Exterior Line.

Fort Gilmer was actually the tip of a large salient in the Intermediate Line where the north-south line turned ninety degrees to run east-west and skirt around the headwaters of a small tributary of Cornelius Creek. Then the line ran north and northwest to the main stream. Inside the fort were five companies of the 15th Georgia plus fragments of several other commands and two heavy guns, one of them a very heavy 64-pounder. The men of two batteries of light artillery manned the line between the fort and the creek. But when the Federals were seen advancing, DuBose rushed more Georgia infantrymen over from Fort Johnson, and Gregg sent his entire Texas Brigade, which arrived just ahead of the attacking Federals.

Foster, who had never commanded a division in battle before, and a brigade only once, led his three badly depleted brigades forward in one long line, two ranks deep. They had to cross a mile of ground out by three ravines full of brush and brambles, then a bare cornfield, then two lines of abatis. The Federals crossed the first ravine with only slight disruption to their formation, but when they reached the open ground between it and the next ravine they were hit by Rebel artillery fire from the front and right. They ran for the cover of the next ravine, but it did not protect them from the flanking fire. So they hurried on to the final ravine. There Foster let the men catch their breath and dress their ranks. "Death fairly reveled in that third ravine," one of them wrote. "Shells hissed and exploded about our ears incessantly, and crushed heads and mangled bodies thickly strewed our pathway."[9]

Some of the Federals refused to leave the scanty shelter of the last ravine, but the rest climbed out of the ravine and rushed with a cheer across the cornfield that sloped up to the earthen walls of the fort. The Confederate infantry now opened fire and the artillery switched from shell to cannister. Scores of men went down and the rest were stopped. They had sense enough to know better than to try to return fire. Instead, they turned and ran back to the cover of the ravine. Birney sent one regiment forward from Paine's division, the 5th United States Colored Troops, and when it reached the front Foster's men joined them in a second charge.

"The hissing and howling and screaming of the missiles," a member of Daggett's brigade remembered, "mingled with the shouts of the attacking party, the yells of the rebels, and the groans of the wounded, were horrible beyond description. The leaves of corn, cut by flying shot, floated before our eyes continually, and fell to earth in showers. Many a poor fellow near me was struck the second time before he reached the ground with his first wound. We had passed a little log house, and were within forty paces of the abatis of the fort, when a whirlwind seemed to rush across our front. The line disappeared as though an earthquake had swallowed it. The fatal hissing increased in volume a hundred fold. Perfectly bewildered, those who remained standing halted. The ground was covered with our slain, and we had come thus far with fixed bayonets and without firing a shot. Every one recoiled, and Foster, who was still with us, ordered a retreat. The rebels stood in crowds upon the parapet of their fort, shouting at us in derision."[10]

The 3rd Brigade got as far as the chevaux de frise but could not get through it. One regiment of the 3rd Brigade took shelter behind the little log house. The other two brigades did not even get that far. But the 5th USCT did, and went on to within a hundred yards of the Rebel trenches. There they flung themselves to the ground but found that even lying down they were unprotected from the deadly Confederate fire. In good order they slowly fell back to the shelter of the last ravine. Colonel Galusha Pennypacker's 2nd Brigade of Foster's division also fell back in good order, but the other two lost much of their formation as they withdrew. About 400 of Foster's men were killed or wounded in the charge and about 100 from the single regiment of black troops. Confederate losses were very light, except for another heavy gun wrecked by the force of its own recoil.

Even as the Federals withdrew, at about 2:30 p.m., the Rebels were reinforced by the arrival of Major General Charles Field, who commanded the division that Gregg's and DuBose's brigades belonged to, along with another of his brigades. This unit of five Alabama regiments, known as Law's Brigade, was under the temporary command of Colonel Pinckney D. Bowles. It had come by train from Petersburg as far as

Drewry's Bluff, then had double-quicked across the bridge to Chaffin's Bluff and on to Fort Gilmer, a total of five miles, only slowing to a normal walk occasionally, and arriving just as another Union attack began.

William Birney led three regiments of United States Colored Troops up the New Market Road from the Exterior Line at about 2 p.m. They soon turned off the road into the woods to the west and came out opposite the north-south Confederate defenses between Fort Gregg and Fort Gilmer. By the time they got into position, Foster's division was already retreating. Like his brother, the corps commander, this Birney also committed his units to attack piecemeal. First he sent Captain Edward Babcock's 9th USCT forward before the other two regiments were ready. One of Babcock's company's had been detached. He deployed four of his remaining companies as skirmishers and the other five in line of battle, and they advanced into the southern end of the same cornfield that Foster had crossed. The Confederate artillery promptly turned its attention to this new threat, hitting it with a crossfire that shook the Federal troops. After crossing half of the field, Babcock ordered his men to lie down while he went to report to his brigade commander. Birney ordered him to renew the assault, but in Babcock's absence his regiment had already advanced again, and by the time he returned it was already defeated and retreating to the cover of the woods.

Next, Birney sent forward Major George Wagner with four companies of his more experienced 8th USCT. They advanced somewhat to the south of the 9th USCT and got to within 250 yards of Fort Gregg before the Rebel fire brought it to a halt. They remained there while Wagner brought up another four companies but even with this reinforcement they could advance no farther but merely returned the Confederate fire as best they could. By then the 7th USCT had arrived and Birney sent it in. However, either its commander, Colonel James Shaw, or the staff officer sent to deliver the order, misunderstood what Birney wanted. He intended for the 7th to attack with four companies in skirmish line backed up by the rest of the regiment in line of battle, as had the 9th. But Shaw understood that he was to attack with the four companies of skirmishers alone, and this he proceeded to do.

Captain Julius Weiss led the four companies, about 200 men, into the cornfield. The Confederate artillery switched to this new target but, with the help of the fire of the 8th USCT, they took their losses and came on. The Rebel infantry waited until the attackers were very close and then hit them with a staggering volley from front and flank. Sixty or seventy Federals went down before this fire and the artillery fire that had proceeded it, but the rest pressed on, breaking into a run. There was no abatis on this side of the fort, and the attackers stormed into the dry moat, where they were trapped. They had no ladders with which to scale the sloping earthen ramparts.

Some clambered up by hand and some were boosted up by their comrades, but they were all shot as they reached the top. Three times the blacks made concerted efforts to climb the wall, and three times they were driven back. Captain Weiss was wounded in the first attempt. Then the Federals tried to return the Rebel fire, but soon the survivors were forced to seek the cover of a blind spot that could not be reached by rifle fire. The Confederates then fashioned hand grenades by cutting the fuses short on cannon shells and lobbing or rolling them into the moat. After the second of these exploded, the last one hundred survivors finally surrendered, but even then their ordeal was not over. Southern soldiers were invariably enraged by the sight of blacks in arms. Several Federals were killed after they surrendered and others were abused. Two thirds of them eventually died in prison.

---

1. *Official Records*, 42:II:1107.
2. Sommers, *Richmond Redeemed*, 62.
3. *Official Records*, 42:I:794.
4. Sommers, *Richmond Redeemed*, 75.
5. Porter, *Campaigning With Grant*, 300.
6. Sommers, *Richmond Redeemed*, 77.
7. Porter, *Campaigning With Grant*, 302.
8. Sommers, *Richmond Redeemed*, 81.
9. Ibid., 85.
10. Ibid., 86.

CHAPTER THIRTEEN

Shouting the Battle Cry of Freedom

29–30 September 1864

Just as the last of William Birney's attacks ended in disaster, yet another ill-timed Federal advance began. Grant had left Heckman with orders to attack in conjunction with the 10th Corps but he failed to get started until Foster's and Birney's attacks on Fort Gilmer had already been repulsed. The last organized brigade in the 18th Corps sector was Colonel James Jourdan's 1st Brigade of Heckman's 2nd Division, and now its three regiments advanced from Battery No. 10, on the Exterior Line just north of Fort Harrison, toward Fort Gregg. The Confederate artillery switched its fire to this new target and stopped most of the brigade. But a small party led by the color bearer of the 55th Pennsylvania actually got inside the fort before being overwhelmed by DuBose's Georgians. However, a corporal from the 158th New York managed to capture and get safely away with the flag of the 20th Georgia.

After the repulse of this attack the battle on this part of the field degenerated into a fire fight between the Rebel artillery and the various

Federal infantry units still hugging the ground in the cornfield, who were backed up by a battery of Union 12-pounder guns on the New Market Road. In this contest the Federal riflemen seemed to be holding their own, silencing at least one Confederate gun in the Intermediate Line. But at about 4 p.m. fire from the Rebel gunboats forced the Union battery to withdraw. Late that afternoon the left flank of the 8th USCT started to give way, but William Birney shifted the 7th to its relief and reinforced the 9th with the 29th Connecticut, which had been late to arrive at the front.

At noon Grant had sent a message to Butler saying, "If our troops do not reach Richmond this afternoon, my opinion is that it will be unsafe to spend the night north of the enemy's lower bridge. I think it advisable to select a line now to which the troops can be brought back to-night, if they do not reach Richmond." At 1:35 p.m. he wrote to Butler that "if General Birney has not been successful in carrying the works in his front, I think it will be advisable to move out to" the Darbytown Road. Confederate reinforcements had been spotted moving north, which showed, Grant said, "that all must be done to-day that can be done toward Richmond." However, Meade assured the general-in-chief that Lee could have sent no more than Hoke's Division to the north side of the James, and at 3:50 p.m. Grant told Butler to "hold all the ground we can to-night, and feel out to the right in the morning. This is not intended to prevent as rapid a push forward to-night as can be made." Just before leaving Deep Bottom to return to City Point at 4:45 Grant wrote to Butler that "if the enemy do not re-enforce by more than a division we will give them another trial in the morning, flanking instead of attacking works."[1] While Grant's chief engineer, Brigadier General John G. Barnard, began laying out a defensive line, Butler sent Terry's division and the 1st Battalion of the 4th Massachusetts Cavalry north to the Darbytown Road. Butler evidently meant for these troops to join with Kautz's cavalry for an attack upon the Intermediate Line, but, of course, Kautz had already moved farther north and Terry could not find him. Instead he captured a few Confederates who told him that strong Rebel forces were in the area. So he deployed his troops across the road and sent out scouts in search of the Union cavalry or the Confederate opposition. Neither one was found, but the afternoon was spent in this futile effort.

On the south side of the James, the Confederate infantry had spent the morning and early afternoon shifting units around in an effort to find ways to man the defenses with fewer men and thus free others to move north of the river. Much of the Union infantry had been prepared since 4 a.m. to march out of its defenses and attack the Confederate supply lines, but Meade was waiting for the Rebels to weaken themselves by sending substantial forces north, and so far he was not convinced that they had. At about 3 p.m. he sent a brigade of infantry from the 5th Corps beyond the west end of his defenses to reconnoiter the Squirrel Level Line, where he knew that at least two brigades of Confederate infantry had been stationed. The brigade moved westward along the Poplar Spring Road and soon encountered Rebel pickets, driving them back for a mile. Beyond Poplar Spring Church, near Peeble's farm, they were fired on by Southern artillery, and a large force of skirmishers backed by an infantry line of battle was seen advancing toward its flank. Having thus satisfied himself that the Confederates still held the area in strength, the brigade commander returned his force to the Union defenses.

Meanwhile, at 3:30 p.m., Meade had, as we have seen, already told Grant that he doubted that more than Hoke's Division had left the Petersburg front to reinforce Richmond and that he would not send out his infantry that afternoon. However, he would "be prepared to advance at daylight tomorrow."[2] Unknown to Meade, shortly after the Union brigade fell back the Rebel infantry, two brigades of Major General Henry Heth's division of A. P. Hill's 3rd Corps, turned over their trenches on the Squirrel Level Line to the cavalry and marched for the main defenses of Petersburg. There they bivouacked for the night, ready to take the place of the troops that had gone to the north side should the Federals attack Petersburg the next day.

At about 4 p.m. Wade Hampton ordered Matthew Butler to attack the Union pickets on the north side of Hatcher's Run. He wanted to find out just how many Federals were over there. The Union picket line could not stand up to such a force and fled to the protection of the rest of their brigade on Wyatt's plantation, followed closely by Matt Butler's dismounted troopers. The Confederates were soon hit by fire from a section of Union horse artillery, but the Rebels also brought up a pair of guns, and soon a lucky shot blew up an ammunition box and disabled one of the Federal cannon, sending up a cloud of smoke that was seen all the way back at the Union defenses around Globe Tavern.

At that, Butler led his division forward while the Rebel artillery turned its attention to the Union troopers. The center of the Northern line started to waver, but Colonel Charles H. Smith, commander of the 2nd Brigade, sent a battalion of the 1st Maine to strengthen it and the Union line held. At about 5:10 p.m. the Confederates fell back. Ten minutes earlier, Meade, who had seen the smoke from the explosion of the ammunition box, had dispatched a brigade of infantry from the 5th Corps to Gregg's aid.

Rebel reinforcements were also on the way, however, and they arrived first. Hampton had ordered Rooney Lee to bring one of his brigades down from where both had been waiting outside Petersburg all day, and it arrived just before sunset and was put in position on the Confederate right. Then all three Rebel brigades made a dismounted attack on Smith's one Union brigade. Lee's reinforcements drove back the Union left, capturing one regimental commander. Two Pennsylvania regiments in the center were almost surrounded, but a counterattack by another battalion of the 1st Maine opened an escape route and the entire Northern brigade fell back to some hastily built defenses in the Wyatts' yard, where it was joined by the infantry brigade rushed down from Globe Tavern. By then it was dark, and Hampton made no further attacks.

All day Robert E. Lee had been urging Ewell to counterattack and recapture Fort Harrison, but the latter never felt that he had enough troops to take the offensive. Lee had finally arrived on the north side of the James at around 3 p.m. and had set up temporary headquarters at Mrs. Chaffin's house. He had taken preliminary steps toward evacuating Petersburg should it become necessary. These included having a pontoon bridge laid across the Appomattox River west of Petersburg to facilitate any withdrawal of his forces there, and the evacuation of all military hospitals in the city. Ewell had evidently returned to Richmond by the time Lee arrived at Chaffin's. Field was there and he wanted to attack Fort Harrison immediately, but Lee saw that the defenders were exhausted and that only two brigades of reinforcements had arrived by then, so he told Field to wait.

Shortly before dark, as he was riding along behind the lines, Lee came upon a solitary young soldier. He asked the boy why he was so far from his unit and was told that he had been sent to fill his company's canteens from a well. "Well, hurry and catch up," Lee told him; "they will need you by daylight."[3]

About then a couple of regiments of Stannard's Union division made one last attack along the Diagonal Line, and some inexperienced Virginia heavy artillerymen fled from Fort Hoke, abandoning it to the Federals. However, yet another work, Fort Maury, still barred the way to the James, manned by Montague's ad hoc brigade from Pickett's Division and backed up by fire from a gunboat in the river. Stannard decided that the rest of the line could not be taken and fell back to Fort Harrison after spiking or carrying off the guns and making at least some attempt to damage the earthworks. At about 5:30 p.m., before this job was

completed, Montague's brigade plus some of Hughs' Tennesseans counterattacked. This only served to hasten Stannard's withdrawal from the
Diagonal Line. But when the Confederates tried to go on and retake
Fort Harrison three Union cannon blasted them with cannister and most
of Stannard's division barred their path. The Rebels fell back and the
fighting was at last over on this front for the day.

Also at about 5:30 p.m., Kautz's cavalry finally left its hiding place in
the woods where the Charles City Road and Williamsburg Road met
just east of the Intermediate Line and headed north again. Kautz had
intended to turn into the next road, which was less than two miles to
the north, but he was not traveling with the head of his column and the
commander of his lead brigade waited until it had gone yet another
couple of miles before turning to the west again. It was after midnight
when the Union troopers again approached the Intermediate Line. It was
a cloudy night and the darkness prevented the defenders from seeing the
Federals, but it also kept the cavalrymen from seeing what they were up
against. They blundered into the abatis, which broke up their formation,
and in the confusion they began to fire at each other. This alerted the
Confederate militia in the defenses, who fired at the muzzle flashes in
the darkness, adding to the general confusion. Kautz called off the attack
and, leery of spending the night so far from the main body of the Union
army, led his tired troopers back to the south.

At the end of the day, William Birney's, Foster's, and Paine's men fell
back, under the cover of a skirmish line, to the Exterior Line, where
they were soon joined by Terry's division. The Confederates followed
only with a skirmish line, which gathered up the rifles that had been left
in the cornfield, along with two flags that had been abandoned. Some of
the wounded black soldiers were bayoneted by these Rebels. Stannard's
division held Fort Harrison, while Heckman's division extended a short
way to the south along the Varina Road to protect the left flank of the
army. The Federals still held their conquests of the early morning: the
New Market Line, Fort Harrison, and the Exterior Line south of the
New Market Road, but they had squandered the rest of the day in unco-
ordinated attacks without achieving anything further. Still, they had
hopes for the next day.

South of the James, Wade Hampton's cavalry broke contact with David
Gregg's Federal troopers at about 9 p.m. and pulled back to the west.
The picket line was reestablished along Arthur's Swamp, the main body
of Matt Butler's division returned to its camps south of Hatcher's Run,
while Rooney Lee took his brigade back to the Boydton Plank Road to

rejoin his other one. By then the Union infantry brigade that had come to the cavalry's support had returned to the defenses around Globe Tavern, so Gregg brought his 1st Brigade up from Reams's Station to take over the new defenses at Wyatt's plantation, leaving only the 1st New Jersey Cavalry to hold that brigade's former positions. Then Gregg took the exhausted 2nd Brigade back to within a half-mile of the western end of the Union infantry defenses to get some rest.

The foot soldiers in those trenches were surprised to hear distant cheers to the east come rolling ever closer down the line that night, until word finally reached them of the capture of Fort Harrison by the Army of the James. Then they too raised three cheers that resounded in the darkness of the early autumn night.

East of Petersburg, where the opposing lines were close, nervous troops engaged in vicious little fire fights throughout the night of 29–30 September—fights which each side thought had been started by the other. Sharpshooters were busy all night in places, and a noisy but ineffectual mortar duel flared up for a while, followed by an even noisier general exchange of artillery and rifle fire. Each side half expected an attack by the other. Major General Winfield Scott Hancock, the able commander of the Union 2nd Corps, which held the right of the line, reported to Meade that the Rebels seemed to be massing just north of the Appomattox for a possible crossing behind his right rear.

At 11:15 p.m. Meade sent a dispatch to Grant outlining these and other signs that the Confederates were still holding Petersburg in force, adding: "I do not see indications sufficient to justify my making an attempt on the South Side Railroad . . . I can throw a force out to Poplar Spring Church, and engage the enemy, if you deem advisable, but this will only be extending our lines without a commensurate object, unless the engaging the enemy is so deemed." But Grant was not so easily dissuaded, fearing, perhaps, that inactivity on Meade's part might lead to a Rebel concentration against either Butler or Sheridan. He replied fifteen minutes later with orders for the Army of the Potomac to delay its advance until 8 a.m. on the thirtieth, by which time he should be back from conferring with Butler about prospects north of the James. "When you do move out," he said, "I think it will be advisable to maneuver to get a good position from which to attack, and then if the enemy is routed follow him into Petersburg, or where circumstances seem to direct. I do not think it advisable to try to extend our line to the South Side road, unless a very considerable part of the enemy is drawn across the James, and then only when we are able to withdraw Butler's force rapidly and send it to you."[4]

Up in the Shenandoah Valley, Sheridan was writing to Grant: "This morning I sent around Merritt's and Custer's divisions, *via* Piedmont, to burn grain, &c., pursuant to your instructions. My impression is that most of the troops which Early had left passed through the mountains to Charlottesville. Kershaw's division came to his assistance, and, I think, passed along the west base of the mountain to Waynesborough. The advance of my infantry is at Mount Crawford, eight miles south of Harrisonburg. I will go on and clean out the Valley. I am getting twenty-five to forty prisoners daily, who come in from the mountains on each side and deliver themselves up. From the most reliable accounts, Early's army was completely broken up and is dispirited. It will be exceedingly difficult for me to carry the infantry column over the mountains and strike at the Central road. I cannot accumulate sufficient stores to do so, and think it best to take some position near Front Royal, and operate with the cavalry and infantry. I will, however, stay here for a few days . . . The country from here to Staunton was abundantly supplied with forage and grain, &c."[5] Sheridan was wrong on at least a couple of counts. Early's army was not "completely broken up," nor had it crossed to the east side of the Blue Ridge. Nor did Sheridan explain why, if the country was "abundantly supplied with forage and grain," he could not "accumulate sufficient rations." The truth seems to be that Sheridan did not have the courage to cut loose from his supply line as Grant had done in his Vicksburg campaign and as Sherman would soon do in Georgia.

Lincoln was also writing to Grant that day, and Sheridan was his subject: "I hope it will lay no constraint on you, nor do harm in any way, for me to say I am a little afraid lest Lee send re-enforcements to Early, and thus enable him to turn upon Sheridan." Grant answered this telegram the same day, sometime after returning from his look at affairs north of the James. "I am taking steps," he said, "to prevent Lee sending reenforcements to Early by attacking him here. Our advance is now within six miles of Richmond and have captured some very strong enclosed forts, some fifteen or more pieces of artillery and several hundred prisoners. Although I have been at the front I can give no estimate of our losses, about 600 wounded men however have been brought in."[6]

Down in Georgia on that 29th day of September another Union division was sent north to help protect Sherman's line of supply and hold down the areas already conquered. General Thomas, commander of the Department of the Cumberland, which included the areas most immediately threatened, was also sent north. "I take it for granted," Sherman wrote to Halleck that day, "that Forrest will cut our road, but think we can prevent him from making a serious lodgment. His cavalry will travel a hundred miles where ours will ten. I have sent two divisions up to Chattanooga and one to Rome, and General Thomas started to-day to drive Forrest out of Tennessee. Our roads should be watched from the rear, and I am glad that General Grant has ordered reserves to Nashville. I prefer for the future to make the movement on Milledgeville, Millen, and Savannah. Hood now rests twenty-four miles south, on the Chatta-hoochee, with his right on the West Point road. He is removing the iron of the Macon road. I can whip his infantry, but his cavalry is to be feared."[7]

In addition to the two Union divisions coming up from Chattanooga, there were 3,000 cavalrymen marching east from Memphis, and 1,300 infantry steaming up the Tennessee River on transports to converge on Forrest. Also, Major General Lovell Rousseau, the Federal commander in middle Tennessee, was moving troops by rail from Pulaski via Nash-ville around to reinforce the rail line between Murfreesboro and the tunnel through the Cumberland Mountains at Cowan, a section already guarded by some 3,150 troops.

Forrest sent two small detachments ahead of his main force to tear up track on both sides of Tullahoma, but the damage they did was repaired within a day. Learning that the Nashville & Chattanooga Railroad was well defended and that strong forces were converging on him from several directions, Forrest decided that attacking that line would be "hazardous and unwise." He reported to Richard Taylor that he would instead "go where there was prospect of accomplishing more good."[8] He sent one of his division commanders, Brigadier General Abraham Buford, with over half of the total force and the only remaining artillery, to the south with orders to capture Huntsville, Alabama, and to damage the railroad between that town and Decatur before crossing back to the safety of the south side of the Tennessee River. Forrest himself, with the rest of his command, turned back to the west to distract the Federals from Buford and to see what further damage he could do to the Nashville & Deca-tur Railroad.

Out in Missouri on 29 September, Thomas Ewing's column from Pilot Knob reached Harrison, 35 miles east of Rolla. There Ewing decided to make a stand against his pursuers. His infantry had already outmarched Marmaduke's cavalry, which had given up the chase from exhaustion. Marmaduke himself rode on with Shelby, whose division kept up the pursuit. But when the two Rebel generals discovered that Ewing had called a halt and that his troops were busily throwing up breastworks of fence rails and railroad ties, they decided that an assault, even if success-ful, would be more costly than it would be worth. So they turned back, leaving behind a token force which tried to bluff Ewing into surrendering with a threat to massacre his men if he did not, but he refused.

The campaign was not going well for Sterling Price. Long before this, perhaps even before the attack on Fort Davidson, Price had realized that St. Louis was too heavily defended for him to capture. The attack on Fort Davidson had not only cost him between 10 and 15 percent of his force in casualties, but had badly shaken the morale of Fagan's and Marmaduke's divisions. Then the fruitless pursuit of Ewing had given Rosecrans and his other forces valuable time to prepare for the Confederates' approach. Price, who was still back at Pilot Knob, after sending some of Shelby's troopers in a feint toward St. Louis, started marching toward Jefferson City, capital of the state.

In Virginia, southeast of Richmond, Ben Butler's Union infantry spent much of the night of 29–30 September digging. Stannard's men started to dig a new line of trenches on the western crest of the hill upon which Fort Harrison sat, so as to defend it from counterattack. And they tore down some of the nearby barracks to provide a clearer field of fire and to provide lumber to shore up the new trenches. The heavy Confederate guns were removed and their own light field pieces were put in place. Stannard's division was shifted farther south as part of a move to extend the left flank, and Paine's division of black troops took over the Fort Harrison hill. William Birney's brigade of blacks held the sector stretching a mile and a half from Fort Harrison to the New Market Road.

The captured portion of the Exterior Line was modified to better defend against an attack from the opposite direction while a new east-west trench was dug to protect the Union right just north of the New Market Road. However, outposts were strung along the Exterior Line all the way to the Darbytown Road, while the 4th Massachusetts Cavalry patroled all the way up to the Charles City Road. At around 6 a.m. the 10th Corps commander had his brother's brigade close up to the left and moved Foster's division to the south side of the New Market Road. Colonel Henry M. Plaisted's 3rd Brigade of Terry's division was taken from reserve to fill the gap thus opened.

All this digging and moving about kept the Federals from getting much rest. "The instant we halted," Colonel Ripley remembered, "the men dropped in their tracks as though shot. In a few moments along would come the order 'side step to the right and close a gap with such a Brigade.' We would kick, prick, and pound the almost insensible men up, and side-step, halt and drop. Then would come another order from the other direction, 'side step to the left' or 'march forward' or 'backward' until at last we got the engineers satisfied and we thought we were going to sleep. Instead of that shovels and pickaxes were passed along, and we dug like beavers all night, until by morning for two miles or more we presented to the enemy a fairly strong breastwork with five redoubts in it manned by light batteries."[9]

At 9:10 p.m. Butler sent a request to Grant for the loan of a corps from Meade's Army of the Potomac. But at 11 p.m. the general-in-chief refused. Meade was about to launch his own attack at the opposite end of the long Union line and needed every man he had. If Lee had not sent sizable reinforcements north of the James, Butler's forces should be safe. If Lee had sent large reinforcements north of the James he may have so weakened his position south of the river as to allow Meade to capture Petersburg, which would free up most of the Army of the Potomac. "If so," Grant told Butler, "I can send two corps, using railroads and steam-boats for the infantry."[10] And this should allow them to arrive in time to save the Army of the James even from a large-scale attack.

Throughout the night Confederate reinforcements did arrive north of the James. The rickety railroad between Petersburg and Richmond could only carry one brigade to Drewry's Bluff at a time. But besides the rest of Field's Division, the four brigades of Major General Robert F. Hoke's division of the Department of North Carolina and Southern Virginia, reinforced by one brigade from Major General Cadmus Wilcox's division of the 3rd Corps, had crossed by daylight on the thirtieth. Hoke's force was placed in reserve along the Osborne Turnpike just north of the entrenched camp. Informed by John Gregg that headquarters wanted his division to make a night attack to recapture Fort Harrison, Field spent much of the night maneuvering his three fresh brigades into position, only to be informed by Anderson that no night attack was intended after all. Field then pulled his troops back to the vicinity of Fort Gilmer, where they bivouacked for the rest of the night.

Several batteries of light artillery from various sectors of the Petersburg front had also crossed the river, and Brigadier General Edward Porter Alexander, acting chief of artillery of the Army of Northern Virginia, arrived to take personal charge of all the guns. A brigade of Local Defense Forces, consisting of workers in defense industries and government agencies who were turned out for emergencies, had also reached the front. Even more reinforcements were expected: the rest of Wilcox's Division, Rooney Lee's cavalry division, and another battalion of artillery.

At 5 a.m. on the thirtieth Butler and Grant met at Deep Bottom, where they conferred for three hours. They decided that it would be best for the Army of the James to stay on the defensive that day. Also, Butler learned from the general-in-chief that the latter had given Ord thirty days leave to recuperate at home. So Butler appointed his friend and chief engineer, Major General Godfrey Weitzel, just returned from reconnoitering Fort Fisher in North Carolina, to command the 18th Corps.

At about 7:30 a.m. on the 30th, Kautz's cavalry returned from its fruitless jabs at the northern portions of the Intermediate Line and took position at the northern end of this line, near the Darbytown Road. Although Kautz had accomplished little on his sojourn, at least his return relieved Butler's and Grant's minds about the safety of his small force. Around 8 a.m. Butler, still worried about the center of his line north of Fort Harrison, ordered another shift of his troops. As part of this move Paine's black troops had to abandon the fort that they had worked all night to improve, and Stannard's men occupied it once again. After this move had been made, Butler realized that by shifting to his right he had weakened his left flank and his connection down the Varina Road with Deep Bottom. So an hour later he ordered another wholesale shift which involved withdrawing Paine's division, returning it to the 18th Corps, and placing it on the vulnerable left. But somebody forgot to tell Paine, and he refused to move.

Just after returning to City Point, at about 9 a.m., Grant wrote to Butler: "Reconnaissances might be made toward the Charles City Road, and preparations made to move out that way in a day or two if thought advisable, breaking for a time all connection with the river. I do not say this will be advisable, but get such information as you can about roads, &c."[11] Success south of the James could make such a move desirable.

While Butler's Federals spent the morning improving their defenses and shifting about, the Confederate commanders spent the time reconnoitering and planning a counterattack. "General Lee, with Ewell, Anderson, and a number of other officers, and some of our staff, was examining a new line of defense with that trained engineer's eye of his, Ewell riding by him," wrote Colonel Moxley Sorrel, chief of staff of the 1st Corps. "The latter was so good a horseman that his one leg was equal to most riders' two, but his horse stumbling, down came both—an awful cropper. I made sure the General's head and neck were cracked. He was picked up, no bones broken, but an 'object' about the head; scratched, bruised, torn and bloody. Lee instantly ordered him back to Richmond and to stay there until completely well. In two or three hours he was again on the lines, and such a sight! Painfully comical it was. He had gone to the hospital, where the bald head and face were dressed. He returned swathed in bandages from crown of head to shoulders. Two little apertures for his piercing eyes and two small breathing spaces were all that was left open for the Lieutenant-General. Quite indifferent, however, to such mishaps, he was sharp about his work and lisping out directions as usual."[12]

At about 11 a.m. three Confederate ironclads in the James River opened fire on the Union lines and an hour later another gunboat joined in the bombardment. Most of their shells fell short. An attempt to increase the range by using more gunpowder caused one Rebel gun to burst. General Alexander, the Confederate chief of artillery, tried to get the big guns on target by signaling corrections to the gunboats, but he only succeeded in bringing their fire down on himself and his spotters and barely escaped with his life. Soon the navy gave up. Porter's field artillery opened fire at about 1 p.m. Some mortars and a few of the big guns in the defenses also joined in. They fired deliberately for twenty minutes and then intensively for 25. But they fired too high, and most of the shells passed harmlessly over the Federal front lines, serving only to chase off some engineers in the rear and to produce a great deal of noise and smoke, which hung over the field in the humid, windless air.

Under the cover of the fire and smoke, Anderson moved the Confederate infantry into position to attack Fort Harrison. Field's three fresh brigades were placed side by side in line of battle near Fort Johnson, facing south. His left brigade, Bowles' Alabamans, straddled the eastern wall of the fortified camp. The other two, Brigadier General G. T. "Tige" Anderson's Georgians in the center and Brigadier General John Bratton's South Carolinians on the right, formed in the cover of some woods. However, Anderson's plan called for the center brigade to move out first then halt halfway to the fort and let Bratton's move in behind it. Meanwhile, Hoke's Division formed in a gully only four or five hundred yards west of the fort with three brigades in the front line and two in a second line. Since Field's brigades had about twice as far to go, they advanced first.

At 1:45 p.m. Tige Anderson's men emerged from the woods. When they saw this, the Federals in the fort moved to face this threat, leaving only a thin picket line facing the Diagonal Line and maintaining the connection with Heckman's division to their left. Very little entrenching had been done on the sector now threatened by Field's advance and in the few minutes that remained to them, Stannard's men were only able to erect a parapet of logs and earth about a foot high. Then they deployed into a dense formation three ranks deep. The commander of the only Union guns in the fort reported that he had fired off all his ammunition in dueling with the Rebel guns, so Stannard ordered them out. Weitzel promised to send another battery to take their place. But before these guns could arrive, Anderson's Georgians reached the slight depression in the middle of the field where they were supposed to lie down and wait for the other two brigades. However, contrary to the plan, they did not stop. Instead, they broke into a charge. Evidently no one had explained the plan to the men, and now they were taking matters in to their own hands.

Seeing this, Field ordered his other two brigades to hasten forward and try to catch up. But they could not. Bowles' men were delayed by some Union pickets in a lunette on the camp's eastern wall, and Bratton's men had too far to go. Hoke, on the other hand, decided not to advance until the scheduled hour of 2 p.m. despite this unexpected development.

Stannard ordered his men to hold their fire until the Rebels emerged from the brush-filled depression at the foot of the hill. As they watched the onrushing Rebels approach, one Federal soldier suddenly burst into song. It was the kind of thing that could only happen in that highly romantic Victorian era. "Yes, we'll rally 'round the flag, boys, we'll rally once again/Shouting the Battle Cry of Freedom." The Union color bearers unfurled their flags and the troops all joined in on the chorus: "The Union forever, hurrah! boys, hurrah!/Down with the traitor, up with the star,/As we rally 'round the flag, boys, rally once again,/Shouting the Battle Cry of Freedom."[13] Then the Georgians started up the hill.

The front rank of the dense Union formation blasted them with a volley, then took loaded rifles from the other ranks and blasted them again and again while Paine's men poured an enfilading fire into their left flank. A few of the Georgians hit the dirt to find what cover they could, while the rest broke and ran in disorder for the shelter of the woods they had so recently left, disrupting Bratton's pursuing South Carolinians and carrying some of them along as well. The rest of Bratton's men then went up the hill, only to receive the same treatment as had been dealt to the Georgians, along with the additional fire of three rifled field guns that had deployed in the fort by then. "No musketry was used until we got within 200 yards of the fort," a South Carolina colonel remembered; "but now there issued forth from the frowning parapet a furious storm of bullets such as would appall the stoutest heart. The noise sounded like the magnified roar of a thousand kettle drums."[14] That colonel and about thirty men managed to get to within about sixty yards of the Federals but then, like all the others who still lived, had to fall back toward Fort Johnson. They left behind the colors of the 6th South Carolina and over 300 casualties.

Among the Union casualties was Stannard, who received a wound that would cost him an arm and any future military glory. He was briefly succeeded by Colonel Cullen, who had only succeeded to brigade command the day before. But Weitzel soon shifted Colonel James Jourdan with two of his regiments from Heckman's division into the fort, and that officer, being senior to Cullen, took command.

Then it was Hoke's turn. But he too failed to coordinate the actions of his various units, and only the two brigades on his left actually advanced. Even these did not maintain their proper alignment, for Clingman's Brigade of North Carolinians, under Colonel Hector M. McKethan, in the front line, outdistanced Brigadier General Alfred H. Colquitt's Georgians in the second line. They climbed out of their gully and crossed a small hill with a Rebel yell, then crossed the headwaters of Cole's Run and started up the hill toward Fort Harrison. The first Union volley was too low, and only kicked up dust in front of the charging Confederates. But the second volley struck home. "Our line was entirely broken . . . literally from the men being cut down by piles by the terrific fire," one Tarheel recorded. A Union officer agreed, saying, "We mowed them down like grass."[15]

Many of McKethan's men took what cover they could among the brambles in the slight depression at the base of the hill. Colquitt's troops, seeing their fate, fell back to the shelter of the gully from which they had advanced. Lee himself tried to get them to advance again, but to no avail. "I had always thought General Lee was a very cold and unemotional man," One Confederate wrote, "but he showed lots of feeling and excitement on that occasion; even the staid and stately 'Traveller' caught the spirit of his master, and was prancing and cavorting while the General was imploring his men to make one more effort to take the position for him."[16]

Colonel McKethan made his way to the rear to appeal for aid for his men, but the North Carolinians would have to stay put until dark, almost three hours away. However, as dusk descended the sharpshooter battalion of Stannard's division went out and gathered them in, along with some of Field's men and even some of the Rebel artillerymen who had been wounded the day before. They gave up without resistence, and over 200 prisoners were taken. Almost two thirds of McKethan's men had been killed, wounded, or captured, and all eight of their flags were either captured or destroyed by the men to keep them from being taken. "The brigade is literally cut to pieces," wrote one North Carolina officer; "another such a fight will certainly wipe us out."[17]

"General Lee was more worried at this failure," General Alexander, the artillery commander, wrote, "than I have ever seen him under similar circumstances." One of McKethan's adjutants wrote of seeing Lee "with a face on him as long as a gun barrel."[18] That evening Pemberton, the

Northern-born Confederate who had surrendered Vicksburg the summer before, asked Lee if he did not still intend to retake the fort at whatever cost. "General Pemberton," Lee replied, "I made my effort this morning and failed, losing many killed and wounded. I have ordered another line provided from that point and shall have no more blood shed at the fort unless you can show me a practical plan of capture; perhaps you can. I shall be glad to have it."[19]

---

1. *Official Records,* 42:II:1110–1111.
2. Ibid., 42:II:1093.
3. Freeman, *R. E. Lee,* 3:502.
4. *Official Records,* 42:II:1094.
5. Ibid., 43:II:209–210.
6. Ibid., 43:II:208.
7. Sherman, *Memoirs,* 619.
8. Henry, *"First With the Most" Forrest,* 359.
9. Sommers, *Richmond Redeemed,* 121–122.
10. *Official Records,* 42:II:1111.
11. Ibid., 42:II:1142.
12. Sommers, *Richmond Redeemed,* 133.
13. Ibid., 140–141.
14. Ibid., 142.
15. Ibid., 145.
16. Freeman, *R. E. Lee,* 3:504.
17. Sommers, *Richmond Redeemed,* 148.
18. Ibid.
19. Freeman, *R. E. Lee,* 3:504.

CHAPTER FOURTEEN

A Pretty Little Fight

30 September 1864

At 8:25 a.m. on the final day of September the key on the military telegraph at the headquarters of the Army of the Potomac began to click out a message from Grant at City Point: "General Butler's forces will remain where they are for the present, ready to advance, if found practicable. You may move out now and see if an advantage can be gained. It seems to me the enemy must be weak enough at one or the other place to let us in."[1]

Meade in turn began to transmit orders to David Gregg and his cavalry, Parke, commander of the 9th Corps, and Warren, commander of the 5th Corps. It was 9:20 a.m. by the time full instructions reached the headquarters of the 9th Corps: "General Warren is ordered to move out the Poplar Spring Church road and endeavor to secure the intersection of the Squirrel Level road. The commanding general directs that you move out after and co-operate with him in endeavoring to secure a position on the right of the enemy's position. Try to open a route across the swamp to vicinity of Miss Pegram's, below Poplar Spring Church, and take post on Warren's left. Gregg will be directed to move out to Wilkinson's."[2] What Meade wanted was for both infantry corps to overrun the Squirrel Level Line and reach the Boydton Plank Road while Gregg's cavalry covered the infantry's left flank from any interference by Hampton's Confederate horsemen. What he did not know was that the Union maps of the area into which these forces were about to advance were hopelessly inaccurate.

At about 9 a.m. the troops of the 5th Corps begin to march westward from the Union entrenchments around Globe Tavern. Warren decided to leave all his wagons behind in the defenses at first. "The movement," his orders said, "will determine very soon whether or not the wagons, &c., will be needed. They can then be sent for."[3] This allowed the infantry of the 9th Corps to follow immediately behind the 5th Corps artillery, but even so it was 10 a.m. before the tail of Warren's column cleared the defenses and Parke's began to file out. In all, twelve brigades of infantry and ten batteries of artillery were in the column, totalling 20,000 men. By the time the last gun in the 9th Corps rolled out of the defenses it was noon. The head of the column, meanwhile, marched along a narrow country road where dense woods soon closed in on both sides. Warren put his pioneers to work at constructing a parallel road to ease his logistical problems. The leading Federals crossed the north-south Vaughn Road and as they approached Poplar Spring Church Warren sent the 18th Massachusetts ahead as skirmishers, soon reinforced by parts of three other regiments and the corps' sharpshooter battalion.

Major General Gouverneur K. Warren, then 34, was the youngest of Meade's corps commanders now that Sherdan was off in the Valley. He had graduated from West Point in 1850, standing second in his class, and had gone into the engineers. At the start of the war he had transferred to the volunteers as lieutenant colonel and then colonel of the 5th New York, the famous Duryea's Zouaves. After commanding a brigade in most of the early battles of the Army of the Potomac, he had served as the chief engineer of that army at Gettysburg, where he had saved the army on the second day of battle by taking upon himself the responsibility of diverting troops to protect an eminence on the left flank known as Little Round Top.

Facing what he called "the anxiety of responsibility," however, was not his long suit.[4] Meade had promoted him to corps command after Gettysburg, and his career at that level had been checkered. At Spotsylvania, Grant had come close to firing him and had kept a wary eye on him ever since. "He was a man of fine intelligence," Grant later wrote, "great earnestness, quick perception, and could make his dispositions as quickly as any officer, under difficulties where he was forced to act." But he had one fatal flaw. "He could see every danger at a glance before he had encountered it."[5] In short, he was too cautious.

Warren later complained to Meade that the practice of leaving some of the troops to hold the defenses and striking out with only part of the army made "the commander at each point apprehensive of being greatly outnumbered by the enemy, which is always practicable for him to do . . . and thus inevitably produce want of boldness and vigor on our part, unless we neglect more than any of us are willing to do."[6] What he failed to see was that the troops left in the entrenchments were also threatening the Confederate defenses opposite them and thus forcing Lee to keep a sizable part of his army away from the area of Warren's operations. A more valid question would have been to wonder why Meade did not personally command this advance by two thirds of his army, leaving his able chief of staff, Major General Andrew A. Humphreys, or the equally capable Hancock to command the third that was left behind on the defensive. Instead, Meade spent the vital hours between 9 a.m. and noon visiting with Hancock and riding from his headquarters to Globe Tavern, which was as far west as he went. He took Humphreys with him and left his adjutant general, Major General Seth Williams, in charge of his headquarters. Warren, Parke, and Gregg were left to cooperate as best they could without anyone at the front to coordinate their activities.

Meanwhile, Warren's skirmishers ran into a few Confederate pickets and slowly pushed them westward. "We advanced cautiously through the thick brush and undergrowth," one of them recorded; "one could scarcely see two rods, not knowing what moment we should receive a volley from the concealed foe. Our boys had had a taste of this in the Wilderness and were pretty cautious."[7] But the Rebel pickets, members of Dearing's Brigade of cavalry from the Department of North Carolina and Southern Virginia, put up little fight, falling back to the entrenchments near the Squirrel Level Road. Dearing himself was ill at the time, and his three regiments were under the temporary command of their senior colonel, Joel Griffin of the 8th Georgia.

Northwest of Poplar Spring Church the Federal skirmishers finally emerged from the woods into the cleared fields of a farm belonging to someone named Peeble. Beyond the abandoned farm buildings the line of Confederate defenses could be seen. They ran more to the west than the south there, but due west of the buildings they turned almost due south and crossed Arthur's Swamp, where the woods closed in again, before turning to the southwest. A battery of Rebel guns began to throw shells at the advancing Northerners, who had no way of knowing that this artillery was backed up by only about 1,000 dismounted troopers in two regiments of not-very-experienced Confederate cavalry.

The dense thickets along the various branches of Arthur's Swamp slowed the deployment of the leading Union division, Brigadier General Charles Griffin's 1st Division of the 5th Corps. And the Union artillery could not find a place in which to deploy to return the Rebel fire. While Griffin's three brigades filed across a mill dam and deployed in the shelter of a ravine containing a branch of Arthur's Swamp, Warren sent his other division, Brigadier General Romeyn B. Ayres' 2nd, north on the Vaughn Road to protect the right flank of the expedition. This move cleared the road for the 9th Corps, and the head of its column reached Poplar Spring Church just after noon, or about the time that its tail was clearing the Union defenses near Globe Tavern. Parke's lead division, Potter's 2nd, went into reserve around Poplar Spring Church while it sent one regiment to work on the construction of a parallel road farther south.

At 1 p.m. the three brigades of Griffin's division left the cover of their ravine and began to advance. If they had moved straight ahead, to the west, their right would have been enfiladed by Fort Archer on the Rebel line, for that line ran diagonally across the open field. Griffin, therefore, planned a maneuver that was as complicated as the one the Confederates were making just then 24 miles to the north in their unsuccessful attempt to retake Fort Harrison. Griffin's orders called for each of his brigades to make a half right wheel as it emerged from the ravine. This would align the leading brigade for a direct attack on the fort with each succeeding brigade coming in behind the other. But this maneuver also broke down almost as soon as it started. The exact cause was long debated. Evidently some regiments were reluctant to advance and others were reluctant to be left behind, and what had been planned as three neat lines soon degenerated into a hodge-podge of individual units moving at various speeds. "Never mind about keeping the men in line," Griffin told one of his officers, "tell them to go and they will go if only you will let them."[8]

Griffin knew his men well. They rushed across the 700-or-so yards of open field, the 20th Maine leading the rush and "whooping like so many demons," as one eyewitness said.[9] "You may not believe it," a Union officer wrote, refering to an action later in the day, "but the cheering is half the battle when we charge."[10] The Confederate skirmishers fired once and ran for the entrenchments behind them. As soon as they were out of the way the main line of dismounted troopers opened fire, along with the battery of Rebel guns. This fire checked one Union regiment and slowed another, but the rest kept on coming. "The charging column pressed steadily, earnestly, persistently forward," a Northern war correspondent wrote. "Rebel shell and bullets had no dismaying effect."[11] Unable to stop the Federal charge, the Southern battery began to limber up its guns and pull them out of the entrenchments. Union pioneers rushed ahead to hack a path through the chevaux de frise and then the main force swarmed through and over the parapet.

The 20th Maine, on the Union left, still led the race, and Lieutenant Albert E. Fernald was way out in front of the rest of that regiment. He got into the fort just as the Rebel gunners were hitching up the last of their guns and his drawn revolver soon convinced them to stop. The dismounted Confederate cavalrymen had by then begun to retreat, some up the line to the north, others into the woods to the west. Some of them opened fire on the lone lieutenant, but they only succeeded in hitting a couple of the horses, making it impossible to withdraw the last gun even if Fernald's revolver was not aimed at the driver's head. The colonel of the 16th Michigan was shot as he led his men over the parapet, but the entire Union division soon entered the entrenchments, capturing some sixty Rebels along with the gun, which turned out be one the Southerners had taken from Hancock's 2nd Corps at Reams's Station the month before. "A more magnificent charge was never made by any troops in any war," Warren later bragged to a newspaper correspondent.[12]

Colonel James Gwynn, commander of the 3rd Brigade, following his men in, was injured when his horse fell on him as it tried to climb the sloping wall of the fort, so Major Ellis Spear of the 20th Maine took charge of the brigade. Griffin had better luck and was greeted by his men with loud cheers. But he could see that a number of Confederates and a couple of guns were rallying around a small earthwork to the west, where the Church Road entered the woods. So he sent his men to take that too. They no longer had any formation to speak of, but, led by the zouaves of the 155th Pennsylvania, they, as one of them put it, went "rolling over the field like a large wave."[13] There was a brief, fierce fight, and the Rebels decided to continue their retreat, taking their guns with them. Then Griffin regrouped his 1st Division in and around Fort Archer.

The 1st Brigade of Potter's 2nd Division of the 9th Corps moved to the north along the Confederate defenses in line of battle, following some of Griffin's skirmishers to the abandoned Fort Bratton. Then the brigade took up position running south from there along the defenses to connect with Griffin's men at Fort Archer. Potter's other brigade took up position in the captured defenses west of Griffin's division. The other division Parke had with him, Brigadier General Orlando B. Willcox's 1st, was used to extend the Union line even farther west and then to connect back to the main stream of Arthur's Swamp to protect the left flank of the expedition. As on the north side of the James the day before, after initially seizing a key position, the Federals, instead of exploiting their breakthrough, were content to defend what they had taken.

A few detachments and pickets, however, were sent to find out what the Rebels were up to. Some of these pushed all the way down to Fort MacRae at the southwestern end of the Squirrel Level Line without finding any Confederates. But a few mounted Rebels were seen lurking in the woods beyond. Some of Griffin's men pushed on westward from the little earthwork where they had fought Dearing's cavalry for the second time and found it regrouping again in the woods. And two of Griffin's regiments roved on beyond Fort Bratton and found part of Dearing's other regiment, the 4th North Carolina Cavalry, pushed it on up the line, and by 2 p.m. had taken the next major work, Fort Cherry. There they were joined by more of Griffin's men, but by then Confederate infantry was beginning to press them and it was all they could do to hang onto what they had taken. The Federals had accomplished something, however, that they did not yet know about. Shortly before 2 p.m. two brigades of the Confederate 3rd Corps that were already north of the Appomattox and on their way to Chaffin's farm were ordered to reverse their march and return to Petersburg to help meet this new threat.

Meanwhile pickets from Ayres' 2nd Division of the 5th Corps had pushed on up the Vaughn Road and had linked up with Griffin's skirmishers east of the captured entrenchments. Then Ayres tied his skirmish line in with cavalry pickets to form a continuous line connecting Fort Cherry on the Squirrel Level Line with Fort Wadsworth in the Union defenses around Globe Tavern. Leaving one regiment to back up this thin line, Ayres took the rest of his division up the Poplar Spring Road to Peebles' farm and then up the captured defenses to Chappell's, which was about half way between Fort Bratton and Fort Cherry. His leading brigade reached there sometime between 3 and 3:30 p.m., relieving the brigade of Potter's division that had been placed on Griffin's right.

David Gregg and his Union cavalry had not been idle. At 9 a.m. he had moved out with his 1st Brigade, while his 2nd Brigade, still worn out from its fight of the day before, was spread out to hold down the positions it and the other brigade had previously held. Gregg followed the same route that his troopers had followed the day before. The resistance was stiff at first, but by early afternoon the Rebel cavalry had again withdrawn to the south side of Hatcher's Run. Again Gregg established detachments to watch the crossings of that stream, satisfied that as long as Hampton's troopers remained on the south bank they were not interfering with the Union infantry.

Meade, however, feared that if Hampton was not fighting Gregg or Warren or Parke he must be up to something, such as another raid against the rear of the Army of the Potomac, which was defended in the cavalry's absence only by some engineers and the troops assigned to the Provost

Marshal General—the equivalent of military policemen. So now he ordered the infantry commanders in the defenses facing Petersburg to be ready to defend against an attack on their rear. At 2:25 p.m. he asked Grant's headquarters to send patrols out from City Point to detect any Confederate moves against that vital point. At the same time he informed Grant that Warren had overrun the Squirrel Level Line. A few minutes later, Meade finally left Globe Tavern and rode to the front. There he found the 9th Corps ready to advance and he ordered it to press on to the Boydton Plank Road and ordered Warren to send Griffin's division to cover its right flank. At 3 p.m. the advance resumed.

After returning from his conference with Butler at Deep Bottom that morning, Grant remained at his City Point headquarters all day in order to remain in contact with both of his armies. That did not do him much good, however, for neither Butler nor Meade bothered to keep him posted. Around 12:30 or 1 p.m. Seth Williams forwarded an intelligence report that refugees from Petersburg claimed that the Confederate army had laid five or six pontoon bridges over the Appomattox "to facilitate the falling back to a new line about three miles to the rear of the river." Then word finally came of Griffin's success. At 3 p.m. Grant sent a reply to Meade saying, "If the enemy can be broken and started, follow him up closely. I can't help believing that the enemy are prepared to leave Petersburg if forced a little." A quarter of an hour later he added that "if the enemy's cavalry has left Gregg's front he ought to push ahead, and if he finds no obstacle turn his infantry."[14] What Meade saw as a threat—Hampton's absence—Grant saw as an opportunity.

Parke's leading division, Potter's 2nd, marched northwest from Peeble's farm, crossed Pegram's farm, and deployed in line of battle at the southern edge of the open fields of Jones' farm. On the other side of these fields the Federals could see what appeared to be another formidable line of Confederate entrenchments running from northeast to southwest. They did not know it, but these defenses were far from complete and had only been started a few days before.

While Potter's two brigades deployed, Parke brought up Willcox's 1st Division. One of his brigades was placed in echelon behind Potter's left flank while his other two remained in reserve on Pegram's farm. All of the 9th Corps artillery remained farther back at Peeble's farm. With his troops in position, Parke seems also to have been overcome with caution. He made no move to attack the defenses on the other side of the fields, which barred his way to the Boydton Plank Road. Warren rode forward and urged Parke to advance, but he could not order him to do so since

Parke was senior to him on the list of major generals. Nor did Warren send Griffin's division to join Parke's right, as Meade had ordered. At about 5 p.m., however, Parke finally decided to attack. "I was ordered," Potter said, "to push on with my whole force as rapidly as practicable, without reference to any one else."[15]

But the consequences of the Federals' delays were finally catching up with them. By the time Potter's skirmishers engaged the Rebels on Jones' farm, those two brigades of Confederate infantry that had been returned from north of the Appomattox were filing into the defenses. They were Brigadier General James H. Lane's and Brigadier General Samuel MacGowan's brigades of Wilcox's Division of the 3rd Corps. (The Union Willcox had two l's, the Confederate one.) The sharpshooter battalions of both brigades were sent forward where they were concealed in the ravine just south of the entrenchments through which flowed the upper fork of Old Town Creek. From there, backed by the fire of guns in the defenses, they launched an attack upon Potter's skirmishers, the dismounted troopers of the 2nd New York Mounted Infantry. Surprised by this sudden reversal from attackers to defenders, most of the New Yorkers ran for the protection of Potter's main line. About 30 of them made a stand around Jones' house but were surrounded and captured.

What had worked for the skirmishers might work for the main force. The Confederate Wilcox could see that the Union main line did not advance to support its skirmishers and that it had, instead, begun to dig in along the northern edge the woods that separated Jones' farm from Pegram's. He decided to exploit the Federals' timidity. A counterattack might not only save this final line of defense for the Boydton Plank Road but regain the Squirrel Level Line as well. He therefore advanced both of his brigades to the cover of the same ravine, where they waited for the arrival of two brigades of Heth's Division of the 3rd Corps—the same two that had been withdrawn from the Squirrel Level Line the day before—who had been ordered to follow him. Heth arrived almost immediately, but ahead of his troops. As the senior Confederate officer present he assumed overall command on the field and approved Wilcox's plan. He also arranged for Hampton's cavalry, which had been assembling in the area, to attack the Federals' left when the infantry struck their front.

But before Heth's two brigades could be deployed in support of Wilcox's two, Potter resumed his advance. His two brigades, however, not only failed to coordinate their advance but the two brigade commanders failed to coordinate their own units. In fact, both brigades, composed of numerous but sadly depleted regiments, were deployed in two lines, and both commanders left their second-line units behind as they advanced with their front lines. The left brigade failed to advance as far as the right one. The brigade of the Union Willcox's division that had been in echelon behind Potter's left had not been informed that Potter was advancing and its view of the advance was blocked by a field of sorghum. Consequently, it stayed in place.

Nevertheless the 1,200 or 1,300 Federals who did attack recaptured the Jones house and pushed the two Rebel sharpshooter battalions through an orchard and back toward the ravine where the main Confederate line lay hidden. But their formation was disrupted in passing the buildings and fences and the 6th New Hampshire on the Union left turned its flank to the ravine as it obliqued to its right to close a gap. This target was too tempting to let pass. The colonel of the 33rd North Carolina led his regiment out of the ravine to strike the exposed flank and the attack was taken up by the rest of Lane's Brigade, then MacGowan's Brigade. "They advanced in splendid, unbroken lines," a Union officer reported. The Union left flank crumbled and then, as the Rebels overlapped their right, the rest of the line also collapsed. The Federal brigade commanders called up some of their second-line units but by the time they came up the front line soldiers were running for their lives, and the reinforcements were swept up in the rout. A few rallied around the Jones buildings but like the skirmishers before them were overwhelmed, while the rest fled for the protection of the sketchy defenses they had started in the edge of the woods. The Rebels gave chase and caught the fleeing Yankees in a crossfire that "piled the ground with their bodies," as one South Carolinian put it.[16]

A Vermont regiment that had been left behind mistook the routing Federals for charging Confederates and fired into members of their own brigade. After this reception most of the routing troops could not even be rallied in their own defenses but fled on to Pegram's farm. Then the Rebels hit the Vermonters as they were fixing bayonets, killed their commander, and swept them and the few men who had rallied out of their defenses.

The other brigade of Potter's division, which had not advanced so far, was ordered to withdraw, but its commander, Colonel John I. Curtin, was off on a personal reconnaissance and did not get the word. So his brigade stayed put. Most of Wilcox's Confederates turned to the west through the woods that separated Jones' farm from Pegram's and rolled up the second line of Curtin's brigade a regiment at a time from their right. Most of these Federals retreated in fairly good order to the west, where they joined the brigade of the Union Willcox's division that had been echeloned behind Potter's left. The commander of that brigade, Brigadier General John F. Hartranft, was the best in the corps. Humphreys, who had not remained back at Peeble's with Meade but had ridden to the front, sent him an order to fall back. But Hartranft and his men had not been able to see what had befallen Potter's leading brigade and he obeyed, as he later put it, "very slowly."[17] He fell back about 100 yards and formed a new line just north of an east-west road, sending a couple of regiments across Arthur's Swamp to protect his left from Hampton's cavalry, while the refugees from Curtin's second line formed in a depression on his right.

The Confederates soon attacked this force, with Lane's brigade assaulting the refugees while Hampton's cavalry threatened the left flank. "Men fell on all sides like autumn leaves," a Union officer wrote. Reluctantly Hartranft ordered a retreat but before his men could break contact the refugees began to break ranks and run, "each man doing his level best," as one of them put it, "to preserve a life for future usefulness to his country."[18] The Rebels captured 124 men there, most of them German immigrants who had recently been sent as reinforcements to the 35th Massachusetts. And Hartranft lost nearly 200 men, mostly captured, including two colonels. But he led the remainder out of the closing pincers in fairly good order to join the rest of Willcox's division on Pegram's farm.

Colonel Curtin returned from his personal reconnaissance to find that the three regiments of his front line were engaged with Confederates from Heth's Division on their right while his second line was being swept away. The front line soon gave way as well and retreated to the west, stopping twice to blast the pursuing Rebels with a volley. By then the second line had been routed and the Confederates who had defeated it turned back to the north, threatening to surround the three remaining regiments, which continued to move west. Then a gun from a battery of Confederate horse artillery moved forward from the defenses and opened fire on them. One gun was not enough to deter the Federals, however, considering what was closing in on them from the east and south. But just as they were about to overrun the cannon Rooney Lee led two dismounted regiments of his cavalry forward from the Confederate defenses to rescue the gun and cut off the retreat of Curtin's three regiments. Only 53 Federals managed to escape the closing Rebel net. Among them was Curtin, whose Kentucky thoroughbred outran his pursuers until killed while jumping a fence. Curtin flew over the dying animal's head, and over the fence, and kept right on going. Over 600 men were captured, along with over 1,000 rifles and two flags. Another one was destroyed by the Federals to prevent its capture. All this was in addition to 700 men captured from Potter's other brigade and from Hartranft.

Even while Curtin's three regiments were being surrounded and captured, the main body of the Confederate infantry continued southward down the Pegram House Road in pursuit of Potter's and Hartranft's routing Federals. The Rebels were somewhat disorganized by their victorious charge, but MacGowan, one of Wilcox's brigade commanders, "thought it best not to dampen the ardor of victorious pursuit by stopping to reform."[19] However, as MacGowan's South Carolinians emerged from the woods which separated Jones' farm from Pegram's they encountered Colonel Samuel Harriman's 1st Brigade of Willcox's Union division drawn up in line of battle on a fairly high east-west bald hill in the middle of Pegram's fields.

As soon as the retreating remnants of Potter's division had passed through Harriman's line, continuing their flight to the south, the 34th New York Battery galloped up, unlimbered its four 3-inch rifles in front of Harriman's infantry, and began to pound the Rebels with cannister fire. The Rebels were slowed but not stopped, and after firing a couple of rounds from each gun the artillerymen limbered up and fell back just in time to keep their guns from being captured. Harriman's men also fell back in good order before the oncoming Confederates. But when the Rebels gained the high ground and started down after the Federals one of Harriman's regiments, the 13th Ohio Cavalry serving as infantry, panicked and, as Harriman reported, "fled ingloriously from the field," carrying a green Wisconsin battalion with it.[20]

Harriman's other three regiments fell back in good order to a fence enclosing Pegram's yard. Again the Union guns were exposed to capture, but six companies of the 7th Rhode Island rushed to their support and slowed the Rebel advance again with brisk volleys. "For God's sake, move up and help that little Seventh Rhode Island," Potter cried to the refugees of his own division, but they did not respond.[21] The guns were saved, however, and joined Harriman in Pegram's yard. The Rhode Islanders fell back to the farm house, where they were joined by a few other odds and ends from Potter's division on Harriman's right. Hartranft's brigade took position west of Pegram's house. The retreating 13th Ohio Cavalry tore through his lines, sweeping one of his regiments away in the rout, but the general managed to rally the retreating Wisconsin battalion to take its place. Potter appealed to Willcox for help in extending his line farther to the right, or east, and the latter responded by sending his remaining brigade, Colonel Napoleon B. McLaughlen's 3rd, which deployed into line, fixed bayonets, and advanced into position. When it got there it discovered Griffin's division of the 5th Corps already in place on its right, blocking the Church Road and extending into the woods beyond.

When news of the disaster that had befallen the 9th Corps had reached Peebles farm, either Meade or Warren had finally sent Griffin forward to cover its right, as it had originally been supposed to do in the advance. Griffin's men had heard the heavy firing ahead coming closer to them and had seen Potter's routed units coming back out of the fight, a sight that disgusted, rather than demoralized, them. They probably considered themselves far superior to such troops and were not surprised to be called upon to save them. "General Griffin entered into the spirit of the occasion," one of his men remembered, "and soon formed us into line on a low crest of land covered with a scattering growth of wood. The enemy must advance in our front, and climb up the ascent."[22]

But the 9th Corps troops on the left were the first to be tested when MacGowan's South Carolinians led the Confederate advance. McLaughlen's newly arrived troops blasted the Rebels' left, Hartranft's units fired on their right, and Harriman's brigade plastered them from the front, and they fell back, most of them too disorganized by their advance and retreat to be of any further use that day. The Rebel artillery then tried to intervene, but a battery that galloped forward was so shot up by the Union infantry that it withdrew without ever unlimbering its guns. Long range artillery support proved to be more effective. A single shell exploding in the midst of the 20th Maine, in Griffin's division, took out a dozen men. And shells striking the rails of the fence in Pegram's yard showered deadly splinters in all directions, forcing the little 4th Rhode Island to fall back.

Two of MacGowan's regiments then advanced again, getting right up to the fence the Federals had abandoned, but the Union artillery blasted them. "Our batteries put grape and canister into them like rain," one Pennsylvanian wrote, "and killed a great many of them."[23] Unable to advance farther and fearing that falling back was also too risky, the South Carolinians hit the dirt and sought what cover they could find where they were.

Next came Lane's North Carolinians, who attacked to the east of MacGowan, striking the Union line where the 5th Corps and 9th Corps connected. The fire of three Federal brigades combined to drive them back. One regiment renewed the attack and got to within 100 yards of the Union line but could go no farther. When these Rebels retreated, four companies of the 4th Rhode Island which had been caught between the lines and hiding in a cornfield took this chance to fall back to the safety of the main line.

To the east of Lane was Brigadier General James J. Archer's Brigade of Heth's Division. It had been sent down the Church Road, east of the Pegram House Road, but its advance had been slowed by the swampy ground around the headwaters of the upper fork of Old Town Creek and what one of its officers called "the almost impassable jungle of tangled briers, grape-vines, and alder bushes."[24] By the time they emerged from all these difficulties, Lane's Brigade had already been repulsed. Some of Archer's men had evidently stopped to plunder a Union camp they had passed through, and some had put on captured blue trousers, coats, or caps. In the fading light of dusk, some Northern officers thought that they were more routing Federals from the 9th Corps, but their men were not deceived and despite orders to hold their fire met the Confederates with a devastating volley that brought them up short. The Rebels returned fire and then came on again. Some of them actually closed with the Federals, who were spread out into little more than a heavy skirmish line. For half an hour the two forces slugged it out at close range.

"And then amid it all," wrote one of Spear's men, "General Griffin came along, resolute, heroic, impressive, with assuring words and comforting promises of help. The wavering lines stiffened; strong men were strengthened and the weak made strong. From now on it was his fight, and his presence in inspiring the men was almost equal to the promised support of his batteries."[25] Griffin had indeed called forward the battery that had followed him from Peeble's farm. The general told its commander to unlimber his guns right up with the infantry. "My God, General," the artillery captain replied, not recognizing the thin formation as the main battle line, "do you mean for me to put my guns out on that skirmish line?" Griffin was an old artilleryman and had commanded a battery himself in the early days of the war. "Yes," he said, "rush them in there; artillery is no better than infantry, put them in the line, and let them fight together."[26]

That they did. Before the fight was over the four 12-pounder Napoleons fired off almost all the cannister ammunition they had, saving three rounds per gun for emergencies, and they mangled the Confederate ranks. The Southerners tried charging the guns once and got to within 50 yards but could go no farther. Finally they fell back to the protection of the edge of the woods between Pegram's and Jones's fields and continued the fire fight from there. The Union gunners then loaded double shots and pounded the woods with deadly results, and then another battery was brought up and added its fire to the contest. At that the Rebels withdrew into the woods out of sight. By then it was dark, and, except for some sniping and long-range artillery duelling, that was the end of what the ever-belligerent Humphreys called "a pretty little fight."[27]

When Meade told Griffin that his men should entrench, he replied, "I don't need any breastworks; I can whip the whole rebel army with my little division." But, as a member of the 20th Maine noted, "entrenchments were made, notwithstanding this remarkable fact."[28]

1. *Official Records*, 42:II:1118.

2. Ibid., 42:II:1137.

3. Ibid., 42:II:1103.

4. Sommers, *Richmond Redeemed*, 243.

5. Grant, *Memoirs*, 2:445.

6. *Official Records*, 42:III:20.

7. Sommers, *Richmond Redeemed*, 245.

8. Ibid., 253.

9. John J. Pullen, *The Twentieth Maine: A Volunteer Regiment in the Civil War* (New York, 1957), 231.

10. Sommers, *Richmond Redeemed*, 293.

11. Trudeau, *The Last Citadel*, 212.

12. Ibid.

13. Sommers, *Richmond Redeemed*, 255.

14. *Official Records*, 42:II:1119.

15. Ibid., 42:I:579.

16. Sommers, *Richmond Redeemed*, 281.

17. Ibid., 284.

18. Ibid., 285.

19. Ibid., 289.

20. Ibid., 291.

21. Ibid.

22. Pullen, *The Twentieth Maine*, 233.

23. Sommers, *Richmond Redeemed*, 299.

24. Ibid., 301.

25. Ibid., 303.

36. Pullen, *The Twentieth Maine*, 233.

27. Sommers, *Richmond Redeemed*, 284.

28. Pullen, *The Twentieth Maine*, 234.

CHAPTER FIFTEEN

Charging the Yankees in the Rain

30 September–1 October 1864

Buford's part of Forrest's raiding force arrived outside Huntsville, Alabama, on the afternoon of the thirtieth and sent in a demand for the garrison's surrender. But the Union commander, Brigadier General R. S. Granger, told him "to come and take it as soon as you get ready." Buford sent another threat that said he would attack "tomorrow morning from every rock, house, tree and shrub in the vicinity," signing it "N. B. Forrest, Major General." It was a bluff that had worked many times before, but this time it did not. Granger was in charge of the area that Forrest had been doing so much damage to on his current raid and, according to one of his officers, he was "feeling very badly. He was surprised. The railroad under his charge is seriously injured and he has lost 3,000 to 4,000 of his command. These are hard blows for an officer to stand up under." Granger had taken all he was about to and was determined to resist. He and his men worked all night barricading the streets of the town and strengthening his little fort with cotton bales. But Buford had no intention of really attacking what was evidently a strong and well manned position, and he marched away to the west the next morning.[1]

Lieutenant General Ambrose Powell Hill, commander of the Confederate 3rd Corps, was in charge of the Petersburg front while Lee was north of the James. Six weeks before he had foiled one of the Federal's many westward moves toward the city's communications by threatening their left, or outer, flank and then rolling up their right. The current situation looked promising for a repeat of that successful one-two combination. While most of his available forces had been dealing with the advance of the 9th Corps on the thirtieth, a probe down the Squirrel Level Line had retaken Fort Cherry against light opposition. Hill concluded from this that the Federals were weak on that flank. Another reason for a strike at the Union right was that it was easier to get at. Also, such a move kept the Rebel troops closer to their main line of defenses in case they were needed there or needed a safe refuge into which they could retreat. With all this in mind, and not content to remain on the defensive and let the Yankees keep what they had taken, Hill withdrew Heth's two brigades from Jones' farm and brought them back into the city's main defenses. From there, if all went well, they could join with Heth's other two brigades for an attack down the Squirrel Level Line that could retake all that had been lost the day before. Meanwhile, Wilcox's two brigades stayed behind on Jones' farm. From there they would threaten the Union front again while Hampton's cavalry threatened their left.

Actually the Federals were not weak on their right. They had not contested the Confederate recapture of Fort Cherry because they just did not consider that area important enough to fight for it. Instead, they had withdrawn to Fort Bratton and had constructed a new line of entrenchments running southeastward from there almost to their old defenses around Globe Tavern. Ayres' relatively fresh division of the 5th Corps still held the western part of this line, while a brigade from Brigadier General Samuel Crawford's 3rd Division of the 5th Corps and some artillery were brought out from the original defenses to man the part of the line where the north-south Vaughn Road passed through it roughly halfway between the Squirrel Level Road and the defenses around Globe Tavern. It was replaced in the old defenses by one of three big new regiments that had just arrived from the North. Warren was, in fact, more worried about the possibility of a Rebel attack on the Globe Tavern area, which, if successful, would reopen the Weldon Railroad. He therefore sent some of his artillery from the mobile force back to the defenses that night.

At about 9 p.m. Meade returned to Globe Tavern and telegraphed the news of the day's operations to Grant. "I do not think it judicious," he concluded, "to make another advance tomorrow unless re-enforced or some evidence can be obtained of the weakening of the enemy." Only then did Grant learn that things had not been going smoothly south of the Appomattox. He nevertheless was not as pessimistic about accomplishing more as Meade was. Ten minutes later he replied: "You need not advance tomorrow, unless in your judgment an advantage can be gained, but hold on to what you have, and be ready to advance. We must be greatly superior to the enemy on one flank or the other, and by working around at each end, we will find where the enemy's weak point is. General Butler was assaulted three times this afternoon, but repulsed all of them. I will direct him to feel up the Darbytown road to-morrow."[2]

Meade returned to his own headquarters by train at about 10:30 p.m. At 11:45 p.m. he ordered Warren and Parke to advance the next morning to see what the Rebels were up to. At midnight he so informed Grant. Fifteen minutes later Humphreys expanded the instructions to Parke and Warren: "General Butler has Field's and Hoke's divisions and part of Pickett's before him. Lee may send away more troops from this side of the Appomattox. If your reconnaissances show the enemy to have left your front, and the indications are that he has sent off more troops against Butler, it is advisable that you get onto the Boydton Plank road. If you deem it practicable, advance to and make a lodgment on it."[3] At the same hour Humphreys sent orders to Gregg to advance at dawn beyond the 9th Corps' left flank. He also took action on an earlier suggestion of Grant's and ordered Hancock to pull a division out of his inactive 2nd Corps line and put it in reserve, prepared to join Warren and Parke pending the results of their reconnaissances in the morning.

At about 11 p.m. the three Union divisions on Pegram's farm began to fall back to or near the captured Squirrel Level Line on Peeble's farm. There, after an exhausting day of marching and fighting, without much to eat or tents to protect them from the rain, they spent much of the night digging in the mud before they could finally rest. Perhaps worse than these physical discomforts was the humiliation felt by Potter and his troops. "To say that there was a general feeling of shame and disgust . . . would weakly characterize the expressions used," one wrote. "Miserable in body and mentally filled with regret and anger," another wrote, "we sullenly counted the hours of that dreary night."[4] In addition to several regiments on picket duty, they left behind Colonel John Hofmman's 3rd Brigade of Crawford's 3rd Division of the 5th Corps, which had been attached to Ayre's 2nd Division most of the day until sent to reinforce Griffin's 1st about dark. This relatively fresh unit dug in near Pegram's house to serve as a reserve for the pickets.

Neither Parke nor Warren was happy with the orders for another advance that reached them at about 5 a.m. on the first day of October. Parke replied that he would "do the best I can to acquire the desired information," but considering the losses of the day before and the strength the Rebels had shown, he would "much prefer making ourselves secure in our present position."[5] It was somewhat later when the order to advance reached David Gregg. At 6 a.m. he informed his commander that Davies' 1st Brigade had spent most of the night reconnoitering to the west and that he had not yet issued rations and forage for his men and horses but that he would carry out these new orders as soon as possible.

All day during the thirtieth Hampton's cavalry had blocked Davies' path to the west, but shortly after dark the Rebels had withdrawn and Davies had seized the opportunity to see what lay to the west. However, in the dark of that rainy night he had seen very little and it had taken five hours to advance a mile and half to a crossroads that lay about halfway to the Boydton Plank Road. There the Federals had run head-on into a brigade of South Carolina cavalry commanded by Brigadier General John Dunovant. The latter had been sure that the road he was traveling on was securely in Confederate hands, proclaiming: "There is no danger on this road; I will be the advance guard myself tonight." Even when the general had been challenged by an Ohio captain at the head of Davies' column he had assumed it was a Confederate picket from another brigade. "I am Dunovant; let me pass," the general had answered.

"I don't know you," had been the reply. "Dismount, one of you, and advance and give the countersign."

"I tell you, I am Dunovant. Let me pass," the general had repeated, beginning to get hot under the collar.

"Damn Dunovant!" the Union officer had shot back, "We don't know you; if one of you do not dismount and come up here and let us know who you are, we will fire."

By that time almost everybody else in the Rebel column had realized that they had run into Yankees, but not Dunovant. He had ordered Captain Andrew Pickens Butler, cousin of his division commander, Brigadier General Matthew C. Butler, to advance and persuade what he thought were some stubborn Georgians to let them pass. The captain had insisted that they must be Northerners.

"Are you afraid, sir?" the general had demanded.

"I am not afraid," Butler had replied, "but I am gone up," he had added as he dismounted and started down the road.[6]

He had almost been right. He was over seven feet tall and the Federals had thought at first that he had disobeyed their instructions to dismount, but he had managed to convince them in time and had merely been captured instead. This had confirmed to both sides that they were facing enemies, and a brief firefight had ensued, causing little damage in the dark, before both sides had fallen back. Dunovant's main loss had been his standing with his own men and with his division commander.

By dawn on the first day of October the rain had stopped, but the sky was still cloudy and threatening. A. P. Hill had been assembling Heth's division throughout the night and at first light the Rebel infantry began to advance down the Squirrel Level Road until they reached the picket line of the Confederate cavalry watching this sector. And by 6:45 a.m. they had taken up positions ready to attack while Hill reconnoitered and waited for Wilcox to get the Yankees' attention. At about 7 a.m. Wilcox started McGowan's Brigade down the Church Road from Jones' farm and led Lane's Brigade down the Pegram House Road. At the southern edge of the woods that separated Jones' farm from Pegram's, both brigades deployed into line of battle just out of sight of Hofmann's Union brigade and began to build light defenses, while a battery of four 12-pounder Napoleon guns deployed on Lane's right.

Farther to the right, Hampton brought up Rooney Lee's division and most of Dearing's Brigade, while at least one of his regiments moved along a road known as Route 673 and reoccupied Fort MacRae at the southern end of the Squirrel Level Line. This had been abandoned by the Federals. Warren's two 5th Corps divisions and Potter's of the 9th Corps occupied that line from Fort Bratton on the northeast, or right, down to Arthur's Swamp. But Willcox's 9th Corps division had built a new line somewhat behind that one. It began near Peeble's house and ran more to the south and crossed the swamp before turning back to the east at the Clements house, where Route 673 met the Squirrel Level Line.

The Federals detected the build-up of Confederate forces north of them along the Squirrel Level Line and Warren and Parke easily concluded that it presaged an attack. This suited them fine because, as they reasoned, if Hill was strong enough to attack them that meant he had not sent further reinforcements north of the James. And that, in turn, relieved them of the responsibility of advancing their own forces. "I expect a hard time," Warren told Humphreys when he reported to headquarters at 8 a.m. that he expected to be attacked.[7]

A few minutes later, Heth's four brigades began to advance in two lines of two brigades each. Ayres' skirmishers—regulars and zouaves—put up a stiff fight but were eventually forced to give ground. But when Hill found Ayres' main line dug in across his path he stopped to reconnoiter and brought up his artillery to soften up the Union defenses. Meanwhile, the Confederate Wilcox, upon hearing the sound of firing on Heth's front, sent his two brigades forward while his artillery enfiladed Hofmann's position on Pegram's farm. Rebel sharpshooters soon overran some advanced Union rifle pits, but Hofmann's main line was almost immediately ordered to fall back. However, the left of his line did not get the word and many of his men there were captured when their defenses were overwhelmed from front and flank. Other Rebels mistook these prisoners for a Union counterattack and fired into them, killing a few and wounding a few of their captors. Wilcox, who was riding to the front just then, was also almost hit by a Confederate bullet.

When he came in sight of the main Union position on Peeble's farm, Wilcox knew he could not hope to take it with his two brigades, but he did not need to try. All that had been asked of him was to distract Federal attention from Heth's attack farther east. He therefore contented himself with sending his sharpshooters into the woods between Pegram's and Peeble's farms to skirmish with the Yankees and with bringing up a battery of artillery to carry on a leisurely long-range duel with the Union guns. The Confederate main force was kept out of sight in Hofmann's old lines at Pegram's.

Hofmann's brigade, meanwhile, after regrouping on Peeble's farm, was sent to the right to reinforce Ayre's for the expected Confederate attack down the Squirrel Level Line. Ayre's used it to extend his own line to the east until it connected with the force covering the Vaughn Road, Brigadier General Edward Bragg's 1st (Iron) Brigade of Crawford's 3rd Division of the 5th Corps. Parke and Warren had, in the meantime, convinced Gregg that he need not bother carrying out Meade's orders for him to reconnoiter beyond the Union left, for, as he reported to headquarters at 8:30 a.m., "The object of the intended reconnaissances has been fully accomplished—the enemy found."[8] So, after posting some troopers to cover the left of Parke's line, he started to withdraw his main force to McDowell's plantation at the junction of the Vaughn and Wyatt roads. Before he could do so, however, he received word that at about 9 a.m. Young's Brigade of Matthew Butler's Rebel cavalry had driven off the 1st Maine Cavalry, which had been left to guard that point, and had captured the key junction.

Not knowing where Gregg's Union troopers had gone, Matt Butler was content to hold what he had taken, and he called up Donovant's Brigade to help out, as well as a battalion of troopers who, having previously lost their horses, were serving temporarily as infantry until they could get more. Gregg, on the other hand, was not content with the status quo. He was determined to recapture the road intersection at McDowell's. However, before he could launch a counterattack he heard heavy firing to the north, indicating that the infantry was under attack. So he decided to wait until he learned of the outcome.

It was just after 9 a.m. when Heth sent Brigadier General William MacRae's brigade forward in a reconnaissance in force. He suspected that Hill's entire plan was based on a false premise. He was evidently not facing a weak flank of the Union position but a strongly manned, formidable-looking line of entrenchments, and he wanted to investigate it more fully before he launched an all-out attack. However, his two right regiments did not know that this was only a reconnaissance in force. They thought that they were really supposed to assault the Union works. With a Rebel yell they surged forward. MacRae tried to slow them but could not; he tried to stop them but could not. The clouds suddenly burst into a downpour of driving rain that quickly turned the already sodden field into even deeper mud, but on they went. Then Ayres' Federals fired a well-aimed volley that tore at their ranks and finally stopped their advance. The Confederates tried to advance again but could not, and soon they were streaming for the rear and the cover of the woods from which they had advanced. One Rebel said that they came out of this battle "the worst cut up they have been in the whole campaign."[9]

No sooner had MacRae's men retreated than two more of Heth's brigades, Archer's and Brigadier General Joseph Davis's, advanced. But when the brigade in front began to oblique to its right the two collided. The 2nd Maryland Battalion was forced out of its position in Archer's line. It regrouped behind some farm buildings but advanced no farther. The 22nd Virginia Battalion refused to advance at all in what it considered a suicide mission. The rest of Archer's Brigade did advance, but the deadly fire of Ayres' Federals cut these regiments to pieces and they too went streaming back to the cover of the woods. Davis' Brigade suffered the same fate. "Oh, it was an awful time Saturday," one of them wrote, "charging the Yankees in the rain through the woods and swamps and thickets, and the balls flying, thick and fast in every direction, and men getting killed, and wounded hollering all over the woods."[10] Heth's fourth brigade was never ordered to advance. Instead, Hill ordered the entire force to withdraw back up the Squirrel Level Line to the vicinity of Fort Cherry. Right behind them came Ayres' skirmishers, howling like fiends, to drive off Heth's rear guard and reestablish their picket line, but the Union main force remained in place behind its defenses.

However, once he was certain that the Union infantry had beaten off Heth's attack, David Gregg set off with his cavalry to retake the key road junction at McDowell's that Matt Butler had seized in his absence. His return evidently surprised the Confederate troopers even more than his departure had done, and a squadron of skirmishers sufficed to retake the intersection. Brigadier General Pierce Young's Brigade of Butler's Division fell back about a half-mile down the Vaughn Road to its intersection with the Squirrel Level Road at Wilkinson's plantation. Gregg's skirmishers followed the Rebels along the Vaughn Road from the high ground around McDowell's down through yet another branch of Arthur's swamp and tried to drive them from Wilkinson's as well. But Young's Georgians rallied there behind some earthworks on the high ground around the plantation buildings and fought off their pursuers. Then they counterattacked. Fighting on foot, they drove the Yankee skirmishers back across the swamp and back up the hill to McDowell's.

However, by then most of Davies' 1st Brigade of Gregg's division had arrived. Davies had his men dismount also. Then they advanced and drove the Georgians back down into the swampy valley between the two plantations. But just then Dunovant's Brigade finally arrived to reinforce Young's. "Young was cursing and storming in that stentorian voice of his, which could be heard for half a mile," one of Dunovant's men wrote. "'Hold your ground down there, you damned scoundrels,' was one of his mildest expressions. The men were fighting gallantly against heavy odds, as we could plainly see, and I remember well how indignant I was at General Young, much as I admired him, for cursing them so outrageously."[11]

However, with Dunovant's arrival, the initiative changed sides again. Matt Butler ordered the South Carolinians to attack the Union right. Dunovant dismounted two of his three regiments and led them down the hill from Wilkinson's, across the swampy ground and up the hill toward the Federals. But his right failed to connect with Young's left and one Union regiment penetrated this gap and moved to get behind the South Carolinians while another assaulted their left flank, and the Rebels fell back across the swamp and back up the hill to the defenses at Wilkinson's. Again the Federals followed the retreating Confederates, and again they were repulsed.

Finally the seesaw battle settled into a stalemate. The 10th New York Cavalry and at least part of the 6th Ohio began to dig in west of the swampy stream, at the foot of the slope up to Wilkinson's, as a bridgehead and an advanced line of defense. Davies told these two regiments that if attacked they should hold on as long as possible and then fall back to a line of defenses that the 1st Massachusetts Cavalry was digging on the east side of the stream. If this, too, could not be held, they could retreat to the protection of the rest of the brigade on the high ground around McDowell's house, where the four guns of Battery A of the 2nd U.S. Artillery were deployed to cover the area between the two plantations. Hampton brought up a second Confederate battery and a slow, deliberate artillery duel passed the time while both sides improved their defenses.

Having regained possession of the key intersection at McDowell's and with the understanding that the Union infantry did not intend to attack that day, Gregg was content to hold what he had with Davies 1st Brigade while he spread Smith's 2nd Brigade in detachments to connect that position with Parke's infantry to the northwest and with the old defenses around Globe Tavern to the northeast. But at around 10 a.m. Meade sent orders to Parke for him to renew the offensive as soon as Mott's division of the 2nd Corps could join him. Parke forwarded this to Gregg and told him to report to Peeble's farm in person. Gregg protested that for him to abandon McDowell's would allow the Rebel cavalry to move up the Vaughn Road and get into the rear of the Union infantry along the Squirrel Level Line. Meanwhile, Gregg's reports of the morning's activities had reached army headquarters, and at 2 p.m. Humphreys sent Gregg permission to attack from where he was. "If you can occupy an equal or greater force of the enemy than your own, and keep them from joining those we attack, it will be equivalent to joining the attack here," he wrote, "particularly if you beat them."[12] But before this dispatch reached Gregg he was already at Peeble's farm, where he conferred with Meade, Humphreys, Parke, and Warren.

Hampton, on the other hand, was not content to remain on the defensive. He felt that the Federals' position, especially that of the advanced guard west of the swamp between the two plantations, gave him a chance to strike them a telling blow. Therefore he led two Virginia regiments of Rooney Lee's division forward to the Squirrel Level Road, then down it and a country lane to bring them onto the right flank of the 10th New York. Due to poor roads and precautions against ambush or revealing their own presence, it would be 3 p.m. before they were in position. Hampton ordered their brigade commander to attack with mounted companies in front, followed by a dismounted line and sent orders for Matt Butler to strike the Yankee front when he heard the Virginians' Rebel yell, using dismounted troopers in front backed up by mounted units. This was a good plan, but it quickly fell apart. The Virginians failed to take the country road that led to the 10th New York's flank and instead came in on Butler's left, making him think that he was about to be attacked himself until he discovered at the last minute that these were fellow Confederates approaching his flank, not Yankees.

Nevertheless, Young's brigade advanced against the New Yorkers and the 6th Ohio, who, as previously arranged, fell back across the swampy stream to the 1st Massachusetts' position, although a group of mounted Rebels swept down on them as they were crossing a narrow causeway and captured 46 Federals. Further Confederate advances were beaten off by the 1st Massachusetts and by the other two regiments as they formed up in this second line. The Southerners fell back to the works just abandoned by the Federals and engaged them in a vicious firefight for half an hour while shells from the opposing batteries flew back and forth over their heads.

Matt Butler now ordered Dunovant to flank the Yankees out of this second line. "During this conversation," an orderly remembered, "I had noticed that Dunovant had seemed to be very impatient, and when Butler gave him this order, he saluted and replied: 'Oh, General, let me charge 'em, we've got 'em going and let us keep 'em going.' Butler said, 'General, I am afraid I will lose too many men.' 'Oh, no we won't,' answered Dunovant, 'my men are perfectly enthusiastic and ready to charge, an' we've got the Yankees demoralized, one more charge will finish 'em. Let me charge them.' Then I saw Butler's face change. He had been calm and unmoved till then, but as Dunovant said this, his face flushed, his eyes seemed to grow darker (I was looking him directly in the face not five feet from him) and in a voice short, sharp, and stern, he called to Dunovant, 'Charge them, sir, if you wish.'"[13]

Dunovant gave the order, but his men hung back. He repeated the order with more emphasis, and this time they rose from their defenses and ran toward the creek, Young's men joining them on their right. Dunovant galloped ahead of them, but as his horse charged across the causeway the Federals fired a volley that toppled the general from his saddle. His foot caught in the stirrup and he was dragged until his saddle turned, releasing the foot. By then he was quite dead, and his men, seeing him fall, retreated.

The Rebel guns advanced from Wilkinson's to the captured defenses, but they still could not drive off or silence the lone Union battery on the high ground at McDowell's. The men of both sides again settled down in their trenches, seeking protection from enemy shells and bullets, as well as the rain that continued to fall, "soaked to the skin . . . ," as one of them recorded, "and shivering all the time with cold."[14]

Hampton was not ready to give up, however. He and Butler reverted to the plan of flanking the second Yankee line. The two Virginia regiments confronted the Union right, north of the Vaughn Road, while Dunovant's Brigade, now under Lieutenant Colonel William Stokes, faced the rest of the enemy line, and Young's Brigade was moved to the far right, beyond the headwaters of the little swampy stream, to turn the Federal left. To complete the arrangement, Hampton sent orders for Rooney Lee to bring two more of his regiments forward and turn the Union right. While Hampton waited for these reinforcements, however, some of Stokes' troopers broke and ran for the rear, but Hampton and Butler personally rallied them and sent them back to their defenses.

Time dragged by and still Rooney Lee did not appear with his reinforcements. Finally, near 5 p.m., Hampton decided to go ahead without them and sent his men forward in a dismounted charge. The three Federal regiments merely withdrew up the hill to McDowell's, where they took up positions in the main Union line, which ran north to south north of the Vaughn road but bent to the southeast to the south of it. A lone 12-pounder Napoleon gun was stationed in the road itself, while another and two 3-inch rifles were deployed on higher ground about 100 yards behind the dismounted troopers.

While Gregg and Davies inserted the three regiments that had fallen back into their main line, Hampton made his arrangements for the final attempt to capture the key intersection and open the way into the rear of the Union infantry. He sent Young's Brigade farther to the southeast to get onto the left flank of this new Yankee line and the rest of his units straight up the hill. As these men emerged from some woods into the clearing in front of the Union position they were surprised by a blast from the lone gun in the road, but the Northern troopers held their fire until the Rebels had closed to within 50 yards of their defenses. Then they cut loose with a hail of artillery, carbine, and revolver fire that "rattled through the underbrush like hailstones," as one Confederate put it.[15] The Rebels were stopped in their tracks.

Hampton brought up his artillery for close-range support, but even that could not silence the Union fire. In fact it seemed to become even more deadly than before, and the Southerners fell back to the cover of the brow of McDowell's hill. They rested and reformed there for half an hour and then advanced again, only to meet the same fate. A third time they tried to advance, and a third time they were repulsed. "The fight . . . was terrific . . . ," wrote a reporter for the New York *Herald*. "Time and again [the Confederates] . . . charged up to within a few feet of the line, when they would receive such a deadly shower of bullets and shot as would send them staggering back."[16] After the third repulse, the 10th New York lept over its defenses and counterattacked, driving the

Rebels back 200 yards before returning to its position. Butler's men took cover in the woods and refused to charge again.

Hampton still would not give up. Young's Brigade was finally in position and he sent it forward to attack the Union left. These Georgians easily drove in the pickets of the 1st New Jersey Cavalry, who were watching this flank, but they unknowingly bypassed the pickets' reserve, Company C of that regiment. These Union horsemen drew their sabers and revolvers and charged the Rebels from the rear, throwing them into confusion and almost capturing Young in the process, before escaping to the cover of their main line. One of Young's staff officers was taken, and when he met Davies he could think of nothing better to talk about than the rain, commenting that it was "fearfully bad weather for moving about and for cavalry fighting." "Yes," said Davies, "you people were not content in your camps, but must come out here for a fight, and I guess you got one."[17] By the time Young's men were reformed and renewed their advance the rest of the 1st New Jersey had been moved into place to block them and the Union guns had been turned to face them. The Georgians were easily repulsed, and finally Hampton gave up, ordering a general withdrawal to Wilkinson's hill as darkness came at last. And that night he retreated even farther.

Warren and Parke remained on the defensive the rest of the day, but Meade was still interested in advancing. The night before, he had given orders for Hancock to withdraw a division from his trenches and to spread his other two to cover the front thus abandoned. The division chosen was Brigadier General Gershom Mott's 3rd, which contained most of the units that had made up the old 3rd Corps before that organization had been discontinued six months previously. Mott's was now the largest division in Hancock's 2nd Corps, since the other two had been in more hard fights and taken more losses in the last few weeks. All in all it was also the best led of the three. Mott himself was no military genius. In fact, he had performed so badly during the Wilderness and Spotsylvania campaigns that he had been reduced to brigade commander again. But since then he had made considerable progress and was now considered quite competent. Moreover, he had the best three brigade commanders in the 2nd Corps.

Meade had given orders for this division to be transported to Globe Tavern via the Military Railroad that ran from City Point behind the Union lines to that place. This line had only been completed less than three weeks before, however, and this was the first time such a large troop movement had been attempted on it. Communications broke down somewhere along the chain of command, and the trains were not ready when the troops were. Consequently, the latter spent a lot of time standing around in the rain waiting while various combinations of engines and cars were scraped together and hurried along. It took all afternoon to forward Mott's units in unequal fragments to the end of the line and for them to march from there to Peeble's farm. Meade refused to commit them to battle piecemeal, and it was dark before the entire division had arrived. He therefore gave up and rode back to headquarters, issuing orders for Parke to advance as soon as possible the next morning with his own two divisions plus Mott's to outflank the Rebels on Pegram's farm and advance to the Boydton Plank Road at last. Warren was also ordered to advance but no route or objective was specified for him. Characteristically, Warren responded with a long critical essay on the way things were being done and how it could be done better, which contained some good points but hardly put him in good stead at army headquarters.

While most of Hill's infantry withdrew that night into the main defenses of Petersburg, in order to be ready to move to the north side of the James if necessary, half of Meade's army was camped in the mud and rain west of Globe Tavern. Most of the Federals would have been glad to have returned to the relative comfort of their elaborate entrenchments on the old front, even though that included the occasional dangers of plunging mortar shells. "We bivouac for the night in a large woods," wrote one of Mott's brigade commanders, "surrounded by big fires kindled everywhere; we go to sleep prepared for the following day—and a battle which will probably put a goodly number of us to sleep for their final sleep."[18]

---

1. Henry, *"First With the Most" Forrest*, 360.

2. *Official Records*, 42:II:1121.

3. Ibid., 42:III:17.

4. Sommers, *Richmond Redeemed*, 318.

5. *Official Records*, 42:III:25.

6. Sommers, *Richmond Redeemed*, 322–323.

7. *Official Records*, 42:III:18.

8. Ibid., 42:III:27.

9. Sommers, *Richmond Redeemed*, 334.

10. Ibid., 335.

11. Ibid., 338.

12. *Official Records*, 42:III:28.

13. Sommers, *Richmond Redeemed*, 344.
14. Ibid., 345.
15. Ibid., 348.
16. Trudeau, *The Last Citadel*, 215.
17. Sommers, *Richmond Redeemed*, 350.
18. Ibid., 377.

CHAPTER SIXTEEN

Intrench and Hold What You Can

1–2 October 1864

Out in Tennessee that first day of October, the force of Confederate raiders led personally by Forrest reached the Nashville & Decatur Railroad again about noon, this time at the village of Spring Hill. From there they turned south. Wood accumulated along the railway for fueling the engines was instead placed on the tracks and set on fire so that the heat would warp the rails. The Union garrisons of three blockhouses surrendered that afternoon. Their defenses and the bridges they were built to guard were then burned. A fourth, however, refused to surrender, despite the disparity in numbers between the opposing forces. Since he had no artillery with him, Forrest could not blast the defenders out of their blockhouse, so he sent ten volunteers under cover of darkness that night to set fire to the bridge they guarded, then marched south to Columbia.

A bit farther south, Buford's part of the raiding force tore up a section of the east-west Memphis & Charleston Railroad that took a Union division coming up from Atlanta by train all that night to fix. That afternoon Buford approached Athens, Alabama, where the raid had begun a week before.

A Federal cavalry raid was called off that day. Union generals Ammen and Gillem, whose forces had been working their way up the east Tennessee valley toward the vital Confederate saltworks in southwestern Virginia, received orders from Sherman to call off their operation. Sherman wanted to concentrate as much of his cavalry as possible against Forrest. Ammen sent off three daring couriers to carry copies of the order overland to General Burbridge, who was converging on the same objective from eastern Kentucky.

Down in Georgia on that first day of October, John Bell Hood began to move his army of Tennessee to the north bank of the Chattahoochee River. While Sherman remained idle in Atlanta waiting for Grant or Canby to open a supply port for him on either the Atlantic or Gulf coast, Hood was bidding to seize the initiative by attacking Sherman's thin railroad lifeline. If he could cut it and keep it cut for long enough, Sherman would be forced to retreat and give up some, or all, of the territory he had worked so hard to gain during the summer. Even the threat of cutting Sherman's supply line should draw the Union army northward away from Atlanta. This plan had been approved, perhaps even originated, by Confederate president Jefferson Davis, with the provision that should Sherman cut loose from the railroad and march for either coast Hood was to follow him and attack the rear of his column.

Sherman wired Grant that same day: "Hood is evidently across the Chattahoochee, below Sweetwater. If he tries to get on our road, this side of the Etowah, I shall attack him; but if he goes to the Selma & Talladega road, why will it not do to leave Tennessee to the forces which Thomas has, and the reserves soon to come to Nashville, and for me to destroy Atlanta and march across Georgia to Savannah or Charleston, breaking roads and doing irreparable damage? We cannot remain on the defensive."[1] In short, Sherman was proposing that if Hood pulled off into Alabama, out of reach from Atlanta, in order to threaten Sherman's supply line, why should not Sherman cut loose from that line and march to the east coast, leaving the job of defending Tennessee to Thomas?

In the Shenandoah, Jubal Early's Army of the Valley was also on the move that day, marching westward through the rain from the Blue Ridge out into the middle of the Valley so as to block any further progress by Sheridan. At least some of his subordinates were not happy about this move. One of his officers wrote a letter of complaint to Governor William "Extra Billy" Smith of Virginia, saying that they "marched all day through the hardest, coldest, and bleakest storm of the season; winter has few more severe days." He claimed that "unless it was imperative it was cruel and injudicious—cruel, because a great many of the command are shoeless and without blankets, and injudicious, because the Quartermaster states that shoes enough to supply the army were expected at Waynesboro." All in all, the officer told Smith—who as a political general before he was elected governor never got on well with Early—the troops wanted a new leader. "The army once believed him a safe commander, and felt that they could trust to his caution, but unfortunately this has proved to be a delusion."[2]

Unknown to Early, Sheridan did not mean to advance any farther up the Shenandoah, but he was equally ignorant of Early's move from Waynesboro out into the Valley. That evening he wrote to Grant: "My judgment is that it would be best to terminate this campaign by the destruction of the crops, &c., in this valley, and the transfer of the troops to the army operating against Richmond. If the Orange and Alexandria Railroad is opened, it will take an army corps to protect it. If the Front Royal Road is opened, it will take as many troops to protect it, as there is no enemy in the Valley to operate against. Early is, without doubt, fortifying at Charlottesville, holding Rockfish Gap. It is no easy matter to pass these mountain gaps and attack Charlottesville, hauling supplies through difficult passes, fourteen miles in length, and with a line of communication from 135 to 145 miles in length, without the organization of supply trains, ordnance trains, and all the appointments of an army making a permanent advance. At present we are organized for a raid up the Valley, with no trains except the corps trains. All the regimental trains had to be used as supply wagons to subsist us as far as this place, and can't do it at that. I am ready and willing to cross the Blue Ridge, but know from present indications that the enemy will strongly fortify at Charlottesville and Gordonsville, and that these places cannot be taken without the expenditure of a largely superior force to keep open the line of communication. With my present means I cannot accumulate supplies enough to carry me through to the Orange and Alexandria Railroad."[3]

Sheridan also replied to Grant's order to send either Wilson or Torbert to command Sherman's cavalry. He informed the general-in-chief that he was sending Wilson as "the best man for the position."[4] More than likely, the truth was that he much preferred to keep Torbert, who was a personal friend, and that he was quite happy to be rid of Wilson, whom he did not particularly like. Also, it is likely that Torbert did not want to leave the East. For Wilson, the move was a promotion. For Torbert it would not have been. So apparently everybody was happy with the change, even Sherman, who had asked for either Gregg or Wilson and had not mentioned Torbert.

Sheridan promptly cancelled the transfer of Custer to the command of Averell's old 2nd Cavalry Division of the Department of West Virginia and instead assigned him to succeed Wilson in command of the 3rd Division of the cavalry that had been brought from the Army of the Potomac. Both moves turned out to be good ones. While Wilson had never shone as a division commander, he soon became an excellent cavalry corps commander, the best the Union ever had in the West throughout the war. Meanwhile, Custer soon turned what had been a lackluster outfit into the best cavalry division in the East. "Wilson was universally considered to be an unlucky man," one member of the division later recalled. "We never went into a fight but that we expected to be beat. We neither had confidence in him or ourselves, but with Custer . . . we never began but we felt sure of victory."[5]

General Lee sent a note through the lines to Grant on that first day of October: "With a view of alleviating the sufferings of our soldiers, I have the honor to propose an exchange of the prisoners of war belonging to the armies operating in Virginia, man for man, or upon the basis established by the cartel."[6] The general exchange of prisoners had broken down some months before, and the Confederacy was feeling the manpower pinch.

On the north side of the James River that day the Union 18th Corps engaged in an exchange of artillery fire with the Confederates opposite them, while the Rebel gunboats in the river occasionally threw a shell its way, but neither side attempted to attack the other. Both were content to work at improving their defenses, bring up ammunition and other supplies, and find what shelter they could from the rain. But at 8:30 a.m. Butler ordered Birney's 10th Corps to reconnoiter up the Darbytown Road and penetrate the Intermediate Line if possible. About an hour later Birney pulled two brigades of Terry's division out of the trenches into a reserve position, but it was not until about 11:15 a.m. that, satisfied that the Rebels would probably not attack his defenses, he sent them, under Terry, northward to the Darbytown Road, and at 1:25 p.m. they linked up with Kautz and one brigade of his cavalry for an advance to the northwest along that artery. Colonel Samuel Spear's 2nd Brigade of Kautz's cavalry, along with a pair of horse artillery guns, advanced along the parallel Charles City Road a bit farther north to protect the main column's flank. Kautz's troopers easily brushed aside the few Confederate horsemen they encountered, while Terry's infantry found nothing to fight but the rain, some fog, and plenty of clinging mud.

In the two days since the Federals had first crossed to the north side of the James in force, Richmond had been in a state of turmoil. When word had reached the city on 29 September that Fort Harrison had fallen, the greatest panic of the war had struck the Confederate capital. Not only had every organization of reserves and militia been called out but, as a clerk in the Rebel war department recorded, "squads of guards were sent into the streets everywhere with orders to arrest every able-bodied man they met, regardless of papers; and this produced a conster-nation among the civilians. The offices and government shops were closed, and the tocsin sounded for hours, by order of the Governor, frighting some of the women."[7]

Only one of the city's newspapers managed to put out an edition on the 30th because so many of their employees had been impressed into service. "Guards everywhere," the war department clerk recorded, "on horseback and on foot, in the city and at the suburbs, are arresting pedestrians, who, if they have not passes . . . are hurried to some of the depots or to the City Square . . . and confined until marched to the field or released."[8] Two members of the Confederate cabinet were among those thus rounded up, although they were released before they saw any action.

By the first of October, as Kautz and Terry approached, such methods had greatly strengthened the Rebel forces in the Intermediate Line. And at 4 p.m., the diarist clerk noted, "a furious cannonade has sprung up on the southeast of the city, and seemingly very near to it. It may be a raid. The firing increases in rapidity, mingled, I think, with the roar of small arms. We can hear distinctly the whistle of shot and shell, and the detonations shake the windows."[9]

The opening blasts of Confederate artillery drove back the first Federal probes of the Intermediate Line where it was met by the Darbytown Road. The north-south line turned briefly to the northeast there, where it was known as Fort Atkinson, before turning to the north again. Then a battery and a half of Union guns unlimbered in an open field and returned fire, knocking out a Rebel 12-pounder with a direct hit, but Terry soon ordered them back into the cover of the woods along the road. Then he sent Colonel Joseph Abbott's 2nd Brigade forward with four of its regiments, all armed with Spencer repeating rifles, deployed in a mile-long skirmish line and with the 16th New York Heavy Artillery in line of battle backing them up. Under heavy artillery fire, the North-erners easily drove the Rebel skirmishers before them, but the muddy cornfield they had to cross was a more serious obstacle, threatening to pull the shoes off the feet of the running soldiers. Rain-swollen Almond

Creek was an even greater obstacle, but they managed to slosh through it, and then a slightly smaller tributary as well. From the thickets bordering the northwest edge of this second stream they could see the defenses of the Intermediate Line from 600 to 800 yards away across another open field. The Confederate artillery stepped up its rate of fire as the Federals reached this open ground, and Terry ordered the brigade to take cover in the shelter of the trees and the gully through which the stream flowed.

Farther north, Spear's brigade of Union cavalry followed the Charles City Road to where it joined the Williamsburg Road just east of the Intermediate Line. Rebel skirmishers put up a fight outside of the defenses there until one squadron of the 7th South Carolina Cavalry panicked, forcing the rest of the regiment to fall back into the entrenchments. Spear then brought up his two guns, but they were no match, in the open, for the more numerous Rebel guns behind prepared defenses and they soon gave up the unequal contest. Terry concluded that the Intermediate Line was too well defended on both roads to be carried by his small force and that he had done all that could be expected in the way of a reconnaissance. He therefore ordered a withdrawal, and at 5 p.m. Abbott's brigade began to pull out of its sheltering gully, recrossed the swollen streams and muddy cornfield under the fire of the Confederate guns, and returned down the Darbytown Road. The other infantry brigade, the cavalry, and the artillery followed, and Kautz sent orders for Spear to fall back along the Charles City Road, which he did after throwing a few long-range artillery shots at the city of Richmond. These Federals had come as close to the Southern capital as any Union troops would get for another six months. "It was a dreary, tiresome night march back to camp," one Union officer recorded, "and no particular relief when we got there—for we had to lie down in the mud and water, making the best shift of it we could, hungry, cold, and tired."[10]

Behind them, the Confederate artillery, unaware that the Federals had withdrawn, continued to bombard the woods. And the local defense regiments, made up mostly of the men hastily impressed into the ranks, although hurrying to the point of danger, failed to arrive in time for the battle. Perhaps it was just as well, for, as the commander of one of them wrote: "The men were found to be deserting rapidly. Provost guards were thrown out as skirmishers and they left also; non-commissioned officers were sent after them and doubtless got lost, as we never saw them again. The commissioned officers were worked to death, and when, at night, after a most wearisome march, we corralled our regiment . . . the captains and lieutenants were worn down and the command reduced by near two hundred men. We thought we were disgraced, until we learned that our regiment had been kept together better than either of the other three."[11] Arriving not long after these amateurs, came two veteran brigades, along with generals Field and Anderson.

After receiving reports from both Butler and Meade on the day's activities, Grant told the former that he should pull back his right flank in case Lee should try to repeat his maneuver of 1862 of bringing the Army of the Valley down to Richmond to attack the Union flank. He said this line should cover either Deep Bottom or Aiken's Landing and be held by one corps while the other was withdrawn into reserve. Then, at Butler's request, he sent two officers from his staff to lay out the line to be occupied. Meanwhile, Butler, Birney, and Weitzel studied the information gained by Terry's reconnaissance. For one thing, it confirmed the accuracy of a map that had recently been taken from a Confederate officer. For another, it indicated that only second-class troops held the Intermediate Line above Fort Gilmer.

Burler therefore wanted to take his entire Army of the James and punch through that line into Richmond itself. He asked Grant to send a corps from Meade's army to hold the proposed defensive line while he did just that. But no such force could possibly cross the James soon enough to allow Butler to make the advance the next day, so Grant vetoed the idea. Thus the second day of October was spent, on the north side, in laying out the new line of defenses while the troops continued to occupy and improve the line they already held. Across the way, Lee's troops also spent the second improving their defenses, especially a new line through what had been the middle of the entrenched camp.

That day, Grant answered the note Lee had written the day before about exchanging prisoners: "I could not of a right accept your proposition further than to exchange those prisoners captured within the last three days and who have not yet been delivered to the Commissary-General of Prisoners. Among those lost by the armies operating against Richmond were a number of colored troops. Before further negotiations are had upon the subject I would ask if you propose delivering these men the same as white soldiers?"[12]

South of Petersburg, the rain finally ended during the night, and Sunday, 2 October, although overcast and foggy, dawned hot and relatively dry, with a hint that some sunshine might appear later in the day. By 5:30 a.m. Mott's Federal division was under arms and massed for an advance, but it was left waiting for an hour and a half while its commander conferred with Parke, Willcox, and Potter to plan the Union advance. It was decided that Potter's 2nd Division of the 9th Corps would advance northward to Pegram's farm again to threaten whatever Confederate force remained in that area. Willcox's 1st Division was to wheel to its right and come up on Potter's left. Mott's 3rd Division of the 2nd Corps would have the key role. It was to move westward along Route 673 past the southwestern end of the Squirrel Level Line until it came to the Harmon Road, then turn north toward the Boydton Plank Road. Warren would support these operations only by sending each of his three divisions, including the one back around Globe Tavern, forward to probe whatever was in their fronts. Otherwise, the 5th Corps would remain on the defensive. But Warren's troops were not ready to move yet, and it was 7:45 a.m. before orders were issued to his divisions.

Mott's division began its march just before 7 a.m. Since it had the farthest to go, it was just as well that it started first. When it reached Route 673 its skirmish line was reinforced to three regiments and was backed up by the rest of Brigadier General Byron Pierce's 2nd Brigade in line of battle. Behind that came Colonel Robert McAllister's 3rd Brigade, in column of battalions, which threw out more and more units as skirmishers to guard the column's left flank as it advanced. Last but not least was Brigadier General Philip Regis DeTrobriand's 1st Brigade. The Union skirmishers easily drove pickets from the 3rd North Carolina Cavalry through the woods and thickets and into the safety of Fort MacRae at the southwestern end of the Squirrel Level Line. Then Pierce's and McAllister's brigades deployed side by side and advanced across clear ground toward the fort and its adjoining trenches. The Confederates knew that they could not hold against such a force and retreated to the northwest to the final defensive line in front of the Boydton Plank Road.

Mott was somewhat at a loss when he found that the Rebels were not present in force. Not knowing where they were or what they were up to was even worse than charging well defended works would have been. He decided that, without knowing where the Confederates were, it would be too risky to continue westward and turn up the Harman Road, as planned, as this would expose his right, or northern, flank to a possible counterattack. He therefore decided to move directly north up a country lane in search of the enemy. This would keep his division closer to the potential aid of Parke's two divisions and still outflank any Rebels on Pegram's farm.

It took a while to reassemble the units that had lost their formations while charging through the abatis of the Squirrel Level defenses and to get them aligned for an advance in a new direction with the three brigades deployed side by side. More time was lost in checking out the surrounding area for signs of the enemy. By then the day was "hot and sultry, and the men perspired as much as in the hottest weather of summer." The muddy ground and the dense woods impeded and delayed the advance. "We had to get through the thickets after the manner of

wild boars," General DeTrobriand remembered, ". . . by breaking the
branches to make way."[13] Confederate troopers were encountered again
about three quarters of a mile up the road in some light earthworks on
the farm of a C. Smith. But there were still far too few of them to stand
up to a full Union division, and they fell back before Mott's skirmishers.
Nevertheless, by the time the Federals had pushed on another quarter
of a mile to where their little farm lane met up with the Harman Road,
it was nearly noon.

Meanwhile, Parke's two divisions had advanced shortly before 8 a.m.
from Peeble's farm toward Pegram's. And his skirmishers soon discovered that the Southerners had abandoned that position also. Parke's plans
for his own units were thus as upset as those for Mott's division. He
was too cautious to send his main line beyond Pegram's onto Jones's
farm, so he held it in the woods south of Pegram's until his skirmishers
had probed farther north. At about 9:30 a.m. he finally brought his main
force forward to Pegram's house and formed it in an east-west line across
the middle of the cleared fields with one brigade pulled back on the left
to guard that flank until Mott caught up. Then Parke decided not to go
any farther until Meade had been consulted.

Warren found that the Confederates had also withdrawn from before
two of his three divisions. A signal detachment in an observation tower
at Globe Tavern reported to Crawford that Hill's main line of defenses
to the north of him were still well manned, so that division did not
advance, although Crawford held his units in readiness to do so in case
Hill's defenses should be weakened. At about 9:30 a.m. it was discovered
that no Rebels remained in front of Griffin's division, and it advanced
to take position on Parke's right. And when Ayres discovered that only
a small force of Rebels remained in the Squirrel Level Line north of him,
he sent one brigade at about 10 a.m. to chase them into Fort Cherry.

At 10:15 a.m. Meade arrived at Globe Tavern from his headquarters
farther east, and there he studied the reports from the front. He had
come to place himself at the head of his troops for a battle just beyond
his new position along the Squirrel Level Line and hoped to defeat the
Confederates whom he had presumed were still holding Pegram's farm
and then pursue them until he had reached the Boydton Plank Road, or
the Southside Railroad, perhaps even to the upper Appomattox. Signifi-
cantly, engineers with six trains of pontoons were already on their way
from City Point. But when he found that the Rebels had withdrawn,
presumably into the highly developed semi-circular defenses of Petersburg, he was uncertain what to do next.

At 11 a.m. he reported the situation to Grant by military telegraph.
"The inference is," he said, "the enemy refuse battle outside their works,

to which they have retired awaiting attack. Without your orders I shall not attack their entrenchments, but on being satisfied they are not outside of them I will take up the best position I can, connecting with the Weldon railroad and extending as far to the left as practicable, having in view the protection of my left flank, and then intrench. I should be glad to know your views and orders." Ten minutes later the lieutenant general replied from Deep Bottom, where he had gone to confer with Butler: "Carry out what you propose in dispatch of 11 a.m.—that is, intrench and hold what you can, but make no attack against defended fortifications." A little while later, after returning to City Point, he added: "You may shorten the line to the extent you deem necessary to be able to hold it. All you do hold west of the Weldon road be prepared to give up whenever the forces holding it are necessary to defend any other part of the line."[14]

At around 11:45 a.m. Ayres decided to rid his forces of the annoying Rebel sharpshooters who were pestering them from Fort Cherry and sent his advanced brigade to drive them away and capture the fort. This was easily done, but the Rebels counterattacked. However, the Union skirmishers, armed with Spencer repeating rifles, handily repulsed this move.

While the Federals hesitated and then decided to go over to the defensive, A. P. Hill began to gather his mobile reserves, which he now knew were no longer needed north of the James River, and he sent them to man the line that paralleled and protected the Boydton Plank Road. MacRae's Brigade of Heth's Division arrived just in time to repulse Mott's skirmishers, who, seeing the Confederates approach, had tried to beat them to the entrenchments. MacRae's Brigade was soon joined on its left by Davis' and Brigadier General John R. Cooke's brigades of the same division, while its right was covered by Brigadier General Rufus Barringer's brigade of Rooney Lee's cavalry division. These troops, plus gunners of attached batteries of light artillery and other units farther east, set to work at improving the incomplete entrenchments.

Meanwhile, Mott's main line of battle came up. But Mott was even more puzzled by the Confederates' presence here than he had previously been by their absense farther south. From what he had been told by Parke and Warren, he had expected to find the Rebels out in the open and to turn their flank. Instead, he found them manning prepared breastworks which extended well beyond his own left. So he assumed a defensive position in the edge of the woods south of the Southern defenses, refused half of DeTrobriand's brigade on his left to face west, and extended a skirmish line to cover his left rear all the way back to C. Smith's.

At about 1 p.m. Parke's two 9th Corps divisions and Griffin's division of the 5th Corps advanced through the woods to the edge of Jones's fields and came within sight of the Confederate entrenchments guarding the Boydton Plank Road. Parke called a halt and, as the Rebel artillery began to throw shells their way, he ordered his men to dig in. At the same hour Meade arrived at Pegram's and soon made his way to Griffin's front, where various officers gathered around him to report. A shot from a Rebel cannon passed between Meade and his chief of staff, Humphreys, who were both mounted and only a foot or two apart. It took off part of Humphrey's horse's tail, grazed Meade's boot near the knee, passed between Griffin and another general, who were standing a few feet in front of Meade, and buried itself in the ground five feet behind them, covering them and their staff officers with dirt. Fortunately for them, it did not explode. "It is extraordinary, for it is almost impossible to have fired a shot into such a crowd without hitting some one," Humphreys wrote. "A more wonderful escape I never saw," Meade told his wife; "at first I thought my leg was gone, as I felt and heard the blow plainly, but it only rubbed the leather of my riding boot without even bruising the skin."[15] The army commander completed his inspection of the front and confirmed Parke's decision not to attack the Confederate defenses.

At around 2:30 p.m. Ayres decided that his advance brigade occupying Fort Cherry was serving no purpose, so he ordered it to withdraw back down the Squirrel Level Line. But the presence of that force at Fort Cherry during the day had caused Hill to hold Wilcox's Division in the main defenses for fear of a further advance. Farther east, Bragg's Iron Brigade, stationed on the Vaughn Road, worked to link Ayres' position with Globe Tavern by means of a new line of entrenchments.

At the opposite end of the Union line, Gregg's cavalry had been prepared all day to defend the Federal left. But when no Confederate attack came he sent out part of his 2nd Brigade to locate Hampton's cavalry. An attempt to cross Hatcher's Run was almost certain to stir up something, and, sure enough, they soon encountered both of Butler's brigades and one of Rooney Lee's. This much larger force slowly pushed the reluctant Federals back up the Vaughn Road, but the latter made a stand in some woods and Hampton decided to let them go in peace since he and his men might be needed at any moment to reinforce the final defenses of the Boydton Plank Road.

In midafternoon Parke ended the stalemate on the main front by ordering Willcox and Mott to make a reconnaissance in force against the Rebel defenses to find out just how well they were manned. Mott assigned this job to Pierce, commander of his 2nd Brigade. He was to advance against the Confederate works where they were crossed by the main branch of

Arthur's Swamp. Pierce moved four regiments into the ravine of a small tributary of the swamp and placed them under Lieutenant Colonel George Zinn of the 84th Pennsylvania. When they were ready, they rushed from the cover of their ravine into the open field leading to the Rebel works. Almost immediately they were struck by enfilading artillery fire from their left and concentrated rifle fire from MacRae's Brigade of Heth's Division. Their pace slackened, but the Federals continued to advance. However, the closer they got to the Rebel entrenchments the more severe was the fire and the slower they advanced, until they were finally stopped about 50 yards short of the defenses. Satisfied that the works were held in force, Zinn knew that the object of his reconnaissance had been achieved, and he ordered his men back to the safety of the ravine. Just then he went down with a serious leg wound, but his men carried him safely off the field.

While this advance was being repulsed, Mott received instruction from Meade by way of Parke "not to run any great risk, but to take up a line and intrench."[16] At 5:15 p.m. Mott received orders to disengage from the enemy and fall back to Pegram's, which he did successfully. There his division took up position facing west and southwest along Arthur's Swamp to protect the left and left rear of the new line that Meade had decided to hold. That night the pontoons that had been brought forward in case they were needed to bridge the Appomattox were sent back, but some of the engineers who had brought them were sent to help build a redoubt at the northwestern tip of the new line. The battle was over and the armies around Richmond and Petersburg once more settled into a routine of siege warfare.

"We have withstood the great shock of Grant's grand army—and still we stand," wrote the Richmond *Examiner,* and it dismissed the Union gains as insignificant. "Instead of Richmond, the enemy got Battery Harrison," which it said was on "the outer or third line of the fortifications around Richmond. It is in no wise essential to the strength of any other battery." Nor did the paper profess to be impressed by Grant's strategy. "It is, in fact, his single trick—his sole manoeuver—a demonstration on the north side to make Lee weaken himself on the Petersburg line, and then a sudden dash to the left flank—always to the left." A correspondent for the New York *Herald* saw things differently: "Our line has been lengthened a mile and a half; we have driven the enemy from his strong works only recently put up . . . We are nearer Petersburg, and now securely threatening the Southside Railroad."[17] As Lee told Wade Hampton: "If the enemy cannot be prevented from extending his left, he will eventually reach the Appomattox and cut us off from the south side altogether."[18]

The pendulum of war began another change of direction as the guns fell relatively quiet around Petersburg and Richmond again. Each spring since the war began, the Union forces, by dint of their superior numbers and equipment, had taken the initiative and set out on various campaigns, East and West. Usually, before the summer was over, at least some of their drives would run out of momentum and the Confederates would seize the initiative in at least some theaters, regaining at least part of what had previously been lost. In 1864 that swing of the pendulum did not really get under way until early October. And that year it lacked one prominent feature of the previous two. Robert E. Lee and the Army of Northern Virginia would not be taking part. There would be no third battle of Bull Run, no third crossing of the Potomac. Lee and his army remained pinned in the defenses of Richmond and Petersburg by the ever-threatening proximity of the armies of the Potomac and the James, and by the persistent, tenacious drive of Ulysses S. Grant.

---

1. Sherman, *Memoirs*, 620.
2. Pond, *The Shenandoah Valley in 1864*, 194, n. 1.
3. *Official Records*, 43:II:249.
4. Ibid.
5. Starr, *The Union Cavalry in the Civil War*, 2:294.
6. *Official Records*, Series 2, 7:906–907.
7. John B. Jones, *A Rebel War Clerk's Diary* (New York, 1866), 427.
8. Ibid., 428.
9. Ibid., 429.
10. Sommers, *Richmond Redeemed*, 170.
11. Ibid., 165.
12. *Official Records*, Series 2, 7:909.
13. Sommers, *Richmond Redeemed*, 382.
14. *Official Records*, 42:III:36.
15. Sommers, *Richmond Redeemed*, 397–398.
16. Ibid., 405.
17. Trudeau, *The Last Citadel*, 216–217.
18. Freeman, *R. E. Lee*, 3:505.

PART THREE

COUNTER-OFFENSIVES

"I cannot guess his movements as I could those of Johnston, who was a sensible man and only did sensible things."

—Major General William Tecumseh Sherman

CHAPTER SEVENTEEN

The Needless Effusion of Blood

2–5 October 1864

At Winchester, up in the Shenandoah Valley, Captain Elisha Hunt Rhodes of the 2nd Rhode Island attended services at the Episcopal church with a couple of other officers on that second day in October, "it being the only one in use," as he told his diary, "the others having been taken for hospitals. This church has a fine organ and a choir. The music was good, and we enjoyed it, but the sermon was a little rebelious. The rector was trying to prove that people should receive all afflictions as from the hand of God and stated that no matter how diabolical the agents sent might be, the people should remember that the Lord sent them. (How are you diabolical Yanks?) He prayed for all Christian rulers. I hope this included Jeff Davis, for he certainly is in need of prayer. There were several Rebel officers present who belong in prison, but were paroled for the day in order that they might attend church. I wonder if the Rebels would do as much for us, if we were prisoners. The sacrament of the Lord's Supper was administered, and one Union soldier (a Private) partook. Most of the ladies were dressed in black, and it seemed almost like a funeral. Several families lost friends in the late battle, and the whole city is in mourning. It made me sad to see the people so sorrowful and weeping, but when I remembered that they brought their troubles upon themselves and that the women encouraged the men to make war on the Government, I could not help feeling that their punishment was just."[1]

Out in Missouri that day, Sterling Price's raiding Confederates reached the Missouri River at the town of Washington, fifty miles west of St. Louis. In Tennessee that morning, Buford's Rebel raiders bombarded Athens, Alabama, and then demanded that the new garrison surrender. But the Federals refused and Buford dared not linger in the area too long with so many Union forces converging on him. He withdrew toward Florence, where he could cross back to the safety of the south side of the Tennessee River. Forrest's own detachment, meanwhile, burned some small trestles south of Columbia, Tennessee, and gathered up cattle and other supplies from the area. But Union commanders from Sherman and Thomas on down felt that at last they had a very good chance of finally catching Nathan Bedford Forrest.

However, an even larger force was now threatening Sherman's supply lines, for Hood's entire Army of Tennessee had moved northward west of Atlanta with the object of cutting the railroad between that city and Chattanooga. The Rebels reached the railway that day near the villages of Big Shanty and Kennesaw Water Tank and began tearing up track. At Augusta, Georgia, that same day Confederate president Jefferson Davis met with General Beauregard and placed him in command of a new Division of the West, consisting of Hood's Army and Department of Tennessee and Taylor's Department of Alabama, Mississippi and East Louisiana. Beauregard's job was to coordinate the two departments but not to interfere with their actual operations unless physically present with the troops. It was a difficult assignment and not calculated to bring military glory to Beauregard, but he preferred it to being, as he had been, what amounted to a corps commander under Lee.

In southwestern Virginia that day, after fighting their way over some of the roughest terrain in North America against increasing resistence, the Union forces under Burbridge approached the town of Saltville. Word had not reached them that Ammen's and Gillem's forces coming up from east Tennessee had turned back in response to orders from Sherman. So they did not know that all Rebels in the area were now free to concentrate against them.

Burbridge had with him two brigades composed of Kentucky cavalry

and mounted infantry regiments and one brigade that consisted of an
Ohio and a Michigan cavalry regiment plus one regiment of U.S. Colored
Cavalry, part of another, and an assortment of black recruits for other
units. Brigadier General John Echols, in temporary command on the
Confederate side, pending the return of Major General John C. Breckinridge from his sojourn with the Army of the Valley, had with him or on
the way a number of Kentucky and Virginia cavalry and mounted infantry units, some Virginia Reserves (old men and young boys), and what
was left of three brigades that had become detached from Wheeler's
Cavalry Corps of Hood's Army of Tennessee. These were commanded
by Brigadier General John S. Williams.

Dawn came late as clouds lingered over Saltville, and these trapped the
cool night air near the ground. The Federals seemed to be in no great
hurry, despite the fact that their supplies were running low, but they
eventually pushed the Rebel delaying force, the 4th Kentucky Cavalry,
down both banks of the North Fork of the Holston River and then
across to the east side. The mixed brigade of black and white regiments,
under Colonel Robert Ratliff of the 12th Ohio, continued to press the
Confederates while the two brigades of Union Kentuckians moved on
down the west bank. But the Confederates rallied on the front slope of
Sanders Hill and stood off Ratliff's advance for fifteen minutes, which
allowed time for the Rebel brigade commander, Colonel Henry L. Giltner, to bring up the 64th Virginia Infantry and the 10th Kentucky
Mounted Rifles. When the 4th Kentucky finally gave way, Giltner
stopped the Union pursuit with a countercharge by another 10th, the
10th Kentucky Cavalry Battalion. By the time the Rebels reformed on
the crest of Sanders Hill they could see the first of Williams' troopers
filing into the breastworks on Chestnut Ridge behind them. And behind
that ridge lay the town of Saltville.

Also nearby, on the back side of Sanders Hill, was the 13th Virginia
Reserve Battalion. Giltner rode to it and tried to persuade it to join his
troops on the crest of the hill. But Brigadier General Felix Robertson,
one of the brigade commanders from Wheeler's lost troops, had sent a
veteran officer to serve as an adviser to these Reserves and he was reluctant to have them join Giltner without the approval of Robertson, who
had wanted them to join him on Chestnut Ridge. The commander of
the battalion, Lieutenant Colonel Robert Smith, however, had been unwilling to do that. It was Ratliff, the Federal, who unknowingly settled
this impasse. First he sent skirmishers against Giltner's position on the
crest of Sanders Hill, and when these were repulsed he sent his entire
brigade in line of battle. Soon Giltner's troops retreated past the reserve
battalion, across Cedar Run, and up Chestnut Ridge, where they took

position on Robertson's left, along the bluffs that bordered a loop of the river.

By then General Williams—known as "Cerro Gordo," presumably after the Mexican War battle—had arrived at Saltville. He sent Colonel George Dibrell's Brigade of his force to take position on Robertson's right and his own small brigade, under Colonel William Breckinridge, cousin of the departmental commander, to Giltner's left. Four late-arriving companies of Smith's 13th Reserves held the extreme left flank, and another small reserve battalion, Lieutenant Colonel Robert T. Preston's 4th, was spread along the river bank to keep an eye out for any flanking move by the Yankees. Echols was still at department headquarters at Abingdon, waiting for General Breckinridge's return, so Williams was in command of the 2,500 to 3,000 Confederates at Saltville.

It was about 11 a.m. and the clouds were gone when Ratliff's line of battle came down the south side of Sanders Hill and struck Smith's battalion of reserves. To the surprise of everyone on both sides, these old men and boys did not turn and run. They stood and for a few minutes tried to slug it out with five times their number. But gradually they were pushed down the hill and across Cedar Branch. Maintaining their cohesion, they then retreated up Chestnut Ridge and took position between Robertson and Giltner, leaving twenty or more dead and wounded behind and as many more as prisoners.

Ratliff's three Union regiments skirmished with Robertson's and Dibrell's Confederates, but paused to reform before crossing the briar-choked ravine of Cedar Branch and starting up Chestnut Ridge. As they emerged from the briars the Rebels at the top of the ridge, some driven to a frenzy of hatred at their first sight of black soldiers, poured a deadly fire into them. An enraged Southern lieutenant climbed over the breastworks and charged downhill all alone, armed only with a revolver. When he was killed, his brother, another lieutenant, followed, and he was badly wounded. But Ratliff's men could not reach the top of the ridge on their own, and the only help they were getting was long-range fire from some mountain howitzers on the slope of Little Mountain, across the Holston.

One brigade of the Union Kentucky troops, under Colonel Charles Hanson, was working its way down the Holston toward a ford guarded by Colonel Breckinridge, while the other, under Brigadier General Edward H. Hobson, swept across an open tableland known as Broddy's Bottom heading straight for the main ford of the river. The water in the ford was higher than usual, due to recent rains, but the Federals splashed across, pushing back part of Giltner's brigade in the process. Then they pushed over the ridge south of the stream, where they encountered the 10th Kentucky Mounted Rifles and the 64th Virginia Mounted Infantry.

These forces also fell back to another bit of high ground in the middle of Elizabeth Cemetery. From there they traded volleys with the larger Union force at a range of 50 paces.

Giltner knew that his men could not hold on for long, and he rode to nearby Church Hill, where he found the 4th Virginia Reserve Battalion. Their commander, Lieutenant Colonel Robert T. Preston, agreed to loan Giltner half of his little battalion. This small force trotted down the road and up the hill to the cemetery. There they got off one volley before they bolted and ran, taking most of Giltner's men with them. But again the 10th Kentucky Cavalry Battalion saved the rest of the brigade by mounting a countercharge. This one cost its colonel his life, but Hobson's Federals fell back.

Soon thereafter, the remaining Union brigade, Hanson's, strengthened by two of Hobson's regiments, probed at the river downstream, searching for a place to cross. For three hours they floundered around in the river, but the Confederates held a high bluff on the south side of the stream from which they inflicted repeated casualties on these Federals without taking any losses themselves. Hanson himself was among those hit. But then what had begun to look like a stalemate was suddenly broken when Robertson's Brigade began to retreat from Chestnut Ridge and the 12th Ohio Cavalry charged up after them. Dibrell pulled back his left flank to face this new danger and refused to give ground. By then the sun was beginning to set, and both sides were running low on ammunition for their rifles and carbines. But they drew their revolvers and continued to blast each other at close range for another thirty minutes. Pistol ammunition and daylight ran out at about the same time, and a stalemate it was after all.

But then a cheer was heard to ripple from one end of the Confederate line to the other. Possibly it was brought on by news that the small brigades of Cosby, Duke, and Vaughn had arrived from east Tennessee. More likely it was caused by the arrival of General Breckinridge. Rebel prisoners told Burbridge that the cheering hailed the arrival of Breckinridge with a whole division of troops, although in truth he brought none at all. But, fearing that it was true, the Union commander ordered Ratliff's and Hanson's brigades to fall back on Hobson's. This decision might have been influenced by his knowledge that the Confederates hated him for the iron fist with which he had ruled Kentucky. As one Rebel put it, "no power or authority at Saltville could have saved his life" had he been captured.[2]

His fears were further enhanced by a timely attack on his led horses and pack animals by two companies that had been cut off from Giltner's command. Dozens of campfires and 18 huge bonfires were lit to make the Southerners think that they were going into camp. Instead, the Federals began to retreat toward Kentucky that night. Burbridge turned command of the column over to Hobson and hurried on ahead. Evidently he was not very popular with his own troops either, for news of the change of command was met with "outbursts of joy and many expressions of confidence."[3]

At 8 p.m. on 2 October eight men walked into Brawner's hotel in Port Tobacco, Maryland, a small county seat southeast of Washington, D.C. They were Lieutenant Walter Bowie and seven of his men, who had been dispatched five days before by Mosby, from his guerrilla battalion, to capture Governor Bradford of Maryland. But getting his 25 men and their horses across the broad Potomac River without being detected by the Federal army or navy had proved too difficult, so Bowie and two of his men had slipped across to reconnoiter and had been told by a sympathetic civilian that there was a small detachment of the 8th Illinois Cavalry quartered at the courthouse in Port Tobacco. Bowie sent for five more of his men to join him, and they all sat around the hotel that evening drinking with blockade runners and waiting for midnight. When that hour finally arrived they walked over to the courthouse and easily captured the sleeping Federals. Then they saddled up eight of the Union horses and rode north until dawn, when they holed up with some Southern sympathizer, quite possibly Dr. Samuel Mudd, who later figured in the flight of John Wilkes Booth.

On that third day of October Lee responded to Grant's note asking if his proposed exchange of prisoners included Union colored troops: "In my proposition of the 1st instant to exchange the prisoners of war belonging to the armies operating in Virginia I intended to include all captured soldiers of the United States of what ever nation and color under my control. Deserters from our services and negroes belonging to our citizens are not considered subjects of exchange and were not included in my proposition. If there are any such among those stated by you to have been captured around Richmond they cannot be returned." Grant replied the same day: "In answer I have to state that the Government is bound to secure to all persons received into her armies the rights due to soldiers. This being denied by you in the persons of such men as have escaped from Southern masters induces me to decline making the exchanges you ask. The whole matter, however, will be referred to the proper authority for their decision, and whatever it may be will be adhered to."[4]

That same day, Grant received Sheridan's letter written on the first explaining why he did not think he could proceed any farther south. Grant was content to trust Sheridan's judgment and replied immediately: "You may take up such position in the Valley as you think can and ought to be held, and send all the force not required for this immediately here. Leave nothing for the subsistence of an army on any ground you abandon to the enemy. I will direct the railroad to be pushed toward Front Royal, so that you may send your troops back that way. Keep all of Crook's forces and the new troops that have been sent to you."[5] Believing Sheridan's report that Early had left the Valley, Grant expected at least the return of Kershaw's Division of infantry and Rosser's Laurel Brigade of cavalry to Lee and warned his subordinates to keep a close watch to prevent being surprised by such Confederate reinforcements. The railroad Grant mentioned being pushed to Front Royal was the Manassas Gap Railroad. Halleck, seeing Sheridan's report, had suggested that the parties then repairing the Orange & Alexandria Railroad in anticipation of Sheridan advancing toward Charlottesville be moved to that road instead, in order to connect to the lower Valley, and Grant had approved.

Down in Georgia, Hood sent Lieutenant General A. P. Stewart's corps of his Army of Tennessee toward the towns of Big Shanty and Acworth on Sherman's supply line, the Atlantic & Western Railroad leading north to Chattanooga, on that third day of October. With his other two corps and what was left of his cavalry he continued marching north and camped that night between Dallas and Lost Mountain, in an area Sherman had fought his way through four months before on his way south. Sherman had at first thought that Hood was heading for Alabama with the hope of eventually retaking Tennessee and had been inclined to ignore him and march for the east coast. But that day he realized that Hood was aiming for the railroad in his immediate rear, and, in the hope of catching and defeating him, started after him.

He left Major General Henry W. Slocum's 20th Corps of Thomas' Army of the Cumberland to hold Atlanta and the bridges across the Chattahoochee River. Thomas himself reached Nashville that day to take charge of its defense against Forrest and possibly Hood. Sherman had with him Thomas' other two corps, the 4th and 14th, commanded by Major General David S. Stanley and Brigadier General Jefferson C. Davis, Howard's Army of the Tennessee, with the 15th and 17th Corps, commanded by Major General Peter J. Osterhaus and Brevet Major General Thomas E. G. Ransom, and the Army of the Ohio, also known as the 23rd Corps, commanded by Brigadier General Jacob D. Cox in the absence of Schofield. He also had two small divisions of cavalry, under brigadier generals Judson Kilpatrick and Kenner Garrard.

"We had strong railroad guards," Sherman wrote, "at Marietta and Kenesaw, Allatoona, Etowah Bridge, Kingston, Rome, Resaca, Dalton, Ringgold, and Chattanooga. All the important bridges were likewise protected by good block-houses, admirably constructed, and capable of a strong defense against cavalry or infantry; and at nearly all the regular railroad-stations we had smaller detachments intrenched. I had little fear of the enemy's cavalry damaging our roads seriously, for they rarely made a break which could not be repaired in a few days; but it was absolutely necessary to keep General Hood's infantry off our main route of communication and supply."[6]

Jefferson Davis, President of the Confederate States, stopped in Columbia, capital of South Carolina, that day on his way back to Richmond after his visit to Hood's army. He received an enthusiastic welcome from the people of that city, and he offered them reason to hope that the war would soon take a turn for the better. "If there be any who feel that our cause in in danger," he said, "that final success may not crown our efforts, that we are not stronger today than when we began this struggle, that we are not able to continue the supplies to our armies and our people, let all such read a contradiction in the smiling face of our land and in the teeming evidences of plenty which everywhere greet the eye. Let them go to those places where brave men are standing in front of the foe, and there receive the assurance that we shall have final success and that every man who does not live to see his country free will see a freeman's grave." As for the Army of Tennessee, "I am able to bear you words of good cheer. That army has increased in strength since the fall of Atlanta. It has risen in tone; its march is onward, its face looking to the front. So far as I am able to judge, General Hood's strategy has been good and his conduct has been gallant. His eye is now fixed upon a point far beyond that where he was assailed by the enemy. He hopes soon to have his hand upon Sherman's line of communications, and to fix it where he can hold it. And if but a half, nay, one-fourth, of the men to whom the service has a right, will give him their strength, I see no chance for Sherman to escape from a defeat or a disgraceful retreat."[7]

When the fog at Saltville began to break up at about 8 a.m. Giltner's Brigade took up the pursuit of the retreating Union forces. Meanwhile, Robertson's Brigade circled around to the south in an attempt to get ahead of the Federals and block their path at Richlands. Williams, with his own brigade, marched toward another gap in the mountains even farther south, and the newly arrived brigades of Cosby and Duke also took round-about routes.

Meanwhile other Rebels, notably Dibrell's Tennesseans and the Virginia reserves, roamed over the battlefield, collecting abandoned weapons, bringing in the wounded, and burying the dead. Rumors that wounded and captured black soldiers were massacred in large numbers that day soon made their way into both Southern and Northern newspapers, some putting the number as high as 150 or 155. A courier on Giltner's staff later claimed to have seen Dibrell's men "shooting every wounded negro they could find," claiming it was "bang, bang, bang, all over the field, negroes dropping everywhere."[8] His testimony is suspect and certainly exaggerated. However, a Union surgeon, who had been left behind to tend the wounded on Sanders Hill, later testified that five of his black patients were taken out of his hospital and shot by "several armed men, as I believe soldiers in Confederate service," and there is no reason to doubt his account.[9] These and up to seven other men appear to have been murdered that day. General Breckinridge later tried to find out who was responsible for these acts, but the exigencies of the war made it impossible to conduct a thorough investigation and the blame was never fixed.

Up in the Shenandoah Valley that afternoon Lieutenant John Meigs, a topographical engineer on Sheridan's staff, and two orderlies were returning to camp at Harrisonburg. Near the village of Dayton they overtook three other riders. All six men were wearing waterproof ponchos over their uniforms, and as they were a mile and a half behind Union lines Meigs assumed the other three men were also Federal soldiers. Only when they were at very close range did he discover his error. They were Rebels. Each side demanded that the other surrender, shots rang out, and Meigs and one of the orderlies fell. The other orderly got away and raced back to Sheridan's headquarters to report that Meigs, son of Union Quartermaster General Montgomery Meigs and a favorite of Sheridan's, had been shot "without even a chance to give himself up."[10] The Confederates were three privates from Rosser's Laurel Brigade, which had recently arrived in the Valley as a reinforcement from Lee, and according to their later account Meigs had fired first, severely wounding one of them in the groin.

Sheridan, however, assumed that the three Rebels were some of Mosby's guerrillas and that Meigs had been ambushed, so he decided to strike back in retaliation. The next morning he sent an aide to fetch Custer and ordered the new commander of his 3rd Division of cavalry to burn every house within five miles of the spot where Meigs had been killed. This would have included the entire village of Dayton. According to an artist who was hanging around headquarters at the time, Custer vaulted into the saddle and exclaimed, "Look out for smoke."[11] But when a few houses nearest to the site of the shooting had been set on fire Sheridan relented and sent orders for Custer to stop the burning but to round up all able-bodied males in the area as prisoners.

At 4 a.m. on 4 October, Lieutenant Bowie and his seven men from Mosby's battalion reached Bowie's father's plantation, about halfway between Washington and Annapolis, near the present town of Bowie, and spent the day resting up. That night, joined by Bowie's brother, Brune, who had been at home recuperating from a wound, they camped at Collington. Bowie left them there, telling them he was going on into Annapolis alone. But when he returned he said that the mission to capture Governor Bradford was cancelled because the governor was too well guarded. The authors of the very well reasoned book *Come Retribution*, which concerns the evidence linking the Confederate government to the assassination of President Lincoln, suggest that Bowie's real mission might have been connected with Captain Conrad's proposed kidnapping of Lincoln. They do not say so, but it is even conceivable that Bowie went alone not to Annapolis but to Washington, perhaps to contact Conrad. The rest of his band might have been told that it was Bradford they were after, not Lincoln, in order to prevent a leak in case any of them were captured. Whether the others were in on it or not, it could be that postwar accounts of the raid gave it a fictitious objective in order to cover up the real one, which it would have been too dangerous to have admitted in the aftermath of the assassination.

Down in southwestern Virginia by the evening of 4 October, when Giltner, Williams, and Robertson all arrived at the town of Liberty Hill without having caught up with Hobson's Union column, the pursuit was called off. Hard marching had kept the retreating Federals ahead of all attempts to cut them off, while the 11th Michigan Cavalry, acting as rear guard, had kept the Confederates behind them at bay, although this had cost the regiment's colonel his life. Nevertheless, the Union troops had another ten days of hard marching ahead of them as the temperature dropped below the freezing point and snow began to fall on them there in the mountains.

The weather that day was considerably warmer in Bahia, on the northeast coast of Brazil. The USS *Wachusetts* was at anchor in the harbor there. This screw sloop—a sister ship of the *Kearsarge* which had sunk the CSS *Alabama* off Cherbourg, France, four months before—had been scouring the South Atlantic for months, tracking down rumors of another Confederate raider, the *Florida*. So far, however, all the *Wachusetts* had accomplished was to partially reassure the captains of numerous American ships in the area that they were not completely at the mercy of Rebel cruisers. But at 7:15 on the evening of 4 October, shortly after darkness had fallen, a lookout reported a trim, low, twin-stacked sloop of war slipping quietly into the bay, and it soon came to anchor a stone's throw from the Union vessel. The captain of the *Wachusetts*, Commander Napoleon Collins, dispatched a longboat to take a close look at this newcomer and could scarcely believe its report. His new neighbor at berth in this neutral port was none other than the long-sought *Florida*.

The CSS *Florida* had been secretly built to order for the Confederate Navy in the yard of William C. Miller and Sons at Liverpool, England, and had put to sea in March 1862 posing as the peaceful merchantman *Oreto*. At Nassau, in the Bahamas, she had rendezvoused with another ship that had brought her her armament and ammunition. Then she had slipped past Union blockaders into the port of Mobile, Alabama, where she had taken on a full crew. She had run the blockade again on the night of 15 January 1863, putting to sea to raid Federal commerce, and for the next twenty months, including six months laid up in a French dockyard, she had taken 37 prizes. Only the *Alabama* had been more ruinous to the maritime commerce of the United States. Now she rode quietly at anchor in the tropical Brazilian port next to her Federal antagonist, and the law of nations said that there was nothing Napoleon Collins could do about it.

In Georgia on 4 October, Stewart's Corps of Hood's Army of Tennessee captured a Union garrison of about 170 men at Big Shanty and about 250 at Acworth, both on the railroad leading north from Atlanta. One of Stewart's divisions, Major General Samuel G. French's, was sent up the track to destroy the bridge over Allatoona Creek. It was then to proceed to the village of Allatoona Pass, where the rails emerged from the Allatoona Mountains. There it was to fill the pass with logs, dirt, and debris to block the track. When his division reached the bridge, French dropped off one regiment, the 4th Mississippi, and one cannon to capture the blockhouse there and he continued on to Alatoona Pass with the rest, arriving there at around 3 a.m. on the fifth. He dropped off some more artillery on a hill about 1,200 yards south of the pass with two regiments of infantry to support them and took the rest of his division toward the ridge west of the railroad cut, but it was daylight by the time all his units were in position.

Meanwhile, Sherman had perceived the danger to Allatoona and had sent orders to Brigadier General John M. Corse, whose 4th Division of the 15th Corps was at Rome, to the west of Allatoona, to reinforce the key village. The telegraph wires were down between Atlanta and Rome, but the order was relayed by signal flag from one Union garrison to another. Allatoona was held by a small brigade of 890 men, commanded by Lieutenant Colonel John E. Tourtellotte, but Corse had arrived before daylight with another small brigade, 1054 men, under Colonel Richard Rowett. The high ground west of the village was then held by Rowett's command and included an earthwork known as the Star Fort because of its shape. Tourtellotte's brigade held the high ground east of the railroad. In between was the village of Allatoona, which, in addition to seven or eight houses and stores, included warehouses containing over a million rations of bread for Sherman's armies.

French did not know that the garrison had been reinforced, and believing that he had the Federals badly outnumbered he decided, after a preliminary bombardment, to see if they would bow to the inevitable. Major David W. Sanders was sent to the Union works with a surrender demand: "Sir: I have placed the forces under my command in such positions that you are surrounded, and to avoid a needless effusion of blood I call on you to surrender your forces at once, and unconditionally. Five minutes will be allowed you to decide. Should you accede to this, you will be treated in the most honorable manner as prisoners of war."[12] But as Sanders returned to the Rebel lines a soldier called out to him, "Is it surrender or fight?" Sanders answered, "Fight."[13] Corse had replied: "Your communication demanding surrender of my command I acknowledge receipt of, and respectfully reply that we are prepared for the 'needless effusion of blood' whenever it is agreeable to you."[14]

"Reaching Kenesaw Mountain about 8 a.m. of October 5th (a beautiful day)," Sherman wrote, "I had a superb view of the vast panorama to the north and west. To the southwest, about Dallas, could be seen the smoke of camp-fires, indicating the presence of a large force of the enemy, and the whole line of railroad from Big Shanty up to Allatoona (full fifteen miles) was marked by the fires of the burning railroad. We could plainly see the smoke of battle about Allatoona, and hear the faint reverberation of the cannon."[15] Sherman then sent the 23rd Corps to try to get between Allatoona and Hood's main force at Dallas, while the rest of his forces moved straight up the railroad. But Allatoona was still a day's march away.

"The signal-officer on Kenesaw reported that since daylight he had failed to obtain any answer to his call for Allatoona," Sherman wrote; "but, while I was with him, he caught a faint glimpse of the tell-tale flag through an embrasure, and after much time he made out these letters— 'C.,' 'R.,' 'S.,' 'E.,' 'H.,' 'E.,' 'R.,' and translated the message—'Corse is here.' It was a source of great relief, for it gave me the first assurance that General Corse had received his orders, and that the place was adequately garrisoned."[16] The reply was sent: "General Sherman says hold fast; we are coming."[17]

French had three small brigades which, after dropping off the two detachments, totaled about 3,200 men. He sent Brigadier General Claudius W. Sears' Brigade of Mississippians north so it could approach the Federals from the northwest down the railroad; Brigadier General Francis Marion Cockrell's Missouri brigade was positioned to attack from the west, along the ridge of Allatoona Mountain; Brigadier General William H. Young's Texas Brigade was in support somewhat farther back and in between the other two. Cockrell's men advanced and drove some of Rowett's Federals from one line of defenses but could not budge them from a second line. Young's Texans then joined the attack, and in hand-to-hand combat drove the Federals from the second and then a third position and into the Star Fort. Meanwhile, Sears' Brigade drove the rest of Rowett's men into the same work.

"Now from out the woods and up from the valley they came," wrote an officer on Corse's staff; "a solid mass of sombre brown and clouded gray; no vacant places in their steady ranks; their artillery on each flank keeping up a constant roar . . . Our artillery answers theirs . . . They open with musketry and we reply . . . Oh, that Sherman or night might come! The Springfields were getting so hot that they could scarcely be handled and those who manned the parapets were told off in relays so that one half could continue the firing and the others allow their guns to cool." Not all of Rowett's men were firing the standard issue Springfield muzzle-loading rifle, however. The 7th Illinois was armed with the 15-shot Henry repeater, forerunner of the famous Winchester, which the men had bought at their own expense. It was an investment that paid good dividends that day. "They had both a destructive and a moral effect upon the enemy, who were now thrown into confusion and for a moment wavered, but soon rallied and with magnificent courage again breasted the storm," the same officer wrote.[18]

Rowett, Tourtellotte, and Corse were all wounded, and the colonel of one of the Union regiments was killed. But the position was held. At about noon French received word from the Rebel cavalry that the Federals were coming up the railroad from Atlanta in heavy force and had already retaken Big Shanty. The Confederate troops were running low on ammunition, and any replenishments would have to be carried up the side of the mountain about a mile by hand. "The enemy," Sherman wrote, "(about 1.30 p.m.) made a last and desperate effort to carry one of the redoubts, but was badly cut to pieces by the artillery and infantry fire from the other, when he began to draw off, leaving his dead and wounded on the ground."[19] Among the wounded who were captured was General Young.

"Under the circumstances," French reported, "I decided to withdraw, however depressing the idea of not capturing the place after so many had fallen, and when in all probability we could force a surrender before night; yet, however desirous I was of remaining before the last work and forcing capitulation, or of carrying the place by assault, I deemed it of more importance not to permit the enemy to cut my division from the army."[20]

It was one of the hardest fought battles of the war, with the Federals reporting 707 casualties and the Confederates 799. In all, about 30 percent of the men engaged were killed, wounded or missing. Much was made in the Northern press of the determined resistance of Corse's small force. That and Sherman's message soon served as the inspiration for a popular hymn titled "Hold the Fort, For I Am Coming."

President Jefferson Davis made another speech that day, this time at Augusta, Georgia. With generals Beauregard and Hardee standing by, he told a cheering crowd, "We must beat Sherman, we must march into Tennessee . . . we must push the enemy back to the banks of the Ohio."[21]

In the Shenandoah that day, 5 October, Sheridan received Grant's message giving him permission to end his advance up the Valley. That much was welcome. But he was not happy with the idea of using the Manassas Gap Railroad. In his reply, sent on the seventh, he said: "I would have preferred sending troops to you by the Baltimore and Ohio Railroad. It would have been the quickest and most concealed way of sending them. The keeping open of the road to Front Royal will require large guards to protect it against a very small number of partisan troops; it also obliges me to have a pontoon train, if it is to be kept open, to bridge the Shenandoah, to keep up communication with Winchester; however, in a day or two I can tell better."[22]

Before the day was out, Mosby demonstrated what was wrong with trying to use the railroad to Front Royal. He sneaked up on the workmen, and the Federal soldiers who guarded them, near the town of Salem, east of the Blue Ridge, posted two howitzers on a hill south of the town, and opened fire. Workmen and soldiers alike fled to Rectortown where there was a Union garrison, leaving the track unfinished and strewing the ground with their tools, their weapons, and anything else that impeded their flight. Mosby followed, and for two days he laid siege to Rectortown while detachments of his men wreaked more destruction on the railroad, especially by derailing trains.

1. Rhodes, *All For the Union*, 188–189.
2. William Marvel, "The Battle of Saltville: Massacre or Myth?" *Blue & Gray Magazine*, August 1991, 50.
3. Ibid.
4. *Official Records*, Series 2, 7:914.
5. Ibid., 43:II:266.
6. Sherman, *Memoirs*, 621.
7. Foote, *The Civil War*, 3:609–610.
8. Marvel, "The Battle of Saltville: Massacre or Myth?" 52.
9. Ibid., 51.
10. Roy Morris, Jr. *Sheridan: The Life and Wars of General Phil Sheridan* (New York, 1992), 208.
11. Urwin, *Custer Victorious*, 193.
12. Sherman, *Memoirs*, 623.
13. William R. Scaife, *The Campaign for Atlanta* (Atlanta, 1990), 99.
14. Sherman, *Memoirs*, 623.
15. Ibid., 622.
16. Ibid.
17. Scaife, *The Campaign for Atlanta*, 101.
18. Ibid., 99–100.
19. Sherman, *Memoirs*, 624.
20. Scaife, *The Campaign for Atlanta*, 100.
21. E. B. Long with Barbara Long, *The Civil War Day by Day*, (Garden City, 1971), 580.
22. *Official Records*, 43:II:308.

CHAPTER EIGHTEEN

The Time I Was Killed

5–7 October 1864

Military authorities in Indiana arrested a prominent Copperhead, Lambdin P. Milligan, on that fifth day of October for conspiring against the United States, giving aid and comfort to its enemies, and inciting others to insurrection.

In northern Alabama that day, the Confederate raiders under Forrest's personal command reached the rain-swollen Tennessee River at Florence. Buford's part of the force was already there, busily ferrying its wagons and artillery across the mile-wide river. High winds were stirring up choppy waves, however, which threatened to swamp the flatboats and skiffs the Rebels were using. Then came word that one of the Union infantry divisions sent up from Georgia by Sherman, Brigadier General J. D. Morgan's 2nd Division of the 14th Corps, was approaching from the east. Forrest sent one regiment to hold the Federals off while the boats were moved farther west. And for the rest of the day and all that night the difficult and dangerous work of ferrying the troops across the river continued. But there were still about 1,000 men on the north bank on the afternoon of the sixth. Leaving detachments behind to delay the Federals, Forrest ordered the rest to swim their horses across about seventy yards of water to a large, wooded island. From there they could continue ferrying while hidden from enemy view by the trees.

As the last boat prepared to leave the island, Forrest made the rounds of his picket posts and found four of his men who had been forgotten. "I thought I would catch some of you damned fools loafing back here in the cane as if nothing was going on," he said. "If you don't want to get left all winter on this island you had better come along with me; the last boat is going over right away." One of the four troopers remembered that "when we reached the boat we were all made to take our turn at the oars and poles, and do our share of the work in ferrying across the river. The general, evidently worried and tired out, was on the rampage and was showing considerable disregard of the third commandment. There happened to be standing in the bow of the boat a lieutenant who took no part whatever in the labor of propelling the craft, noticing which, Forrest said to him: 'Why don't you take hold of an oar or pole and help get this boat across?' The lieutenant responded that he was an officer, and did not think he was called on to do that kind of work as long as there were private soldiers sufficient to perform that duty. As the general was tugging away with a pole when the reply was made, he flew into a rage, and holding the pole in one hand, with the other he gave the unfortunate lieutenant a slap on the side of the face which sent him sprawling over the gunwale and into the river. He was rescued by catching hold of the pole held out to him, and was safely landed in the boat, when the irate general said to him: 'Now, damn you, get hold of the oars and go to work! If I knock you out of the boat again I'll let you drown.' Forrest's rough and ready discipline was effectual; the young officer made an excellent hand for the balance of the trip."[1]

In the Shenandoah Valley, Sheridan put his army on the march back to the north again. Or at least the infantry and the artillery marched. The cavalry lingered behind to seize all livestock, destroy all food and forage, and burn every mill, barn, and haystack across the thirty-mile-wide valley as it swept from Harrisonburg toward Strasburg. The Rebel troopers who followed them, incensed at this new Yankee outrage, had a new commander. Tom Rosser, who had been a close friend of Custer at West Point not so long before, had arrived with his Laurel Brigade, composed of regiments which had originally fought in the Valley under Turner Ashby and Stonewall Jackson. Rosser, already being heralded as the Savior of the Valley, was given temporary command of the wounded Fitzhugh Lee's division of cavalry. Under Rosser's direction the Confederate horsemen snapped at the Federals' heels and harassed their rearguard to the best of their ability.

In Indianapolis that day the military tribunal met to resume the trial of several Copperheads, including Harrison H. Dodd, Grand Commander of the Sons of Liberty in Indiana, Dr. William A. Bowles, the group's military commander for that state, Judge Joshua F. Bullitt, Grand Commander for Kentucky, James Barrett, Grand Commander for Missouri, the newly arrested Milligan, and several others. Dodd's lawyer had previously been granted a postponement in order to prepare his defense after his motion to dismiss the charges on the grounds that the military lacked jurisdiction had been denied.

Dodd was so influential in Indiana politics that, since he objected to being kept in jail, he had been allowed to occupy a room on the upper floor of the Indianapolis post office on his promise not to try to escape. The other defendants were held at a military prison, whose commandant might well have wished that they were being lodged at the post office as well, since Bowles' wife proved to be a tremendous pest. When she was not berating or insulting the commandant, she was trying to break her husband out. Once she had been found to be carrying a package full of shiny new bowie knives. On another occasion she had tried to smuggle $1,250 in cash into the prison, presumably for bribing guards. And a much-folded scrap of paper had been found in Bowles' cell which, along with an indecipherable signature and a number of hieroglyphics, said: "The revolvers have all been distributed. Our Society meets tonight here. Great excitement prevails over your arrest. Shall I distribute the balance of the revolvers and rifles to Davis and Granger? Some of our men here are not supplied as yet. I think you should supply them at once . . ."[2]

Excitement did indeed prevail. A crowd of hundreds of people milled around outside the building where the trial was to take place, kept at bay by soldiers, while shouting "that Bowles and Dodd and the rest must be freed or they would have vengeance."[3] Inside, the courtroom was also packed with friends of the defendants. Once the members of the military tribunal had entered and been seated, the Judge Advocate pressed five charges against the defendants: conspiracy against the government of the United States; aiding and abetting those in rebellion against the authority of the United States; inciting insurrection; disloyal practices; and violation of the laws of war. All of these charges were tied to the defendants' membership in the Order of American Knights and the Sons of Liberty, secret societies which had as their purpose "the overthrow of the Government; holding communication with the enemy; conspiring to seize munitions of war stored in the arsenals and to free the rebel prisoners in the North, and attempting to establish a Northwestern Confederacy."[4]

Dodd pleaded not guilty to it all, and the prosecution summoned its first witness. The defendants sat in horror and amazement to see that it was Felix G. Stidger, known to them as the Grand Secretary of the Kentucky Grand Council of the Sons of Liberty, but, it developed, known to the Union army as Corporal Stidger, a former clerk to the adjutant general of the 14th Corps. For two hours Stidger related how he had infiltrated the Copperhead organization and described much of its inner workings and past history, with special emphasis on a meeting held the previous June during which many of the defendants had proposed the murder of another Union spy. He was followed by a number of other witnesses, including a New York arms merchant who described how he had sold revolvers and ammunition to the group and shipped them under the guise of Sunday school books. Another told of the group's plans to kidnap Governor Oliver P. Morton of Indiana and to kill him if he resisted.

A recess was then taken until the next day. But when the court opened on 7 October the Judge Advocate announced that Dodd had escaped at 4 a.m. by sliding down a rope "furnished by his immediate friends."[5] It was found that a ball of heavy twine had been smuggled into his room not long after he had returned from the trial. He had then used the twine to draw up one end of a heavy rope, which he had tied to his bed before climbing down it and getting away.

His escape touched off even more excitement than had his arrest, coming as it did just four days before state elections in Indiana and some other Northern states. The War Democrats accused the Peace Democrats of arranging Dodd's escape. The Peace Democrats said it was all a plot by Governor Morton, a Republican, and Colonel Carrington, until recently the commander of the District of Indiana, to destroy the Democratic Party. Carrington, in turn, issued a statement to the *Indianapolis Journal* that claimed that Dodd's escape was an admission of guilt. "Innocent men do not do so," he said. "The act confesses the guilt." He appealed to the voters, saying, "The traitors intend to bring war to your homes. Meet them at the ballot box while Grant and Sherman meet them in the field."[6] Meanwhile, little effort was made to recapture Dodd, who met with Confederate secret agent Captain Thomas Hines and made his way to Canada.

Two Quakers owned a well-stocked little store in the tiny village of Sandy Spring, Maryland, just a few miles due north of Washington, D.C. One of these men lived in a house behind the store with his nephew and two store clerks, and just before midnight, 6–7 October, Lieutenant Walter Bowie and his small band of Rebels, recently joined by a new recruit, aroused these men and captured them. But while the Confederates were helping themselves to new boots and whatever else suited their fancies, one of the clerks slipped out of a window and spread the news of this raid, and as the Southerners rode off he fired at them. By dawn a posse of seventeen men from Sandy Spring was in pursuit of the raiders, while word was sent to alert the Union cavalry at Rockville to the southwest. At 8:30 a.m. the posse caught up with Bowie's men, who were sleeping in a pine grove three miles north of Rockville. In the confused gunfight that followed there were only two casualties: a horse that was shot in the eye, and Walter Bowie, who was shot in the face by a double-loaded shotgun. Bowie was left by his men at a nearby farmhouse, and his brother stayed to take care of him. Bowie died about noon, and the brother was captured, but the rest of the little band got away and somehow made it safely across the upper Potomac back to Mosby in Virginia.

Out in Missouri, Price's Confederate column, which had turned away from well-defended St. Louis to follow the Missouri River westward, approached the state capital, Jefferson City. Along the way the Rebels pillaged the countryside, filling their large train of wagons with food and plunder, while the flanks and rear of the column became, in the words of one disapproving Confederate officer, a "rabble of deadheads, stragglers and stolen negroes on stolen horses" which gave the army the appearance of a "Calmuck horde." Governor Reynolds also disapproved. "It would take a volume," he said, "to describe the acts of outrage; neither station, age, nor sex was any protection. Southern men and women were as little spared as Unionists; the elegant mansion of General Robert E. Lee's accomplished neice and the cabin of the negro were alike ransacked . . . the clothes of a poor man's infant were as attractive spoil as the merchant's silk and calico or the curtain taken from the rich man's parlor; ribbons and trumpery gee-gaws were stolen from milliners, and jeweled rings forced from the fingers of delicate maidens whose brothers were fighting in Georgia in Cockrell's Confederate Missouri brigade."[7]

On the seventh a fairly large Union force moved out of Lexington to meet these Rebels, but Fagan's Division drove the Federals back into the city's defenses, and Price's army occupied the hills overlooking the capital in the river valley below, fully expecting to storm the defenses the next day.

In Virginia, on the evening of the seventh day of October, three armed men walked into Emory & Henry College, which had been turned into a hospital. They ascended the stairs to the top floor and burst into the room where wounded Federals from Saltville were being kept. With candles held aloft the three men went from bed to bed searching for black soldiers. Two were found, and both were shot where they lay.

Even as Forrest's raiders escaped the jaws of the trap the Union commanders had hoped to close upon them and were ferried to the southern bank of the Tennessee River, General John Bell Hood was asking Richard Taylor, Forrest's boss, to send him on another raid into Tennessee. Meanwhile, when Sherman learned, on the morning of 7 October, that French's Confederate division had withdrawn from in front of Allatoona and that the location of Hood's entire army was unknown, he was unsure of what to make of it. Fearing that the Rebels might be doubling back for a surprise attack on Atlanta, he telegraphed a warning to Slocum, whose 20th Corps still held that city. Then when he learned that Hood had instead continued to the north, he complained: "I cannot guess his movements as I could those of Johnston, who was a sensible man and only did sensible things."[8]

He considered Corse's conduct sensible enough, however. That officer had reported by telegraph: "I am short a cheekbone and an ear, but am able to whip all hell yet."[9] That day Sherman published an order in which he commended the defense of Allatoona and held it up as an example "to illustrate the most important principle in war, that fortified posts should be defended to the last, regardless of the relative numbers of the party attacking and attacked . . . Commanders and garrisons of the posts along our railroad are hereby instructed that they must hold their posts to the last minute, sure that the time gained is valuable and necessary to their comrades at the front."[10]

In southeastern Virginia, General Robert E. Lee was not yet reconciled to the loss of Fort Harrison and the Exterior Line of Richmond's fortifications. He determined to try once again to break the Union hold on that line, and the plan he came up with was vintage Lee. The left, or south, flank of Butler's Army of the James, held by Weitzel's 18th Corps, was anchored on the James River, or near enough to it to make it assailable only from the front. But the Union infantry line stretched to the north only as far as the New Market Road. Beyond that, Kautz's small cavalry division stretched away to the Darbytown Road and on to the Charles City Road. But such a small force could not hope to hold such a long line against a sizable, determined attack. It was little more than a picket line, reinforced here and there by small reserves.

This, obviously, was the vulnerable portion of Butler's line. Therefore, Lee quietly withdrew Field's and Hoke's divisions from the defenses in front of Butler's infantry and replaced them with the local defense forces. Most of the veteran infantry was placed on the Darbytown Road, while Gary's brigade of cavalry, from the Department of Richmond, backed up by the small Florida Brigade from Field's infantry, was formed on the parallel Charles City Road farther north. These forces would attack down that road, break Kautz's thin line, and turn to the south to take in flank the Federals on the Darbytown Road while Field attacked them in front. With this part of the Union line demolished, Field's infantry would also wheel to its right and take Butler's Union infantry in flank and rear while Hoke attacked its front. If that Union flank collapsed, the entire line could be peeled away from the Exterior Line like peeling the skin from a tangerine.

Lee was uncharacteristically nervous in the early hours of 7 October. At 1:30 a.m. his aide, Colonel Charles Venable, came to Brigadier General E. Porter Alexander, artillery commander of the 1st Corps, with word that Lee was impatiently waiting for the latter to bring up his guns and was "mad enough to bite nails." Venable and Alexander tried to explain to the commander that they were sure he had told them the day before that he wanted the guns to move at 2 a.m., but Lee would have none of it. "One o'clock was the hour, Sir, at which I said I would start!" he exclaimed with what Alexander described as "a very severe emphasis." Then Lee asked if a guide had been found for the artillery. "No, general," Alexander answered, "as the subject was not mentioned I supposed no guide would be needed, and I would only have to follow you." The subject was argued back and forth for a while, tempers stretching politeness to the breaking point. "It was the one time in all the war," Alexander wrote, "when I saw him apparently harsh and cross."[11] Riding over to where Field's Division was preparing, he asked one of his staff officers if the troops were ready to attack. "None but the Texas brigade, General," the officer replied. "The Texas brigade is always ready," Lee remarked, half in pride for his Old Guard, half in irritation at the rest.[12]

The Federals knew that something was up. "Deserters from the enemy had anounced an attack as contemplated for Friday morning," a Union chaplain wrote, "and arrangements were made to receive it."[13] There was not, however, a whole lot that Kautz could do to strengthen his position. He had, he estimated, only 1,700 men to cover a line as long as that covered by the 18th Corps and the 10th Corps combined. This small force was spread out along the old Exterior Line entrenchments. But much work was necessary to modify these earthworks, which had been designed by the Confederates to defend against an attack from the east, to make them suitable for defense against an attack from the west. However, the limited number of shovels and picks were still being used by the infantry, farther south, who had been given priority. When Kautz had complained about this to Butler, "He replied that the cavalry had legs and could run away."[14] Even running away, however, might not be all that easy, for the Rebel engineers had laid out their line so that it overlooked low, swampy ground that would have impeded an advance. Now that swamp lay behind the Union defenders to impede a retreat.

One thing that Kautz could, and did, do was to send a small detail, led by Captain George F. Dern, to watch the Confederates and give warning of any attack. It "was near daylight," one of these Federals remembered, "when all of a sudden . . . [the enemy] camps were astir."[15] In the bivouac of Gary's Brigade, Colonel Alexander Haskell, commander of the 7th South Carolina Cavalry, was moving among his men with encouraging words: "Officers," he said, "I expect you to lead your men. Men, I hope you know your duty too well not to follow your officers."[16] The day before, that regiment had received brand new sabers and Haskell had ordered the men to sharpen them that night. That morning, Haskell led an advance party of 200 men forward along the Charles City Road, only to run into a spoiling attack launched by Union Colonel Samuel P. Spear, commander of Kautz's 2nd Brigade, which was manning the part of the Union line north of the Darbytown Road.

South of that road was Kautz's 1st Brigade, under Colonel Robert M. West. And each brigade was backed up by a battery of four 3-inch guns of the horse artillery. On the Darbytown Road front, stubborn Federal dismounted troopers in skirmish formation held up Field's advance for almost an hour. One Confederate participant called this "the hardest fight that we have Ever bin in Since the war." But slowly the power of the Confederate numbers began to overwhelm the thin Union line. "By the time we realized that we were to be attacked in force," Kautz wrote, "it was too late to get out of the pocket in which we had been placed by the commander of the Army of the James."[17]

Field had deployed G. T. Anderson's brigade on the right of the Darbytown Road and Bratton's on the left, with Gregg's Texans in support on the road. Anderson's attack was repulsed, but Bratton's men advanced through heavy timber and drove off the 400 or so Union troopers who had opposed them. Kautz said that his men, "unused to foot service . . . fell back in some confusion," and added that it was "impossible to rally them." One of his men said that they had "but one course open—flight." The Union formation disintegrated, and as Kautz put it, "Those who did not want to be captured had to go." The cavalrymen took recourse, as Butler had suggested, to their legs. "A few of them had chosen this arm of the service on account of its mobility," a Union infantryman noted, "and now, when danger threatened, they seemed to think no one was more entitled to its advantages than themselves."[18]

Just then, Gary's Rebel troopers, finally freed from their melee with Spear's attackers, charged into the flank and rear of the retreating Federals. Colonel Haskell himself "sent three of the vandels to their long home," as one Rebel horseman put it. As the Union artillery pulled out, the leading gun became mired in the swamp, blocking the way for all the others, and the gunners had to abandon all eight pieces to be captured by the Rebels. Kautz himself and a small party of Federals came upon a group of wagons being attacked by Haskell and some of his Confederate horsemen and "had a little private battle of our own at about 20 paces." Haskell shot two of Kautz's aides and was taking aim at the general himself when he in turn was shot by a Union trooper. "The ball entered my left eye," Haskell later wrote, "and came out behind the left ear. I believe I felt the sensation of death." A Federal cried out, "We have killed the General!" meaning Haskell. "As I fell heavily to the ground," the Rebel officer remembered, "I said to myself, with a sort of grim mental smile, 'Only a Colonel, Gentlemen, only a Colonel.'"[19]

The Union infantry of the 10th Corps, just south of Kautz's position, was alerted between 6 and 7 a.m. by the increasing noise of battle to the north of them that a serious attack was under way. David Birney, the 10th Corps commander, who was less than two weeks away from death by malaria, got up from his sick bed to meet this threat to his right. He shifted units from his left to man the northern part of Fort Harrison so that he could withdraw all three brigades of Terry's division from the main line and place them in an east-west line facing north. Colonel Francis B. Pond's 1st Brigade held the left, connecting with the main line in strong works that had previously been built to protect this flank, with an open field to its front. Abbott's 2nd Brigade held the center, and Plaisted's 3rd Brigade held the right, which was in a deep woods with defenses that consisted only of rude and hastily constructed rifle pits. All three brigades sent out skirmishers, and at about 10 a.m. the sound of their fire indicated that the Confederates were coming their way.

As a Northern reporter wrote, "The rebels . . . had discovered, as they supposed, the right of our infantry line, and the cavalry being stampeded, they now pressed on in what seemed to them the shortest route to pass our right and strike in our rear."[20] Reforming Field's division into a line three brigades wide facing south had taken time. While the infantry was thus engaged, Alexander put his artillery into action. The open nature of the terrain gave him, he said, "the only opportunity I ever had, in action, to use that beautiful manouevre in artillery drill of 'Fire advancing by half battery.' One half of a battery stands and fires, while the second half advances a short distance, when it also halts and opens fire . . . So they go, alternately, one half always firing and the other advancing." The Union artillery returned fire, and a Federal shell struck the muzzle of a Rebel gun, killing one gunner and wounding four others, not a hundred yards from where General Lee was sitting on his horse. "At them boys!" one of the wounded Confederates yelled, raising a shattered limb. "Let's give the Yankees one more shot before the surgeons get hold of my arm."[21]

As Field's Division finally began its advance against Birney's infantry, Lee's plan seemed to be working and, according to Alexander, he was "now in the pleasantest mood in the world." His men were in good spirits as well. "Just as the infantry rose for the charge," Alexander wrote, "we blew up one of the enemy's caissons, which raised a general hurrah along our line and I felt sure we were about to smash them." The Confederates "came tearing through the woods yelling like demons," one of Terry's Federals remembered. In fact, they came on so fast that most of the Union skirmishers did not have time to get out of their way, so "many lay flat on their faces and let the charging column pass over them." But then the main line of Terry's units, many men of which were armed with Spencer repeating rifles, opened fire, as Alexander wrote, "with a roar which told its own story of its deadly power."[22]

On the Union right, where the defenses were weakest, one Federal regiment, the 100th New York, broke and ran. Many of its members' enlistments had already expired and they were not willing to risk life and limb when they were so close to getting home alive. But the regiment was soon rallied and the "enemy was handsomely repulsed," as Plaisted put it, "leaving his dead within a few yards of my line." One of Perry's Floridians said, "We had gone as near as we could, and nothing remained for us to do but to fall back." Another Rebel, who was wounded and later captured, said that he and others "hugged the ground like lizards." One of Bratton's South Carolinians said, "It was the heaviest fire we ever was under. We got up within forty yards of the enemy and was ordered to halt, our line being cut down so fast it was thought advisable to halt and await reinforcements, but the support did not come up and we was compelled to fall back." "Hoke's division was to have supported us by engaging the enemy on our right," a Texan declared, "but they did such a poor job of it that the Yankees had abundant leisure and opportunity to concentrate their strength against us." Alexander said merely that "Hoke's line . . . never moved. I never knew why."[23]

A young soldier in a blood-streaked uniform came up to Lee to plead for reinforcements. "If you don't send some more men down there," he said, "our boys will get hurt sure." Lee asked him if he was wounded and was told that he was. "I'm shot through both arms, General, but I don't mind that, General! I want you to send some more men down there to help our boys."[24] But it was too late. Gregg's Texans, on the Confederate right, charged Pond's brigade, on the Union left, where the defenses were strongest. When the Federals opened fire with their Spencers, "the noise was like appalling peals of thunder," as a watching Union cavalryman observed. "The Texans swayed to the earth like cut grain."[25]

"A short time later," a regimental commander in Bratton's Brigade reported, "we were withdrawn, abandoning all the ground we had gained in the morning." Lee had finally reconciled himself to the loss of the Exterior Line. "I trust the importance of the repeating rifle . . . will be fully appreciated," one Federal officer wrote, "as I do not believe the same number of men armed with any other piece would have held the enemy in check for a moment." It was, as one South Carolinian described it, "another terrible fight." A wounded Texan said, "History will likely call it a reconnaissance in force, but to me and fifty or a hundred others of the Texas Brigade who lost their lives or were wounded, it was a desperate assault by a small force upon well-manned earthworks." Among the dead was General Gregg, shot through the neck. Four of his men braved the enemy fire to wrap his body in a blanket and carry it away. Bratton was severely wounded. And Colonel Haskell of the Rebel cavalry, who had been shot through the eye, was also carried off the field. He went through a long spell of what he called brain fever and had to almost learn to talk all over again, but he resumed command of his regiment four months later. He always referred to this day as "the time I was killed."[26]

In far-off South America, when the CSS *Florida* had sailed into Bahia, the Brazilian admiral in command of the port had granted her a stay of 48 hours for repairs. Her commander, Lieutenant C. M. Morris, had been instructed to anchor between the USS *Wachusett* and the Brazilian flagship. With the assurance that he had the protection of international law and the Brazilian government, Lieutenant Morris and several of his officers had left the ship and gone off to attend the opera. Half of the crew had been given shore leave as well. Collins, commander of the *Wachusett*, sent Morris a challenge, by way of the United States Consul in the port, to a fight outside the three-mile limit. Morris replied that he would be pleased to engage the *Wachusett* if they should meet on the open sea, but he declined to make an appointment to duel with the *Wachusett*, as the *Alabama* had with the *Kearsarge*.

With that, Collins made up his mind to attack the *Florida* in port regardless of the international complications. That ship's escape from Mobile had been made possible by another Union officer's too strict adherence to the niceties of international law, refusing to fire on her because she was flying a British flag. Collins, on the other hand, had already shown a disposition to place the exigencies of war ahead of the rights of neutrals. Two years before he had seized a British ship off an uninhabited island in the Bahamas.

Collins regarded the *Florida* as a pirate ship. Further, he knew that the Brazilian government, unlike the British and French, had not recognized the Confederacy as a belligerent. But despite this the Brazilian government had in the past allowed the CSS *Alabama* to violate Brazilian neutrality without protest when the Rebel ship transferred coal from a captured Union ship at the Brazilian island Fernando de Noronha. Further, the *Alabama* had sallied out of that port to seize two more Union ships and had actually towed one of them into that port.

So, after dark on the sixth of October, Collins sent a whaleboat to reconnoiter the *Florida*. When the boat returned he cut it loose, for the noise of hoisting it back on board might have alerted the Rebel ship. Then at 3 a.m. on the seventh, in the still of the night, the *Wachusett* slipped her cable and, under a full head of steam, rammed into the *Florida*. Collins had hoped to sink the raider without firing a shot and then to head straight out to sea. But the Rebels had heard him coming and began to turn, and his ship struck the Confederate only a glancing blow that only carried away her mizzen mast and main yard while cutting down her bulwarks on the starboard quarter. Thinking that the blow had indeed been mortal, Collins was backing out to let his victim sink when the Rebels opened small arms fire at his ship. The Federals responded in kind, and then, contrary to Collins' orders, his first officer fired two heavy guns into the *Florida*. The senior officer aboard the Confederate ship at the time was Lieutenant T. K. Porter. In response to a Federal demand, he boarded the *Wachusett* and surrendered his ship, protesting at the same time against this attack in a neutral port. Collins then had a hawser attached to the *Florida* so he could tow her.

The sound of firing had alerted the Brazilians, and the admiral sent an officer to check on the situation. Collins assured the officer that he would do "nothing more" to disturb the peace of the port.[27] So when the *Wachusett* started out to sea the Brazilians thought the two American ships were returning to their berths. When they finally realized that the Federal ship was towing the Confederate raider they opened fire from a distant fort and sent three ships to give chase, but the *Wachusett* soon outdistanced them, taking with her the Rebel ship, seven Confederate officers, and 58 men.

The next morning, 8 October, the British ship *Sea King* sailed from London. At the same time another ship, the *Laurel,* sailed from Liverpool full of guns, munitions, supplies, and sailors with which to turn the *Sea King* into another Rebel raider, to be known as the CSS *Shenandoah*.

---

1. Henry, *"First With the Most" Forrest*, 363.
2. Horan, *Confederate Agent*, 150.
3. Ibid.
4. Milton, *Abraham Lincoln and the Fifth Column*, 311–312.
5. Horan, *Confederate Agent*, 151.
6. Milton, *Abraham Lincoln and the Fifth Column*, 314.
7. Castel, *General Sterling Price*, 222–224.
8. Foote, *The Civil War*, 3:612–613.
9. Ibid., 612.
10. Sherman, *Memoirs*, 625.
11. Noah Andre Trudeau, "Darbytown Road Debacle," *America's Civil War*, May 1992, 32–33.
12. Douglas Southall Freeman, *R. E. Lee* (New York, 1935), vol. 3:508.
13. Trudeau, "Darbytown Road Debacle," 30.
14. Ibid., 32.
15. Ibid., 33.
16. Ibid., 30.
17. Ibid., 33.
18. Ibid.
19. Ibid., 34.
20. Ibid.
21. Ibid., 35.
22. Ibid.
23. Ibid., 35–36.
24. Freeman, *R. E. Lee*, 3:509.
25. Trudeau, "Darbytown Road Debacle," 36.
26. Ibid.
27. Clarence Edward Macartney, *Mr. Lincoln's Admirals* (New York, 1956), 250.

CHAPTER NINETEEN

Or Get
Whipped
Yourself

8–11 October 1864

On the eighth day of October, Judge Advocate General Joseph Holt, who was head of the Bureau of Military Justice, issued a public report on the Copperhead conspiracy and its ties to the Confederacy and to the Democratic party in the North. It was published in the newspapers just in time to influence the elections that some states held in October.

At Emory & Henry College in Virginia, where two wounded black soldiers had been murdered in their beds, Confederate surgeon James Murfree had obtained a guard to protect the rest of his patients. But, on the eighth, armed men appeared again and overwhelmed the guard. They stalked through the wards in broad daylight calling for three Union officers by name and announced that they intended to kill all three. Murfree managed to hide two of the Federals, but when he heard shots he rushed out to find that a man he later identified as a Confederate guerrilla Champ Ferguson had shot the third, a Union lieutenant, in the forehead.

Out in Missouri that day, Price's raiding Confederates were again heading west. The defenses and defenders of Jefferson City had appeared to be too strong to risk attacking them, and in his report Price claimed to have positive information that there were 15,000 Federals in the city. What was worse, from his standpoint, was that Rosecrans, the Union department commander, was sending Major General Alfred Pleasonton after him with 7,000 cavalrymen and, perhaps even worse, A. J. Smith and 8,000 veteran infantrymen, who had recently defeated Forrest down in Mississippi. Price also learned that Major General Samuel R. Curtis, commander of the Federals' Department of Kansas, was busily accumulating troops to meet him when he reached the Missouri-Kansas border. Therefore, he decided to hurry on to the west to strike Curtis before he was ready. Along the way he would pass through friendly territory, where he hoped to pick up many recruits and enough weapons to arm his unarmed men. As Price departed, Pleasonton arrived at Jefferson City, to take charge of its 5,000 actual defenders, and he sent Brigadier General John B. Sanborn to follow the Rebels with 4,100 Union cavalrymen.

On the ninth the Confederates reached Boonville, forty miles upriver from Jefferson City. There they were welcomed by the pro-Southern citizenry, and many of the young men joined Price's ranks. That same day, Bloody Bill Anderson's guerrillas raided the town of Otterville on the Missouri Pacific Railroad. The Union sergeant whom Anderson had captured at Centralia and set aside for some unnamed special treatment had been carried about ever since by Anderson's band, which had dispersed once when some Federals got after it with artillery and then had reassembled later. But three days before, while the guerrillas had been busy fording a river, Sergeant Goodwin had calmly walked away without being noticed.

In Georgia on the ninth, Sherman finally reached Allatoona. There he found that Corse's report about losing a cheekbone and an ear had been a slight exaggeration. In fact, he found that officer with only a small bandage which covered nothing worse than a scratch where he had been grazed by a bullet. "Corse," Sherman laughed, "they came damned near missing you, didn't they?"[1]

Union scouts reported that day that Hood's army was heading west, toward Rome, Georgia. Sherman telegraphed Grant that day: "It will be a physical impossibility to protect the roads, now that Hood, Forrest, Wheeler, and the whole batch of devils, are turned loose without home or habitation. I think Hood's movements indicate a diversion to the end of the Selma and Talladega Railroad, at Blue Mountain, about sixty miles southwest of Rome, from which he will threaten Kingston, Bridgeport, and Decatur, Ala. I propose that we break up the railroad from Chattanooga, and that we strike out with our wagons for Milledgeville, Millen, and Savannah. Until we can repopulate Georgia, it is useless to occupy it, but the utter destruction of its roads, houses, and people will cripple their military resources. By attempting to hold the roads, we will lose 1,000 men monthly, and will gain no result. I can make the march, and make Georgia howl. We have over 8,000 cattle and 3,000,000 of bread, but no corn; but we can forage in the interior of the State."[2]

In the Shenandoah Valley, Early's Confederates continued to follow Sheridan's Federals as they slowly withdrew to the north, burning everything of value as they went. "When this is completed," Sheridan had reported to Grant, "the Valley, from Winchester up to Staunton, ninety-two miles, will have but little in it for man or beast."[3] "The burning parties distributed across the Shenandoah swept it with the fire of desolation," a Rebel captain wrote. "Every home was visited, the proud mansion and the humble cottage feeling alike the blasting and savage hand of war."[4] Merritt's division alone reported that in ten days it destroyed 630 barns, 47 flour mills, 4 saw mills, 1 woolen mill, 3 iron furnaces, 2 tanneries, 1 railroad depot, 1 locomotive, 3 boxcars, 4,000 tons of hay, straw and fodder, half a million bushels of wheat and oats, 515 acres of corn and 560 barrels of flour, and drove off 3,300 head of livestock. It was against orders to burn houses, but many were destroyed anyway.

Not only did this reduce the ability of the Shenandoah Valley to supply Early's and Lee's armies but it also affected the morale of the Confederate soldiers and civilians. For one thing, Richmond received an urgent appeal that the men of the region be exempted from conscription. The presiding justice of Rockingham County wrote, "Many who are liable are without a pound of meat, bread, or anything to live on, to say nothing of firewood. It will require the daily and hourly exertions of the poor and those who have been burnt out to procure a scanty subsistence to sustain life during the winter. When the soldier now in the army learns that his neighbor, on whom his family have leaned for support during all this war, is himself called into service, and his family (his wife and little children at home) are sure to suffer, *he will become uneasy in his place,* and will weigh the duty he owns his family; and what the promptings of nature would be is not difficult to determine . . . We have no slave labor, and this call taxes our principal working force. What is to become of a corn crop? What is to become of any spring crop?"[5]

All this destruction infuriated the soldiers of Early's army, who considered such things as outside the customs of civilized warfare. "I try to restrain my bitterness at the recollection of the dreadful scenes I witnessed," wrote Major Henry Kyd Douglas, a Confederate staff officer, after the war. "I rode down the Valley with the advance after Sheridan's retreating cavalry beneath great columns of smoke which almost shut out the sun by day, and in the red glare of bonfires, which, all across that Valley, poured out flames and sparks heavenward and crackled mockingly in the night air; and I saw mothers and maidens tearing their hair and shrieking to Heaven in their fright and despair, and little children, voiceless and tearless in their pitiable terror. I saw a beautiful girl, the daughter of a clergyman, standing in the front door of her home while its stable and outbuildings were burning, tearing the yellow tresses from her head, taking up and repeating the oaths of passing skirmishers and shrieking with wild laughter, for the horrors of the night had driven her mad."[6]

"The people here are getting sick of the war," Sheridan told Grant, "heretofore they have had no reason to complain, because they have been living in great abundance." The chaplain of the 121st Ohio wrote home that "war is terrible in its effects, but the Rebels should have anticipated this before they ventured to test its scathing scourges." One Confederate found among the ruins a plank upon which some Federal had written, "Remember Chambersburg."[7]

The Rebels were furious, but so were the Yankees, or at least the troopers of Merritt's and Custer's cavalry divisions were. Throughout the sixth, seventh, and eighth of October they had been stung by the attacks of the vengeance-seeking Southerners and yet they had been forbidden by Torbert's orders to counterattack. Their job was the work of destruction. Custer finally got so fed up with the situation that on the eighth he took it upon himself to turn back and threaten to get between Rosser's pursuing division and the Confederate infantry, which had fallen behind and was 25 miles back. Rosser saw what his old West Point buddy, Custer, was up to and managed to block his move and retire to the south side of a stream called Tom's Brook. His men, seeing the countless campfires of the Union army north of them, suggested that they continue to withdraw until their infantry could catch up. But Rosser was the new Savior of the Valley. He would not retreat.

Sheridan heard the firing that afternoon, and he rode back to find out what it was all about. When Custer and Merritt told him, he went looking for Torbert. Custer had told him that Rosser had captured one of his wagons, loaded with runaway slaves, and a traveling blacksmith's forge from one of his batteries. Sheridan, however, seems to have gotten the impression that an entire battery and a wagon train had been captured. That evening, riding through a thunderstorm, he found his chief of cavalry ensconced in a commandeered mansion where he and his staff had just finished a fine turkey dinner. "Well, I'll be damned!" he roared as he burst into the room. "If you ain't sitting here stuffing yourselves, general, staff, and all, while the Rebels are riding into our camp! Having a party, while Rosser is carrying off your guns! Got on your nice clothes and clean shirts! Torbert, mount quicker than hell will scorch a feather!" Back at Sheridan's headquarters, a mere tent not a mansion, there was more of the same. The staff officers had sense enough to keep their distance, but one heard Sheridan's closing remark. "I want you to go out there in the morning and whip that Rebel cavalry or get whipped yourself."[8]

At first light on 9 October Merritt's 1st Division was heading south on the Valley Turnpike and Custer's 3rd Division on the Back Road farther west. Merritt encountered Lomax's Division at Woodstock and deployed his three brigades side by side, but he seemed to be content to await developments on the Back Road. Custer's column easily drove in Rosser's pickets and found his main force holding the high ground south of Tom's Brook. There was a line of dismounted Rebel troopers at the base of the ridge protected by stone walls and piles of fence rails and a second, stronger, line was posted behind similar defenses near the top. On the crest was a mounted reserve and a battery of six guns. It was, overall, a strong position, and Rosser had 3,500 men in his three brigades, compared to 2,500 in Custer's two.

The Confederate artillery opened a plunging fire on the Federals, and Custer placed his four cannon on a pair of knolls on each side of the Back Road to return this fire, but their ammunition turned out to be defective. One Rebel shell exploded six feet in front of a Union gun, and fragments from the explosion killed or wounded every member of its crew and broke a spoke on one of its wheels. But the Federal artillery returned the favor, disabling one of the Southern guns.

Meanwhile, Custer deployed three regiments of his 1st Brigade in a heavy, mounted skirmish line, supported by the other two regiments. His 2nd Brigade was massed in reserve. Then the flamboyant young general in his bright red tie and his flowing yellow hair galloped out into the open ground between his division and Rosser's Confederates, where he could easily be seen by every man of both sides. He swept his large hat from his head down to his knee in a dramatic gesture, bowed in the saddle, and shouted, "Let's have a fair fight, boys! No malice!"[9]

Rosser pointed to his old West Point friend and turned to his staff. "You see that officer down there? That's General Custer, the Yanks are so proud of, and I intend to give him the best whipping today that he ever got. See if I don't."[10]

But while he was apparently grandstanding, Custer was also getting a closer look at Rosser's position. And he quickly spotted its weakness: neither obstacles nor men covered its left flank. While his skirmishers and artillery kept the Rebels busy, he sent two regiments from his 2nd Brigade and one from his 1st to circle around and get on that exposed flank. With the rest of his command he would charge across Tom's Brook to pin the Confederates in place until the three detached regiments could strike. Just as he had his men in position he saw more Federals coming up on his left. Spotting the red ties that the men had adopted in imitation of his own, he told his officers, "There is my old Michigan Brigade on the flank." Then, pointing toward the Confederate position with his sword, he yelled, "Now go for it!"[11] The bugles blared, the band struck up "Yankee Doodle," and eight regiments of mounted men moved forward, first at a walk, then a trot, and then at the gallop, sabers waving. Just as Rosser's Confederates were taking aim at this huge target, the sound of gunfire and cheering broke out behind them and the three flanking regiments came charging down on their undefended left, threatening to cut them off from their own horses. The Rebels broke and ran for their mounts, then rode for their lives, and the jubilant Federals chased them for two miles.

When Lomax heard the firing receding southward over on the Back Road he knew that Rosser was retreating and he had to follow suit to avoid being outflanked. However, this forced him to give up his defensive position south of Tom's Brook and brought his two brigades into open country around the town of Woodstock. But Lomax's men had no sabers or pistols, only muzzleloading rifles. "The consequence is," as Early explained to Lee, "that they cannot fight on horseback, and in this open country cannot successfully fight on foot against large bodies of cavalry; besides, the command is and has been demoralized all the time. It would be better if they could all be put into the infantry; but if that were tried I am afraid they would all run off."[12]

Lowell's Reserve Brigade charged Jackson's Brigade on Lomax's right while Devin's 2nd Brigade attacked Johnson's. Lomax's entire front crumbled and streaked for the rear. "The success of the day," Merritt wrote, "was now merely a question of the endurance of horseflesh." And for twenty miles his troopers chased Lomax's fleeing Confederates. "Each time our troopers came in view," Merritt said, "they would rush on the discomfited rebels with their sabers, and send them howling in every direction." The pursuit only ended when the Rebel cavalry reached the protection of Early's infantry at Rude's Hill, near New Market. One of these foot soldiers said that Lomax's men came galloping up the turnpike, "some without arms, some without hats, some without jackets, and some without sensibility."[13] Along the way, Merritt captured 42 wagons, 3 ambulances, 4 cannon, 4 caissons, 5 forges, 25 sets of harness, 68 horses and mules, 52 prisoners, a wagonload of Enfield rifles, and the battleflag of the 34th Virginia Cavalry Battalion.

Over on the Back Road, however, Rosser was able to rally a brigade and his artillery along a belt of trees and their fire soon stopped Custer's disorganized pursuers. Rosser then led a countercharge with another brigade that forced the Federals to retreat for half a mile. There the Union gunners unlimbered their pieces and checked this Rebel counterattack. Rosser then deployed his men and guns in defensive positions in the woods, while Custer reorganized his men for another attack. While he was busy at this one of Torbert's staff officers arrived to inform him that Merrit had routed Lomax's Division, capturing five guns. "All right," Custer shot back, "hold on a minute and I'll show you six."[14] He called to his bugler to sound the charge, and his line leapt forward. Rosser made the mistake of standing on the defensive to receive it instead of countercharging.

"Before this irresistible advance," Custer wrote, "the enemy found it impossible to stand. Once more he was compelled to trust his safety to the fleetness of his steed rather than the metal of his saber. His retreat soon became a demoralized rout. Vainly did the most gallant of this affrighted herd endeavor to rally a few supports around their standards and stay the advance of their eager and exultant pursuers, who, in one overwhelming current, were bearing down everything before them. Never since the opening of the war had there been witnessed such a complete and decisive overthrow of the enemy's cavalry."[15]

Up the Valley they raced, the Rebels fleeing for their lives and the Federals hot on their heels, bowling over anybody who tried to stem their pursuit. The color bearer of the 1st Vermont Cavalry was seen to lower his flag staff like a lance and skewer one Confederate who did not run fast enough. More conventional weapons dispatched many another. Among the victorious Union troopers, that day would always be remembered as the Woodstock Races. And when it was over, Custer had his six guns, along with many caissons, wagons, ambulances, and prisoners. One of his captures turned out to be Rosser's headquarters wagon, and inside a trunk he found his old friend's dress coat and hat. That night he wrote Rosser a note asking him to have his tailor cut his next coat a little shorter, as this one did not quite fit him right. The next day he proudly wrote to his wife that "Genl. Torbert has sent me a note beginning 'God bless you.'"[16] Soon, every officer and enlisted man in the 3rd Division was wearing a bright red tie.

A veteran colonel in the Laurel Brigade, who had never cared much for Rosser anyway, blamed the Confederate defeat on the Savior of the Valley: "Rosser's head seemed to be completely turned by our success, and in consequence of his rashness, and ignorance of their numbers, we suffered the greatest disaster that had ever befallen our command, and utterly destroyed the confidence of the officers of my brigade in his judgement—they knew that he would fight and was full of it, but he did not know when to stop, or when to retire." However, the acerbic tongue of Jubal Early, who never trusted his cavalry anyway, had the final word. "I say, Rosser, your brigade had better take the grape leaf for a badge," he quipped that night. "The laurel is a running vine."[17]

But Early was more worried about Sheridan's next move than he was about the defeat of his cavalry. As he wrote to Lee that day, "the question now is, what he intends doing." He figured that Sheridan had three options: to cross the Blue Ridge and advance against the Virginia Central Railroad and eventually Richmond; to send some of his troops to Petersburg; or to stay in the lower Valley to protect the Baltimore & Ohio and to prevent Early from again conducting raids into Maryland and Pennsylvania. He thought that if his opponent tried to operate on the east side of the Blue Ridge that he could defeat him. "But what shall I do if he sends re-enforcements to Grant or remains in the lower Valley?" It would be hard for Early to confront the Federal if he chose the latter option because he could not draw supplies from the part of the Valley that Sheridan had just devastated. "I will have to rely on Augusta for my supplies, and they are not abundant there."[18]

The next day, the tenth, Sheridan's army renewed its withdrawal northward down the Valley. Emory's 19th Corps and Crook's 8th bivouacked that night north of Cedar Creek, between that stream and Middletown. But Wright's 6th Corps continued on through Middletown and turned eastward on the road to Front Royal, beginning its return to the Army of the Potomac. Custer's and Merritt's cavalry divisions went into camp that night at Fisher's Hill. Powell's 2nd Cavalry Division was holding Front Royal, and Sheridan paid it a visit that day. He went there to issue instructions for that division to move through the Blue Ridge at Chester Gap for a small-scale version of the raid to Gordonsville and Charlottesville that Grant had hoped he could make with his entire army.

Out beyond the Appalachians, Sherman had not given up hope that his various forces in the area could corner Nathan Bedford Forrest, and he told Thomas to "give such orders as will dispose of Forrest and break his railroad from Tuscumbia back toward Corinth."[19] One of the Union forces counted on to help accomplish this consisted of 1,300 men and a battery of four guns belonging to Major General Cadwallader C. Washburn's District of West Tennessee, who were steaming up the Tennessee River on four transport boats escorted by two navy gunboats. They were commanded by Colonel George B. Hoge, who had orders from Washburn to "land at Eastport, move rapidly out on the line of railroad near Iuka, and break up the road and destroy bridges . . . After doing this hold Eastport." Washburn added that he should "approach Eastport with care so as not to be ambuscaded."[20]

At 1:30 p.m. on the tenth the Union transports tied up to the bank at Eastport and ran out their stage planks while the two gunboats anchored in midstream to cover the landing of the troops. But when about two thirds of the Federals were ashore two brigades of Forrest's men and a pair of guns opened a vigorous, accurate, and unexpected fire upon them. They were "ambuscaded" after all. The result was mass confusion among the Union troops. Shells went plunging through the gunboats and set fire to two of the transports, even as many of the soldiers tried to scramble back on board to avoid the rifle fire. Then, according to Colonel Hoge's report, the naval commander declared that "we must get the transports away at once, be going with them." Hoge disagreed, but "in spite of all I could do, the boats backed out, parting their lines, leaving about two-thirds of the command on shore." The naval commander, however, said that the troops on shore "broke and fled pell-mell down the river. The battery of four guns was abandoned." And, according to him, "the gunboats were ready to assist in any movement that the colonel commanding might have suggested for the recovery" of the guns.[21] At any rate, most of the troops worked their way downstream through the briers along the river's edge until they were out of range of the Rebel guns, where they were picked up by one of the transports, which twice put in to the bank to collect them. But that ended yet another attempt to "dispose" of Bedford Forrest.

Over in Georgia that day, Sherman sent a telegram to Grant: "Hood is now crossing Coosa River, twelve miles below Rome, bound west. If he passes over to the Mobile and Ohio road, had I not better execute the plan of my letter sent by Colonel Porter, and leave General Thomas with the troops now in Tennessee, to defend the State? He will have an ample force when the reinforcements ordered reach Nashville." Grant replied the next day, the eleventh: "Does it not look as if Hood was going to attempt the invasion of Middle Tennessee, using the Mobile and Ohio and Memphis and Charleston roads to supply his base on the Tennessee River, about Florence or Decatur? If he does this, he ought to be met and prevented from getting north of the Tennessee River. If you were to cut loose, I do not believe you would meet Hood's army, but would be bushwacked by all the old men and little boys, and such railroad guards as are still left at home. Hood would probably strike for Nashville, thinking that by going north he could inflict greater damage upon us than we could upon the rebels by going south. If there is any way of getting at Hood's army, I would prefer that, but I must trust to your own judgment. I find I shall not be able to send a force from here to act with you on Savannah. Your movements, therefore, will be [i]ndependent of mine; at least until the fall of Richmond takes place. I am afraid Thomas, with such lines of road as he has to protect, could not prevent Hood from going north. With Wilson turned loose, with all your cavalry, you will find the rebels put much more on the defensive than heretofore."[22]

Sherman reached Kingston that day, where he had telegraphic communication in several directions. "From General Corse, at Rome, I learned that Hood's army had disappeared," Sherman later wrote, "but in what direction he was still in doubt; and I was so strongly convinced of the wisdom of my proposition to change the whole tactics of the campaign, to leave Hood to General Thomas, and to march across Georgia for Savannah or Charleston, that I again telegraphed to General Grant: 'We cannot now remain on the defensive. With twenty-five thousand infantry and the bold cavalry he has, Hood can constantly break my road. I would infinitely prefer to make a wreck of the road and of the country from Chattanooga to Atlanta, including the latter city; send back all my wounded and unserviceable men, and with my effective army move through Georgia, smashing things to the sea. Hood may turn into Tennessee and Kentucky, but I believe he will be forced to follow me. Instead of my guessing what he means to do, he will have to guess at my plans. The difference in war would be fully twenty-five per cent. I can make Savannah, Charleston, or the mouth of the Chattahoochee (Appalachicola). Answer quick, as I know we will not have the telegraph long.'"[23]

Grant did answer quickly. That night he wired back, "If you are satisfied the trip to the sea-coast can be made, holding the line of the Tennessee River firmly, you may make it, destroying all the railroad south of Dalton or Chattanooga, as you think best."[24] But he was not quite quick enough. "General Sherman informed me long after the war," Horace Porter wrote, "that he did not receive this reply, which was accounted for, no doubt, by the fact that his telegraph-wires were cut at that time."[25] Meanwhile, Grant ordered ships to be loaded with supplies, ready to sail for Ossabaw Sound below the mouth of the Savannah River as soon as word was received that Sherman had started across Georgia.

Grant's personal chief of staff, Brigadier General John A. Rawlins, had now returned from a medical leave, although he was not cured of the tuberculosis that would eventually kill him. Rawlins was seriously opposed to Sherman's plan to march across Georgia and never missed an occasion to speak against it. Horace Porter, having been the one sent to confer with Sherman, became the chief spokesman in favor of it. "And many evenings were occupied in discussing the pros and cons of the contemplated movement," Porter wrote. "The staff had in fact resolved itself into an animated debating society. The general-in-chief would sit quietly by, listening to the arguments, and sometimes showed himself greatly amused by the vehemence of the debaters."[26]

One evening it was suggested that Grant should instruct Sherman to hold a council of war on the subject, whereby Sherman's principal subordinates would vote on what to do. But Grant said, "No; I will not direct any one to do what I would not do myself under similar circumstances. I never held what might be called formal councils of war, and I do not believe in them. They create a divided responsibility, and at times prevent that unity of action so necessary in the field . . . There is too much truth to the old adage, 'Councils of war do not fight.'"[27]

"One night the discussion waxed particularly warm," Porter said, "and was kept up for some time after the general had gone to bed. About one o'clock he poked his head out of his tent and interrupted Rawlins in the midst of an eloquent passage by crying out: 'Oh, do go to bed, all of you! You're keeping the whole camp awake.'"[28]

Also on the eleventh, Powell's 2nd Cavalry Division of the Department of West Virginia departed Front Royal to begin its raid east of the Blue Ridge. And that morning Sheridan received further instructions from Halleck. "General Grant directs me to say," the chief of staff wrote, "that you had better, at all events, retain the Nineteenth Corps, and that the time of sending the Sixth Corps and a division of cavalry must be left to your judgment."[29] Supplies, Halleck said, would continue to be sent by way of Martinsburg, and added that repair work on the Manassas Gap Railroad would continue unless Sheridan decided against its use as a future supply line.

Sheridan informed Halleck that night that he would "hold on to the Sixth Corps for a day or two, to watch the developments."[30] He added that work on the railroad should be stopped and that when the 6th Corps did move it would march on its own feet. And he ordered Major General Christopher C. Augur, commander of the Department of Washington, to withdraw his men, who had been guarding the railroad workers, to Manassas Junction or Bull Run. "He could not complete the railroad to Front Royal without additional force from me," he later explained to Halleck, "and to give him that force to do the work and transport

[Wright's] troops by railroad to Alexandria would require more time than to march across, via Ashby's Gap."[31]

He also informed the chief of staff of the raid that Powell was setting off on, saying that, in bowling terms, it "may make a ten-strike," and adding that "at all events, it will spread consternation, and may force everything out of the Valley and onto the railroad. If I do not have to send a division of cavalry to Petersburg, I probably can keep the enemy running from the Valley to the railroad and from the railroad to the Valley."[32]

Merritt's and Custer's divisions crossed to the north side of Cedar Creek that day and camped alongside the 8th and 19th corps, while the 6th Corps remained at Front Royal. The first heavy frost of the autumn whitened the ground that morning. Soldiers from Ohio voted that day, and Sheridan and Crook, both being from that state, cast their ballots at the polls of the 36th Ohio in Colonel Rutherford B. Hayes' division of the 8th Corps. Hayes himself was in the race for congressman from Ohio, but he refused to go home and campaign, saying, "Any officer fit for duty who at this crisis would abandon his post to electioneer for a seat in Congress, ought to be scalped."[33]

County and state elections took place in Ohio, Indiana, and Pennsylvania, and the results ran strongly in favor of the Republicans. This augured well for the possibility of Lincoln's reelection the following month. In Indiana, Governor Morton was reelected and the Republicans gained four Congressional seats. In Pennsylvania they gained three seats, breaking what had been an even division of its delegation. They also gained three seats in Ohio, leaving the Democrats with only two congressmen to their seventeen. Hayes was elected, beginning his rapid rise to the Presidency.

Out in Missouri that day, Price was joined by Bloody Bill Anderson and his bushwhackers, still riding with human scalps dangling from their bridles. Price made them get rid of the scalps, but welcomed their help and accepted a brace of silver-mounted pistols from Anderson. Then he dictated an order for "Captain" Anderson to return to the north side of the Missouri River and "permanently destroy" the North Missouri Railroad.[34] He also sent orders for "Colonel" Quantrill to wreck the Hannibal & St. Joseph Railroad, not realizing that Quantrill no longer commanded more than six or seven men. Anyway, the order was never received.

Missouri was on Grant's mind that day. He was not happy with the pursuit of Price's raiders and placed the blame on Rosecrans, whom he had never cared for. "On reflection," he wired Secretary of War Stanton that day, "I do not know but that a proper regard for the present and future interests of the service demands the removal of Rosecrans and the appointment of a subordinate general in his place. In conversation I said that I doubted the propriety of making any change during present complications, but present movements of Hood's army, especially if he should go on to the Mississippi River, may make it necessary to have a commander in Missouri who will cooperate. The best general now in Missouri to take that command would be General J. J. Reynolds, if he is there; if not, then Mower would come next. Probably more activity could be insured by sending Sheridan to Missouri, place Meade where Sheridan is, and put Hancock in command of the Army of the Potomac. I send this more to get your views before anything positive is done than to ask the change at once. It ought to be made, however, as soon as what is thought best can be agreed upon."[35]

Far to the northeast, in the town of Philipsburg in Lower Canada (now the province of Quebec), a pair of handsome, well-dressed young men arrived at the Lafayette Hotel that day. They had breakfast and then asked the clerk whether the newspaper from St. Albans, Vermont, had arrived. It had not. Several times that afternoon the same two men returned to ask the clerk the same question, and finally the taller of the two asked the clerk how far it was from Philipsburg to St. Albans. He was told that it was fifteen miles. Also throughout the day several more well-dressed young men arrived at the hotel. They were all well-mannered and soft-spoken, but no one thought very much about the coincidence. After dinner that evening, one by one, they all gathered in one room, and the tall man spread a map on the floor.

He was Confederate lieutenant Bennett H. Young of the 8th Kentucky Cavalry. He had been captured in the summer of 1863 on Morgan's raid north of the Ohio but had escaped from Camp Douglas in Chicago and had made his way to Canada before the end of the year. There he had convinced Confederate commissioner Clement C. Clay that it would be possible to launch raids into the United States from Canada with the handful of Rebel soldiers who had, like him, made their way there after escaping from various prisoner-of-war camps. Young had then sailed to Richmond, where he had convinced the officials of the Confederate government to support such activities, and then had returned to Canada.

He had been among the Confederate agents who had met the Copperhead leaders in Chicago in August and had then gone to Ohio to see if the prisoners of war at Camp Chase might be freed by a raid from Canada. But he had not been able to round up enough men of the right quality for the venture, so he and Clay had selected the town of St. Albans for their first raid. They would rob the town's three banks and those of the smaller nearby villages of Sheldon and Swanton and then return to the safety of neutral British North America. Their objective was to divert Northern forces from the main war fronts by forcing the Federal government to station military units all over the North to protect against more such raids. Every Yankee soldier guarding a bank or a town or a bridge in New England or New York or anywhere along the border was one less available to fight in Virginia or Georgia, Missouri or Mississippi.

After they had studied the map and gone over their plans, Lieutenant Young opened his carpetbag and showed his men forty small bottles of Greek fire, a liquid mixture of phosphorous and other ingredients designed to ignite on contact with the air. In pairs, they would all make their way to St. Albans by various routes and means of transportation and reconvene there at the American House hotel on the evening of the seventeenth. Then he would distribute these vials among them. "After we visit the banks," he said, "we'll burn the town."[36]

1. Foote, *The Civil War*, 3:612.
2. *Official Records*, 39:III:162.
3. Ibid., 43:II:308.
4. Thomas A. Lewis, *The Guns of Cedar Creek* (New York, 1988), 97.
5. Pond, *The Shenandoah Valley in 1864*, 200.
6. Douglas, *I Rode With Stonewall*, 302.
7. Wert, *From Winchester to Cedar Creek*, 158–159.
8. Lewis, *The Guns of Cedar Creek*, 99.
9. Urwin, *Custer Victorious*, 199.
10. Lewis, *The Guns of Cedar Creek*, 101.
11. Urwin, *Custer Victorious*, 199.
12. *Official Records*, 43:I:559.
13. Wert, *From Winchester to Cedar Creek*, 164.
14. Lewis, *The Guns of Cedar Creek*, 103.
15. *Official Records*, 43:I:521.
16. Urwin, *Custer Victorious*, 202.
17. Lewis, *The Guns of Cedar Creek*, 104.
18. *Official Records*, 43:I:559.
19. Ibid., 39:III:190.

20. Henry, *"First With the Most" Forrest*, 364.
21. Ibid.
22. Grant, *Memoirs*, 2:595–596.
23. Sherman, *Memoirs*, 628–629.
24. Grant, *Memoirs*, 2:597.
25. Porter, *Campaigning With Grant*, 318.
26. Ibid., 314–315.
27. Ibid., 316.
28. Ibid., 315.
29. *Official Records*, 43:II:327.
30. Ibid., 43:II:340.
31. Ibid., 43:II:346.
32. Ibid., 43:II:340.
33. Grant, *Memoirs*, 2:341.
34. Castel, *William Clarke Quantrill*, 196.
35. *Official Records*, 41:III:773.
36. Horan, *Confederate Agent*, 168.

CHAPTER TWENTY

Be Ready to Move

12–18 October 1864

On 12 October 1864 Roger B. Taney, Chief Justice of the United States Supreme Court, died at the age of 87. He had been born only eight months after the country's declaration of independence, and he had been the chief justice since Andrew Jackson had appointed him in 1836. It was he who had delivered the majority opinion in the key Dred Scott case of 1857, which had declared that Congress had no right to prohibit slavery in the territories.

That same day, Rear Admiral David Dixon Porter assumed command of the North Atlantic Blockading Squadron, which was the largest, most important command in the United States Navy, including, as it did, all the ships in Chesapeake Bay, the James River, and down the east coast. What is more, there was another big job in the works for this squadron, something more interesting than maintaining the blockade and running errands for the army up and down the James River.

Back in August, Porter had been in Washington on navy business when his brother-in-law, Assistant Secretary of the Navy Gustavus Fox, had invited him to participate in a meeting with Navy Secretary Gideon Welles at the home of then-Postmaster General Montgomery Blair. There they had gone over the navy's plans for a joint operation to close the port of Wilmington, North Carolina, which it had long wanted to undertake but had never been able to get the army's cooperation for. However, General Grant had taken an interest in the project on the condition that a more aggressive naval commander could be found than Admiral Samuel P. Lee, who had then been the commander of the North Atlantic Blockading Squadron, which had naval jurisdiction over the Wilmington area and would have to provide the ships for any such expedition. Welles had originally intended to appoint Farragut to this command, but the hero of Mobile Bay's poor health had precluded the appointment, and so it was offered to his foster brother, Porter, instead. Porter had done a good job as commander of the gunboats on the Mississippi and its tributaries, where he had worked with Grant during the Vicksburg campaign the year before, and Grant considered him an acceptable commander for the move against Wilmington. The operation had originally been scheduled for early October, but Grant's double offensive against Richmond and Petersburg in late September had forced its postponement.

Lee was writing a long, fatherly letter to Early that day, saying, among other things, that if Sheridan detached part of his troops to reinforce Grant "you had better move against him and endeavor to crush him . . ." And he reminded the commander of the Army of the Valley that "I have weakened myself very much to strengthen you. It was done with the expectation of enabling you to gain such success that you could return the troops if not rejoin me yourself." He still thought this was possible, saying, "With your united force it can be accomplished," and adding, "I do not think Sheridan's infantry or cavalry numerically as large as you suppose; but either is sufficiently so not to be despised and great circumspection must be used in your operations."[1]

Meanwhile, Secretary of War Stanton was not yet convinced that the Manassas Gap Railroad should not be opened. However, since Mosby's men continued to attack the trains and the working parties and then blend in with the civilian population, Stanton issued orders through Halleck that day for every house within five miles of the tracks to be destroyed, except those of persons known to be friendly to the Union cause.

Stanton also replied to Grant's telegram about the command in Missouri that day, saying: "Whatever your judgment dictates as best in view of the western operations now developing, will have my cordial acquiescence. Sheridan is no doubt the best man, but his presence here will spare to you thousands of troops that would be required by any other commander. Have you considered what, if anything, would be accomplished by sending Hooker to the field as division commander, including Missouri, and, if you choose, Kansas and Arkansas, or either of them. I have no wish on this point, but only suggest it for consideration, if you have not already thought of it."[2]

Grant replied before the day was out: "I agree with you that Sheridan cannot well be replaced in his present position. I have also considered well the matter of sending Hooker to Missouri, and on mature reflection do not believe he will do. We want there a man who will push the enemy with vigor without waiting to get up supplies from a given base. There are no better men to command a division in such a pursuit of an enemy than Smith and Mower, who are already there. To give a proper head is now the question. After thinking over all the generals who can possibly be spared, I have made up my mind that Crook is the man to send. I would recommend General Logan for Crook's place. He is an active, fighting general, and under Sheridan will make a first-class commander for that department."[3]

Down in Georgia that day, the twelfth, Hood's Army of Tennessee appeared outside Resaca, on the Atlantic & Western Railroad, and Hood sent in a note to the garrison's commander: "I demand the immediate and unconditional surrender of the post and garrison under your command, and, should this be acceded to, all white officers and soldiers will be parolled in a few days. If the place is carried by assault, no prisoners will be taken." Colonel Clark Weaver, who held Resaca with the small 2nd Brigade of the 3rd Division of the 15th Corps, replied: "I am somewhat surprised at the concluding paragraph, to the effect that, if the place is carried by assault, no prisoners will be taken. In my opinion I can hold this post. If you want it, come and take it."[4]

Hood did not have the town surrounded, and reinforcements from Kingston managed to slip in from the other side. And when Sherman learned that Hood had turned to the north and attacked his supply line again, instead of heading west into Alabama, he sent more reinforcements by train. "I thought of interposing my whole army in the Chattooga Valley," he later wrote, "so as to prevent Hood's escape south; but I saw at a glance that he did not mean to fight, and in that event, after damaging the road all he could, he would be likely to retreat eastward by Spring Place, which I did not want him to do."[5] Sherman therefore turned all of his forces toward Resaca, reaching there that night, where he learned that Hood, desiring no more repulses such as the one suffered at Allatoona, had made no assault, contenting himself with a bit of skirmishing and with destroying the railroad that day and the next all the way up to

Tunnel Hill, about seventeen miles away. And on the thirteenth he captured the garrison at Dalton, the 44th Regiment of U.S. Colored Troops.

Grant received a telegram on the thirteenth that had been sent by Secretary of War Stanton the day before: "The President feels much solicitude in respect to General Sherman's proposed movement and hopes that it will be maturely considered. The objections stated in your telegram of last night impressed him with much force, and a misstep by General Sherman might be fatal to his army. This much the President directed me to say to you, when I saw him this evening, and although I find on reaching the office that you now think better of the plan, you should know how he feels on a point so vital."[6]

Grant replied: "On mature reflection, I believe Sherman's proposition is the best that can be adopted. With the long line of railroad in rear of Atlanta Sherman cannot maintain his position. If he cuts loose, destroying the road from Chattanooga forward, he leaves a wide and destitute country to pass over before reaching territory now held by us. Thomas could retain force enough to meet Hood by giving up the road from Nashville to Decatur and thence to Stevenson and leave Sherman still force enough to meet Hood's army if it took the other and most likely course. Such an army as Sherman has (and with such a commander) is hard to corner or capture."[7]

Stanton sent a copy of Grant's reply to Sherman, along with these comments: "You will see by General Grant's dispatch that your plans are approved by him. You may count on the co-operation of this Department to the full extent of the power of the Government. Supplies will be forwarded with the utmost dispatch to the points indicated. Whatever results you have the confidence and support of the Government."[8]

The weather had turned cool in the Shenandoah Valley, causing Sheridan's men to break out their overcoats. But their camp on the north side of Cedar Creek was otherwise pleasant and peaceful. Emory's two divisions of the 19th Corps were camped on the northwest side of the Valley Turnpike and the two small divisions of Crook's 8th Corps were bivouacked on the southeast side. The 6th Corps was still over at Front Royal, waiting for Sheridan to decide whether to send it on to Petersburg or not. There was no expectation of any annoyance from the Confederates, whose cavalry had been keeping a respectful distance since Custer and Merritt had turned on it at Tom's Brook. Early's infantry was thought to be over on the east side of the Blue Ridge somewhere, probably guarding Charlottesville and Gordonsville. The day before, the

Union cavalry and Thoburn's 1st Division of the 8th Corps had made reconnaissances toward Strasburg without seeing any sign of the Rebels.

But they were there. Early's army had marched north from Rude's Hill the day before. Now, on the thirteenth, it marched on past Fisher's Hill, where it had suffered its second defeat the month before, to Hupp's Hill, between Strasburg and Cedar Creek, for a reconnaissance in force. Why this was necessary is hard to say, since the Confederates had a signal station up on Shenandoah Peak, the highest of the three peaks at the northeast end of Massanutten Mountain. From there, 1,700 feet above the floor of the Valley, every detail of the Union camp could be seen. At any rate it was evidently not Early's intention to reveal the presence of his army, for he kept Gordon's Division hidden in some woods atop Hupp's Hill and the rest of his infantry hidden behind the ridge, allowing only a small portion of his cavalry to be seen. But this concealment was soon nullified by the decision of a subordinate somewhere in the Rebel chain of command. For a battery of Confederate artillery had opened fire on the Union camp, kicking the Federal troops out of their complacency.

In the 8th Corps' camp, five officers of the 34th Massachusetts were stretched out in a shelter tent playing cards when, at about noon, came the distant boom! boom! of artillery fire. At first they thought little of it. But then came another boom! boom! "This time accompanied by the whizzing of a shell which struck the ground midway between the tents and regimental headquarters," as one of them wrote. "From General Crook on down," a staff officer remembered, "it was as unlooked for as lightning out of a clear sky, for not a mother's son of us dreamed of the enemy being within 50 miles of Cedar Creek."[9]

Crook sent Thoburn's two small brigades, totaling perhaps 2,000 men, to drive off this annoying Rebel battery and what looked like only a small supporting force of infantry or dismounted cavalry. They crossed Cedar Creek and started up Hupp's Hill across the land of a farmer named Stickley, becoming separated from each other by a wooded spur of the main ridge. Colonel George D. Wells' 1st Brigade of Thoburn's division was on the Union left. Colonel Thomas M. Harris's 3rd Brigade was on the right. As the opposing infantry forces came in sight of each other, Wells' Federals ran forward to the cover of a low stone wall and opened fire. Brigadier General James Conner, commanding the leading Rebel brigade, was hit by this first volley, the bullet shattering his knee. His command fell to the colonel of one of the regiments, but he was mortally wounded minutes later, leaving a major as the highest ranking officer in the brigade. That brigade, however, was backed up by the rest of Kershaw's Division, while Harris' Federals were facing Gordon's entire division. Wharton's Division was coming up on Gordon's left, while Ramseur's and Pegram's divisions were farther back. Seeing that he was up against a far superior force, Thoburn ordered his two brigades to fall back. Harris got the order and promptly obeyed, but Wells did not receive it. Evidently the horse carrying the courier who carried the order was killed, and Wells stayed in place.

Soon Confederates were seen to be advancing against the little brigade's right flank from the wooded ridge that kept Wells from seeing that Harris had withdrawn. At first these Rebels were driven off, but more and more of them kept coming. Finally the order to retreat reached Wells, but before he could execute it he went down with a bullet through his chest. The staff officers tried to carry him off the field but he told them it was no use, ordering them to take his money and his watch and save themselves. Wells' men broke and ran but the Confederate pursuit was soon stopped by Union artillery fire from north of Cedar Creek, which brought an end to the small battle.

That night the Federals probed Hupp's Hill again, only to find that the Rebels had gone. What remained to be seen was how far and for how long. As Civil War battles went, this one was not very impressive. Fewer than 200 men were killed, wounded, or captured on each side. But it had far-reaching consequences, for it alerted Sheridan to the fact that Early's army had followed him down the Valley.

Sheridan had just ordered Wright's 6th Corps to march from Front Royal toward Alexandria as the first leg on its return to Petersburg and had written to Grant: "Information received from Colonel Powell, at Sperryville, reports Early or Longstreet, I do not yet know which, is in command, but think Early is, with the bulk of his force at Craig's Creek, between Brown's Gap and Waynesborough. I object to the opening of the railroad and an advance on the old Rapidan line, on account of the waste of fighting force to protect railroads, and the additional waste of force, as some would have to be left in this valley. You see how many troops might then be rendered unavailable. I believe that concentration at vital points, and the destruction of subsistence resources, to be everything; but do not let my views influence your better judgment. I believe that a rebel advance down this valley will not take place."[10]

Then he received a dispatch from Halleck, who forwarded Grant's instructions for him to "keep up as advanced a position as possible toward the Virginia Central road, and be prepared with supplies to advance on that road at Gordonsville and Charlottesville at any time the enemy weakens himself sufficiently to admit of it. The cutting of that road and of the canal would be of vast importance to us."[11] Halleck added that this advanced position "must be strongly fortified and provisioned. Some point in the vicinity of Manassas Gap would seem best suited to all purposes. Colonel Alexander of the Engineers, will be sent to consult with you, as soon as you connect with General Augur."[12]

Sheridan replied: "If any advance is to be made on Gordonsville and Charlottesville, it is not best to send troops away from my command, and I have therefore countermanded the order directing the Sixth Corps to march to Alexandria. I will go over and see General Augur and Colonel Alexander, and communicate with you from Rectortown."[13] Halleck then directed Augur to continue to repair the Manassas Gap Railroad.

But, after the little battle of Stickley's farm had revealed that Early's army was in his immediate vicinity, Sheridan cancelled his trip to Rectortown and ordered the 6th Corps to join the rest of his forces along Cedar Creek. The courier carrying this order caught up with Wright just as his corps was about to ford the Shenandoah River, and by noon the next day, the fourteenth, it was going into camp north of the 19th Corps, from which point it could support either of the other two corps or again march away without disrupting the front line near the creek.

Early's inadvertent attack, Halleck's persistent efforts to continue the work on the Manassas Gap Railroad, and Grant's fixation on a campaign against the Virginia Central were not Sheridan's only problems. Shortly after midnight of 13–14 October, Mosby and 84 of his men slipped past Union pickets not far west of Harper's Ferry. "It was a lovely night, bright and clear, with a big Jack Frost on the ground," Mosby remembered. They soon made their way to the track of the Baltimore & Ohio Railroad. One of his men had a timetable from the line, so Mosby knew that a westbound passenger train was due to come along in a few minutes. The Rebels pulled a rail loose where the track ran through a deep cut through a hill and waited to see the result. "I preferred derailing the train in a cut to running it off an embankment," Mosby later explained, "because there would be less danger of the passengers being hurt." Still, he reasoned that if some were injured it would not be his fault. "People who travel on a railroad in a country where military operations are going on take the risk of all these accidents of war," he wrote. Besides, he added, "I was not conducting an insurance business on life or property."[14]

Mosby and his men had been riding all day and they were tired, so, except for a few videttes who were sent out to keep watch, they were all soon so fast asleep that they did not even hear the train approach. But they were soon aroused by the sound of a crash and an explosion as the engine ran off the track and its boiler burst, filling the air with red-hot cinders and escaping steam. "A good description of the scene can be found in Dante's 'Inferno,'" Mosby said.[15]

His men seemed to be stunned by the sudden crash, so Mosby hobbled along the railroad cut—a Union soldier's horse had stepped on his foot in a recent skirmish—and pushed them down the bank, ordering them to pull out the passengers and to set the cars on fire. But his men soon reported that one of the cars was full of German immigrants on their way west and that they would not come out. They did not understand a word of English and had no idea what was going on, but they had through tickets and intended to keep their seats. Mosby told his men to "set fire to the car and burn the Dutch, if they won't come out." They took a bunch of copies of the *New York Herald* that were on their way to Sheridan's troops, spread them around, and applied matches to them. "The Germans now took in the situation and came tumbling, all in a pile, out of the flames," Mosby wrote.[16]

While he and most of his men were helping the passengers up the steep banks of the cut, two of his men reported to Mosby that they had found a couple of paymasters from the Union army on board with satchels of greenbacks for paying off Sheridan's men. Without stopping to count the loot, Mosby sent a lieutenant and two or three men to ride on ahead with the satchels to their rendezvous east of the Blue Ridge. "Whether my men got anything in the shape of pocketbooks, watches, or other valuable articles, I never inquired," Mosby wrote, "and I was too busy attending to the destroying of the train to see whether they did."[17] One female passenger appealed to Mosby for protection on the grounds that her father was a Mason. A male passenger thought that he should be due special consideration because he was a member of a certain aristocratic church in Baltimore. But all such appeals were in vain. Mosby blamed it all on the Union commander at Harper's Ferry. "General Stevenson will not guard the railroad and I am determined to make him perform his duty," he told the distraught passengers.[18]

"We left all the civilians, including the ladies, to keep warm by the burning cars," Mosby wrote, "and the soldiers were taken as prisoners." Then the Rebels rode off into the night. Among the Union soldiers captured was a young lieutenant recently immigrated from Germany, who had been on his way to join his regiment in Sheridan's army. Mosby noticed him because of his fancy uniform, "a fine beaver-cloth overcoat; high boots, and a new hat with gilt cord and tassel." So he struck up a conversation with him. "We have done you no harm. Why did you come over here to fight us?" Mosby asked. "Oh, I only come to learn de art of war," the dapper young lieutenant replied. Mosby then rode on up to the head of the column, for he knew that Federal patrols were about and he was afraid the column would have to fight before it got away. But pretty soon the German officer came trotting up to join him. Only now the Federal was not quite so resplendent. "One of my men had exchanged his old clothes with him for his new ones, and he complained about it. I asked him if he had not told me that he came to Virginia to learn the art of war." The lieutenant affirmed that he had. "Very well," Mosby said, "this is your first lesson."[19]

Before they reached the Shenandoah River a civilian brought word to the Rebels that a Captain Blazer was searching the area for them. Blazer was a Union officer in charge of a special anti-guerrilla detachment armed with Spencer repeating carbines. When the Confederates learned that "Old Blaze," as they called him, was about, they were eager for a fight. And they soon came upon the Federals' trail and saw their campfires where they had spent the night. Mosby said that he could not restrain his men, and that they rushed into the camp "as reapers descend to the harvests of death." But Blazer and his men were gone. "He was a bold but cautious commander," Mosby said, "and had left before daybreak."[20]

Before noon the guerrilla band had crossed the Blue Ridge and rendezvoused with the men carrying the satchels full of greenbacks. Mosby had his men dismount and form line and then the money was counted before them and divided equally among them without distinctions of rank. "My command was organized under an act of the Confederate Congress to raise partisan corps," Mosby explained; "It applied the principle of maritime prize law to land war. Of course, the motive of the act was to stimulate enterprise."[21] They found that they had made off with $173,000, which amounted to over $2,000 each. That was, in those days, quite a bit of stimulation. Later that same day, Captain William Chapman crossed the Potomac with two companies of Mosby's Rangers and attacked the Baltimore & Ohio Railroad and the Chesapeake & Ohio Canal in Maryland.

Powell's division of Union cavalry returned from its raid east of the Blue Ridge that day. It had come no closer to the Virginia Central Railroad than Amissville, a full 35 miles north of Gordonsville. About all that had been accomplished was the collection of some livestock, the hanging of one of Mosby's men in retaliation for the alleged murder of a Union soldier, and the burning of the house, barn, and outbuildings belonging to another member of Mosby's battalion who was reputedly one of the murderers.

That day Sheridan received another dispatch from Halleck: "The Secretary wishes you to come to Washington for consultation, if you can safely leave your command. General Grant's wishes about holding a position up the Valley as a basis against Gordonsville, etc., and the difficulty of wagoning supplies in the winter, may change your views about the Manassas Gap road." Secretary Stanton also wrote to Sheridan directly: "If you can come here, a consultation on several points is extremely desirable. I propose to visit General Grant, and would like to see you first."[22]

The next day, the fifteenth, Sheridan received another message from Grant: "What I want is for you to threaten the Virginia Central Railroad and canal in the manner your judgment tells you is best, holding yourself ready to advance if the enemy draw off their forces. If you make the enemy hold a force equal to your own for the protection of those thoroughfares, it will accomplish nearly as much as their destruction. If you cannot do this, then the next best thing to do is to send here all the force you can. I deem a good cavalry force necessary for your offensive as well as defensive operations. You need not, therefore, send here more than a division of cavalry."[23] Sheridan then ordered Merritt's division to Front Royal that night with the intention of sending it, backed up by Powell's division, across the Blue Ridge on a more powerful raid to the Virginia Central. He rode along with it as far as Front Royal on the first leg of his trip to Washington to meet with Stanton.

The funeral for Chief Justice Taney was held in Washington that day, the fifteenth. Lincoln's secretaries, in their joint multi-volume history of his presidency, wrote that Taney "was a man of amiable character, of blameless life, of great learning, of stainless integrity; yet such is the undiscriminating cruelty with which public opinion executes its decrees, that this aged and upright judge was borne to his grave with few expressions of regret, and even with a feeling not wholly suppressed that his removal formed a part of the good news which the autumn had brought to the upholders of the Union."[24] Republicans had, for almost four years, been looking forward to the chance to appoint their first chief justice, but it had appeared for a while as if they would never get their chance. "No man ever prayed as I did that Taney might outlive James Buchanan's term," a Republican Senator had quipped, but he said that he had begun to worry that he had overdone it.[25]

Since Taney's death all kinds of recommendations had been pouring in on President Lincoln as to his successor. Most often mentioned was Salmon P. Chase, only recently forced to resign as Secretary of the Treasury. Some urged his appointment. Others warned against it. Reporter Noah Brooks happened to bring up the subject with the president and saw his formerly gay and cheery visage lengthen. "With great seriousness he pointed to a pile of telegrams and letters on his table, and said: 'I have been all day, and yesterday and the day before, besieged by messages from my friends all over the country, as if there were a determination to put up the bars between Governor Chase and myself.' Then, after a pause, he added: 'But I shall nominate him for Chief Justice, neverthe-less.' It was therefore with amusement that I learned from one of Chase's most ardent friends, about an hour later, that 'Lincoln was not great enough to nominate Secretary Chase as Chief Justice'; and with inward satisfaction I bore in silence much contumely and reproach from Chase's fast friends."[26]

Rumors had reached Richmond that the Federals were planning a move against Wilmington, North Carolina. The Confederate commander there was Major General William Henry Chase Whiting, who was a capable engineer and had constructed formidable fortifications over the past cou-ple of years that so far had kept the U.S. Navy at bay. But he had difficulty in getting along with others, had performed poorly during Beauregard's defense of Petersburg from Butler, and was rumored to be overindulging in alcohol or narcotics. To further complicate matters, Whiting's district was in the Department of Southern Virginia and North Carolina, which had been Beauregard's command until he had recently been sent to coordinate Hood's Army of Tennessee and Richard Taylor's department. No one had been assigned to replace Beauregard in North Carolina. Now, on the fifteenth of October, President Davis made a move which he hoped would solve at least some of these problems. Without removing him from his job as nominal commanding general of the entire Confederate Army, Davis appointed General Braxton Bragg to the temporary command of the forces in North Carolina. Few others in the Confederate Government had Davis' faith in Bragg, and the gen-eral feeling seems to have been that while they feared that the move would lead to the loss of Wilmington it might be worth it to get Bragg away from Richmond.

The next morning, the sixteenth, Secretary of War Stanton and Secre-tary of the Treasury Fessenden arrived at City Point to pay Grant a visit. "They came at once to headquarters," Horace Porter wrote, "were warmly greeted by General Grant, and during their short stay of two days were profuse in their expressions of congratulation to the general upon the progress he had made with his armies." Grant took them to visit Butler's Army of the James that afternoon, and Porter went along. "Stanton," he said, "did most of the talking." The secretary of war was glad to get away from his desk and out of doors, saying that he felt "like a boy out of school." He then gave what Porter called "a graphic description of the anxieties which had been experienced for some months at Washington on account of the boldness of the disloyal element in the North and the emissaries sent there from the South." He also "spoke with much earnestness of the patient labors and patriotic course of the President. There had been rumors of disagreements and unpleasant scenes at times between the distinguished Secretary of War and his chief; but there evidently was little, if any, foundation for such reports, and certainly upon this occasion the Secretary manifested a genuine personal affection for Mr. Lincoln, and an admiration for his character which amounted to positive reverence." Sheridan's name soon came up in the conversation, in complimentary terms. "Yes," Grant said; "Sheridan is an improvement upon some of his predecessors in the valley of Virginia. They demonstrated the truth of the military principle that a commander can generally retreat successfully from almost any position—if he only starts in time."[27]

At Front Royal that morning, a courier caught up with Sheridan with a message from General Wright, who had been left in command of the army camped at Cedar Creek: "I enclose you dispatch which explains itself. If the enemy should be strongly re-enforced in cavalry, he might, by turning our right, give us a great deal of trouble. I shall hold on here until the enemy's movements are developed, and shall only fear an attack on my right, which I shall make every preparation for guarding against and resisting." A Union signal station had observed a Confederate signal being wig-wagged from the peak of Massanutten Mountain to Early's headquarters at Fisher's Hill. Consulting a captured Rebel code book, the signal officers had deciphered the message, which said: "Lieutenant-General Early: Be ready to move as soon as my forces join you and we will crush Sheridan. LONGSTREET, Lieutenant-General."[28]

Sheridan correctly interpreted this signal as a ruse. Longstreet, in fact, was still recuperating from the wound he had received in the Wilderness back in May and had no forces with which to join Early, although Sheridan did not know that. Sheridan assumed, correctly, that the purpose of the message was to discourage him from returning troops to Petersburg. But, as it happened, none were being sent yet anyway. However, he promptly called off the cavalry raid, sending Merritt's division back to the main camp along Cedar Creek just in case Wright might need it and leaving Powell's division to cover Front Royal. He sent Wright word of what he was doing with instructions for what to do in his absence: "The cavalry is all ordered back to you; make your position strong. If Longstreet's dispatch is true, he is under the impression that we have largely detached. I will go over to Augur, and may get additional news. Close in Colonel Powell, who will be at this point. If the enemy should make an advance, I know you will defeat him. Look well to your ground, and be well prepared. Get up everything that can be spared. I will bring up all I can, and will be up on Tuesday, if not sooner."[29] Then he continued on toward Washington, escorted by the 2nd Ohio Cavalry.

That night, Rosser was sent down the Back Road, with his cavalry and a brigade of infantrymen riding double behind his troopers, for a surprise attack on the camp of what he thought was a Union cavalry brigade that was somewhat isolated from the rest of Sheridan's army. Actually, it was Custer's entire division. The attack was successful except that Custer had moved and all that was captured in the camp was a picket reserve of 50 men.

Forrest began moving units into western Tennessee on the sixteenth. They were to move up from Mississippi and Alabama by various routes, sweeping up deserters, stragglers and supplies along the way. His ultimate objective was the Union supply base at Johnson City on the Tennessee River. This was a key point in Sherman's supply line, where freight was transferred from river steamers to the Nashville & Northwestern Railroad for shipment to Nashville. When his forces were assembled he would attack it.

Over in Georgia that day, Sherman was telegraphing Thomas at Nashville: "Send me Morgan's and Newton's old divisions. Reestablish the road, and I will follow Hood wherever he may go. I think he will move to Blue Mountain. We can maintain our men and animals on the country." The next day, the seventeenth, Sherman reached LaFayette, where Hood had recently been reported, only to find him gone. There he received Thomas' reply: "Schofield, whom I placed in command of the two divisions (Wagner's and Morgan's) was to move up Lookout Valley this A.M., to intercept Hood, should he be marching for Bridgeport. I will order him to join you with the two divisions, and will reconstruct the road as soon as possible. Will also reorganize the guards for posts and block-houses . . . Mower and Wilson have arrived, and are on their way to join you. I hope you will adopt Grant's idea of turning Wilson loose, rather than undertake the plan of a march with the whole force through Georgia to the sea, inasmuch as General Grant cannot cooperate with you as at first arranged." (Wilson, of course, was the new cavalry commander sent out for him from Sheridan. Mower was a very capable infantry division commander, one of Sherman's favorites, who had been campaigning with A. J. Smith and was being sent for duty with Sherman's main army.) Sherman then telegraphed to Schofield at Chattanooga: "Hood is moving south via Summerville, Alpine, and Gadsden. If he enters Tennessee, it will be to the west of Huntsville, but think he has given up all such idea. I want the road repaired to Atlanta; the sick and wounded men sent north of the Tennessee; my army recomposed; and I will then make the interior of Georgia feel the weight of war. It is folly for us to be moving our armies on the reports of scouts and citizens. We must maintain the offensive . . . Notify General Thomas of these my views. We must follow Hood till he is beyond the reach of mischief, and then resume the offensive."[30]

"After striking our road at Dalton," Sherman wrote in his memoirs, "Hood was compelled to go on to Chattanooga and Bridgeport, or to pass around by Decatur and abandon altogether his attempt to make us let go our hold of Atlanta by attacking our communications. It was clear to me that he had no intention to meet us in open battle, and the lightness and celerity of his army convinced me that I could not possibly catch him on a stern-chase. We therefore quietly followed him down the Chattooga Valley to the neighborhood of Gadsden, but halted the main armies near the Coosa River, at the mouth of the Chattooga, drawing our supplies of corn and meat from the farms of that comparatively rich valley and of the neighborhood.

"General Slocum, in Atlanta, had likewise sent out, under strong escort, large trains of wagons to the east, and brought back corn, bacon, and all kinds of provisions, so that Hood's efforts to cut off our supplies only reacted on his own people. So long as the railroads were in good order, our supplies came full and regular from the North; but when the enemy broke our railroads we were perfectly justified in stripping the inhabitants of all they had. I remember well the appeal of a very respectable farmer against our men driving away his fine flock of sheep. I explained to him that General Hood had broken our railroad; that we were a strong, hungry crowd, and needed plenty of food; that Uncle Sam was deeply interested in our continued health and would soon repair these roads, but meantime we must eat; we preferred Illinois beef, but mutton would have to answer. Poor fellow! I don't believe he was convinced of the wisdom or wit of my explanation."[31]

On that same seventeenth day of October, Beauregard officially assumed command of the new Military Division of the West. Unknown to him, Hood had already abandoned the plan that he and President Davis had approved. Instead of continuing to attack Sherman's line of supply in northern Georgia, or fighting Sherman when he came up to protect it, Hood now planned, without informing anyone higher up the chain of command, to invade Tennessee.

In the Shenandoah, Early had been hoping that Sheridan would continue to withdraw down the Valley. He considered the Cedar Creek position a strong one for the Union army, and he hoped that "we would be able to get at him in a different position, but he did not give any indications of an intention to move, nor did he evince any purpose of attacking us, though the two positions were in sight of each other."[32] The Federals could stay where they were indefinitely, but the Confederates could not, because they could not draw enough supplies from the burned out area immediately behind them and because they were too far from the nearest railroad for their limited number of wagons to shuttle supplies from it. Therefore, they either had to withdraw or advance, and in order to advance they had to drive Sheridan from his camp at Cedar Creek. Early decided to attack.

On the morning of the seventeenth, Gordon was sent with one brigade of his division on a reconnaissance to Hupp's Hill for a close inspection of the Union position. Early wanted to know whether or not it was entrenched, and Gordon returned with word that it was. "As I was not strong enough to attack the fortified position in front," Early later explained, "I determined to get around one of the enemy's flanks and attack him by surprise if I could."[33] Pegram was sent to examine the Union right, or northwestern, flank, while Gordon and Captain Jed Hotchkiss, the army's topographical engineer, were sent to have a look at the other flank from the signal station atop Massanutten Mountain.

The weather remained crisp and clear in the Valley, and conditions for observation of the Union army's camp along Cedar Creek were ideal. "A fine day," as Jed Hotchkiss called it, and the view was perfect.[34] "It was," Gordon said, "an inspiring panorama." But the climb to the top of the mountain took hours of clambering "through tangled underbrush and over giant boulders and jutting cliffs." It was well worth the effort, however, for with their field glasses, the Confederates could see every detail of the enemy camp below. "I could count, and did count, the number of his guns," Gordon said. "I could see distinctly the three colors of trimmings on the jackets respectively of infantry, artillery and cavalry, and locate each, while the number of flags gave a basis for estimating approximately the forces with which we were to contend in the proposed battle."[35]

Below the observing officers the North Fork of the Shenandoah River coiled around the base of Massanutten Mountain from west to east, while Cedar Creek flowed down from the north and northwest in lazy zigzags to join the river just below them. The nearest Union formation was Thoburn's 1st Division of the 8th Corps, camped on a low hill in the middle of a westward-pointing V of Cedar Creek, just beyond the point where it met the river. The 2nd Division of the 8th Corps, now under Rutherford Hayes, was about a mile farther to the northeast, just beyond the bridge where the Valley Turnpike crossed Cedar Creek. Due east of

Hayes' camp was a new formation that was probably unknown to the Rebels: Colonel John H. Kitching's Provisional Division. This was a collection of units from the Department of Washington, most of which had not yet arrived at that time. Only a small detachment of its 1st Brigade and the 6th New York Heavy Artillery were on hand, and some reports therefore refer to Kitching as commanding a brigade rather than a division. Just to the northwest of Hayes' division, on the other side of the turnpike, were the two divisions of Emory's 19th Corps. And about a mile farther north or northeast, just west of the village of Middletown, were the three divisions of Wright's 6th Corps. Another mile north was the camp of Merritt's 1st Division of cavalry, and Custer's 3rd Division was about a mile and half northwest of Merritt.

This deployment indicated that Sheridan assumed that his left was protected by the river and the mountain. He had therefore deployed the vast majority of his powerful and mobile cavalry on the right to discourage any attack on that flank. However, the area between Thoborn's division and the mountain was guarded only by what Gordon called "a very small detachment of cavalry on the left bank of the river, with vedettes on their horses in the middle of the stream."[36] "It required, therefore, no transcendent military genius," Gordon said, "to decide quickly and unequivocally upon the movement which the conditions invited." He was sure that if a surprise attack could be made on the Union left "the destruction of Sheridan's army was inevitable."[37] Hotchkiss drew a map of the Union positions and then the Confederate officers made their way back down the mountain. It was dark by then, and Hotchkiss had dinner with Gordon before making his report to Early.

Pegram also came to headquarters to report on the possibilities of attacking the Union right, which he had been reconnoitering. "I told him General Gordon had a plan to propose," Hotchkiss recorded, "and stated the substance of it to General Early and showed him the map, as I did not wish his judgment to be forestalled by General Pegram."[38] Early was impressed, and since Pegram reported that the banks of Cedar Creek on the Union right were steep and that an attack on that flank would not be profitable, there was no reasonable alternative, other than to retreat without a fight. All that remained to be done was to find a route by which a large force could get between the Union left and Massanutten Mountain without being discovered. Gordon and Hotchkiss were assigned that task, for which they were allowed the morning of the eighteenth, while Pegram went to the top of Massanutten Mountain to have another look at the Union camp.

Sheridan stopped off at Rectortown on the morning of the seventeenth for a brief meeting with General Augur, and there he received a message from Halleck: "General Grant says that Longstreet brought with him no troops from Richmond, but I have very little confidence in the information collected at his headquarters. If you can leave your command with safety, come to Washington, as I wish to give you the views of the authorities here."[39] Sheridan was worrying about being away from his army, "But after duly considering what Halleck said, and believing that Longstreet could not unite with Early before I got back, and that even if he did Wright would be able to cope with them both, I and my staff, with our horses, took the cars for Washington, where we arrived on the morning of the 17th at about 8 o'clock."[40] He proceeded to the War Department and as soon as he met Secretary Stanton, just back from City Point, he asked that a special train be ready at noon to take him to Martinsburg, the nearest town to his army on the railroad, for he wanted to be able to get back to Cedar Creek as soon as possible.

"He at once gave the order for the train," Sheridan said, "and then the Secretary, Halleck, and I proceeded to hold a consultation in regard to my operating east of the Blue Ridge. The upshot was that my views against such a plan were practically agreed to, and two engineer officers were designated to return with me for the purpose of reporting on a defensive line in the valley that could be held while the bulk of my troops were being detached to Petersburg. Colonel Alexander and Colonel Thom, both of the Engineer Corps, reported to accompany me, and at 12 o'clock we took the train."[41]

They arrived at Martinsburg about dark. Waiting for them there was the escort of 300 cavalrymen that Sheridan had ordered before leaving Cedar Creek. They spent the night there and started up the Valley Turnpike the next morning, the eighteenth. "Colonel Alexander was a man of enormous weight," Sheridan wrote, "and Colonel Thom correspondingly light, and as both were unaccustomed to riding we had to go slowly, losing so much time, in fact, that we did not reach Winchester till between 3 and 4 o'clock in the afternoon, though the distance is but twenty-eight miles."[42]

As soon as they arrived at the headquarters of Colonel Edwards, whose brigade of the 6th Corps was garrisoning the town, Sheridan sent a courier to Cedar Creek to bring him a report of the situation there. Then he took Colonel Alexander out on the heights west of Winchester so that he could make up his mind about fortifying the area. By the time that this was done it was dark, and when they got back to Colonel Edwards' headquarters, where they would spend the night, the courier had returned with word that all was quiet along Cedar Creek, and that a brigade of the 19th Corps would make a reconnaissance of the Confederate position the next morning.

Confederate lieutenants Young and Hutcherson checked into the American House hotel in St. Albans, Vermont, on the morning of the seventeenth, and after lunch they strolled around the town of some 5,000 citizens—fairly large for that era. They visited each of the three banks they planned to rob and noted that several horses could be found at the Fuller Livery Stable near their hotel. Mr. Fuller, Young noticed, seemed suspicious when they asked him about the best roads to Sheldon. That evening, Young met an attractive young woman and charmed her into joining him for dinner and a walk to the village green afterwards, during which they discussed theology. Young was a former divinity student and could quote the Bible extensively. Hutcherson disapproved of Young's flirtation with this Yankee woman, but the latter countered that he had learned something useful. "We can use the village green to hold our prisoners. Two mounted men with revolvers can guard the whole square."[43]

Throughout the next day, the rest of Young's men arrived, some by train, some on horseback, and checked into the American House and various boarding houses around town. That afternoon, Young strolled again with his new lady friend among the gold and crimson oaks and maples on the village green. And that evening they had one more walk in the crisp autumn air. When he returned from this third walk, Young gathered his raiders for a final discussion of their plans. All of his men had by then inspected the banks on one pretext or another, and they all had made themselves familiar with the roads out of town. Each man had one or two revolvers and plenty of ammunition. The time for robbing the three St. Albans banks was set for 3 p.m. the next day, and the bottles of Greek fire were distributed. Four men who had arrived by train would need horses for the escape, but they could take some from Fuller's. "Be sure the livery stable is burned," Young told them.[44]

At 9:30 p.m. on the eighteenth of October John Wilkes Booth checked into the St. Lawrence Hall hotel in Montreal, the unofficial Confederate headquarters in that city. He was there for ten days, and is known to have met with two different Confederate agents. One was Patrick C. Martin, a native New Yorker and Baltimore liquor dealer who was involved in smuggling contraband of war to the Confederacy. Through Martin, Booth arranged to ship his theatrical wardrobe south. Martin also gave Booth a letter of introduction to William Queen, an old doctor who lived on the edge of a swamp in Charles County, Maryland, on the lower Potomac southeast of Washington, who would help Booth set up an escape route out of Washington for the proposed capture of President Lincoln. The other Rebel agent Booth is known to have met was George

N. Sanders, one of the Confederate commissioners and a strong believer in political assassination, who, while American consul in London, had advocated the killing of Louis Napoleon "by any means, and by any way it could be done."[45]

1. *Official Records*, 43:II:892.
2. Ibid., 41:III:774.
3. Ibid., 41:III:801.
4. Sherman, *Memoirs*, 630.
5. Ibid., 629.
6. *Official Records*, 39:III:222.
7. Ibid., 39:III:239.
8. Ibid., 39:III:240.
9. Lewis, *The Guns of Cedar Creek*, 108.
10. *Official Records*, 43:II:345–346.
11. Ibid., 43:II:339.
12. Ibid., 43:II:345
13. Ibid., 43:II:355.
14. John S. Mosby, *The Memoirs of Colonel John S. Mosby* (Bloomington, Ind., 1959), 313–314.
15. Ibid., 314.
16. Ibid., 315–316.
17. Ibid., 317–318.
18. Kevin H. Siepel, *Rebel: The Life and Times of John Singleton Mosby* (New York, 1983), 126.
19. Mosby, *Memoirs*, 318.
20. Ibid., 320.
21. Ibid.
22. *Official records*, 43:II:355.
23. Ibid., 43:II:363.
24. Nicolay and Hay, *Abraham Lincoln*, 9:385.
25. Ibid., 386.
26. Noah Brooks, *Washington in Lincoln's Time* (New York, 1958), 122–123.
27. Porter, *Campaigning With Grant*, 304–306.
28. *Official Records*, 43:II:389.
29. Ibid., 43:II:389–390.
30. Sherman, *Memoirs*, 631–632.

31. Ibid., 632.
32. Early, *War Memoirs*, 438.
33. Ibid.
34. *Official Records*, 43:I:580.
35. Lewis, *The Guns of Cedar Creek*, 121.
36. Ibid.
37. Ibid., 122.
38. *Official Records*, 43:I:580.
39. Sheridan, *Memoirs*, 2:65.
40. *Official Records*, 43:II:386.
41. Sheridan, *Memoirs*, 2:66.
42. Ibid., 2:67.
43. Horan, *Confederate Agent*, 169.
44. Ibid.
45. Tidwell, Hall and Gaddy, *Come Retribution*, 331.

CHAPTER TWENTY-ONE

And Yet the Soldiers Slept

18–19 October 1864

In the Shenandoah Valley on the eighteenth, General Gordon and Captain Hotchkiss went in search of a route that the Confederates could take which would get them past the left flank of Sheridan's army undetected during the night, so that a surprise attack could be launched on the morning of the nineteenth. By midday they had found it. There was a narrow trail along the edge of Massanutten Mountain and southeast of the river that led to a ford that could be used to get well beyond Thoburn's Union division for an attack on Hayes's and Kitching's commands. Along this trail infantry could march single file hidden from the view of the Federal army by trees, ridges, and the dark of night. Gordon estimated that if a large column started from Fisher's Hill at sundown it could be in position to attack by dawn. The two officers evidently borrowed some work clothes and corn knives at a nearby farm and went into the field near the river, cutting corn while taking a close look at the enemy pickets before reporting back to Early.

Tuesday, 18 October, in the Shenandoah was what one Union soldier called a "superb specimen of an autumn day."[1] Another said it "was such a day as few have seen who have not spent an autumn in Virginia—crisp

315

and bright and still in the morning; mellow and golden and still at noon; crimson and glorious and still at the sunsetting; just blue enough in the distance to soften without obscuring the outline of the mountains; just hazy enough to render the atmosphere visible without limiting the range of sight."[2] As usual, the Federals were up at 2 a.m. and standing at arms until daylight. After breakfast some of them had an hour of drill and some even held a dress parade. But most of them spent another leisurely, peaceful day in camp. Some regiments received pay that day and some received new uniforms. Most received mail. And that evening, various bands played patriotic and sentimental tunes.

Crook sent Harris's brigade back to Hupp's Hill on another reconnaissance that day, and it reported that the Rebels were gone. Harris meant only that there were no Confederates around Hupp's Hill, but Wright, who was in charge during Sheridan's absence, seems to have interpreted the report to mean that the Rebels were gone from their camp at Fisher's Hill. For this or some other reason, and despite Sheridan's warning to be prepared for a Confederate attack, Wright cancelled the precautionary order that had been responsible for the troops getting up at 2 a.m. They would be allowed to sleep a little later on the nineteenth. However, he ordered Emory to send a brigade of the 19th Corps up the turnpike the next morning and Torbert a brigade of cavalry up the Back Road. Both were to keep going all the way to Fisher's Hill or until they found the Rebels.

Captain Henry DuPont, chief of artillery in Crook's 8th Corps, was worried about the isolation of three of his batteries on the Union left with nothing but Thoburn's little division to protect them and a steep ravine between them and the rest of the army. DuPont kept asking who was guarding the space between Thoburn's position and Massanutten Mountain. "The invariable reply was that our left was protected by Powell's cavalry division," he said, "which was not at all satisfactory to me as nobody seemed to be informed as to its exact position: I even went so far as to ride out beyond our left to try to locate it but returned after going some distance and seeing nothing."[3] Actually, one of Powell's brigades, Colonel Alpheus Moore's 1st, was stationed at Buckton Ford, which was over two miles down the river from Thoburn's camp. The other brigade of Powell's division was even farther away, around Front Royal. Only Moore's videttes were covering the space between his main camp and Thoburn's pickets.

Colonel Stephen Thomas, commander of the 2nd Brigade of the 1st Division, who was the officer of the day in the 19th Corps, evidently saw Gordon and Hotchkiss in their farm clothes pretending to be cutting corn, without, of course, knowing who they were, and he felt there was something suspicious about the urgency of their conversation and the way they pointed now and then to various parts of the Union position. He reported his suspicions to Emory and then to Wright, but these two were more worried about their right than their left. Anyway, he was told, the reconnaissance the next morning would find out what was going on.

At 2 p.m. there was a meeting at Early's headquarters of all the Confederate division commanders except Pegram, who had not yet returned from the top of the mountain. Despite past differences with Gordon, Early put him in temporary charge of all three of the divisions from the 2nd Corps for a move along the route he and Hotchkiss had discovered to get around the Federal left. Early himself, with Kershaw's and Wharton's divisions and all the artillery, meanwhile, would advance along the turnpike through Strasburg and would attack up that road as soon as Gordon's corps was engaged. Payne's Brigade of Rosser's cavalry—already guarding the area between the river and Massanutten Mountain—would go with Gordon's infantry and make a dash for the Union headquarters in an attempt to capture Sheridan, while the rest of Rosser's Division would attack on the other flank in an effort to pin down the Union cavalry while the infantry camps were being overrun. Lomax's cavalry, which was over in the Luray Valley, was to "move by Front Royal, across the river, and come to the Valley Pike, so as to strike the enemy wherever he might be, of which he was to judge by the sound of the firing."[4] Altogether, it was the kind of bold, unlooked-for flanking move and surprise attack that had paid off very handsomely in the past for the team of Lee and Stonewall Jackson. Perhaps it would work now for their old subordinates, Jubal Early and John Gordon. Anyway, desperate times called for desperate measures.

Rosser and Gordon would both attack at 5 a.m. on the nineteenth, just before daylight. Kershaw and Wharton would move up to Strasburg during the night and wait until Gordon was engaged before attacking. The men were to carry two days' rations, and everyone was to leave canteens and swords in camp in order to minimize the noise generated by the moving columns. The artillery would wait back at Fisher's Hill, for fear that the sound of its wheels on the macadamized road would alert the Federals, but once the attack started it was to gallop for Hupp's Hill.

Gordon started his three divisions moving at around 8 p.m., about an hour after dark and just as the moon rose. Couriers from headquarters were stationed at every fork in the path to make sure that no one took a wrong turn. The bright moon gave the men enough light to follow the narrow trail, although there was only room for them to go single file.

As Gordon put it, "With every man, from the commanders of the divisions to the brave privates under them, impressed with the gravity of the enterprise, speaking only when necessary and then in whispers, and striving to suppress every sound, the long gray line like a great serpent glided noiselessly along the dim pathway above the precipice."[5] A captain in the 13th Virginia found himself on familiar ground and said he recognized every tree. "I used to hunt squirrels and partridges all over these grounds," he wrote, "but now I was hunting men, and found game plentiful."[6]

A Union lieutenant remembered that the evening of the eighteenth was "milder in its temperature than some of the autumn nights that had preceded it." And he remembered lying out on the turf, with a group of comrades, admiring the view of the distant Blue Ridge and the closer Massanutten Mountain when, at about 10 p.m., "there came from one of the upper slopes of Massanutten a series of flash-lights that looked for the moment as if a group of shooting stars had been suspended over the tree tops. 'The Rebs are signalling again,' was the word."[7] He and his friends thought that enemy forces of considerable size and on a mission of some importance must be on the move if they had to relay signals by lights on Shenandoah Peak. But the Federals were confident that their own commanders had things well in hand.

The 2nd Ohio Cavalry, in Custer's division, was one of the regiments that had received mail on the eighteenth. A major in that outfit remembered the close of that day. "The letters were all read and their contents discussed; the flute had ceased its complaining; the eight o'clock roll-call was over; taps had sounded; lights were out in the tents; cook fires flickered low; the mists of the autumn night gathered gray and chill; the sentinels paced back and forth in front of the various headquarters; the camp was still—that many headed monster, a great army, was asleep. Midnight came, and with it no sound but the tramp of the relief guard as the sergeant replaced the tired sentinels. One o'clock, and all was tranquil as a peace convention; two, three o'clock, and yet the soldiers slept."[8]

Finally Gordon's column came down off the side of the mountain into the bottom lands near the river. Farm roads were plentiful there but the posted couriers kept the men on the right road. However, there was one fork where no courier had been placed because a log had blocked the wrong road anyway, leaving only the proper road open. Gordon felt that something was wrong when he came to this fork, but he could not decide what it was. The men marched on, but he could not shake the feeling that something was wrong, so he stopped the column and sent a staff officer back to check at a nearby farm house. Sure enough, the farmer had moved the log during the day in order to use the road he had wanted. "On such small things sometimes hang the fate of great battles," Gordon later wrote.[9]

Meanwhile, Pegram returned from his trip up the mountain and reported to Early that he had discovered what he thought were Union entrenchments constructed since Gordon and Hotchkiss had examined the position the day before. "And he suggested," Early wrote, "the propriety of attacking the enemy's left flank at the same time Gordon made his attack, as he would probably have more difficulty than had been anticipated."[10] Early agreed and decided to send Kershaw's Division across Cedar Creek just above its mouth, at Bowman's Mill, to attack Thoburn's camp at the same time that Gordon attacked Hayes's and Kitching's. At 1 a.m. on the nineteenth Kershaw's and Wharton's divisions began their march, and at Strasburg Kershaw turned off to the right onto the road to Bowman's Mill while Wharton continued along the turnpike to Hupp's Hill with orders to keep his men out of sight of the Union camp until the attack began. He was then to support the artillery when it caught up and to capture the turnpike bridge over Cedar Creek.

Gordon's soldiers were again put on the right road and marched on. Eventually someone spotted two Union pickets up ahead, and the column was halted while a few men led by an experienced scout crept up on these Federals to surprise them. The Rebels were the ones who were surprised, however, when they fell upon the dreaded pickets only to discover that they were just a pair of small cedar trees.

Again the three divisions marched on, and when the head of the column approached Bowman's Ford over the North Fork of the Shenandoah the men lay down, waiting for the column to close up. Despite the delays they were ahead of schedule. Fog was starting to cover the river and its banks by then and the moon was going down, but the Confederates could still make out the figures of some of the Union cavalry videttes guarding the ford. And this time, they were real. "In the still starlit night," Gordon remembered, "the only sounds heard were the gentle rustle of leaves by the October wind, the low murmur of the Shenandoah flowing swiftly along its rocky bed and dashing against the limestone cliffs that bordered it, the churning of the water by the feet of the horses on which sat Sheridan's faithful pickets, and the subdued tones of half-whispers of my men as they thoughtfully communed with each other as to the fate which might befall them each in the next hour. The whole situation was unspeakably impressive."[11]

Gordon and Ramseur sat on an outcrop of rock and talked quietly. Ramseur, who was only 27 although he looks older in his wartime photograph, had just learned three days before that he was a father. The message had come by way of the army signal stations on Massanutten Mountain, but it had neglected to mention whether the child was a boy or a girl. Now he told Gordon that he hoped that this coming battle would be a decisive one so that he could take leave to go home and see his wife and baby. He was certainly going to do his best to make it so. And when he left Gordon to rejoin his men he said quietly, "Well, General, I shall get my furlough today."[12]

Colonel Thomas, officer of the day in the 19th Corps, had not been reassured by Wright's plans to send out a reconnaissance in the morning, and he stayed in the saddle all that night, prowling around and checking on things. He made a midnight inspection of the pickets, and then rode alone out into the no-man's land beyond, watching and listening. As he made his way down a ravine someone suddenly called out, "Surrender, you damned Yankee!" He replied, "No, sir! It's too early in the morning!"[13] Wheeling his horse he dug in his spurs, and made his way up the steep side of the ravine as bullets spattered around him. He got safely back into the Federal lines, unsure of whether he had run into Confederate pickets or something more.

The officer of the day in the 8th Corps, Lieutenant Colonel Luther Furney, was not so lucky. He went out to investigate strange sounds and did not come back, for he was taken prisoner.

When all of his infantry had caught up, Gordon sent Payne's 300 cavalrymen ahead, and they plunged down the bank of the Shenandoah into the cold water and quickly overran the Union videttes, who retreated to the east, toward their own brigade, leaving the rear of Crook's infantry unprotected. Payne's troopers then continued on their mission to find Sheridan's headquarters and capture the Federal commander. It was these Virginians who captured Furney. Behind them, Gordon's infantry forded the chest-high stream and trotted up the country road on the other side. A mile and a half north of the ford, at the J. Cooley house, Gordon formed his three divisions into lines of battle and wheeled them to the left, facing northwest. His own division was on the left and Ramseur's on the right, with Pegram's in a second line behind Gordon's.

On a knoll overlooking Bowman's Mill, less than a mile away, General Early and Kershaw's Division were also in position, waiting for the appointed hour. From the northeast, Early heard a rumbling sound, like the wheels of cannon. "It's all up with us!" he cried out. "We are discovered, and that is the enemy's artillery."[14] Captain Hotchkiss reassured him, and in a few minutes the sound faded. It had only been some Union wagons moving north. Then, at about the same time that Payne's troopers charged forward, Early gave Kershaw the word, and the latter sent his leading brigade, Colonel James P. Simms' 520 Georgians, forward to deal with Thoburn's pickets. The rest of his division followed in column of fours. Farther up Cedar Creek, Wharton's infantry, and much farther, Rosser's cavalry, were also in their assigned positions. Rosser also advanced at the designated hour, sending Wickham's Brigade forward on foot and his own Laurel Brigade mounted, headed for Torbert's camps.

The 2nd Battalion of the 5th New York Heavy Artillery, serving as infantry, was manning the picket line of Thoburn's division that night, and its men had been hearing strange sounds off to the east, toward Massanutten Mountain, since midnight. Its commander reported this to brigade headquarters, and then, at about 4 a.m., the New Yorkers heard the firing at Bowman's Ford when Payne's Rebel cavalry overran the Union videttes there, but they did not know what it was all about. At 4:45 a.m. some of Payne's troopers brushed into some of the artillerymen in the dark and the Federals fired a ragged volley in their direction, but the Rebels disappeared without replying.

Farther up Cedar Creek, Company A of the 128th New York formed part of the picket line for the 19th Corps, holding what was called the Stonewall Post south of the creek near the turnpike. In the pre-dawn darkness these New Yorkers also felt that something was wrong. Three times one of the company's two lieutenants hailed the pickets of the 8th Corps but received no answer. Soon his men reported that the woods beyond them seemed to be alive with Rebels. Not long after that, however, the post was visited by the brigade's officer of the day, Lieutenant Colonel Alfred Neafie. He told the company's two officers not to be concerned if they heard firing to the east, for a brigade would be making a reconnaissance at first light, only minutes away, and any shooting would, no doubt, be due to its advance. At about the same time, farther downstream, the heavy artillerymen caught a glimpse through the fog of Kershaw's infantry fording the creek. They fired but again there was no response. However, before they knew what was happening, they were overrun by Simms' Georgians, and 309 of the 349 New Yorkers were captured. After the rest of his men had crossed the creek, Kershaw formed his division just below the fortified hill where Thoburn's division was camped.

Lieutenant Colonel Thomas F. Wildes was now the commander of Thoburn's 1st Brigade. When he heard the firing on the picket line he sent his men into their defenses, sent his wagons to the rear, and sent out his skirmishers. The latter "soon met the enemy advancing silently through the woods." Meanwhile, Wildes and a few of his staff officers rode over to Harris' brigade, on their right, and found the men there still asleep. "Some good, vigorous efforts were made to arouse them," Wildes said. "There stood the guns of the battery with only a sentinel over them, and only a man now and then of the infantry or artillery could be roused up enough to ask 'What's up?' or, 'Who the hell are you?'" A captain on Wildes' staff found Colonel Harris himself asleep in an ambulance half a mile from his lines. When the captain reported the danger to him, Harris "raised himself slightly in his bed and answered, 'That cannot be.'" Wildes and his staff returned to their own brigade, "which we had scarcely reached before the storm burst in front and on both flanks."[15]

At 5 a.m. Kershaw sent his four brigades forward in an attack that echeloned to the left, and they double-quicked up the hill and plunged into the abatis in front of Thoburn's defenses. A major in Payne's cavalry was more than a mile east of Kershaw's attack and riding north when he heard its opening volley. "It was not ushered in by a few preliminary shots, as was generally the case," he wrote, "but it was a prolonged roll, without cessation, for apparently five minutes. After the volley was over the echo of it seemed to roll back and forth over the Valley a half dozen or more times. When it had once died away it would return to you again from another direction." An officer in Kershaw's last brigade said, "We could see the enemy in great commotion, but soon the works were filled with half-dressed troops and they opened a galling fire upon us. The distance was too great in this open space to take the works by a regular advance in line of battle, so the men began to call for orders to 'charge.' Whether the order was given or not, the troops with one impulse sprang forward."[16]

"The mist and fog was so heavy," Colonel Wildes said, "that you could hardly see the length of a regiment."[17] His men held on as best they could, but their efforts were nullified by the poor fight put up by Harris's sleepy men. One Confederate said that these Federals were panicky and fired without taking aim and could not stop the oncoming Rebels. Simms' Georgians poured through a gap between the two Union brigades where one of Harris's regiments was not yet in position, and turned left to outflank Harris's other regiments one at a time and send them scurrying for the rear. A Pennsylvania battery of six 10-pounder guns was next in line, and it was overrun without ever firing a shot because the Rebels followed so closely behind the retreating Federals.

When the Confederates attacked, Captain DuPont, chief of the 8th Corps artillery, made his way to Battery B, 5th U.S. Artillery at the extreme right end of Thoburn's line. The battery commander, Lieutenant Brewerton, said he had his six 3-inch rifles loaded with cannister, but he could not see the enemy because of the fog. DuPont told him to open fire anyway. At what, the lieutenant asked. DuPont told him to fire to the left, toward the sound of battle, and soon two of the guns were adding their bass notes to the crackle of musketry and the high-pitched yell of the Rebels. The Confederates answered almost immediately with guns they had captured from the Pennsylvania battery farther down the line.

Realizing that the position could not be held and that there was no time to bring up the battery's horses and hitch them to the guns, DuPont told Brewerton to "hold his ground until he could see the forms of the enemy approaching." Then he was to "run the pieces down the hill by hand, abandoning the limbers."[18] DuPont then rode to the bottom of the hill, where he found the excited teams being harnessed, and he told the drivers to abandon the caissons but to hitch the teams to the caissons' limbers and be ready to hitch these to the guns when they were rolled down the hill by the gunners. Then he galloped up the next ridge to check on an Ohio battery.

Behind him, Brewerton turned his guns to fire into the Georgians who had breached the line to his left until they were within 25 yards of his guns, then he sent both men and guns tumbling down the hill. One gun was caught in some bushes and had to be spiked and abandoned, and Brewerton himself was captured, but the rest of his battery got away. Simms' Georgians had outrun the rest of Kershaw's Division, and "there being no troops either on our right or left," Simms reported, "I thought it prudent to fall back to the captured works and await the arrival of other troops."[19]

Wildes' right regiment, nearest the breach in the line, was also outflanked and it quickly disintegrated. His other two regiments, the 116th and 123rd Ohio, were hit on both flanks and from the front all at the same time, but managed to extricate themselves while maintaining reasonable order. The still-lingering fog helped the Federals get away. The two Ohio regiments reformed in some timber behind their original position, but they were soon driven out and retreated toward Rutherford Hayes' position.

One Rebel officer, in the last brigade to reach the Union defenses, said that the hill upon which these were built was above the fog and that by then there was enough light to see for a mile or more across a treeless plateau. "Tents whitened the field from one end to the other for a hundred paces in rear of the line, while the country behind was one living sea of men and horses—all fleeing for life and safety," he said. And he added that "men, shoeless and hatless, went flying like mad to the rear, some with and some without their guns."[20] Colonel Thoburn was somewhere down in that mass of fleeing soldiers, waving his sword and trying to stem the tide of defeat, when he was shot dead. The rout of his division had taken only about a quarter of an hour.

Pursuit of the defeated Federals was delayed as Kershaw's men stopped to help themselves to what the Yankees had left behind. A Rebel captain remembered seeing "costly blankets, overcoats, dress uniforms, hats, caps, boots and shoes all thrown in wild confusion over the face of the earth." While such goods were appreciated by the ragged Confederates, what really caught their attention was the uneaten breakfast that had been abandoned by Thoburn's men. "Good gracious, what a feast we had," another captain remembered. To the half-starved Rebels it seemed that there was every kind of food they could possibly want in that camp. "Five- and ten-gallon camp kettles on the fire were full of boiling coffee," he said, and that was an item particularly prized in the blockaded South. "We got some of the good things, filled our tin cups with the coffee, and moved on after the Yankees, eating, drinking, and feeling big and brave."[21]

The heavy firing that marked Kershaw's attack on Thoburn served notice on the rest of the Union army that a battle was under way. A captain on Emory's staff, John W. DeForest, was having breakfast with Brigadier General Cuvier Grover, the commander of the 2nd Division of the 19th Corps, when the "shrill prolonged wail of musketry broke forth, followed by scream on scream of the Rebel yell." A captain in the 8th Vermont said that he "was awakened at the first signs of day by a terrific clap of thunder and sprang into a sitting position and listened." He could tell that the sound came from the 8th Corps' camps. "I listened for the yell of our men, but alas, it never came; instead, the Yi Yi Yi! of the Confederates—it seemed to me as if our whole left were enveloped, enfolded, by this cry. It was like the howl of the wolves around the wagon train in the early days on the great prairies."[22]

Captain DeForest said that in the "unexpected and astounding clamor" he and General Grover "silently exchanged a glance of surprise and comprehension." Then the general turned to an aide and said, "in his usual gentle, monotonous voice, 'Tell the brigade commanders to move their men into the trenches.'" It was his division that was to have conducted the reconnaissance to Fisher's Hill that morning, so his men were already up and ready, and they were in their defenses in a matter of minutes. DeForest hastened to the 19th Corps headquarters and found General Emory "just up, coatless and hatless and uncombed, shouting for his horse and his orderlies. He was more excited and alarmed than would have seemed necessary to an ignoramus in warlike matters." Emory sent DeForest on to Wright's headquarters to report that Crook's corps was being attacked in force. "As I rode away," the captain remembered, "I heard him grumbling, 'I said so; I knew that if we were attacked, it would be there.'" Wright, still at 6th Corps headquarters even though he was in temporary charge of the whole army, was just preparing to mount when DeForest rode up. "He knew what I had to tell him, but he listened to my brief message patiently and replied with the formal courtesy of the regular army, 'Give my compliments to General Emory and say that I will be with him shortly.'"[23]

A lieutenant on Thoburn's staff came galloping up to Colonel Rutherford Hayes, congressman elect, who had only recently succeeded to command of the 2nd Division of the 8th Corps, to report that a Rebel attack was driving the 1st Division from its defenses. But, like Emory and Wright, Hayes did not really need a staff officer to tell him that things were going terribly wrong over there. Thoburn's men could be seen through the fog running for the protection of his own position or of the 19th Corps'. And behind them could be heard the screams and shouts of Kershaw's men and the steady tread of their advance.

Hayes had just ordered his 1,445 men to fall in and was about to form a battle line when Crook rode up. He was followed shortly by Wright, and then Emory, all come to see what was going on. Emory sent orders for the 2nd Brigade of the 1st Division of the 19th Corps, commanded by Colonel Stephen Thomas—the same who had been the corps' officer of the day—to come over to the turnpike to form a connecting link between that corps' defenses and Hayes' two small brigades. And Wright sent for two divisions of his 6th Corps to reinforce this new line, but it would take some 20 minutes for them to arrive. On Hayes' left was Kitching's little provisional command of about 1,000 men. One of Hayes' regiments was still on picket duty, and another, the 9th West Virginia, was camped a half a mile to the southeast, where it had been working on the new entrenchments that had worried Pegram. Now both units were out there somewhere in the fog, and so, apparently, were an awful lot of Rebels. Hayes wrote that "the firing in our front and both on our right and left flanks told plainly enough that the rebels were rapidly advancing." Nevertheless, Wright later reported that he had "felt every confidence that the enemy would be promptly repulsed."[24]

Kershaw's Division had assaulted Thoburn's isolated position just as the last of Gordon's divisions was crossing the river. When all three of these had completed their deployment near the Cooley house they stepped off on their advance to the west, Gordon and Ramseur in front, Pegram behind, and without any skirmishers. Soon they came to the camp of the 9th West Virginia, the lone regiment of Hayes' division which had been working on the new entrenchments. These Federals were caught completely by surprise by the huge force of Confederates materializing out of the fog. "They jumped up running," one Rebel remembered, "and did not take time to put on their clothing, but fled in their night clothes, without their guns, hats or shoes."[25] And the Rebels pressed on to the west.

When Captain DuPont reached the Ohio battery on the next ridge behind Thoburn's old position, he saw Wharton's skirmishers coming along the turnpike toward the bridge over the creek. He ordered two of the Ohioans' 12-pounder Napoleons to fire at these skirmishers, while the other two were sent to some high ground about a quarter of a mile to the east to try to slow the Confederate pursuit of Thoburn's routed men. DuPont was surprised to see Wharton's advance come to a halt, not realizing, perhaps, that those Rebels faced not only his two guns but the entrenchments of the 19th Corps on the other side of the turnpike. He was also surprised when the other two guns soon came rushing back again after having found themselves almost face to face with Rebels advancing from the east. DuPont said that until then he had not realized "the extensive scale upon which the Confederate turning movement was being carried out nor the vigor with which it was being pressed."[26] He and his gunners fled north to the turnpike and along it to Kitching's defensive line, which they joined. DuPont's work in delaying the Rebel attack and saving as many guns as he did eventually brought him a promotion and a Congressional Medal of Honor.

Hayes rode over to check on Kitching's command. Kitching himself, although only 25, had led brigades of heavy artillerymen serving as infantry in the Army of the Potomac. But the troops in his small force that day had never seen combat. Hayes, recently turned 42 and a veteran of many campaigns in the Shenandoah and West Virginia, asked the younger colonel if he thought he could hold on. "Oh, yes," Kitching answered, "I shall have no trouble. This is a good position, and I can hold on here if you can hold on down there." Hayes was a bit irritated at the younger man's presumption. "You need not feel afraid of my line," he replied. "I will guarantee that my line will stand there."[27]

But as Hayes turned to go back to his own division he saw Gordon's 9,000 screaming Rebels come charging out of the fog from the east and saw his own troops break and run.

In his report, Wright said: "With the other troops brought up, this supporting division was in good position to offer sturdy battle, with every prospect of repulsing the enemy, and aided, as it soon would have been, by the rest of the force, the chances were largely in our favor. Here the battle should have been fought and won, and long before midday the discomfited enemy should have been driven across Cedar Creek stripped of all the captures of his first attack, but from some unexplained cause the troops forming this part of the line would not stand but broke under a scattering fire, which should not have occasioned the slightest apprehension in raw recruits much less in old soldiers like themselves."[28] But survivors from Thoburn's division had come fleeing through Hayes' lines with tales of the disaster that had befallen them, and their fear must have been contagious. So when Gordon's large battle line then appeared unexpectedly out of the fog from an unexpected direction, Hayes' men suddenly decided that discretion was the better part of valor.

Hayes' troops joined Thoburn's in retreat, but an officer in that brigade of the 19th Corps that Emory had sent for noted as he advanced that the retreating men of the 8th Corps were not frantic or excited but "only stolidly, doggedly determined to go to the rear . . . They passed around us, through our ranks, and almost over us, insistent, determined. They heeded none of our cries to 'Turn back!' 'Make a stand!' but streamed to the rear."[29]

Hayes himself galloped after his troops, but his horse was shot out from under him, tumbling head over heels and throwing the future president to the ground so hard that he was briefly knocked unconscious. Some of his men carried word to the rear that he had been killed. When he came to, he had a sharp pain in one ankle but found that he could walk. Some Rebels then yelled for him to stop, which led to the discovery that he could even run, and he escaped into the concealment of a grove of trees. "The names they called me reflected disrespect upon my parentage," Hayes later complained.[30] But his troubles were still not over, for next he was struck in the head by a spent musket ball. This caused no real damage, however, and eventually he caught up with his staff, borrowed a horse, and began to gather the men of his division near army headquarters, a mansion called Belle Grove, behind the 19th Corps camps.

To the left of Hayes' division, Kitching's small command and the four 12-pounders of the Ohio battery that DuPont had brought over held up

Ramseur's Division for a while, knocking veteran brigade commander Cullen Battle out of the war with an incapacitating wound. But this small force could not be expected to stand up to such odds for long and Du-Pont ordered his guns to move once more. They retreated across the turnpike and Meadow Brook, which paralleled it on the northwest side, and unlimbered again. Kitching went down with a wound that soon cost him a leg and eventually his life, and his troops joined the general flight to the north and west. Only half an hour had passed since the opening of the battle.

---

1. Wert, *From Winchester to Cedar Creek*, 174.
2. Lewis, *The Guns of Cedar Creek*, 143.
3. Ibid., 141.
4. Early, *War Memoirs*, 441.
5. Wert, *From Winchester to Cedar Creek*, 175–176.
6. Lewis, *The Guns of Cedar Creek*, 146.
7. Ibid., 141.
8. Urwin, *Custer Victorious*, 206.
9. Lewis, *The Guns of Cedar Creek*, 160.
10. Early, *War Memoirs*, 442.
11. Lewis, *The Guns of Cedar Creek*, 161.
12. Ibid.
13. Ibid.. 142.
14. Ibid., 189.
15. Ibid., 192.
16. Ibid.
17. Wert, *From Winchester to Cedar Creek*, 180.
18. Lewis, *The Guns of Cedar Creek*, 194.
19. Wert, *From Winchester to Cedar Creek*, 183.
20. Lewis, *The Guns of Cedar Creek*, 194.
21. Ibid., 194–195.
22. Ibid., 197.
23. Ibid., 197–198.
24. *Official Records*, 43:I:158.
25. Lewis, *The Guns of Cedar Creek*, 200.
26. Ibid., 197.

27. T. Harry Williams, *Hayes of the Twenty-Third: The Civil War Volunteer Officer* (New York, 1965), 300.

28. *Official Records,* 43:I:160–161.

29. Williams, *Hayes of the Twenty-Third,* 301–302.

30. Wert, *From Winchester to Cedar Creek,* 186.

CHAPTER TWENTY-TWO

Glory Enough For One Day

19 October 1864

Colonel Wildes, with the only two regiments of Thoburn's division that had maintained their organization, had tried to join Hayes' division before it too was routed, but had kept running into Confederates. So they had been forced to move over toward the turnpike, where they encountered Emory. The general knew that he needed to buy time in which to prepare his 19th Corps to face in a new direction and meet both Kershaw's and Gordon's attacks. So he ordered Wildes to charge the woods 300 yards back the way he had just come, which he knew were full of Rebels. The two Ohio regiments faced about and formed line of battle.

"Every officer and man in our little band knew he was going to meet overwhelming numbers in those woods," Wildes wrote, "but they never hesitated. Fixing bayonets, we started on the way back down the hill from the pike, and as we started to ascend to the woods raised the old yell and dashed forward. Just after we started, General Wright rode out in front and most gallantly led the charge." Wright did not mention this episode in his report, perhaps because by then he realized that it was a foolhardy thing for an army commander to do. "We advanced close to the edge of the woods," Wildes wrote, "where we met with a terrible fire and a countercharge from ten times our number, which swept us back again to the pike. General Wright was wounded in the face, and came back bleeding freely. He displayed great personal courage, but gallant as he and the men who followed him were, they were obliged to give way before the awful fire they met at the edge of the woods. Falling back again to the pike, we found the 19th Corps changing front to the rear along down the pike."[1]

Colonel Thomas' brigade of the 19th Corps was just coming into place to connect the 8th Corps line with the 19th Corps defenses when Hayes' men broke and ran. Now Emory threw it at the advancing Rebels in order to buy more time for his corps to form a new line facing east. "I never gave an order in my life that cost me so much pain," Emory said later. Thomas formed up his three regiments, some 800 men, and advanced against those same woods full of the Confederates of Gordon's Division. A private in the 8th Vermont said that "as the great drops of rain and hail precede the hurricane, so now the leaden hail filled the air, seemingly from all directions, while bursting shell from the enemy's cannon on the opposite hill created havoc on our only flank not yet exposed to the rebel infantry." The Federals got in one volley before there was "a sudden rush of the enemy from every direction, in their yellowish suits, breaking through even the short intervals between the commands, forced each regiment to fight its own battle as the swarming enemy broke upon it with almost resistless fury. Suddenly a mass of rebels confronted the flags, and with hoarse shouts demanded their surrender. Defiant shouts went back. 'Never! Never!' And then, amid tremendous excitement, commenced one of the most desperate and ugly hand-to-hand conflicts over the flags that has ever been recorded. Men seemed more like demons than human beings, as they struck fiercely at each other with clubbed muskets and bayonets." Over half the men in the brigade were killed or wounded in that brief fight. "It was useless to stand against such fearful odds," the Vermont private said, "neither could such frightful butchery be endured longer; and the regiment, now almost completely surrounded by dense masses of rebel infantry, was for a few moments tossed about as a leaf in the small, fitful circle of a whirlwind, and then by a mighty gust lifted from the ground and swept from the field, but not without the flags."[2]

The brigade reformed a couple of hundred yards farther back. Captain DeForest of Emory's staff joined it there and said that "this second stand was too near a victorious and advancing enemy to result in anything but a little more useless bloodshed. A semicircle of dropping musketry converged on the new position, for Early's reserve under Wharton had just got within range, and its skirmishers were raking us from the south.

Our men were apparently bewildered, and did not know which way to face, and could not be brought to fire."[3] What was left of the brigade was ordered to retreat to the north, along the turnpike.

Two regiments of Emory's left-most brigade were moved to face to the east and a Rhode Island battery was placed at the end of this new line, but the rest of the 19th Corps, as Captain DeForest remembered, "continued for the present at the breastworks, guarding against an expected attack in force from the south; for none of us could yet believe that Early's main body was in our rear and that our fortified plateau had become a trap, sure to ruin us if we did not skip out of it." The two regiments, the 156th and 176th New York, had just moved to their new positions when Kershaw's troops came charging out of the fog "in masses," as a lieutenant in the 176th put it, adding that the Rebels "were so sure of their advance that they could even afford in part to disregard the portion of our line that was most immediately to be reached, and to press their way northward with the view of occupying the pike and of cutting off the retreat of our division." The Rhode Island guns hit the Confederates with a murderous fire, but they came on. "A desperate hand-to-hand fight ensued on the left of the brigade line," the commander of the 156th reported. "The enemy had planted their colors on our works and were fighting desperately across them, meeting with a stubborn resistance, while they swarmed like bees around the battery on our left and rear. The enemy rushed upon, seized, and attempted to capture the colors of the 156th and 176th New York."[4] The New Yorkers were able to save their flags by ripping them from their poles, but the two regiments were soon driven from their position.

Before these two regiments were overwhelmed, Emory brought most of the rest of his corps over to extend their line to the north. But Gordon's three divisions soon attacked this line's front, while the collapse of the two New York regiments exposed its right flank to Kershaw's Division. One by one the Federal brigades were overpowered, and both the new line and the old quickly collapsed. Only the 1st Brigade of the 1st Division still maintained its organization. Its commander, Colonel Edwin P. Davis, divided it into two lines to serve as a rear guard and buy time for the others to get clear. He put two regiments in an advanced line and his other four regiments and a battery of guns on a knoll behind them. "We who commanded companies," wrote a captain in one of the front-line regiments, "walked up and down their front, exhorting the men to stand firm to the fiery shock that was approaching. There is, at such times, a dead weight of suspense at a soldier's heart, which is perhaps harder to bear than the fury of battle itself." When the pursuing Rebels appeared out of the fog the Federals staggered them with "a withering volley." But it was a hopeless struggle as the Confederates swarmed around the two regiments shouting, "Surrender! you sons of b——s!"[5] The front two regiments ran for the cover of the second line, but it also collapsed and ran for the rear, leaving three guns behind, and reduced to the same disorganized state as the 8th Corps had been, the 19th Corps streamed past army headquarters at Belle Grove.

"Here were Crook and his staff, Hayes and his staff, and a large number of officers," Colonel Wildes wrote, "striving with might and main to stem the tide of disaster."[6] Wildes and his two battered Ohio regiments joined this makeshift line, bringing it up to about 1,500 men. "A great many line and staff officers took muskets and lay down in the ranks of the men, while all mounted officers used their holster revolvers," Wildes said, and he estimated that fully one fourth of the Federals in this line were officers. "We checked the advance of the enemy, and pushed him back a short distance, and I think the very hardest and most stubborn fighting of the day took place here. We were fighting Kershaw's and Wharton's rebel divisions." Crook's adjutant, normally a quiet, studious fellow, raged up and down just behind the line on a conspicuous white horse until Confederate bullets finally found him, but, as Wildes said, "the position was held for over half an hour, which gave time for the trains to move out of the way."[7]

While this battle was going on, efforts were being made by headquarters personnel to save the ammunition and supply wagons that were parked between Belle Grove and Middletown, as well as their own maps and papers. They had just gotten the wagons started on what Captain DeForrest called a "wretched country road" toward Winchester when he saw one of Payne's Rebel cavalrymen dash up and shout, "Here! Bring that train this way." A guard replied, "What the hell have you to do with this train?" and shot him.[8]

Colonel Thomas and his brigade of the 19th Corps also stopped to help defend the wagons until they could be moved across Meadow Run, a stream that paralleled the turnpike on its northwest side. He also stopped a number of retreating 8th Corps troops and got them to help him. Seeing General Crook ride by, the Colonel reported to him what he had done. "All right," was all the preoccupied general said, and then he "rode away as he came," a private noted, "unattended by even an orderly."[9]

Gordon's Confederates continued to advance to the west, passing through what was left of the wagon park, and soon came to the steep ravine of Meadow Run. They found many Federals at the bottom of it, seeking shelter from their fire. "Poor fellows!" a Georgian in Gordon's Division said. "It looked like murder to kill them huddled up there where they could not defend themselves, while we had nothing to do but load and shoot. At the first volley most of those who were not killed or wounded began a scramble to ascend the steep side of the ravine, catching to bushes and any object that offered help. Their knapsacks on their backs presented a conspicuous target for our rifles, and I was surprised as I crossed the ravine to see how few of them were killed."[10]

Captain DeForest was with the retreating 19th Corps. "Random bullets tossed up whiffets of dust from the hard-trodden earth," he said, "and their quick, spiteful *whit-whit* sang through an air acrid with the smoke of gunpowder. Here and there were splashes of blood, and zigzag trails of blood, and bodies of men and horses. I never on any other battlefield saw so much blood as on this of Cedar Creek. The firm limestone soil would not receive it, and there was no pitying summer grass to hide it."[11]

A captain in Kershaw's Division looked back at about 7:30 a.m. at Belle Grove and the overrun Union camps. "What a sight!" he said. "Here came stragglers, who looked like half the army, laden with every imaginable kind of plunder—some with an eye to comfort had loaded themselves with new tent cloths, nice blankets, overcoats, or pants, while others, who looked more to actual gain in dollars and cents, had invaded the sutler's tents and were fairly laden down with such articles as they could find the readiest sale for. Some of the favorites were tin cups and frying pans. "I saw one man," he said, "with a stack of wool hats on his head, one pressed in the other, until it reached more than an arm's length above his head."[12]

Emory reformed his men on Red Hill, some three quarters of a mile west of Belle Grove. But between them and the pursuing Confederates, the three veteran divisions of Wright's 6th Corps were taking position on another hill. Captain DeForest heard one 19th Corps straggler tell another, "The bloody Sixth is going in. *They'll* stop these blasted cusses. They say that, by Jesus, *they'll* hold 'em."[13]

The two divisions of the 6th Corps that Wright had ordered forward with the original intention of reinforcing Hayes' line were Wheaton's 1st and Ricketts' 3rd. However, since Wright was in temporary command of the Army of the Shenandoah, Ricketts took temporary command of the corps and Colonel J. Warren Keifer took temporary command of the 3rd Division. These divisions consisted of only two brigades each. Normally the 1st Division had three, but its 3rd Brigade, which included Captain Elisha Hunt Rhodes' 2nd Rhode Island, was still garrisoning Winchester. The two divisions had crossed to the east side of Meadow Run (also called Meadow Brook) onto the field west of Belle Grove when their lines were disrupted by fleeing soldiers from the 19th Corps. The wagon train was pounding down the road toward Middletown and Winchester, and just beyond it, as a Colonel Moses Granger in the 3rd Division wrote, a "thin line of blue, facing southeast, was firing at clumps of men in gray east of the turnpike." It was a very confusing situation, especially with the fog limiting visibility. "Unable to see the ground for over a hundred yards," a major said, "unable to fix the position of other troops, each command was in a measure isolated." And "the heavy and continuous firing, the rebel yells, the swarms of fugitives, the whizzing musket balls, the roar of the enemy's guns (which, having crossed the creek after Wharton, were now opening along the pike) and the shriek and burst of their shells told only of disaster."[14]

Wright ordered Rickets to move the 6th Corps to the left in order to try to head off the Confederate attack. The corps' 24 guns were wheeled into action en masse, almost as they had stood in camp, and opened fire whenever they were not blocked by fleeing wagons or soldiers. They had no clear targets because of the fog, but fired as best they could at the noise of battle. The two divisions that had advanced now recrossed Meadow Run and formed on each side of the artillery, the 3rd Division on the right and the 1st on the left. Colonel Granger said that "it was at once apparent that the line was wrongly placed. The ground sloped upward from us to the edge of the plateau. The enemy ascending from the run (which turning southwest separated us from Belle Grove) could lie down and use that edge as a breastwork from which to fire at us in open ground. So I, at once, ordered my two regiments forward." Granger's Federals soon collided with part of Kershaw's division and, after a brief struggle, drove the Rebels back down the slope toward Belle Grove. During the ensuing respite, Granger watched clumps of Confederates moving north along the turnpike. General Wright came along and questioned Granger about the situation and then rode on, looking "serious, but not discouraged."[15]

Without waiting for orders from Wright or Ricketts, the commander of the 2nd Division of the 6th Corps, Brigadier General George Washington Getty, moved his three brigades behind the 1st Division to extend the line to the north and east. They were fired upon by Rebel skirmishers over on the east side of Meadow Run, so Getty formed his men in line along the west side of the ravine and ordered his skirmishers forward to clear the woods on the other side, which they did. The sun had risen at last, but it was more hinderance than help to the Federals. "The newly risen sun, huge and bloody," a major in the 1st Division wrote, "was on their side in more senses than one. Our line faced directly to the east, and we could see nothing but that enormous disc, rising out of the fog, while *they* could see every man in our line, and could take good aim."[16]

"A little after sunrise we had captured nearly all of the Union artillery," Gordon wrote; "we had scattered in veriest rout two thirds of the Union army; while less than one third of the Confederate forces had been under fire, and that third intact and jubilant. Only the Sixth Corps of Sheridan's entire force held its ground. It stood like a granite breakwater built to beat back the oncoming flood; but it was also doomed unless some marvelous intervention should check the Confederate concentration which was forming against it." Colonel Carter, Early's chief of artillery, asked Gordon how far he intended to push the pursuit before he stopped to regroup, for he knew that many of the men had been marching all night and fighting all morning. "I am going through the town," Gordon said, meaning Middletown, "and stop beyond it." Carter offered to dispose of the 6th Corps with his guns alone, saying, "General, you will need no infantry. With enfilade fire from my batteries I will destroy that corps in twenty minutes."[17] Gordon knew better, and he kept the men moving. Kershaw advanced against the 3rd Division, supported by two of Ramseur's brigades, and Gordon's own division attacked the 1st, while the rest of Ramseur's, with Pegram's in close support, hurried down the turnpike to get at Getty's division.

Colonel William Emerson, commander of the 1st Brigade of the 3rd Division, ordered his men to lie down while "troops, artillery and wagons went pouring through our lines. It being quite foggy, it was difficult to tell when our troops were through and the enemy commencing to come. As soon as satisfied on that point, the brigade commenced firing." Corporal Augustus Buell, a cannoneer in a regular army battery, said that his captain ordered his guns to fire cannister, "but there was such a jam of wagons and other debris in our immediate front that we had to wait for them to clear the way, and when we did open, the enemy was pretty close to us." Twice the 3rd Division counterattacked and drove Kershaw's Rebels back, but they returned again. Then Colonel Emerson's brigade suddenly came under fire from its right, where only moments before some reformed troops from the 19th Corps had been. "I ordered up support from the second line," he said, "but the fire was so heavy the men could not be held there."[18] Emerson ordered a withdrawal, but when he saw Kershaw's men overrun a nearby Union battery he ordered the 10th Vermont to recapture it. This regiment was joined by the 6th Maryland from Keifer's other brigade, and together they counterattacked and, after some severe hand-to-hand combat, managed to bring off three of the guns. The others were disabled. But both brigades of the 3rd Division were still forced to retreat.

Confederates kept working around Keifer's right, between the high ground and Cedar Creek, while continually attacking or threatening his front, and the 3rd Division was continually forced to give ground. The artillery and the 1st Division, also under constant pressure from the front, had to fall back to avoid being outflanked. A soldier in the 1st Division said, "The tide of battle was stayed for a while, but they poured a withering fire upon our brigade, and Lamb's gunners and our men were falling fast. We maintained our position for nearly half an hour, until the fog lifted and revealed our position to be perilous in the extreme."[19]

When confederates overran a Rhode Island battery to the right of the 1st Division, the division commander, Brigadier General Frank Wheaton, brought over his 1st Brigade from the left of his line. These three New Jersey regiments counterattacked, retook the guns, and held off the Rebels long enough for the artillerymen to haul them to safety. But while they were doing so other Confederates came through the part of the line they had been taken from and outflanked Wheaton's other brigade and routed it. The New Jersey troops managed to get out in time, but just barely, leaving one of their flags behind when nobody saw the color bearer fall.

On the corps' left, or eastern, flank, Getty had just advanced the 2nd Division's main line across Meadow Run, hoping to block the Valley Turnpike running toward Middletown. "At this juncture," he reported, "observing the troops on the right falling back in confusion, and running through the artillery of the corps, and heavy lines of rebel infantry pressing in that direction, I withdrew the division to the west side of the creek, about 300 yards, to a strong crest, semi-circular in form and partially wooded. The second line was moved up and extended the first, it being necessary to cover as much ground as possible. The right flank of the division was entirely uncovered; on the left, however, where the crest was refused parallel to and bordering the run, a skirmish line of Bidwell's brigade (Third), which held that flank, was extended along the height and connected with a skirmish line of a portion of Merritt's cavalry on the left rear."[20] This cavalry was Devin's brigade of Merritt's 1st Division and Moore's brigade of Powell's 2nd Division, which had ridden to the sound of the guns and circled around Middletown to take position on the Union left.

Couriers from Gordon had already brought reports to General Early of the brilliant success of his turning movement and of Kershaw's flank attack, and Early's own trip up the turnpike past the litter of the routed Union forces confirmed these reports. A staff officer reported that the normally dour general's face "became radiant with joy." At about 8 a.m., as the sun was finally burning away the morning fog, Early reached the front. "Ah," he said, "the Sun of Middletown!" mocking how Napoleon had greeted the sun that had risen over his victory in the fog at Austerlitz, "The Sun of Middletown!"[21]

When Early and his staff rode up to Gordon on the turnpike just south of Middletown, he said, "Well, Gordon, this is glory enough for one day. This is the 19th. Precisely one month ago today we were going in the opposite direction." Gordon later claimed to have answered, "It is very well so far, general; but we have one more blow to strike, and then there will not be left an organized company of infantry in Sheridan's army." Of course, this was written well after the event, when Early and Gordon had even more to disagree about than ever. "No use in that," he claimed that Early replied; "they will all go directly." Gordon formally relinquished command of the field, but before riding off to resume direct command of his division he supposedly replied, "That is the Sixth Corps, General. It will not go unless we drive it from the field." But Early was not impressed. "Yes, it will go too, directly," he said.[22]

The withdrawal of Getty's division—now the only Union infantry still resisting—was followed closely by the Confederates, and no sooner were the Federals established in their new position than they were attacked again. First, part of Kershaw's Division hit the point where Colonel James Warner's 1st Brigade, on the right, joined Brigadier General Lewis A. Grant's 2nd Brigade. "Getty's veterans cooly held their fire until the enemy was close upon them," a Union major said, "then delivered it in their very faces, and tumbled the shattered ranks down the hill, pursued to the foot by Warner's two right regiments." But by then the Confederate artillery was unlimbering along the turnpike, and its fire sent Warner's men scrambling back up the hill. Then Ramseur's and some of Pegram's men struck the area where Lewis A. Grant's 2nd and Brigadier General Daniel Bidwell's 3rd Brigade came together. "On the rebels came, through the woods, with a vigor that promised success," a Union major wrote. Then the Federal artillery opened up. "I kept her muzzle down," cannoneer Buell said, "so that every round threw dirt in their faces, but there was no stopping them."[23]

For once the Confederates had a skirmish line out in front, and the skirmishers, instead of making way for their main line, kept on coming and engaged the artillerymen in hand-to-hand combat. But infantrymen from Lewis Grant's crack Vermont Brigade drove the Rebels out at bayonet point. The battery commander desperately tried to limber up his guns and get them away, but a fierce volley from the main Confederate line, at a range of about 200 feet, felled nearly every horse and driver.

The surviving artillerymen, corporal Buell among them, managed to get away with two of their guns.

Grant's and Bidwell's brigades were also forced to give ground, but they did so grudgingly and in good order. A panic seemed to strike two of the Vermont regiments momentarily, but their officers soon restored order. "At this critical juncture," one officer wrote, "a shell struck General Bidwell as he sat on his horse holding his men to their work; he was a man of remarkably large frame, and the missile tore through his shoulders and lungs, bringing him heavily to the ground." His successor, Lieutenant Colonel Winsor French, yelled to his men, "Don't run till the Vermonters do!" Thus inspired, one officer said, "the troops sprang to their feet, dressed their line, fixed bayonets, moved forward a few paces to and over the crest, and met the enemy at 30 yards with so well-aimed a volley, so thundering a cheer and so suddenly and spontaneously a rush forward that he fell back in great confusion."[24]

After parting with Gordon, Early rode forward on the turnpike trying to see the Union position for himself, despite the fog and gunsmoke. "But I soon came to Generals Ramseur and Pegram," he wrote, "who informed me that Pegram's division had encountered a division of the 6th corps on the left of the Valley Pike, and, after a sharp engagement, had driven it back on the main body of that corps, which was in their front in a strong position. They further informed me that their divisions were in line confronting the 6th corps, but that there was a vacancy in the line on their right which ought to be filled. I ordered Wharton's division forward at once, and directed Generals Ramseur and Pegram to put it where it was required."[25]

A courier brought word to Getty that General Ricketts had been wounded during the attacks on the 1st and 3rd divisions and that Getty was now in temporary command of the 6th Corps. That did not seem to matter much, since his division was the only part of the corps—indeed the only infantry in the army—that was still fighting. But Getty went through the formality of placing Lewis Grant, no kin to the general-in-chief, in temporary command of the 2nd Division.

Corporal Buell was impressed with this Vermont general, especially with his calmness in the middle of a great battle. As Buell and the other gunners of his battery—they had lost all their officers—were bringing off their rescued guns, Grant rode up and asked them politely whether or not they still had any ammunition. When they replied that they did, he led them to a position on the left of Bidwell's—now French's—brigade, overlooking Meadow Run and Middletown. The position was already under a terrific fire of musketry, as well as cannister fire from a Rebel battery. In "a natural and pleasant tone of voice," Buell said, the general told the gunners to "go in battery here and attend to those folks coming out of the village; the men on your right will support you. Now, boys, give 'em the best you've got."[26] Then he calmly rode away.

The Rebels coming out of Middletown were Wharton's Division, three small but fresh brigades. French's men gave them the same treatment they had given Ramseur's and Pegram's men. "Again the troops rose to their feet, dressed their ranks and gripped their muskets, with bayonets fixed," wrote the same officer who had described their previous fight. "And again, at the critical moment, just as the charging line, straining up the hill, gained the summit, the steady veterans countered upon it with a terrific threefold blow, a sudden, deadly volley, a fierce charge and a mighty shout, and dashed it in pieces down the ridge."[27]

Captain DuPont, the 8th Corps artillery chief, said this attack by Wharton was Early's fatal error: "The battle in any event was lost to the Confederates from the moment that Wharton was ordered to support Ramseur and Pegram in their assault upon Getty's division, not only for the reason that it then and there became apparent that the morale of Getty's troops was still unimpaired and that his men could not be driven an inch farther by frontal attacks, but also because the very heavy casualties in the three hostile divisions seem to have made Early much more circumspect."[28]

"In a very short time," Early wrote, "and while I was endeavoring to discover the enemy's line through the obscurity, Wharton's division came back in some confusion, and General Wharton informed me that, in advancing to the position pointed out to him by Generals Ramseur and Pegram, his division had been driven back by the 6th corps, which, he said, was advancing. He pointed out the direction from which he said the enemy was advancing, and some pieces of artillery, which had come up, were brought into action. The fog soon rose sufficiently for us to see the enemy's position on a ridge to the west of Middletown, and it was discovered to be a strong one. After driving back Wharton's division he had not advanced, but opened on us with artillery, and orders were given for concentrating all our guns on him."[29]

"The enemy now brought up his batteries," Getty reported, "and concentrated on the division a severe fire of artillery, but being sheltered by the ground the loss from this cause was lighter than could have been expected. After holding this position for over an hour, it at length became necessary to withdraw the division, the enemy having turned the right and opened a flank and reverse fire upon the line. Obliquing to the right to gain the pike, the division retired in perfect order, marching slowly and making several halts, to a position about a mile north of Middletown, where a new line was established, with the left resting on the pike, connecting with Merritt's cavalry, already in position on the east side of the pike, and slight rail breast-works were thrown up. The line of skirmishers was strengthened and the farther advance of the enemy checked."[30]

Gordon was forever after embittered by the way Early seemed to fritter away all the advantages that had been won by his plan and attack. "We halted, we hesitated, we dallied," he said, "firing a few shots here, attacking with a brigade or a division there, and before such feeble assaults, the superb Union corps retired at intervals and by short stages."[31]

Throughout the morning, Gordon, Early, and Wright as well, seem to have forgotten all about the cavalry.

Firing on the picket line had awakened Custer at 4 a.m. and he had roused one regiment and sent it to support his outposts. But Rosser had been content to seize a ford over Cedar Creek far upstream from the infantry battle and to hold it. When firing was heard to the south, in the infantry camps, both Custer and Merritt got the rest of their men up, and when Torbert arrived from Belle Grove he found everybody ready, but they had nothing to do. Wright was an infantry officer and in the heat of battle it did not seem to occur to him to call upon these two cavalry divisions to take part in the battle to the south.

Merritt deployed his headquarters escort, the 5th U.S. Cavalry, and his staff officers across the fields north of Middletown in an effort to keep stragglers from leaving the field, but with only limited success. Devin's brigade of Merritt's division was then used for the same purpose, first behind the 6th Corps and then on its left, where it was joined by Moore's brigade of Powell's 2nd Division. Merritt and Torbert both were with Devin, both hoping for orders to get into the fight, but no such order came. Meanwhile, four of the best brigades in the cavalry were kept idle. Merritt's other two brigades, Lowell's Reserve Brigade plus Custer's old Michigan Brigade, now under Colonel James H. Kidd, were watching Rosser's two brigades, which were doing nothing. The two brigades of Custer's 3rd Division were still in camp, mounted and poised for action. But no action came their way.

Finally, one of Torbert's aides came galloping up to Custer with a report of the disaster that had befallen the infantry and orders to put his division in on the 6th Corps' right, where the Rebel flanking moves had forced the corps to retreat. On his own initiative, Custer sent two regiments across the Valley Turnpike to try to stem the tide of retreat, then he put the rest of his division in line of battle on Getty's right, and Custer's horse artillery dueled with the Rebel guns. This put an end to the Confederate turning movements on that flank, but soon the other flank was threatened and Wright sent orders for Custer to move around to the left. Custer left three regiments to protect the right flank, just in case, and took the rest, plus his guns, to a position behind the left of Devin's brigade, just east of the turnpike.

At around 9 a.m. Colonel Charles Russell Lowell, commander of the Reserve Brigade in Merritt's division, rode over to have a talk with Colonel Kidd of the Michigan Brigade. Both were feeling anxious about the obviously deteriorating situation over in the infantry camps and their own enforced idleness. Lowell, who was 29 but looked much younger, was a nephew of the poet James Russell Lowell and the scion of one of the first families of Massachusetts. He had graduated at the top of the Harvard class of 1854. Early in the war he had, like Custer, served on McClellan's staff. Then he had been made colonel of the 2nd Massachusetts Cavalry and commander of a brigade that consisted of that regiment and a couple of New York cavalry regiments in the Department of Washington and had taken part in the pursuit of Early after the latter's raid on the capital. Sheridan had been so impressed with his abilities that he had put him in command of the regulars of the Reserve Brigade and was reportedly thinking of jumping him over several heads to make him his new chief of cavalry. Kidd, on the other hand, had come up through the ranks of the 6th Michigan Cavalry to succeed Custer when the latter was given command of first the 2nd Division and then the 3rd just a few weeks before.

Now Russell pointed out that his orders were to support the Michigan Brigade, if needed. Kidd replied that no support was needed. "The enemy had been easily checked," he later wrote, "and, at the moment, had become so quiet as to give rise to the suspicion that they had withdrawn from our front, as indeed they had." Then Kidd said that, judging by the sounds of battle, the Union infantry was retreating. Lowell said that it seemed that way to him as well. Then, after a pause, Lowell announced that he was going to go see if he could help. Kidd, brand new to brigade command, asked for advice: "Colonel, what would you do if you were in my place?" Lowell said, "I think you should go too. Yes, I will take the responsibility to give you the order."[32]

The two brigades made their way to the southeast, heading for the sound of guns, and soon came to a large plateau about a mile behind Getty's embattled division. From there, Kidd said, "The full scope of the calamity which had befallen our arms burst suddenly into view. The valley and intervening slopes, the fields and woods, were alive with infantry, moving singly and in squads. Some entire regiments were hurrying to the rear, while Confederate artillery was raining shot and shell and spherical case among them to accelerate their speed." Yet the troops did not appear to be routed, he said. "It did not look like a frightened or panic stricken army, but like a disorganized mass that had simply lost the power of cohesion. They were chagrined, mortified, mad at their officers and themselves—demoralized; but after all, more to be pitied than blamed."[33]

The two mounted brigades, in column of fours, passed the 1st Division of the 19th Corps, which had reformed to Getty's right. General William Dwight, that division's normal commander, was under arrest because of a running quarrel he had been having with Grover and Emory over his report on the battle of the Opequon, but he was with his troops that morning and saw the horsemen ride by. "They moved past me, that splendid cavalry," he wrote; "if they reached the Pike, I felt secure. Lowell got by me before I could speak, but I looked after him for a long distance. Exquisitely mounted, the picture of a soldier, erect, confident, defiant, he moved at the head of the finest body of cavalry that today scorns the earth it treads." Colonel Carter's Rebel artillery soon found this compact target. "One shell took an entire set of fours out of the Sixth Michigan," Kidd wrote. "Not a man left the ranks. The next set closed up the gap."[34] Off to the left they could see Custer's division taking position behind Devin's left, and soon an order arrived from Merritt for them to continue across the turnpike and join the rest of the cavalry.

After Wharton's Division had been repulsed by Getty, Early sent it to protect his right from Devin's and Moore's cavalry, backing it up with Wofford's Brigade of Kershaw's Division, which had become separated from its other brigades. Orders were sent for Gordon and Kershaw to again attack Getty's right, but, before they could, the latter had made his withdrawal to the north of Middletown, which Early attributed to the bombardment by the Confederate artillery. "Ramseur and Pegram advanced at once to the position from which the enemy was driven," Early wrote, "and just then his cavalry commenced pressing heavily on the right, and Pegram's division was ordered to move to the north of Middletown, and take position across the Pike against the cavalry."[35]

By then a staff officer had returned and reported to Early that he had delivered the attack order to Kershaw but that the latter had informed him that his division was too scattered to make the attack. The staff officer said that he had not even delivered the order to Gordon because he had seen that neither Kershaw's nor Gordon's division was in condition to execute it. Therefore, as soon as Pegram moved to the right, Early ordered Kershaw to take his place. "I then rode to Middletown," Early said, "to make provision against the enemy's cavalry, and discovered a large body of it seriously threatening that flank, which was very much exposed."[36]

While the 1st and 3rd divisions of the 6th Corps were taking position on Getty's right and Kershaw's and Gordon's rebel divisions, which had fallen behind due to Getty's last withdrawal, were advancing to catch up with the rest of Early's army, Merritt's cavalry, especially Lowell's brigade, began a series of short, sharp charges. The horsemen would gallop up and apply their revolvers and sabers to any Rebels who did not fall back fast enough, then gallop back, reform, and come on again. Early claimed that "several charges of the enemy's cavalry were repulsed," but he sent off a message to Lomax, who had not yet appeared, "requiring him to move to Middletown as quickly as possible."[37] Lomax, however, never got the message, and anyway he had Powell to contend with. Merritt said that his line "advanced nearly to Middletown, driving the enemy before it through the open country." But he added that "this advance was intended more as an offensive-defensive movement than one looking to a final victory."[38]

When he thought he had advanced far enough, or as far as he could, Lowell, who had already had a horse shot out from under him during those charges, had his men dismount and take cover behind a stone wall on the edge of the town. From there they used their Spencer repeating carbines to hold off Wharton's and Wofford's skirmishers, who repeatedly tried to dislodge them, while the cavalry in general suffered from the attention of Carter's massed guns. Merritt said that the artillery fire was "truly terrific; it has seldom been equalled for accuracy of aim and excellence of ammunition." The Union horse artillery and other guns tried to suppress the Confederate fire, but "were overpowered at times by weight of metal and superior ammunition."[39]

Colonel Wildes, whose two Ohio regiments were now with "the remnant of our little corps still clinging to the left," reforming behind Getty's division, said, "We could see the cavalry driving back the rebel hordes, which was the first ray of hope and grain of encouragement we had received during the morning. But the day was lost, as all felt, and the army directed its attention to saving its trains and preventing the enemy from getting complete possession of the Pike and cutting us off from Winchester." Nevertheless, Wildes noted, "The enemy appeared content with his victory, and was now making no attempts to force us further back."[40]

"So many of our men had stopped in the camp to plunder . . . ," Early reported two days later, "the country was so open, and the enemy's cavalry so strong, that I did not deem it prudent to press farther, especially as Lomax had not come up. I determined, therefore, to content myself with trying to hold the advantages I had gained until all my troops had come up and the captured property was secured."[41]

"We waited," Gordon later complained, "waited for weary hours. Waited till the routed men in blue found that no foe was pursuing them and until they had time to recover their normal composure and courage; waited till Confederate officers lost hope and the fires had gone out in the hearts of the privates."[42]

"The battle and the day wore on together," wrote a colonel in Custer's division. "The sulphurous cloud that overhung the field, and the dense volumes of dust that rose behind the wheeling batteries and the charging troops, contrasted grimly with the sweet light of that perfect October day as it could be seen beyond the limits of the battlefield."[43]

Another of Custer's officers, a major sitting his horse near the Valley Turnpike, also took a moment to look around at more distant scenes. And looking down the road behind him he saw a rider coming hard, covered with dust and followed by a knot of other riders. Each time this distant rider passed a group of Union fugitives he would wave his cap and shout something. Then the stragglers would cheer and toss their caps in the air, grab their weapons, and turn back toward the fighting. And there was absolutely no doubt in the cavalry officer's mind about who this distant rider could be.

---

1. Lewis, *The Guns of Cedar Creek*, 201.
2. Ibid., 204–206.
3. Ibid., 206.
4. Ibid., 207.
5. Wert, *From Winchester to Cedar Creek*, 194.
6. Lewis, *The Guns of Cedar Creek*, 208.
7. Ibid., 209.
8. Ibid., 208.
9. Ibid., 209.
10. Ibid., 200–201.
11. Ibid., 211.
12. Ibid.
13. Ibid.
14. Ibid., 214.
15. Ibid., 216.
16. Ibid., 218.

17. Ibid.
18. Ibid., 219.
19. Ibid.
20. *Official Records*, 43:I:193–194.
21. Lewis, *The Guns of Cedar Creek*, 223.
22. Ibid.
23. Ibid., 224.
24. Ibid., 226–227.
25. Early, *War Memoirs*, 444–445.
26. Lewis, *The Guns of Cedar Creek*, 229.
27. Ibid.
28. Wert, *From Winchester to Cedar Creek*, 209–210.
29. Early, *War Memoirs*, 445.
30. *Official Records*, 43:I:194.
31. Lewis, *The Guns of Cedar Creek*, 238.
32. Ibid., 231.
33. Ibid.
34. Ibid., 232.
35. Early, *War Memoirs*, 446.
36. Ibid.
37. Ibid.
38. Lewis, *The Guns of Cedar Creek*, 237.
39. Ibid., 238.
40. Ibid.
41. *Official Records*, 43:I:562.
42. Lewis, *The Guns of Cedar Creek*, 239.
43. Ibid., 238–239.

CHAPTER TWENTY-THREE

We'll Whip
Them Yet!

19 October 1864

Sheridan had been awakened that morning at Winchester by an officer on picket duty who had come to his room to report that artillery fire could be heard coming from the direction of Cedar Creek. The general asked the officer if the firing was continuous or only desultory, and he said it was not a sustained fire but irregular and fitful. "It's all right," Sheridan said, "Grover has gone out this morning to make a reconnoissance, and he is merely feeling the enemy."[1] Sheridan tried to go back to sleep, but he was too restless, so he got up and got dressed. Before long the picket officer came back and reported that the firing, which could be heard from his line on the heights outside of town, was still going on. Sheridan asked him if it sounded like a battle and he said it did not, so the general again assumed that it was caused by the scheduled reconnaissance. Nevertheless, he went downstairs and had the preparation of his breakfast hurried and ordered the horses to be saddled and ready.

"We mounted our horses between half-past 8 and 9," Sheridan wrote, "and as we were proceeding up the street . . . I noticed that there were many women at the windows and doors of the houses, who kept shaking their skirts at us and who were otherwise markedly insolent in their demeanor, but supposing this conduct to be instigated by their well-known and perhaps natural prejudices, I ascribed to it no unusual significance." At the edge of town he stopped for a moment and he could hear the sound of artillery firing in an unceasing roar. "Concluding from this that a battle was in progress," he said, "I now felt confident that the women along the street had received intelligence from the battlefield by the 'grape-vine telegraph,' and were in raptures over some good news, while I as yet was utterly ignorant of the actual situation."[2]

He rode for a while with his head down, listening intently, trying to locate and interpret the sound, and finally concluded that the sound of firing was moving north, indicating that his army was falling back. At Mill Creek, about a half-mile south of Winchester, his escort fell in behind him, "When, just as we made the crest of the rise beyond the stream, there burst upon our view the appalling spectacle of a panic-stricken army—hundreds of slightly wounded men, throngs of others unhurt but utterly demoralized, and baggage-wagons by the score, all pressing to the rear in hopeless confusion, telling only too plainly that a disaster had occurred at the front." He talked to some of the fugitives, and "they assured me that the army was broken up, in full retreat, and that all was lost; all this with a manner true to that peculiar indifference that takes possession of panic-stricken men."[3]

Sheridan sent orders to Colonel Edwards to stretch his troops across the valley and stop all fugitives. Then he considered what he ought to do next. He thought about letting the army retreat to Winchester, where it could form a new line, but that was just not his style. He was always a general who led from the front and who preferred the offense to defense. So he rode on. Soon his chief commissary officer rode up and gave him a fuller report of what had happened in his absence from the army. Sheridan then took two of his aides, Major George "Sandy" Forsyth and Captain Joseph O'Keefe, and twenty men from the escort and rode for the front, leaving the rest to do what they could about stopping the stragglers, wagons, etc.

Sheridan's big black horse, Rienzi, ate up the ground with what Sandy Forsyth called "his long swinging gallop, almost a run, which he seemed to maintain so easily and endlessly—a most distressing gait for those who had to follow far." Were it not for the difficult pace and the anxiety about the fate of the army, it would have been a beautiful ride. "It was a golden sunny day," Forsyth remembered, "that had succeeded a densely foggy October morning. The turnpike stretched away, a white, dusty line, over hill and through dale, bordered by fenceless fields, and past farmhouses and empty barns and straggling orchards. Now and then it ran through a woody copse, with here and there a tiny stream of water crossing it, or meandering by its side, so clear and limpid that it seemed to invite us to pause and slake our thirst as we sped along our dusty way. On either side we saw, through the Indian-summer haze, the distant hills covered with woods and fairly ablaze with foliage; and over all was the deep blue of a cloudless Southern sky, making it a day on which ones' blood ran riot and he was glad of health and life."[4]

Before long Sheridan found the road blocked by wagons and wounded men, so he had to take to the fields. When the wagons and wounded were out of the way he returned to the road, finding it thickly lined with unhurt men who, having gone far enough to the rear to be out of danger, had stopped, without any organization, and had begun to boil coffee. "Come on back, boys!" he shouted. "Give 'em hell, God damn 'em! We'll make coffee out of Cedar Creek tonight!"[5] The men abandoned their coffee, threw up their caps, grabbed up their rifles, and turned to follow him south with enthusiasm and cheers. He took off his cap, making it easier for the men to recognize him, and with his two aides rode well in advance of his escort. "I already knew," he later wrote, "that even in the ordinary condition of mind enthusiasm is a potent element with soldiers, but what I saw that day convinced me that if it can be excited from a state of despondency its power is almost irresistible."[6]

To those along the road he said, "If I had been with you this morning this disaster would not have happened. We must face the other way; we will go back and recover our camp." A demoralized infantry colonel shouted back, "The army's whipped!" and kept going north. "You are," Sheridan answered, "but the army isn't."[7] Most mounted officers who saw him, however, galloped out on either side of the pike to tell the men farther from the road that Sheridan had returned, and they, too, turned their faces toward the enemy and marched back toward the sound of battle. "As he galloped on," Forsyth wrote, "his features gradually grew set, as though carved in stone, and the same dull red glint I had seen in his piercing black eyes when on other occasions the battle was going against us, was there now."[8]

Just north of Newtown, about halfway between Winchester and Middletown, he met a chaplain who was digging his heels into a jaded horse and making for the rear with all possible speed. Sheridan asked him how things were going at the front. "Everything is lost; but all will be right when you get there," he replied. "Yet notwithstanding this expression of confidence in me," Sheridan remembered, "the parson at once resumed his breathless pace to the rear."[9] At Newtown the streets were so crowded that he had to detour around the village. There he saw young Major William McKinley of Crook's staff—the future president—who spread the news of his return throughout the refugees in the town. Just south of Newtown Sheridan spotted a large body of troops about three quarters of a mile west of the turnpike. These turned out to be the 1st and 3rd divisions of the 6th Corps. And then he learned that the 19th Corps was a little farther to the right and rear. But he did not stop, for he wanted to find the troops who were nearest to the enemy.

James E. Taylor, an artist for a news magazine, was near the turnpike behind Getty's division when he heard "murmurs like the breaking of a surge on a far off shore. Nearer it grew. Grew louder and swelled to a tumult. Cheers—the cheers of the stragglers." "There we stood," wrote one of Getty's officers, "driven four miles already, quietly waiting for what might be further and immediate disaster, while far in the rear we heard the stragglers and hospital bummers, and the gunless artillerymen actually cheering as though a victory had been won. We could hardly believe our ears."[10]

Finally, at about 10:30 a.m., halfway between Newtown and Middletown, Sheridan came upon the 2nd Division of the 6th Corps. Torbert, however, was the first officer he saw. "My God! I am glad you've come," the cavalry commander said.[11]

Sheridan found Getty's division posted on the reverse slope of some slightly rising ground, behind some breastworks made of fence rails. Jumping his horse over this barricade he rode to the crest, took off his cap so that his soldiers would recognize him, and said, "Men, by God, we'll whip them yet! We'll sleep in our old tents tonight!" The men cheered, shouted, and stamped their feet. "Instantly," one of Getty's staff officers said, "a mighty revulsion of feeling took place. Hope and confidence returned at a bound. No longer did we merely hope the worst was over, that we could hold our ground until night, or at worst make good an orderly retreat to Winchester. Now we all burned to attack the enemy, to drive him back, to retrieve our honor and sleep in our old camps that night. And every man knew that Sheridan would do it."[12]

"But close at the heels of Sheridan's horse rode his orderly," General Lewis Grant remembered, "a little fellow scarcely more than a boy. His animal was small, and how he managed to keep up with his chief the entire distance is something remarkable." This orderly's job was to carry Sheridan's personal flag, a swallow-tailed guidon with a white star on red in the top half and a red star on white below, to mark his location wherever he went. When the general's big horse skidded to a stop, the young trooper "turned with him and halted almost simultaneously at the proper distance behind. A general cheer went up by those who saw the incident and our men shouted as much for the little orderly as they did for Sheridan."[13]

The general then returned to the rear of the 2nd Division where, as he put it, "a line of regimental flags rose up out of the ground." This was the remnant of the 8th Corps. Behind the flags, where Sheridan failed to notice them, Rutherford Hayes had collected over a thousand men of that corps. Soon he found Crook and Wright talking together nearby, and dismounting he threw his arms around his old friend Crook. "What are you doing way back here?" he teased. As the man who had been in charge, Wright answered for them both. "Well, we've done the best we could," he said as he gripped Sheridan's hand. "That's all right," Sheridan replied. A few seconds later Emory rode up and said that his troops were ready to cover the retreat of the army. "Retreat, hell!" Sheridan answered. "We'll be back in our camps tonight." Wright then gave him a hurried account of the day's events, and Sheridan ordered Wright's and Emory's divisions brought up on line with Getty's division, on its right.[14]

Next, Sheridan rode over to where the cavalry was posted on Getty's left, east of the turnpike. When Custer saw him ride by he galloped after him, and when he caught up with him he threw both arms around the little general's neck and hugged him as though he were a long-lost brother. "Looks as though we are gone up today," Custer said. "The right will prevail," Sheridan assured him, and Custer, like so many others, immediately caught the commander's enthusiastic optimism. "We will go back to our old camps to-night or I will sacrifice every man in my division," he said, "and I will go with them."[15]

Sheridan sent Sandy Forsyth to ask Lowell if he could hold his position on the northern edge of Middletown for forty minutes. The answer was positive, but when asked whether he could extend that to sixty minutes, he said only, "I will if I can."[16] Meanwhile, Sheridan found a point from which he could get a good view of the front, and after studying the situation he ordered Custer's division to move back to the right flank. Then he returned to the spot behind Getty's division which he had designated as his new headquarters. Here he had Rienzi unsaddled and replaced by his spare horse, a gray named Breckinridge for his former owner who had lost him at the battle of the Opequon the month before.

When Sheridan saw Kiefer's and Wheaton's divisions coming up, in obedience to his previous order, he went to show them just where he wanted them placed. He ordered Wright to resume command of the 6th Corps and Getty of his 2nd Division, and restored the arrested Dwight to the command of the 1st Division of the 19th Corps, and by the time that corps was put in position between the 6th Corps and a little stream called Middle Marsh Brook he had decided that it was time to return to the vantage point he had found east of the turnpike to have another look at what the Rebels were up to.

They were in what one Union officer called an "immensely strong" position protected "by the heavy stone walls which lined the old furnace road and bordered the fields, and by a stone mill at the crossing of the road and brook. Open ground, which must be crossed by an attacking force without cover, extended in front. There was every reason to expect, and Sheridan did expect, that Early with his victorious troops rested and reformed and deployed and united in one strong battalia, would move onward to the attack at any moment."[17]

Sandy Forsyth now suggested that, while most of the troops knew that he had returned, not all that many had actually seen him yet. So he rode down the entire length of the infantry line, again carrying his cap in his hand to allow the men to see him clearly, and they greeted him with a great cheer. "It was a thrilling spectacle, as dramatic as the ride from Winchester," wrote newspaper artist James Taylor. "The sight of that little man instantly inspired confidence in the men and threw them into a perfect frenzy of enthusiasm," a surgeon remembered. "I'll get a twist on these people yet!" Sheridan shouted, referring to the Confederates. "We'll raise them out of their boots before the day is over!"[18] His confidence was so contagious that, as a major in the 19th Corps put it, "no more doubt, or chance for doubt existed; we were safe, perfectly and unconditionally safe, and every man knew it."[19] Of course, he did not mean that they felt individually safe from harm, but collectively safe from defeat. They might die, but they could not lose. By then it was past noon.

Colonel Lowell, riding up and down behind his troopers who were holding the stone wall north of Middletown, was worried about what the Rebels opposite him were up to, and he rode forward to have a closer look. Suddenly he was flung backward on his horse, twisting to his left. Another officer caught him and eased him to the ground. Lowell could not speak, but he gestured to his chest, and when the officer pulled open his coat to inspect the wound a flattened, distorted bullet fell out. It had evidently struck something else first and then ricocheted into his chest. It had not broken the skin, but it had stunned him badly directly over lungs that had been ravaged by tuberculosis. He began to cough up blood, could not stand, and could speak only in a whisper, but he refused to leave the field. He was lain behind some cover and draped with a staff officer's coat, but he did not plan to stay down for long. When he could talk, he said he would return to the saddle in time to join the counterattack which he knew was coming. He said he was not hurt bad. "It is only my *poor* lung," he said.[20]

As Custer returned to the right flank, he sent ahead to learn the situation there and found out that Rosser's Confederate troopers had finally bestirred themselves and were advancing. However, they did not seem to know that most of the Union cavalry had been withdrawn to the other flank, and the three regiments Custer had left to cover the right had been able to slow them up considerably. Now Rosser was massing his two brigades for an all-out attack, but Custer, with his usual keen eye for hidden approaches, took one of his brigades to a position "almost in rear of and overlooking the ground upon which the enemy had massed his command."[21] From there his battery of horse artillery opened fire at close range and he charged with three mounted regiments. The Rebels retreated in haste, while Custer formed a line two miles long stretching back to the infantry's right flank, and the two old friends, Custer and Rosser, only skirmished with each other through the early afternoon.

A staff officer then brought Custer word that Sheridan was preparing for a general attack by his entire line, in which he wanted Custer to participate. So the latter gradually closed up his division to the left. "Before this disposition was completed," Custer wrote, "the mounted skirmishers of the enemy were seen advancing over the ridge . . . I was compelled for the time at least, to break my connection with the infantry on my left, in order to direct my efforts against the force of the enemy now approaching on my right." Again Custer charged with three regiments while his battery provided fire support, and again the Rebels fell back toward Cupp's Ford. "It was apparent," Custer wrote, "that the wavering in the ranks of the enemy betokened a retreat, and that this retreat might be converted into a rout. For a moment I was undecided. Upon the right I was confident of my ability to drive the enemy's cavalry with which I was then engaged across the creek; upon the left my chances of success were not so sure, but the advantages to be gained, if successful, overwhelmingly greater; I chose the latter."[22] Again he left three regiments to watch Rosser's cavalry while he wheeled the rest of his division into column and led it off to the left. The officer in charge of the three regiments was ordered to push the Rebels along and then to send two of them to rejoin the rest of the division as soon as possible.

The Confederate infantrymen were getting anxious for something to happen. Some thought that they should retreat with their spoils to a safer position—Fisher's Hill perhaps. Others were for continuing to advance, but hardly anyone seemed to favor staying where they were. Colonel Carter, the Confederate chief of artillery, came to General Early and "explained that the troops were eager to go ahead, and I have been questioned all along the line to know the cause of the delay. Every practical fighting man in our war knows that troops scattered and panic-stricken cannot be rallied in the face of hot and vigorous pursuit." Wharton later wrote that he "supposed we were arranging for a general movement to the front, and expected every minute orders to advance; but no orders came, and there we stood—no enemy in our front for hours except some troops moving about in the woodland on a hill nearly a mile in our front. I have never been able to understand why General Early did not advance, or why he remained in line for four or five hours after the brilliant victory of the morning."[23]

The reasons Early later gave for neither continuing the attack nor withdrawing to Fisher's Hill were: the presence of large and undamaged Union cavalry units threatening his flanks, and the numbers of his own men who had fallen out of ranks to plunder the Federal camps. The battles of the previous month had taught Early a healthy respect for Sheridan's powerful cavalry both in attack and pursuit. And he was worried by his own weakness in that arm, especially by the absence of Lomax, who had still not shown up. Further, he seems to have been deceived by the movements of large parts of the Union cavalry from the west to the east and back again and did not realize that he was seeing, and hearing reports of, the same units in different places as they moved around.

As for the number of his men who left the ranks to plunder the Union camps, the evidence seems to indicate that, although many men picked up valuable articles of food and clothing as they passed through the camps, not very many frontline troops fell out for very long. Wharton later said, "It is true that there were parties passing over the field and perhaps pillaging, but most of them were citizens, teamsters and persons attached to the quartermaster's and other departments, and perhaps a few soldiers who had taken the wounded to the rear." A Confederate chaplain said that "they were men who in large numbers had been wounded during the summer's campaign, who had come up to the army for medical examination, and who came like a division down the pike behind Wharton, and soon scattered over the field and camps and helped themselves. They were not men with guns."[24]

"As soon as I had regulated matters on the right so as to prevent his cavalry from getting in rear of that flank," Early said, "I rode to the left for the purpose of ordering an advance. I found Ramseur and Kershaw in line with Pegram, but Gordon had not come up. In a short time, however, I found him coming up from the rear, and I ordered him to take position on Kershaw's left, and advance for the purpose of driving the enemy from his new position—Kershaw and Ramseur being ordered to advance at the same time." By then, however, Custer had returned to the Union right or Confederate left. "As the enemy's cavalry on our left was very strong," Early continued, "and had the benefit of an open country to the rear of that flank, a repulse at this time would have been disastrous, and I therefore directed General Gordon, if he found the enemy's line too strong to attack with success, not to make the assault."[25]

At about 1 p.m. Gordon's Division began advancing through some woods toward the 19th Corps' left. Sheridan saw it coming and ordered Lewis Grant's crack Vermont Brigade over from Getty's division of the 6th Corps to take up position behind Emory's line as a reserve. Sandy Forsyth, stationed with the 19th Corps to keep Sheridan posted, could hear the Rebels coming through the woods, then "we caught a glimpse of a long gray line stretching away through the woods on either side of us, advancing with waving standards, with here and there a mounted officer in the rear of it. At the same instant the dark blue line at the edge of the woods seemed to burst upon their view, for suddenly they halted, and with a piercing yell poured in a heavy volley, that was almost instantly answered from our side, and then volleys seemed fairly to leap from one end to the other of our line, and a steady roar of musketry from both sides made the woods echo again in every direction." Captain DeForest said that the troops of the 19th Corps "were apparently somewhat dismayed at discovering that the enemy showed a willingness to renew the battle; and while the fusilade lasted I noted some ominously gloomy faces. 'They are not going to fight well,' said one of our staff officers sadly. 'They haven't recovered their spirits. They look scared.'"[26]

As it turned out, however, they did not have to put up much of a fight. "The uproar lasted several minutes, and then I was told that the column had retreated," DeForest said.[27] So despite his later complaining about Early's lack of fight, Gordon was scared off by the sight of Yankees behind hastily constructed defenses and did not drive home the attack. As Early later wrote, "The advance was made for some distance, when Gordon's skirmishers came back, reporting a line of battle in front behind breastworks, and Gordon did not make the attack. It was now apparent that it would not do to press my troops further . . . I determined, therefore, to try and hold what had been gained, and orders were given for carrying off the captured and abandoned artillery, small arms and wagons."[28]

"That's good! That's good!" was Sheridan's response when told that the Confederate attack had been driven back. "Thank God for that! Now then, tell General Emory if they attack him again to go after them, and to follow them up, and to sock it to them, and to give them the devil."[29] But the Rebels did not attack again, and neither did the Federals. Impatience finally overcame Sandy Forsyth, and he rode back to Sheridan's headquarters, where he was astonished to find the general "half lying

down, with his head resting on his right hand, his elbow on the ground."
Asked why he had come, Forsyth said, "It seems to me, general, that
we ought to advance; I have come hoping for orders." Too late he realized
that he should not talk that way to the commanding general. Sheridan
"half sat up, and the black eyes flashed. But gradually an amused look
overshadowed the anxious face, and the chief slowly shook his head.
'Not yet, not yet; go back and wait.'"[30]

Forsyth returned to the right and sat down under a tree behind the
19th Corps, where the men were themselves stretched out "listlessly and
sleepily" on the ground, and soon he thought he saw at least one reason
why Sheridan was waiting: "Every now and then stragglers—sometimes
singly, oftener in groups—came up from the rear, and moving along
back of the line, dusty, heavy-footed and tired, found and rejoined their
respective companies and regiments, dropping down quietly by the sides
of their companions as they came to them, with a gibe or a word or two
of greeting on either side, and then they, too, like most of the rest,
subsided into an appearance of apathetic indifference."[31] The army was
growing stronger even as it rested.

But after another hour of this, Forsyth grew anxious, rode out to the
front without being able to see what the enemy was up to, and then went
back and tried Sheridan again. "Not yet, not yet," he was told. "Go
back and wait patiently." After another hour he walked out to the picket
line for another look and kept going until he could see what the Rebels
were up to. He found that they had a strong skirmish line in front of
their main line along Old Forge Road, and he watched them "piling up
stones and rails on the prolongation of a line of stone fences, evidently
expecting an advance from our side and preparing for it."[32] Again he
returned to Sheridan.

"I had been supposing all day," Sheridan later wrote, "that Longstreet's troops were present, but as no definite intelligence on this point
had been gathered, I concluded, in the lull that now occurred, to ascertain something positive regarding Longstreet; and Merritt having been
transferred to our left in the morning, I directed him to attack an exposed
battery then at the edge of Middltown, and capture some prisoners.
Merritt soon did this work effectually, concealing his intention till his
troops got close enough to the enemy, and then by a quick dash gobbling
up a number of Confederates. When the prisoners were brought in, I
learned from them that the only troops of Longstreet's in the fight were
of Kershaw's division, which had rejoined Early at Brown's Gap in the
latter part of September, and that the rest of Longstreet's corps was not
on the field. The receipt of this information entirely cleared the way for
me to take the offensive, but on the heels of it came information that

Longstreet was marching by the Front Royal pike to strike my rear at Winchester, driving Powell's cavalry in as he advanced. This renewed my uneasiness, and caused me to delay the general attack till after assurances came from Powell denying utterly the reports as to Longstreet and confirming the statements of the prisoners."[33]

The courier who had delivered this information from Powell had just left headquarters when Sandy Forsyth returned. "It's all right now!" Sheridan exclaimed, then he asked the time. When he was told that it was 3:40 p.m. he said, "So late! Why, that's later than I thought!" Then he issued orders for a general attack all along the line with the 19th Corps, if possible, to wheel to its left and push the Rebels toward the turnpike while the 6th Corps went straight in. The 8th Corps was to be kept in reserve, and the cavalry was to hit both flanks. Sheridan rode over to explain his orders to Getty, on the left of the infantry line, in person. He was probably not yet aware of the decisive part that Getty had already played in that day's action when he told him, "Do well in this movement, General, and I will see that you are properly recognized." Getty was deeply offended and replied icily, "General Sheridan, I always do well—the best I can, at all events."[34]

The attack orders worked their way down the chain of command, from corps to division to brigade to regiment, until they reached the men in the ranks. "Everywhere along the line of battle," Sandy Forsyth wrote, "men might be seen to stoop and retie their shoes; to pull their trousers at the ankle tightly together and then draw up their heavy woolen stockings over them; to rebuckle and tighten their waist-belts; to unbutton the lids of their cartridge-boxes and pull them forward rather more to the front; to rearrange their haversacks and canteens, and to shift their rolls of blankets in order to give freer scope to the expansion of shoulders and an easier play to their arms; to set their forage caps tighter on their heads, pulling the vizor well down over their eyes; and then, almost as if by order, there rang from one end of the line to the other the rattle of ramrods and snapping of gunlocks as each man tested for himself the condition of his rifle." When all this had been done, the men leaned on their weapons and waited for the order to advance. And finally it came: "'Attention!' rings down the line. 'Shoulder arms! Forward! *March!*' And with martial tread and floating legs the line of battle is away." As one Federal soldier later put it, "they felt that glory or defeat, the salvation or ruin of the country, depended upon the issues of that moment." Some however, probably had less lofty motivations. One of them was heard to say at the time that "we may as well whip them tonight; if we don't we shall have to do it tomorrow. Sheridan will get it out of us some time.'"[35]

1. Sheridan, *Memoirs*, 2:69.
2. Ibid., 2:71–73.
3. Morris, *Sheridan*, 213.
4. Lewis, *The Guns of Cedar Creek*, 245–246.
5. Sheridan, *Memoirs*, 2:75–77.
6. Ibid., 2:81.
7. Morris, *Sheridan*, 213.
8. Lewis, *The Guns of Cedar Creek*, 248.
9. Sheridan, *Memoirs*, 2:81.
10. Lewis, *The Guns of Cedar Creek*, 249.
11. Sheridan, *Memoirs*, 2:82.
12. Lewis, *The Guns of Cedar Creek*, 250.
13. Ibid.
14. Ibid., 250–251.
15. Urwin, *Custer Victorious*, 211.
16. Lewis, *The Guns of Cedar Creek*, 253.
17. Ibid.
18. Ibid., 255.
19. Morris, *Sheridan*, 216.
20. Lewis, *The Guns of Cedar Creek*, 254.
21. *Official Records*, 43:I:523.
22. Ibid., 43:I:523–524.
23. Lewis, *The Guns of Cedar Creek*, 257.
24. Ibid., 258–259.
25. Early, *War Memoirs*, 447.
26. Lewis, *The Guns of Cedar Creek*, 260.
27. Ibid.
28. Early, *War Memoirs*, 447–448.
29. Lewis, *The Guns of Cedar Creek*, 260.
30. Ibid., 261.
31. Ibid.
32. Ibid.
33. Sheridan, *Memoirs*, 2:88.
34. Lewis, *The Guns of Cedar Creek*, 262.
35. Ibid., 263.

CHAPTER TWENTY-FOUR

The Johnnies Are Whipped All to Pieces

19 October 1864

Colonel Kidd, at the head of the Michigan Brigade of cavalry on the far left of the Union line, had a good view from the high ground east of the turnpike: "It was a glorious sight to see that magnificent line sweeping onward in the charge. Far, far away on the right it was visible. There were no reserves, no plans for retreat, only one grand, absorbing thought—to drive them back and retake the camps. Heavens, what a din! All along the Confederate line, the cannon volleyed and thundered. The Union artillery replied. The roll of musketry became incessant."[1]

Merritt's cavalry advanced on the Union left against Wharton's infantry on the Confederate right. The troopers trotted across a ravine and up onto a broad plateau where they were hit by deadly artillery fire. The regulars of the Reserve Brigade were in the front line and Colonel Lowell, mounted again as he had promised, was well out in front of everyone, as usual, defying death in order to give courage to his men. But he was soon hit by another bullet, and this one found a more vital organ than his bad lung. It severed his spine and knocked him to the ground paralyzed. As they had done off and on all afternoon, his men wheeled their horses and galloped back to the cover of the ravine, followed by Kidd's and Devin's brigades, there to reform for another try.

However, their brief retreat exposed the left flank of Getty's infantry to enfilading fire from the Rebel artillery to the east. These troops were under orders to advance slowly, in order to give the 19th Corps time to drive in the Confederate left, and they were caught out in the open by this crossfire. French's—formerly Bidwell's—3rd Brigade was on the left end of Getty's line and took the brunt of this fire and it soon fell back to its starting position. To Getty's right, Keifer's 3rd Division also pulled back, taking part of Warner's brigade of Getty's division along. But the rest of that brigade plus Lewis Grant's Vermonters in the center of Getty's line would not retreat. They took cover behind a low stone wall that happened to be in just the right place and just long enough to cover their front. From there, as an admiring Federal major wrote, they, "with the utmost coolness, opened so well-sustained and effective a hail of musketry on the gray forms crouching behind the stone walls in front that their fire visibly slackened."[2] On the right of the 6th Corps line, Wheaton's 1st Division was also brought to a halt but also refused to fall back. Beyond Wheaton, Grover's 2nd Division of the 19th Corps also stalled after driving Rebel skirmishers from a stone wall. Grover went down with a wound, and his place was taken by Brigadier General Henry Birge, commander of his 1st Brigade.

Merritt's three cavalry brigades charged forward again just as half of the 6th Corps was falling back. This time they crossed the plateau and two more ravines and got as far as the fence behind which Wharton's skirmishers crouched before the concentrated fire of Confederate guns and rifles forced them to retreat again. While they reformed in the nearest ravine, Colonel French obtained Getty's permission to forget about a slow advance, and his brigade on the left of the infantry line advanced again, this time at the double-quick. When it came abreast of Lewis Grant's men, the Vermonters joined the attack. Under this pressure from the front, and sensing that something was wrong over on the Confederate left, Ramseur ordered his four brigades to fall back a couple of hundred yards to another stone wall. The withdrawal almost turned into a rout, but the Rebel officers managed to maintain order and get some of the men reformed in their new position. Getty sent staff officers to his right to make contact with the 1st Division, but found that Kershaw's Division was still holding its original line over there.

On the Confederate left, Gordon had been worried about what he called "a long gap, with scarcely a vedette to guard it, between my right and the main Confederate line." He sent several staff officers to inform Early of this dangerous situation and finally went to see the general himself to urge him to send reinforcements to fill the gap or else to either concentrate his force on a shorter line or withdraw to a better position. "He instructed me to stretch out the already weak lines and take a battery of guns to the left. I rode back at a furious gallop to execute these most unpromising movements." A colonel in Kershaw's division later wondered where Gordon expected Early to find any reinforcements for the left, "as our whole force was on the front, and every inch of the line menaced. And how could 'concentration or withdrawal' have been effected in the open country, in the presence of such cavalry? There was nothing to be done but to fight where we stood."[3] However, the real gap on the Confederate left was not between Gordon's division and Kershaw's, but between Evans' Brigade, Gordon's left-most unit, and the rest of his division. This gap, however, proved to be of advantage to the Rebels at first, for, Custer's Union cavalry was off chasing Rosser and Evans' brigade was beyond the right flank of the Federal infantry.

The 19th Corps advanced at the same time as the 6th, down through the woods through which Gordon's men had recently advanced and withdrawn. Soon the Federals came to an open field partly covered with small bushes, and several hundred yards beyond, crowning a slight crest on its farther side, was a low line of fence rails and loose stones which marked the Confederate line. "A deep roar broke upon the summer stillness," a Union surgeon remembered, "in which the very skies seemed to quake. Then an overpowering torrent of shells, grape and bullets tore through the devoted ranks, with murderous effect, followed by a stifling, acrid cloud of smoke, which hovered over the assailants and dimmed the horrid sight."[4]

Fortunately for the Federals, Gordon's men were aiming too high and did less damage than would normally have been the case. The Union line returned a volley and then resumed its advance. In the lead was the brigade which Colonel Stephen Thomas had led that morning, but with Dwight's return to command of the division Brigadier General James McMillan had returned to command of the brigade. Another Rebel volley was more damaging than the first, but still the Federals advanced, fixing bayonets as they went, and a final rush carried them over the defenses with a triumphant shout as Gordon's men gave way, retreating but not broken, stubbornly contesting every inch of ground. Then Evans' Brigade came crashing in on the Union right flank, throwing McMillan's brigade into confusion. However, the Federals swung around to face this new threat, swept their new front with repeated volleys, and then charged. "The enemy broke in great confusion and ran to the south and west," a Union captain wrote, and he noted that the Federals took "grim satisfaction in knowing that the swath was being cut through the identical divisions from which we received the combined assault at early dawn."[5]

As the Union line was facing back toward its original front, Sheridan came dashing up on his big gray charger and ordered McMillan to close up to the left in order to reconnect with the main infantry line, but to delay any further advance until Custer's cavalry was back in position on his right. Just then Custer himself came riding up, again threw his arms around Sheridan's neck, and announced that his division was preparing to join the attack. While Custer returned to complete his preparations, Sheridan rode among the 19th Corps infantrymen, telling them, as a surgeon remembered, "Lie down right where you are, and wait until you see General Custer come down over those hills, and then (he raised himself in the stirrups and made an impulsive gesture with both hands) by God, I want you to *push* the rebels!"[6]

They did not have long to wait. Soon 2,000 Union horsemen came pounding over the hills, overrunning three detached companies from Evans' Brigade who, stretched out in a skirmish line, had been trying to form a connection with Rosser's cavalry before Custer chased off the latter and McMillan's infantry had defeated Evans. Custer's objective was not the flank of Gordon's infantry. As he later reported, "The design was to gain possession of the pike in rear of the enemy, and by holding the bridge and adjacent fords cut off his retreat."[7]

"We caught sight for a moment of the dashing Custer, that prince of horsemen, on an opposite eminence toward the setting sun," said a private in McMillan's brigade, "as he started with his famous division on that fierce charge which did not end till long after dark."[8] The Rebels of Gordon's Division also saw Custer's troopers coming. One yelled, "Great God! We're flanked; now every man for himself!" and another cried, "Run, boys, run! The Yankee cavalry are right on to us!"[9]

The 19th Corps sprang up with a cheer and rushed forward. "This time the rebels offered scarcely any resistence," the surgeon recorded, "but at the first onset broke and ran like a herd of stampeding cattle. From that moment all organization in either army was entirely lost. Among our men, those who had the greatest wind and the strongest legs were soon far ahead of their comrades, in this exciting and exhilarating chase. Yet all moved along in the current, as fast as they could, and every heart pulsated with intense delight. Mounting some elevated spot before them, they observed in the valley a spectacle that caused them to laugh and scream with joy. They saw thousands of rebels indiscriminately mingled together, wearily jogging along, exhibiting nothing but their butter-nut-colored backs, hurling away their guns and knapsacks in their fright, their courage all oozing out at the ends of their toes, and not even daring to turn around and respond to the fire of the boys."[10]

While some of Emory's men pursued Gordon's fleeing troops, others turned against those who were still standing, "to pour in a fearful fire on their exposed flank," Sandy Forsyth said. "The enemy was gallantly holding his line behind some stone fences, but flesh that is born of woman could not stand such work as this."[11] Gordon said that "regiment after regiment, brigade after brigade, in rapid succession was crushed and, like hard clods of clay under a pelting rain, the superb commands crumbled to pieces."[12]

Wright ordered the 3rd Division of the 6th Corps to charge Kershaw's front, and when it went forward, so did Wheaton's 1st Division. Even so, a Rebel captain claimed, Kershaw's men were holding their ground until "someone raised the cry and it was caught up and hurried along like all omens of ill luck, that 'the cavalry is surrounding us.' In a moment our whole line was in one wild confusion, like pandemonium broke loose. If it was a rout in the morning, it was a stampede now. None halted to listen to orders or commands. Like a monster wave struck by the head-land, it rolls back, carrying everything before it by its own force and power, or drawing all within its wake."[13]

"We pursued with avenging haste," wrote a Union chaplain, "cheering as we ran, so loud that the voice of cannon mingling with the clattering of musketry, seemed only the distant echo of our tumultous joy, pushing rapidly over the four miles they had driven us, without an instant's relief, with no thought of their further resistance—they a flying mob, we a shouting and exulting host, pursuing. We chased them to Cedar Creek, over which, after one look of mock defiance, expressed by the angry zips of a thousand bullets, those who could escaped."[14]

As the Confederate army fell apart from left to right, the next to go were Ramseur's Division—or what was left of it after it had fallen back before Getty's attack—and one last brigade of Kershaw's. Ramseur had just asked a major commanding a regiment in Kershaw's remnant whether he could hold on until dark, an hour away, and was riding away after receiving a positive answer when his horse was shot out from under him. He took the horse of a courier, but he had hardly more than mounted when it too was shot from under him. With some difficulty, he found another horse and had just put his foot in the stirrup to mount it when a bullet struck Ramseur in the right side and penetrated both of his lungs. His men saw him fall and their line began to unravel. In an attempt to avoid further panic, staff officers got the young general onto a horse and, propping him up to make it look like he was not too badly hurt, bore him away toward the turnpike. There, out of sight of his men, they put him in an ambulance heading south.

"Every effort was made to stop and rally Kershaw's and Ramseur's men," Early wrote, "but the mass of them resisted all appeals, and continued to go to the rear without waiting for any effort to retrieve the partial disorder . . . Pegram's and Wharton's divisions, and Wofford's brigade had remained steadfast on the right," Early wrote, "and resisted all efforts of the enemy's cavalry, but no portion of this force could be moved to the left without leaving the Pike open to the cavalry, which would have destroyed all hope at once. Every effort to rally the men in the rear having failed, I now had nothing left to me but to order these troops to retire also. When they commenced to move, the disorder soon extended to them, but General Pegram succeeded in bringing back a portion of his command across Cedar Creek in an organized condition, holding the enemy in check, but this small force soon dissolved. A part of Evans' brigade had been rallied in the rear, and held a ford above the bridge for a short time, but it followed the example of the rest."[15]

North of Cedar Creek the pursuit was anything but feeble. For the infantry, it was now what a Union staff officer called "a race and a chase, not a battle, and the very men who had in the morning so ingloriously fled were now the first in the chase—their legs were always good." But there was another part of the pursuit that was far more ominous to the retreating Rebels. "As the tumult of battle died away," Gordon wrote, "there came from the north side of the plain a dull, heavy, swelling sound like the roaring of a distant cyclone, the omen of additional disaster." Not only was Custer's division charging into the Confederate rear in the hope of cutting off the retreat, but with the withdrawal of Wharton's and Pegram's Rebels, Merritt's division came pounding down on the opposite flank. "As the sullen roar from the horses' hoofs beating the soft turf of the plain told of the near approach of the cavalry," Gordon said, "all effort at orderly retreat was abandoned."[16]

Custer could see that the Confederates were retreating so fast that he was not going to get to the turnpike bridge in time to cut them off, so instead he headed for a ford about a half mile upstream and out of sight of the fleeing Rebels. The speed at which it was moving had so extended his column, however, that only two regiments crossed the creek with Custer, the 1st Vermont and the 5th New York. He reformed them on the south side, and they made sure that their carbines and revolvers were loaded.

Not far south of Cedar Creek, Confederate officers started putting together a rear guard. "A breastwork of rails was thrown together, colors planted, a nucleus made, and both flanks grew longer and longer, with wonderful rapidity," said a pursuing 6th Corps officer, Lieutenant Theodore Vaill. "That growing line began to look *ugly*, and somewhat quenched the ardor of the chase. It began to be a question in many minds whether it would not be a point of wisdom to 'survey the vantage of the ground' before getting much further. But just as we descended into the intervening hollow, a body of cavalry, not large, but compact, was seen scouring along the fields to our right and front, directly toward the left flank of that formidable line on the hill."[17]

This compact body of cavalry was the 1st Vermont of Custer's force. The Rebels greatly outnumbered it, but once again they found themselves attacked by infantry in the front and cavalry on the flank. "General Pegram came," said staff officer Henry Kyd Douglas, "and, believing we would be overrun, unfortunately ordered the line to retire. As it proceeded to do so, the enemy came at us with a rush. The few of us who remained could make little resistance and were virtually run over."[18] The Rebels fired a wild volley and tried to run. "The enemy when we struck them were in a dense body, covering several acres," wrote the commander of the 1st Vermont, "and the broken and disorganized rushed upon those in better order, so that all were thrown into confusion. My men with carbines, lying along the side of their horses' necks, fired point blank upon this mass. At one point some of the enemy fell and others fell over them until the ground for the distance of nearly half an acre was covered with a struggling mass of fallen men."[19]

While this was going on, Devin arrived with the leading regiment of Merritt's cavalry, the 6th New York, and charged into the other flank. Then Captain DuPont galloped up with nine guns, threw them into battery on high ground overlooking Cedar Creek and opened fire. "Almost every shell exploded in the midst of the crowded masses before us," he wrote. "Field pieces and caissons, wagons and ambulances, were abandoned by their drivers and dashed along the road in wild confusion, damaging or destroying each other by collisions, while swarms of the retreating enemy left the road and scattered through the fields."[20] The infantry of the 6th Corps continued to advance up the hill, but as Lieutenant Vaill said, "When we reached the top there was no enemy there!"[21]

Both Custer and Devin, after pausing briefly to reorganize their small forces, continued up the turnpike toward Strasburg in the gathering darkness. A 6th Corps staff officer said that "the broad macadamized limestone highway, compacted like a solid rock, resounded and re-echoed under the iron-shod hoofs of the galloping squadrons in the ears of the beaten and flying rebels as if ten thousand Yankee troopers, sword in hand, were thundering down upon their defenseless heads. Dropping their muskets by thousands, abandoning their guns and teams in the road, the terrified fugitives scattered right and left, seeking refuge in the fields and woods, as the charging column with ringing hoof beats and clashing scabbards and shout and cheer and carbine shot went thundering past."[22]

"That which hitherto, on our part, had been a pursuit after a broken and routed army now resolved itself into an exciting chase after a panic-stricken, uncontrolable mob," Custer reported. "It was no longer a question to be decided by force of arms, by skill, or by courage; it was simply a question of speed between pursuers and pursued; prisoners were taken by hundreds, entire companies threw down their arms and appeared glad when summoned to surrender."[23]

Gordon tried to put together another rear guard on Hupp's Hill, where the turnpike ran "immediately on the edge of one of those abrupt and ragged limestone cliffs down which it was supposed not even a rabbit could plunge without breaking its neck." He soon disproved that supposition, however. Union cavalry charged in from three directions at once, and Gordon shouted for his men to save themselves. Then, "wheeling my horse to the dismal brink, I drove my spurs into his flank, and he plunged downward and tumbled headlong in one direction, sending me in another. How I reached the bottom of that abyss I shall never know."[24] Both the general and the horse lay unconscious for a while. When they came to they limped along to the south.

"Half a mile beyond Strasburg," a 6th Corps officer said, "the pike crosses a small creek by a wooden bridge only 30 feet long. The left-hand or lower side of this bridge was broken down, but over half of it remained intact and afforded ample and safe room for anything on wheels. Some frightened teamster in his haste had driven too close to the broken side of the bridge, running his wheels on that side off the sound part, and left the wagon half upset, hanging on the edge, the lower wheels dangling over the broken planks and the stream. A single sturdy shove would have thrown it over and cleared the way. But this trifling obstruction, which any man who kept his head could have cleared away in a few minutes, blocked the whole retreating column of guns and trains behind it, by which the road was jammed full for a long distance in an almost solid mass." Traffic was backed up on the turnpike for about a mile, right through Strasburg and up to Hupp's Hill. "Whole batteries were found standing in the pike, the horses all harnessed and ready to move at the word, but the drivers and cannoneers had fled. Ambulances, filled with wounded, had become jammed and locked together, and were abandoned. Wagons were overturned in the gutters, scattering their contents in every direction. The men stumbled over great piles of debris, or walked around innumerable heaps of dead horses and men."[25]

The cavalry pressed on through the darkness, lit here and there by a burning wagon. But Custer turned command of his two leading regiments over to Colonel William Wells, commander of his 2nd Brigade, while he turned back to look after the rest of his division. Wells and the two leading regiments did not turn back until they approached Fisher's Hill, where it was assumed that the Rebels would make a stand. There they captured one last piece of Confederate artillery, which brought the total for the two regiments to 45, along with five battle flags, numerous wagons, ambulances, horses, mules, and prisoners. Many of the latter, however, got away again in the darkness.

Before the last Confederate had crossed Cedar Creek the Union clerks and orderlies and staff officers had returned to Belle Grove and started hauling the corpses and litter out of the yard and erecting their tents again. Captured guns and wagons soon began to arrive, and they were parked in neat rows in front of the house. Sheridan came in after having gone as far as Strasburg, and before long he saw a familiar figure ride up. "You have done it for me this time, Custer," he said. And he reached up and pulled the cavalry general off his horse. Then the younger man reciprocated. A lieutenant who happened to be there remembered that "Custer seizing Sheridan around the waist lifted him high up and in wild glee danced and whirled him around and around, completely lost to military deportment in his intoxicating joy, exclaiming as their tears mingled, 'By God, Phil, we've cleaned them out of their guns and got ours back!'"[26]

The wounded Ramseur was brought in and given a room in the mansion. His ambulance had been among the numerous captures. Sheridan's chief medical officer and a captured Confederate doctor both examined his wound and agreed that it was mortal. They made him as comfortable as they could and gave him laudanum for his pain. Sheridan came in to awkwardly offer his assistance to the dying man. Generals Custer and Merritt and Captain DuPont, all of whom had known him at West Point, paid him a visit, but he scarcely responded, except to complain when DuPont thoughtlessly sat on the edge of his bed. He lingered on through the night, talking with one of his staff officers who had also been captured about his wife and newborn baby, whom he would never see, and he died the next morning.

About a mile away, Colonel Lowell lay dying in a house in Middletown, where his men had carried him as soon as the village was captured. A surgeon from his brigade found him stretched out on a table, paralyzed from the shoulders down. "Four others were lying desperately wounded on the floor," he remembered. "One young officer was in great pain. Lowell spent much of his ebbing strength helping him through the straits of death. 'I have always been able to count on you, you were always brave. Now you must meet this as you have the other trials—be steady— I count on you.'"[27] He dictated messages to his friends, gave a few final orders for his brigade, with the surgeons help scribbled a last few words to his wife, sent the surgeon out in the yard to care for some wounded Confederates, and died as dawn approached.

To the Union soldiers who stayed on the north side of Cedar Creek, the day-long battle seemed to end with startling abruptness, "like a dream from which one is suddenly awakened," as Captain DeForest put it. "The field was deserted by the Rebels, and our infantrymen were dragging back to their camps in perfect peace." It was a field of victory, but it was not a pleasant sight. "Dead and wounded men, dead and wounded steeds, dismounted guns, shattered caissons, broken muskets, and pools or splatters of blood," DeForest said, showed "that the dragon of war had lately passed that way. Of the wounded a few lay still and silent; here and there one uttered quavering cries expressive of intense agony; others groaned from time to time, gently and patiently."[28] Colonel William Emerson, commander of the 1st Brigade of the 1st Division of the 6th Corps, said that his brigade "went to its position of the morning, got its breakfast, and encamped, satisfied that it had done a good day's work before breakfast."[29]

Corporal Charles M. Burr of the 2nd Connecticut Heavy Artillery in the same division had been shot in the leg when his division had first been driven back, and he had been lying on the field all day, watching the world go by. First the attacking Rebels had gone past him. Then a Southern officer had stopped to help him put a tourniquet on his leg. "Next came the noble army of stragglers and bummers," Burr wrote, "with the question, 'Hello, Yank, have you got any Yankee notions about you?' and at the same time thrusting their hands into every pocket." After that, detachments of Confederates appeared to gather up discarded weapons and equipment into wagons and to place wounded Rebels into ambulances. The wounded Federals, including Burr, were left where they were. Later, a curious civilian came by but passed on without offering any assistance. Then three boys came, and they, at least, gave Burr some water. For hours Burr lay there, listening to the sounds of battle grow more distant. However, by mid-afternoon "the tide of travel began to turn. The noble army of stragglers and bummers led the advance—then the roar of battle grew nearer and louder and more general, then came galloping officers and all kinds of wagons, then the routed infantry, artillery and cavalry, all mixed together, all on a full run, strewing the ground with muskets and equipments. Then came the shouting boys in blue and in a few minutes Pat Birmingham came up and said, 'Well, Charley, I'm glad to find you alive. I didn't expect it. We're back again in the old camp, and the Johnnies are whipped all to pieces.'"[30]

---

1. Lewis, *The Guns of Cedar Creek*, 265.
2. Ibid., 268–269
3. Ibid., 271.
4. Ibid., 273.
5. Ibid., 274–275.
6. Ibid., 275.
7. *Official Records*, 43:I:524.
8. Lewis, *The Guns of Cedar Creek*, 277.
9. Urwin, *Custer Victorious*, 212–213.
10. Ibid., 213–214.
11. Lewis, *The Guns of Cedar Creek*, 278.
12. Wert, *From Winchester to Cedar Creek*, 234.
13. Lewis, *The Guns of Cedar Creek*, 278.
14. Urwin, *Custer Victorious*, 214.
15. Early, *War Memoirs*, 448–449.
16. Lewis, *The Guns of Cedar Creek*, 281.
17. Ibid., 282.
18. Douglas, *I Rode With Stonewall*, 304.
19. Lewis, *The Guns of Cedar Creek*, 283.
20. Ibid.
21. Ibid., 282.
22. Ibid., 284.
23. *Official Records*, 43:I:525.
24. Lewis, *The Guns of Cedar Creek*, 284.
25. Ibid., 285–286.
26. Ibid., 288.
27. Ibid., 290.
28. Ibid., 286.
29. Ibid., 287.
30. Ibid., 286.

CHAPTER TWENTY-FIVE

We Don't Give a Damn For Your Neutrality

19–20 October 1864

"The 19th day of October 1864 was fine and the wind blew from southwest," wrote Lieutenant James I. Waddell. He was a Confederate naval officer aboard the British-registered ship *Laurel*, off Madeira, a Portuguese island near the coast of Morocco. He and the *Laurel* were waiting with supplies, armament, and crew to rendezvous with the steamer *Sea King* and turn her into another Rebel high seas cruiser. The night before, a mysterious-looking steamer had come in sight, and now she appeared again. "So soon as the *Laurel* drew near the steamship," Waddell wrote, "I saw on her port quarter three words in large white letters, *Sea King, London*. Each of us asked himself instinctively, what great adventures shall we meet in her? What will be her ultimate fate? . . . The *Shenandoah*, late the *Sea King*, was commissioned on the ocean the

19th day of October 1864 under the lee and on the north side of the islands known as the Desertas, a few miles from the island of Madeira. She was anchored in 18 fathoms and the *Laurel* came to and was lashed alongside of her. The little nook was smooth, the day bright and cheering, and we felt it a harbinger of success."[1]

A group of Marylanders living in the District of Columbia went to the White House that night to serenade President Lincoln in celebration of the passage of their state's new constitution prohibiting slavery. "Most heartily do I congratulate you, and Maryland, and the nation, and the world upon the event," Lincoln said in response. "I regret that it did not occur two years sooner, which I am sure would have saved to the nation more money than would have met all the private loss incident to the measure. But it has come at last, and I sincerely hope its friends may fully realize all their anticipations of good from it; and that its opponents may, by it's effects, be agreeably and profitably, disappointed.

"A word upon another subject.

"Something said by the Secretary of State in his recent speech at Auburn, has been construed by some into a threat that, if I shall be beaten at the election, I will, between then and the end of my constitutional term, do what I may be able, to ruin the government.

"Others regard the fact that the Chicago Convention adjourned, not *sine die*, but to meet again, if called to do so by a particular individual, as the intimation of a purpose that if their nominee shall be elected, he will at once seize control of the government. I hope the good people will permit themselves to suffer no uneasiness on either point. I am struggling to maintain government, not to overthrow it. I am struggling especially to prevent others from overthrowing it. I therefore say, that if I shall live, I shall remain President until the fourth of next March; and that whoever shall be constitutionally elected therefor in November, shall be duly installed as President on the fourth of March; and that in the interval I shall do my utmost that whoever is to hold the helm for the next voyage, shall start with the best possible chance to save the ship.

"This is due to the people both on principle, and under the constitution. Their will, constitutionally expressed, is the ultimate law for all. If they should deliberately resolve to have immediate peace even at the loss of their country, and their liberty, I know not the power or the right to resist them. It is their own business, and they must do as they please with their own. I believe, however, they are still resolved to preserve their country and their liberty; and in this, in office or out of it, I am resolved to stand by them.

"I may add that in this purpose to save the country and its liberties, no classes of people seem so nearly unanamous as the soldiers in the field and the seamen afloat. Do they not have the hardest of it? Who should quail while they do not?

"God bless the soldiers and seamen, with all their brave commanders."[2]

Out in Missouri on the nineteenth, the van of Price's raiding Confederates collided at Waverly, twenty miles east of Lexington, with a small division of 2,000 Federals. This was composed of troops sent ahead by Major General Samuel R. Curtis, commander of the Department of Kansas, to slow up the Rebels' westward advance and allow him time to gather in outlying garrisons and organize the Kansas militia just being called out. The commander of this advance brigade was Major General James G. Blunt, recalled from a campaign farther west against the Cheyennes and Arapahos to meet this invasion. The Federals retired to the west side of the Little Blue River, which they prepared to defend, while Pleasonton's Union cavalry nipped at Price's heels and A. J. Smith's veteran infantry paralleled his march to the south.

Down in Georgia that day, Sherman was busy on the telegraph again. To Halleck, in Washington, he said: "Hood has retreated rapidly by all the roads leading south. Our advance columns are now at Alpine and Melville Post-Office. I shall pursue him as far as Gaylesville. The enemy will not venture toward Tennessee except around by Decatur. I propose to send the Fourth Corps back to General Thomas, and leave him, with that corps, the garrisons, and new troops, to defend the line of the Tennessee River; and with the rest I will push into the heart of Georgia and come out at Savannah, destroying all the railroads of the State. The break in our railroad at Big Shanty is almost repaired, and that about Dalton should be done in ten days. We find abundance of forage in the country."[3]

To his chief quartermaster, then at Chattanooga, he wired: "Go in person to superintend the repairs of the railroad, and make all orders in my name that will expedite its completion. I want it finished, to bring back from Atlanta to Chattanooga the sick and wounded men and surplus stores. On the 1st of November I want nothing in front of Chattanooga except what we can use as food and clothing and haul in our wagons. There is plenty of corn in the country, and we only want forage for the posts. I allow ten days for all this to be done, by which time I expect to be at or near Atlanta."[4]

He also telegraphed to his chief commissary, at Atlanta: "Hood will escape me. I want to prepare for my big raid. On the 1st of November

I want nothing in Atlanta but what is necessary for war. Send all trash to the rear at once, and have on hand thirty days' food and but little forage. I propose to abandon Atlanta, and the railroad back to Chattanooga, to sally forth to ruin Georgia and bring up on the sea-shore. Make all dispositions accordingly."[5]

Lieutenant General James Longstreet, the same whose name had been used by Early in an attempt to bluff Sheridan, was actually returned to duty on that nineteenth day of October, but at Richmond, not in the Shenandoah Valley. He had been wounded on the second day of the battle of the Wilderness at the opening of Grant's campaign against Lee, accidentally shot by his own men, just as Stonewall Jackson had been almost exactly a year before, but in his case the wound was not fatal. He still had not recovered the use of one arm, but he resumed command of the 1st Corps of Lee's Army of Northern Virginia that day. In his absence, that corps had been ably, if not brilliantly, commanded by Lieutenant General Richard H. Anderson. Now Anderson was given command of a new 4th Corps, composed of the troops from Beauregard's old Department of Southern Virginia and North Carolina, namely Hoke's and Johnson's divisions and some artillery. However, Hoke's Division was still north of the James, while Johnson's and most of the artillery were south of the Appomattox in the defenses of Petersburg. Longstreet was also given overall command of all the troops defending Richmond north of the Appomattox River. This included Field's Division of his 1st Corps, Hoke's Division of Anderson's new corps, and Ewell's Department of Richmond, all north of the James and at Drewery's Bluff, plus Pickett's Division of the 1st Corps holding the lines across the base of the Bermuda Hundred peninsula between the James and Appomattox.

The nineteenth of October was a bright and clear autumn day in St. Albans, Vermont. The morning passed peacefully and quietly in the small New England city, while far to the south battle was raging near the banks of Cedar Creek in Virginia. But early that afternoon lieutenants Young and Hutchinson removed their long overcoats to reveal what Young always thereafter insisted were Confederate uniforms, although nobody else seemed to recognize them as such. Some said that Young was wearing a plum-colored shirt. Anyway, Young stood on the steps of the American House, drew a Colt revolver from inside his jacket, and shouted, "This city is now in the possession of the Confederate States of America."[6] Those who saw and heard him laughed. Everyone knew that the Confederate States were far, far away, and so was the war.

Young repeated his statement while four of his men formed a mounted line at the north end of Main Street and charged down the street with a wild Rebel yell, brandishing their revolvers and scattering locals in all directions. The other Rebels, dismounted, then ran into the street. Young walked to the First National Bank; Hutchinson and three other Rebels walked across the street to the Franklin County Bank, and Caleb Wallace and two others went to the St. Albans Bank. Wallace and his companions easily cleaned out the St. Albans Bank and then locked the clerk in the vault. A few minutes later a depositor who had been watching the Rebels through the window, went in, found the key in the vault, and let the clerk out again. Together, the clerk and the customer went to the window and watched the further activities of the Confederate raiders.

In the Franklin County Bank the clerk looked up as Hutchinson and his three men walked in and greeted them politely. Hutchinson asked what the bank was paying for gold and was told that it did not deal in gold and was referred to a Mr. Armington down the street. "Well, the hell with Mr. Armington," Hutchinson said, pointing his revolver at the clerk. Just then the bank's president came out of the back room. Hutchinson forced both men to raise their right hands and take an oath of loyalty to the Confederate States, after which they were made to sit on chairs behind the bank's counter while Hutchinson and his men took the securities, gold, and currency out of the vault and stuffed them into large carpetbags. Then the president and the clerk were pushed into the back room, and when the former protested against such "rough treatment" he was told, "Well, you people in the North are treating the people of the South in the same manner."[7]

As Young walked into the First National Bank, revolver in hand, a man who was coming out of it saw him and shouted, "They're robbing the bank!"[8] Young ordered the man taken prisoner, but it took quite a struggle to subdue him. One of the Rebels suggested shooting the fellow, but Young would not allow the shooting of an unarmed man. Eventually the man was taken to the village green, where a number of other local citizens who got in the way were being taken. Young's experience inside the bank was similar to Hutchinson's, or at least it started out to be. He asked about gold, was referred to Armington, said he could not wait, pulled his revolver, pushed the clerk into a chair, and told his men to clean out the vault.

Just as this was done, a smiling man in a fur hat came in and started telling the clerk how four strangers had stared at him as he had entered the bank, but he failed to notice anything unusual taking place inside. He turned out to be none other than Mr. Armington. "Ah, the gentleman who buys gold," Young said. "The same," he was told. "Would you care to buy some, sir?" Young asked. "Certainly. Have you any to sell?" Young pointed with his toe to the carpetbag full of loot. "Yes, sir, right here." Armington, still unaware that the bank was being robbed, asked the clerk for the Boston *Journal*, scanned the financial columns, and quoted the price for gold. Young said that would be satisfactory and proceeded to sell him some of the gold he had just stolen from the bank. "It was only afterwards that I learned he was one of the party," Armington later explained.[9]

There was a good reason for Young's deal with Armington, for the gold that was not sold turned out to be a heavy burden to place on the Rebels' mounts. "Hearing the commotion," Leonard Cross, the town's photographer, came outside in time to see Young struggling with one of the heavy carpetbags full of gold. "What are you celebrating here, young man?" Cross asked. "This," the irritated Young replied, drawing his revolver and firing over Cross's head. The photographer dived back into his shop and slammed the door behind him. Young sent Wallace and two others to the edge of town to intercept any farm wagons coming or going and to bring back their horses. He also sent Hutchinson to Fuller's livery stable. "My God, what are you doing?" Fuller demanded. "Stealing your horses," Hutchinson replied.[10]

Fuller ran inside to get his gun, and when he came out into the street he could see Lieutenant Young, shouting orders to his men, a perfect target. Fuller took careful aim and pulled the trigger, but instead of an explosion there came only the annoying click of a misfire. Again he pulled the trigger, and again came only a click. While Fuller reloaded, the Rebels moved up the street, but he followed, hugging the sides of the buildings and using narrow alleyways to remain unnoticed. Again he saw Young. Again he took aim and pulled the trigger. Again the gun only clicked. Jumping back into an alley he hurriedly reloaded again, and he came out just as Young was standing in his stirrups, shouting, "I am an officer of the Confederate service. I have been sent here to take this town. The first one who offers resistance will be shot."[11] While he was making his little speech, Fuller took careful aim at him again, pulled the trigger again, and again the gun answered with only a click. He threw it away and walked back to his livery stable.

Other local citizens also decided to fight back. A man fired at Young from an upper window but missed. Young shot back and hit the man, who slumped across the sill, badly wounded. Another man fired from a porch, but fired too high. Hutchinson shot him in the chest, and two other men dragged him into the house. "I think I'm hurt bad," the wounded man said. "I had better go to the drug store."[12] Supported by his two friends, he calmly walked down the street past the Rebels, who were now blazing away in a regular skirmish with townspeople, and entered Dutcher & Son's drug store. There he quietly died.

Someone shot Hutchinson's hat off. Looking around he spotted a man near the door of the Franklin County Bank. "Give me your hat," he demanded. "I'll be damned if I do," was the answer. Hutchinson pointed his cocked revolver at the man and demanded the hat again. The man took off his hat, stuck it under his coat, and took off running down the street. At Hutchinson's order, one of the Rebels jumped down from his horse and gave chase on foot, bringing the man down with a flying tackle. After a terrific struggle he finally managed to drag the man to his feet, tear open his coat, and pull out the hat. He handed the badly battered item to Hutchinson, who put it on. After all that trouble it proved to be too small, but Hutchinson wore it anyway. The civilian and the Rebel started for the village green, but the Yankee insisted on a slow and dignified pace. The Confederate tried to make him hurry, but the Vermonter replied, "I'll be darned if a Rebel will make me," and the trooper, having had one taste of Yankee stubborness, decided not to make an issue of it.[13]

Nineteen-year-old Captain George Conger of the 1st Vermont Cavalry in Custer's division, who was home on leave, began to organize the resistance. He found a horse and began to ride through the town shouting, "We have a lot of Rebel raiders here. Let's catch them. Get your guns." Men began to join him in twos and threes and soon they were sniping at the Southerners from behind trees and from the windows of buildings in the best minute-man tradition—except that they failed to hit anybody. As their numbers increased they became bolder, and Conger formed them in a line across Main Street. The mounted Rebels charged this line with blazing revolvers and broke it up. But as soon as the Confederates turned back, the Northerners reformed. At Young's order, the Rebels rode down Main Street and threw their vials of Greek fire at various buildings, including the American House. Some of the bottles failed to explode. Others flared up and then died out, but enough of them worked to make Young and his men think that they had set fire to the town. Then Young shouted, "That's all, men, the ball is over. Break up."[14] And they turned and galloped out of town. However, with no Rebels there to chase away the firefighters, the burning buildings were easily saved.

Conger and Fuller rounded up some horses, and within ten minutes a posse of fifteen men galloped after the Rebels. "Once out of town," Conger later testified, "it was a running fight. We pressed them hard."[15] Just outside of Sheldon the Confederates came to a bridge over a river which was blocked by a farmer's wagon crossing with a load of hay.

Much valuable time was lost while they waited for the wagon to get out of their way. But once the Rebels got across the bridge they turned the hay wagon over upon it and set the hay on fire to block pursuit. Then, as prearranged, they broke into small parties and headed for the border, passing the First National Bank of Sheldon, one of their intended targets, at a gallop. Twice Conger's posse caught up with small bands of the Rebels, but both times the Confederates turned about and charged, scattering the untrained civilians.

Young and Wallace reached the Canadian line at about 9 p.m. There they allegedly changed from their uniforms into civilian clothes and proceeded to Montreal. But the next day, the twentieth, Young learned that several of his men had been captured at Phillipsburg by the posse, which had crossed into Canada after them, and he decided to go to them. When Hutchinson, who had joined him by then, protested, Young replied, "I am their leader. Their cause is my cause. I alone had the authority and command of the raid."[16]

He strapped on his pair of revolvers and rode south. That evening he stopped at a farmhouse a few miles north of Phillipsburg, whose owner agreed to feed him and his horse and put him up for the night for five dollars. Unknown to him, the Federal posse had stopped at the house earlier and had warned the farmer to be on the watch for any Rebel raiders seeking shelter. Now he sent a farmhand to find Conger. After supper Young was dozing in a chair by the fire when he awoke to find the room full of shouting Yankees, all aiming guns at his head. As calmly as he could, he pointed out that they were violating British neutrality, but Conger replied, "I'm not interested in any damn laws or in Great Britain either."[17]

Conger later said that it was all he could do to keep the posse from stringing up Young from the farmer's hayloft. Instead they put him in a wagon with a rope around his neck and started back to Vermont. They kept cocking their pistols and pointing them at Young and telling him how they would like to blow his brains out. He was sure that he would be hanged as soon as they got him back to St. Albans. When Conger, who was driving, turned to say something to the men riding on either side of the wagon, Young lunged at him, catching him in the stomach with his knee. Conger fell, and Young grabbed the reins and turned the horses toward Phillipsburg. The Federals were startled at first, but soon recovered, and their horses easily overtook the wagon about a half-mile down the road. Young tried to jump down and get away, but the Vermonters pounced on him and started pounding him with their fists, boots, and guns.

Before they had done him any really serious injury a British major came onto the scene and demanded to know what was going on. "This is the leader of the Rebels who robbed our banks," Conger said. "He tried to escape." Young, with blood running down his face, said through swollen lips that he was on British soil and entitled to protection and that his captors intended to take him to the United States against his wishes, without authority, and in violation of British neutrality and British law. The officer said that seven other Confederates captured earlier at Phillipsburg were to be escorted back to the states and turned over to the Union authorities at 10 the next morning and he suggested that they take Young to Phillipsburg to join the others. Conger thought this was reasonable, but some of the other Vermonters wanted to keep Young while they had him and take him back to St. Albans that night. The major said that to do so would be to violate British neutrality. "We don't give a damn for your neutrality," one of the Yankees said. "But you will respect our arms, sir," the major replied. "If you leave with this prisoner I shall send a company of regulars to bring him back."[18]

This threat won the argument. They took Young to the barracks at Phillipsburg and turned him over to a British captain, who, along with his soldiers, showed a lot more sympathy for Young than for the posse. The major disappeared, the captain ordered the Yanks off his post, escorted by British regulars who took delight in dropping their rifle butts on American toes, and Young and his men were lionized by the British, who listened admiringly to Young's recounting of their adventures and brought them beer and ale and plates of food. And, it turned out, there was no arrangement for returning the prisoners to Vermont the next day. Instead, they were taken that night to St. John's, where there was an even larger garrison of British regulars.

Grant answered another letter from Lee regarding prisoners of war on 20 October. Some time before, Ben Butler had learned that the Confederates were using black soldiers recently captured from his army to rebuild and extend the fortifications at Fort Gilmer. Butler, the Union commissioner for the exchange of prisoners in Virginia, had, in retaliation, put a hundred Confederate prisoners of war to work on the canal he was constructing at Dutch Gap on the James River and he had sent word to the Confederate commissioner of what he was doing and why. Since Butler had previously been outlawed by proclamation of President Davis, the Confederates refused to answer him directly. Instead, Secretary of War James Seddon passed the whole question over to Lee, along with a lengthy discussion of the Confederate position on the entire subject of prisoner exchange, and instructed him to take up the matter with Grant:

"All negroes in the military or naval service of the United States taken by us who are not identified as the property of citizens or residents of any of the Confederate States are regarded as prisoners of war, being held to be proper subjects of exchange . . . Negroes who owe service or labor to citizens or residents of the Confederate States, and who through compulsion, persuasion, or of their own accord, leave their owners and are placed in the military or naval service of the United States, occupy a different position . . . It has been uniformly held that the capture or abduction of a slave does not impair the right of the owner to such slave, but that the right attaches to him immediately upon recapture . . . and I am instructed to say that all such slaves when properly identified as belonging to citizens of any of the Confederate States, or to persons enjoying the protection of their laws, will be restored like other recaptured property to those entitled to them . . .

"The negroes recently captured by our forces were sent to Richmond with other Federal prisoners. After their arrival it was discovered that a number of them were slaves belonging to citizens or residents of some of the Confederate States, and of this class fifty-nine, as I learn, were sent with other negroes to work on the fortifications around Richmond until their owners should appear and claim them. As soon as I was informed of the fact . . . I ordered them to be sent into the interior . . . It only remains for me to say that the negroes employed upon our fortifications are not allowed to be placed where they will be exposed to fire . . . I have now, in accordance with my instructions, respectfully to inquire whether the course pursued toward our prisoners, as set forth in the accompanying letters, has your sanction, and whether it will be maintained."[19]

Grant replied: "Understanding from your letter of the 19th that the colored prisoners who were employed at work in the trenches near Fort Gilmer have been withdrawn, I have directed the withdrawal of the Confederate prisoners employed in Dutch Gap Canal. I shall always regret the necessity of retaliating for wrongs done our soldiers, but regard it my duty to protect all persons received into the Army of the United States, regardless of color or nationality. When acknowledged soldiers of the Government are captured they must be treated as prisoners of war, or such treatment as they receive inflicted upon an equal number of prisoners held by us. I have nothing to do with the discussion of the slavery question, therefore decline answering the arguments adduced to show the right to return to former owners such negroes as are captured from our Army.

"In answer to the question at the conclusion of your letter, I have to state that all prisoners of war falling into my hands shall receive the kindest possible treatment consistent with securing them, unless I have good authority for believing any number of our men are being treated otherwise. Then, painful as it may be to me, I shall inflict like treatment on an equal number of Confederate prisoners."[20]

To both sides the treatment of captured black soldiers was both a question of principle and of strategy. The Confederacy, regarding slavery as natural and legal, felt obligated to its citizens to return their property. At the same time, it hoped to place the blame for the breakdown in the exchange of prisoners upon the Lincoln administration and thus to encourage the families and friends of white Federal soldiers suffering in prison camps to vote it out of office. The Federals, especially Secretary of War Stanton, were content to let the prisoners of both sides stay prisoners, for they could get other men to replace them in the ranks and the Confederates could not. And the issue of the treatment of black soldiers brought principle into line with expediency. It was a very touchy issue for both sides and some of its features are well illustrated by a letter sent to President Lincoln that day by the Chicago Board of Trade. This body was concerned "that a large number of Federal soldiers are languishing in Southern prisons, especially at Andersonville, Ga., destitute of shelter from rain and from the burning rays of the sun, without sufficient clothing to cover their nakedness; and that they are famishing with hunger that would gladly be appeased by the flesh of horses and of mules, and are consequently dying in untold numbers, pray you to effect an honorable exchange of prisoners without delay, or to retaliate by subjecting rebel prisoners to the same treatment in all respects . . .

"It is not too much to say that nothing in the conduct of the war presents so great an obstacle to those who would otherwise volunteer, and nothing will cause the drafted soldier to take such reluctant steps to the field so much as the dread of the horrors of Southern prisons." This was a very good point, but these patriotic businessmen also touched upon a good reason not to exchange prisoners when they said: ". . . prisoners taken by us are clothed, fed, and as comfortably cared for as are our own men, and when an exchange is made we give them soldiers hale and hearty, ready to again enter the field and give us battle, but receive in return men pale and emaciated, fit only for the hospital."[21] They unknowingly exaggerated the care received by Confederates in Northern prisoner of war camps, but the point was a valid one. Neither side was intentionally cruel to the white prisoners in their hands, but their arrangements for feeding and housing such numbers as were forced upon them by the breakdown of the exchange cartel were inadequate in the extreme, especially in the South.

"At three o'clock on the afternoon of October 20," Horace Porter wrote, "General Grant was sitting at his table in his tent, writing letters. Several members of the staff who were at headquarters at the time were seated in front of the tent discussing some anticipated movements. The telegraph operator came across the camp-ground hurriedly, stepped into the general's quarters, and handed him a despatch. He read it over, and then came to the front of the tent, put on a very grave look, and said to the members of the staff: 'I'll read you a despatch I have just received from Sheridan.' We were all eager to hear the news, for we felt that the telegram was of importance. The general began to read the despatch in a very solemn tone. It was dated 10 p.m. the night before: "'I have the honor to report that my army at Cedar Creek was attacked this morning before daylight, and my left was turned and driven in confusion, with the loss of twenty pieces of artillery. I hastened from Winchester, where I was on my return from Washington, and joined the army between Middletown and Newtown, having been driven about four miles."' Here the general looked up, shook his head solemnly, and said, 'That's pretty bad, isn't it?' A melancholy chorus replied, 'It's too bad, too bad!' 'Now just wait till I read you the rest of it,' added the general, with a perceptible twinkle in his eye. He then went on, reading more rapidly: "'I here took the affair in hand, and quickly united the corps, formed a compact line of battle just in time to repulse an attack of the enemy's, which was handsomely done at about 1 p.m. At 3 p.m., after some changes of the cavalry from the left to the right flank, I attacked with great vigor, driving and routing the enemy, capturing, according to last reports, forty-three pieces of artillery and very many prisoners. I do not yet know the number of my casualties or the losses of the enemy. Wagon-trains, ambulances, and caissons in large numbers are in our possession. They also burned some of their trains. General Ramseur is a prisoner in our hands, severely, and perhaps mortally, wounded. I have to regret the loss of General Bidwell, killed, and Generals Wright, Grover, and Ricketts, wounded—Wright slightly wounded. Affairs at times looked badly, but by the gallantry of our brave officers and men disaster has been converted into a splendid victory. Darkness again intervened to shut off greater results . . ."' By this time the listeners had rallied from their dejection, and were beside themselves with delight. The general seemed to enjoy the bombshell he had thrown among the staff almost as much as the news of Sheridan's signal victory."[22]

Grant ordered a salute of 100 shotted guns fired to honor Sheridan's victory in the same way as he had Sherman's capture of Atlanta. Then he sent off a telegram to Stanton in which he said: "Turning what bid fair to be a disaster into a glorious victory stamps Sheridan what I have always thought him—one of the ablest of generals."[23] In conversation with his staff, Grant said, "Sheridan's courageous words and brilliant deeds encourage his commanders as much as they inspire his subordinates. While he has a magnetic influence possessed by few other men in an engagement, and is seen to best advantage in battle, he does as much beforehand to contribute to victory as any living commander. His plans are always well matured, and in every movement he strikes with definite purpose in view. No man would be better fitted to command all the armies in the field."[24]

In Washington that day, the twentieth, in a move apparently already planned before the receipt of the good news from the Shenandoah Valley, President Lincoln issued a proclamation setting aside the last Thursday in November as a national day of Thanksgiving.

1. James I. Waddell, C. S. S. Shenandoah: The Memoirs of Lieutenant Commanding James I. Waddell (New York, 1960), 92–94.
2. Basler, ed., The Collected Works of Abraham Lincoln, 8:52–53.
3. Sherman, Memoirs, 633.
4. Ibid., 633–634.
5. Ibid., 634.
6. Horan, Confederate Agent, 170.
7. Ibid.
8. Ibid., 171–172.
9. Ibid., 172–173.
10. Ibid., 173.
11. Ibid., 174.
12. Ibid.
13. Ibid., 174–175.
14. Ibid., 175–176.
15. Ibid., 176.
16. Ibid., 177.
17. Ibid.
18. Ibid., 178–179.
19. Official Records, Series 2, 7:1010–1012.
20. Ibid., Series 2, 7:1018–1019.
21. Ibid., Series 2, 7:1014–1015.
22. Porter, Campaigning With Grant, 306–308.
23. Lewis, The Guns of Cedar Creek, 292.
24. Porter, Campaigning With Grant, 308.

CHAPTER TWENTY-SIX

Then Fight It Is

20–25 October 1864

Out in Missouri on the twentieth, Price's raiding Confederates were still heading westward along the south bank of the Missouri River. After driving Blunt's delaying force through Lexington, Price was resting in a meadow ten miles east of Independence, lying on a carpet, sipping a toddy, and watching his men ride past, when a squad of horsemen rode up from the west and turned into the field where he was resting. After speaking to an orderly, the leader of this group approached and said he had some prisoners, who were from Lawrence, Kansas. "Who are you, young man?" Price asked. "I am George Todd," he was told. "Are you Captain Todd?" the general asked, remembering that he had commissioned a guerrilla by that name. "Yes, sir."[1] The prisoners, glad to get out of Todd's hands alive—a rare accomplishment—answered Price's questions. They said that Blunt commanded the force in his immediate front, along the Little Blue River, but claimed that Curtis was putting together a much larger force farther west at the Big Blue, just east of Kansas City.

The next day, Friday, the 21st, was cool and foggy. The last of Price's men pulled out of Lexington, while Todd, with about six of his bushwhackers, scouted ahead of the van of the column, Marmaduke's Division. Riding to the crest of a hill about noon, Todd stopped to examine the terrain ahead when a shot rang out and he fell to the ground unconscious and choking on his own blood, which was streaming from a wound in his neck caused by a bullet from a Spencer rifle or carbine. Within an hour he was dead.

Marmaduke's Division, in the lead, managed to drive off some of Blunt's men who were trying to burn a bridge over the Little Blue, and with the help of Shelby's Division, drove the Federals through Independence in four hours of house-to-house fighting. The elated Price issued a proclamation that he would take Sunday dinner at Fort Leavenworth, Kansas. Curtis, however, did not think so. He had fortified the ridge west of the Big Blue and thought he could block Price's advance there with his volunteers and such of the Kansas militia as had consented to cross the state line into Missouri. And, if Pleasonton would only push hard enough from the east, Price would be trapped between the Big Blue, the Little Blue, and the Missouri.

How, though, could Curtis communicate this plan to Pleasonton, what with Price's entire army separating the two Union forces? A member of the Kansas militia, Daniel W. Boutwell, volunteered to float down the Missouri that night to carry a message to Pleasonton. Boutwell set off in a boat after dark and drifted past Price's right flank. When he grounded on a sand bar he climbed out on the south bank and soon found Union soldiers all right. However, they were not Pleasonton's troopers but some of Blunt's men who had been cut off by Price's advance. They were hiding in the woods near the river waiting for the Rebels to move on to the west and for Pleasonton's Federals to come along.

Sherman's army reached Gaylesville, Alabama, near the Coosa River west of Rome, Georgia, that day, and there he ended his pursuit of Hood. Someone else, however, did finally catch up with Hood that day. Beauregard, supposedly in command of all the Confederate West, had expected to find Hood and his army at Blue Pond, Alabama, but instead had found only Wheeler's cavalry there. Hood, he was informed, had moved 27 miles farther west to Gadsden, down the Coosa from Gaylesville, and for the first time Beauregard learned that Hood was planning to invade Tennessee.

He proceeded to Gadsden, and there, far into the night, the two generals studied their maps and discussed the proposed campaign. Beauregard later claimed to have opposed the plan, but his correspondence with Richmond at the time shows something bordering on enthusiasm. The Confederates overestimated the damage that had been done to the railroad between Chattanooga and Atlanta and calculated that it would take Sherman at least five weeks to repair it. If, during that period, Hood could cross the Tennessee at Guntersville, some 40 miles north of Gadsden, and hit the railroad between Nashville and Chattanooga, they could force Sherman to keep retracing his steps. This plan seemed feasible, and Hood decided to start moving north the next day. Beauregard insisted, however, that Wheeler's cavalry should stay behind to keep an eye on Sherman, although Hood could take with him most of Brigadier General W. H. "Red" Jackson's cavalry division, which was not a part of Wheeler's corps. Wheeler was reinforced by one of Jackson's three brigades and by a brigade of Kentucky infantry that was being mounted on horses that had been captured from or abandoned by the Federals. Beauregard did send an order to Taylor for Forrest to join Hood with his cavalry, but he evidently did not understand that Forrest was then already far away in western Tennessee.

There were further convolutions in Hood's plan that shaded off into the realm of wishful thinking. He meant to recapture Nashville, resupply his army from union depots there, fill his ranks with new recruits and conscripts from Tennessee and march into Kentucky. He said that if this caused Sherman to fall back to cover his communications in Tennessee then he would defeat him, after which he could either send reinforcements or take his entire army to help Lee against Grant. Or if Sherman marched for the Gulf or Atlantic coast instead, then Hood could reach Richmond or Petersburg at least two weeks before Sherman could join Grant. After he and General Lee defeated Grant, Hood added, they could "either march upon Washington or turn upon and annihilate Sherman."[2]

Defeating Sherman is something he had already tried several times, without success, and one cannot help but think that he hoped that the Union army would march for the coast and away from him. However, transferring all or any sizable part of his army to Virginia would not have been an easy matter and would have involved, at the very least, clearing the Federal garrisons out of eastern Tennessee. Otherwise he would not have had a secure supply line for such a move. And the Confederates were having a hard enough time supplying the troops they already had in Virginia without adding another large army to the area. It was, nevertheless, quite similar to the kind of grandiose schemes that Beauregard himself was fond of proposing, and he seems to have fallen for it.

In Indiana that day, the military commission that had been trying Cooperhead Harrison Dodd before he escaped, having found him guilty in absentia, proceeded with similar charges against other Sons of Liberty leaders in military custody. Some of the Copperheads promptly turned state's evidence against their fellows, confirming the testimony of Federal secret agent Felix Stidger.

In Washington that evening, a torchlight parade passed through the grounds in front of the White House, where a large celebrating crowd had gathered and kept up a continual blaze of light with rockets, Roman candles, etc. The fireworks lit up the upper windows and portico of the mansion, where President Lincoln stood with his young son Tad. After the procession had left the grounds, the crowd called loudly for the president to speak, and finally he consented to make a few remarks. "I was promised not to be called upon for a speech to-night," he said, "nor do I propose to make one. But, as we have been hearing some very good news for a day or two, I propose that you give three hearty cheers for Sheridan. While we are at it we may as well consider how fortunate it was for the Secesh that Sheridan was a very little man. If he had been a large man, there is no knowing what he would have done with them. I propose three cheers for General Grant, who knew to what use to put Sheridan; three cheers for all our noble commanders and the soldiers and sailors; three cheers for all people everywhere who cheer the soldiers and sailors of the Union—and now, good night."[3]

The next day, the 22nd, Lincoln sent Sheridan a telegram: "With great pleasure I tender to you and your brave army, the thanks of the Nation, and my own personal admiration and gratitude, for the month's operations in the Shenandoah Valley; and especially for the splendid work of October 19, 1864."[4]

Things remained quiet around Richmond and Petersburg. Major Joe Bowers, of Grant's staff, in writing to a fellow staff officer that day, summed up the situation very well: "We are busy doing nothing, positively nothing, and I confess to you that I see no prospect of our doing anything for some time to come. Everything is at a dead lock. We have men enough to make our present positions safe, but none with which to get up 'side shows' or inaugurate new movements. We are not receiving reinforcements to any considerable extent. The accessions are barely sufficient to make up for losses in battle and by expiration of enlistments . . . We hear of many men in rendezvous, but they don't come and it is evidently not the intention of the Government to send them until after the election. Everything now hinges on the elections."[5]

Down in Alabama, Hood's Army of Tennessee marched north out of

Gadsden on 22 October, headed for the Tennessee River at Guntersville. However, before the day was out, he changed his mind, without informing Beauregard, and decided to cross the river farther west, later claiming that it was too well guarded by the Federals in the Guntersville area.

Out in Missouri that day, Curtis' Federals took up position behind the Big Blue River. The Federal line was formidable, with breastworks and abatis on a ridge overlooking the stream and manned by about 4,000 veterans and an equal number of raw Kansas militiamen, but it was not long enough. That morning, Blunt, whose veterans held the right end of the line, sent Colonel Charles R. Jennison's small brigade farther south to Byram's Ford to prevent the enemy from crossing there. Unknown to them, the entire Confederate army planned to cross there.

After learning that Curtis would be holding the Big Blue in force to prevent him from moving farther west, Price decided to send Colonel Sydney Jackman's brigade of Shelby's Division to feint in that direction while the rest of the army turned to the southwest, toward Little Santa Fe, crossing the Big Blue at Byram's Ford. At about 11 a.m., Price's van, under Shelby, reached the ford, but Jennison's small command, reinforced by some of the militia, beat back every attempt to cross until about 3 p.m., when the Confederates got across the river on both Union flanks and forced the Federals to retire. Then Shelby drove Jennison nearly to Westport, Missouri, which is now part of Kansas City. But, reinforced by another small brigade under Colonel Thomas Moonlight, the Federals counterattacked and forced Shelby to retreat in turn, although not very far. However, Byram's Ford had been cleared, and Price's immense train of some 500 wagons had crossed the river and rumbled off to the southwest, while Curtis had to give up the Big Blue line and retreated to Westport with his whole force.

Meanwhile, militiaman Boutwell, who had floated down the Missouri with a message from Curtis, finally met up with Pleasonton that morning. Assuming that Curtis was holding the Confederates at the Big Blue, the cavalry leader moved Brigadier General John McNeil's brigade forward, and it drove Fagan's rear guard out of Independence, capturing 400 Rebels and two guns in the process. Rosecrans, Pleasonton's boss, also "supposing the enemy could not cross the Big Blue in the face of Curtis," suggested by telegraph that Pleasonton leave McNeil's brigade to harass Price's rear guard and take his other three brigades south to join A. J. Smith so that the combined force could fall upon Price when he turned south.[6] Instead, Pleasonton did almost exactly the opposite.

He ordered McNeil to march that night for Little Santa Fe, while he not only kept the rest of his force pushing westward, but persuaded Rosecrans to order Smith to turn north and reinforce the cavalry for the drive across the Big Blue.

Meanwhile, without waiting for the infantry to reach him, Pleasonton decided to "push them all night," since, as he wrote in his report, "the enemy seemed to be in haste." That evening Colonel Edward F. Winslow's brigade, veterans of Grierson's campaigns against Forrest in Mississippi, pushed Fagan's Division, reinforced by part of Marmaduke's, six miles to the Big Blue River. "Notwithstanding the almost impenetrable darkness of the night, they rushed upon us with a reckless fierceness that I have never seen equaled," wrote one of Marmaduke's colonels.[7]

Eventually, the Rebels were all driven across the Big Blue, where Marmaduke's Division took over what had been Jennison's defense at Byram's Ford, while farther west Fagan and Shelby faced Curtis near Brush Creek, south of Westport. Pleasonton's artillery kept up a steady fire on Marmaduke's Rebels until after midnight, to at least keep them from getting a good night's sleep. Off to the west, the nervous Kansas militiamen had finally moved two or three miles into Missouri, and they too were kept awake by this bombardment, knowing that it probably meant a battle in the morning—the first battle for most of them and the last morning for some. "I'd rather hear the baby cry," one married militiaman complained.[8]

That night, Shelby convinced Price that he and Fagan should attack Curtis the next morning while Marmaduke held off Pleasonton. Then they could all turn against the latter for a classic Napoleonic double victory from a central position.

At his headquarters in Independence that night, Pleasonton ordered Brigadier General Egbert B. Brown's 1st Brigade to attack at dawn across the Big Blue at Byram's Ford.

Curtis met with his senior commanders that night in a parlor at the Gillis House hotel in Kansas City. He was ready to retreat to Fort Leavenworth, well into Kansas, and in fact had already ordered his wagons to head there, but the militia officers had talked him into holding this council of war. Curtis said he did not know how a general could be expected to fight with such a command as his. He had only 4,000 trained troops and he did not trust the militia. He was not even sure that they would obey his orders.

The Kansans were furious. They urged and pleaded with the old general to stand and fight but could not convince him. Finally, at about 2 a.m., some of them took General Blunt aside and suggested that he arrest Curtis and assume command. "Gentleman, that is a serious thing to do,"

Blunt said. "Yes, but not so serious as for this army to run away like cowards and let Price sack Kansas City and devastate southern Kansas," said Captain Samuel Crawford, who was a candidate for governor of that state. "Will the army stand by me?" Blunt asked. "Yes, and we will stand by you while making the arrest," he was told. Blunt walked over to where Curtis was arguing with Senator James Lane. "General Curtis, what do you propose to do?" he asked. Curtis seemed uncertain at first, then, perhaps sensing what was afoot, said, "General Blunt, I will leave the whole matter to you. If you say fight, then fight it is."[9]

"The 23rd of October dawned upon us clear, cold, and full of promise," Jo Shelby wrote. Both sides had decided to attack on the western front of this two-front battle, but the Federals stepped off first. At about 3 a.m. they advanced and crossed Brush Creek, an east-west tributary of the Big Blue, crunching through ice that was as thick as window glass, and moved into the frosted woods on the south side. Curtis rode out to Westport from Kansas City to climb up onto the roof of the Harris House hotel, which had been pro-slavery headquarters in the old prewar bleeding-Kansas days. From there he had a clear view of the field through his telescope. At 8 a.m. his men ran into Shelby's and Fagan's Confederates moving in the opposite direction. "Inch by inch and foot by foot they gave way before my steady onset," Shelby reported. "Regiment met regiment and opposing batteries draped the scene in clouds of dense smoke."[10] Seeing his line giving ground and hearing Pleasonton's artillery begin its morning bombardment across the way, Curtis called for his horse.

Pleasonton, in the mean time, rode out from Independence to Byram's Ford to watch Brown's brigade make its attack, only to find, when he got there, that it had not yet moved. The dapper Pleasonton, who always carried a riding crop, now shook this item in Brown's face and, with a volley of oaths, demanded to know why he had not advanced at dawn as ordered. Brown, saluting with his one good arm, said that Winslow's brigade had been in the way. Pleasonton was not impressed. "You are an ambulance soldier and you belong in the rear," he told Brown and put him under arrest. Then he proceeded to arrest Brown's senior colonel, James McFerran, "whose regiment was straggling all over the country, and he was neglecting to prevent it."[11] "Who is next in command here?" he shouted. Someone said that would be Colonel John F. Phillips of the 7th Missouri State Cavalry. "Where is he?" Pleasonton demanded. "Here I am," Phillips answered. He was sitting on the ground changing his boots in anticipation of crossing the Big Blue. "What are you doing down there on the ground?" Pleasonton wanted to know. "I am getting ready to lead my men into that fight down there," the colonel replied. "If you want a fight you shall have it," Pleasonton said. "You take charge of this entire brigade and go down there and put those people out."[12]

Brown was not the only one who had failed to follow Pleasonton's orders, however. McNeil had been told to be at Little Santa Fe by daylight, but dawn found him and his brigade where Brown's should have been, at Byram's Ford, where he had stopped to feed his horses. However, he had resumed his cautious advance in time to be gone when Pleasonton arrived there.

Meanwhile, Pleasonton threw his other three brigades at Byram's Ford. Phillips ordered a battery to provide covering fire, and at around 8 a.m., just as Curtis was colliding with Shelby and Fagan, he led his brigade toward the ford over the Big Blue. A cannon shell exploded in the water behind Phillips and blew a trooper and his horse to shreds, but his men continued to wade across the chest-high stream, holding their carbines and ammunition above their heads. When they were across they found their path blocked by the abatis and Marmaduke's Rebels firing at every man who exposed himself. Phillips ordered his men to lie flat under the cover of the abatis and sent a detail back to get axes. Then, covered by the fire of the artillery, they chopped a path through the barrier, and Lieutenant Colonel Thomas Crittenden ordered his regiment to advance on hands and knees while other Federals fired volleys at the Rebel works and a nearby cabin being used by Confederate sharpshooters.

A trooper brought back word that Crittenden was dead, so Phillips started forward to personally take over at the front. Among the dead sprawled in the roadside gullies and stumps Phillips recognized a captain, the back of whose head had been blown off. The colonel stopped and took some letters from the dead man's pocket, including one to his fiancee. Farther along the road he came to a young lieutenant whose breast was torn open and who tried to salute him even as he slumped to the ground. Finally he came to Crittenden, who was lying on the ground unconscious. His face was pale and his hand was clutching his side. Phillips opened Crittenden's coat and shirt and saw a black spot on his stomach, but the skin was not broken. A ricocheting bullet had struck a wallet in his vest pocket which was stuffed with about an inch of paper money. This had been enough to stop the bullet, although the force of the impact had knocked Crittenden out. Phillips held up the senseless man's head and poured a sip of peach brandy into his mouth, and his eyes opened. Soon Crittenden stood up and stumbled on up the hill to the head of the draw where his men had stopped after gaining their objective. Marmaduke's Confederates had retreated. In the distance to the west, across the treeless plateau between the Big Blue River and Brush Creek, the Federals could see what looked like 20,000 men. While they gazed in wonder at this sight, Pleasonton rode up and pointed to the distant figures. "Rebels, rebels, rebels," he shouted, "fire, fire, you damned asses."[13]

On the other side of the battlefield, Curtis had gone riding up and down his line of volunteers and militiamen, preparing them to counter-attack Shelby, when an old man rode up and said he lived in the neighborhood and that a nearby gulch would provide a hidden way through the Rebel lines. Curtis ordered Blunt to take his veterans up this gulch and then told Major General George Deitzler, commander of the Kansas militia, to have his entire line ready to advance as soon as Blunt's men opened fire. Blunt's veterans emerged from the gulch at about 11 a.m. between Shelby's left-most brigade, Colonel Jeff Thompson's, and his other two and they started firing into the flanks of both forces. Shelby's men fell back and Deitzler's Kansans advanced.

Shelby formed his division, minus Thompson's Brigade, on a low ridge overlooking a sloping valley of farm land covered mostly with brown, dead grass. A Union battery unlimbered on the opposite hill and began to bombard Shelby's new line, but Colonel J. H. McGhee, commander of a regiment of Arkansas cavalry, decided to put an end to this harassment. Forming his mounted regiment in battalion front, he led it forward to capture those guns. However, Colonel Jennison ordered a countercharge by Captain Curtis Johnson's Company E of the 15th Kansas Cavalry and a squadron of the 2nd Colorado Cavalry. As the two masses of charging horsemen converged, McGhee and Johnson zeroed in on each other. McGhee fired his revolver and hit Johnson in the arm, but the Union captain shot the Rebel colonel through the heart, and after a brief melee of slashing sabers and blazing revolvers, the Arkansans retreated to the protection of Shelby's main line.

When he heard that Pleasonton's Federals had crossed the Big Blue and driven off Marmaduke's Division, Price realized that he was in danger of being surrounded. The most immediate threat was to his train of supply wagons, and he ordered everybody to fall back and protect the wagons, which in turn were ordered down the road to Little Santa Fe that followed the state line between Missouri and Kansas. Marmaduke's men were already retreating in that direction, and Fagan's Division, whose flank and rear were threatened by Marmaduke's retreat, also fell back. Shelby sent Jackman's Brigade back at about noon, and it was soon met by an order from Fagan to come to his assistance, for, as Shelby put it, "the entire prairie in his front was dark with Federals."[14] But both Jackman and Fagan were driven back.

"Now, my entire rear was in possession of the enemy," Shelby wrote, "and the news was brought that Thompson was fighting for dear life at Westport. Withdrawing him as soon as possible, and with much difficulty, for he was hard pressed, I fell back as rapidly as I could." When he came to the road to Little Santa Fe, Shelby saw that the prairie "was covered almost by a long line of troops which at first I had supposed to be our own men. This illusion was soon dispelled . . . I knew the only salvation was to charge the nearest line, break it if possible, and retreat rapidly."[15] In this way, Shelby broke through the encircling Federals and followed the rest of Price's army south, but many of his best men were left behind, dead, wounded, or captured.

It was about 1 p.m. when the van of McNeil's Union brigade, the 7th Kansas Cavalry, topped a ridge at Hickman Mills and looked down on a road to the west of the base of the ridge. It was filled with Price's immense wagon train, guarded by only a meager escort. The Kansans could probably have overwhelmed the guard and captured the prize of the campaign, but the 7th's commander, Major Francis M. Malone, did not seize his opportunity. Instead, he sent an orderly back to find General McNeil and inform him that the enemy had been found. An hour had passed by the time the word reached McNeil and he reached the ridge. He ordered his men to charge, but by then the Confederates had deployed some artillery and a large number of dismounted men in a position to rake the flank of the Federals if they rode toward the wagons. Many of those Rebels were without weapons, but McNeil had no way to know that. The remainder of his brigade was still a mile back down the road, and McNeil decided to cancel the attack. Instead, as Pleasonton wrote in his report of the battle, he "contented himself with some skirmishing and cannonading, and the train escaped."[16]

That evening, the Union commanders met at a farmhouse to decide on what to do next. As was so often the case after a large battle in the era of black-powder gunsmoke, it was raining. Governor Carney of Kansas and General Dietzler both urged that the militiamen be discharged, and Curtis agreed. Pleasonton, who was ill, also wanted to take his troops home. Many of his regiments were of Missouri militia, and they, like their Kansas counterparts, wanted to get home in time to vote in the approaching election. He also complained that Winslow's brigade, which had been hurried to him from Arkansas, especially needed rest, and most of his troops had not eaten since noon the day before. The

Kansans were raw levees, untrained and on foot, but the Missourians were experienced cavalrymen, and Curtis, feeling that it was their duty to mount a pursuit of "a much demoralized enemy," persuaded Pleasonton to stay.[17]

Up in Canada, Caleb Wallace, who was one of the St. Albans raiders who had been captured, managed to send a telegram to Confederate commissioner George Sanders at Montreal: "We are captured. Do what you can for us."[18] So Sanders went to St. Johns on the 23rd.

In the Shenandoah Valley on the 23rd, Assistant Secretary of War Charles A. Dana left Harper's Ferry at about 5 a.m., heading south. "It was a distance of about fifty miles to Sheridan, and by riding all day I got there about eleven o'clock at night. Sheridan had gone to bed, but in time of war one never delays in carrying out orders, whatever their nature. The general was awakened, and soon was out of his tent; and there, by the flare of an army torch and in the presence of a few sleepy aides-de-camp and of my own tired escort, I presented Sheridan his commission as major general in the regular army. Sheridan did not say much in reply to my little speech, nor could he have been expected to under the circumstances, though he showed lively satisfaction in the Government's appreciation of his services, and spoke most heartily, I remember, of the manner in which the administration had always supported him."[19]

Down around Petersburg that evening, Meade suggested to Grant that they make another attempt to cut the last supply lines into Petersburg. Scouting reports and the interrogation of Rebel prisoners indicated that a large section at the lower end of the new Confederate line of defenses running down to Hatcher's Run was still little more than lines scratched in the dirt by Rebel engineers. The next day, the 24th, Grant replied with a telegram to Meade: "Make your preparations to march out at an early hour on the 27th to gain possession of the South Side Railroad, and to hold it, and fortify back to your present left. In commencing your advance, move in three columns, exactly as proposed by yourself in our conversation of last evening, and with the same force you proposed to take."[20]

Since the battle of the Crater Grant had preceded all of his attacks around Petersburg with moves north of the James. This time he would vary the routine slightly by making both moves simultaneously. He told Butler, on the 24th, "I wish you to demonstrate against the enemy in your front." But he added, "I do not want any attack made by you against intrenched and defended positions, but feel out to the right beyond the front, and, if you can, turn it." As usual, the primary purpose of Butler's move would be to "prevent reenforcements going from the north side of James River to Petersburg."[21]

Sherman was still camped at Gaylesville, Alabama, on that 24th of October, because he had not yet learned that Hood had left Gadsden. He issued orders that day reorganizing his cavalry. Sheridan had sent him Wilson, whom Grant said would improve Sherman's mounted troops by fifty percent. Grant had also suggested that Sherman send Wilson with most of his cavalry to make the raid through Georgia alone. "But," Sherman later wrote, "I had not so much faith in cavalry as he had, and preferred to adhere to my original intention of going myself with a competent force."[22] Instead he intended to build up one large division of cavalry to take with him, under the command of Kilpatrick, transferring horses from the other divisions to get it ready. "I know that Kilpatrick is a hell of a damn fool," Sherman said, "but I want just that sort of a man to command my cavalry on this expedition."[23]

Previously, Sherman's cavalry had been divided administratively between his three armies. Most of the horsemen he had taken with him into Georgia had belonged to Thomas' Army of the Cumberland, and Stoneman's division had belonged to Schofield's Army of the Ohio. But these had all reported directly to Sherman without a real cavalry corps commander, although Thomas did have a chief of cavalry on his staff. Both of those commands also had large mounted forces helping to protect various rear areas, such as Nashville, eastern Tennessee, and Kentucky, while most of the cavalry of Howard's Army of the Tennessee was in Washburn's District of West Tennessee, organized as a small corps under Brigadier General Benjamin H. Grierson. Now Wilson was appointed chief of cavalry of Sherman's entire Military Division of the Mississippi, and most of the mounted units in that entire command would be organized into one large cavalry corps, of which Kilpatrick's would be the 3rd Division. Wilson, with the rest of the corps, would remain in Tennessee to help Thomas defend it from Hood, and he drafted the order himself for the establishment of his corps. It gave him the authority "to make such dispositions and arrangements as . . . [he] might think best for getting the largest possible force into the field and inflicting the greatest possible damage upon the enemy."[24]

In the Shenandoah Valley that day, fate was much less kind to another Union cavalry officer. Brigadier General Alfred Duffié, whose 1st Cavalry Division of the Department of West Virginia had been reduced to a mere training command, was captured near Winchester by Mosby's rangers.

Out along the Missouri-Kansas border, the 24th was a wet and windy day. Curtis and Pleasonton, riding in the same ambulance, followed Price's trail south with 7,000 troopers. It was a trail "marked by broken wagons and caissons, discarded rifles and blankets, bits of harness and debris, and by sick, wounded, and exhausted Confederates lying by the wayside waiting to be captured."[25] Colonel Phillips' brigade led Pleasonton's column, which was on the east. Blunt, with his own veteran 1st Brigade, was a little to the west. Colonel Moonlight, with the 2nd Kansas Brigade, moved to try to get around Price's column and beat it to Fort Scott, which would otherwise be in danger from the large Rebel force. They did not catch up with the tail of the Rebel column until after dark, but they harried the Confederate rear guard half the night.

The next morning, the 25th, they came upon the Rebels just as they were completing the crossing of the Marais des Cygnes River—the Mary Dasun, as one soldier spelled it. Price deployed Marmaduke's Division on the prairie south of the river. There was a brief skirmish, but Phillips and Blunt got into an argument about who should have the glory of making the real attack, and while the two tired commanders bickered the Confederates got away, although they left a couple of cannon behind. However, twelve miles farther south Price had to cross Mine Creek, a deep stream with high banks, and while his numerous wagons filed across the ford he deployed Marmaduke's and Fagan's divisions in mounted line north of the creek. Price, meanwhile, sent Shelby's Division off in an attempt to capture Fort Scott and its supplies.

Captain Crawford, the candidate for governor of Kansas, with a small party of men, was the first to come upon the two Confederate divisions, whose eight cannon soon began to fire. The next Federals to arrive were two brigades of Pleasonton's force, one commanded by Phillips and the other by Lieutenant Colonel Frederick W. Benteen, who had succeeded Colonel Winslow when the latter had been wounded on the 23rd and who would figure in Custer's last stand twelve years later. Crawford was joined by a few Kansas militiamen who were still with the pursuers, but Blunt was nowhere to be seen. Finally, Crawford rode over to Phillips and said, "I never liked to be fired upon, let's charge them."[26] Phillips was willing, and so was Benteen, although their combined force of 2,500 to 2,600 men was up against about two or three times as many Rebels.

Benteen's brigade charged first, headed straight for the middle of Marmaduke's line, and Phillips' was just seconds behind it, aiming for Fagan's left flank. The Confederates fired one volley from their muzzleloading rifles, and Benteen's front line faltered, but Major Abial Pierce, commander of the 4th Iowa in the second line, led his men on through the first line and slammed into Marmaduke's Division with sabers swinging, and, as one Iowan wrote, "it all fell away like a row of bricks." At the same time Phillips' men struck Fagan's flank, and the whole Confederate line disintegrated as the Rebels rode for their lives to get across Mine Creek. Benteen reported that the "enemy was completely routed and driven in the wildest confusion from the field."[27]

The eight Confederate guns were captured, along with Brigadier General William Cabell, one of Fagan's brigade commanders, and four colonels, along with some 560 other Rebels. So was Marmaduke, whose horse became frightened and threw him. Private James Dunlavy of the 3rd Iowa Cavalry captured him, not sure whether to believe that what looked like a portly old farmer in blue jeans was really a major general. Dunlavy took him to Curtis, who was still in his ambulance, to turn in his high-ranking prisoner. "How much longer have you to serve?" Curtis asked Dunlavy. "Eight months, sir," the private replied. The general turned to his adjutant, "Give Private Dunlavy a furlough for eight months," he said.[28]

"A number of prisoners taken in this fight were dressed in our uniform," Colonel Phillips wrote, "and in obedience to existing orders from department headquarters, and the usages of war, they were executed instanter."[29]

Price rode back to see what was going on at the rear and saw Marmaduke's and Fagan's men "retreating in utter and indescribable confusion."[30] He sent a courier pounding across the prairie with orders to "tell General Shelby that he alone can save the army."[31] Shelby came galloping back, and with Fagan's help managed to put together a rear guard and protect the retreat of the wagons and the disorganized units. Fortunately for the Rebels, the Federals, who were as tired and hungry as they were, did not press their advantage. Pleasonton, with about half of his forces, turned off to the west to Fort Scott for rest and supplies, despite Curtis's objections. That night Price burned about a third of his wagons to make it easier to get away with the rest.

On that 25th day of October, General R. E. Lee wrote a strange, interesting letter to President Davis in response to one he had received from the president by way of Confederate scout and spy Benjamin F. Stringfellow. It pertained to some unspecified project proposed by Reverend Kinsey John Stewart, a Virginian who had recently returned from Canada. Stewart had passed through Maryland at about the same time as Lieutenant Bowie's mysterious expedition and had crossed the lower

Potomac in a basket boat he had made from saplings and some rubberized cloth he had bought in Baltimore and proceeded to report to President Davis. A couple of days before, he had visited General Lee, who now wrote to Davis as follows: "Mr. Stringfellow has just handed me your note enclosing one from Mr. Steward—Mr. S. said upon your advice he had come to consult me upon a project he had in view, especially as to its morality.—I gave him opinion as far as I understand it & thought from what he said he had not determined to undertake it, but that it would depend upon an interview he would have with you. I know so little of Mr. S. that is his capacity for such an undertaking as he intimated rather than explained that when Mr. Stringfellow first came to me I told him, as I have written to Genl Fitz Lee, that I could give him no advice or recommendation as to his course—He must make up his own opinion as to what he should do—Col: E. G. Lee has just called on me on the same subject, having been referred to me by Mr. Steward—as Mr. S. told me, what I very well knew, that his project must be kept a profound secret, I could neither explain it to Mr. Stringfellow or Col. Lee even as far as he had unfolded it to me—In fact I have not a high opinion of Mr. Stewarts Discretion, & could not advise any one to join him in his enterprize. I had inferred that his companions were to be taken from Canada, until I got a note from Genl Fitz Lee, asking if he must send some half dozen of his men to Mr. S—To take a party of men from here seems to me to ensure failure & I could not recommend it. I supposed he would make up his mind as to what he would do & arrange his party in his own way.—I have had nothing to do with it—I return Mr. Stewarts letter."[32]

The authors of *Come Retribution* make a good case for Stewart's involvement in, perhaps even the origination of, the Confederate plot to capture President Lincoln so as to trade him for a large number of their men held in Union prison camps. It would be hard to find another possible secret operation upon which an ordained minister would seek General Lee's opinion of its morality, unless it be actual assassination. Stewart evidently wanted to borrow some men, perhaps experienced scouts, from Fitz Lee's cavalry but was turned down. Stewart did go on to visit Colonel Edwin G. Lee at Staunton, who was in charge of the Virginia reserves in the Shenandoah Valley, and then returned to Canada by again crossing the Potomac below Washington in a small boat.

General Lee added a postscript to his letter to President Davis: "Upon reperusal of your note I perceive you ask my advice—I do not think Mr. Stuart by his habits life etc. qualified for the undertaking he proposes— It was on this account that I could not advise others to join him. He may be an entirely different man from what I suppose him & the best fitted for the business, but I do not know it—I know nothing of the means or information at his disposal & can form no opinion as to his probable success."[33]

In Canada on the 25th, George Sanders returned to Montreal from visiting the St. Albans raiders in St. Johns. He did not check into the Ottawa House hotel, where he had been staying before this brief trip. Instead, he checked into the St. Lawrence Hall, where John Wilkes Booth was still living just down the hall. Eight Confederate officers in civilian clothes left Toronto the next day heading for New York. Their mission was to set a series of fires as a diversion so that Copperheads could seize control of the city as the first step in setting up a Northeastern confederacy which would ally itself with the South.

---

1. Monaghan, *Civil War on the Western Border*, 325.
2. Foote, *The Civil War*, 3:617.
3. Basler, ed., *Collected Works of Abraham Lincoln*, 8:58–59.
4. Ibid., 8:73–74.
5. Catton, *Grant Takes Command*, 369.
6. Starr, *The Union Cavalry in the Civil War*, 3:512.
7. Ibid., 3:515.
8. Monaghan, *Civil War on the Western Border*, 329.
9. Ibid., 331.
10. Daniel O'Flaherty, *General Jo Shelby: Undefeated Rebel* (Chapel Hill, 1954), 222.
11. Starr, *The Union Cavalry in the Civil War*, 3:517.
12. Monaghan, *Civil War on the Western Border*, 332.
13. Ibid., 334.
14. O'Flaherty, *General Jo Shelby*, 223.
15. Ibid.
16. Starr, *The Union Cavalry in the Civil War*, 3:520.
17. Ibid., 519.
18. Tidwell, Hall and Gaddy, *Come Retribution*, 333.
19. Charles A. Dana, *Recollections of the Civil War*, (New York: 1898), 217–218.
20. Humphreys, *The Virginia Campaign*, 294.
21. Trudeau, *The Last Citadel*, 223.
22. Sherman, *Memoirs*, 634–635.
23. Foote, *The Civil War*, 3:622.

24. Starr, *The Union Cavalry in the Civil War*, 3:534.
25. Ibid., 3:520.
26. Monaghan, *Civil War on the Western Border*, 338.
27. Alvin M. Josephy, Jr., *The Civil War in the American West* (New York, 1991), 384.
28. Monaghan, *Civil War on the Western Border*, 339.
29. Starr, *The Union Cavalry in the Civil War*, 3:521, n. 58.
30. Josephy, *The Civil War in the American West*, 384.
31. O'Flaherty, *General Jo Shelby*, 224.
32. Tidwell, Hall and Gaddy, *Come Retribution*, 278–279.
33. Ibid., 279.

CHAPTER TWENTY-SEVEN

It Was a Terrible Place to Charge

26–27 October 1864

On 26 October, Richard Taylor sent off a courier with Beauregard's order for Forrest to join Hood as soon as he finished his raid in western Tennessee, but Forrest had ridden north out of Jackson, Tennessee, two days before. Hood, that day, was approaching Decatur, Alabama, on the south bank of the Tennessee River. He hoped to cross the river there, but first he would have to overcome the Union garrison in the town. However, Colonel Charles Doolittle's bold and judicious use of his 18th Michigan repulsed the Confederates' first efforts to storm the defenses, and Brigadier General R. S. Granger arrived that night with reinforcements.

Sherman learned that same day of the appearance of a large force of Confederate infantry at Decatur. He immediately ordered a reconnaissance down the Coosa River, which went almost to Gadsden and discovered that Hood's army was indeed gone, except for some of Wheeler's cavalry. "I then finally resolved on my future course," he wrote, "which was to leave Hood to be encountered by General Thomas, while I should carry into full effect the long-contemplated project of marching for the sea-coast, and thence to operate toward Richmond."[1]

He calculated that Thomas had about 4,000 men under Granger at Decatur and Huntsville; Brigadier General John T. Croxton's brigade of about 2,500 cavalry from his own Army of the Cumberland; Colonel Horace Capron's brigade of about 1,200 cavalry from Schofield's Army of the Ohio; and Brigadier General Edward Hatch's division of about 4,000 cavalry from Washburn's District of West Tennessee, all watching the crossings of the Tennessee; plus from 8,000 to 10,000 new recruits and about the same number of civilian employees of the Quartermaster's Department at Nashville, who could be used to man that city's powerful defenses; about 5,000 men at Chattanooga under General Steedman; another 5,000 at Murfreesboro under Rousseau; and about 10,000 dismounted cavalrymen whom Wilson was collecting at Louisville and Nashville, where he was getting them remounted as rapidly as possible. However, these forces were all scattered, many of them disorganized, and few of them firstline veteran troops. But A. J. Smith's 8,000 to 10,000 veteran infantrymen from the 16th Corps could be brought from Missouri now that Price had been dealt with, and Sherman decided to send Thomas one corps from his Army of the Cumberland. Thomas asked for Davis's 14th, which had been his own corps before he was promoted to army command, but Sherman gave him Stanley's 4th Corps, 15,000 men, instead.

The next day, the 27th, Beauregard, somewhat irritated at Hood for changing plans without consulting him, caught up with Hood outside of Decatur, where the latter was preparing to lay siege to the Union defenses. For a day and half the two generals debated whether or not the Federal force was too strong to be attacked.

A force of about 150 Union militia under Major Samuel P. Cox approached the camp of Rebel guerrilla Bloody Bill Anderson not far north of the Missouri River that morning. A local woman had brought Cox word of Anderson's location. After driving the Rebel pickets through the nearby town of Albany, Cox had most of his men dismount and advance cautiously into the woods concealing the camp and sent a mounted squad to flush out the bushwhackers. This worked, for Anderson's men all mounted up and chased these mounted Federals down a narrow road through the woods, and when they came in sight of the dismounted men they charged with a Rebel yell, firing their revolvers. However, the Union men stood their ground and returned an accurate, steady fire that caused the guerrillas to retreat in confusion—all except

Anderson and one other. Both of them rode right through the Union line, but two bullets hit Anderson in the back of the head and he toppled backward off his horse while his companion got away. Anderson's men fought hard to recover their commander, and one of them was killed while attempting to drag him away with a lariat. But Cox's men eventually drove them off.

Anderson was dead. Among the items found on his body were six revolvers, a photograph of himself, a mirror, a pocketbook containing $600 in gold and Federal greenbacks and some Confederate money, a small Rebel flag, and some orders from General Price. The militiamen put his body in a wagon and took it to the county seat, Richmond, where it was placed on display at the courthouse after the local photographer had taken a picture of it. After a while they cut off the head and stuck it on top of a telegraph pole as a warning to other bushwhackers, then dragged the headless body through the streets behind a horse, before burying it in the local cemetery.

In the pre-dawn darkness of 27 October, large formations of Union troops assembled in the rain south of Petersburg and southeast of Richmond. On the Petersburg front, Meade had pulled well over 75 percent of his infantry out of the defenses facing Petersburg for a serious effort to extend his reach to the west. North of the James, Butler was preparing to use over half of his available infantry for another probe of Richmond's Intermediate Line of defenses. The two army commanders had come up with similar plans. Both would make tentative frontal attacks near the ends of the two Confederate lines, where they were thought to be the weakest. If these attacks broke through, well and good. If not, they would serve as diversions to keep the Rebels from interfering with attempts by other forces to get completely around these flanks.

Butler's plan was for Terry's 10th Corps, holding his right, to move farther north, cross White Oak Swamp, and hit the Intermediate Line between the New Market and Charles City roads while over half of Weitzel's 18th Corps, taken from his left, would, with Kautz's cavalry, move even farther north to the Williamsburg Road and attack along it, where Confederate defenders were believed to be few, if not nonexistent. Meade's plan was somewhat more complex. Most of Parke's 9th Corps would move from its position on the Union left to attack the supposedly unfinished Rebel works between Peeble's farm and Hatcher's Run. Meanwhile, two thirds of Hancock's 2nd Corps, which had already been withdrawn from the trenches on the far right, would march southwest down the Vaughn Road, cross Hatcher's Run, and turn to the northwest to cut the Boydton Plank Road and, if possible, go on to the Southside

Railroad. Most of Warren's 5th Corps would be placed in between the other two corps, ready to support whichever line of advance seemed the most promising.

Both plans were the sort that, if boldly executed, might, with a reasonable amount of good luck, achieve decisive results. If all went well south of the Appomattox, the last supply lines into Petersburg would be cut, and both that city and Richmond would soon have to be abandoned. If Butler's plan succeeded, Richmond might even fall immediately. In war, however, there are always risks. Neither plan was likely to lead to the kind of disaster that would shake Grant's hold on either city, but either or both could easily lead sizable Union forces into deadly traps that would demoralize the troops, expand the casualty lists, and thus hurt Lincoln's reelection chances.

Humphreys, Meade's chief of staff, later pointed out two problems that the Army of the Potomac faced from the start. For one: "It was a dark, rainy morning, and the movement in the wooded ground was necessarily delayed, so that the enemy were not taken by surprise."[2] For another: "We were ignorant of the topography of the country to be passed over."[3] Substantially the same could be said for the Army of the James, although it had somewhat more familiarity with the terrain since it would be moving through country that had been fought over during McClellan's Peninsula campaign two and a half years before.

Considering that time was ultimately in his favor, Grant could afford to err on the side of caution. If these attacks did not bring about the fall of Richmond and force Lee out into the open, there would eventually come chances to try again, and the fewer losses taken now the sooner another attempt could be made and the better its chances of success would be. There was also the national election to consider, which was only ten days away. As Grant's military secretary, Adam Badeau, wrote, "The enemies of the nation in the North were certain to exaggerate every mishap. Success at the polls was just now even more important than a victory in the field, and it would have been most unwise to risk greatly on this occasion."[4]

Butler was an extremely ambitious politician who would like nothing better than to be the general who took Richmond. Such glory might well be a ticket to the White House. So Grant's aide, Cyrus Comstock, was sent to keep an eye on Butler. As Comstock put it, that general was "most unscrupulous and would stop at nothing to carry out his ends."[5] Meade was, if anything, inclined to be too cautious, but, as Grant was always more sanguine about the Petersburg front than the north side of the James, he would personally supervise that front this time. Lee, on the other hand, was always more worried about the Richmond front and rode out to witness the operations there, once it was known that the Federals were up to something, although he gave Longstreet a free hand in conducting those operations. "His idea," Longstreet wrote long afterwards, "was that the north side was the easier route of Grant's triumphal march into Richmond, and that sooner or later he would make his effort there in great force."[6]

Parke moved out at about 3:30 a.m. with the bulk of each of his three divisions, leaving only 1,500 men to hold his defenses. He led the other 11,000 men of his 9th Corps across to the south side of Arthur's Swamp and turned westward on Route 673, heading straight for the new extention of the Confederate line he had run into the month before. Warren left 2,500 men to hold his part of the defenses and with the other 11,000 followed Parke's column, worried that almost 4,000 of his men were so new and untrained that they had never fired a musket, even in practice. At about the same time, Hancock, with 10,000 men in two divisions of his 2nd Corps, headed down the Halifax Road, turned west at Wyatt's Crossing to the Vaughn Road, and followed it south to the crossing of Hatcher's Run. Just beyond, he would turn west along the Dabney's Mill Road. Gregg, with most of his cavalry division, about 3,000 troopers, moved down the Halifax and Stage roads and crossed Rowanty Creek at Monk's Neck Bridge, just southeast of where that stream was formed by the confluence of Hatcher's Run and Gravelly Run, then turned west to cover Hancock's left flank.

In order to keep the columns from being too encumbered, no wagons were allowed to accompany the troops, only a few pack animals, and the infantrymen carried four days' rations in their haversacks. "The morning was dark and gloomy," wrote Grant's aide, Horace Porter, "a heavy rain was falling, the roads were muddy and obstructed, and tangled thickets, dense woods, and swampy streams confronted the troops at all points. The difficulties of the ground made the movements necessarily slow."[7] At 7:30 a.m. Humphreys, Meade's chief of staff, sent Parke a message urging him to "push ahead more rapidly and get into position."[8] But Parke and his men were doing the best they could. The terrain was so confusing that when the lead brigade stopped to form its skirmish line it deployed facing north instead of west, and about a half an hour was lost getting it realigned in the right direction. The lost minutes did not matter much, however, for when the line was formed and the Federals advanced—with Griffin's 1st Division of the 5th Corps on Parke's left—it soon found that the unfinished nature of the Confederate defenses was greatly exaggerated. As Humphreys put it, "General Parke and General Warren, driving in their pickets, found their intrenchments to consist of breastworks, with abatis and slashing, and held with such force as not to justify an attempt to carry them."[9]

By then it was nearly 9 a.m., and at about that hour Grant and Meade with a large party of staff officers, couriers, etc., arrived at the Clements house at the southwest corner of the Union defenses around Poplar Spring Church, near the south bank of Arthur's Swamp. Meade promptly sent a message to Hancock advising him that Parke's advance was blocked by strong defenses and that there was "no chance of his getting into them."[10] Humphreys, who had ridden ahead, had already realized that Parke's way was blocked, but hearing that Hancock's was not, he had already ordered Warren to send support to the 2nd Corps. But while Humphreys went to report what he had done to Meade, Warren decided to make a personal reconnaissance "to ascertain the practicability of forcing the enemy back."[11] As Grant's military secretary later put it, "Warren never seemed to appreciate the tremendous importance, in battle, of time. He elaborated and developed, and prepared, as carefully and cautiously and deliberately in the immediate presence of the enemy as if there was nothing else to do, and, while he was preparing and looking out for his flanks, the moment in which victory was possible usually slipped away."[12]

Warren got back from his reconnaissance just in time to meet Grant and Meade. The latter also ordered Warren to support Hancock, but specified that his men were to cross to the south side of Hatcher's Run and advance up the west bank of that stream, thus filling the space between Griffin's division, north of the stream, and Hancock's corps on the road about a mile south of it. Leaving two brigades of Ayres' 2nd Division to support Griffin, Warren took Crawford's 3rd Division and the other brigade of Ayres' across Hatcher's run. When this force reached a position across the stream from the end of the defenses blocking Parke and Griffin, it was to attack it. Grant and Meade hoped that this flank attack would drive off the defenders and allow Parke and Griffin to resume their advance. The head of Crawford's column crossed Hatcher's Run at Armstrong's Mill at 11:45 a.m.

Hancock's two divisions had encountered some Georgia cavalry defending the ford across Hatcher's Run behind some earthworks and abatis, and the Federals' first attempt to cross was driven back, so an entire brigade was deployed and waded across. The water was up to the men's armpits and they had to carry their rifles and cartridge boxes over their heads, but they charged over the breastworks and drove off the Georgians. About a mile beyond the ford, Hancock's column turned right onto the Dabney's Mill Road, a mere path through thick woods that was barely passable for the artillery.

To the southeast, Gregg's cavalry encountered only a few pickets at Monk's Neck Bridge, and these were easily scattered. Gregg learned that Rooney Lee's cavalry was in camp about three miles to the south and that Matthew Butler's division was to the west. Gregg's troopers pressed on to the west near the south bank of Gravelly Run to the Vaughn Road, then soon turned north on the Quaker road. But a mile and a half up that road they found the Quaker Bridge over Gravelly Run defended by Wade Hampton with a pair of guns and some of Dearing's Brigade of cavalry on high ground. And at about the same time another force of Rebel cavalry attacked their rear guard. However, the Confederates in their front gave ground when they learned that they were in danger of being cut off by Hancock's infantry moving westward behind them. Gregg got his column across the bridge as quickly as possible, then burned it behind him and pushed on up the Quaker Road to its intersection with the critical Boydton Plank Road, which was reached before 1 p.m., and where he found Hancock had already arrived.

By then, Hancock's infantry, following its much shorter route, had pushed across the Boydton Plank Road and had driven off a battery of artillery that had been firing on it from Burgess' Tavern, where the White Oak Road left the Boydton Plank Road. This was about a quarter of a mile north of the Dabney's Mill Road, which Hancock had followed, and ran westward not far to the south of Hatcher's Run. Hancock had just ordered Mott's 3rd Division of the 2nd corps to follow this White Oak Road toward the Southside Railroad when he received instructions from Meade to halt at the Boydton Plank Road. Meade evidently did not want Hancock to get too far off to the west until Crawford could turn the Rebels away from the line that was blocking the progress of Parke's and Griffin's troops. Otherwise, Hancock would be too far separated from the rest of the army.

North of the James, Butler's troops also moved out in the morning rain. William Birney's division of U.S. Colored Troops formed the left end of the 10th Corps' new line that stretched northward from the defenses Terry had held against Lee's attack on 7 October. In the center of the line, stradling the Darbytown Road, was Foster's 1st Division, and on the right, stretching up to and across the Charles City Road, was Brigadier General Adelbert Ames' 2nd Division. Once the line was formed, it moved forward, some of the troops having to make their way through what one of Birney's officers called "almost impassable undergrowth," and at about daylight the Federals encountered the Confederate pickets. "The skirmishers easily pushed the rebels back," one Union soldier remembered, "but at length came upon their earthworks and were suddenly checked by a galling fire."[13]

Meanwhile, Weitzel's 18th Corps column was marching farther north by a zig-zag route to the east of Terry's advancing line. But, like their comrades in the Army of the Potomac farther south, these Federals were delayed by poor roads and bad weather. The column moved out at 5 a.m., but it was 8 a.m. by the time it reached the Darbytown Road and 10 when it came to the Charles City Road. There it found Kautz's cavalry, commanded in his absence by Colonel Robert West. For some reason, the cavalry had turned west onto the Charles City Road instead of continuing to the north. "Where they were to have been ahead two or three hours," one of Weitzel's officers complained, "to have shrouded our march in a cloud of Cavalry dust, we actually ran over them and had to wait for them to get out of the way." On the other hand, Terry's infantry was not on the Charles City Road in the strength that Weitzel had expected. The latter sent off a note to Butler saying he supposed that the commander wanted him to continue to the north anyway but asking for orders just in case. Butler replied that he should indeed continue as planned, which he did, preceded by Colonel Samuel Spear's brigade of the cavalry, and at about 1 p.m. the head of the column finally reached the Williamsburg Road. "You understand now that I am entirely lost from Terry," Weitzel warned Butler.[14]

On the Petersburg front, Crawford's division of the 5th Corps was deployed on the south side of Hatcher's Run with its right flank on the bank of that stream, and it began advancing at about 12:30 p.m. But the dense low growth of trees and bushes and the crooked course of the stream caused serious delays. To make matters worse, a large tributary was mistaken for the main stream, causing the entire division to move in the wrong direction. When the mistake was discovered it was not easily rectified, because the Confederates had slashed the trees and brush along the tributary, making it even harder to cross than it otherwise would have been.

Crawford had made very little progress by the time that Grant and Meade reached the Boydton Plank Road, at about 1:30 p.m. There they found that not only was the enemy opposing any further advance to the west but that he was also disputing the crossing of Hatcher's Run at Burgess's Mill. "His troops were strongly posted," Horace Porter wrote, "with a battery in position directly in front of the head of Hancock's corps, and another about eight hundred yards to our left. Unless this force on the opposite side of the stream could be driven back, our lines could not be thrown forward for the purpose of making the contemplated movement." The two commanders, along with Hancock, rode out toward the front for a closer look, but their large contingent of staff officers and orderlies soon attracted the fire of the Rebel guns. "The whistling of projectiles and the explosion of shells made the position rather uncomfortable," Porter remembered.[15]

"This is pretty hot," Meade said; "it will kill some of our horses."[16] But it did worse than that. One orderly was killed and two others were wounded. "It looked at one time as if the explosion of a shell had killed General Meade," Porter said, "but fortunately he escaped untouched. A little speck of blood appeared on Hancock's cheek after the bursting of a shell. It was probably caused by a bit of gravel being thrown in his face."[17] Most of the officers withdrew to where they were covered from the artillery fire, while some of the staff officers were sent out to reconnoiter. But the reports brought back were conflicting, "General Grant sits upon a rock," a cavalry officer wrote, "at the foot of a huge tree— His orderly and Horse near him—and about him stood Generals Meade, Hancock, Gregg and Mott . . . There was high tension easily to be seen."[18] Finally Grant decided to go see for himself.

Taking only one aide with him, Lieutenant Colonel Orville Babcock, he rode to within a few yards of the bridge that carried the Boydton Plank Road over Hatcher's Run. "Before he had gone far," Horace Porter wrote, "a shell exploded just under his horse's neck. The animal threw up his head and reared, and it was thought that he and his rider had both been struck, but neither had been touched." However, with both sharpshooters and artillery firing, the watching officers and orderlies were "expecting every moment to see the general fall," Porter said. Then Grant's horse got one foot caught in a loop of downed telegraph wire. "Every one's face now began to wear a still more anxious look," Porter said. "Babcock, whose coolness under fire was always conspicuous, dismounted, and carefully uncoiled the wire and released the horse. The general sat still in his saddle, evidently thinking more about the horse than himself, and in the most quiet and unruffled manner cautioned Babcock to be sure not to hurt the animal's leg. The general soon succeeded in obtaining a clear view of the enemy's line and the exact nature of the ground, and then, much to our relief, retired to a less exposed position."[19]

One of his aides chided Grant for exposing himself to such danger and, with a smile, the general said, "Well, I suppose I ought not to have gone down there." But he had found out what he wanted to know. "The rebels were evidently in force north of the creek, with strong defenses," Adam Badeau, wrote. "Their entrenched line extended far beyond the point at which it had been supposed to turn to the north. . . . The contemplated movement was thus impracticable."[20] But if the Federals could not attack, perhaps the Confederates would oblige. Thus Grant told Hancock to keep his troops where they were until noon the next day in the hope of provoking an attack. Then, with the assurance that Crawford was connecting with Hancock's right flank, at about 4 p.m. Grant and Meade rode away.

"General Grant then took a narrow cross-road leading down to the Run to the right of Hancock's corps," Horace Porter wrote; "but it was soon found that there were no troops between our party and the enemy, and that if we continued along this road it would probably not be many minutes before we should find ourselves prisoners in his lines. There was nothing to do but to turn around and strike a road farther in the rear. This, as usual, was a great annoyance to the general, who expressed his objections, as he had done many a time before, to turning back. We paused for a few minutes, and tried to find some cross-cut; but there was not even a pathway leading in the proper direction, and the party had to retrace its steps for some distance. General Grant was now becoming anxious to get in telegraphic communication with Butler, and he rode on to a point on the military railroad called Warren Station, reaching there about half-past five p.m."[21]

On the north side of the James, Weitzel had reached the Williamsburg Road by a little after 1 p.m. and by a bit before 2 p.m. he had completed an examination of the Confederate defenses in his front. "I found them," he said, ". . . defended by only three pieces of artillery and a small body of dismounted cavalry." But it took him nearly two hours to deploy his troops and probe the Rebel position. "Weitzel," one of his men later wrote, "if he was to attack at all, took too much time to reconnoiter and get into position." He did, however, send Colonel John Holman's brigade of U.S. Colored Troops even farther north, to the Nine Mile Road. Holman was to advance along it "until he should come within sight of the enemy's line, and then to halt and report to corps headquarters."[22] When Weitzel finally did attack, at about 3:30 p.m., he did so with only two of his seven brigades.

Meanwhile, Lieutenant General James Longstreet, now in charge of the Confederate defenses north of the Appomattox, had realized that Terry was only feinting to keep him busy and "that some other was the point of danger, which must mean the unoccupied lines beyond White Oak Swamp." So he ordered Field's Division out of the lines and up to the Williamsburg Road and Hoke to spread his division to take over Field's position as well as his own. "When the head of General Field's column got to the Williamsburg road the enemy's skirmishers were deployed and half-way across the field approaching our line," Longstreet said. "Just behind the trenches was a growth of pines which concealed our troops until a line of sharp-shooters stepped into the works. Their fire surprised the enemy somewhat, as they had seen nothing but part of Gary's cavalry, and their skirmish line gave up the field for their heavy infantry.

"The opening in front of the breastworks was about six hundred yards wide and twelve hundred in length, extending from the York River Railroad on the north to a ditch draining towards the head of White Oak Swamp on the south. About midway of the field is a slight depression or swale of five or six feet depth. Quickly following the repulse of the skirmish line, and just as Field had adjusted the infantry and artillery to their trenches, came the Eighteenth Corps bursting into the open and deploying on both sides of the road in solid ranks. They were at once in fair cannister range, and soon under the terrific fire of a solid line of infantry,—infantry so experienced that they were not likely to throw as much as one bullet without well-directed aim. At the first fire they began to drop, and they fell more rapidly until they reached the swale, when the entire line dropped to the ground. They had just enough cover there for their bodies as they spread themselves closely to the ground, but not enough to permit them to load or rise to deliver fire without exposing their persons to our fire. To attempt to retreat would have been as disastrous as to advance; so they were entrapped."[23]

On the Union left, just south of the Williamsburg Road, another Federal brigade advanced over the prostrate forms of the force clinging to the cover of the swale. Colonel Ripley, commander of one of the brigades hugging the ground, watched this fresh force as it "almost vanished" into the storm of Confederate fire. "I never saw such magnificent musketry firing," he said. Nevertheless, the new brigade got to within 150 yards of the Rebel defenses. "Here the line became so broken and cut up as to prevent its pushing forward any further, and the men fell upon the ground for protection," a Union officer reported.[24]

Longstreet ordered Gary's cavalry to come in on the flank of the Federals pinned down by his infantry and artillery fire and force their surrender. But before Gary could execute this order he received a report of Federals advancing on the Nine Mile Road. That was Holman's brigade. The Rebel cavalry turned back to stop it, but before they got there the squadron and two guns that had been left to guard the Nine Mile Road were driven off by the 1st U.S. Colored Troops with the loss of one cannon. However, when Gary's main force returned, he sent it forward in a dismounted charge that struck Holman's line in the flank and drove it back, recovering the lost gun.

Holman's attack had at least served to divert Gary's cavalry long enough for many of the Federals in the swale to escape under the cut of the York River Railroad on their right and down the dry ditch on their left. One young Texan in Field's Division clambered over the breast-works and started after them. When his captain told him to get back in the trenches he said, "But, Captain, these slow-going generals of ours are going to sit still until night comes, and let those Yankees get away."[25] The soldier not only continued his advance but many others joined him, and soon several hundred Federal prisoners were brought in.

About a half-hour after Weitzel's attack began, Terry launched one of his own between the New Market and Charles City roads, "the object being to ascertain the strength of the enemy and his position." One of his men said, "It was a terrible place to charge, through thick woods." Another said that "it was useless and against the judgment of our officers. But old Beast Butler ordered it, and it must be done." General Foster, the division commander, reported that the assaulting columns "were met with a severe fire of grape and canister and after advancing to within about eight rods of the enemy's works it was found impracticable to proceed." A private said, "We was ordered to halt and lay flat on the ground. We lay a few moments and the grape and canister flew over our heads till it made everything rattle. . . . I tell you it took the tree tops off like nothing."[26]

As soon as it was dark, both Terry and Weitzel withdrew their troops, although Terry maintained his position up as far as the Darbytown Road, and they began the long march back to the south. "This march," Weitzel said, "owing to the rain, the intense darkness, the muddy and narrow roads, was the most fatiguing and trying one that ever I have known troops to undertake." One of his men said, "Everything is mixed to-gether. Utter confusion reigns; teams, artillery, ambulances and infantry all jumbled together, and all heavily loaded; mud and water in many places knee-deep in the roads, the night pitchy dark, the rain pouring in torrents . . . wagons are tipped over and smashed . . . horses and mules ugly, drivers hurrying, noisy, swearing, quarreling, mad."[27] Weitzel's men finally went into bivouac near the Charles City Road.

Cyrus Comstock, Grant's aide sent to watch Butler, was livid: "Grant's order was imperative that corps commanders should be in-structed not to attack entrenched defended lines. . . . This order was not obeyed, at least in spirit—the spirit of Butler's written & verbal orders being to do something." Weitzel, however, took the responsibility. "I did more than I was ordered to do," he confessed. "I knew my orders were simply to make a demonstration. I probably made a more lively demonstration than was intended."[28]

South of Petersburg, after Grant and Meade left, Hancock decided to secure the Boydton Plank Road bridge over Hatcher's Run. He sent his 2nd Division, then under the temporary command of Brigadier General Thomas W. Egan, to accomplish this, supported by McAllister's 3rd Brigade of Mott's 3rd Division. At the same time, he sent two regiments of Pierce's 2nd Brigade of the 3rd Division into the woods to see what had become of Crawford, whose division had still not linked up with Hancock's right. Mott's other brigade, DeTrobriand's 1st, was guarding the corps' left flank, facing to the northwest. The rest of Pierce's brigade was supporting a pair of guns posted on a ridge midway between Egan and DeTrobriand, facing north. One regiment of Gregg's cavalry was with Egan, one of his two brigades was on DeTrobriand's left, and the other was guarding the rear, facing southwest across the Boydton Plank Road.

Responsibility for the Confederate defenses south of the Appomattox rested primarily with Lieutenant General A. P. Hill, commander of Lee's 3rd Corps. Johnson's Division of R. H. Anderson's new 4th Corps held the left end of the line, where it was closest to the Federals, and Hampton's cavalry held the far right, but all the rest of the defenses of Petersburg were manned by the three divisions of Hill's corps. Hill was too sick to leave his headquarters that day, so he left tactical control to the commander of the division at the threatened right end of his line, Henry Heth, who also happened to be the senior division commander in the corps. Heth had command of his own four brigades, two brigades of Cadmus Wilcox's division, Dearing's Brigade of cavalry, and about 600 to 800 dismounted cavalrymen who were manning the extreme right end of the defenses northeast of Hatcher's Run. And when it was known that the Federals were advancing, Hill sent three brigades of Major General William Mahone's division to reinforce him, but it was 3 p.m. by the time the first two of these arrived. Nevertheless, Heth decided that the only way to get the Union forces off the critical Boydton Plank Road was to attack immediately, so to the two brigades that Mahone had brought up he added one of his own and directed Mahone to cross Hatcher's Run on a dam downstream from the bridge and to attack Hancock's flank by way of a blind path through the dense woods. Meanwhile, Heth would attack across the bridge with one brigade of his own infantry plus Dearing's cavalry. Hampton had Matthew Butler's cavalry division blocking the White Oak Road, which led to Five Forks and the Southside Railroad, and Rooney Lee's division pressing up the Boydton

Plank Road from the southwest. As soon as they heard the sound of Mahone's assault, both cavalry divisions would also attack, so that Hancock's force would be hit from three sides, while to the fourth side, the south, was nothing but woods.

At about 4:30 p.m., just after Egan's Union division had begun its attack on the bridge and the two regiments from Pierce's brigade had just disappeared into the woods to the east, the gunfire in that direction rose to a heavy roar, leaving Hancock no doubt that the enemy was advancing. The two regiments were quickly scattered, the rest of Pierce's brigade was pushed to the west, toward the Boydton Plank Road, and the two guns it had been supporting were overrun. Many prisoners were captured, as were the colors of three regiments. And Hampton's two cavalry divisions also surged forward in dismounted attacks. The Federals were surrounded and they knew it. When Hancock ordered one unit to start digging some defenses, one puzzled soldier asked, "General, which way will you have them face?"[29]

But neither Rooney Lee nor Matthew Butler could make much headway, and Hampton lost two of his own sons in Butler's attack, one killed and one wounded. Soon it was Mahone's turn to find himself surrounded. As one of his men put it, they "discovered that we had only knocked a gap out of the Yankee line and that the two ends were closing together behind us." McAllister's brigade, which had been supporting Egan's attack on the bridge, just did an about-face and attacked Mahone's right, followed by Egan's division. "We charged down the hill," McAllister wrote; "the enemy became panic-stricken and gave way. We rushed on and received the enemy's front and flank fire. We wavered and fell back. The enemy took courage and followed. We reformed and rolled in the musketry upon them." Some of Gregg's cavalry turned about and charged Mahone's left while DeTrobriand also faced his brigade about and charged the Rebels' front, "driving the enemy before us," he wrote, "and clearing the whole of the open field." The two lost guns were recaptured, along with the flags of two North Carolina regiments, and Mahone's force fell back the way it had come. One Virginian remembered that when "our men fell back into the woods from which they made this assault, many lost their way in the thick undergrowth, some being captured, others narrowly escaping capture."[30] Then, with Mahone disposed of, Hancock turned his and Gregg's men back to face Hampton's two divisions, and they too were repulsed.

When Meade learned of the attack on Hancock he sent Ayres' division of the 5th Corps to reinforce him, but it had gone only as far as Armstrong's Mill on Hatcher's Run, just upstream from the Vaughn Road, and Crawford's division had still not closed the gap between itself and

Hancock's men, when darkness finally put an end to the fighting on this front. The question remained whether it was best to have Hancock stay where he was or withdraw during the night. "If you think that with Crawford and Ayres joined to your troops you can attack successfully," Hancock was told, "the commanding general desires you to do so. If not, you can withdraw as directed, and during the night if you consider best." Hancock checked on his various commands, including Gregg's, riding through the rainy darkness with Meade's son and aide. And he concluded that, because most of his units were low on ammunition, especially Gregg's cavalrymen with their breechloaders and repeaters, and because the single muddy logging road past Dabney's Mill could not be counted on to bring him both the ammunition he needed and the reinforcements, and because that road was vulnerable to Confederate attack, it would be best to retreat. "Reluctant as I was to leave the field," he wrote, "and by so doing lose some of the fruits of victory, I felt compelled to order a withdrawal rather than risk disaster by awaiting an attack in the morning only partly prepared."[31]

At about 10 p.m. Mott's division led Hancock's infantry back down the rain-soaked Dabney's Mill Road, where the mud was ankle- and sometimes knee-deep, while Gregg's cavalry, after repairing the bridge it had destroyed earlier, fell back down the Quaker Road. By 1 a.m. the last picket had been withdrawn, but due to a lack of ambulance wagons, 250 wounded men had to be left behind, along with the surgeons taking care of them.

As the fighting came to a close at one end of the Petersburg front, it flared up at the other, as Federal patrols probed the Confederate defenses where they were close together, to make sure that they were still manned. At dusk a Union captain led a party of 100 men across no-man's land, through the abatis, drove in the Rebel pickets, and captured a strong work in the Confederate line near where the battle of the crater had been fought three months before. They were driven out by Rebel reinforcements, but not before capturing more than a hundred Confederates, including four officers. At 8:30 p.m. a Union lieutenant colonel led 130 men into no-man's land opposite Fort Sedgwick and captured part of the Rebel picket line. This set off a "furious cannonade" that lasted all night. "During this expedition," one Federal complained, "not an officer or man of the regiment had a moment of sleep."[32]

"It was evident," Humphreys wrote, "that we must extend our intrenchments more to the left before advancing to the South Side Railroad, so as to give us more and better roads to move the infantry columns on." But he complained that the Federals could have accomplished much more that day if the 5th Corps had followed the 2nd Corps to the Boydton Plank Road. "We could have carried the high ground on the north bank of Hatcher's Run at Burgess's mill easily and thus have turned Lee's right, and most probably have secured a footing on the South Side Railroad. But the attempted movement up Hatcher's Run failed of any favorable result. It kept two-thirds of our force at the right of Lee's intrenchments substantially doing nothing, when the two-thirds should have been at the movable end of the column."[33]

However, Grant, ever the optimist, found some good in the day's results. "To-day's movement has resulted, up to the time I left, only in a reconnaissance in force," he told his staff. "I had hoped to accomplish more by means of it, but it has at least given us a much more thorough knowledge of the country, which, with its natural and artificial obstacles, is stronger than any one could have supposed."[34]

---

1. Sherman, *Memoirs*, 636–637.
2. Andrew A. Humphreys, *The Virginia Campaign of '64 and '65.* (New York, 1883), 296.
3. Ibid., 299.
4. Trudeau, *The Last Citadel*, 242–243.
5. Ibid., 225.
6. James Lonstreet, *From Manassas to Appomattox: Memoirs of the Civil War in America* (Philadelphia, 1903), 579.
7. Porter, *Campaigning With Grant*, 309.
8. Trudeau, *The Last Citadel*, 231.
9. Humphreys, *The Virginia Campaign*, 296.
10. Trudeau, *The Last Citadel*, 231.
11. Ibid., 232.
12. Ibid., 227.
13. Ibid., 228.
14. Ibid., 229.
15. Porter, *Campaigning With Grant*, 309–310.
16. Trudeau, *The Last Citadel*, 242.
17. Porter, *Campaigning With Grant*, 310.
18. Trudeau, *The Last Citadel*, 242.
19. Porter, *Campaigning With Grant*, 310–311.
20. Trudeau, *The Last Citadel*, 242.
21. Porter, *Campaigning With Grant*, 311–312.
22. Trudeau, *The Last Citadel*, 237–8.

23. Lonstreet, *From Manassas to Appomattox*, 577–578.
24. Trudeau, *The Last Citadel*, 240.
25. Ibid.
26. Ibid., 241.
27. Ibid., 247–248.
28. Ibid., 248.
29. Ibid., 245.
30. Ibid., 247.
31. Ibid., 249.
32. Ibid., 251.
33. Humphreys, *The Virginia Campaign*, 300.
34. Porter, *Campaigning With Grant*, 312.

CHAPTER TWENTY-EIGHT

Impossibilities Are for the Timid

26–28 October 1864

At about 9 p.m. on the 26th of October a small steam-powered launch came alongside the USS *Otsego*, on blockade duty in Albemarle Sound, North Carolina. The launch was there to pick up men from that vessel who had volunteered for a very dangerous secret mission. As the men were descending the ship's ladder an eager young face appeared at the taffrail. "Lieutenant Cushing!" the young man called in a stage whisper. "I'll pay you ten thousand dollars if you'll let me go along!"

Lieutenant William B. Cushing, commander of the expedition, laughed. "You haven't got it," he answered.

"But I'd give it to you if I did," came the reply.

"Who is that—is that Ensign Gay?" Cushing asked. "If it is, you're on—I need another madman on this expedition."

The young officer clambered down the ladder with a laugh. "Acting Ensign Thomas S. Gay reporting, sir," he said. "The only ten-thousand-dollar ensign in the fleet."[1]

The launch chugged across the sound, but the Federals had misjudged the tide, and as they entered the Roanoke River they ran aground. It was 2 a.m. on the 27th by the time they had freed themselves and set off up the stream again. But they had not gone 500 yards when they saw the dim silhouette of a picket launch loom out of the darkness. "Who goes there!" came the hail. Cushing feared at first that they had been discovered by Rebels, but it turned out to be a Union army tug on picket duty. The tug drew alongside and two Federal soldiers boarded the launch. It was not until they recognized Ensign Gay that their suspicions were allayed. By the time the army's boat was gone, it was 3 a.m. by Cushing's watch, and he ordered Ensign William L. Howarth, his second-in-command, to turn back. If the launch's engine was loud enough to be heard by the army's picket boat it would surely be heard by the Confederates long before it reached their objective. They would try again the next night, and meanwhile ship's carpenters could box in the engine to muffle the noise.

William Barker Cushing was a few days short of his 22nd birthday in October 1864. He had attended the Naval Academy at Annapolis, but he had been forced to resign during his final year, evidently due mostly to some practical jokes he had played on his Spanish instructor. However, when the Civil War had come the navy had needed all the officers it could get, and he had been appointed an acting master's mate, and he was determined to make the most of this second opportunity. "Where there is danger in the battle, there will I be," he had told a relative, "for I will gain a name in this war."[2] Soon he had been promoted to lieutenant after helping to capture a blockade runner while serving aboard the USS *Minnesota*. When he had been transferred to the waters off North Carolina he had begun to build a reputation as a daring, resourceful officer by a series of forays into Rebel territory.

In November 1862 he had led a raid up New River Inlet. In January 1863 he had surprised and captured an earthwork at Little River with a force of 25 men. In February 1864 he had taken twenty men in two boats and rowed past Fort Caswell in the dark, landed at Smithville, and raided the headquarters of General Louis Hebert. The general had been lucky enough to be away at the time, but the Federals had captured one of his staff officers. In June Cushing had taken a party of fifteen men in a cutter nearly as far as Wilmington. Then they had hidden in a swamp during the day and had come out at night to reconnoiter the obstructions below the city. At dawn they had landed again and captured a courier carrying mail out of Fort Fisher. Before this raid was over he had also examined the Confederate ironclad *Raleigh*, confirming that it had been disabled.

"Cushing's hazardous undertakings were sometimes criticized as useless," Admiral David Dixon Porter, Cushing's new boss, wrote after the war, "but there was more method in them than appeared on the surface, and important information was sometimes obtained, to say nothing of the brilliant example of courage and enterprise which they afforded to others."[3] Assistant Secretary of the Navy Gustavus Fox had told Porter's predecessor, Admiral S. P. Lee, "You notice the Department never finds fault with these exploits. I believe they ought to be encouraged. To be sure, the people will say, when he is captured, 'Damn fool!' The Department will not.'"[4]

Now Cushing had volunteered to deal with the navy's greatest worry: the Confederate ironclad *Albemarle*. Back in April this iron monster had steamed down the Roanoke River from the cornfield where she had been built, chased the Union navy's wooden gunboats away, and helped the Confederate army capture a sizable Federal garrison at Plymouth, North Carolina. This had allowed the Rebels to regain control of a sizable region in the northern part of that state which provided much-needed supplies for Confederate forces. In the process, the *Albermarle* had sunk the USS *Southfield*, a wooden gunboat, and killed Commander C. W. Flusser, who had been one of Cushing's instructors at Annapolis and his closest friend in the navy. "I shall never rest until I have avenged his death," Cushing had said when he learned of Flusser's death.[5]

A couple of weeks later the *Albemarle* had come down the river in an attempt to get into the sounds so that it could help the Confederate army recapture New Berne, North Carolina. She had been attacked by several Union wooden gunboats, and one of them had even rammed her. Although neither the ramming nor the fire of all their guns could do her much damage, her commander had decided that she did not steer well enough to take her into the sounds and had retired up the river to Plymouth.

Since then there had been an uneasy stalemate in the waters of North Carolina. The Confederates were reluctant to take further risks with their only ironclad in the area, for its loss might well entail the recapture of Plymouth by the Federals. The latter, meanwhile, worried that the Rebel ram might steam down the Roanoke at any time and scatter their helpless wooden ships. So they racked their brains trying to come up with some way to destroy her. The easy answer would have been to use some of their own ironclads, but these all drew too much water to make it over the bar into the sound. Then they considered sending in a tug with a torpedo (what we would call a mine today), but they could not see any way for it to get close enough. The only possibility seemed to be a small boat raid to either capture her or blow her up. Admiral Lee's thoughts had naturally turned to Lieutenant Cushing.

Cushing had jumped at the chance. He had drafted a plan which Admiral Lee had approved, and in July he had been sent to Washington to sell it to the Navy Department. Assistant Secretary Fox, on the other hand, had been reluctant to approve the plan. He had considered it unlikely to succeed and likely to cost the navy the services of a very daring and resourceful young officer. But the fact had remained that the *Albemarle* must be destroyed and that there had been no other plan available. And there had been reports that the Rebels were building two more ironclads up the Roanoke, under the protection of the first. So Fox had sent Cushing to the Brooklyn navy yard to pick out his boats.

Cushing had chosen two open launches about 45 feet in length with small, low-pressure engines and screw propellers. "A 12-pounder howitzer was fitted to the bow of each," Cushing later explained, "and a boom was rigged out, some fourteen feet in length, swinging by a goose-neck hinge to the bluff of the bow. A topping lift, carried to a stanchion inboard, raised or lowered it, and the torpedo was fitted into an iron slide at the end. This was intended to be detached from the boom by means of a heel-jigger leading inboard, and to be exploded by another line, connecting with a pin, which held a grape shot over a nipple and cap."[6] It sounds complicated, and it was, but Cushing tested the device several times in the Hudson River and found that it worked, although he had to make sure that the lanyard that released the torpedo and the trigger line that set it off were pulled at exactly the right moments and not too hard. And, of course, it would not do to get the two lines mixed up or pull them in the wrong order.

The two boats had been sent by the canal route to Chesapeake Bay with Ensign Howarth in charge of one and Ensign Andrew Stockholm in charge of the other. Cushing, meanwhile, had gone south by train, after obtaining permission for a brief visit to his home in Fredonia, New York. There he had told no one what he was up to except his mother. "I will succeed, Mama," he had said, "or you will not have any Will Cushing."[7] His older brother, Alonzo, had already been killed—at the age of 22—when his battery of light artillery had been overrun by Pickett's charge on the third day of battle at Gettysburg, Pennsylvania, the summer before. On his way south, Cushing had stayed with his cousin, George White, at New York. "Cousin George," he had said, "I am going to have a vote of thanks from Congress, or six feet of pine box by the time you hear from me again."[8]

Meanwhile, Ensign Stockholm had been captured and his boat had been destroyed when engine trouble had forced him to put into a cove on the Virginia coast and he had run into a patrol of Confederate home guards. Cushing had caught up with Howarth and the other boat in Hampton Roads and, with considerable difficulty, had taken it through the Chesapeake and Albemarle Canal, thirty miles of which were unprotected by any Union troops. On 23 October they had reached Roanoke Island, a Federal base in Albemarle Sound, where they had learned that an inaccurate account of the plan to destroy the *Albemarle* had recently appeared in a newspaper. They had also learned that the month before five enlisted men had tried to blow up the ironclad by carrying two 100-pound torpedoes across a swamp on stretchers, but they had been spotted when they had tried to swim across the Roanoke River with them and had retreated under a hail of rifle and pistol fire. The Confederates were bound to be on their guard.

Nevertheless, Cushing and Howarth had been determined to go on, and the next day they had reported to Commander W. H. Macomb, who was in charge of the Union ships in the North Carolina sounds, and asked for more men to fill out their expedition. Macomb had sent word to the commanders of his various ships that volunteers were needed for a very dangerous mission. A large number had volunteered, some even offering a month's pay for the privilege. The boredom of blockade duty probably had something to do with their eagerness. The fact that word had leaked out about who would be leading them had also helped. When the volunteers had been winnowed down to a select few, Cushing had gathered all of his men on the afterdeck of Macomb's ship, the *Shamrock*. "Not only must you not expect, but you must not hope to return," he had told them. "I can promise you nothing but glory, death or, possibly, promotion. We will have the satisfaction of getting in a good lick at the rebels, that is all."[9] When asked who still wanted to go, all twelve had stepped forward.

Leaving Howarth to explain the plan to the volunteers, Cushing had gone to Macomb's cabin to interview Ensign Rudolph Sommers, who had just completed a series of small-boat reconnaissances of the *Albemarle*. In fact, he had just returned, exhausted, from the latest one the night before, during which his boat had been detected. Part of his crew had been captured, and he had spent four hours in the water under fire. He had told Cushing that the ram was tied up along the water front at Plymouth, eight miles up the Roanoke River, which was about 150 to 200 yards wide. There were up to 4,000 Confederate soldiers in the area on both sides of the river, he had said, and about a mile below the ironclad was the wreck of the USS *Southfield*, submerged to the hurricane deck, where the Rebels had evidently posted a picket guard. It would be impossible to surprise them. "Impossibilities are for the timid," Cushing later said.[10] At the end of their two-hour discussion, Sommers had asked Cushing to take him along. "But you can't even walk!" Cushing had replied. Sommers had smiled and said, "If I *could* walk I'd like to go."[11] Then had come the abortive attempt of the 26th.

At noon on the 27th, while ships' carpenters were boxing the engine on Cushing's launch, three escaping slaves were found swimming out to the fleet, and when it was discovered that they had information about the *Albemarle* they were brought to the *Shamrock*. There they were interrogated by Cushing and Howarth for an hour. The slaves confirmed that the Rebels did have a picket guard on the wreck of the *Southfield*. What was more, they said that the Confederates had a schooner anchored near the wreck which had a lieutenant and 25 men with a cannon and with rockets for signaling to the ironclad. After a conference with Commander Macomb and his first officer, Lieutenant Duer, it was decided that the launch would tow a cutter with twelve or fifteen men. When they reached the *Southfield*, the cutter would be cast off and the men would capture the schooner while the launch steamed on up the river. Even if the men failed to capture the schooner they would divert Confederate attention from the launch.

Then the crew of the *Shamrock* was lined up on deck. "I want eleven men and two officers to accompany Lieutenant Cushing on a dangerous expedition, from which probably none will return," Lieutenant Duer told them. "None but young men without encumbrances will be accepted. Those who wish to volunteer will step over to this side." All 275 men stepped over. "I thought so," Commander Macomb said. "Pick your men."[12] Duer chose his best and bravest, with Acting Master's Mate Wilson D. Burlingame and Acting Gunner William Peterkin as their leaders. They were then issued weapons, but it was not until their cutter had been attached to Cushing's launch at about 8:30 p.m. that they were told, out of hearing of the rest of the crew, just what it was that they had volunteered for.

Clouds darkened the sky that night and although the air temperature was around 65 degrees the water was a good ten degrees cooler, and chilling showers of rain occasionally fell. By the time the launch, towing the cutter, entered the mouth of the Roanoke River the rain was falling harder, but the men shivered in silence, for they had been warned not to talk or even whisper. The engine had not only been boxed but a tarpaulin had been tucked around it to further block its sound. When one of the men started coughing Ensign Howarth muffled him with his coat. "Good for you, Mr. Howarth," Cushing whispered when he returned. "I'll muffle you, sir, if you say another word," Howarth replied.[13]

In order to maintain silence, Cushing, standing in the forward half of the launch where he could see, had arranged a number of signals that would avoid the necessity for spoken orders. In his left hand he held the two lines that controlled the torpedo, whose boom was now swung around to the stern to keep it out of the way. In his right he held three other lines. One led to the wrist of Ensign Gay, who was on the deck at the bow. When Cushing pulled that line, Gay would swing the boom into place. Another line led to the ankle of Engineer William Stotesbury. One pull would be the signal for more speed, two pulls would mean stop the engine. The third line led to the howitzer, but it would be attached to Howarth when the time for action approached. Howarth would man the gun and receive firing orders from Cushing by means of that line. Cushing had worked out a method for keeping the different lines straight in his mind so that he would not pull the wrong one by mistake, but the success of the entire mission depended upon his ability to keep a clear head.

A few miles up the river the banks crowded in closer and were covered with large trees that blocked out the sky and increased the darkness. Cushing could no longer see the stern of the launch and was only aware of Engineer Stotesbury from the twitching of his line as he tended the engine. To his left Cushing could just make out the peak of Howarth's cap where he stood by the howitzer. Between the two young officers was Acting Master's Mate John Woodman, near the wheel because of his knowledge of the river. At the wheel was Samuel Higgins, one of the original crew who had brought the launch down from Brooklyn. Behind Cushing was Assistant Paymaster Francis H. Swan, another old friend of his who had talked his way on board at the last minute. In the stern was a pair of firemen, ready to set the cutter loose in case of an accident.

At 2 a.m. Cushing, calculating that they must be nearing the wreck of the *Southfield,* took out his handkerchief and waved it. This was the signal for the men in the cutter to take their places with oars poised in case they were challenged. Faint sounds of movement from that direction indicated that they had seen the signal and were getting ready. Suddenly there was a jerk on the line from Ensign Gay up on the bow. He had spotted the schooner up ahead, and soon Cushing could see it also. They were headed straight for it. Cushing leaned down and gave the wheel a quarter turn, and slowly, while the Federals all held their breaths, the launch and the cutter passed between the schooner and the wreck, within thirty feet of the latter. They could hear voices, and once a match flared up and quickly went out, but they had not been spotted. Soon they were around a bend and beyond immediate danger.

Cushing did not give the three tugs on the line to Stotesbury's ankle that would have been the signal to cast off the cutter. He had not expected to get past the picket undetected, but he did have a plan in mind for just such an event. If they could approach the *Albemarle* undetected they would not use the torpedo. "I now thought that it might be better to board her," he wrote, "and 'take her alive,' having in the two boats twenty men well armed with revolvers, cutlasses, and hand-grenades. To be sure, there were ten times our number on the ship and thousands near by; but a surprise is everything, and I thought if her fasts were cut at the instant of boarding, we might overcome those on board, take her into the stream, and use her iron sides to protect us afterward from the forts. Knowing the town, I concluded to land at the lower wharf, creep around, and suddenly dash aboard from the bank."[14] He even had a U.S. flag with him so he could run it up to let the Union fleet know that the monster had changed sides. Not only would this be an even greater triumph than sinking the ironclad, but it would be safer as well. For if he had to use the torpedo most of the attackers would probably be killed or captured in the ensuing fight, but if they once got control of the ironclad they would be safe inside it from anything the Rebels could throw at them.

After a few minutes of suspense, the launch came around another bend in the river and there against the faint light of the sky ahead was the dark, square shape of the ironclad, and they still had not been seen. Cushing turned the wheel sharply and the two boats headed into the bank. Then he saw the wharf jutting into the water about a hundred yards from the looming silhouette of the *Albemarle*, and he headed for that. Howarth looked at him and nodded, and Cushing knew that he understood what he planned. It was nearly 3 a.m. and they were within minutes of capturing the pride of the Confederate navy right out from under the Rebels' noses when a dog barked at these unknown intruders, waking up a dozing sentry on the ironclad. "Who's there?" came the challenge, "Who goes there?" In the flash of an instant Cushing dropped the boarding plan and pulled hard on the line leading to the engineer's ankle. Then he realized that there was no longer any need for silence. "Ahead fast!" he called, and turning to the cutter he cried, "Cast off Peterkin, and go down and get those pickets on the schooner!"[15]

With the drag of the cutter gone and Stotesbury pouring on all steam, the launch leaped forward, headed straight for what Cushing called "the dark mountain of iron" in front of it. From the *Albemarle* came the sound of the alarm rattle like the screech of an angry bird. "A heavy fire was at once opened upon us," Cushing wrote, "not only from the ship, but from men stationed on the shore. This did not disable us, and we neared them rapidly."[16] "Who's there? Who's there?" the sentry repeated, even though his comrades were firing constantly now. The defenders seemed to be somewhat confused, Cushing thought.

He was more worried by the darkness than the enemy fire at that point, for it was hard for him to see any details on the ram. But when the launch was within fifty yards of its target the Confederates solved that problem for him by lighting a huge bonfire they had prepared for just such occasions so that they could see what they were up against. "By its light I discovered the unfortunate fact that there was a circle of logs around the *Albemarle*." Cushing wrote, "boomed well out from her side, with the very intention of preventing the action of torpedoes."[17] These logs had just been placed there the day before, after Lieutenant Sommers' reconnaissance. The *Albermarle's* captain had heard about the arrival of a steam launch at Roanoke Island and had correctly deduced the general idea of the Federal plan. Realizing that this dark, rainy night would provide good cover for a Union attack, he had also doubled the guard aboard his ship. It was not enough.

Ignoring the Rebels' fire, Cushing ran the launch in close for a good look at the logs. His only chance, he decided during that brief examination, was to circle back around and strike the logs squarely at full speed. He hoped that they had been in the water long enough to become slimy and that the launch's momentum would carry it over the slippery logs and within reach of the *Albemarle*. He knew that once over the logs his boat would never get out again, but escape was not important to him at the moment. He spun the wheel and ordered full speed, noticing the look of disbelief on Howarth's pale face as he did so. "As I turned," he wrote, "the whole back of my coat was torn out by buckshot, and the sole of my shoe was carried away. The fire was very severe." At Cushing's order, Ensign Gay swung the boom around into place, and during a lull in the firing as the launch came around the ram's captain called after it, demanding to know what boat it was. "All my men gave comical answers," Cushing wrote, "and mine was a dose of canister from the howitzer."[18]

"In another instant we had struck the logs and were over," Cushing said, "with headway nearly gone, slowly forging up under the enemy's quarterport. Ten feet from us the muzzle of a rifle gun looked into our faces, and every word of command on board was distinctly heard."[19] John C. Howard had a good view of the launch from the cutter, which had not yet gone very far on its way downriver. "The launch never went over the boom," he said. ". . . the boat's bow struck the boom with such force that it was forced in the water and the boat overlapped it two or three feet. The launch's bow was thus suspended in the air, and her stern was well set in the water."[20]

But the launch was near enough to the ironclad for Cushing's purpose, "and I ordered the boom lowered until the forward motion of the launch carried the torpedo under the ram's overhang. A strong pull of the detaching-line, a moment's waiting for the torpedo to rise under the hull, and I hauled in the left hand, just cut by a bullet."[21] The position of the torpedo in relation to the ram's hull had to be carefully judged, and the line to the trigger pulled not only at just the right instant but with neither too much nor too little force. But he must have done it just right. "The explosion took place at the same instant that 100 pounds of grape, at 10 feet range, crashed among us," Cushing wrote, "and the dense mass of water thrown out by the torpedo came down with choking weight upon us."[22] But the ironclad's big gun could not be depressed quite enough to hit her attackers. Howard, watching from the cutter, said that "the shot passed directly over the launch, and the air pressure was such as to force the launch, boom and all under water."[23]

It was suddenly silent after the bang of the torpedo, the blast of the big gun, and the splash of water thrown up by both. Then some Rebel called out, "Surrender or we will blow you out of the water!" Cushing looked down at his left hand and saw that it was bleeding freely where it had been clipped by a bullet just as he pulled the firing line to the torpedo. "Surrender!" the Rebels called out again. "Never!" Cushing replied. "I'll be damned first!" He threw off his sword, his revolver, his frock coat, and his shoes. "Men, save yourselves," he cried, and dived into the river.[24] "Three men followed him," Howard observed from the cutter.[25] "It was cold," Cushing said, "long after the frosts, and the water chilled the blood, while the whole surface of the stream was plowed up by grape and musketry, and my nearest friends, the fleet, were twelve miles away; but anything was better than to fall into rebel hands, so I swam for the opposite shore."[26]

Most of the men in the launch did surrender. Ensign Gay had dived into the water after Cushing. "I had not proceeded far from the boat," he later wrote, "when I fell in with Acting Ensign William L. Howarth on a log, unable to proceed farther without assistance. Having a life preserver with me, I gave it to him and returned to the boat to procure another, not knowing how far I might have to swim, and at the same time I destroyed two boxes of ammunition and several carbines. I had not gone far the second time when I found myself chilled, and after a severe struggle I regained the circle of logs, where I found several of the crew, with a boat from the ram in charge of Lieutenant Roberts. We were all taken on shore and marched to the prison."[27]

The captain of the *Albemarle*, A. F. Warley, said that when the torpedo went off, "I heard a report as of an unshotted gun, and a piece of wood fell at my feet. Calling the carpenter, I told him a torpedo had been exploded, and ordered him to examine and report to me, saying nothing to any one else. He soon reported 'a hole in her bottom big enough to drive a wagon in.' By this time I heard voices from the launch: 'We surrender,' etc., etc., etc. I stopped our fire and sent out Mr. Long, who brought back all those who had been in the launch except the gallant captain and three of her crew, all of whom took to the water. Having seen to their safety, I turned my attention to the *Albemarle* and found her resting on the bottom in eight feet of water, her upper works above water. That is the way the *Albemarle* was destroyed, and a more gallant thing was not done during the war."[28]

One Confederate, writing to give a friend the news of the sinking of the *Albemarle*, said, "The torpedo burst and blew a great hole in her some 6 feet long, sinking her almost instantly. She is now lying at the bottom of the Roanoke River. The crew lost everything they had, bed clothing and everything. Some lost their hats and shoes, and some even came out in their shirts and drawers, barefooted. We are in an awful condition."[29]

Cushing was a strong swimmer and soon was beyond the area lit by the Confederates' bonfire. He struck out toward the opposite shore, but as he neared it he heard one of his crewmen—it was Samuel Higgins, who had been at the wheel—give a "great gurgling yell" and go under. Boats had put out from the bank carrying Rebels with torches who shot at anything that moved in the water, and one, attracted by Higgins' cry, was coming toward Cushing. He held his breath and swam under water for as long as he could. When he came up for air the boat was far behind him. "I heard my own name mentioned," he said, "but was not seen." It occurred to him that the Confederates would also be watching the bank opposite the ironclad, so he turned and swam downriver.[30]

Soon he decided he had gone far enough for it to be safe for him to go ashore. "This time, as I struggled to reach the bank, I heard a groan in the river behind me, and, although very much exhausted, concluded to turn and give all the aid in my power to the officer or seaman who had bravely shared the danger with me. . . . Nearing the swimmer, it proved to be Acting Master's Mate Woodman, who said that he could swim no longer. Knocking his cap from his head, I used my right arm to sustain him, and ordered him to strike out. For ten minutes at least,

I think, he managed to keep afloat, when, his physical force being completely gone, he sank like a stone."[31]

"Again alone upon the water," Cushing wrote, "I directed my course toward the town side of the river, not making much headway, as my strokes were now very feeble, my clothes being soaked and heavy, and little chop-seas splashing with choking persistence into my mouth every time I gasped for breath. Still, there was a determination not to sink, a will not to give up; and I kept up a sort of mechanical motion long after my bodily force was in fact expended." At last he touched soft mud and realized that he had reached the bank. "And in the excitement of the first shock I half raised my body and made one step forward; then fell, and remained half in the mud and half in the water until daylight, unable even to crawl on hands and knees, nearly frozen with my brain in a whirl, but with one thing strong in me—the fixed determination to escape."[32]

"It must be remembered," John C. Howard said, "that the troops and the artillery began firing into the bosom of the river immediately after the explosion of the torpedo. The balls pattered on the water like a shower of hail. . . . We, in the *Shamrock's* cutter, however, pulled into the heaviest of the shower, and, strange to say, not a bullet or a shot struck us or the boat." The Confederate pickets on the *Southfield* were too busy trying to figure out what was happening up at Plymouth to notice the cutter pull alongside. "If they had preserved a particle of pluck, they could have murdered us all," Howard claimed, "as we were not in a position to defend ourselves."[33] But the Rebels surrendered without a fight, and the Federals proceeded on down the river.

At dawn, Cushing found himself in a point of swamp that entered the suburbs of Plymouth, and not forty yards from a Confederate fort. The sky was clear and the warmth of the rising sun restored some of his strength, while its light showed that the town was swarming with soldiers and sailors like ants whose nest had been disturbed. "It was a source of satisfaction to me," he wrote, "to know that I had pulled the wire that set all these figures moving, but as I had no desire of being discovered my first object was to get into a dry fringe of rushes that edged the swamp; but to do this required me to pass over thirty or forty feet of open ground, right under the eye of a sentinel who walked the parapet."[34]

Cushing waited until the sentry turned the other way and then made a dash for the rushes, but he was only halfway across the open space when the sentinel turned back again. Cushing dropped to the ground between two paths out in the open. The sentry failed to notice him, however, probably because his mud-covered clothes blended so well with the ground on which he lay, even though he was close enough to tell that the Rebel's eyes were brown and that he needed a shave. Cushing lay perfectly still, flat on his back, waiting for a chance to move again. Soon a group of four Confederates, two of them officers, came down one of the paths and passed so close to him that they almost stepped on his arm. They were talking about the events of the night before and were wondering "how it was done," entirely unaware that the man who could best answer their question was lying at their feet.[35] On the other hand, their conversation failed to answer the question that was burning in Cushing's mind: had he been successful; had he destroyed the *Albemarle*?

This incident convinced him that he had to get into cover, so he began to crawl on his back by digging in his heels and his elbows. It took an hour of this to get him out of sight. "For five hours then, with bare feet, head, and hands, I made my way where I venture to say none ever did before, until I came at last to a clear place, where I might rest upon solid ground. The cypress swamp was a network of thorns and briers that cut into the flesh at every step like knives; frequently, when the soft mire would not bear my weight, I was forced to throw my body upon it at length, and haul myself along by the arms." Cushing's hands and feet were raw by the time he reached the clearing, but his difficulties were far from over. A working party of Rebel soldiers was nearby, engaged in sinking some schooners in the river to obstruct the channel. "I passed twenty yards in their rear through a corn furrow," Cushing said, "and gained some woods below. Here I encountered a negro, and after serving him twenty dollars in greenbacks and some texts of Scripture (two powerful arguments with an old darkey), I had confidence enough in his fidelity to send him into town for news of the ram."[36]

Cushing did not send the man for food or water or weapons, but for news. More than anything, he wanted to know if the *Albemarle* had been destroyed. The old man was back within an hour. "She is dead gone sunk," he said, "and they will hang you, massa, if they catch you."[37] Invigorated by this confirmation of his success, Cushing stood up, patted the old man on the back, and started off down the bank of the stream. Soon the swamp was so thick that he could not see ten feet and had only the sun for a guide. "About 2 o'clock in the afternoon I came out from the dense mass of reeds upon the bank of one of the deep, narrow streams that abound there, and right opposite to the only road in the vicinity. It seemed providential, for, thirty yards above or below, I never should have seen the road, and might have struggled on until, worn out and starved, I should have found a never-to-be-discovered grave. As it was, my fortune had led me to where a picket party of seven soldiers were posted, having a little flat-bottomed, square-ended skiff toggled to the

root of a cypress-tree that squirmed like a snake in the inky water."
Cushing watched the Rebels until they moved a few yards away to eat.
Then he slipped into the water, keeping a big tree between them and
himself, and swam silently over to the boat. He cast it loose and floated
behind it for about thirty yards until a bend in the stream blocked him
from the view of the soldiers. Then he climbed into the little skiff and
"paddled away as only a man could whose liberty was at stake."[38]

"Hour after hour I paddled," he wrote, "never ceasing for a moment,
first on one side, then on the other, while sunshine passed into twilight
and that was swallowed up in thick darkness only relieved by the few
faint star rays that penetrated the heavy swamp curtain on either side.
At last I reached the mouth of the Roanoke, and found the open sound
before me. My frail boat could not have lived in the ordinary sea there,
but it chanced to be very calm, leaving only a slight swell, which was,
however, sufficient to influence my boat, so that I was forced to paddle
all upon one side to keep her on the intended course. After steering by
a star for perhaps two hours for where I thought the fleet might be, I at
length discovered one of the vessels, and after a long time got within
hail. My 'Ship ahoy!' was given with the last of my strength, and I fell
powerless, with a splash, into the water in the bottom of my boat, and
awaited results. I had paddled every minute for ten successive hours,
and for four my body had been 'asleep,' with the exception of my arms
and brain."[39]

The ship that he had found was the gunboat *Valley City.* All anyone
on board it knew about the events upriver was what the men in the
Shamrock's cutter had been able to tell when they had reached the fleet
that morning. They had not been sure whether the attack had been successful, and they had supposed that Cushing was dead. It was near midnight when officers on the *Valley City* heard a hail from a small boat.
Fearing that it was a Confederate attack in retaliation for the Union
assault on the *Albemarle,* they sounded general quarters and slipped the
vessel's cable. But when no attack developed, they sent Acting Ensign
Milton Webster in an armed boat to investigate. The boat approached the
little skiff and found a man lying half conscious in its bottom. Nobody in
the boat knew him. But Webster slung him up the ladder onto the ship
and laid him out on the deck.

The commander of the *Valley City,* Acting Master J.A.J. Brooks,
looked down at the wet figure just as he opened his eyes. "My God,
Cushing," he said, "is that you?"

"It is I," he answered.

"Is it done?" Brooks asked.

"It is done," he said, trying to manage a smile.[40]

1. Ralph J. Roske and Charles Van Doren, *Lincoln's Commando: The Biography of Commander W. B. Cushing, USN* (New York, 1957), 223.

2. Foote, *The Civil War*, 3:592–593.

3. Roske and Van Doren, *Lincoln's Commando*, 219.

4. Ibid., 15.

5. Ibid., 200.

6. W. B. Cushing, "The Destruction of the 'Albemarle'" in *Battles and Leaders*, Vol. 4, 634.

7. Roske and Van Doren, *Lincoln's Commando*, 217.

8. Ibid., 218.

9. Ibid., 222.

10. Cushing, "The Destruction of the 'Albemarle,'" 635.

11. Roske and Van Doren, *Lincoln's Commando*, 223.

12. Ibid., 225.

13. Ibid., 226.

14. Cushing, "The Destruction of the 'Albemarle,'" 635–636.

15. Roske and Van Doren, *Lincoln's Commando*, 230.

16. Cushing, "The Destruction of the 'Albemarle,'" 636.

17. Ibid.

18. Ibid., 637.

19. Ibid.

20. Roske and Van Doren, *Lincoln's Commando*, 235.

21. Cushing, "The Destruction of the 'Albemarle,'" 637.

22. Ibid.

23. Roske and Van Doren, *Lincoln's Commando*, 235.

24. Ibid., 233.

25. Ibid., 235.

26. Cushing, "The Destruction of the 'Albemarle,'" 637.

27. Roske and Van Doren, *Lincoln's Commando*, 244.

28. A. F. Warley, "Note on the Destruction of the 'Albemarle,'" in *Battles and Leaders*, Vol. 4, 642.

29. Ibid., 235–236.

30. Cushing, "The Destruction of the 'Albemarle,'" 637–638.

31. Ibid., 638.

32. Ibid.

33. Roske and Van Doren, *Lincoln's Commando*, 244.

34. Cushing, "The Destruction of the 'Albemarle,'" 639.

35. Ibid.
36. Ibid.
37. Roske and Van Doren, *Lincoln's Commando*, 241.
38. Cushing, "The Destruction of the 'Albemarle,'" 639–640.
39. Ibid., 640.
40. Roske and Van Doren, *Lincoln's Commando*, 242–243.

CHAPTER TWENTY-NINE

The Pleasure of Exchanging Shots

28 October–4 November 1864

Lieutenant Cushing was given a little brandy and water and then a few crumbs of bread and a little rest, but within an hour of reaching the deck of the *Valley City* he was on his way to the *Shamrock* to report to Commander Macomb. "When I announced success," Cushing wrote, "all the commanding officers were summoned on board to deliberate a plan of attack."[1] For with the *Albemarle* eliminated there was little to prevent the Union ships from steaming up the Roanoke and attacking Plymouth. Then Cushing set on the deck of the *Shamrock* and watched rockets arching across the sky, fired off by the Union ships in celebration, and listened to cheer after cheer ring out across the water. He had indeed made a name for himself in the navy. He would eventually receive the thanks of Congress, promotion to lieutenant commander—making him the youngest officer of that grade in the navy—and $56,000 in prize money, although it was nine years before he received all of the latter. As Admiral Farragut, no stranger to courage himself, later told Secretary of the Navy Welles, "While no navy had braver or better officers than ours, young Cushing was the hero of the War."[2]

Out beyond the Mississippi, while Curtis's and Pleasonton's Federals rested at Fort Scott, Kansas, Price's retreating Confederates had swung back into Missouri and made a forced march to Carthage, where they in turn had rested for a day. Then the Rebels resumed their march on the morning of the 28th, heading for the crossings of the Arkansas River, over a hundred miles away. But twenty miles down the road, at Newtonia, Missouri, the pursuing Federals caught up with the tail of the Confederate column again. Shelby's men were catching some badly needed sleep south of the town while the rest of the army marched by when Blunt, leading the Union pursuers, saw the dust of the moving column and rode hard to get around the Rebels and cut them off. However, he ran into Shelby's exhausted troopers instead. The Federals "drove in our pickets quite briskly," Shelby reported, "and came charging on with their usual vitality. Dismounting every man of my division, I formed my line of battle just in time to meet the onset."[3] Soon it was Blunt who was cut off, and after a two-hour fight he finally cut his way out with the help of one of the two brigades Pleasonton had left with the pursuing column. Wild Bill Hickock, a Union spy who had been riding with Price during the entire campaign, was able to slip away during the confusion of the battle to report to the Federals.

Of Shelby, Price wrote in his report that "I consider him the best cavalry officer I ever saw." Even higher praise came from Pleasonton, who had held his own in Virginia with the likes of Hampton, Fitzhugh Lee and Jeb Stuart. He said that Shelby was "the best cavalry general of the South."[4] This was the final clash between Price and his pursuers, although Curtis continued on down into Arkansas by what he considered a short cut in an attempt to head off the retreating Rebels.

In Tennessee on the 28th, Brigadier General Abraham Buford, with the leading division of Forrest's troops coming north out of Jackson, emplaced guns along the north-south stretch of the Tennessee River, backed up by his cavalry units. Two 20-pounder Parrott rifles, somewhat larger than the average field piece, had been sent by rail from the defenses of Mobile and Buford implaced them in the old abandoned Confederate works known as Fort Heiman, across from Fort Henry, where U.S. Grant had begun his rise to fame almost three years before. Two field pieces were set up a few hundred yards farther north, downstream. These four guns were backed up by Brigadier General Hylan B. Lyon's Kentucky brigade. Col. Tyree H. Bell's Tennessee brigade and two more field pieces were stationed five miles upstream (south) at Paris Landing.

This stretch of the river was an important part of Sherman's supply line. Steamboats would bring supplies from the Ohio River up the Tennessee to Johnsonville, where special facilities had been built to transfer their cargoes to the Nashville & Northwestern Railroad for shipment to Nashville.

A little after sunset four Union steamboats came down the river, from the direction of Johnsonville, and Buford's men were eager to try out their ambush. Buford was not. "Keep quiet, men, keep quiet," he told them, "don't fire a gun. These are empty boats going down for more supplies for Sherman's army. I want a loaded boat, a richer prize. Just wait until one comes up the river, and then you may take her if you can."[5]

In New York that day, three Confederate officers from the group that had left Toronto two days before met with James A. McMaster, publisher and editor of the weekly *Freeman's Journal and Catholic Register*, who was to be their liaison with the Copperheads in the city. McMaster had been alerted by a note from Jacob Thompson in Toronto to expect these callers. He compared the handwriting on that letter to that on the letter of introduction they presented him to make sure they were genuine.

The Confederates were using the names Maxwell, Stanton, and Williams, but in reality they were Lieutenant Colonel Robert M. Martin, Captain Robert C. Kennedy, and Lieutenant John W. Headley. Martin and Headley, like many of the Rebels operating out of Canada, were former members of John Hunt Morgan's Kentucky cavalry, and both had been sent to Canada by the Confederate government the month before to aid in the series of uprisings and raids that were being planned and initiated from there. Kennedy was from Louisiana. He had been captured while carrying dispatches for his West Point classmate, Joe Wheeler, commander of the Cavalry Corps of the Army of Tennessee, and had only recently escaped from Johnson's Island Military Prison, near Sandusky, Ohio, and had made his way to Canada.

The Confederate plan seems to have been somewhat muddled. While they talked of burning Northern cities in retaliation for Sheridan burning crops and barns in the Shenandoah, either in an attempt to deter the Union army from using such tactics again or simply as revenge, the original objective of the group sent to New York was to set a series of fires to divert the attention of the police and the small garrison in the city so that local Copperheads could seize control of the city and release the Confederate prisoners from Fort Lafayette. Following the success of this revolution, delegates from New York, New Jersey, and all the New England states would be invited to a convention in New York City to form a confederacy that would ally itself with the South and with a northwest confederacy which was also in the works. At the very least, such activities would divert Union forces away from the fronts in Virginia, Georgia, and Tennessee. New York City was fertile soil for such ideas. The city's political leaders were all of the peace-at-any-price wing of the Democratic Party, who saw the war in strictly political terms. If the Republicans were for it, they were against it. If not pro-slavery they were at least anti-abolition, primarily on racist grounds.

The Confederates and McMaster did not get very far in their plotting that afternoon, however, for Colonel Martin, watching the street outside the newspaper office, soon spotted a man he recognized as someone he had recently seen in Toronto. McMaster was able to identify the man as Sergeant John S. Young, chief of detectives of the New York Police Department. NYPD detectives were often used by the Federal government as counterespionage agents, which would explain his recent presence in Toronto. The four men quickly agreed to adjourn their meeting until the next day, somewhere else.

Elsewhere in the city on that same day, Major General John A. Dix, a War-Democrat political general who commanded the Department of the East, was composing his General Order No. 80, which would appear in the New York papers over the next couple of days. He had received a warning that Confederate agents were cooking up something for New York to coincide with the presidential election. Maybe it would take the form of election fraud or maybe it would be something along the lines of the recent raid on St. Albans, Vermont. In an attempt to prevent this or at least deter it, he ordered all Southerners within his department to register their presence with the army immediately, and "those who fail to comply with this requirement will be regarded as spies or emissaries of the insurgent authorities in Richmond, and will be treated accordingly."[6] This order was probably more for the record than to be taken seriously, for there were from 10,000 to 50,000 Southern refugees in New York City alone and if they all tried to register before election day his small garrison there would not be able to handle the paper work, let alone guard the city at the same time.

John Wilkes Booth left Montreal that morning after going to the Ontario Bank the day before to deposit $455 and purchase a bill of exchange, which was that era's approximation of a traveler's check. The head teller later testified that Booth was introduced at the bank by "Mr. P. C. Martin," the Confederate agent engaged in smuggling contraband of war

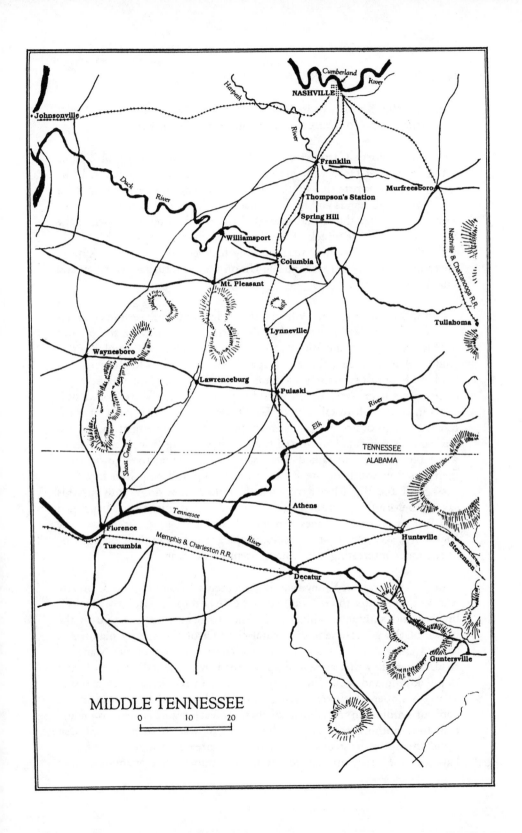

MIDDLE TENNESSEE

0   10   20

to the South.[7] Booth was in New York by the 29th, where he signed a document related to disposing of his oil properties in Pennsylvania.

Down in North Carolina on the 29th, Commander Macomb's ships got under way at 11:15 a.m. and proceeded up the Roanoke River. Lieutenant Cushing wrote that by then he "was well again in every way, with the exception of hands and feet, and had the pleasure of exchanging shots with the batteries that I had inspected the day before."[8] But when the Federals reached the wreck of the *Southfield*, they found that they could not get past the schooners that Cushing had seen the Rebels sinking in the channel the day before, and the Union vessels returned to Albemarle sound for the night.

Out in Missouri on the 29th, the two brigades that Rosecrans had left with Curtis, McNeil's and Sanborn's, turned back, leaving the pursuit of Price to Curtis's and Blunt's forces from the Department of Kansas. And on that same day, the War Department sent orders to Rosecrans to send A. J. Smith's infantry to Thomas at Nashville. Not satisfied that mere orders from Washington would pry these troops loose from Rosecrans in time to forestall Hood, Grant directed his own chief of staff, Rawlins, to go out to St. Louis and expedite their movement to Tennessee. Smith's veterans had missed their chance to bag Price's entire force when Pleasonton had talked Rosecrans into diverting them away from their position south of the Rebels to come up and help him force the passage of the Big Blue River, which he had then done with just his cavalry before the infantry could get there. What might have happened had Price's retreating forces run into these 8,000 or so veterans of the Vicksburg, Red River, and Tupelo campaigns blocking their path is one of the more interesting might-have-beens of the war.

In the Shenandoah Valley that day, Lieutenant Colonel John S. Mosby was writing a letter to General Lee, to be carried to the latter by Mosby's brother and adjutant, William: "I desire to bring through you to the notice of the government the brutal conduct of the enemy manifested toward citizens of this district since their occupation of the Manassas road. When they first advanced up the road, we smashed up one of their trains, killing and wounding a large number. In retaliation they arrested a large number of citizens living along the line, and have been in the habit of sending an installment of them on each train. As my command had done nothing contrary to the usages of war, it seems to me that some attempt at least ought to be made to prevent a repetition of such barbarities. During my absence from the command, the enemy captured six of my men, near Front Royal; these were immediately hung by order and in the presence of General Custer. They also hung another lately in Rappahannock. It is my purpose to hang an equal number of Custer's men whenever I capture them. There was passed by the last U.S. Congress a bill of pains and penalties against guerillas, and as they profess to consider my men within the definition of the term, I think it would be well to come to some understanding with the enemy in reference to them. . . ."

Lee added an endorsement to this letter: "I do not know how we can prevent the cruel conduct of the enemy toward our citizens. I have directed Colonel Mosby through his adjutant to hang an equal number of Custer's men in retaliation for those executed by him." Secretary of War Seddon added: "General Lee's instructions are cordially approved. In addition, if our citizens are found exposed on any captured train, signal vengeance should be taken on all conductors and officers found on it, and every male passenger of the enemy's country should be treated as prisoners."

That same day, Captain Walter E. Frankland of Mosby's command, with 106 men, made the mistake of attacking 200 troopers of the 8th Illinois Cavalry without the advantage of surprise, and the Rebels were routed with the loss of four men killed, five wounded, and nine captured. "Nobody who fought against the Eighth Illinois could ever think of them as anything but brave and gallant soldiers," one ranger later told his young son when the latter claimed that all Yankees were cowards.[9]

Out in Tennessee that morning, the patience of Buford and his Confederate gunners was rewarded when the steamboat *Mazeppa* came up the Tennessee River with a barge in tow. It took only three rounds from the lower batteries to disable her, and she drifted to the opposite bank, where she was abandoned by her crew. A Rebel soldier, stripped naked except for the pistol strapped around his neck, paddled across the river on a plank to take possession of the expedition's first prize. He used the steamer's yawl to bring back a line, and the Confederates pulled the *Mazeppa* to the western bank of the Tennessee. On the steamer and her barge Buford found 700 tons of supplies for the Union army, including 9,000 pairs of shoes, as well as blankets, winter clothing, and some food and drink. "Plenty of meat, boys," General Buford told his men after looking over the cargo, "plenty of hard-tack, plenty of shoes and clothes for the boys, but just enough brandy for the General!"[10] No sooner than these supplies were unloaded and hauled away from the river bank than three light Union gunboats came down the river, but the fire of the Rebel guns soon drove them back.

The next day, the steamer *Anna*, coming downstream, fell into the Rebel trap. Buford, who wanted to take her whole, hailed her and promised not to fire on her if she would put into the bank. The Federal captain promised to round to at the lower landing, but instead put on all steam and got away, although she arrived at Paducah badly damaged by the Rebel guns when they realized what she was up to.

The sound of this firing attracted the Union gunboat *Undine*, which had escorted the *Anna* from Johnsonville to within a few miles of where Buford ambushed her. She cleared for action and steamed toward the sound of guns, but she was only a light gunboat of the type the Federals called tinclads because they only carried enough armor to protect against small arms fire. After a fight of slightly less than an hour, four Confederate shots had penetrated her gun casemates, she had lost four dead and three wounded, a shell had knocked the fire out of her furnace, another had shot off the escape pipe, and she was becoming unmanageable. However, she was able to get to a point in the river that was not reachable by either the guns at Paris Landing or those at Fort Heiman, and she was using her broadside of four 24-pounder howitzers to return the small arms fire of Rebel troopers when the transport *Venus* came down the river. *Undine* tried to warn her off, but the *Venus* kept coming, got by the lower battery, and came to anchor under the protection of the *Undine's* guns. About twenty minutes later another transport, the *Cheeseman*, came down the river and also ignored *Undine's* signals until her steam pipe was shot off. Then she ran into the west bank and surrendered to the Rebels.

Brigadier General James R. Chalmer's 1st Division of Forrest's corps arrived that day with two more batteries of field guns, and these were both positioned above Paris Landing. Meanwhile, Colonel Edmund W. Rucker found a way that guns could be moved through the thick brush along the bank to a spot that would bear on the *Undine* and the *Venus*. Two guns were put in this position and opened fire on the gunboat at 3:10 p.m. By 4 p.m. it had been run into the east bank and been abandoned and the *Venus* had surrendered. As the Confederates were taking possession of these two prizes another gunboat, the *Tawah*, came steaming downriver, attracted by the sound of firing. She anchored a mile and a half upriver, out of range of the Rebel field pieces, and began to shell the upper battery. Chalmers tried moving his guns to shorten the range, but the *Tawah* just moved upriver, staying out of range.

Even farther up the Tennessee River on that 30th of October the advance elements of Hood's Army of Tennessee reached Tuscumbia, Alabama, near the northwestern corner of that state, and a few Confederates even crossed to the north side of the river and occupied Florence. Meanwhile, the tail of Hood's column was just marching away from Decatur that day, giving up on any attempt to capture its reinforced Union garrison.

That same day, the Federal 4th Corps left Chattanooga, headed for Pulaski, Tennessee, on the railroad between Nashville and Decatur, Alabama. Sherman, who was back at Rome, Georgia, learned from Thomas that the new troops promised by General Grant were coming forward very slowly and decided to further reinforce him by sending him Schofield's 23rd Corps of 12,000 men. "I then knew," Sherman later wrote, "that General Thomas would have an ample force with which to encounter General Hood anywhere in the open field, besides garrisons to secure the railroad to his rear and as far forward as Chattanooga. And moverover, I was more than convinced that he would have ample time for preparation; for, on that very day, General R. S. Granger had telegraphed me from Decatur, Alabama: 'I omitted to mention another reason why Hood will go to Tuscumbia before crossing the Tennessee River. He was evidently out of supplies. His men were all grumbling; the first thing the prisoners asked for was something to eat. Hood could not get any thing if he should cross this side of Rogersville.' I knew that the country about Decatur and Tuscumbia, Alabama, was bare of provisions, and inferred that General Hood would have to draw his supplies, not only food, but of stores, clothing, and ammunition, from Mobile, Montgomery, and Selma, Alabama, by the railroad around by Meridian and Corinth, Mississippi, which we had most effectually disabled the previous winter."[11]

Over in North Carolina on the 30th, a reconnaissance by the USS *Valley City* had determined that the block ships in the Roanoke River could be bypassed by taking a channel known as Middle River. So Commander Macomb's ships threaded their way through it that day—shelling Plymouth across the intervening neck of land in the process—and passed into the Roanoke River above Plymouth, where they lay at anchor that night. Lieutenant Cushing was not there to take part in this move, however, for he left that day for Hampton Roads, carrying his personal report of his expedition to Admiral Porter.

At 9:30 a.m. the next day, the 31st—the day Nevada joined the Union as the 36th state—Macomb's vessels formed up in line astern. The USS *Commodore Hull* had the lead, because, being a converted ferry boat, she had guns that could fire forward. The *Whitehead*, which had arrived with stores just before the attack, was lashed to the *Tacony*, and the tugs *Bazley* and *Bell* to the *Shamrock* and *Otsego*, to provide power in case of damage to the engines of the larger vessels. Soon after 11 a.m. the fleet was engaged with the Rebel batteries, which were supported by rifle fire from rifle pits and houses. After an hour of spirited action at close range, the *Shamrock* planted a shell in the Confederate magazine, which blew up. The Rebels hastily abandoned their defenses, and in a short time Plymouth was once again in Union hands.

"On the 31st of October," Sherman wrote, "General Croxton, of the cavalry, reported that the enemy had crossed the Tennessee River four miles above Florence, and that he had endeavored to stop him, but without success. Still, I was convinced that Hood's army was in no condition to march for Nashville, and that a good deal of further delay might reasonably be counted on. I also rested with much confidence on the fact that the Tennessee River below Muscle Shoals was strongly patroled by gunboats, and that the reach of the river above Muscle Shoals, from Decatur as high up as our railroad at Bridgeport, was also guarded by gunboats, so that Hood, to cross over, would be compelled to select a point inaccessible to these gunboats. He actually did choose such a place, at the old railroad-piers, four miles above Florence, Alabama, which is below Muscle Shoals and above Colbert Shoals."[12] At all times except during very high water, navigation of the Tennessee River was split into two parts by these shoals—areas of shallow rapids just to each side of Florence. There were Union gunboats in both stretches, above and below, but neither could interfere with the crossing of the river between them.

Forrest arrived in person on the last day of October at the scene of Buford's and Chalmer's successes against the Union boats in the Tennessee River and decided to form his own navy. The *Cheeseman* was too badly damaged to use and was unloaded and burned, but the other two boats were taken over. The two 20-pounder Parrott rifles were mounted on the *Venus* to turn her into a gunboat, and volunteer crews were put aboard her and the *Undine*, with Lieutenant Colonel William A. Dawson on the *Venus* as commodore of the fleet and Captain Frank M. Gracey, an old Cumberland River steamboat man, in command of the *Undine*.

The next day, 1 November, the two boats started up the river, but first Colonel Dawson told Forrest that he wanted a promise that "if we lose your fleet and come in on foot, you won't curse us out about it."[13] Chalmers' men moved ahead of the boats and Buford's followed along behind them, forcing their way through thick brush and sharp briers along the muddy bank on a rainy day while the newly converted sailors, with little to do but watch the world float by, teased them with expressions of mock sympathy. The troopers ashore replied with elaborate warnings about what would happen when Union gunboats showed up. But the boats were under strict orders to stay between the upper and lower batteries moving along the bank.

They tied up that night near the railroad bridge at Danville and did not encounter any Federals until the next day at 3:30 p.m., about six miles north of Johnsonville. That's when the dire predictions of the landsmen proved all too true. The *Venus* had not only got out ahead of the shore batteries but of the *Undine* as well. She was swept into a bend of the river and found herself confronted by the *Tawah* and another gunboat, the *Key West*. The Federals attacked immediately and aggressively, driving the undergunned, inexperienced *Venus* ashore, where her crew abandoned her and the two 20-pounders to the enemy. The *Undine* tried to come to her rescue but was driven back downstream, although she was not followed.

On 2 November Sherman received a telegram from Grant, sent the day before: "Do you not think it advisable, now that Hood has gone so far north, to entirely ruin him before starting on your proposed campaign? With Hood's army destroyed, you can go where you please with impunity. I believed and still believe, if you had started south while Hood was in the neighborhood of you, he would have been forced to go after you. Now that he is far away he might look upon the chase as useless, and he will go in one direction while you are pushing in the other. If you can see a chance of destroying Hood's army, attend to that first, and make your other move secondary."[14]

To this Sherman answered: "If I could hope to overhaul Hood, I would turn against him with my whole force, then he would retreat to the southwest, drawing me as a decoy away from Georgia, which is his chief object. If he ventures north of the Tennessee River, I may turn in that direction, and endeavor to get below him on his line of retreat; but thus far he has not gone above the Tennessee River. General Thomas will have a force strong enough to prevent his reaching any country in which we have an interest; and he has orders, if Hood turns to follow me, to push for Selma, Alabama. No single army can catch Hood, and I am convinced the best results will follow from our defeating Jeff. Davis's cherished plan of making me leave Georgia by maneuvering. Thus far I have confined my efforts to thwart this plan, and have reduced baggage so that I can pick up and start in any direction; but I regard the pursuit of Hood as useless. Still, if he attempts to invade Middle Tennessee, I will hold Decatur, and be prepared to move in that direction; but, unless I let go of Atlanta, my force will not be equal to his."[15]

During the day, Sherman transferred his headquarters from Rome to Kingston, Georgia, since the break in his railroad around Dalton had been repaired. Evidently he had done some more thinking about Grant's ideas, for from there he sent him another telegram: "If I turn back, the whole effect of my campaign will be lost. By my movements I have thrown Beauregard (Hood) as well to the west, and Thomas will have ample time and sufficient troops to hold him until the reenforcements from Missouri reach him. We have now ample supplies at Chattanooga and Atlanta, and can stand a month's interruption of our communications. I do not believe the Confederate army can reach our railroad-lines except by cavalry-raids, and Wilson will have cavalry enough to checkmate them. I am clearly of opinion that the best results will follow my contemplated movement through Georgia."[16]

But before Grant received either of these two wires he had changed his mind: "I dispatched you . . . advising that Hood's army, now that it had worked so far north, ought to be looked upon now as the 'object.' With the force, however, that you have left with General Thomas, he must be able to take care of Hood and destroy him. I do not see that you can withdraw from where you are to follow Hood, without giving up all we have gained in territory. I say, then, go on as you propose."[17]

On that same second day of November, U.S. Secretary of State William Seward sent a warning to the mayors of New York, Albany, Buffalo, Chicago, Detroit, Cleveland, Philadelphia, New Haven, Providence, Boston, Portland, Portsmouth, Salem, and Newburyport, Massachusetts: "This Department has received information from the British Provinces to the effect that there is a conspiracy on foot to set fire to the principal cities in the Northern States on the day of the Presidential election. It is my duty to communicate this information to you."[18] That same day the Confederate officers in New York City were introduced by McMasters to the private secretary of Horatio Seymour, governor of the state of New York and a Democrat, who assured the elated Rebels that the governor would remain neutral during the insurrection they and the Copperheads were planning.

The next day, 3 November, the *Undine* steamed up to the head of Reynoldsburg Island about noon, two miles north of Johnsonville, Tennessee, daring the three Union gunboats there to come out and fight. But Lieutenant E. M. King, commanding the Union flotilla, rightly suspected that the now-Confederate gunboat was trying to draw the Federals to within reach of the Rebel guns on the river bank below, and he declined this challenge, although it was repeated three times. Meanwhile, despite the continuing rain, Forrest was getting his men and guns into position to cut off Johnsonville from both above and below and some of them onto the muddy bottom land across from the giant Union depot.

Farther south, Hood was still engaged in moving his army to the north bank of the Tennessee near Florence and in gathering in supplies. The rain was swelling the river, which was not making the job any easier. By then Beauregard had agreed to Hood's new strategy. Since he was now too far west to go after the railroad between Nashville and Chattanooga, Hood would cross the river, move into middle Tennessee, join up with Forrest, and see what Sherman would do. Beauregard had little choice but to go along at this late date and, with Richard Taylor, he worked to do what he could to improve Hood's supply situation. The Confederates regarded indications that Union troops were moving up from Georgia as evidence that their plan was working and that sooner or later Sherman would have to give up Georgia in order to protect Tennessee. The arrival of the Federal 4th Corps at Pulaski, Tennessee, that day confirmed their assessment.

Schofield reached Nashville the next day, the fourth, having gone ahead of his troops for the purpose of discussing arrangements with Thomas. "This assignment of the Twenty-third Corps to duty under General Thomas had been at Schofield's own suggestion, and was agreeable, therefore, to both officers," one of Schofield's division commanders, Jacob D. Cox, said in a history he later wrote of the campaign. "Schofield's departmental command covered East Tennessee and part of Kentucky, and his presence saved the necessity of any change in the organization there. But still stronger motives were found in the fact that the strength of the Twenty-third Corps had been reduced below ten thousand men present for duty, by the casualties of the campaign, and the opportunity would thus be given it to recruit the two divisions already belonging to it, while a third division of new troops was ordered to join it when the new levies should reach the front. Schofield also believed that the campaign in Tennessee was to be an important one, full of varied military problems and contingencies, and that he could be quite as useful there as in any other field of operations."[19]

At 8 a.m. on 4 November, Lieutenant King of the Union navy, with the *Tawah*, *Key West*, and the *Elfin*, came down the Tennessee River, while at the same time Lieutenant Commander Le Roy Fitch came upriver from the north with six more gunboats. Caught between these two overwhelming forces, Captain Gracey abandoned the *Undine* and burned her.

The Federals were not able to intimidate the land batteries, however.

Two guns were positioned above the head of Reynoldsburg Island and two more a little below, covering a narrow chute where the channel passed between the island and the west bank. The upper battery, Lieutenant King reported, was "too much for us."[20] Out of a total of thirty shots fired in twenty minutes the Rebels put ten shells through the *Key West's* upper works, seven through her berth deck, and two through her hull, and King's flotilla withdrew to Johnsonville. The larger force downriver kept firing until 11 a.m., but did not even try to steam up the narrow, tortuous channel.

While the Union gunboats were being fought to a draw, Forrest continued to emplace guns in a natural levee opposite Johnsonville behind camouflaging boughs that blended with the thick underbrush along the bank. When all was ready and the guns opened fire at 2 p.m. there were 3 gunboats, 11 transports, and 18 barges at the wharves across the river. And on the bank, 20 feet higher than the western shore, were bulging warehouses, acres of supplies in open storage piled ten feet high and covered only by tarpaulins, and two freight trains being put together for a run to Nashville. The Federals did not have any idea what the Rebels were up to until the shells began to rain down upon them.

For forty minutes the ten Confederate guns concentrated their fire on the boats. Bursting boilers soon spewed scalding steam on unsuspecting crews and some vessels were set afire. Some of these, out of control, drifted into other boats and set them alight as well. Lieutenant King decided that his gunboats had no chance and he ordered them and all the transports burned to keep them out of Rebel hands.

Next the Confederates turned their attention to the eastern riverbank, and the bursting shells and sparks from the burning boats soon turned the warehouses and stacks of supplies into acres of roaring flames. One warehouse contained hundreds of barrels of liquor, and when it caught fire the barrels burst, sending rivers of blue flames running down the hill into the river. Within two hours the entire complex was on fire. One Union officer said the scene "beggared description; it was awfully sublime." The Confederates were enjoying themselves so much that Forrest himself took a turn as gunner with the battery nearest the town, with General Buford and Colonel Bell serving in his crew, "handling, loading and firing the piece with the enthusiasm of boy cannoneers on a Fourth of July." When a shot was reported as being too high, Forrest told his highranking crew to "elevate the breech of that gun a little lower!"[21] That night the Confederate troopers started south to join Hood's army.

In Washington that day, President Lincoln approved the location of the first hundred miles of the Union Pacific Railroad—west of Omaha, Nebraska—which four and a half years later would connect with the Central Pacific to complete the first transcontinental railroad.

---

1. Cushing, "The Destruction of the 'Albemarle,'" 640.
2. Roske and Van Doren, *Lincoln's Commando*, 303.
3. O'Flaherty, *General Jo Shelby*, 224.
4. Foote, *The Civil War*, 585.
5. Henry, *"First With the Most" Forrest*, 372.
6. Nat Brandt, *The Man Who Tried to Burn New York* (Syracuse, 1986), 85.
7. Tidwell, Hall and Gaddy, *Come Retribution*, 334.
8. Cushing, "The Destruction of the 'Albemarle,'" 640.
9. Virgil Carrington Jones, *Ranger Mosby* (Chapel Hill, 1944), 221–223.
10. Henry, *"First With the Most" Forrest*, 372.
11. Sherman, *Memoirs*, 637–638.
12. Ibid., 638–639.
13. Henry, *"First With the Most" Forrest*, 374.
14. Sherman, *Memoirs*, 639.
15. Ibid., 639–640.
16. Ibid., 640.
17. Ibid., 640–641.
18. Brandt, *The Man Who Tried to Burn New York*, 87–88.
19. Jacob D. Cox, *The March to the Sea, Franklin and Nashville* (New York, 1882), 7–8.
20. Henry, *"First With the Most" Forrest*, 376.
21. Ibid., 378.

CHAPTER THIRTY

Very Far from Being Certain

4–9 November 1864

On the morning of 4 November, Ben Butler arrived in New York. In July 1863 that city had been the scene of extremely violent draft riots that had only been quelled when veteran troops had been sent from the Army of the Potomac. Now, Secretary of War Stanton was taking no chances. He was sending the soldiers first. There were rumors that Butler had brought 15,000 troops with him to make sure that there were no disorders in conjunction with the presidential election in the nation's largest city. Actually he had fewer than 3,500, but the rumor was almost as good as the soldiers.

Butler set up his headquarters at the Fifth-Avenue Hotel but his entourage was so large that there were not enough rooms there, so he later moved to a 12-room suite at the new Hoffman House. One of those rooms was turned into a telegraph center with 60 wires running into it, keeping the general in direct touch with every police station and polling place in the city and every major city in the state, as well as the War Department in Washington.

Most of Butler's regiments were from New York state, and this created a legal difficulty. Not knowing that they would soon be sent to New York, they had already voted by absentee ballot, which meant that they could not legally be in the state on Election Day without voiding their votes. Butler put this problem on hold by stationing them at army posts in Brooklyn and on Staten Island which were on Federal land and thus not legally part of the state of New York. Butler declined to call out the militia, saying, "If they were called out they would be under arms, and in the case of difficulty it was not quite certain which way all of them would shoot." And he warned that any armed forces found in Manhattan on Election Day would be treated "as enemies."[1]

In an order issued the next day, Butler declared that he and his troops were there to preserve the peace, to protect public property, to prevent disorder, and to ensure calm and quiet. Democrats were charging that the soldiers were there to interfere with the election, but Butler replied that, to the contrary, they were there to see that nobody interfered with it, saying, "Let every citizen having the right to vote act according to the inspiration of his own judgment freely. He will be protected in that right by the whole power of the Government if it shall become necessary."[2]

On that same fifth of November, the Confederates who had raided St. Albans, Vermont, and been captured in Canada were taken to Montreal to face charges of robbery, arson, and treason, despite United States Secretary of State William H. Seward's demands for their extradition to the United States.

Due to Forrest's attack on Johnsonville, Tennessee, and the Federals' fears that he would cross the river to complete his work, the van of the 23rd Corps, as it came up from Georgia, was rushed in that direction, and on the fifth of November Schofield, with his leading brigade, arrived at Gillem's Station, on the railroad between Nashville and Johnsonville. On the sixth, Schofield marched from there to Johnsonville, and two of his brigades were stationed there for a few days under a division commander with orders to fortify the place, while Schofield returned to Nashville.

It was cool but sunny in the Shenandoah Valley on Sunday morning, 6 November. Mosby and some of his men lined up 27 captured Union soldiers in a hollow near Rectortown, and 27 slips of paper were folded and thrown into a brown felt hat. Seven of them had numbers on them and the other twenty were blank. Each prisoner was made to take a slip from the hat and the seven who drew the numbered slips were to be hanged in retaliation for seven rangers that Custer and Powell had hanged. One of the seven who drew numbered slips, however, was a young drummer boy, and Mosby ordered his release. So another drawing was held to fill his place. Then the seven doomed men were put on horses and led off toward Sheridan's camps with a small group of guards. Mosby wanted the executions to take place as near to Sheridan's lines as possible. Two of the seven, however, soon received a reprieve, for Captain R. P. Montjoy, bringing in a new batch of prisoners, recognized two of the original bunch as fellow Masons. He ordered their release and substituted two of his own prisoners in their places. Mosby did not learn of this until later, and when he did he was furious. "Remember, Captain, in the future," he told Montjoy, "that this command is not a Masonic lodge!"[3]

By the time the prisoners and their escort were approaching Berryville it was raining and dark, and one of the prisoners had already managed to escape. So the Confederates decided to stop and get the job over with. "The first man was gotten up," wrote one of the Federals, Sergeant Charles Marvin, "his hands tied behind him, a bedcord doubled and tied around his neck; he was marched to a large tree beside the road, from which a limb projected. He was lifted in the air, the rope taken by one of the men on horseback and tied to the limb, and there he was left dangling. Two more were treated in the same manner. It took some considerable time and our executioners were becoming uneasy . . . and they decided . . . to shoot the balance of us, as 'this hanging is too damned slow work.'"[4]

The three remaining Federals were lined up, a revolver was pointed at each, and the command was given to fire. Sergeant Marvin heard the men on each side of him shot, but the revolver pointed at him only clicked. Taking advantage of the Confederates' momentary confusion, Marvin struck his would-be executioner as hard as he could and ran for his life into the dark, rainy night. He got away, but his five companions were not so lucky. The two who were shot were not killed, but they were badly wounded. One had an eye and part of his head blown away but lived. The other had only a shattered elbow. They and the bodies of the three who were hanged were found the next morning. One of them bore a note, evidently written ahead of time: "These men have been hung in retaliation for an equal number of Colonel Mosby's men hung by order of General Custer, at Front Royal. Measure for measure."[5]

"If my motive had been revenge," Mosby wrote, "I would have ordered others to be executed in their place. I did not. I was really glad they got away as they carried the story to Sheridan's army which was the best way to stop the business. My object was to prevent the war from degenerating into a massacre."[6]

Down in Georgia on the sixth, Sherman took a few minutes to send congratulations to Sheridan: "I have been wanting to write to you for some days, but have been troubled by an acute pain in my shoulder resulting from recent exposure. I wish to assure you of the intense interest I feel in your personal and official success. If I have not caused the burning of as much gunpowder as our mutual friend Grant in your honor, I can assure you that our army down in Georgia have expended an equal amount of yelling and noisy demonstration at your success. I notice particularly the prominent fact that you in person turned the tide in the recent battle of Cedar Creek. You have youth and vigor, and this single event has given you a hold upon an army that gives you a future better than older men can hope for. I am satisfied, and have been all the time, that the problem of this war consists in the awful fact that the present class of men who rule the South must be killed outright rather than in the conquest of territory, so that hard, bull-dog fighting, and a great deal of it, yet remains to be done, and it matters not whether it be done close to the borders, where you are, or farther in the interior, where I happen to be; therefore, I shall expect you on any and all occasions to make bloody results. I beg to assure you of my warm personal attachment and respect."[7]

He also sent a long dispatch to Grant. He said, in part: "On the supposition always that Thomas can hold the line of the Tennessee, and very shortly be able to assume the offensive as against Beauregard, I propose to act in such a manner against the material resources of the South as utterly to negative Davis' boasted threat and promises of protection. If we can march a well-appointed army right through his territory, it is a demonstration to the world, foreign and domestic, that we have a power which Davis cannot resist. This may not be war, but rather statesmanship, nevertheless it is overwhelming to my mind that there are thousands of people abroad and in the South who will reason thus: If the North can march an army right through the South, it is proof positive that the North can prevail in this contest, leaving only open the question of its willingness to use that power. Now, Mr. Lincoln's election, which is assured, coupled with the conclusion thus reached, makes a complete, logical whole. Even without a battle, the result operating upon the minds of sensible men would produce fruits more than compensating for the expense, trouble, and risk." After a long discussion of possible objectives and routes, he said, "I will not attempt to send couriers back, but trust to the Richmond papers to keep you well advised. I will give you notice by telegraph of the exact time of my departure. General Steedman is here to clear the railroad back to Chattanooga, and I will see that the road is broken completely between the Etowah and the Chattahoochee, including their bridges, and that Atlanta itself is utterly destroyed."[8]

The Copperhead plot to seize control of New York was only a small part of the uprising planned for Election Day. For weeks Captain Tom Hines (who evidently had a temporary commission as major general), the Confederacy's top agent working with the Copperheads, had been traveling in various disguises throughout what was known in those days as the Northwest, trying to repair the damage done by the arrest of most of their leaders that summer. The only high-ranking Copperhead left in the Chicago area was Charles Walsh, brigadier general of the Illinois organization. But Walsh assured Hines that this time there would be no holding back and that his men were armed "and ready to shed blood."[9]

Colonel Ben M. Anderson had been sent to Missouri and had reported distributing arms to 300 men who were ready to march into southern Iowa and burn as many towns and villages as possible. Along with New York, Boston and Cincinnati were to be burned. In Chicago, the plot once again revolved around a plan to free the Rebel prisoners of war at Camp Douglas, who with the local Copperheads would form the nucleus of a new army whose ranks would be swollen by Confederates freed from other prisons, such as Rock Island, and by Copperheads from down state and from Indiana, Missouri, and other states. Colonel George St. Leger Grenfel, a British adventurer, had already been sent to reconnoiter Rock Island Prison while pretending to be hunting quail in the area, and he was now waiting at the Richmond House hotel in Chicago to make his report.

At about the time that Colonel Martin and his party had left Toronto for New York, Hines had left the same city for Chicago along with several others, including Colonel Vincent Marmaduke, Richard T. Semmes (brother of Raphael Semmes who had commanded the Confederate cruiser *Alabama*), and Lieutenant J. J. Bettersworth. Other agents were sent to the far southern end of Illinois, the area between the Mississippi and Ohio Rivers, known as "Egypt," which was very pro-Southern. They took enough money with them to be able to bring about 1,500 Copperheads to Chicago as the strike force for the attack on Camp Douglas. And word was slipped to the prisoners so they would know what to do and when.

This was necessary, of course, but it was also the plan's undoing. There were 8,000 to 9,000 prisoners in Camp Douglas, many of whom had been conscripted into the Rebel army in the first place, and there were bound to be some among them who did not want to risk their lives in an escape or in a return to combat, or whose devotion to the Confederacy was weak for some other reason. What's more, the Union commander of the prison, Colonel Benjamin J. Sweet, was an intelligent and resourceful officer who was in that noncombat position only because of a wound he had received at the battles around Chattanooga the year before. Sweet not only had spies among the prisoners but in the city outside the gates and even in downstate Illinois. One of his agents was J. Winslow Ayer, a patent medicine salesman who had infiltrated the Sons of Liberty. Another was Secret Service agent Tom Keefe, who had been watching Hines in Toronto and had ridden in the seat behind him on the train to Chicago but had not arrested him in the hope that he would lead him to the local conspirators. Instead, Keefe had lost track of Hines, but he brought word to Sweet that Hines was in Chicago and planning a revolt.

Inside the camp, Sweet had a pair of Rebel lieutenants from Texas who gave him details of the plot. One of these, James T. Shanks, had, on one of Morgan's raids, captured the Union colonel who had later become Sweet's predecessor in command of Camp Douglas. And when Shanks had become a prisoner there he had been befriended by the colonel and appointed camp clerk in the medical department. Soon he had developed a romance with a young Chicago widow who was a member of the ladies' society that brought fruit and cigars to the prisoners, and the colonel had allowed Shanks to leave the prison twice a week, with a guard, to court the lady. When Sweet had taken over he had continued this practice. Then, after learning about the plot to break the prisoners out, Sweet had arranged to let Shanks escape by hiding in the wagon of the local peddler who collected the camp's garbage.

Word from someone in the prison was smuggled out to Hines that Shanks was not to be trusted, and Hines managed to pass this on to all the Rebel officers except Lieutenant Bettersworth. Shanks got to Bettersworth first, telling him that Hines had sent him to pick him up. Instead, Shanks took the young lieutenant to the home of his pretty widow, got him drunk, and wormed from him the names and locations of all the Confederate agents, which he promptly carried to Sweet.

The Federal authorities had been planning to wait until the last minute to break up the plot in order to increase their chances of capturing all the ringleaders and to give the latter time to thoroughly incriminate themselves. But on Sunday, 6 November, Sweet thought it was time to move. The Rebels were onto Shanks, Sweet had most of the details of the plot, and he had reports that hundreds of suspicious persons had arrived in town. So he wrote a dispatch to his superior, Brigadier General John Cook, commander of the District of Illinois. "The city is filling up with suspicious characters," he said, "some of whom are known to be escaped prisoners, and others who were here from Canada during the Chicago convention plotting to release the prisoners of war at Camp Douglas." He added that he had "only 800 men all told, to guard between 8,000 and 9,000 prisoners. I am certainly not justified in waiting to take risks, and mean to arrest these officers if possible, before morning. The head gone, we can manage the body." In addition to the Rebel agents, he said he planned to seize "two or three prominent citizens who are connected with these officers, of which the proof is ample."[10] He sent this by special courier to Cook's headquarters at Springfield since he did not trust the telegraph. (It was later learned that Hines had given the telegrapher at Camp Douglas $1,000 to provide him with copies of all official telegrams.)

Three parties of 100 men each, under Colonel Skinner of the 8th Regiment of the Veteran Reserve Corps, were sent out, one to patrol the city and the other two to raid specific places and to arrest known spies. Grenfel was the first one rounded up. The Federals found him at the Richmond House, sipping brandy by the fire with his hunting dog at his feet. They put the colonel in leg irons and hauled him out into the cold, rainy night. Three and half years later he escaped from Fort Jefferson in the Dry Tortugas and was never heard from again, presumably dying in his little row boat before reaching land. The troops sent to the center of the city rounded up about 100 Confederate soldiers, Copperheads, and bushwhackers from "Egypt" before midnight.

Judge Buckner S. Morris, treasurer of the Sons of Liberty, was arrested at his home, and in the wee hours of the morning Colonel Skinner and his men surrounded the home of Charles Walsh, brigadier general of the Sons of Liberty. They broke down the door after what the Chicago *Tribune* called "a great deal of trouble," and arrested Walsh, Richard Semmes, Captain George Cantrill, Colonel Ben Anderson, and several other Confederates. Walsh's home was only about a block from Camp Douglas and it was being used to store the weapons needed for the attack that would break the prisoners out. The Federals found 210 double-barrelled shotguns loaded with "the largest buckshot," 350 Colt revolvers, 100 Henry repeating rifles, 13,000 rounds of ammunition, 344 boxes of caps for the shotguns and revolvers, two kegs of gunpowder, molds for making cartridges, and boxes of knives, hooks, and spears.[11]

At about 1:30 on the morning of the seventh a patrol approached the home of Dr. Edward W. Edwards, where Hines was thought to be staying. The doctor was attending his wife, who was suffering from diphtheria, when he heard the soldiers approach the house and saw the Union officer swing down from his horse. Quickly he alerted Hines. "Have you a large box mattress?" Hines asked. "Yes. Mrs. Edwards is sleeping on it," the puzzled doctor replied. "Please show it to me at once," Hines said, grabbing up his revolver and dagger from under his pillow. While the soldiers banged on the front door, Dr. Edwards guided Hines to his wife's room, and while Edwards held a lamp and the covers, Hines split open the side of the mattress with his dagger, crawled inside with his weapons, and made another slit in the bottom to provide himself with air. "Let them in, Doctor," he said.[12]

Edwards went down and opened the door for the soldiers, and they searched the house, soon finding Colonel Marmaduke still in bed. Neither Edwards nor Hines had thought to warn him. Hines evidently did not care much for Marmaduke anyway. Perhaps he was justified. When the Union troops burst in, the colonel reached for his revolver, but a soldier clubbed him with the butt of his rifle. Maybe that explains why Marmaduke was stupid enough to ask Edwards, "Did they get Hines?" thus confirming for the Federals that the ringleader was indeed on the premises. However, search as they would, they could not find him.[13] They pulled clothes out of closets and looked under the beds, even the one on which Mrs. Edwards lay tossing in fever, but finally gave up, leaving Edwards under house arrest, with two sentries by his door, so he could continue to look after his wife.

The next day, friends of Dr. Edwards received word that his wife was not expected to live, and in twos and threes they called at the house to pay their last respects. The Union sentries, warmed by glasses of whiskey provided by the good doctor, expressed their sympathy and huddled out of the way under the eaves, trying to stay dry. They did not bother to look under each umbrella as the sorrowful visitors came and went, nor did they bother to count them. Had they done so, they would have found that the gentleman who left with Mary Walsh, daughter of the brigadier general of the Sons of Liberty, was not the man with whom she had arrived.

In New York on 7 November, McMaster informed the Confederate officers that the Copperhead leaders in the city had held a meeting and decided, because of the presence of Butler and his troops, to postpone their revolt. Once the election was over the soldiers would be sent back to Virginia, and that is when they would strike. Then the news reached New York that afternoon of the arrest of the Copperheads and Confederates in Chicago, further dampening the spirits of the would-be revolutionaries. Nevertheless the eight Rebel officers stayed on in New York, keeping an eye on Ben Butler, and waiting for the withdrawal of his troops.

The arrests on the night of the sixth-seventh did not end all Union fears for Chicago. On the seventh the provost marshal at Danville, Illinois, sent a telegram to Major General Joseph Hooker, commander of the Northern Department, which included all the northwestern states, reporting rumors that "Forrest has been in disguise alternately in Chicago, Michigan City and Canada for two months; has 14,000 men, mostly from draft, near Michigan City. On 7th of November, midnight, will seize telegraph and rail at Chicago, release prisoners there, arm them, sack the city, shoot down all Federal soldiers, and urge concert of action with Southern sympathizers." Hooker expressed the opinion that the rumor was "all stuff."[14] But to be on the safe side he ordered troops he had sent from Springfield to Chicago to remain there through Election Day, sent 500 troops from Indianapolis and a regiment from St. Louis, and finally went to Chicago himself, while the governor of Illinois called out the militia. In actuality, of course, Forrest was in Tennessee, heading south to join Hood after his attack on Johnsonville. Schofield, meanwhile, decided that day to send no more of his troops to Johnsonville even as the last of them were loading onto trains to head north from Georgia.

The trial of the St. Albans raiders got under way in Montreal at 10 a.m. on that seventh day of November. They were defended by J. G. K. Houghton, one of Canada's most prominent attorneys. But during the proceedings, smiling, debonair George Sanders bustled about the courtroom, whispering to Lieutenant Young, giving orders to Houghton, even telling the clerks of the court when to close the doors. The trial was promptly adjourned for thirty days to give the defendants time to obtain official copies from the Confederate War Department in Richmond of their commissions and orders in order to prove that their depradations were acts of war.

In Richmond on the seventh, the second Confederate Congress gathered for its second session. The message it heard from President Davis was optimistic. He deprecated the loss of Atlanta, saying, "There are no vital points on the preservation of which the continued existence of the Confederacy depends. There is no military success of the enemy which can accomplish its destruction. Not the fall of Richmond, nor Wilmington, nor Charleston, nor Savannah, nor Mobile, nor of all combined, can save the enemy from the constant and exhaustive drain of blood and treasure which must continue until he shall discover that no peace is attainable unless based on the recognition of our indefeasible rights."[15] He called for a general militia law and an end to most exemptions from conscription. He also recommended that the government purchase slaves for use in non-combat jobs in the army. He concluded by saying that his administration favored a negotiated peace, but only with independence, not "our unconditional submission and degradation."[16]

Far to the southwest, Price's Army of Missouri, or what was left of it, after veering into Indian Territory—now Oklahoma—to avoid the Federals at Fort Smith, crossed the Arkansas River on 7 November. But even then the Confederates' march was not over. Many of them had already deserted or had just fallen behind looking for food or were unable to keep up. Entire regiments and brigades of Arkansas troops were allowed to go home on the understanding that their officers were to bring them back within Confederate lines during the month of December "if possible." The rest of the army was not so lucky. According to Major John Edwards of Shelby's staff: "After crossing the Arkansas the worst stage of misery came upon the army, and the sufferings were intense. Horses died by thousands; the few wagons were abandoned almost without exception; the sick had no medicines and the healthy no food; the army had no organization and the subordinate officers no hope. Bitter freezing weather added terrors to the route and weakness to the emaciated, staggering column. Small-pox came at last, as the natural consequence, and hundreds fell out by the wayside to perish without help and be devoured by coyotes without a burial."[17]

Curtis's pursuing Federals came upon a broken and abandoned carriage that day that was said to be Price's own. And Curtis noticed that the "elm trees for miles had been stripped to furnish food for the starving multitude."[18] At 11 a.m. the next day, the eighth, the head of the Union column reached the Arkansas River and learned that the Rebels had crossed the day before. Curtis decided that it would be both useless and dangerous to continue the pursuit and called it off at last.

Down in Georgia on 8 November, Sherman received a telegram Grant had written the day before: "I see no present reason for changing your plan. Should any arise, you will see it, or if I do I will inform you. I think every thing here is favorable now. Great good fortune attend you! I believe you will be eminently successful, and, at worst, can only make a march less fruitful of results than hoped for." "Meantime," Sherman wrote in his memoirs, "trains of cars were whirling by, carrying to the rear an immense amount of stores which had accumulated at Atlanta, and at the other stations along the railroad; and General Steedman had come down to Kingston, to take charge of the final evacuation and withdrawal of the several garrisons below Chattanooga."[19]

On the morning of Election Day, 8 November, not a soldier was visible on the streets of New York, but everybody knew they were there. The result, as Ben Butler telegraphed to President Lincoln at noon, was "the quietest city ever seen."[20] In Chicago there was considerably more excitement, as the mayor called upon citizens to enlist in the Home Guards for three days to protect the city from any further Confederate or Copperhead plots. The Home Guards were armed with rifles and revolvers taken from the Copperhead arsenal, and some of them were a little trigger happy, but nobody seems to have been hurt and no Copperhead revolt or Confederate attack materialized. Hines managed to get out of town without being caught, although Mary Walsh, who had helped get him out of Dr. Edward's house, was arrested that day.

The voting in the camps of the various Union armies went smoothly and quietly. Horace Porter said that the soldiers in southern Virginia favored Lincoln over McClellan by a ratio of three to one. From down in Georgia Congressman/General Frank Blair, who was back at the head of the 17th Corps in Sherman's army after stumping for Lincoln in his home state of Missouri, wired to Washington, "The vote in this army to-day is almost unanimous for Lincoln. Give Uncle Abe my compliments and congratulations."[21]

In Washington, "the day of the presidential election in November 1864 was dark and rainy," reporter Noah Brooks remembered. "About noon I called on President Lincoln, and to my surprise found him entirely alone, as if by common consent everybody had avoided the White House." The Cabinet had met that morning, but only Navy Secretary Welles and Attorney General Bates had been there. Secretary of War Stanton was home sick, Secretary of the Treasury Fessenden was meeting with New York financiers about ways to float a new loan, and the rest had gone to their home states to vote. "I spent nearly all the afternoon with the President," Brooks wrote, "who apparently found it difficult to put his mind on any of the routine work of his office, and entreated me to stay with him." Lincoln made no attempt to hide his anxiety over the results of the election. "I am just enough of a politician," the president said, "to know that there was not much doubt about the Baltimore convention; but about this thing I am very far from being certain."[22]

No one could pass that much time with Lincoln without hearing an amusing story, and Election Day was no exception. The president told Brooks how his young son Tad had come bursting into his office that morning wanting his father to come watch the soldiers "voting for Lincoln and Johnson." The guards at the White House were from the famous Pennsylvania Bucktails regiment, and their votes were being taken by a commission from their state. Lincoln went to the window to watch and noticed that the pet turkey, whom Tad had saved from the dinner table the year before, was also watching the proceedings with interest. "Does he vote?" the president teased. "No," the boy shot back, "he is not of age."[23]

Brooks came back that evening and with the president and one of his secretaries walked over to the War Department in the rainy darkness. Lincoln always went to the War Department telegraph office whenever he was waiting for news from the battlefield, and the battle that raged in the nation's ballot boxes that day was perhaps the most important contest of the war. As he entered the telegraph room he was handed a message from John W. Forney, editor of the Philadelphia *Press*, claiming that Lincoln would carry that city by 10,000 votes. "Forney is a little excitable," Lincoln said.[24] A moment later a wire came from Baltimore indicating a lead of 15,000 in that city and 5,000 in the state for the Union ticket, and in another minute there was a telegram indicating a good lead in Boston. Lincoln asked that the latter figure be confirmed, fearing a clerical error, but it was correct.

Assistant Secretary of the Navy Gustavus Fox was there, exulting over the defeat of Congressman Henry Winter Davis, a radical Republican from Maryland who had not only given Lincoln many difficulties over reconstruction of the conquered Southern states but had always given the navy a hard time. "You have more of that feeling of personal resentment than I," Lincoln said. "Perhaps I have too little of it; but I never thought it paid. A man has no time to spend half his life in quarrels. If any man ceases to attack me I never remember the past against him."[25]

Reports came in much slower after that first flurry because the rain storm interfered with the telegraph. By the time Assistant Secretary of War Charles Dana arrived at 8:30 p.m. Stanton was there, up from his sick bed, and he and Lincoln were in his office. Major Thomas Eckert, supervisor of military telegraphs, would bring in the returns and Stanton would read them. Then Lincoln would look them over and comment on them. During a lull the president called Dana over. "Dana, have you ever read any of the writings of Petroleum V. Nasby?" he asked. "No, sir," Dana said; "I have only looked at some of them, and they seemed to be quite funny." "Well," Lincoln said, "let me read you a specimen," and he pulled out a thin yellow pamphlet from his breast pocket and began to read aloud.

"Mr. Stanton viewed these proceedings with great impatience, as I could see," Dana wrote, "but Mr. Lincoln paid no attention to that. He would read a page or a story, pause to consider a new election telegram, and then open the book again and go ahead with a new passage. Finally, Mr. Chase came in, and presently somebody else, and then the reading was interrupted. Mr. Stanton went to the door and beckoned me into the next room. I shall never forget the fire of his indignation at what seemed to him to be mere nonsense." Stanton, who had no sense of humor, considered Lincoln reading what he considered "balderdash" while the destiny of the country was being decided was something akin to Nero fiddling while Rome burned. He could not understand that it was the safety valve of humor that saved Lincoln from the pressures of responsibility and the natural despondency of his melancholy temperament.[26]

All evening the reports that straggled in over the fragile telegraph were favorable. One came in that Lincoln was ahead in New York state by 10,000 votes, but he refused to believe it. Soon Horace Greeley wired that the lead in New York was 4,000 and Lincoln said that was a lot more reasonable. By midnight it was pretty certain that he would carry New York, Pennsylvania, Maryland, Ohio, Indiana, Michigan, Wisconsin, and the New England states. Lincoln was concerned that his home state of Illinois had not been heard from, nor the states west of the Mississippi, but it was almost certain that he had been reelected, "and the few gentlemen left in the office congratulated him very warmly on the result," Brooks said. "Lincoln took the matter very calmly, showing not the least elation or excitement, but said that he would admit that he was glad to be relieved of all suspense, and that he was grateful that the verdict of the people was likely to be so full, clear, and unmistakable that there could be no dispute."[27]

At about 2 a.m. on the ninth, a messenger arrived from the White House with word that a crowd was serenading outside his window. So he walked home and in answer to repeated calls made a little speech in which, after some preliminaries, he said: "I earnestly believe that the consequences of this day's work, if it be as you assure me and as now seems probable, will be to the lasting advantage, if not to the very salvation, of the country. I cannot at this hour say what has been the result of the election; but, whatever it may be, I have no desire to modify this opinion—that all who have labored to-day in behalf of the Union organization, have wrought for the best interests of their country and the world, not only for the present, but for all future ages. I am thankful to God for this approval of the people. But while deeply grateful for this mark of their confidence in me, if I know my heart, my gratitude is free from any taint of personal triumph. I do not impugn the motives of any one; but I give thanks to the Almighty for this evidence of the people's resolution to stand by free government and the rights of humanity."[28]

The full results were not known for some time, but Lincoln carried every state except New Jersey, Kentucky, and Delaware, winning 212 electoral votes to McClellan's 21, with 55.09 percent of the popular vote, 2,203,831 to 1,797,019. McClellan resigned his commission in the army and started making plans for a trip to Europe.

The next day, the ninth, Lincoln told Noah Brooks: "Being only mortal, after all, I should have been a little mortified if I had been beaten in this canvass before the people; but the sting would have been more than compensated by the thought that the people had notified me that my official responsibilities were soon to be lifted off my back." Lincoln also told Brooks a curious story which the reporter wrote down in the President's own words, as nearly as he could remember them, immediately after he told it: "It was just after my election in 1860, when the news had been coming in thick and fast all day and there had been a great 'hurrah, boys,' so that I was well tired out, and went home to rest, throwing myself down on a lounge in my chamber. Opposite where I lay was a bureau with a swinging glass upon it. . . , and looking in that glass I saw myself reflected nearly at full length; but my face, I noticed, had *two* separate and distinct images, the tip of the nose of one being about three inches from the tip of the other. I was a little bothered, perhaps startled, and got up and looked in the glass, but the illusion vanished. On lying down again, I saw it a second time, plainer, if possible, than before; and then I noticed that one of the faces was a little paler—say five shades—than the other. I got up, and the thing melted away, and I went off, and in the excitement of the hour forgot all about it—nearly, but not quite, for the thing would once in a while come up, and give me a little pang as if something uncomfortable had happened. When I went home again that night I told my wife about it, and a few days afterward I made the experiment again, when (with a laugh), sure enough! the thing came back again; but I never succeeded in bringing the ghost back after that, though I once tried very industriously to show it to my wife, who was somewhat worried about it. She thought it was a 'sign' that I was to be elected to a second term of office, and that the paleness of one of the faces was an omen that I should not see life through the last term."[29]

Captain Thomas N. Conrad, who had been keeping an eye on Lincoln's movements for the Confederte kidnapping plot, was still in Washington when John Wilkes Booth arrived from New York that day.

---

1. Brandt, *The Man Who Tried to Burn New York*, 89.
2. Nicolay and Hay, *Abraham Lincoln*, 9:373–374.

3. Siepel, *Rebel*, 129.
4. Ibid.
5. Ibid., 130.
6. Ibid.
7. *Official Records*, 43:II:552–553.
8. Ibid., 39:III;660–661.
9. Horan, *Confederate Agent*, 181.
10. Milton, *Abraham Lincoln and the Fifth Column*, 331–332.
11. Horan, *Confederate Agent*, 191.
12. Ibid., 192.
13. Ibid., 193.
14. Henry, *"First With the Most" Forrest*, 380.
15. Foote, *The Civil War*, 3:624.
16. Long, *The Civil War Day by Day*, 583–594.
17. Castel, *General Sterling Price*, 247–248.
18. Ibid., 248.
19. Sherman, *Memoirs*, 643.
20. Nicolay and Hay, *Abraham Lincoln*, 9:375.
21. Ibid., 9:379.
22. Brooks, *Washington in Lincoln's Time*, 195–196.
23. Ibid., 196.
24. Nicolay and Hay, *Abraham Lincoln*, 9:376.
25. Ibid., 9:377.
26. Dana, *Recollections of the Civil War*, 227–228.
27. Brooks, *Washington in Lincoln's Time*, 197.
28. Basler, ed., *The Collected Works of Abraham Lincoln*, 8:96.
29. Brooks, *Washington in Lincoln's Time*, 199.

PART FOUR

GEORGIA AND TENNESSEE

"It surely was a strange event—two hostile armies marching in opposite directions, each in the full belief that it was achieving a final and conclusive result in a great war."

—Major General William Tecumseh Sherman

CHAPTER THIRTY-ONE

Grant Is Waiting for Us

9–16 November 1864

On that ninth day of November, up in the northeast corner of Tennessee, Brigadier General Alvan C. Gillem learned that Breckinridge was advancing with a Confederate force from southwestern Virginia that was reportedly much larger than his own brigade. Gillem therefore sent out patrols in various directions and retreated with his main force to Greeneville. From there he sent reports of the situation to Andrew Johnson at Nashville, military governor of Tennessee and vice president-elect of the United States, whom he considered his immediate superior since his brigade was designated as the Governor's Guard, and to Brigadier General Jacob Ammen at Knoxville, commander of the 4th Division of the 23rd Corps, part of Schofield's Department of the Ohio, which garrisoned east Tennessee. That evening Gillem's patrols returned with word that the Confederates were still advancing, and feeling that the position at Greeneville was not suitable for defense against superior numbers, Gillem fell back farther, to Bull's Gap.

Most of Schofield's 23rd Corps was moving through Nashville that day on its way to Pulaski, Tennessee, and Forrest's Confederate cavalry continued to move south toward Corinth, Mississippi, where it would turn to the east to join Hood at Florence, Alabama. At Kingston, Georgia, Sherman was organizing his remaining forces into two wings that day. Only one of his three department/army commanders was still with him in Georgia: Oliver O. Howard, commander of the Army of the Tennessee. That force, sometimes referred to after this as the Right Wing because the Department of the Tennessee was being discontinued, now consisted of only two corps since the 16th had been broken up: Peter Osterhaus' 15th and Frank Blair's 17th. Meanwhile, most of Howard's department, the rear-area garrisons in west Tennessee and Mississippi, was redesignated the Department of Mississippi and transferred from Sherman's Military Division of the Mississippi to Canby's Military Division of West Mississippi. (Western Kentucky was transferred to the Department of the Ohio.) The other two corps still with Sherman, Jefferson C. Davis' 14th and Henry Slocum's 20th, were part of Thomas's Army of the Cumberland, but since Thomas was back at Nashville they needed an overall commander at the front. Slocum was the senior of the two and got the job, and the two corps became known unofficially as the Army of Georgia or the Left Wing. Thomas was left with full authority over the Military Division of the Mississippi in Sherman's absence.

It is interesting that the two wings of Sherman's western army were commanded by two generals who had been corps commanders in the Army of the Potomac until they and their men had come west after Chickamauga. Succeeding Slocum in command of those very troops, the 20th Corps, was Brigadier General Alpheus S. Williams, Slocum's senior division commander.

Kilpatrick's 3rd Division of Wilson's new Cavalry Corps of the Military Division of the Mississippi would report directly to Sherman during the coming campaign, for which Sherman had a total of 52,796 infantrymen, 4,961 cavalrymen, and 1,788 artillerymen in his field force.

Assistant Secretary of War Dana wired Sherman that day about a newspaper story that had annoyed Secretary Stanton: "Yesterday's Indianapolis Journal says: 'Officers from Chattanooga report that Sherman returned to Atlanta early last week with five corps of his army, leaving two corps in Tennessee to watch Hood. He destroyed the railroad from Chattanooga to Atlanta, and is sending the iron into the former place. Atlanta was burned, and Sherman is now marching for Charleston, S.C.'" Sherman answered with what Dana called "two characteristic dispatches." The first said, "Dispatch of 9th read. Can't you send to Indianapolis and catch that fool and have him sent to me to work on the forts? All well." The second said, "If indiscreet newspaper men publish information too near the truth, counteract its effect by publishing other paragraphs calculated to mislead the enemy, such as 'Sherman's army has been re-enforced, especially in the cavalry, and he will soon move several columns in circuit, so as to catch Hood's army'; 'Sherman's destination is not Charleston, but Selma, where he will meet an army from the Gulf,' etc." In response, Dana wired Major General A. P. Hovey at Indianapolis: "In compliance with the request of Major-General Sherman, the Secretary of War directs that you ascertain what persons furnished the information respecting Sherman's alleged movement published in the Indianapolis Journal of the 8th inst. You will arrest them and send them under guard to such point in the Department of the Cumberland as Major-General Thomas may prefer, where they will be employed in hard labor upon the fortifications until General Sherman shall otherwise order."[1] But Hovey never found the person responsible.

"On the 10th of November the movement may be said to have fairly begun," Sherman wrote. "All the troops designed for the campaign were ordered to march for Atlanta, and General Corse, before evacuating his post at Rome, was ordered to burn all the mills, factories, etc., etc., that could be useful to the enemy, should he undertake to pursue us, or resume military possession of the country."[2]

In Montreal that day, George Sanders issued a statement which the Canadian newspapers carried on their front pages. He claimed that General Dix, commanding the Union army's Department of the East, was sending an expedition to Canada to seize the St. Albans raiders and return them to the United States by force. The British garrison was put on alert, with the cavalry prepared to mount at a moment's notice. The United States denied the claim, of course—it was pure fabrication—but Sanders charged that Stanton had backed down because he was afraid of the British. As a result, the raiders were more popular in Canada than ever.

"On the 10th of November," Horace Porter wrote, "enough was known at headquarters to make it plain that Lincoln was elected." That night Grant sent a telegram to Halleck asking him to "congratulate the President for me for the double victory. The election having passed off quietly, no bloodshed or riot throughout the land, is a victory worth more to the country than a battle won . . ."[3]

"On the night of November tenth," Noah Brooks wrote, "an impromptu procession, gay with banners and resplendent with lanterns and transparencies, marched up to the White House, and a vast crowd surged around the main entrance, filling the entire space within the grounds as far as the eye could reach from the house. Martial music, the cheers of people, and the roar of cannon, shook the sky. Tad, who was flying around from window to window arranging a small illumination on his own private account, was delighted and excited by the occasional shivering of the large panes of glass by the concussion of the air produced when the cannon in the driveway went off with tremendous noise. The President wrote out his little speech, and his appearance at 'the historic window' over the doorway in the portico was the signal for the maddest cheers from the crowd, and it was many minutes before the deafening racket permitted him to speak."[4]

Lincoln's secretaries, in their biography of him, said this speech, "while it has not received the world-wide fame of certain other of his utterances, is one of the weightiest and wisest of all his discourses." One of them stood beside him, holding a candle, while he read the speech he had jotted down. "Not very graceful," Lincoln commented on this arrangement, "but I am growing old enough not to care much for the manner of doing things." When the noise of the crowd finally abated enough to allow him to be heard, he said: "It has long been a grave question whether any government, not *too* strong for the liberties of its people, can be strong *enough* to maintain its own existence, in great emergencies.

"On this point the present rebellion brought our republic to a severe test; and a presidential election occuring in regular course during the rebellion added not a little to the strain. If the loyal people, *united,* were put to the utmost of their strength by the rebellion, must they not fail when *divided,* and partially paralized, by a political war among themselves?

"But the election was a necessity.

"We can not have free government without elections; and if the rebellion could force us to forego, or postpone a national election, it might fairly claim to have already conquered and ruined us. The strife of the election is but human-nature practically applied to the facts of the case. What has occurred in this case, must ever recur in similar cases. Human-nature will not change. In any future great national trial, compared with the men of this, we shall have as weak, and as strong; as silly and as wise; as bad and good. Let us, therefore, study the incidents of this, as philosophy to learn wisdom from, and none of them as wrongs to be revenged.

"But the election, along with its incidental, and undesirable strife, has done good too. It has demonstrated that a people's government can sustain a national election, in the midst of a great civil war. Until now it has not been known to the world that this was a possibility. It shows also how *sound,* and how *strong* we still are. It shows that, even among candidates of the same party, he who is most devoted to the Union, and most opposed to treason, can receive most of the people's votes. It shows also, to the extent yet known, that we have more men now, than we had when the war began. Gold is good in its place; but living, brave, patriotic men, are better than gold.

"But the rebellion continues; and now that the election is over, may not all, having a common interest, re-unite in a common effort, to save our common country? For my own part I have striven, and shall strive to avoid placing any obstacle in the way. So long as I have been here I have not willingly planted a thorn in any man's bosom.

"While I am deeply sensible to the high compliment of a re-election; and duly grateful, as I trust, to Almighty God for having directed my countrymen to a right conclusion, as I think, for their own good, it adds nothing to my satisfaction that any other man may be disappointed or pained by the result.

"May I ask those who have not differed with me, to join with me, in this same spirit toward those who have?

"And now, let me close by asking three hearty cheers for our brave soldiers and seamen and their gallant and skilful commanders."[5]

At a meeting next day, the eleventh, the president had a surprise for his cabinet. "Gentlemen," he said, "do you remember last summer I asked you all to sign your names to the back of a paper of which I did not show you the inside? This is it. Now, Mr. Hay," he said, handing the paper to his secretary, "see if you can get this open without tearing it." It took some doing, but when the paper was opened Lincoln read it: "This morning, as for some days past, it seems exceedingly probable that this Administration will not be reelected. Then it will be my duty to so cooperate with the President-elect as to save the Union between the election and the inauguration; as he will have secured the election on such grounds that he cannot possibly save it afterward."

"You will remember," Lincoln said, "that this was written at a time six days before the Chicago nominating Convention, when as yet we had no adversary, and seemed to have no friends." He said that he had resolved, in the case of McClellan's election, to see the general and to try to agree on a policy that would bring a rapid end to the war. "And the General would answer you 'Yes, Yes,'" Stanton replied, "and the next day when you saw him again and pressed these views upon him, he would say, 'Yes, Yes'; and so on forever, and would have done nothing at all."[6]

Napoleon Collins, captain of the USS *Wachusetts*, steamed into Hampton Roads that day with the CSS *Florida* still in tow.

In eastern Tennessee on the eleventh, Basil Duke's (formerly John Hunt Morgan's) brigade of Breckinridge's Confederates pushed the Union rear guard back upon Gillem's main Union position at Bull's Gap while Vaughn's Brigade was sent to circle around and get behind the Federals. Gillem was aware of Vaughn's move and telegraphed an appeal to Ammen at Knoxville for reinforcements to keep his line of retreat open.

In the Shenandoah Valley on the eleventh, Early's Confederate forces, having left their bivouacs at New Market the day before, probed Sheridan's position. There had been rumors that Sheridan was detaching troops to send to Petersburg, but they were not true. Early found that the Federals had pulled back from Cedar Creek to Kernstown, where they were entrenching. This was the position Sheridan had selected for defending the lower Valley, and the Winchester & Potomac Railroad was being put back in service between Stephenson's Depot and Harper's Ferry to serve as his supply line.

Sherman and Thomas exchanged long messages on the 11th. Thomas heard that day that A. J. Smith's forces had begun to reach Paducah, Kentucky, where the Tennessee River meets the Ohio, so there was no doubt that they would get to Nashville long before Hood could get there from Florence, Alabama. Thomas was, as Sherman put it, "perfectly satisfied with his share of the army."[7] That same day, Thomas sent Schofield to take command at Pulaski, where his 23rd Corps was in the process of joining the 4th. The next day, Sherman left Kingston for Atlanta. At about noon he and his staff reached Cartersville, where they sat on the porch of a house near the road to rest. His telegraph operator got the wire down from a nearby pole and attached it to a small pocket instrument which he held in his lap. He called Chattanooga and in reply received a message for Sherman relayed from Thomas at Nashville:

"Your dispatch of twelve o'clock last night is received. I have no fears that Beauregard can do us any harm now, and, if he attempts to follow you, I will follow him as far as possible. If he does not follow you, I will then thoroughly organize my troops, and believe I shall have men enough to ruin him unless he gets out of the way very rapidly. The country of Middle Alabama, I learn, is teeming with supplies this year, which will be greatly to our advantage . . . I am now convinced that the greater part of Beauregard's army is near Florence and Tuscumbia, and that you will have at least a clear road before you for several days, and that your success will fully equal your expectations."[8]

Sherman answered simply, "Dispatch received—all right." Then somewhere up the line some of his men burned a bridge and severed the telegraph line, cutting Sherman off from communication with the rear. "As we rode on toward Atlanta that night," he wrote, "I remember the railroad-trains going to the rear with a furious speed; the engineers and the few men about the trains waving us an affectionate adieu. It surely was a strange event—two hostile armies marching in opposite directions, each in the full belief that it was achieving a final and conclusive result in a great war; and I was strongly inspired with the feeling that the movement on our part was a direct attack upon the rebel army and the rebel capital at Richmond, though a full thousand miles of hostile country intervened, and that, for better or worse, it would end the war."[9]

In east Tennessee on the twelfth, Breckinridge planned a complicated concentric attack upon Gillem's position at Bull's Gap. All of his artillery—six howitzers—and some dismounted cavalry, all under the command of Colonel George B. Crittenden, would demonstrate against Gillem's front to keep him pinned in place; Vaughn's Brigade, having completed its circuit, would attack from the rear; while Breckinridge would personally lead a body of dismounted troopers from various commands, under Lieutenant Colonel Alston, plus Duke's Brigade, temporarily dismounted, up the mountain for a descent upon Gillem's left. In his report of this action, Breckinridge sounds rather proud and perhaps surprised that "the plan was carried out with perfect exactitude, and the enemy actually attacked at the same time in front, flank, and rear."[10]

Gillem reported that his troops slept on their arms on the night of the eleventh-twelfth and were in line of battle by 4 a.m. The Confederate artillery opened fire at dawn, but Gillem, suspecting correctly that this was just a feint to keep his attention, forbid his own guns to return fire. "About 6 a.m.," Gillem said, "our picket on the extreme left was attacked. I immediately concluded that the enemy were endeavoring to turn our extreme left and get in rear of the battery." He ordered the 13th Tennessee Cavalry (Union) to hold the left end of one ridge and six companies of the 8th Tennessee to hold what he called "the other left," meaning, evidently, the left of another ridge. And as more and more Confederates were seen to be massing on this flank, more Federals were sent to reinforce it. "The enemy, led by Generals Breckinridge and Duke, assaulted with great fury," Gillem reported, "many of them actually entering the rude works behind which our troops were posted, but every man knew that if these hills were taken all was lost, fought with desperation, and finally repulsed the enemy, who left 27 dead and many wounded in front of our lines. Some of their dead were inside our breastworks. Whilst this assault was being made a strong force advanced against our front, evidently to prevent our weakening that point by sending re-enforcements to our left. At the same time General Vaughn made an attack in our rear on the Knoxville road. This attack was handsomely repulsed by Colonel Parsons with Ninth Tennessee Cavalry, the enemy leaving 1 captain and 8 privates dead on the field."[11]

Breckinridge said, "The force on the mountain succeeded in carrying a line of works, but the assault as a whole did not succeed, most of the troops being unaccustomed to that mode of fighting."[12] Gillem said, "Although skirmishing and artillery firing continued during the day, the enemy did not again renew the assault. During the entire day I had been anxiously expecting the arrival of a train at Russellville with bread, my men having had none for two days. I dispatched messengers to General Ammen urging him to send me ammunition and bread, and if possible re-enforcements."[13]

In the Shenandoah Valley on the twelfth, as Sheridan put it, "Early's reconnaissance north of Cedar Creek ended in a rapid withdrawal of his infantry after feeling my front, and with the usual ill-fortune to his cavalry; Merritt and Custer driving Rosser and Lomax with ease across Cedar Creek on the Middle and Back roads, while Powell's cavalry struck McCausland near Stony Point, and after capturing two pieces of artillery and about three hundred officers and men, chased him into the Luray Valley."[14]

That same day, one of Mosby's scouts, a frail young man named John Russell, came into the Union lines under a white flag with a message for Sheridan. Custer threatened to hang him in retaliation for his men who had been killed the week before, but Russell reminded him that Mosby still held a hundred Federal prisoners who could be put to death if he was harmed. Finally he had been blindfolded and brought to Sheridan's headquarters. The general waved him to a seat while reading the message he had brought. It said: "Some time in the month of September, during my absence from my command, six of my men, who had been captured by your forces, were hung and shot in the streets of Front Royal, by the order and in the immediate presence of Brigadier-General Custer. Since then another (captured by a Colonel Powell on a plundering expedition into Rappahannock) shared a similar fate. A label affixed to the coat of one of the murdered men declared that 'this would be the fate of Mosby and all his men.'

"Since the murder of my men, not less than 700 prisoners, including many officers of high rank, captured from your army by this command, have been forwarded to Richmond, but the execution of my purpose of retaliation was deferred in order, as far as possible, to confine its operation to the men of Custer and Powell. Accordingly, on the 6th instance, seven of your men were by my order executed on the Valley turnpike, your highway of travel.

"Hereafter any prisoners falling into my hands will be treated with the kindness due to their condition, unless some new act of barbarity shall compel me reluctantly to adopt a line of policy repugnant to humanity."[15]

It was evidently on Saturday, 12 November, that John Wilkes Booth went to Charles County, Maryland, southeast of Washington, to make contact with pro-Confederate Marylanders who would be useful in any get-away after capturing President Lincoln. He delivered the letter of introduction given to him by Patrick C. Miller in Canada to Dr. William Queen after being brought from Bryantown by Queen's son, Joseph. The next morning he went with Queen and his son-in-law, John C. Thompson, to mass at St. Mary's Catholic Church in Bryantown, where Thompson introduced him to another pro-Confederate doctor, Samuel A. Mudd.

"Early on the morning of the 13th," General Gillem reported from east Tennessee, "the firing began along the entire front, but the day wore away without an assault. My ammunition, both for artillery and small-arms, was almost exhausted, and orders were given not to throw away a single shot. The forage in the vicinity having been exhausted, the horses were failing fast, as we were unable to forage except at night. The men having fought for four days without bread or salt, and as I could see re-enforcements of infantry arriving in the enemy's camp, I determined to evacuate the gap on the night of the 13th, but still hoping that ammunition and bread might arrive I sent down beyond Russellville to ascertain. The messenger returned at 7 p.m., not having heard of any train."[16]

The Confederate reinforcements which Gillem had seen were about 600 men under Colonel John B. Palmer from Asheville, North Carolina. "And the same night," Breckinridge reported, "I moved with Vaughn and Duke to turn the enemy's right, Colonel Crittenden following with Colonel Palmer's force, the artillery, and the dismounted men of the other commands. The enemy having foolishly withdrawn his pickets, we passed without opposition or notice through Taylor's Gap, about two miles and a half below Bull's Gap . . ."[17]

"The moon shone brightly," Gillem remembered, "and at 8 p.m. my forces moved out . . ." Leading the way were two companies of his cavalry, then came his wagon train, his artillery, and then most of the rest of his cavalry. "Col. John K. Miller, with the Thirteenth Tennessee

Cavalry and one battalion of the Eighth, was left in our position at the gap to prevent the enemy obtaining a knowledge of our movements until the train should be well on its way. Colonel Miller had orders to move at 10.30 p.m., and act as a rear guard." His column had only gone about four miles and was approaching Whitesburg when Gillem learned that the Confederates were advancing along a parallel road only about two miles away. "I was confident that the rebel commander was ignorant of the real character of my movement," he said.[18] So he ordered his wagons and his artillery, which was out of ammunition, to turn off to the right at Whitesburg and cross the Holston River before turning to the southeast toward Knoxville, and he sent orders for Colonel Miller with the rear guard to do the same, while with the rest of his force he intended to continue on to Russellville, where he expected the Rebels to come out on the main road. He would attack them and hold them there until his wagons and guns were across the river. Then, if necessary, he would fall back and cross the river with the rest of his force.

Just then he received word that a railroad train had arrived at Morristown, southwest of Russellville, with ammunition, provisions, and reinforcements consisting of 600 infantrymen and a battalion of cavalry. This changed his plans. If he fell back across the Holston with his entire force the Rebels would be free to fall upon these reinforcements. The infantry might get away on the train, but the battalion of cavalry could not and would be overwhelmed. On the other hand, he believed that, with their help and the ammunition they were bringing, he could hold off the Rebels, so instead of crossing the river he turned his entire column, wagons, guns, and all, down the road toward Russellville and sent word for the train and the reinforcements to meet him there. But when he got to Russellville there was no sign of the reinforcements.

He therefore ordered Colonel Patton, with two battalions of his 8th Tennessee Cavalry, to hold the intersection of his road with the one the Rebels were following until his wagons and guns got past. Then he moved forward to the intersection with another road and was in the process of posting Colonel Parsons' 9th Tennessee there when he heard the sound of firing from Patton's position. The 8th Tennessee beat off the first attack, but the Confederates came on again and in greater force, driving it back in disorder. However, the tail of the wagon train had safely passed, and the 9th Tennessee held the Rebels in check for about an hour, until its ammunition was all gone.

"In the meantime," Gillem reported, "as the re-enforcement, who were said to be in Morristown, did not arrive on the field, I sent several messengers urging them to come forward, among others Lieut. D. M. Nelson, one of my aides, to whom the commanding officer, Major

Smith, replied that he did not come there to fight but to protect the train. I rode back myself to Morristown and requested Major Smith to move forward and assist in holding the enemy in check. To my surprise he informed me that his entire force was 302 infantry and dismounted cavalry, and that he did not consider that he would be justifiable in moving the train forward or in separating his men from it, but finally agreed to move the train a mile down the Knoxville road and form his men on a crest of the hill. This was done with as little delay as possible, and the artillery posted in a position which commanded the road, to fire away its few remaining rounds of cannister."[19]

The Confederates came on across an open field, 2,500 to 3,000 strong, but when they were within 60 yards the fire of the Union artillery, infantry, and dismounted cavalry drove them back several hundred yards. However, with their ammunition about gone, the Federal troopers then panicked and ran, and the infantrymen joined them. Knowing that his guns were almost out of ammunition and seeing that their supports were rapidly evaporating, Gillem ordered them to fall back as well. But before they had gone more than a few hundred yards, the Rebels charged again and easily broke through the few Federals who were still facing them. "Their entire force charged past us," Gillem said, "without stopping to take prisoners, and continued the pursuit of our forces this side of Morristown, capturing artillery, ambulance and wagon train."[20] The Federals who could get away, including Gillem himself, did not stop until they reached Strawberry Plains, a little northeast of Knoxville. Colonel Miller's rear guard, meanwhile, arrived at Russellville and found the Confederates too numerous to take on alone. After one charge he tried to work around the Rebels, but when he approached Morristown he learned that Gillem and the rest of the command had retreated, so he crossed to the north side of the Holston River and worked his way down to Strawberry Plains.

"The results of this night attack," Breckinridge reported, "were a good many of the enemy killed and wounded, about 300 prisoners, and all his artillery, wagon trains, &c. This force was routed with much confusion, and few of them stopped this side of Knoxville."[21] Gillem said that, "Had my troops behaved with calmness and deliberation I might have been able to have withdrawn with less loss in property, but more in men."[22]

On the next day, the fifteenth, after returning to his New Market camps and having satisfied himself that there was nothing he could do with Sheridan for the time being, Early started Kershaw's Division on its way to rejoin the 1st Corps at Richmond.

Federal troops were also returning to their starting place that day. The first snow of the season was falling on New York as Ben Butler and his troops left the city to return to Virginia. The Confederate officers in the city immediately pressed McMasters and the Copperheads to set Thanksgiving Day, the 24th, as the date for putting their plan into action. Within 24 hours they were told to forget it. There would be no revolt. The Copperheads did not think there was now any chance that the South could win the war, and McMasters personally refused to have any further connection with the plot. The stunned Confederates argued among themselves over whether to go on with their part of the plan, setting fire to the city. In the end they decided to go through with it, as revenge for Sheridan's destruction in the Shenandoah and as a diversion to draw Union troops away from Virginia. In the mean time, the New York Police Department, with only nineteen detectives, discontinued following the Rebel agents as they had failed to come up with anything incriminating against them.

John Wilkes Booth deposited $1,500 in Jay Cooke's Washington bank on 16 November and left for New York to meet his brothers, Edwin and Junius. The three of them would be appearing in a benefit performance of "Julius Caesar" at the Winter Garden Theatre on the 25th to raise money for the Shakespeare Statue Fund.

That same day was the beginning of what was called "the great turkey movement" by Assistant Secretary of War Charles A. Dana. "The presidential election was hardly over before the people of the North began to prepare Thanksgiving boxes for the army. George Bliss, Jr., of New York, telegraphed me, on November 16th, that they had twenty thousand turkeys ready in that city to send to the front . . . From Philadelphia I received a message asking for transportation to Sheridan's army for 'boxes containing four thousand turkeys, and Heaven knows what else, as a Thanksgiving dinner for the brave fellows.' And so it was from all over the country."[23]

There were, however, over 60,000 Union soldiers who would have to harvest their own Thanksgiving dinner. "About 7 A.M. of November 16th," Sherman wrote, "we rode out of Atlanta by the Decatur road, filled by the marching troops and wagons of the Fourteenth Corps; and reaching the hill, just outside of the old rebel works, we naturally paused to look back upon the scenes of our past battles. We stood upon the very ground whereon was fought the bloody battle of July 22d, and could see the copse of wood where McPherson fell. Behind us lay Atlanta, smouldering in ruins, the black smoke rising high in air, and hanging like a pall over the ruined city."[24]

Sherman was determined to leave nothing behind that would be of any use to an enemy army, and the destruction had gone on all the previous day. Fire was first applied to an iron foundry, an oil refinery, and a freight warehouse. "First bursts of smoke," wrote Sherman's adjutant general, Major Henry Hitchcock, "dense, black volumes, then tongues of flame, then huge waves of fire roll up into the sky: Presently the skeletons of great warehouses stand out in relief against . . . sheets of roaring, blazing, furious flames . . . as one fire sinks, another rises . . . lurid, angry, dreadful to look upon."[25] The depot, round house, and machine shops of the Georgia Railroad were fired, and soon the flames spread, helped by Confederate artillery shells that had been stored in one of the machine shops. The Atlanta Hotel, dry-goods stores, theaters, slave markets, the jail, even the fire stations, went up in smoke, along with hundreds of empty houses. When the flames threatened the quarter-masters' and commissaries' warehouses they gave up trying to issue food and clothing to the remaining troops in an orderly fashion and told the men to just take what they wanted before it burned up.

The soldiers soon found a supply of whiskey, and before long the streets were full of drunken men who decided to lend a hand at all this arson. By nightfall the fires were bigger and brighter than ever. A young girl, a member of one of the fifty families remaining in the city, said the soldiers "were going around setting houses on fire where they were not watched," adding that "they behaved very badly." A Union officer confirmed that "drunken soldiers on foot and on horseback raced up and down the streets, while the buildings on either side were solid sheets of flames." He said the scene surpassed "all the pictures and verbal descriptions of hell."[26]

Sherman spent most of that night in the streets with his engineers trying to keep the flames from spreading to any occupied houses. One of his aides recorded the scene: "The heaven is one expanse of lurid fire; the air is filled with flying, burning cinders; buildings covering two hundred acres are in ruins or in flames; every instant there is the sharp detonation or the smothered booming sound of exploding shells and powder concealed in the buildings, and then the sparks and flame shoot away up into the black and red roof, scattering cinders far and wide. These are the machine shops where have been forged and cast the Rebel cannon, shot and shell that have carried death to many a brave defender of our Nation's honor . . . The city, which, next to Richmond, has furnished more material for prosecuting the war than any other in the South, exists no more."[27]

Most of Sherman's troops had marched out of the city on the fifteenth, except for the 14th Corps and the troops in charge of the official destruction. Now, on the morning of the sixteenth, Sherman looked away from the ruined city. "Away off in the distance," he wrote, "on the McDonough road, was the rear of Howard's column, the gun-barrels glistening in the sun, the white-topped wagons stretching away to the south; and right before us the Fourteenth Corps, marching steadily and rapidly, with a cheery look and swinging pace, that made light of the thousand miles that lay between us and Richmond. Some band, by accident, struck up the anthem of 'John Brown's soul goes marching on;' the men caught up the strain, and never before or since have I heard the chorus of 'Glory, glory, hallelujah!' done with more spirit, or in better harmony of time and place. Then we turned our horses' heads to the east . . ."

"The day was extremely beautiful," Sherman wrote, "clear sunlight, with bracing air, and an unusual feeling of exhilaration seemed to pervade all minds—a feeling of something to come, vague and undefined, still full of venture and intense interest. Even the common soldiers caught the inspiration, and many a group called out to me as I worked my way past them, 'Uncle Billy, I guess Grant is waiting for us at Richmond!' Indeed, the general sentiment was that we were marching for Richmond, and that there we should end the war, but how and when they seemed to care not; nor did they measure the distance, or count the cost in life, or bother their brains about the great rivers to be crossed, and the food required for man and beast, that had to be gathered by the way. There was a 'devil-may-care' feeling pervading officers and men, that made me feel the full load of responsibility, for success would be accepted as a matter of course, whereas, should we fail, this 'march' would be adjudged the wild adventure of a crazy fool."

As Sherman and his staff rode eastward "Atlanta was soon lost behind the screen of trees, and became a thing of the past. Around it clings many a thought of desperate battle, of hope and fear, that now seem like the memory of a dream; and I have never seen the place since."[28]

---

1. Dana, *Recollections of the Civil War*, 193–194.
2. Sherman, *Memoirs*, 643–644.
3. Porter, *Campaigning With Grant*, 324.
4. Brooks, *Washington in Lincoln's Time*, 200.
5. Basler, ed., *The Collected Works of Abraham Lincoln*, 8:100–101.
6. Allan Nevins, *The War for the Union* (New York, 1971), Vol. 4, 200.

7. Sherman, *Memoirs*, 644.

8. Ibid.

9. Ibid., 644–645.

10. *Official Records*, 39:I:893.

11. Ibid., 39:I:889.

12. Ibid., 39:I:893.

13. Ibid., 39:I:889.

14. Sheridan, *Personal Memoirs*, 2:98.

15. Jones, *Ranger Mosby*, 227–228.

16. *Official Records*, 39:I:889.

17. Ibid., 39:I:893.

18. Ibid., 39:I:889–890.

19. Ibid., 39:I:890–891.

20. Ibid., 39:I:891.

21. Ibid., 39:I:893.

22. Ibid., 39:I:891.

23. Dana, *Recollections of the Civil War*, 220.

24. Sherman, *Memoirs*, 655.

25. Burke Davis, *Sherman's March* (New York, 1980), 6.

26. Earl Schenck Miers, *The General Who Marched to Hell* (New York, 1951), 220.

27. Ibid., 221.

28. Sherman, *Memoirs*, 655–656.

CHAPTER THIRTY-TWO

All That Devils Could Wish For

16–24 November 1864

Martha Amanda Quillen watched from her home in Decatur, Georgia, that evening as a line of flames approached from the direction of Atlanta. "As far as the eye could reach," she recorded, "the lurid flames of burning buildings lit up the heavens . . . I could stand out on the verandah and for two or three miles watch them as they came on. I could mark when they reached the residence of each and every friend on the road." She heard "the eternal gab of the Yankee army" and saw the flames as outbuildings at each house were set afire. "I heard the wild shout they raised as torch in hand they started for the next house." By watching the fires, she calculated the Federals' rate of approach and "ascertained almost to the very minute when the torch would be set to our own house." Her expectations were somewhat thrown off, however, when a Union officer turned her house into his headquarters and his guards turned away all Federals who approached with torches. Nevertheless, she dreaded the dawn. "I prayed that I might never see the destruction, the deep distress, the morn would reveal to me." But she did live to see the dawn, and many more thereafter. Eventually she managed to take a slightly more philosophical view, but only slightly. "That too has all passed," she said, "and lives only in memory; but no one I hope will ever expect me to love Yankees."[1]

Soldiers of the 2nd Minnesota sprawled on the lawn of a Georgia farmhouse that afternoon while others lined up to get water from a nearby spring and three or four Southern women sat in rocking chairs on the porch of the house and watched nervously. One of the Federals noticed that the ground where he was lying had recently been dug up, and with visions of buried treasure called for his companions to help him uncover whatever cache of gold coins or silver spoons might be buried below. They found a small box, but it gave off a foul odor, and when they opened it they found a dead spaniel. "It looks like poor Curly will get no peace," one of the women on the porch remarked. "That's the fourth time he's been dug up today."[2]

Sherman's two wings marched in different directions. Sherman himself rode with Slocum's left wing, The Army of Georgia, which moved eastward from Atlanta as if headed for Augusta. Howard's right wing, The Army of the Tennessee, marched to the south, toward Macon. Sherman planned this in order to induce the Confederates to send what few troops they had in the state to defend those two points. But eventually both wings would turn toward the center and converge on Milledgeville, the state capital. Kilpatrick's cavalry division preceded Howard's wing toward Macon, and on the sixteenth it encountered some of Wheeler's Confederate cavalry and part of the Georgia militia, under Major General Howell Cobb, in Hood's old defenses at Lovejoy's Station. Kilpatrick's 1st Brigade, under Colonel Eli H. Murray, charged and carried the works, capturing two 3-inch rifles that the Rebels had taken from Stoneman's cavalry on it disastrous raid of three months before. The Rebels retreated in what Kilpatrick called great confusion to Bear Creek Station, where they tried to make a stand, but the 10th Ohio Cavalry charged and broke their formation, driving them to Griffin, fourteen miles away. "Wheeler being disposed of for a time," Kilpatrick reported, "I separated my command, marching on two roads, that the greater amount of cotton, cotton gins, and other valuable property might be destroyed."[3]

On that first night out of Atlanta Sherman camped by the road near Stone Mountain. "The whole horizon was lurid with the bonfires of railties," he wrote, "and groups of men all night were carrying the heated rails to the nearest trees, and bending them around the trunks." His chief engineer had provided tools for ripping up the rails and twisting them when hot. "But the best and easiest way is the one I have described, of heating the middle of the iron-rails on bonfires made of the cross-ties, and then winding them around a telegraph-pole or the trunk of some convenient sapling. I attached much importance to this destruction of the railroad, gave it my own personal attention, and made reiterated orders to others on the subject."[4]

In east Tennessee, Breckinridge's Confederates closed up to the Federal position at Strawberry Plains, just east of Knoxville. "I found strong works on the opposite side of the river," Breckinridge wrote, "manned and furnished with artillery. The flanks of this position were well protected and it was quite unassailable in front by the troops at my command. The enemy received re-enforcements from the garrisons beyond Knoxville and probably a regiment or two from Chattanooga. We had artillery firing and active skirmishing for several days, and General Vaughn, crossing the Holston above, made a demonstration on their rear and burned the railroad bridge over Flat Creek, but I made no serious attack on the position."[5] Union generals, meanwhile, kept the telegraph wires busy in an effort to scrape up reinforcements for east Tennessee. General Steedman was able to send some infantry detachments that had been left behind by Sherman. And Major General George Stoneman, who had recently been exchanged from Confederate captivity and designated second-in-command of the Department of the Ohio to look after it while Schofield was in the field, ordered Brevet Major General S. G. Burbridge, commander of the District of Kentucky, to assemble as many of his mounted units as possible. These would either be sent into east Tennessee to threaten Breckinridge's communications or used to defend Kentucky in case Hood or Forrest got that far.

It was on that same sixteenth of November, while Sherman's army was marching away from Atlanta, that Forrest's cavalry began crossing Hood's pontoon bridge from Tuscumbia, Alabama, to Florence, on the north side of the Tennessee. The day before, Hood had put Forrest in charge of all of the cavalry with his army, which consisted of his own two divisions, under Chalmers and Buford, plus Red Jackson's division. Wheeler's cavalry corps was down in Georgia, keeping an eye on Sherman.

It was not until the seventeenth that Hood and Beauregard received word from Georgia that Sherman had burned Atlanta and the bridge across the Chattahoochee River, thus abandoning his line of supply, and was marching toward Macon with four corps. Up until then they had both thought that Sherman was hastening north from Georgia to Tennessee and that the Federals concentrating at Decatur, Alabama, and Pulaski, Tennessee, were the vanguard of his entire army. They were also aware that reinforcements were coming up the Mississippi from Vicksburg to Memphis and knew that A. J. Smith's divisions were collecting at Paducah. Beauregard now gave Hood two choices: either send troops back to Georgia to defend it against Sherman, or advance immediately into middle Tennessee in the hope that such a move would cause Sherman to turn back to defend that area. Hood chose the latter course, but delays in accumulating supplies meant it would still be a few days before he could move. Beauregard therefore ordered Richard Taylor to send to Georgia any troops he could spare from his Department of Alabama, Mississippi and East Louisiana and to go himself to command all forces in Georgia from his own and Hood's departments.

With the election over, the weather turning bad, and no special operations in the works for the Richmond-Petersburg front, Grant started on the seventeenth on a trip to visit his wife and children, still living at Burlington, New Jersey.

From his headquarters at Corinth, Mississippi, Beauregard issued a call on the eighteenth "To the People of Georgia: Arise for the defense of your native soil! Rally around your patriotic Governor and gallant soldiers! Obstruct and destroy all the roads in Sherman's front, flank, and rear, and his army will soon starve in your midst. Be confident. Be resolute. Trust in an overruling Providence, and success will soon crown your efforts. I hasten to join you in the defense of your homes and firesides." And on the same day, Senator B. H. Hill, at Richmond, also issued a call "To the People of Georgia: You have now the best opportunity ever yet presented to destroy the enemy. Put every thing at the disposal of our generals; remove all provisions from the path of the invader, and put all obstructions in his path. Every citizen with his gun, and every negro with his spade and axe, can do the work of a soldier. You can destroy the enemy by retarding his march. Georgians, be firm! Act promptly, and fear not!"[6]

On his second day out of Atlanta, Slocum's column came to the town of Covington, Georgia. There an old farmer named Jones made his stand on a street corner. When four Union horsemen rode past he blasted one of them out of the saddle. The other three shot him down, of course, and he lay in the street for a long time. When the Union infantry arrived, the soldiers closed up their ranks, the color-bearers unfurled their banners, and the bands struck up patriotic marches. "The white people came out of their houses to behold the sight," Sherman wrote, "spite of their deep hatred of the invaders, and the negroes were simply frantic with joy. Whenever they heard my name, they clustered about my horse, shouted and prayed in their peculiar style, which had a natural eloquence that would have moved a stone."

About four miles beyond the town Sherman camped for the night at the crossing of the Ulcofauhachee River. "And I walked up to a plantation-house close by, where were assembled many negroes, among them an old, gray-haired man, of as fine a head as I ever saw. I asked him if he understood about the war and its progress. He said he did; that he had been looking for the 'angel of the Lord' ever since he was knee-high, and, though we professed to be fighting for the Union, he supposed that slavery was the cause, and that our success was to be his freedom. I asked him if all the negro slaves comprehended this fact, and he said they surely did. I then explained to him that we wanted the slaves to remain where they were, and not to load us down with useless mouths, which would eat up the food needed for our fighting-men; that our success was their assured freedom; that we could receive a few of their young, hearty men as pioneers; but that, if they followed us in swarms of old and young, feeble and helpless, it would simply load us down and cripple us in our great task . . . and I believe that old man spread this message to the slaves, which was carried from mouth to mouth, to the very end of our journey, and that it in part saved us from the great danger we incurred of swelling our numbers so that famine would have attended our progress."[7]

In the Shenandoah Valley that day, the eighteenth, two companies of Mosby's command, under Captain Adolphus "Dolly" Richards, ambushed the special detachment of Union scouts that had been especially organized for the purpose of tracking down Mosby and disposing of him. Three days before, these Federals had ambushed some of Mosby's men near Berry's Ferry, killing two, and that was only the latest blow they had dealt to the rangers' command. Mosby himself was disabled by a very bad cold, but he was determined to turn the tables on these Yankees. Richards trailed the Federal unit to Kabletown then he concealed one company, attacked with the other and then feigned retreat. This was a ploy almost as old as warfare itself, but it worked like a charm. The Northerners pursued the retreating company and ran right into the ambush set by the other, at which point the retreating company whirled about and counterattacked. The Union commander, Captain Richard Blazer, an old Indian fighter who had put his experience to work in tracking down Mosby, temporarily got away with a few of his men, but a fourth of his 100 men were killed and most of the rest were either wounded or captured or both. Three of Blazer's men eventually reached the safety of one of Sheridan's cavalry brigades, bringing word of the disaster that had befallen his command.

Blazer himself was chased and caught by four of Mosby's rangers, one of whom unhorsed him by cracking him over the head with his revolver. One of these four Confederates was Lewis Powell, better known to history as Lewis Payne, who would hang the next spring as one of the conspirators in the assassination of President Lincoln. Blazer's second in command was a Lieutenant Cole. Earlier, Cole had almost killed a captured member of Mosby's battalion by hoisting him off the ground with a rope around his neck in an effort to get information out of him. Now this prisoner, whose name was John Puryear, clubbed his guard, grabbed a revolver, and took off after Cole. By the time he caught up with him, however, the lieutenant had been wounded and had surrendered to another ranger, John Alexander. Puryear rode up to Cole and pointed his revolver in the lieutenant's face and cocked it. "Don't shoot this man. He's surrendered," Alexander yelled. "This son of a bitch tried to hang me this morning!" Puryear cried. "Is that true?" Alexander asked Cole, but while he was waiting for the answer Puryear fired.[8]

Grant's trip to see his family in New Jersey was interrupted that day by a telegram from Brigadier General John A. Rawlins, his chief of staff, back at City Point: "Scouts who left Richmond yesterday afternoon report that the day before all the rolling-stock that could be spared from other railroads was put on the Central and sent north; that wagon trains were sent in the same direction, and that it was understood in the city that they were sent for the purpose of bringing Early back."[9] Rawlins sent a similar message to Sheridan, and the next day Grant wired the latter: "It is reported from Richmond that Early has been recalled from the Valley. If you are satisfied this is so send the Sixth Corps to City Point without delay. If your cavalry can cut the Virginia Central road now is the time to do it."[10]

That same day, the nineteenth, President Lincoln ordered the blockade lifted for the ports of Fernandina and Pensacola in Florida and Norfolk, Virginia, all areas which had been solidly under Union control for quite some time. Meanwhile, Admiral Porter ordered the captured Confederate raider *Florida* moved to Newport News and anchored near the spot where the converted *Merrimac* had sunk the USS *Cumberland* 32 months before. In the process, the cruiser collided with a Union transport, losing her figurehead and her jibboom and scraping her wooden side enough that she began to leak. Perhaps that was just as well, for she was an embarrassment to the Federal government. Captain Collins had, of course, been greeted enthusiastically by his naval comrades when he had steamed into Hampton Roads with his prize the week before, but while the administration silently approved of his actions it could not publicly condone his violation of Brazilian neutrality. And there was little doubt that the courts would require that the vessel be returned intact to the neutral port where she had been seized. "I wish she was at the bottom of the sea," Secretary of State William H. Seward reportedly told Admiral Porter. "Do you mean it?" Porter asked. "I do, from my soul," Seward said.[11]

At Nashville, General Thomas was worried about the non-arrival of A. J. Smith's troops. Rumors indicated that Hood would probably advance into Tennessee soon, and without Smith's divisions Thomas would not be able to put a force in the field large enough to be sure of defeating him, especially since it was taking much longer to reorganize and mount Wilson's cavalry than had been expected. Some of the latter, in fact, was also still on the way from Missouri. On the nineteenth, Thomas sent a dispatch to Smith "or Commanding Officer troops concentrating at Paducah: General: I desire you to use every exertion to get your troops forward to this place by steamer as rapidly as possible. Besides the troops of the Sixteenth Army Corps there should be at Paducah eight regiments of the infantry and one battery of artillery awaiting transportation to this place. Bring them with you, and if all your troops have not yet arrived at Paducah, come with what you have and leave orders for the balance to follow."[12]

The next day, the twentieth, Smith wired Thomas, not from Paducah, but from St. Louis: "All my infantry troops have arrived, and will embark on Tuesday [the 22nd], to comply with your previous order. I have two batteries at Paducah, and will join them to my command; also some 3,000 troops ordered to report to me at that point. Please inform me what disposition I shall make of them. I am informed that Colonel Winslow's cavalry has been ordered by General Curtis to Memphis." Thomas replied that evening: "I wish you to make every exertion to reach this place with all possible dispatch. Bring with you all the troops ordered to report to you at Paducah, as well as all others belonging to your command. You will come to Nashville via the Cumberland River. I have sent an officer with orders to bring Winslow's cavalry to this place without delay."[13]

On 20 November, Grant and his wife, Julia, went on a shopping and sight-seeing trip to New York. The general had not seen the city since he passed through there after graduating from West Point in 1843. They appeared quietly and unannounced at the Astor House hotel, but the news of the general-in-chief's presence spread rapidly. Among the first to recognize him was Lieutenant James T. Harrington, one of the Confederate officers laying plans to burn the city. Lieutenant Headley had just taken a room at the Astor where the Rebel agents now planned to hold their meetings.

Despite a severe rainstorm, leading citizens quickly presented themselves to Grant to pay their respects, and the hotel was soon mobbed by people trying to get a look at him. When the Grants went to their rooms an enthusiastic crowd filled the streets, hoping to catch a glimpse of the general through the windows, and when he dined with Governor Reuben E. Fenton that night guests jumped on chairs and tables to see and cheer him.

That afternoon Rawlins wired him from City Point that a Union agent who had left Richmond the evening before reported that Kershaw's Division was definitely back from the Shenandoah and that the rumor in Richmond was that Sheridan's Union forces had already begun to disembark on the north bank of the James River. That same day Sheridan replied to Rawlins' wire about the railroad being used to take Early's forces to Richmond: "There has been none of the enemy's force within reach in my front for a distance of forty miles since the last advance of Early and his hasty retreat. The report in reference to Early's army having left the Valley entirely is somewhat contradictory. I will comply with the request of the general-in-chief as soon as I can definitely ascertain the true conditions of affairs. Steps have been taken to ascertain the facts of the case."[14]

The next day, the 21st, Sheridan wired Rawlins again: "I have not any positive information. Reports are very conflicting. It was reported to me on the 17th that Early's whole army moved from New Market to Staunton. On the 18th I heard that only one division moved (Breckinridge's old division, commanded by Wharton), and it moved to East Tennessee. On the 18th I received a letter from Early, at New Market. Yesterday I heard that Early's army was moving to Richmond; then again I heard that he was going to Staunton to go into winter quarters. None of my scouts sent out have returned; they must have been captured. I moved out this morning all the cavalry, and will be able to ascertain definitely. Kershaw's division, I think, is not more than 5,000 strong. It must have made very fast time to have gotten to Richmond. It was at Middletown on the 12th, and left that place on the night of the 12th. From Middletown to Staunton is seventy-seven miles, which it had to march. My impression is that Early has gone to Staunton, and will probably go to

Richmond with a portion of his troops. If such is the case I will move the Sixth Corps as rapidly as possible. I would like to be a little more certain than I am at present before I send it off."[15]

In New York on the 21st, women pushed and shoved to get close to Julia Grant when she shopped at A. T. Stewart's, while the general managed to walk a few blocks in civilian clothes with a former staff officer before he was recognized. Then, finding himself surrounded by a crowd, he stepped onto a passing street car to escape. Since there were no vacant seats, the former staff officer asked the conductor to have the passengers sit closer together to make room for General Grant. The conductor just winked and grinned, as if to say, "you can't fool me with that one." So the general quietly took hold of a strap and rode standing with a number of other passengers, glad, one assumes, to be just another unknown tourist for a change.

That same day, the Confederate Army of Tennessee finally advanced from Florence, Alabama, heading into its namesake state. As was the custom in that era, Hood issued an order to be read to all his troops in an attempt to raise their spirits and enlist their best efforts. "SOLDIERS: You march to-day to redeem by your valor and your arms one of the fairest portions of our Confederacy. This can only be achieved by battle and by victory. Summon up in behalf of a consumation so glorious all the elements of soldiership and all the instincts of manhood, and you will render the campaign before you full of auspicious fruit to your country and lasting renown to yourselves."[16]

Hood seems to have had little in the way of a plan, just a vague desire to move the seat of war as far north as possible. It seems unlikely that he could hope to induce Sherman at this late date to abort his march into Georgia and hurry back to defend Tennessee. He was aware by then that Sherman had literally burned his bridges behind him and would find it hard to move north now even if he wanted to. He was aware that Schofield was at Pulaski, Tennessee, with about 15,000 men, but ignored him and headed more-or-less straight for Nashville. His advance was not helped by the fact that an unseasonably early snowstorm hit the area that morning, followed by a hard freeze that night and alternating snows, freezes, thaws, and rains over the next few days. It was a combination that turned the roads to deep-rutted quagmires.

Brigadier General Hylan B. Lyon, who had previously commanded a brigade of Kentucky troops under Forrest, was at Corinth, Mississippi, that day obtaining arms for a new command of recruits and conscripts which he was putting together at Paris, Tennessee, not far south of the

Kentucky line on the west side of the Tennessee River, when he received an order from Hood written three days before. He was to cross the Tennessee and Cumberland rivers with his command somewhere between Paducah, Kentucky, and Johnsonville, Tennessee, and then move southeast up the Cumberland to Clarksville, Tennessee, putting all the mills in the area to work grinding grain for the Confederate army. He was then to destroy the railroads and telegraph lines between Clarksville and Nashville and between Bowling Green, Kentucky, and Nashville. "My command at this time," Lyon later reported, "consisted of 800 men, undisciplined and but poorly organized, and two pieces of artillery (12-pounder howitzers). None of my command had been in the service exceeding four months, and a majority of them but a few days."[17]

While the Confederacy was short on troops in Georgia it had plenty of leaders, and most of them had gathered in Macon, which seemed to be the most vital of the points threatened by Sherman. In addition to Major General Joseph Wheeler, commander of the cavalry corps Hood had left behind, there was Lieutenant General William J. Hardee, commander of the Department of South Carolina, Georgia and Florida, Joseph Brown, governor of Georgia, Howell Cobb, former governor and present major general of Georgia militia, Robert Toombs, former U.S. Senator, former Confederate General, and present adjutant and inspector general of Georgia militia, and Gustavus W. Smith, former New York City street commissioner, former Confederate general, and present major general of Georgia militia. And at dawn on 22 November, Lieutenant General Richard Taylor, commander of the Department of Alabama, Mississippi and Eastern Louisiana, stepped off the train at Macon, where he had been sent by Beauregard.

Taylor was met by Cobb. "We'll ride out and see the defenses," the Georgian said. "I've been up all night, working on them. The Yankees were only twelve miles away at noon yesterday." But Taylor declined. "There's no need to see the trenches," he said, "and I hope you'll stop your workmen and let all of them get warm by the fire—which is where I'm going to stay. Sherman's not coming here. If his advance was twelve miles away at noon yesterday, you'd have seen him last night. He'd have come before you had time to finish the works or remove your stores."[18] Cobb thought Taylor was a lunatic until a messenger brought word during breakfast that Howard's Union column had turned eastward at the last minute.

Hardee had left Macon the night before, because he was more worried about Augusta. He had already sent the 1st Brigade of the Georgia militia there and had ordered G. W. Smith to send another three small brigades, the two regiments of the state line, and an attached battery of artillery to the same point as soon as he could. Smith sent them all eastward that morning toward Griswoldville, on the railroad, with orders to wait there for further instructions, while he stayed behind to arrange for supplies. There, under the temporary command of Brigadier General P. J. Phillips, they blundered into Brigadier Charles C. Walcutt's 2nd Brigade of the 1st Division of the 15th Corps. Walcutt's 1,500 men had been pushing beyond Griswoldville against Wheeler's cavalry in order to protect the rest of the column from harassment, and had taken up a defensive position in the edge of some timber along a slight rise of ground overlooking an open field. Their flanks were covered by a couple of Kilpatrick's cavalry regiments and some swampy ground, and there was more swamp forming a natural obstacle protecting their front. Light breastworks of rails were constructed to protect the men and the two guns stationed with them.

"These preparations were considered sufficient," wrote the 15th Corps commander, Major General Peter J. Osterhaus, "to meet any of General Wheeler's reconnaissances, which he might undertake after finding out that he was no longer pressed,but had to stand a more severe trial. In the afternoon the rebel commander brought forward four brigades of infantry and a battery of artillery, supported by a strong cavalry force, to dislodge General Walcutt from his position. For several hours their attempts were repeated with the greatest possible impetuosity. Their artillery threw a terrific fire into the frail works of Walcutt, while their columns of infantry marched in heroic style to within fifty yards of our line. It was all in vain!"[19]

The Federals had been cooking their lunch, "not dreaming of a fight," as one of them said, when the Rebel militia drove in their pickets and advanced across the open field. Walcutt waited until the Georgians were within 250 yards before giving the order to open fire. His men were veterans of many battles, large and small, and most of them were armed with Spencer repeating rifles, and they quickly cut the Confederate ranks to pieces, but the attackers reformed and came on again. Their own fire was doing little damage, however, for, like most green troops, they were firing too high. The one disadvantage of repeaters was that troops armed with them tended to shoot off all their ammunition too quickly, and this fight was no exception. But the Federals fixed bayonets and prepared to spear any Confederate who dared to enter their breastworks, while the drummer boys were sent to bring up more ammunition.

The Rebels were much closer by the time the repeaters were reloaded and began to bark again. This fire was too deadly for the Georgians to stay where they were or even to safely retreat, so many of them ran for the cover of a ravine fifty yards in front of the Union line. At that range the veteran Federals could hardly miss, and only a few militiamen actually made it to the ravine. A few others took cover out of sight behind some bamboo and gallberry bushes. One of the latter, 16-year-old J. J. Eckles, sat down behind the bushes, took his homemade blanket off his shoulder and unrolled it, shook out several deformed bullets, and counted 27 holes in the cloth.

Finally the militia retreated back toward Macon after losing over 600 men while the Federals lost only 62, including Walcutt, who was wounded by a shell fragment from the Confederate artillery. The Union veterans advanced into the field to gather up the wounded and those Rebels who had been unable or unwilling to retreat. It was then that they discovered the true nature of the enemy they had been fighting. "Old grey haired and weakly looking men and little boys, not over 15 years old, lay dead or writhing in pain," Captain Charles Wills wrote home. "It was a terrible sight," wrote another Federal, Theodore Upson. "Someone was groaning. We moved a few bodies, and there was a boy with a broken arm and leg—just a boy 14 years old; and beside him, cold in death, lay his father, two brothers and an uncle." Upson and some of his friends carried the boy to their campfire and found him a doctor. "I was never so affected at the sight of dead and wounded before," wrote Captain Wills. "I hope we will never have to shoot at such men again. They knew nothing at all about fighting and I think their officers knew as little, or else certainly knew nothing about our being there." One of the young Rebels told his captors, "We never wanted to fight. The cavalry rounded us up and drove us in and made us march."[20] Others told similar stories.

After taking care of the wounded young Georgian, Upson looked after the body of his friend, Uncle Aaron Wolford, the patriarch of the 100th Indiana, who was one of the few Union casualties. The night before, the normally cheerful Wolford had told Upson that he felt that he did not have long to live and had extracted a promise from him to take care of his things and to write to his wife about him. Upson took Wolford's Testament, watch, and money from his pocket to send to his widow and eight children. He split a hollow sycamore log to make Wolford a casket and scratched his name, company, and regiment on a rail to mark his grave. Then he wrote a letter to Mrs. Wolford. "I am afraid she will have hard work to read it," he said, "for I could not help blotting the paper."[21]

Such scenes as the field full of dead and wounded militiamen moved one Federal soldier to write, "There is no God in war. It is merciless, cruel, vindictive, un-Christian, savage, relentless. It is all that devils could wish for."[22]

At Milledgeville, the capital of Georgia, the legislators passed a bill of levy en masse, which made every man of military age in the state a legal part of the state's forces, then fled before Sherman's advancing troops. Several members of the legislature were themselves rounded up by zealous conscription officers at Macon, and it was with some difficulty that they eventually obtained their release on the grounds that they were personally exempt from their own new law. It was bitter cold when, late that afternoon, the 20th Corps marched into town with flags flying and bands playing "Yankee Doodle." Two regiments were posted for guard duty on Capitol Square, and the bands played the "Star-spangled Banner" as they hoisted the stars and stripes above the capitol dome. Sherman himself still rode with the 14th Corps and stopped at what he called "a good double-hewed-log house" a little west of town. "In looking around the room," he wrote, "I saw a small box, like a candle-box, marked 'Howell Cobb,' and inquiring of a negro, found that we were at the plantation of General Howell Cobb, of Georgia, one of the leading rebels of the South, then a general in the Southern army, and who had been Secretary of the United States Treasury in Mr. Buchanan's time. Of course, we confiscated his property, and found it rich in corn, beans, pea-nuts, and sorghum-molasses. Extensive fields were all round the house; I sent word back to General Davis to explain whose plantation it was, and instructed him to spare nothing. That night huge bonfires consumed the fence-rails, kept our soldiers warm, and the teamsters and men, as well as the slaves, carried off an immense quantity of corn and provisions of all sorts."[23]

Up in Tennessee on the 22nd, the Union cavalry brought word to Schofield at Pulaski that, in spite of intensely cold weather and intermittent rain and snow, one corps of Hood's army had advanced northeastward from Florence, Alabama, to Lawrenceburg, Tennessee, due west of Pulaski and just as close to Nashville as Schofield was, while another of Hood's corps was nearing Waynesboro, west of Lawrenceburg, and the third was somewhere in between. Uncertain about just where Hood was going but fearing a raid on his railroad, Schofield decided to spread his forces between Pulaski and Columbia, Tennessee. So that morning he sent Brigadier General Jacob D. Cox's 3rd Division of the 23rd Corps to Lynnville, halfway between Pulaski and Columbia, and it was joined there that evening by Brigadier General George D. Wagner's 2nd Division of the 4th Corps, while the other two divisions of the 4th Corps remained at Pulaski. The other division of the 23rd Corps was still at Johnsonville. Thomas, meanwhile, sent Wilson out from Nashville to take personal command of the cavalry at the front.

General Braxton Bragg, nominal commanding general of the Confederate army and temporary commander of the Department of North Carolina, received orders that day to proceed to Augusta, Georgia, to organize the defense of that city from Sherman's approaching army. Bragg sent off a wire at 9 p.m. to the city's mayor, telling him to "exhort your people to be confident & resolute." To Millege L. Bonham, governor of South Carolina, whose state was just east of Augusta, he telegraphed to "prevail on your men to unite in protecting a sister state. Our cause is one. If Georgia is saved South Carolina cannot be lost. If Georgia be lost South Carolina cannot be saved."[24] While this was true, and fairly obvious, it did not address the problem of just how to save Georgia, or even part of it. The next day, the 23rd, Bragg left Wilmington, North Carolina, which he had only recently been sent to protect from real or imagined invasions, and took half the garrison with him.

Also on the 23rd, General Grant reached Washington for a conference with President Lincoln and Secretary Stanton. On the way he had stopped off at Philadelphia, where he had experienced the same problem with crowds of admirers as he had in New York and had been forced to take refuge in Independence Hall. He had been spirited out a private exit, but had been discovered on his way back to his hotel and his carriage had almost been tipped over by the crowd. One reason for his visit to Washington was to push for the promotion of a number of officers whom he thought had proven their worth. In order to create vacancies for these promotions, he presented Lincoln and Stanton with a list of eight major generals and 33 brigadiers whose services could be dispensed with. "Why, I find that lots of the officers on this list are very close friends of yours," the president said; "do you want them all dropped?" Grant replied, "That's very true, Mr. President; but my personal friends are not always good generals, and I think it but just to adhere to my recommendations."[25]

Among other items discussed was a proposal by Lincoln to send Major General Ambrose E. Burnside to command in Kentucky instead of Burbridge, who was embroiled in a dispute with that state's governor. The year before, Burnside had commanded the Department and Army of the Ohio and had won Lincoln's gratitude by finally achieving his long-sought goal of liberating Union-loving east Tennessee. Burnside had later returned to Virginia to command the 9th Corps during Grant's campaign from the Wilderness to Petersburg, but had been relieved after he and Meade had bungled the battle of the crater. Grant consented to Lincoln's proposal but later changed his mind before it was put into effect.

Stanton's health was still not good, and there were rumors that he might have to retire soon. Lincoln told Grant that if that should become necessary that he would not appoint a new secretary of war without consulting the general-in-chief. Grant said that he doubted anyone could be found for the job who would be as efficient as Stanton. "He is not only a man of untiring energy and devotion to duty, but even his worst enemies never for a moment doubt his personal integrity and the purity of his motives; and it tends largely to reconcile the people to the heavy taxes they are paying when they feel an absolute certainty that the chief of the department which is giving out contracts for countless millions of dollars is a person of scrupulous honesty."[26]

Out in Tennessee, the weather was sunny on the 23rd, for a change, but remained very cold. Hood's Confederate infantry was still toiling northward, but the terrible weather had turned the roads to mud that was so bad that at least some units found better going by marching through the woods. However, Forrest's cavalry, far outnumbering the three brigades of Union horsemen in the area, was ranging far ahead. Forrest himself was riding with Chalmer's Division that afternoon, which was pushing Capron's brigade of Union cavalry ahead of it. Capron's outfit had been part of Stoneman's Cavalry Division of the Army of the Ohio and had been badly cut up during its raid on Macon during the Atlanta campaign. Now it was the 1st Brigade of the 6th Division of Wilson's new Cavalry Corps. The rest of the division was not yet ready for combat, and even this brigade was not in first-class shape. For one thing, many of Capron's men were armed with muzzleloading infantry rifles, which were almost worthless on horseback. "Our rifles after the first volley were about as serviceable to cavalry as a good club," a Union major observed.[27]

In the gathering darkness that evening, Capron's men were making camp along the road to Mount Pleasant, southwest of Columbia, but Forrest was not through with them for the day. Leaving most of Colonel Edmund W. Rucker's brigade to skirmish with Capron's rear guard, Forrest sent one regiment to get around one Union flank while he took his 80-man escort company around the other to get into the Federals' camp. The regiment was not able to get through, but Forrest charged anyway, despite being outnumbered about ten to one. Surprise made up for the Rebels' lack of numbers, however, and Forrest's men stampeded the entire camp as they rode through it with revolvers blazing.

And when the sound of their attack was heard at the front, Capron's rear guard came riding back to the Union camp and into an ambush. Forrest's escort was armed with captured Spencer repeating carbines, and for once the Federals were on the receiving end of their firepower.

The result was tremendous confusion. Forrest himself rode into a party of horsemen he thought were his own, only to discover they were Union soldiers. A Federal officer pointed his revolver at Forrest and pulled the trigger, but the general's adjutant, riding next to him, deflected the gun at the last instant. When the two sides finally sorted themselves out and separated, the Rebels found that they had captured about fifty prisoners, twenty horses, and an ambulance wagon.

Forrest's other two divisions, Buford's and Jackson's, meanwhile, moved to the east that day and discovered that Schofield had evacuated Pulaski. The rest of the 4th Corps had been moved up the road to Lynnville, while Cox's division had been sent to Hurricane, halfway to Columbia.

Down in Georgia that day, the rest of Slocum's Left Wing marched into Milledgeville. Slocum set up his headquarters in the Milledgeville Hotel, and Sherman, still riding with the 14th Corps, made his in the governor's mansion, which was found to be bare of everything except a few pieces of furniture whch must have been too heavy for Governor Brown to move in a hurry. Sherman's staff placed planks across camp chairs to make a table for their meals, and the general slept on the floor.

A large number of Union officers and men convened a rowdy mock session of the state legislature at the capitol building. After some speeches, some drinking, and a noisy debate, the new legislators repealed Georgia's ordinance of secession as "highly indiscreet" and appointed Sherman's entire army as a committee to arrange for the state's return to the Union. But when other soldiers rushed in crying, "The Yankees are coming!" they fled from the building in comic imitation of the real legislators. Other soldiers got into the capitol's library and tossed hundreds of books out the windows onto the wet ground. Some kept volumes which caught their fancy, but others disapproved of what one sergeant called "a very bad exhibition of a very lawless nature." A major, who said he could have picked up a thousand dollars' worth of law books, resisted the temptation. "I should feel ashamed of myself every time I saw one of them in my book case at home," he said. "I don't object to stealing horses, mules, niggers and all such *little things,* but I will not engage in plundering and destroying public libraries."[28]

The Federals took bushels of state currency and gave it to women textile workers who said they had not been paid in months. They were ecstatic over their good fortune until they finally caught on to the joke. The bills had not been signed. The troops also used the worthless money as stakes for some fantastic poker games and found more practical uses for it as well, such as lighting their pipes and kindling their campfires.

The next day, the 24th, was Thanksgiving Day, and Sherman's men feasted well enough on captured pork, beef, and poultry. During their celebrations around their campfires appeared a few ragged men, starved to little more than skin and bones and gazing like wild animals at the relatively well fed and well clothed troops. These were Union soldiers who had escaped from the prisoner of war camp at Andersonville, south of Macon, before or while the Confederates had recently moved them out of Sherman's supposed path. Now, after crossing almost a hundred miles of enemy territory, they wept at the sight of the Stars and Stripes and the plentiful food. The appearance of these escaped prisoners, as well as the tales they told of their suffering in the prison camp, sickened and infuriated Sherman's men, as did other stories reaching their ears just then. It was said that the Rebels had cut the throats of Federals captured near Macon, two of them supposedly surviving to tell the tale because the "Rebs had sliced their throats too far up."[29] Another rumor said that Union soldiers captured by Wheeler's cavalry had been given two choices: taking an oath of allegiance to the Confederacy, or death.

The Federals began marching out of Milledgeville that day amid rumors that the town was to be burned. The state arsenal was destroyed, by Sherman's order, after ammunition found there was dumped in the Oconee River. And female inmates soon set the state penitentiary on fire and escaped. The male inmates and guards had already been inducted into the state military forces. But the rest of the town was spared from fire, although not from plundering. For instance, the pews of the churches on Capitol Square had been chopped up for firewood, the pipe organ at the Episcopal church had been poured full of molasses, and the explosion that destroyed the armory did further damage to the churches.

At least one of the escaped female prisoners soon found the Union soldiers and resumed the profession which had probably landed her in the penitentiary in the first place. A rare case of rape later came to light. The 27-year-old wife of a Confederate officer was raped by two soldiers in her sick bed in her home outside of town. She eventually died in a mental institution.

Up in Tennessee that day, General Schofield had been up all night. He had come to the realization that Hood, or at least a sizable part of Hood's army, was closer to Columbia than was his own main force. And if the Confederates occupied Columbia they would be on the railroad and the turnpike between him and Nashville. The only Union forces at Columbia were parts of three regiments, about 800 men, the leading elements of Brigadier General Thomas Ruger's 2nd Division of the 23rd Corps, the rest of which was still on the way there from Johnsonville. Upon hearing from Capron that a superior force of Confederates was pushing the cavalry back, Ruger wired Schofield to ask for reinforcements. So, at 1 a.m. on the 24th, Schofield ordered his troops to start marching north to Columbia.

Cox, who was the closest to Columbia, received this order at 4 a.m. He was what one admirer called a universal genius, "world famous as an authority on microscopy and cathedral architecture, literator, politician, artist, soldier—everything." Before the war he had been a lawyer and state senator. After the war he became governor of Ohio, secretary of the interior, president of the Wabash Railroad, congressman, and historian. One of his men wrote that "he looks like a lawyer or maybe a preacher. Talks like a professor of higher learning. He is a selfmade soldier of sheer force of character and sense of duty. Conducts the war business with dignity and dispatch."[30] Dispatch was exactly what he showed on the 24th of November. Cox roused his sleeping troops at once, and had them on the road by 5 a.m., without breakfast.

Soon after daylight, Chalmers' Rebel cavalry advanced again, and by 7:30 a.m. Capron's Union troopers were in full retreat toward Columbia. But Cox turned his infantry column off the Lynnville road onto a side road and deployed two brigades and three batteries across the Mount Pleasant-Columbia road and behind Bigby Creek. He was just in time. Capron's retreating horsemen soon thundered past, and Cox's men greeted Chalmers' Confederates with a fire that brought their pursuit to a sudden halt. More of Ruger's division had already reached Columbia from the north after an all-night train ride—although portions of his command were sent by Thomas to watch crossings of the Duck River west of Columbia—and the 4th Corps began to arrive by 10 a.m.

Schofield himself arrived about noon. While the position that Cox and Major General David S. Stanley, commander of the 4th Corps, were busily entrenching north of Bigby Creek was a good one for blocking movement up the Mount Pleasant-Columbia road, there was nothing to keep an army the size of Hood's from outflanking it. That afternoon Schofield ordered the construction of a second line of defenses designed primarily to cover the railroad bridge two miles west of town.

Meanwhile, Jackson's and Buford's divisions of Forrest's cavalry followed Hatch's Union troopers, who rode northward on a road to the west of the one Schofield's infantry had taken. At noon the two forces began a sharp little battle at the town of Campbellsville in which the outnumbered Hatch lost four battleflags. But at sunset the Federals got away, riding toward Lynnville, while the Confederates stayed put at Campbellsville, despite Forrest's urgent orders for them to intercept Schofield's infantry on the Pulaski-Columbia road.

At 10 a.m. on the 24th A. J. Smith, not really aware of exactly how anxiously Thomas was awaiting his arrival at Nashville, finally departed from St. Louis, along with a little 1,300-man division of the 17th Corps he had rounded up at Benton Barracks. Thomas' dispatch sent to Paducah for Smith did not reach there until the 23rd. And it still might be a week before Smith got all his troops to Nashville.

On the 24th Grant sent Thomas a copy of Beauregard's proclamation to the people of Georgia of the 18th, taken from the Savannah newspapers. The Confederate's last sentence ("I hasten to join you in defense of your homes and firesides.") seemed to imply that Hood's army was being sent to Georgia after all. The Federals knew that Beauregard had been placed in command over Hood and Taylor and for quite a while assumed that Beauregard was actually directing Hood's army. It was what they would do—was what Grant and Sherman had both done when given similar commands over multiple departments. So if Beauregard was hastening to the defense of Georgia he must be taking his (Hood's) army with him. And if that were true, then Forrest's recent attacks were mere diversions. "Do not let Forrest get off without punishment," Grant told Thomas.[31]

---

1. Davis, *Sherman's March*, 29.
2. Ibid., 34.
3. *Official Records*, 44:362.
4. Sherman, *Memoirs*, 656–657.
5. *Official Records*, 39:I:893.
6. Sherman, *Memoirs*, 665.
7. Ibid., 657–658.
8. Siepel, *Rebel*, 131.
9. *Official Records*, 43:II:640–641.
10. Ibid., 43:II:645.
11. Foote, *The Civil War*, 3:589.
12. *Official Records*, 45:I:953.
13. Ibid., 45:I:969.
14. Ibid., 43:II:649.
15. Ibid., 43:II:653.
16. Ibid., 45:I:1236.
17. Ibid., 45:I:803.
18. Davis, *Sherman's March*, 52.

19. *Official Records,* 44:83.

20. Davis, *Sherman's March,* 56.

21. Ibid.

22. Foote, *The Civil War,* 3:647.

23. Sherman, *Memoirs,* 662.

24. Judith Lee Hallock, *Braxton Bragg and Confederate Defeat,* Vol. 2 (Tuscaloosa, 1991), 226.

25. Porter, *Campaigning With Grant,* 328.

26. Ibid., 328–329.

27. Wiley Sword, *Embrace an Angry Wind: The Confederacy's Last Hurrah: Spring Hill, Franklin, and Nashville* (New York, 1992), 92.

28. Davis, *Sherman's March,* 64.

29. Ibid., 67.

30. James Lee McDonough and Thomas L. Connelly, *Five Tragic Hours: The Battle of Franklin* (Knoxville, 1983), 33.

31. *Official Records,* 45:I:1014.

CHAPTER THIRTY-THREE

There Was the Wildest Excitement Imaginable

24–26 November 1864

On 24 November Captain Thomas N. Conrad returned to King George County, Virginia, from his mission to watch President Lincoln and learn his habits of movement. There he set up a secret base near the lower Potomac, east of Belle Plain, to help other Confederate agents get across the river.

The same day, Union officers and Secret Service agents made secret arrests of Confederate spies in New York, Cincinnati, St. Louis, Baltimore, Indianapolis, Portland, and Boston. They also confiscated stockpiles of arms, ammunition, and medical supplies, and the plans to a number of Federal buildings, bridges, prison camps, storehouses, arsenals, and shipping centers. The Rebel agents who planned to burn New

509

York City were not, however, among those arrested, nor did they know of the arrests of the others.

Thanksgiving was a lovely Indian Summer day in New York. Church bells rang throughout the town, and families dressed in their best clothes walked near Castle Garden at the Battery. A small bell tinkled as young Lieutenant John W. Headley entered a chemist's shop in a basement near Washington Square. Soon a stocky little man with a dirty white beard emerged from behind a curtain. Headley told the man that Longuemare had sent him to pick up his luggage. Captain Emile Longuemare was another Rebel agent who had preceded the others to New York and who had arranged for this chemist to produce the Greek fire which the others would use. The old man dragged a valise out from behind the curtain. It was four feet long and two or three feet high, and heavier than Headley had expected, and he had to change hands every ten paces as he carried it along the street. He had not taken a taxi and could not find one, so he struggled along with the weighty satchel until he caught a streetcar going up Bowery to Central Park.

"The car was crowded," Headley remembered, "and I had to put the valise in front of me on the floor in the passway, as the seats ran full length on each side of the car. I soon began to smell a peculiar odor—a little like rotten eggs—and noticed passengers were conscious of the same presence. But I sat unconcerned until my getting off place was reached, when I took up the valise and went out. I heard a passenger say as I alighted, 'There must be something dead in that valise.'"[1]

When Headley reached the cottage off Central Park which the Confederates were using as a meeting place, only five others were there. Two of the Rebels had backed out at the last minute. But the remaining six opened the valise and found 144 bottles inside, each filled with four ounces of clear liquid and sealed with plaster of Paris. Experiments performed outside the cottage confirmed that the chemicals worked. It was designed to ignite spontaneously when exposed to the air. However, in order to give the wielder time to get away, it would take a few minutes to catch if the liquid were allowed to soak into some handy flammable material, such as cloth or wood.

Each of the agents had already taken rooms at several of the city's leading hotels. Fires set almost simultaneously in those rooms, it was thought, would soon have all those hotels in flames, which should exceed the capacity of the various volunteer fire companies' firefighting efforts. The flames would then spread, wreaking havoc on much of the city. The hour of 8 p.m. on the 25th was chosen for the setting of the fires. A later hour, after most people were asleep, would probably have increased the time the fires would have to spread before being discovered, but the

Rebels intentionally picked a time when everyone would still be awake "so that the guests of the hotels might all escape," as Headley put it, "as we did not want to destroy any lives."[2] The Confederates put some of the bottles of Greek fire in satchels that they had, packed with newspapers, old clothes, and boots, to be distributed to some of the hotel rooms that night. The rest would be picked up at another meeting the next evening.

By the morning of the 25th a cold wind from the northwest had brought dark clouds and rain to New York. The Confederates feared at first that the rain would spoil their plans, but by noon the sky had cleared. It was another holiday, of sorts: Evacuation Day, commemorating the departure of the British troops from the city at the end of the American Revolution 81 years before. However, stores would not be closed, as they had been the day before for Thanksgiving, and large crowds were expected, and the theaters would be busy that evening, a Friday night. A special attraction at the Winter Garden was a performance of Shakespeare's "Julius Caesar," with Edwin Booth as Brutus, Junius Brutus Booth as Cassius, and John Wilkes Booth as Mark Antony. It was the first time the three Booth brothers had ever appeared together in the same play. Chairs being set up in the aisles were selling for $5 apiece.

At 6 p.m. the Rebel agents met again at the cottage near Central Park and stuffed the rest of the bottles of phosphorus into satchels and pockets. They also had turpentine, rosin, and matches, just in case they were needed. Lieutenant Headley reached the Astor House, on Broadway near City Hall Park, at 6:20 p.m., got his key and went to his room on the top floor. "After lighting the gas jet," he later wrote, "I hung the bedclothes loosely on the headboard and piled the chairs, drawers of the bureau and washstand on the bed. Then stuffed some newspapers about among the mass and poured a bottle of turpentine over it all. I concluded to unlock my door and fix the key on the outside, as I might have to get out in a hurry, for I did not know whether the Greek Fire would make a noise or not. I opened a bottle carefully and quickly and spilled it on the pile of rubbish. It blazed up instantly and the whole bed seemed to be in flames, before I could get out. I locked the door and walked down the hall and stairway to the office, which was fairly crowded with people. I left the key at the office as usual and passed out."[3] However, in his haste he left three bottles of turpentine in the room and a carpetbag which contained the note that had summoned the Confederates to a conference the day before. It was written in Colonel Martin's handwriting on stationery from McDonald's piano shop, a Copperhead contact.

Captain Robert Kennedy went to the New England Hotel and took a room on the second floor under the name George Morse. As soon as he closed the door behind him, he pulled the bedclothes off and piled them and the mattress on the bed, then put a chair on top of them. Uncapping a bottle of Greek fire taken from his carpetbag, he soaked the bedclothes with it, put the remaining bottle in an already bulging pocket of his overcoat, and threw the bag onto the pile. Within five minutes he was hurrying down the corridor as best he could, for he limped due to a wound received at the battle of Shiloh. He slowed as he approached the desk, where he turned in his key and said he was going for a walk.

Ten blocks away, Kennedy went to a room he had taken four days earlier on the fourth floor at Lovejoy's Hotel, opposite City Hall Park. There he repeated the same procedure, except that he piled the bedding in the middle of the floor. Then he went to a room in the same hotel that had been rented by Lieutenant James Chenault and again repeated the procedure, adding towels and drapes to the pile. However, in his haste to get away he left behind an unopened bottle of Greek fire and two vials of turpentine.

Somewhere in the vicinity of Park Row, Kennedy met up with Chenault, who had in the meantime emptied two bottles of phosphorus onto a pile of bedding in a room on the fourth floor of the Howard Hotel on lower Broadway. The two Confederates had not yet heard any fire alarms, so they decided to see what was happening on Broadway, where other officers were at work.

Lieutenants John T. Ashbrook and James T. Harrington were in two separate rooms in the sprawling St. Nicholas Hotel on Broadway at Spring Street. In order to ensure that his fire would spread, Ashbrook dumped a boxfull of matches onto the things he had piled on his bed and soaked the pile with phosphorous. Then he took a candle from the mantel and tossed it onto the pile, walked out, and locked the door. Downstairs he met Harrington, who had followed the standard procedure in his room, and together they walked north on Broadway for a block and a half. There Harrington went into the Metropolitan Hotel, while Ashbrook went on another block or so to the Lafarge House.

Colonel Martin, dressed in the uniform of a Union officer, began with a room on an upper floor at the Fifth-Avenue Hotel. He piled bedding, two chairs, and drawers from the bureau in a corner, threw six cartridges soaked in turpentine into another corner, and tossed more cartridges and some rosin around the room. But in his haste he left three sealed bottles of Greek fire behind. Two blocks away, at the St. James Hotel, he went to room 84 on the third floor, where he made the customary pile of flammable objects, soaked in phosphorus, and scattered matches all around. But again he left several unopened bottles of Greek fire behind.

Next he went to the Belmont Hotel on Fulton Street between Broadway and Nassau. There he evidently saw a Union officer, Lieutenant James Kellogg, signing the register and heard the clerk say the room, number 28, was not made up yet. Kellogg said he would be back after dinner, so Martin went up to room 28 and found the door open. He tossed the linens into a pile and poured several bottles of the incendiary liquid onto them. Again he left several sealed bottles behind.

By 7:20 p.m. Lieutenant Headley was at the Everett House, on Union Square. He had tried to get a room there earlier and when told that none were available had left a valise with the clerk and had said he would try again later. There were still no rooms available, however, so he took his valise and proceeded to the United States Hotel, near the East River. As he arrived there, at about 8:45 p.m., he heard the first fire bells ringing at the City Hall fire tower, northeast of him.

The watchman at City Hall was repeatedly plunging the lever that rang the 23,000-pound bell to alert the volunteer fire companies—one ring for the First District, followed by four rings for the Fourth District—and other fire towers soon picked up and repeated the rings, spreading the call throughout the city. Soon they had to add eight rings for the Eighth District as more alarms came in. The first alarm had come from the St. James, where a guest had smelled a peculiar odor, opened the door of his room, and found the hallway full of smoke. A few minutes later another alarm came from the St. Nicholas. A guest headed for his room on the sixth floor, after passing Ashbrook and Harrington in the lobby, had seen smoke coming from room 174. At almost the same moment a waiter on the fourth floor traced the smell of smoke to rooms 139 and 140, and when he opened the door to 139 the sudden draft of air caused flames to shoot up from the phosphorus within.

At the United States Hotel, Headley was again told that no room was available. The owner, John F. Carlton, was worried about burglars and was suspicious of Headley's light bag. Headley said he only needed a room for one night, and Carlton reluctantly gave him room 172 on the fifth floor. But when Headley came back downstairs only ten minutes later Carlton's suspicions were renewed. He tried to intercept the young Confederate but was too late, for Headley quickly disappeared onto the street. While Carlton tried to decide whether he should search room 172 for burglary tools, Headley headed west.

"As I came back to Broadway," Headley remembered, "it seemed that a hundred bells were ringing, great crowds were gathering on the street, and there was general consternation. I concluded to go and see how my fires were doing. There was no panic at the Astor House, but to my surprise a great crowd was pouring out of Barnum's Museum nearly opposite the Astor. It was now a quarter after nine o'clock by the City Hall tower clock. Presently the alarm came from the City Hotel and the Everett. The surging crowds were frantic. But the greatest panic was at Barnum's Museum. People were coming out and down ladders from the second and third floor windows and the manager was crying out for help to get the animals out. It looked like people were getting hurt running over each other in the stampede, and still I could not help some astonishment for I did not suppose there was a fire in the Museum."[4]

But there was. Kennedy and Chenault had stopped in at P. T. Barnum's to pass a little time. They had climbed to the fifth floor, passing by the exhibitions, until they had come to a window from which they could see up and down Broadway, but at that time there had been nothing to see. They had stopped outside the Lecture-Room, where a performance of the London drama "Waiting for the Verdict" was in progress, when they heard the first alarm bell. Satisfied that their work was beginning to bear fruit, the two Confederates descended the stairs again. Kennedy, who had been drinking, decided that it would be fun to put a real scare into all these Yankees. There was nobody in sight, so he bent down and cracked a bottle of phosphorus against a step, and the wood began to smoke and burn. As he hurried on down the steps he tossed another bottle down the stairwell, but it failed to break. Outside, Chenault went on to Handfield's Hotel, while Kennedy crossed Broadway, dodging between the carriages.

A fist fight had broken out in front of Barnum's admission booth between the doorkeeper and the cashier on one side and four young toughs thought to be members of the Dead Rabbits gang on the other when an usher came running out, flinging open the doors to Ann Street and shouting, "Fire—there's a fire upstairs!" In the Lecture-Room panic seized the audience, and the actors as well. There were cries of "Fire! Fire!" and several people slid down the pillars from the gallery to the parquet.[5] Some women fainted while others screamed in fear and the men fought to get to the exits.

A huge crowd gathered in the street, staring at the flames shooting from the upper windows. A woman appeared on the second-floor balcony and was met by cries of "Don't jump . . . don't jump." She stood there for a moment, silhouetted against the flames, but soon firemen charged through the crowd, knocking people aside, and put a ladder against the building, and the crowd roared in appreciation as a fireman climbed the ladder and rescued the swooning lady in the finest tradition of melodrama. A manager was running through the crowd yelling, "Save the animals . . . save Mr. Barnum's animals," and indeed the roar of a tiger and the trumpeting of a bull elephant could be heard above the noise of the crowd.[6]

Barnum's seven-foot-tall giantess, her black hair streaming wildly behind her, rushed out the front door in terror, tossing aside two men who tried to restrain her. A fire captain and the museum manager were also pushed away and she plunged through the crowd, across Broadway, and into the lobby of the Powers Hotel. She flailed about and cried hysterically that she did not want to be burned, until she was overpowered by five firemen and several spectators long enough for a doctor to administer a sedative. Then she was taken to a room in the hotel while the firemen went back to work, and the blaze was soon brought under control.

Fear spread up and down Broadway, as people in carriages spread word of the fires at the museum and various hotels. People ran in frenzy through the crowded streets in search of safety. Patrolmen spilled from police wagons at various points, billyclubs in hand, ready for anything. Occupants of wooden houses near the fires were evacuated. Alarms continued to come in to the watchtower: the United States Hotel, the New England, Lovejoy's, the Belmont, the Hudson River docks. More than 5,000 firemen and policemen responded during the night with amazing promptness and skill.

Headley, meanwhile, had moved farther west to the docks along the Hudson River. "The vessels and barges of every description were lying along close together," he wrote, "and not more than twenty yards from the street. I picked dark spots to stand in, and jerked a bottle in six different places. They were ablaze before I left. One had struck a barge of baled hay and made a big fire. There were wild scenes here the last time I looked back. I started straight for the City Hall." He edged through the crowd around the Astor House, caught a street car headed uptown, and got off at Bowery Street across from the Metropolitan Hotel to see how Ashbrook and Harrington had fared. But half a block ahead he saw Captain Kennedy, caught up with him, and slapped him on the shoulder. Kennedy crouched and started to draw his revolver until he recognized Headley. "He laughed and said he ought to shoot me for giving him such a scare."[7] The two exchanged reports, and Headley learned at last how the fire at Barnum's Museum had come about.

Ashbrook, by then, was in room 104 on the third floor of the Lafarge Hotel, searching for matches with which to light the gas jet. A servant girl in the hallway had told him there were some in the room, but he could not find any. He stuck his head out in the corridor and asked for her help, and she stepped in, pointed to the box on the mantel, took out a match and lit the gas herself. Twenty minutes later she saw Ashbrook lock the door and go down the stairs. When she passed the door to his

room a few minutes later she saw a light through the transom and concluded that he had left the gas jet on. She was groping for the master
key in her apron when the light from the transom suddenly lit up the
hall like a flash of lightning. She ran to the speaking tube beside the
stairway and shouted down to the office below that the hotel was on fire.

Firemen were pulling a fire engine toward the Lafarge when shouts
suddenly went up from the Winter Garden Theatre next door and a
fashionably dressed crowd poured out of its exits amid shouts of "Fire!
Fire!"[8] Actually the theater was not burning, but a member of the audience had seen firemen arriving at the Lafarge and had told some friends
that the hotel was on fire. People nearby heard only the word "fire"
and panicked. The word spread rapidly through the theater in an ever-
increasing murmur. Soon the audience was standing up, looking about.
A judge in the audience cried out, "Don't panic! There are plenty of
exits!" A police inspector, also in the audience, stood on his seat and
shouted, "It's only a drunken man—keep your seat!"[9] By then the play
had been interrupted and Edwin Booth stood in the center of the stage
with his arms outstretched, calling for order. But the audience was already pushing and shoving and trying to get out.

A very similar scene was taking place at Niblo's Garden, next to the
Metropolitan Hotel two blocks south. Harrington had gone up to the
room there, which he had rented four days before, and poured one bottle
of phosphorus on the bedding and another into a bureau drawer, and it
had begun to smolder right away. In his haste to get out, he left an
unopened bottle behind in a bag, along with some old clothes and boots.
As Harrington was leaving the hotel a woman discovered the fire and
told a chambermaid, who rushed downstairs to tell the proprietor. And
the word soon spread to the theater next door. A sword fight was in full
career on stage as "The Corsican Brothers" reached its climactic moment
when someone in the gallery shouted, "Fire!"[10] The entire audience stood
up and ran for the exits, leaving the stunned actors standing on stage
with swords dangling from their hands.

Kennedy and Headley continued south along Broadway, pushing their
way through the huge crowds which were wild with excitement. Rumors
were shouted back and forth in the streets about fires at this place and
that place and that they had all been set by Rebel spies. This last was, of
course, of greatest concern to the Confederates. "There was the wildest
excitement imaginable," Headley wrote. "There was all sorts of talk
about hanging the rebels to lamp posts or burning them at the stake. Still
we discovered that all was surmise apparently."[11]

As midnight approached, Colonel Martin was at work in a sixth-floor
room at French's Hotel and Kennedy was across Frankfort Street at the

Tammany Hotel. By then they were the only two Rebels still at work. After parting with Headley on Broadway, Kennedy had evidently stopped somewhere for more drinks, for he was drunk when he poured the Greek fire on the bedding in his room at the Tammany. When it did not ignite right away he touched it with a piece of burning paper and it flared up, so he hurried to the door, but when he looked back into the room the fire had gone out. He went back and relit it with a match, and this time the entire room seemed to flare up. He got out as quickly as he could, locking the door behind him, but he had failed to notice that the shutters on his room's window had been open all the time.

From across the street the porter at French's Hotel was showing his new revolver to the bookkeeper. Both saw Kennedy light the fire at Tammany's, and they raced down the stairs and across the street to give the alarm. Neither one thought to take the revolver along. By the time the bookkeeper reached the Tammany it was filling with smoke, a fire engine was there, and guests were running out into the street. He searched through the crowd for the man he had seen through the window while two firemen came out of the hotel carrying a woman and a child who had been asleep in the room next to Kennedy's. The bookkeeper suddenly remembered the army officer he had registered in his own hotel shortly before. He had spoken with a Southern drawl and his hat had lacked the usual ornamentation to go with his uniform. He told the porter to go get his revolver and keep an eye on that officer while he went to get the hotel's proprietor, Richard French.

Meanwhile, Martin, the army officer in question, opened the shutters on his window and looked out. He could see burning bedclothes being tossed out of the windows of the Tammany across the street. He went to the door of his room and looked out into the hall, where he was spotted by the porter and told not to leave his room because he was under suspicion. "You must be mistaken," Martin replied. "I don't want to be disturbed. Get out of the hall." Just then French, the proprietor, arrived. "I think it best you leave," he told Martin. "Do you have any fear of your hotel being set on fire?" Martin asked. "No, but I'd like you to leave," he was told. "Please see the cashier and get your money back. I won't let you stay under any consideration."[12] Martin grabbed his overcoat and hat and left. Several guests told French that Martin's overcoat pockets were bulging and one suggested that he be stopped and searched. French decided to head him off at the cashier's and do just that, but Martin left the hotel without getting his refund and thus got away.

Martin walked down Broadway to the National Hotel. There he heard the clerk discussing the fires with guests and was so alarmed by the subject that the clerk noticed. He gave Martin a room on the first floor but told the watchman to keep an eye on him. However, Martin had had enough of arson for one night. He left a call to be awakened at 6 a.m.

After walking for several hours, Kennedy went to his room at the Exchange Hotel and also went to bed.

Outside, the firebells continued to toll.

Elsewhere, the war went on. In Indiana the trial of Copperheads by a military commission heard its final witness that day, 25 November, and adjourned until 6 December to give the lawyers for the various defendants time to prepare their closing arguments.

The last of Sherman's troops left Milledgeville at about 9 that morning, crossing the wooden toll bridge over the Oconee River. The bridge belonged to a man a Federal officer called "a fat, dirty, lazy-looking citizen," who begged the soldiers not to burn it. He said that, although he had never been more than five miles from the river, he had "allers bin for the Union and wus yet," and added that he was a Mason and deserved protection.[13] It did him no good. The Federals lit fires on the bridge and within ten minutes the blazing timbers were falling into the river.

In Virginia, some command changes were made. General Hancock's old Gettysburg wound was bothering him so much that he had to relinquish command of the 2nd Corps. Meade's chief of staff, Major General Andrew A. Humphreys, was given Hancock's job on the 25th. "His appointment was recognized as eminently fitting," Horace Porter wrote, "and met with favor throughout the entire army."[14]

The next day, on the Confederate side, Lee's oldest son, Major General George Washington Custis Lee, an aide on Jefferson Davis' staff, was directed to report to Lieutenant General Richard Ewell, commander of the Military Department of Richmond for assignment to command a newly formed division. This division, composed mostly of Reserve units, contained most of the infantry in Ewell's department. It was stationed in the trenches southeast of Richmond. The authors of *Come Retribution* speculate that it was also used as a parent unit for regiments recruited in the northern Virginia area through which Lincoln would be brought to Richmond if he could be successfully captured and smuggled across the lower Potomac. Large numbers of men from these regiments could be sent on "leave" to their homes, where they would be on hand to provide protection for the kidnappers. But their units would still be in the lines east of Richmond, and the Federals, who kept close watch on the location of Confederate units, would not know that anything unusual was going on. Custis Lee, as one of Davis' aides, was probably already in on the plan, and therefore would not, like most commanders, wonder why so many of his men were sent off on leave. In fact, he might well have been in charge of the military preparations for covering the kidnappers' escape.

In New York on the 26th, fires continued to break out from delayed combustion of the Greek fire. At 2:30 a.m. the house detective at the Fifth Avenue Hotel, an elegant building of white marble overlooking Madison Square, opened the door of a room and was met with a rush of smoke. A guest at the Howard Hotel several miles to the south found his room was filling up with smoke from a fire in the room next door. Sailors on their way back to their ships docked along the Hudson River after putting out the burning hay on one ship were sent ashore again to help save a barge a block away from the first fire. At the Handfield Hotel, over by the East River, two members of the staff were so busy fighting flames that they could not take time to send for help. At dawn men coming to work at the lumber yard behind the Handfield found piles of wooden beams smoldering, as were stacks of hay at an adjacent stable.

The manager of the Astor House was boasting to some guests at about 9 that morning about how his hotel had escaped the flames. Perhaps he had been lucky, but then his was not the sort of establishment which would cater to arsonists. To be on the safe side he had set up a double watch and had put extra buckets of water at the foot of each stairway, but he had been confident enough to postpone a search of the hotel's 1,000 rooms until this morning, so as not to inconvenience his guests. Just then an employee rushed up and reported that a fire had broken out on the top floor.

Colonel Martin and Captain Kennedy sat in the parlor of the Exchange Hotel that morning, reading the papers. There were only a few incomplete stories at that hour, but both the *Times* and the *Herald* were sure that the fires were due to a Rebel plot. The *Times* said that the police were on the track of several suspects and added that a bag containing phosophorus found at one hotel had burst into flames when it had been opened. A familiar figure walked in, and the Confederates recognized him as "Old" Young, the detective they had seen in Toronto and whom they had seen watching McMasters' office. Young went to the desk and warned the manager to put on extra watchmen until the police were sure the danger had passed, while Martin and Kennedy tried their best to look inconspicuous behind their newspapers. Then Young, who had been up all night, came over and sat down next to Martin, who was still wearing his Union officer's uniform. Kennedy was sure that they were caught. Young noticed that Martin was reading about the fires, and remarked, "I'm looking for who did it, and I'll be damned if I don't get them."[15] Then a policeman came in and told Young that the superintendent wanted him at headquarters and the detective got up and left. Martin turned to Kennedy with a smile of relief.

The Confederates dispersed for a while, planning to meet at the cottage near Central Park at 6 p.m. Later papers had more details, and Martin and Headley read some of them at a restaurant on Broadway. Headley was nervous and insisted that they take a streetcar up to Central Park. A description of him given to the police by the clerk at the United States Hotel was in the *Evening Post's* third edition. However, the police appeared to be on the wrong track, for they had arrested some woman from Baltimore, a former Confederate soldier, and Lieutenant Kellogg, the Union officer who had gone to dinner while Martin fired his unmade room.

So, buoyed by his experience with Young, Martin decided that they would go downtown to McDonald's piano store to get his luggage and then to supper. They hailed a cab at about 4 p.m. and as they passed Union Square it dropped Martin off, while Headley continued downtown to the restaurant to order their supper. But as Martin started down the two steps into the piano shop's vestibule he saw Gus McDonald's niece, Katie, at the window, with a panic-stricken look on her face. Behind her, Martin could see several men, their backs to the street, talking with McDonald. Katie waved Martin away, and he turned and ran to catch up with the cab, not telling Headley what had happened. The lieutenant was nervous enough already. However, the fourth edition of the *Evening Post* told the story. It said that the police had made "an important arrest" of a man who was in possession of "the baggage of the chief conspirator and one hundred and twenty dollars in American gold. He was the confidant of the conspirators." The police, the paper said, believed that the Rebels had already left the city, but "have full descriptions of several of them."[16]

Now Martin was also worried, and he decided that they should get out of town and back to Canada as soon as they could. He and Headley went back to the cottage near Central Park and were relieved when the other four also showed up at the appointed time, for they had been afraid that some of them might have been picked up by the police. Checking the train schedules, they saw that a northbound express on the Hudson River Railroad would leave town at 10:40 p.m. and that sleeper cars would be open for boarding at 9 p.m. at the 30th Street depot at 10th Avenue. They decided to board the train there at that time. Meanwhile, those who had luggage would go get it and they would all meet at the Exchange Hotel.

Ashbrook and Harrington were sent to pick up tickets in advance, presumably because their faces were probably less familiar to any New York detectives who had spent time in Toronto. Then all six men boarded the sleeping car, sitting on a siding, and went directly to their berths. After a porter came through, Martin looked over the car and then passed instructions on to the other five: If anyone came for them they would resist, try to get out the exit at the rear of the car, and get lost in the crowd outside. Finally an engine and other cars were backed into the station and hooked onto their sleeper car, and passengers came swarming down the platform. Among them were several men without luggage who scrutinized everyone boarding the train, but they did not think to check those who were already on board. At 10:40 p.m., right on schedule, the whistle blew and with a hiss of steam the train started out for Albany and points north. The Confederates waited an hour before getting undressed. Then, convinced finally that no detectives were on board, they drifted off to sleep as the train chugged through the night.

---

1. Brandt, *The Man Who Tried to Burn New York*, 101.
2. Ibid., 102.
3. John W. Headly, "The Confederates' Attempt to Burn New York," in *The Blue and the Gray*, Henry Steele Commager, editor, (Indianapolis and New York, 1950), 734–735.
4. Ibid., 735.
5. Brandt, *The Man Who Tried to Burn New York*, 13–14.
6. Horan, *Confederate Agent*, 214.
7. Headly, "The Confederates' Attempt to Burn New York," 735.
8. Brandt, *The Man Who Tried to Burn New York*, 116.
9. Ibid., 14–15.
10. Ibid., 15.
11. Headly, "The Confederates' Attempt to Burn New York," 736.
12. Brandt, *The Man Who Tried to Burn New York*, 118–119.
13. Davis, *Sherman's March*, 67.
14. Porter, *Campaigning With Grant*, 329.
15. Brandt, *The Man Who Tried to Burn New York*, 20.
16. Ibid., 122.

Confound the Cavalry

26–28 November 1864

Major General George Stoneman, chief of cavalry of the Department of Army of the Ohio, had been captured during a raid near Macon before the fall of Atlanta, but he had recently been exchanged, as high-ranking officers often were despite the Union's refusal to make large-scale exchanges. Schofield then appointed him his second in command and put him in charge of his department's garrisons in Kentucky and eastern Tennessee. On the 26th, Stoneman reported that the Confederates under Breckinridge who had recently defeated Gillem's Federals and advanced nearly to Knoxville were then engaged in destroying the railroad in the neighborhood of Bull's Gap. Stoneman had ordered General Burbridge, the Union commander in Kentucky, to concentrate as many mounted men as possible near Cumberland Gap, ready to join him in east Tennessee, where Gillem was reorganizing his own force and Stoneman was gathering infantry and artillery units to hold the important points in the area so that the cavalry could take the offensive against Breckinridge. Stoneman hoped, by a rapid concentration of his cavalry, to reach the Tennessee-Virginia line ahead of the Rebels, cut them off, and beat them to Saltville, or at least to drive them back to Virginia, which would open the way for a raid into North Carolina or even South Carolina. "I submit this for your consideration," he told Schofield, "and if you approve of the idea, please inform me by telegraph. I hope you will not disapprove of it, as I think I can see very important results from its execution. I owe the Southern Confederacy a debt I am anxious to liquidate, and this appears a propitious occasion."[1]

Down in Georgia, Sherman's forces entered a different kind of country when they left Milledgeville and crossed the Oconee River. It was a swampy area of numerous sluggish streams, where the Federals first saw Spanish moss, palmettos, magnolias, sugar cane, and deadly coral snakes. Then they came to higher ground, covered with pine barrens, where farms were small and poor. The right wing, Howard's Army of the Tennessee, continued to tear up the railroad as it moved eastward, and Kilpatrick's cavalry division shifted across the front of the marching infantry columns from the right to the left, where it was to raid toward Augusta and keep the Confederates worried about defending that city for as long as possible. Kilpatrick had been riding in a carriage for several days while recuperating from a wound, but he felt better now and was again on horseback, as he stripped his division down to fighting weight by killing 500 of his weakest horses.

Wheeler's Confederate cavalry, meanwhile, moved to Sherman's front, occupying the town of Sandersville, There, at 3 a.m. on the 26th, a mob, probably consisting mostly of Rebel soldiers angered over the plundering and destruction being wreaked on the countryside by Sherman's men, took a bunch of captured Federals away from their guards and shot them down in a nearby field.

As Slocum's left wing approached Sandersville later that morning Wheeler's troopers put up a brief fight, before falling back. "A brigade of rebel cavalry was deployed before the town," Sherman wrote, "and was driven in and through it by our skirmish line. I myself saw the rebel cavalry apply fire to stacks of fodder standing in the fields at Sandersville, and gave orders to burn some unoccupied dwellings close by. On entering the town, I told certain citizens (who would be sure to spread the report) that, if the enemy attempted to carry out their threat to burn their food, corn, and fodder, in our route, I would most undoubtedly execute to the letter the general orders of devastation made at the outset of the campaign. With this exception, and one or two minor cases near Savannah, the people did not destroy food, for they saw clearly that it would be ruin to themselves.

"At Sandersville I halted the left wing until I heard that the right wing was abreast of us on the railroad. During the evening a negro was brought to me, who had that day been to the station (Tenille), about six miles south of the town. I inquired of him if there were Yankees there, and he answered, 'Yes.' He described in his own way what he had seen. 'First, there come along some cavalry-men, and they burned the depot; then come along some infantry-men, and they tore up the track, and burned it;' and just before he left they had 'sot fire to the well!'"[2]

A 16-year-old widow of a Confederate soldier watched the Federals march in. "It seemed to me the whole world was coming," she wrote. "Here came the 'wood-cutters'—clearing the way before the army. Men with axes on their shoulders, men with spades, men with guns. Men driving herds of cattle—cows, goats, hogs, sheep. Men on horseback with bunches of turkeys, bunches of chickens, ducks and guineas swinging on both sides of the horse like saddle-bags. Then the wagons— Oh! the wagons—in every direction—wagons! wagons!"[3] The 9-year-old daughter of one of the men who had buried the murdered Union prisoners saw Wheeler's troops ride out while bullets splattered against her house, and she also saw the Federals march in. "In a few minutes our house was filled with the surging mass," she later wrote. "In a little while even the table cloth left, and the food disappeared in a second. Fences were torn down, hogs shot, cows butchered, women crying, children screaming, pandemonium reigned. Then the jail, court house, peoples' barns and a large factory that made buckets and saddle-trees were all ablaze."[4]

Not far from Sandersville a Union captain with a party of foragers found two little girls all alone in a remote deserted cabin. One was 5 and the other was about 3 years old, and they were so dirty that the Federals thought at first that they were black children. They were exceedingly shy and would only say, "Mamma gone, Mamma gone."[5] But they were won over by hot food, and soon were fast friends with the soldiers, who built a fire and gave the girls a hot bath and washed and combed their hair. All they had to wear were little dresses made out of cotton sacks with holes ripped in them for their heads and arms, but the Union foragers soon stole complete new wardrobes for them, and since there was nobody else to take care of the girls, the foragers' regiment adopted them, mounted them on pack mules, and took them along to Savannah.

On the night of the 26th, Wheeler's cavalry caught up with Kilpatrick's troopers, who were bivouacked by the railroad near the town of Waynesboro. At about midnight the Confederates made a rare night attack on the Union camp, scattered the pickets, lept over the log barricades, and galloped through the sleeping Federals, capturing several flags, fifty horses, and numerous prisoners, as well as a great many blankets and overcoats. Kilpatrick was at a nearby house, and he and his staff avoided capture only by jumping from a window, leaving behind a pair of attractive black women.

The cavalry battle continued through the 27th, as the Federals fell back from one barricade to another along the road in some of the most furious clashes of cavalry in the war. The Confederates were convinced that they were fighting to save Augusta, and they attacked furiously. Kilpatrick's men were not quite so well motivated, and they continued to give ground slowly until late that night when a division of infantry came to their aid. "Confound the cavalry," a major in this infantry division wrote. "They're good for nothing but to run down horses and steal chickens."[6]

Up in Tennessee it rained all day on the 26th and into the 27th as Hood's Confederate infantry closed up on Schofield's Union position at Columbia. That town was on the south bank of the Duck River, and Schofield had entrenched a line that ran from the river above the town to the river below it. It was a strong position, and Hood had no intention of attacking it. His mind was already ranging ahead to the capture of Nashville as the first step in his campaign to renew the Confederacy's fortunes. Intermittent rain continued to fall on the 27th as the last of his infantry came up and he sent Forrest's cavalry farther east, where he planned to cross the river as soon as possible. When that would be was hard to say. The rain had swollen the river, so that it could not be crossed at the normal fords, and his pontoon train had fallen far behind. This was due mostly to the fact that, because of a shortage of horses and mules, it was being drawn by Texas longhorn steers. That night, as it began to snow, Schofield moved all his forces to the north side of the river and burned the bridge.

In Virginia on the 27th, General Butler invited Admiral Porter to come along on a cruise down the James River on his headquarters steamer, the *Greyhound*. The two had not gotten along well when Butler had been the Union commander in Louisiana in 1862 and Porter had been a subordinate officer in Farragut's fleet on the Mississippi River. But now the two needed to cooperate, not only on the James, but in the planned operation against Wilmington, which both were working on. Butler had invited Porter to lunch a few days before, and now he was showing off his fancy steamship. That was not necessarily a good move, as far as endearing him to Porter was concerned. The *Greyhound*, a captured blockade runner, was said to be the fastest ship on the James, while Porter's flagship, the *Malvern*, was old and slow. As Porter was shown around, he was not only envious of the general's ship but he was disturbed by the lack of security on board her. He was just on his way up to the bridge to report some suspicious-looking civilians who were loitering around the ship's lounge when suddenly the engine room was shattered by an explosion. The ship was enveloped in flames and sank within five minutes. Porter, Butler, Congressman Robert Schenck, and others aboard just barely escaped with their lives. An investigation concluded that the explosion was due to Confederate sabotage, but Porter saw it as another example of Butler's incompetence. "It requires great patience to deal with fools," he said, "and I have no patience to spare."[7]

Another ship sank in the James River that night. The captured Rebel raider, the *Florida*, suddenly went down off Newport News. To the world at large, it was an unfortunate result of her collision with a Union transport a few days before, but Admiral Porter privately confided that he had put an engineer aboard the ship with orders to "open her sea cock before midnight, and do not leave that engine room until the water is up to your chin."[8] With the ship under nine fathoms of water the United States would not have to return her to the neutral port where she had been captured. Two years later, an American gunboat did put into Bahia on the birthday of the Emperor of Brazil and fired a 21-gun salute as a gesture of respect to make up for the *Wachusett's* violation of Brazilian neutrality, but by then the war was long over. Captain Collins was eventually court-martialed and sentenced to be dismissed from the service for that violation, but Secretary of the Navy Welles set aside the verdict, restored Collins to duty, and later promoted him.

Over in West Virginia, Colonel G. R. Latham, commander of the Union garrison at New Creek, sent two small columns toward Moorefield that day, where Rebel partisans were said to be, with orders to "attack, capture, or drive them off."[9] One column, under Lieutenant Colonel Rufus E. Fleming, consisted of 120 men in three companies of cavalry plus one cannon. The other column, commanded by Major Peter J. Potts, consisted of 155 men. Fleming's column was to advance directly on Moorfield while Potts' was to cross over into a different valley and come in on Moorefield from the east. In addition, about 150 state scouts, known as "Swamps," were told to block the valley of the South Fork of the Potomac River south of Moorefield to prevent the Confederates from escaping in that direction. Brigadier General B. F. Kelley, commander of all forces of the Union Department of West Virginia west of Hancock, Maryland, had planned this operation and hoped to thus surround and capture the guerrillas.

However, when Fleming was still five miles from Moorefield his scouts brought him word that Rosser's Division of Confederate cavalry from

Early's army was either in or approaching that town. In fact, Rosser was on his way to attack New Creek when Fleming ran into him. Fleming fell back fighting, but he was handicapped by the fact that two and a half of his three companies were armed only with muzzleloading rifles while the other half a company had only revolvers, and the Rebels outnumbered him so badly that he was soon outflanked and lost his gun, his only wagon and ambulance, and about twenty men. However, the rest of his force got away.

Major Potts' column did not learn of Rosser's presence, and it attacked Moorefield at dawn on the 28th. His force was promptly driven back, so, learning that he was badly outnumbered, Potts circled around to the south, crossed the South Branch, and retreated to the northwest, toward Williamsport. What Potts encountered, however, was only about 1,000 men Rosser had left behind while he advanced with about 2,000 on New Creek. There Colonel Latham had about 500 cavalrymen, mostly dismounted, of which only about 160 were armed (and with condemned weapons at that), and about 200 artillerymen with three field pieces plus four small guns that were mounted in an earthwork known as Fort Kelley. Confederates wearing captured blue overcoats surprised and captured all the Union pickets—who thought they were Potts' men returning—and overran the artillery before the Federals saw through the deception and realized that they were under attack. They were quickly routed, and over 400 of them were captured. The Confederates also captured the field pieces, spiked the garrison artillery, blew up the fort's magazine, cut the telegraph lines, and destroyed almost the entire town of New Creek, including Union storehouses bulging with supplies. "I feel most deeply the disaster," Colonel Latham wrote in his report, "and especially the stigma of a surprise, but without standing picket myself I cannot see that I could have been much more vigilant."[10]

Rosser then sent a detachment of about 300 men five miles farther west to attack the Baltimore & Ohio Railroad at the town of Piedmont. However, the little garrison of 35 men defending the town took up a position that commanded all the important buildings, and its fire prevented the Rebels from doing much damage to the government warehouses and railroad facilities. After three hours of trying, the Confederates rejoined Rosser's main force, which eventually returned to the Shenandoah Valley with 400 or 500 head of cattle and a few sheep that were rounded up in the surrounding area.

That same day, the 28th, Sheridan sent Merritt's 1st Division of the Cavalry Corps east of the Blue Ridge into Mosby's home territory, "for the purpose of destroying all mills, barns, forage, driving off stock, and capturing and dispersing the guerrilla bands."[11] Sheridan told the garrison commander at Harper's Ferry, "Should complaints come in from the citizens of Loudoun County tell them that they have furnished too many meals to guerrillas to expect much sympathy."[12]

The Confederate officers who had set the fires in New York returned to Toronto on the night of 28 November and reported to Commissioner Jacob Thompson. They blamed their lack of success on the Greek Fire, which was not nearly so effective as they had expected it to be. "Their reliance on the Greek Fire has proved a misfortune," Thompson reported to Secretary of State Judah P. Benjamin. "It cannot be depended on as an agent in such work. I have no faith whatever in it, and no attempt shall hereafter be made, under my general directions with any such material."[13]

However, the fire marshall of New York, after examining the contents of two bottles found at the Fifth-Avenue Hotel, felt that the fault was not with the chemicals but with the arsonists. "The chemist had done his work sagaciously," he wrote, "but in carrying out the plan a blunder was committed which defeated the anticipated results. In each case the doors and windows of the room were left closed, so that when the phosphorus ignited, the fire only smoldered from the want of oxygen necessary to give it activity, thus affording an opportunity for its detection before much harm was done." The New York *Times* said, "The plan was excellently well conceived, and evidently prepared with great care, and had it been executed with one-half the ability with which it was drawn up, no human power could have saved the city from utter destruction . . . the best portion of the city would have been laid in ashes."[14]

All of the New York papers, Unionist and Copperhead alike, condemned the Confederate attack, and most would have agreed with the *Herald*, which said, "The wretches who would have destroyed all our principal hotels but one by fire, and caused the death of their harmless occupants, deserve no pity, and should they be detected, as we have no doubt they will be, should be hung up in as brief a space as possible and as soon as the law will permit."[15] The mayor announced a reward that day of $25,000 for the arrest and conviction of the arsonists, but the board of supervisors reduced it to $5,000. However, the Hotel-Keepers Society also offered a reward, set at first at $3,000 but later raised to $20,000.

Down in Georgia, Sherman's army continued to wreak havoc on the state. The treatment the civilians in his path received depended a great deal upon the character of the individual soldiers they encountered. A good illustration was the case of the elderly Canning family, whose plantation was visited by Union foragers on the 28th. The first Federals they met offered to pay for food, advised Mrs. Canning to move her meat indoors for safekeeping, and even helped her to carry it to her house. "I began to think they were not so bad after all," she said.

But as more and more Federals arrived they invaded her house and demanded to know how long since the Rebels had passed. She refused to answer. "You goddam old bitch, why don't you answer me?" one of them demanded.

"Don't you know Southern women know no such persons as 'Rebs'?" another said.

"Then will you please tell me, ma'am, how long since the last Confederate soldier passed here?"

"General Wheeler's men have been passing for several days," she said, "and some of them went by this morning. I expect they're waiting for you down in the swamp."

More soldiers dragged Mr. Canning outside. "We just want you to show us where you hid the syrup," one of them said. The old man said he could not walk so far, so they hoisted him onto a mule and led him to the swamp. Now, old man, where's your gold?" they demanded.

"I've got none," he told them. "I just came down here for a short stay. All our money's at home in the bank."

"That tale won't do," they said. "Your wife went to Macon and brought it down, a whole trunkful of gold and silver. Your nigger man said he could hardly lift it. Now where's it at?"

"No. You're wrong," he said. "I have none."

So they tied a rope around his neck, slung it over a tree limb, and hoisted him off the ground until he was almost unconscious. Then they lowered him and demanded the gold again, but again he denied having any. They repeated the procedure, but still he maintained his story. "I'm an old man, and at your mercy," he said. "You can kill me, but I won't die with a lie on my lips. I've got no gold. I have a gold watch at the house, but nothing else."

They swung him up again and dropped him even harder than before, and he blacked out briefly. "We like to have carried that game too far," one of them said. Then they put him back on the mule and took him back to the house.

"Give them my watch," he told his astonished wife.

"Why?" she asked. "They've no business with your watch."

"Give it to them and let them go," he said. "I'm almost dead." She gave the looters the watch and they went out to her yard, where they forced the overseer's wife to lead them to the family's buried table silver.

That night the old man had a very high fever, his tongue was swollen and parched, and he was bleeding from his nose and ears. But Mrs. Canning could not help him. "The Yankees had cut all the well ropes and stolen the buckets, so there was no water nearer than half a mile." They were saved by a "rough-looking man from Iowa," a soldier who found a bucket and brought her some water and gave her some brown sugar and parched coffee. "I never appreciated a cup of coffee more than I did that one," she said.

When the soldiers had all gone, the Cannings took a look around. "We could hardly believe it was our home. One week before it was one of the most beautiful places in the state. Now it was a vast wreck. Gin-houses, packing screws, granary—all lay in ashes. Not a fence was to be seen for miles . . . the army had turned their stock into the fields and destroyed what they had not carried off. Burning cotton and grain filled the air with smoke, and even the sun seemed to hide its face."[16]

---

1. *Official Records*, 45:I:1074.
2. Sherman, *Memoirs*, 667–668.
3. Davis, *Sherman's March*, 76.
4. Ibid., 75.
5. Ibid., 78.
6. Ibid., 84.
7. Rod Gragg, *Confederate Goliath: The Battle of Fort Fisher* (New York, 1991), 44.
8. Foote, *The Civil War*, 3:590.
9. *Official Records*, 43:I:654.
10. Ibid., 43:I:661.
11. Ibid., 43:I:671.
12. Ibid., 43:II:687.
13. Ibid., 43:II:934.
14. Brandt, *The Man Who Tried to Burn New York*, 128–129.
15. Ibid., 132.
16. Davis, *Sherman's March*, 84–86.

CHAPTER THIRTY-FIVE

The Most Critical Time I Have Ever Seen

28–30 November 1864

In Tennessee on the morning of the 28th, Schofield telegraphed to Thomas, back at Nashville: "My troops and material are all on the north side of Duck River; the withdrawal was completed at daylight this morning without serious difficulty. Cox holds the ford in front of Columbia, and Ruger the railroad bridge, which I partially destroyed. Stanley is going into position a short distance in rear of Cox. I think I can now stop Hood's advance by any line near this, and meet in time any distant movement to turn my position. I regret extremely the necessity of withdrawing from Columbia, but believe it was absolute; I will explain fully in time." Fifteen minutes later he added, "I am in doubt whether it is advisable, with reference to future operations, to hold this position or to retire to some point from which we can move offensively. Of course we cannot secure the river here. I could easily have held the bridge head at the railroad, but it would have been useless, as we could not possibly advance from that point. Please give me your views and wishes." Ten minutes after that he added, "I have all the fords above and below this place well watched and guarded as far as possible. Wilson is operating with his main force on my left. The enemy does not appear to have moved in that direction yet to any considerable distance. I will probably be able to give you pretty full information this evening. Do you not think the infantry at the distant crossings below here should now be withdrawn and cavalry substituted? I do not think we can prevent the crossing of even the enemy's cavalry, because the places are so numerous. I think the best we can do is to hold the crossings near us and watch the distant ones."[1]

Hood discovered that morning that Schofield had retreated to the north bank of the Duck River during the night and had burned the bridge behind him, but the weather had turned warm and clear, the river was falling, and that day three columns of Forrest's cavalry—Jackson's Division, Chalmers with Rucker's Brigade, and Colonel Jacob Biffle's small brigade—crossed to the north side at fords from three to seven miles east of Columbia. However, Buford's Division, moving even farther to the east, ran into stiff opposition from Capron's Union brigade, which was guarding the ford at Hardison's Mill on the Lewisburg Pike to Franklin and Nashville. It was Hood's plan to follow his cavalry with two of his infantry corps and one division of another and to get between Schofield and Nashville. S. D. Lee would be left south of the river with two of his divisions and most of the army's artillery to demonstrate against Schofield's front. That afternoon the pontoon train arrived and Hood's engineers began laying their bridge across Davis's Ford, four miles east of Columbia.

Wilson was now on hand in personal charge of the Union cavalry, and he notified Schofield shortly after 2 p.m. that the Confederate cavalry was across the river. Then he began concentrating Hatch's division and Croxton's brigade at Hurt's Crossroads, five miles north of Hardison's Mill, where they began erecting barricades across the macadamized Lewisburg Pike. But because of this concentration of the Union cavalry, there was little opposition to the other Confederate crossings. And Brigadier General Lawrence S. Ross's Texas brigade of Jackson's Division, once across, moved to the east and at sunset attacked the rear of Capron's Union brigade guarding the ford at Hardison's Mill. Capron and his reserve, the 7th Ohio Cavalry, were routed after a brief, spirited engagement. But Major J. Morris Young of the 5th Iowa Cavalry led the rest of the brigade, which was cut off, on a wild, saber-swinging charge in the dark through Ross's Texans to escape.

At about the same hour, 5:30 p.m., Schofield received a message Wilson had written an hour before. It said that Forrest's cavalry seemed to be en route to Spring Hill, a town several miles north of Columbia on the macadamized road leading from there to Franklin and Nashville. "You had better look out for that place," he said.[2] In response, Schofield only ordered Stanley to send two brigades of Brigadier General Nathan Kimball's 1st Division of the 4th Corps north to guard the supply wagons, which were parked where Rutherford Creek crossed the Franklin Pike, less than half way to Spring Hill.

Also at about that time, Brigadier General Thomas J. Wood, commander of the 3rd Division of the 4th Corps, complained to Stanley: "I am informed that the cavalry has been withdrawn from our left, and my pickets report that two regiments of rebel cavalry have crossed the river. It will be necessary to have cavalry watch those fords, as infantry cannot do it, and as the country is open the whole rebel army may be over on our left flank without hindrance." Later he expanded upon his complaint: "It seems to me a little strange that General Schofield does not intimate what measures he proposes to adopt to protect ourselves and guard our trains, and still more strange that he does not initiate such measures at once, as the enemy, according to his own statement, has crossed the river in force. It is perfectly patent to my mind, if the enemy has crossed in force, that General Wilson will not be able to check him. It requires no oracle to predict the effect of the enemy's reaching the Franklin pike in our rear. I have ordered Captain Bartlett, my inspector, to take two companies of the Fifty-first Indiana, numbering in the aggregate about 150 men, and post them on a very commanding eminence nearly a mile to the east of our left flank, and whence the approach to us from the ford can be watched, with orders to observe well and give timely notice of any movement of the enemy in that direction." He suggested that two brigades of Kimball's division should be moved to his left at once, otherwise, if the Confederates should attack that flank "we could not extricate our trains, possibly not ourselves."[3] Consequently, Stanley only sent one of Kimball's brigades to Rutherford Creek and told the other to wait until daylight.

A half-hour after receiving Wilson's message, Schofield received one from Thomas saying that he had heard from Grant that Savannah newspapers claimed Forrest was expected to attack Sherman's rear and that Breckinridge was already on his way to Georgia from east Tennessee. "If this proves true, General Grant wishes me to take the offensive against Hood, and destroy the railroad into Virginia with Stoneman's force, now beyond Knoxville. General Smith will certainly be here in three days, when I think we will be able to commence moving on Hood, whether Forrest goes to Georgia or remains with Hood."[4]

At 8 p.m. Stanley received instructions from Schofield to send a force up the river to find out what the Rebels were up to on the left, but either Stanley or Wood decided that it was too dark to send out such a reconnaissance. The two companies Wood had previously sent out would have to suffice.

At 1 a.m. on the 29th, Wilson wrote a dispatch to Schofield that contained the first definite information about what Hood's infantry was up to. Interrogation of two of Forrest's men who had been captured revealed not only that all of the Rebel cavalry was north of the Duck River but that the infantry was to follow on pontoon bridges that were expected to be ready at 11 p.m. on the 28th. "I think it very clear that they are aiming for Franklin, and that you ought to get to Spring Hill by 10 a.m. I'll keep on this road and hold the enemy all I can . . . There may be no strong advance of the enemy's cavalry til the infantry have crossed, which will be between now and daylight. Get back to Franklin without delay, leaving a small force to detain the enemy. The rebels will move by this road toward that point." Somehow the rider carrying this message did not get through to Schofield, however, and at 3 a.m. another copy had to be sent, marked "Important, Trot!!"[5]

An hour later Wilson decided that he was not satisfied with his position at Hurt's Crossroads, so he ordered his troopers to move north about five miles along the Lewisburg Pike to the village of Mount Carmel. At dawn on the 29th, Jackson's Division of Forrest's cavalry, itself about as large as the forces Wilson had concentrated so far, attacked Croxton's brigade, which was Wilson's rear guard. Croxton had to dismount several regiments to fight off the aggressive Rebels.

Wilson's courier had to go by way of Spring Hill, for a total distance of about twenty miles, and it was 7 a.m. by the time he finally delivered the 1 a.m. message to Schofield. The latter did not care for Wilson telling him what to do, but he agreed with the gist of what he said, and he immediately ordered one of his own divisions (Ruger's 2nd) and two of Stanley's to Spring Hill and the wagon train to move to that place from Rutherford Creek. Before 8 a.m. he received two messages that Thomas had sent from Nashville the night before. In the first, Thomas expressed the hope that Schofield could hold on where he was until A. J. Smith's troops arrived, but in the second, written after he had heard about the Confederate crossing of the river, he said that, unless Wilson could drive them back, Schofield would have to fall back to the north bank of the Harpeth River at Franklin.

Then the Rebel artillery opened a heavy bombardment from south of the Duck River at Columbia, which seemed to contradict the notion that Hood's infantry was crossing the river farther east. Uncertain of what was really going on, unwilling to fall back if he did not have to, and lacking any timely information from Wilson's cavalry, Schofield suspended Ruger's move and told Stanley to take only one division to Spring Hill (Brigadier General George D. Wagner's 2nd) as an escort for the wagon train, stopping Kimball's 1st Division at Rutherford Creek. He also ordered Wood to make a reconnaissance up the river to find out whether the Confederate infantry had really crossed over. This was conducted by Colonel P. Sidney Post's 2nd Brigade of Wood's 3rd Division of the 4th Corps, and Schofield himself rode with it for a few miles before returning to his headquarters, leaving his aide and chief engineer, Captain William J. Twining, to ride with Post.

Colonel Datus Coon's 2nd Brigade of Hatch's 5th Division of Wilson's cavalry was just approaching Mount Carmel at 9 a.m., and Capron's brigade, now the 1st of the 6th Division, was already in the town and building barricades from fence rails when Chalmer's Division of Forrest's cavalry came charging out of some nearby trees screaming and yelling "like legions of wild Comanches."[6] While Jackson had harassed the Federals from the rear, Chalmers had circled around and gotten in front of them. Coon's troopers were veterans who had fought Forrest's men down in Mississippi, and most of them were armed with Spencer repeating carbines. They dismounted, opened fire, and drove Chalmer's troops back long enough for Hatch's other brigade to come up. Behind Hatch came Croxton's brigade, the 1st of the 1st Division, and behind it came Jackson's Rebels, still pursuing. Croxton's men had just taken position behind a garden fence when the Confederates launched another attack, but they were soon driven back into the cover of the trees.

By 10 a.m. the firing had died down and Wilson's aide sent off a note to Schofield telling him that the Union troopers had been driven back to Mount Carmel and would soon fall back even farther but that so far they had been fighting only cavalry. Wilson was worried that the lull in the fighting meant that Forrest was moving around to the north of him again, and he was determined to keep the Confederates from getting between him and Nashville. He therefore ordered Hatch to move north again and for his men not to mount up for the first two miles so they would be ready to drive off any attack. But no attack came.

Hood's infantry had not crossed the river during the night, as Wilson had expected. The first light of dawn had been streaking the eastern sky

by the time Major General Patrick Cleburne's crack division of Cheatham's Corps led the way. It was 7:30 a.m. before it was all across, and
it was 9:30 a.m. on a beautiful fall day by the time the tail of the column
was on the north side. Hood himself rode with Cleburne's Division. He
was strapped to the saddle as usual, his wooden leg jammed into the
stirrup, his crippled arm hanging useless, and a pair of crutches strapped
to the saddle. He told a chaplain that morning, while the troops were
crossing the pontoon bridge, that he would "press forward with all possible speed and . . . would either beat the enemy to Nashville or make
them go there double quick."[7]

Wilson had also been wrong about the infantry's crossing place and
objective. He had told Schofield that Hood's bridges were just east of
Huey's Mill, which was only a little southwest of Hardison's Mill and
the Lewisburg Pike, and that the Rebels would advance along that road
to Franklin. But in fact the pontoons were laid at Davis's Ford, only a
couple of miles east of Columbia, and Hood planned to take them along
a country road to Spring Hill. Wilson's cavalry was on the wrong road
and much too far north to interfere with or even detect this move.

About a mile north of the river Hood stopped to summon his local
guide because he noticed that the road they were following did not seem
to conform to the map he was using. This map was evidently a copy of
a Federal map which the Confederates had found in Columbia the day
before. According to it, Spring Hill was only twelve miles from Davis's
Ford, but the scout, who had been born and raised in the area, explained
to the general that the road they were following was one of the oldest
and worst in the county and that it twisted and turned to follow property
lines, making the actual distance much longer. (In fact, it was over seventeen miles.) Hood was surprised and concerned but there was little he
could do but press on.

He was soon hit with another surprise. Major T. E. Jameson, another
resident of the area, had been sent forward with the advance guard with
orders to report any difficulties encountered by the head of the column,
and at about 10 a.m. he rode back to advise the general that they had
been fired on by Union skirmishers up ahead. Hood's scout soon came
back with the added information that from a nearby hill he had seen
Federals deployed in line of battle along a small ravine. Both groups of
Federals belonged to Post's reconnaissance. Hood decided that a range
of hills would screen his march from the Federals' view, but in order to
prevent surprise and to be ready to fight at short notice he put almost
half of Major General John C. Brown's division in skirmish line in the
fields west of the road while the rest of Brown's Division marched in
column through the fields on the east side of the road, ready to form a

reserve behind Cleburne's troops if they should be attacked from the west. The condition of the road was bad enough, but marching through muddy fields and woods soon wore down Brown's troops until they were just dragging themselves along.

Captain Twining notified Schofield of the Confederate presence, but said that an intervening hill prevented him from telling whether the Confederates were moving north or holding their position. Schofield was more worried about a Rebel attack upon his immediate left flank than the possibility that they might be trying to get between him and Franklin. He sent Ruger's 2nd Division of the 23rd Corps from his right to his left to reinforce Wood, but he decided that, except for that and Stanley's two divisions already sent up the road, he would maintain his position just north of the Duck River until dark and only then withdraw to Franklin. Since he did not have enough transportation to take them with him, he had destroyed his pontoon boats when he had crossed to the north bank, so he had to telegraph Thomas to ask that more pontoons be sent from Nashville to Franklin to allow him to cross to the north side of the Harpeth River there. S. D. Lee, commanding the artillery and two divisions of infantry left behind by Hood, saw Ruger's troops withdraw from the Union right and ordered up some pontoons for a crossing of the Duck River on that flank.

At the beginning of the day the only Union troops at Spring Hill had been members of the 12th Tennessee Cavalry, a new, inexperienced regiment of what the Confederates called "homemade Yankees." Most of its men were manning the courier line between Franklin and Spring Hill, and most of the remaining 200 were on picket duty. Then, in the middle of the morning, four companies of the 73rd Illinois Infantry marched into Spring Hill with orders to deploy north of the town and stop any stragglers trying to go farther north. They were followed by the army's huge train of supply wagons, escorted by about 240 men of the 103rd Ohio.

At about 10 a.m. a troop of the 2nd Michigan Cavalry trotted in after having been cut off near the Duck River by the Confederate advance. Its captain alerted Lieutenant Colonel Charles C. Hoefling, commander of the 12th Tennessee, that there were a lot of Rebels in the area, and soon Hoefling's outposts retreated toward the town from a large body of Confederate cavalry. Hoefling sent the Michigan company to back them up and dashed off a note to Schofield that Spring Hill and the wagon train were in danger and that communication with Wilson was cut.

Fortunately for Hoefling, more reinforcements came in at about 11 a.m., consisting of the 3rd Illinois Cavalry and three troops of the 11th Indiana. These units, under Colonel R. R. Stewart of the 3rd Illinois, had been guarding crossings of the Duck River west of Columbia and were on their way to rejoin Hatch's division. They rode eastward out of Spring Hill, dismounted, and started constructing a barricade of logs and fence rails while a few videttes rode farther east. Soon the sound of gunfire indicated that the videttes had run into Rebels.

After faking Wilson into retreating to the north along the Lewisburg Pike, Forrest had left Ross's Brigade of Jackson's Division to follow him and keep up the show of pursuit while with the rest of his command he had turned to the west toward Spring Hill and had driven in Hoefling's pickets. When the Rebels came upon Stewart's troopers, Brigadier General Frank C. Armstrong's Mississippi brigade charged the Union line like a mounted whirlwind but was driven off by unexpectedly heavy fire. Most of the 3rd Illinois was armed with Colt Revolving Rifles, scaled-up versions of the popular handgun, and Stewart's men were veterans of two years of combat.

Forrest dismounted his men and sent them forward again. His line was much longer than Stewart's and the latter fell back to avoid being flanked. Forrest, moving south with part of his command, came to a high hill from which he could see the Columbia-Franklin Pike filled with Schofield's wagons. This was a tempting target, and he ordered a mounted charge by the 21st Tennessee Cavalry of Buford's Division. However, this regiment ran into the lone company of the 2nd Michigan. Its men were also veteran troops—two years before, that company's regiment had been the first command of then-colonel Phil Sheridan— and they were armed with Spencer repeaters. They cut the 21st Tennessee to pieces, wounding its colonel three times in the process, but continued to fall back in conformity with Stewart's command. It took Forrest an hour to push these stubborn Federals back to the outskirts of Spring Hill, by which time detachments of the 103rd Ohio were constructing breastworks of logs and rails behind them and the four companies of the 73rd Illinois were doing the same north of town.

The head of Stanley's column, marching along the Columbia-Franklin turnpike with about 800 wagons and 40 pieces of artillery, was still over two miles from Spring Hill at 11:30 a.m. when a frightened Union cavalryman was brought to General Stanley. He reported that Forrest's cavalry was approaching Spring Hill. A few minutes later, the courier carrying Hoefling's message to Schofield was intercepted, and Stanley took it upon himself to open and read the dispatch, adding an endorsement saying that he had done so and that he would soon be in Spring Hill. At 12:15 p.m. Stanley received a message from Schofield, back at Columbia, telling him that a large enemy force was north of the river and telling him to select a good position at Spring Hill and to reconnoiter to the east and southeast. Instead of the routine job of guarding the wagon train, Stanley suddenly found himself in the middle of a crisis. "It was," he later wrote, "the biggest day's work I ever accomplished for the United States."[8]

Stanley's leading brigade, Colonel Emerson's Opdycke's 1st Brigade of Wagner's 2nd Division of the 4th Corps, began to run, and at 12:30 p.m. it passed the railroad depot and jogged on out the north side of town. There a thin Confederate skirmish line had approached to within 400 yards of the wagon park. But Opdycke deployed two small regiments as skirmishers and the rest of his brigade in line of battle and when they advanced the Rebels faded back and disappeared. Opdycke then formed a half-mile long defensive perimeter covering the north side of Spring Hill.

Meanwhile, the 2nd Brigade of Wagner's division, commanded by Colonel John Q. Lane, moved out to the east side of the town and hastily formed line of battle. When skirmishers from the 28th Kentucky were in position, Lane ordered an advance against Forrest's Confederates, who could be seen on a low hill a half mile east of the town. His 1,600 men passed the hastily constructed breastworks of the Union cavalry and train guards and pushed on up the hill. Armstrong's Mississippians launched a countercharge but were repulsed and then pushed off their hill.

Wagner's 3rd Brigade, commanded by Colonel Luther P. Bradley, was delayed by several batteries of artillery, and Lane had already pushed Armstrong back when it came up on his right at about 2 p.m. It began constructing breastworks of logs and fence rails on a wooded knoll about a half-mile east of the turnpike and well to the southeast of Lane's hill, while Bradley put one regiment in reserve and sent another out as skirmishers. Forrest did not see Bradley's main position under the trees on the knoll but saw his skirmishers advancing and told Chalmers to "drive those fellows off." Chalmers was reluctant to attack them, thinking there must be a large Union force nearby backing up those skirmishers. "I think you are mistaken," Forrest told him. That is only a small cavalry force." Chalmers sent Colonel Tyree Bell's brigade of Buford's Division foward dismounted and it easily pushed the Federal skirmishers back about a half a mile. But then it not only came up against Bradley's main line but was shelled by two batteries of Union artillery positioned along the turnpike and fell back at about 3 p.m. When Chalmers returned to report to Forrest the latter said, rather sheepishly, "They was in there sure enough, wasn't they, Chalmers?"⁹

From interrogation of some of Bradley's skirmishers who had been captured, Forrest learned that at least part of the 4th Corps was in his front, and he decided there was little he could do but skirmish with the Federals and wait for Hood's infantry to show up. Before long his men on the north side of Spring Hill brought him a dispatch from Thomas to Schofield found on a Union courier who had ridden in from the direction of Franklin. It was about twelve hours old and said, among other things: "I desire you to fall back from Columbia and to take up your position at Franklin, leaving a sufficient force at Spring Hill to contest the enemy's progress until you are securely posted at Franklin . . . General A. J. Smith's command has not yet reached Nashville; as soon as he arrives I will make immediate disposition of his troops and notify you of the same."¹⁰

At about 3 p.m., Post's brigade returned from its reconnaissance up the Duck River with two disturbing bits of news for General Schofield: Large formations of Confederates were moving north beyond the Union left flank; and whenever the artillery duel across the Duck died down enough the sound of artillery fire could be heard coming from the direction of Spring Hill. Schofield finally realized that the artillery fire from Columbia was just a feint to keep him occupied and that Hood was not aiming a blow at his immediate left but at his line of communication. At 3:30 p.m. he personally led two of Ruger's brigades north toward Spring Hill.

He was barely on his way when S. D. Lee finally got his pontoons to a ford west of Columbia and started ferrying troops across to the north bank, despite long-range Union artillery fire and the rifle fire of a couple of infantry regiments in some woods about 300 yards away. At about 4 p.m. the Rebels advanced and drove the Federals from the woods and established a firm bridgehead, and by dark Confederate engineers were busily constructing a pontoon bridge across the ford.

Hood also heard the firing at Spring Hill and realized that Forrest had run into Federals there. He had hoped that the cavalry could seize the town without serious opposition. At about 3 p.m.—as Post was reporting to Schofield and Chalmers was blundering into Bradley—the head of Hood's column reached a ford over Rutherford Creek, well upstream from the point where Kimball's 1st Division of the 4th Corps still guarded the Columbia-Franklin Pike. Cheatham's Corps pressed on, wading the swollen stream, but Hood decided to hold Stewart's Corps in reserve at the crossing. According to Stewart, Hood was worried that

Cheatham's column might be "in great danger of being out-flanked and crushed."[11] Hood rode on ahead to the same hill from which Forrest had seen the Union supply wagons. He too saw wagons on the turnpike to the west, but he also saw enemy troops double-timing up the road. The Federals saw him, as well. They did not know who he was but he had the appearance of a general with his staff, and Stanley had his artillery throw a few shells in his direction.

Hood rode back to Cleburne's Division, still leading his column, and had it deploy en echelon, each brigade going into line of battle behind the previous one's left flank so that when it reached the turnpike it could wheel to the left and confront the Federals coming up the road with a solid line of battle. Brigadier General Mark Lowrey's brigade was at the front right, Daniel Govan's in the center, and Hiram Granbury's at the left rear, while Bell's Brigade of Forrest's cavalry covered Cleburne's right even though his men were down to about four rounds of ammunition each. Then Hood rode back to deploy his next division, Major General William Bate's, in echelon on Cleburne's left. Hood told Bate "to move to the turnpike and sweep toward Columbia" and then rode on south to establish headquarters at the Absalom Thompson farm, near the road.[12]

Cheatham, meanwhile, had ridden to the front without seeing Hood or Forrest and he was not informed that Hood had changed his plan. As far as he knew, the objective was still the town of Spring Hill, and the instructions Hood had given to Cleburne and Bate to get across the turnpike south of the town and "sweep toward Columbia" had not been passed on to him. Since, in the absence of Hood, he was the senior Confederate officer on the field, that was a very major omission.

Cleburne's and Bell's men advanced at about 4 p.m. with what Forrest called "a promptness . . . energy, and gallantry which I have never seen excelled."[13] They encountered only a few Union skirmishers until Lowrey's Brigade suddenly came under an intense fire from its right flank. Like Forrest before him, Cleburne had not seen Bradley's brigade until it opened fire. Lowrey swung his regiments around in a right wheel to face this concealed threat, which actually consisted of only one of Bradley's regiments, the 42nd Illinois. Cleburne's advance had swept past Bradley's knoll to the south and only this one regiment, behind a rail fence in an open field south of the wooded knoll on Bradley's right, was in position to fire on it as it passed. Bradley rushed his reserve regiment, the 64th Ohio, to extend this southward-facing part of his line.

Lowrey rode to Cleburne and told him the enemy was about to charge his flank. "I'll charge them!" Cleburne said, raising his fist, and he dashed off to bring Govan's Brigade over, leaving Granbury's Brigade to continue on to the west alone and unaware of what was happening on its right.[14] Soon Cleburne's two brigades not only outflanked the two Union regiments facing them and drove them back but their fire enfiladed Bradley's main line. His units were full of green recruits and when Bradley was carried off the field with a bullet in his left arm his brigade quickly fell apart, fleeing to the north and pursued by Cleburne's veterans, who captured the colors of the 42nd Illinois. But the Rebels were soon stopped by the fire of a line of guns Stanley had posted on a ridge on the outskirts of Spring Hill. "The ground was planted in corn and was very muddy," Stanley wrote, "and if the Johnnies in gray were not hit with artillery missiles, they were covered with mud."[15]

By 4:30 p.m. the tail of the Union wagon train had reached Spring Hill and the turnpike was temporarily clear. At about 5 p.m., as Bradley's brigade was being outflanked, Wagner brought two Napoleon 12-pounder guns clattering down the pike and put them into battery east of the road, supported by his reserve regiment, the 36th Illinois, just in time to dispute Granbury's advance. Granbury soon drove off this small force, but he was recalled by Cleburne. Bradley's forces were regrouping under the cover of the Union artillery, and Cleburne could see part of Lane's brigade being sent to their assistance, so he decided that he needed his entire division to assault the combined enemy forces. Before he could launch his attack, however, Cheatham ordered him to wait until the rest of the corps could be brought up.

At about 5 p.m. Cheatham consulted with Hood but apparently neglected to mention that the objective of his attack was Spring Hill and not the turnpike south of it. Hood send orders for Stewart's Corps to march from its reserve position at Rutherford Creek around to the north of Spring Hill to cut off the Federals' expected retreat.

It was 5:30 p.m. and almost dark by the time Brown's Division was in place on Cleburne's right, and Bate's Division was still advancing against the turnpike, where it had run into the 26th Ohio, which had been left behind by Lane to guard a crossroad. Cheatham ordered Brown to take Spring Hill with the support of Cleburne on his left and Forrest's cavalry on his right. Cheatham himself would go to hurry Bate's Division forward. In the gathering dusk, the sound of Brown's attack would be the signal to Cleburne to do the same. Cleburne waited and listened, but Brown did not attack.

The commander of Brown's right brigade, Brigadier General Otto F. Strahl, reported that his line was outflanked by a line of Federals on a wooded knoll to the east and if he advanced his brigade would be caught in a crossfire. Brown went and had a look for himself and had to agree. With this handicap, plus the absence of his largest brigade, which had not yet caught up, and of Forrest's cavalry, which could not be found, Brown decided that he would not advance until he had consulted with Cheatham, and he sent off two staff officers to find him. Cheatham came and conferred with Brown, approved his course, and rode off to check with Hood. That general had also been listening for the sound of Brown's attack and wondering why it had not been launched. When Cheatham rode up he asked, "Why in the name of God have you not attacked the enemy and taken possession of that pike?"[16] However, he seems to have accepted Cheatham's explanation of the difficulties.

Having been up since 3 a.m. and being tired after his long ride, Hood had a sumptious dinner and several drinks and was in bed in a guest room at the Thompson farm by 9 p.m.

Unknown to the Confederates, the Federals on Brown's flank were only one regiment plus one company that Lane had sent out. But placed where they were in the gathering darkness, they were as valuable as a division. Their move onto Brown's flank was only possible because Forrest had withdrawn his men at about 4:30 p.m. due to their lack of ammunition and to their exhaustion after fighting all day. He evidently did not know that Cheatham was counting on him to protect Brown's flank.

It was just after dark when Schofield, at the head of Ruger's division, approached Spring Hill. When the Federals came within two miles of the town, Ruger put his leading brigade, Colonel Silas Strickland's 3rd, in line of battle across the pike. Strickland himself rode ahead until he was challenged by a picket. "It's all right, my boy," Strickland answered, "I want to put my brigade in position here." Only then did he learn that the picket was a Rebel, and he dashed away just in time to avoid being shot. Ruger then formed his next brigade in line of battle as well, and Schofield assured his men that the Rebels were only cavalry. "Just put your bayonets on and go right through them," he said.[17] But he did not sound very convincing.

Flankers of the 23rd Michigan captured a Confederate captain, one of Granbury's staff officers, who had gone out to see if the passing troops were Bate's men. Evidently that was the prevailing opinion among the Confederates, and Ruger's march was not interfered with. Schofield arrived at Spring Hill at about 7 p.m., where Stanley confirmed that the Federals were in a dangerous fix. Confederates were present in large numbers, and, as Schofield well knew, most of the Union army was still south of Spring Hill.

Soon a locomotive steamed in from the north with more alarming news. It had been pulling a train into Thompson's Station, only a few miles north of Spring Hill, when it was suddenly attacked by Confederate cavalry. The engineer had detached his cars, which had coasted back to the cover of a Union blockhouse by a bridge, while he had raced on through to bring word of the Rebel presence. "Take it all together," Stanley's chief of staff wrote that night, "we are in a very bad situation."[18] The road north had to be reopened or the Federals would be trapped, so at about 9 p.m. Schofield marched on toward Thompson's Station with Ruger's division. Unknown to the locomotive engineer, the Confederates he had seen were Ross's Brigade of Texas cavalry, which, after herding Wilson off to the north, had turned west to Thompson's Station, where it had captured a few wagons moving along the Columbia-Franklin Pike and burned the depot and railroad bridge before riding out again.

Bate's Division had actually pushed to within 200 yards of the Columbia-Franklin Pike before it was recalled by staff officers from Cheatham to go to the support of Cleburne and Brown. At about 6:30 p.m. a major on Bate's staff interrupted Cheatham's conference with Hood to express Bate's reluctance to leave the turnpike and go to the support of Cleburne, but Cheatham told him that Bate would obey the order or put himself under arrest. It was 10 p.m. by the time Bate's Division had found Cleburne's flank in the darkness and gone into bivouac.

At about the same time, Major General Edward Johnson's division of S. D. Lee's corps arrived on the battlefield. It was before that hour when Stewart, on his way to the north of Spring Hill, came to the house where Forrest made his headquarters. He dismounted and went in, hoping to learn more about the army's position. He found Forrest preoccupied with reports that the Federals had left the main turnpike and were bypassing Spring Hill along the more westerly Carter's Creek Pike. When Stewart came out of the house he found his column had been halted in the road and soon learned that one of Cheatham's staff officers had brought orders in Hood's name for the corps to discontinue its move to the north of Spring Hill and go to the support of Brown's Division. He was reluctant at first, but when the officer insisted that he had just come from Hood's headquarters he reluctantly moved his corps to extend Brown's line to the east and went into camp between 10 and 11 p.m.

Many Confederates were puzzled that night about why they did not launch that final attack and cut the Federals' retreat route. Many officers asked Brown why he did not attack, but since he had referred the question to Cheatham and Hood he refused to advance until he received an order to do so. Soon Cheatham returned with Hood's order suspending the attack, and the men were ordered to bivouac where they were, in line. But even then many Confederate officers were not satisfied. A. P.

Stewart went to Hood's headquarters at the Thompson house and woke his commander at about 11 p.m. He explained that he did not understand why he had been ordered to suspend the move to the north of Spring Hill and instead put his corps adjacent to Brown's right flank. It developed that Hood had not realized that Cheatham's line was facing north, toward Spring Hill, instead of west, toward the pike. But it was the middle of the night. Stewart's men were already in camp. Let the men rest. The Yankees would still be there in the morning.

Hood tried to get back to sleep, but he soon had more visitors. Forrest was next. He obtained permission to send Chalmers' Division to check on the report that the Yankees were using the Carter's Creek Pike and to send Jackson's Division to Thompson's Station to block the Columbia-Franklin Pike. As soon as Forrest left, Bate came in to complain to Hood about Cheatham's order that had diverted him to support Cleburne and Brown when he had been about to seize the turnpike. Hood, who was groggy with sleep and perhaps the laudanum he took for the pain of his old wounds, said, "It makes no difference now, or it is all right, anyhow, for General Forrest, as you see, has just left, and informed me that he holds the turnpike with a portion of his forces north of Spring Hill, and will stop the enemy if he tries to pass toward Franklin, and so in the morning we will have a surrender without a fight." He added, perhaps somewhat hopefully, "We can sleep quietly tonight," and went back to bed.[19]

His sleep was interrupted once more, however, this time by a private. In the darkness, this soldier had blundered into the Union lines, where he had seen the turnpike filled with all kinds of traffic and the Union troops moving about in great confusion. He thought that something should be done about this situation and had come to report it to his commander. Hood remained in bed but told his chief of staff, who was sleeping in the same room, to send a note to Cheatham, asking him to "advance a line of skirmishers" and "confuse" the Federals marching along the road.[20] The general went back to sleep and so did his chief of staff, who was so tired that the next day he could not even remember sending the note to Cheatham.

By 10 p.m. the last major Federal unit, Wood's 3rd Division of the 4th Corps, was on the road from the original Union position north of the Duck, following Cox's 3rd Division of the 23rd Corps. Still to come were a couple of Kentucky regiments and some assorted pickets Cox had left behind to make the Confederates think his entire force was still in place. The head of Cox's column approached Spring Hill at about 11 p.m., and an aide on Cox's staff remembered seeing Confederates moving about their campfires only about a quarter of a mile east of the turnpike as the Federals marched past as quietly as they could. Among Wood's unit was a regiment of green troops, the 40th Missouri, accustomed to garrison duty but not to marching and fighting. Its men, like most inexperienced troops, carried a great amount of equipment that veterans had long since discarded as not worth the weight. The clatter of all this extra equipment as they marched by soon alerted some of the nearby Rebel pickets, who fired at the Missourians, causing them to hit the dirt in the middle of the road. When they refused to get up and move on, the next unit, the veteran 13th Ohio, marched right over them. Only then did the Missourians gather enough courage to resume the march. The frightened regiment was known thereafter among Wood's veterans as "the Fortieth Misery."

At about 11:30 p.m. Schofield returned from Thompson's Station with news that the Rebel cavalry there had disappeared at his approach with Ruger's division. Ruger had been left to hold that town, the road to Franklin appeared to be open, and he had sent Captain Twining to Franklin with his headquarters troop to telegraph the situation to Thomas and to see if there was a bridge there yet. Then he issued orders for Cox to march on to Franklin and for the rest of the army to follow. Cox was on the road again by midnight, and by 1 a.m. on the 30th, the huge train of wagons began to roll north. A half-hour later Kimball's division marched up the road from Rutherford Creek, the last major unit of Schofield's army to reach Spring Hill.

Cheatham received the note from Hood's chief of staff in the middle of the night. He had already been given Edward Johnson's detached division of S. D. Lee's corps and had just ordered it positioned south of Bate's Division. When the staff officer returned from having delivered the order for that move, Cheatham sent him back to order Johnson to fulfill this new order from army headquarters. Edward Johnson, better known as "Allegheny," was new to the Army of Tennessee. In early 1862 he had commanded a small force guarding the western approaches to the Shenandoah Valley, where he had gained his nickname. Then he had been wounded and his command had been absorbed into Stonewall Jackson's Army of the Valley, which later became the 2nd Corps of Lee's army. After recovering from his wound, Johnson had commanded a division of that corps through the Gettysburg and Wilderness campaigns and had been captured, along with most of his division, during the battle of Spotsylvania. After being exchanged, he had been sent to Hood.

When he received this latest order, Johnson complained that it was the middle of the night, griped about being attached to a different corps, and asked why Cheatham could not send one of his own divisions to do the job. But he got his men up, and while they were preparing to move he and Cheatham's staff officer rode ahead to see what they were up against. By then it was 2 a.m. and they found the turnpike empty and everything quiet. Johnson grumped about moving his troops beyond Cheatham's flank, where he might become isolated, especially since it was dark and he could not see where he was or what was around him. Besides, if his troops started moving about in the dark they were liable to run into other Confederate units and they might fire into each other. He and the staff officer rode back to Cheatham's headquarters and convinced the corps commander that Johnson's Division could not be safely advanced until daylight.

At about 4 a.m. the two Kentucky regiments and assorted pickets of other units that Cox had left behind marched into Spring Hill, unmolested by either S. D. Lee or the rest of Hood's army. At that same hour Stanley, still busy moving the wagons out of Spring Hill, received word that the Confederates had attacked the head of the wagon train near Thompson's Station and that the entire column had ground to a halt. It had been about midnight by the time that Hood's order to Forrest reached Ross's Brigade to return to Thompson's Station, and it was 2 a.m. by the time the Texans arrived there. That was also the hour that the head of Schofield's wagon train arrived. Ross dismounted three regiments and sent them to within 100 yards of the turnpike, and when they fired a concentrated volley at the passing wagons pandemonium broke loose on the road. Ross's men then ran forward and captured 39 wagons and many of their drivers, and while they were being hauled away Ross deployed his men across the pike, blocking any further passage.

A half-hour later, as some of the wagons were being burned, Union infantry was seen approaching. Standing in the glare of the burning wagons and peering into the darkness, the Confederates did not realize that they were facing only the 35 men of Stanley's headquarters guard, and they mounted up and rode off to the hills to the east, where they could keep an eye on the turnpike and watch for another opportunity to attack undefended wagons. But the next segment of the wagon train was guarded by Kimball's and Wood's divisions marching along on each side of the road. About daylight Ross tried to get at what looked like an unprotected group of wagons by way of a large stand of trees bordering the pike, but his men were driven off by a pair of Union 10-inch guns and chased by the same lone company of Michigan cavalry that had helped to defend Spring Hill from Forrest's attack.

By 5 a.m. Stanley had managed to get the last wagon across the narrow village bridge north of Spring Hill, and Opdycke's brigade of Wagner's division fell in behind as the rear guard just as day was dawning. "To say that night was one of terrible suspense was putting it mildly," one Union soldier said. General Luther Bradley, whose brigade did more fighting at Spring Hill than any other Federals, said, "It was the most critical time I have ever seen. If only the enemy had shown his usual boldness, I think he would have beaten us disastrously."[21]

---

1. *Official Records*, 45:I:1106–1107.
2. Sword, *Embrace an Angry Wind*, 105.
3. *Official Records*, 45:I:1115.
4. Ibid., 45:I:1107.
5. Ibid., 45:I:1143.
6. Sword, *Embrace an Angry Wind*, 112.
7. McDonough and Connelly, *Five Tragic Hours*, 38.
8. Sword, *Embrace an Angry Wind*, 129.
9. Ibid., 122.
10. *Official Records*, 45:I:1137.
11. Sword, *Embrace an Angry Wind*, 124.
12. Ibid., 126.
13. Ibid., 127.
14. Ibid., 128.
15. Ibid., 130.
16. Ibid., 136.
17. Ibid., 143–144.
18. Ibid., 145.
19. McDonough and Connelly, *Five Tragic Hours*, 49.
20. Ibid., 52.
21. Sword, *Embrace an Angry Wind*, 152.

CHAPTER THIRTY-SIX

Let Us Die
Like Men

30 November 1864

At daylight on the 30th of November, General Chalmers, on his way to check the Carter's Creek Pike for Union activity, was shocked to find that all the Federals were gone from Spring Hill. "When I crossed the Columbia pike," he wrote, "I learned to my great astonishment the enemy's whole column had passed up that pike."[1] Contrary to rumor, there did not seem to have been any Federal use of the Carter's Creek Pike, but Chalmers turned to the northeast on that road and headed toward Franklin.

On the opposite flank, Forrest sent Colonel Edward Crossland's Brigade of Buford's Division to move up the Lewisburg Pike toward the same town, while he took Buford's other brigade, Bell's, up the Columbia Pike. At about 8 a.m., six miles up the road, he came upon Jackson's Division, skirmishing with Opdycke's Union rear guard. The Federal brigade was deployed in two lines, screened by skirmishers, and covered by two pieces of artillery. One line would stand fast while the other fell back. Then it would stand fast while the other fell back. In this way, with the help of the two guns, they avoided all Confederate efforts to assault them or outflank them.

There was a considerable delay before the Rebel infantry joined in the pursuit. Stewart's Corps took the lead, followed by Cheatham's, but it was two hours after sunup, or almost 9 a.m., by the time Brown's Division was put on the march. His troops did not yet know that the Federals had escaped. "Everything indicated an immediate attack," wrote Private Sam Watkins. "When we got to the turnpike near Spring Hill, lo! and behold; wonder of wonders! the whole Yankee army had passed during the night."[2] "This state of affairs was, and still is inexplicable to me, and gave us a great disappointment," one of Cheatham's regimental commanders wrote. "I have never," another Rebel said, "seen more intense rage and profound disgust than was expressed by the weary . . . Confederate soldiers when they discovered that their officers had allowed their prey to escape."[3]

When Hood learned that the Federals had slipped past his sleeping soldiers during the night he was absolutely dumbfounded—a condition which was rapidly transformed to anger. "He is as wrathy as a rattlesnake this morning," a staff officer recorded, "striking at everything."[4] Hood, of course, did not consider that any blame attached to himself for Schofield's escape, and he later complained that "the best move in my career as a soldier I was thus destined to behold come to naught."[5] At a breakfast conference with his senior commanders that morning he turned his anger on his generals. He put most of the blame on Cheatham, who in turn tried to blame it all on Brown and Cleburne, neither one of whom was present.

The failure of the Confederate Army of Tennessee to trap Schofield's forces at Spring Hill has been one of the great mysteries and might-have-beens of the Civil War from that day to this. All sorts of theories have been propounded to explain how the Union army could have marched unmolested right past better than two thirds of Hood's army without a fight. Eventually many Confederates came to believe that God just was not on their side. As one aging Rebel later put it, "It seemed then, as it seems now, that a hand stronger than armies had decreed our overthrow."[6]

It is easy enough to find a more earthly reason for the Union escape in Hood's failure to communicate his wishes to Cheatham before riding off to Absalom Thompson's house. Beyond that there were many mistakes by other Confederates, such as Forrest's withdrawal from Cheatham's flank without consulting or advising either that officer or Hood. However, it is also worth considering the possibility that, as George Pickett said when asked who was to blame for the Confederate defeat at Gettysburg, that maybe the Yankees had something to do with it: not just Schofield and Stanley, but Hoefling's troopers and the orphan company of Michigan cavalry, the artillery, Bradley's brigade, and Opdycke's, and Lane's. Especially we should credit Lane and the reinforced regiment he put on Brown's flank that brought the entire Confederate army to a befuddled halt long enough for darkness to put an end to the fight.

Cleburne rode with Brown for a while on the 30th and talked with him about Hood's anger. Cleburne had learned that he was being blamed for allowing the Federals to get away and he was deeply resentful of the charge. He would call for an investigation once the enemy was disposed of, he said. Brown asked him who he thought really was to blame—perhaps fearing that his own name might be mentioned—and Cleburne replied that the responsibility rested with Hood, who had been on the field and informed of the Federals' movements.

S. D. Lee's two divisions and the army's artillery began to arrive at Spring Hill at around 9 a.m., and Lee was as surprised as Hood had been to learn that, due to some "egregious blunder, mistake, or disobedience," the Federals had escaped without a battle.[7] Hood returned control of Allegheny Johnson's division to Lee and said that he did not think Schofield would stop short of Nashville. "If he does," he added, "I can whip him with what I have."[8] After Lee had rested his troops who had just marched in from Columbia, he was to follow with his entire force, including the artillery.

With the rest of his army, Hood followed Schofield toward Franklin. On the way he continued to denounce his generals. Governor Isham G. Harris of Tennessee, who was serving as a volunteer aide on Hood's staff, heard him censure Cheatham "in severe terms."[9] When Hood came upon General Brown on the road that morning he gave him a lecture on the necessity for a retreating army to be attacked immediately by whatever pursuing force could catch it. "If you have a brigade in front as advance guard, order its commander to attack as soon as he comes up with him. If you have a regiment in advance and it comes up with the enemy, give the colonel orders to attack him; if there is but a company in advance, and if it overtakes the entire Yankee army, order the captain to attack forthwith; and if anything blocks the road in front of you today, don't stop a minute, but turn out into the fields or woods and move on to the front."[10]

Schofield arrived at Franklin before daylight and found a telegram from Thomas waiting for him. It was in reply to the one Captain Twining had sent at 1 a.m. to advise Thomas of Schofield's retreat. "Please inform General Schofield that Major-General Smith's troops have just arrived at the levee and are still on boats," it said, "and that it is impossible for them to reach Franklin to-day. He must make strong efforts to cover his wagon train, protecting it against the enemy, and as well to reach Franklin with his command and get in position there. I will dispatch him further in a few hours." To this Schofield replied at 5 a.m.: "If Smith is not needed for the immediate defense of Nashville, I think he had better march for Franklin at once. He could at least cover my wagon train, if I have to fall back from here." A half-hour later he added: "I hope to get my troops and material safely across the Harpeth this morning. We have suffered no material loss so far. I shall try and get Wilson on my flank this morning. Forrest was all around us yesterday, but we brushed him away during the evening, and came through. Hood attacked in front and flank, but did not hurt us."[11]

Schofield also found, upon reaching Franklin, that the pontoons he had asked for had not arrived from Nashville. The bridge that carried the turnpike over the Harpeth River had been destroyed twice during the previous two years, but the railroad bridge was still standing and the river was fordable at a few places. The railroad bridge was narrow and unsuitable for wagons. Nevertheless, Schofield ordered planks, taken from nearby buildings, laid over the tracks so that it could be used, at least by the infantry. The artillery could use one of the fords if its approaches were cut down, but the wagons would have to wait until the turnpike bridge could be rebuilt. The posts of the old bridge were sawed off near the waterline and new crossbeams and stringers were fitted to it.

All of these things took time, and while they were being done the partially obliterated trenches that had been built south of the town the year before would have to be manned to protect the wagons and the bridges. Cox was put in charge of both divisions of the 23rd Corps, and these were used to man and improve the defenses, while the corps artillery was sent across the ford to the north bank of the Harpeth. "In all my intimate acquaintance with him," Cox said of Schofield, "I never saw him so manifestly disturbed by the situation as he was in the glimmering dawn of that morning."[12]

At 9:50 a.m., Schofield wired Thomas again: "My trains are coming in all right. Half the troops are here, and the other half about five miles out, coming on in good order, with light skirmishing. I will have all across the river this evening. Wilson is here, and has his cavalry on my flank. I do not know where Forrest is; he may have gone east, but, no doubt, will strike our flank and rear again soon. Wilson is entirely unable to cope with him. Of course I cannot prevent Hood from crossing the Harpeth whenever he may attempt it. Do you desire me to hold on here until compelled to fall back?"[13]

At about 11 a.m., as Opdycke's brigade approached some high hills a couple of miles south of Franklin it received orders to halt and hold that high ground. The other two brigades of Wagner's division had already stopped east of the road on another hill, where they were allowed to cook and eat breakfast, as was Brigadier General Walter C. Whitaker's 2nd Brigade of Kimball's division of the 4th Corps, which was halted on the north slope of the same hill where Opdycke's men were deployed. The latter did not even get to boil coffee before Forrest's Confederates began advancing against them again, but the three brigades of Rebel cavalry could not budge four brigades of veteran infantry and contented themselves with skirmishing at long range.

A telegram from Thomas reached Franklin at about 11:30 a.m., saying he had received Schofield's wires of that morning. "It will take Smith quite all day to disembark, but if I find there is no immediate necessity to retain him here, will send him to Franklin or Brentwood [nearer Nashville], according to circumstances. If you can prevent Hood from turning your position at Franklin, it should be held; but I do not wish you to risk too much." To this Schofield replied: "I am satisfied that I have heretofore run too much risk in trying to hold Hood in check, while so far inferior to him in both infantry and cavalry. The slightest mistake on my part, or failure of a subordinate, during the last three days might have proved disastrous. I don't want to get into so tight a place again; yet, I will cheerfully act in accordance with your views of expediency, if you think it important to hold Hood back, as long as possible. When you get all your troops together and the cavalry in effective condition, we can whip Hood easily, and, I believe, make the campaign a decisive one; before that, the most we can do is to husband our strength and increase it as much as possible. I fear the troops which were stationed on the river below Columbia will be lost. I will get my trains out of the way as soon as possible, and watch Hood carefully. Possibly I may be able to hold him here, but do not expect to be able to do so long."[14]

By noon the pontoons had finally arrived from Nashville, but Schofield, no longer needing them, ordered them back to Nashville. Just then the tail of the Union wagon train had passed within the defenses of Franklin, the head of the train was beginning to cross the Harpeth River, and the artillery of the 23rd Corps and Wood's division of the 4th Corps had already crossed to the north bank. Also at about that hour Wagner and Whitaker, feeling that their job was done, evacuated their hills and marched toward Franklin. As they pulled out, the head of Hood's infantry column could be seen approaching from the south. Within half an hour, a staff officer found Wagner on the road to Franklin and delivered an order from Stanley to hold the high ground until dark, unless too severely pressed. Reluctantly, Wagner turned his column about and started back.

However, an hour and a half later Wagner abandoned the hill again. He had already been angry that his division, the only that had been engaged the day before, had been left to do rear guard duty all day, and his leg hurt from a fall he had taken earlier. Now he had received no further orders from Stanley, a large force of Confederate infantry had deployed into line in his front, and another large force of Rebels had been seen moving up the Lewisburg Pike toward his left flank. So he marched his division north again. But after going about a mile, still trying to obey the spirit of Stanley's order, Wagner placed his two guns and Lane's brigade on the southern slope of a low, rock-strewn hill, known as Privet Knob or Merrill's Hill, just east of the pike and about a mile south of Cox's defenses. About half a mile farther north he placed Bradley's brigade, now under Colonel Joseph Conrad, on a gentle rise of ground in an uncultivated field east of the pike. Then he told Opdycke to extend Conrad's line on the west side of the pike.

Opdycke had also been growing increasingly angry as the day wore on. Most of his men had not had any sleep for 48 hours and had not had anything to eat all day, and he did not think it was fair that his brigade should always have to be the rear guard. The position that Wagner wanted him to occupy had no natural cover, and he refused to put his men in it. Instead he kept riding north and let his men keep marching. Wagner insisted. Opdycke continued to refuse. Both men were naturally scrappy to start with, and both were already in a bad mood. For fifteen minutes they continued to argue, while all the time Opdycke's men continued to march, and finally, when the column reached Cox's defenses, Wagner gave up. He told Opdycke that his brigade would be in reserve and that if a battle developed he could fight however he thought best. At about 2:30 p.m. Opdycke's men stacked arms well inside the Union defenses, about 200 yards north of a brick farmhouse belonging to Fountain B. Carter, and began to make fires to boil their coffee and cook their belated breakfasts.

Wagner conferred with Cox and they evidently decided that the approaching Confederates would not launch any major attack. It was more likely that they would mask the defenses while crossing the Harpeth either upstream or down to again threaten the Union rear and force Schofield to retreat once more. Wagner should therefore retreat into the defenses only if and when actually compelled to do so. However, Lane sent word that the Rebels were still advancing and threatening his flanks, so Wagner told him to fall back to the position on Conrad's right that Opdycke had refused to fill.

Wagner then rode out to Conrad's position, where he found that officer expecting to receive orders to retreat into the defenses. Since he had not expected to stay on his little rise of ground for very long, he had let his men rest rather than prepare defenses. Wagner took out some of his anger on Conrad, telling him that he wanted no repetition of the way his men had routed the day before at Spring Hill. He was to have his sergeants fix bayonets and force the men to stand and fight. Then, seeing that Lane's men were filing into position on Conrad's right, and sending Lane orders to fall back only if overpowered, Wagner rode back into the defenses, where he evidently tried to cool his temper with liquid refreshment. General Stanley later claimed that Wagner was soon "full of whiskey, if not drunk."[15]

Behind him, Conrad's men began to fortify as best they could. There were no trees to provide logs in the barren field, nor even any fence rails, but some of Conrad's men had brought some shovels with them that they had taken from an abandoned wagon they had passed that morning, and they began to dig. "There was not a particle of doubt in the mind of any man in my vicinity as to what was coming," one of Conrad's officers wrote, and the men began to curse the stupidity of their orders. "What can our generals be thinking about in keeping us out here!" one of them asked an officer. "We are only in the way. Why don't they take us back to the breastworks?"[16] It was a good question.

At around 3 p.m. Schofield received another telegram from Thomas at Nashville. "General Smith reported to me this morning that one division of his troops is still behind. We must therefore try to hold Hood where he now is until those troops can get up, and the steamers return; after that we will concentrate here, reorganize our cavalry, and try Hood again. Do you think you can hold Hood at Franklin for three days longer? Answer, giving your views, and I should like to know what Wilson thinks he can do to aid you in holding Hood." Schofield answered right away: "I have just received your dispatch asking whether I can hold Hood here three days. I do not believe I can. I can doubtless hold him one day, but will hazard something in doing that. He now has a large force, probably two corps, in my front, and seems preparing to cross the river above and below. I think he can effect a crossing to-morrow, in spite of all my efforts, and probably to-night, if he attempts it. A worse position than this for an inferior force could hardly be found. I will refer your question to General Wilson this evening; I think he can do very little. I have no doubt Forrest will be in my rear to-morrow, or doing some greater mischief. It appears to me that I ought to take position at Brentwood at once. If A. J. Smith's division and the Murfreesborough garrison join me there, I ought to be able to hold Hood in check for some time. I have just learned the enemy's cavalry is already crossing three miles above. I will have lively times with my trains again."[17]

It was Jackson's Division of Forrest's cavalry which had crossed to the north side of the Harpeth River, at Hughes' Ford, three miles southeast of Franklin. Ross's brigade of Texans led the way and seized some hills about a half-mile north of the river. But soon the Confederates ran into Hatch's division of Wilson's cavalry. When these Federals dismounted and advanced, Ross ordered the 9th Texas Cavalry to charge. The Texans drove back the Union skirmishers, but Hatch's main line repulsed the charge with heavy loss. Ross sent the 3rd Texas Cavalry to hold off the Federal pursuit, but decided to withdraw to the river.

At about 2:45 p.m. the two Confederate infantry columns came marching over the southern horizon with, as one Federal put it, "the appearance of a huge monster closed in folds of flashing steel."[18] Stewart's Corps was to the east, where it had been shifted to the Lewisburg Pike. Cheatham's Corps came up the Columbia Pike onto the hills Wagner had recently abandoned, and Hood rode alone down the north face of this high ground to a large linden tree. There he took out his field glasses and scanned Franklin. He could see the hundreds of wagons jammed into the small town and hastening across the two rickety bridges and what he considered a makeshift-looking line of entrenchments on the southern edge of town. At last he had caught up with the elusive Federals. Not far away Patrick Cleburne was also studying the Union defenses through his binoculars. "They are very formidable," he told a staff officer.[19]

Cleburne and the staff officer were playing a game of checkers with colored leaves and a board scratched in the dirt when a messenger arrived from Hood summoning his senior generals to a conference at a nearby house. There Hood announced that he had decided to make an immediate frontal attack and asked for comments. Forrest objected vigorously, saying that in his opinion the Union entrenchments could not be successfully assaulted without great loss of life and that this was unnecessary. "General Hood," he said, "if you will give me one strong division of infantry with my cavalry, I will agree to flank the Federals from their works within two hours' time."[20] Hood replied that the Yankees were only making a show of force, not a determined stand.

Cleburne commented that to attack across two miles of open ground against what looked like impregnable defenses was to court disaster. Cheatham agreed that the enemy had a good position and was well fortified. However, Hood had already made up his mind and could not be dissuaded, especially by Cleburne and Cheatham, two men whose timidity, he thought, had been responsible for letting the Federals get away the night before. He feared that this supposed timidity permeated the army, which, he later wrote, "after a forward march of one hundred and eighty miles, was still, seemingly, unwilling to accept battle unless under the protection of breastworks."[21] Hood told his generals that it was better to attack the Federals here at Franklin, where they had had only a few hours to fortify their position, "than to strike them at Nashville where they had been strengthening themselves for three years."[22]

The conference broke up and the generals rode back to their commands. As Cleburne was about to ride off, Hood gave him explicit instructions: "Form your division to the right of the pike, letting your left overlap the same. General Brown will form on the left with his right overlapping your left . . . Give orders to your men not to fire a gun until you run the Yankee skirmish line from behind the first line of works, then press them and shoot them in their backs as they run to their main line; then charge the enemy's works. Franklin is the key to Nashville, and Nashville is the key to independence." When Cleburne returned to his division and gathered his brigade commanders together, Govan, commander of an Arkansas brigade, saw that he was "greatly depressed." When Cleburne had passed on Hood's orders and his brigadiers turned to go, Govan said, "Well, general, there will not be many of us that will get back to Arkansas." Cleburne, who was also from that state, replied, "Well, Govan, if we are to die, let us die like men."[23]

Cleburne's Division and Brown's formed as Hood had instructed. Cheatham's other division, Bate's, formed farther west and was to swing over to the Carter's Creek Pike, where it would be supported by Chalmers' cavalry, and attack up that road. Stewart's three divisions formed well to the east of Cleburne's and, because of the course of the Harpeth River, would advance to the northwest, supported on their right by Buford's Division of cavalry. Each infantry division was to advance in two lines with two brigades on the front line and the remaining one or two on the second line. Most of the Confederate artillery was still on the road with S. D. Lee's corps, and only two batteries of six guns each were at the front. Hood assigned one to each corps and directed that they both be split into two-gun sections that were to be placed in the intervals between the divisions.

For the first time in three years, the Army of Tennessee was attacking out in the open, not in the heavily timbered terrain it was used to. "Very few battlefields of the war," a Union officer wrote, "were so free from obstruction to the view."[24] Now the Confederates marveled at the spectacle of over 20,000 men in gray and butternut brown and bits of captured blue uniforms forming for the attack with fixed bayonets flashing in the sun of an Indian Summer late afternoon. At 4 p.m., at a signal from Cheatham, the troops were called to attention, bugles blew, bands began to play "Dixie" and "The Bonnie Blue Flag," and the men stepped forward with rifles on their right shoulders and battleflags catching the breeze. The sound of their marching feet, said one witness, was like the low, hollow rumble of distant thunder. Rabbits bounded ahead of them, and coveys of quail burst into flight at the Confederates' approach. Even the Federals enjoyed the spectacle of two corps advancing as if on parade. "It was worth a year of one's lifetime to witness the marshalling and advance of the Rebel line," one Union soldier wrote. "Nothing could be more suggestive of strength, discipline, and resistless power."[25]

Just as Cheatham's and Stewart's corps stepped off, S. D. Lee rode up ahead of his troops, surprised to find that Hood was starting a battle. Had he known that such a thing was contemplated, he said, he could have marched his corps faster and arrived in time to participate. Hood seemed unconcerned and merely told Lee to bring up his leading division, Johnson's, and to prepare another to support Cheatham's Corps.

Schofield was at his headquarters in the Alpheus Truett home on the Nashville Pike a half-mile north of the river when he heard that the Confederates were forming line of battle. He and his staff officers clumped up the stairs to a second-story porch on the south side of the house to have a look. With them went 14-year-old Edwin Truett, who begged for a chance to look through somebody's field glasses at the gathering Confederates. A staff officer tried to brush him aside, but Schofield himself let the boy have a look through his binoculars and told him it was a sight he would never see again. Soon the sound of small arms fire echoed across the valley. "For a moment my heart sank within me," Schofield later admitted. He had not expected Hood to attack him here but to try to get around his flank again. The Union army had its back to a river, and if it was forced from its hastily erected defenses it would never be able to cross the river safely. He wondered if he had not made a mistake at West Point when he had encouraged his classmate, Hood, not to give up trying to pass his exams. Now he fired off a message to his quartermaster to "start all your trains, except ammunition, headquarters, and ambulances, to Nashville immediately." Another message went to Wood: "Hold your command in readiness to cover the crossing of the river in case the enemy break our lines on the south side of the river."[26]

The Harpeth River, a tributary of the Cumberland, ran from southeast to northwest, generally, but made a loop around Franklin, on the southwest bank, protecting over half of the circumference of the town. The Union defenses covered the other, southern, half. Cox's 3rd Division of the 23rd Corps, under the temporary command of Brigadier General James W. Reilly, manned the line from the river on the southeast to the Columbia Pike. Ruger's 2nd Division of the 23rd Corps manned the line from there to the Carter's Creek Pike on the southwest of the town, and Kimball's 1st Division of the 4th Corps manned the rest of the line, from there to the river northwest of town. A hole had been left in the main line of defenses where the Columbia Pike came through, for at the time that Cox's men were entrenching the wagons were still using the road. However, a short second line had been constructed behind this opening and it did extend into the road, so that guns or troops stationed there could cover this weak point. Opdycke's brigade of Wagner's division was resting just north of this short inner line, and, of course, a half-mile to the south were Lane's and Conrad's brigades.

Wood's 3rd Division of the 4th Corps had already crossed to the north bank of the Harpeth, where there was an old earthwork known as Fort Granger. Some of the Union artillery was placed in this fort to cover the bridges. Other batteries were posted on high ground east of the river and southeast of Cox's defenses. From there they could rake the advancing Confederate brigades from one flank to the other. Now they opened fire, sending explosive shells across the river to tear gaps in the advancing lines. But the Rebels closed ranks and came on with a spirit and determination that one Federal observer termed "most terrifically beautiful and grand."[27]

The two guns in the advanced Union position with Wagner's two brigades also opened fire, but Rebel sharpshooters on Privet Knob were picking off the Union gunners. The latter stood their losses for a while, but soon they fastened prolonge ropes between their guns and limbers and withdrew at full speed up the turnpike to the main line of defenses. Both Conrad and Lane sent messengers hurrying back to find Wagner. Farther west two Confederate guns took position on another knoll and sent their first shot screaming over the heads of Conrad's men into the main line, where it tore off a cornice near the back porch of the Fountain Carter house and exploded in the yard.

Captain Theodore Cox, General Cox's younger brother and aide, was sitting on that porch talking with another staff officer at the time. Both officers ran to their horses and galloped forward to the gap in the main line where the Columbia Pike entered. There they found General Wagner standing by the side of the road talking with one of the messengers sent back from his front line. The latter was excitedly telling the general that the enemy was about to overwhelm his two brigades and he did not think they should be left out there any longer. "Go back," Wagner told him, "and tell them to fight—fight like hell!" The courier tried to argue, but Wagner cut him short. "Tell Colonel Conrad that the Second Division can whip all hell." As this courier galloped back to the front line, the second messenger, a staff officer, rode up. He too requested permission for the two brigades to withdraw but was also told they would have to stand and fight. "But Hood's entire army is coming," the officer replied. Captain Cox and his friend also tried to reason with Wagner, telling him that General Cox never intended for Wagner's division to fight Hood's whole army alone. Swearing mightily, Wagner threw down the stick he had been using as a cane, so violently that it broke, and roared, "fight 'em," and the intimidated messenger took off.[28]

Just then the two guns retreating from the front line rumbled up the road. A Confederate shell struck the macadamized pike just behind them and caromed over the main Union line and into Franklin as the guns entered the defenses and swung into position behind the second line, covering the entrance. One gunner, his face grimy with powdersmoke, jumped down from a limber and said, "Old Hell is let loose, and coming out there."[29]

By the time the two messengers got back to the front line it was probably too late to withdraw the two brigades anyway, even if Wagner had allowed it. Conrad's and Lane's men held their fire until the Rebels were within 100 yards. Then a sudden shout rang out: "Fire." A rattling fusilade staggered the Confederates, and their advance came to a temporary halt, but their officers quickly got them moving again, and from thousands of throats came the high-pitched Rebel yell. After getting off another shot or two the Federals were starting to use bayonets and gun butts when Captain John Shellenberger, in Conrad's brigade, glanced over his shoulder and saw the front begin to unravel, starting at the turnpike and running along the line like a burning train of gunpowder. He shouted for his company to fall back "and gave an example of how to do it," he said, "by turning and running for the breastworks." With little hesitation, Lane's brigade soon joined the retreat, as did a couple of regiments of skirmishers, belonging to the 23rd Corps, farther west. "Rally behind the works!" someone shouted.[30]

When the Federals turned to run, Cleburne's line fired a staggering volley into their backs. "It seemed as if bullets had never before hissed with such diabolical venom," Captain Shellenberger remembered. "Every one that passed made a noise seemingly loud enough to tear one in two."[31] A soldier watching from the main Union line noticed that many of Conrad's and Lane's men ran crouched low to the ground to escape the withering Confederate fire. They had a half-mile to go before gaining cover, and the Federals were laden with knapsacks, haversacks, blankets, and ammunition, with the Rebels hot on their heels, "the Yanks running for life," as one Confederate put it, "and we for the fun of it, but the difference in the objects are so great that they out run us." Even as the fleetest runners, and those who got a head start, reached Cox's breastworks, those at the back of the pack, who had slowed to a trot or even a walk, were overtaken by the Rebels and seized or knocked down. Shellenberger was among those too winded to make it. "Even with life at stake, I could go no farther," he said. Thinking that his time had come, he remembered his mother telling him not to get shot in the back, so he turned to face his end. He saw an onrushing Confederate raise his rifle, and thought, "I was looking at the man who would shoot me."[32] But the Rebel fired into a nearby cluster of other Federals instead of at him. Shellenberger heard the bullet strike a body and heard the victim groan, and with renewed energy the captain turned and staggered on until he lunged headlong into the ditch at the base of the Union earthworks.

The Confederates were almost as disorganized by their advance as the Federals were by their retreat, and Cleburne's and Brown's Rebels became intermixed with Wagner's men as they all rushed toward the main Union line, funneling toward the point where the Columbia Pike entered the defenses. Cox's men on the main line could not fire because they were afraid of hitting Wagner's men. "We were standing up against the parapet, breathlessly and silently waiting for Lane's and Conrad's men to run in," an officer in Cox's division remembered. "Let's go into the works with them!" some Rebel cried out, and others took up the shout.[33]

From the ditch in front of the defenses Captain Shellenberger could see that the front rank of Rebels was almost as exhausted as he was, but it kept coming. However, just as it began to reach the ditch, Cox's men decided, without orders, that they could not wait any longer to fire. A few scattered shots soon led to a deafening volley that virtually leveled the front rank of Confederates and several retreating Federals as well. All these men lay writhing in agony on the ground, and the men behind them were staggering and reeling like drunks as a great cloud of gunsmoke rolled over them and obscured the scene. And then another wave of Rebels came pushing through the smoke with fixed bayonets. A sudden fear of being pinioned by a bayonet gave Shellenberger the energy to spring to the top of the earthwork and grab the top log with both hands. Evidently some defender on the other side did not notice the color of his uniform and knocked him senseless, for the next thing he knew he was inside the parapet, lying across the body of a Union soldier who, although shot through the head, was still breathing.

Another member of Conrad's brigade, W. A. Keesy, also managed to scramble into the main defenses, "helpless from exhaustion," as he put it. A captain in the 23rd Corps tapped him with his sword and told him to move on. "I will not have my company demoralized by stragglers coming in here," the captain told him. Keesy managed to scramble another 80 or 90 yards and then he took cover "in a little hollow in the ground." From there he looked back and saw the Confederates pouring over the defenses. "On our right the artillery teamsters stampeded," he said. "The ammunition went with the teams and caissons, and the gunners took picks, shovels or anything at hand, and nobly defended the guns." One of the pieces was still loaded, however, and "a large crowd was rushing to the muzzle of the gun. The man with the lanyards tremblingly held his fire until the first rebel in the rush placed his hands upon the muzzle of the cannon to spring over, when he let her go. Like a huge thunder bolt that awful roar and flash went blasting through that crowd of men, annihilating scores! Arms, legs and mangled trunks were torn and thrown in every direction."[34]

Engulfed by a sea of routing Federals and pursuing Confederates and confused by the shouts of Wagner's officers for their men to rally at the rear, some of Cox's regiments, on both sides of the turnpike, also broke and ran, leaving a gap in the line some 200 yards wide. "Boys, we have got to get out of here," a Union lieutenant shouted.[35] Those who did not run were captured, including about 60 men of the 50th Ohio. One of these saw a Rebel private fire point-blank at a Union sergeant sitting nearby who was surrendering. The bullet only sliced across the bridge of the sergeant's nose, however, and a Confederate officer turned and poked his sword in the Rebel private's face and told him that if he even attempted such a cowardly thing again he would cut him down. However, the captured Federal noted that the officer was hit by Union fire before he had taken many more steps. The Federal soldier cowered in the ditch under crashes of musketry that exceeded any he had heard throughout the Atlanta campaign, and while he was lying there two wounded Confederates fell across him, soaking his uniform with their blood.

General Wagner sat on his horse in the middle of the turnpike facing the enemy and shaking his broken stick at the retreating Federals. He cursed them, called them cowards, ordered them to stop, but, even with the help of a passing sergeant, he only managed to rally about twenty men. "Some Zouave officers," Keesy said, "mounted and armed to the teeth, deployed across the pike and flourishing their swords and revolvers, swore terribly that they would shoot the first men who undertook to pass, but all was to no avail. The cyclone of bewildered humanity was not to be stayed in that way."[36]

1. Sword, *Embrace an Angry Wind*, 158.
2. Sam R. Watkins, *Co. Aytch: A Side Show of the Big Show* (Nashville, 1882), 232.
3. Sword, *Embrace an Angry Wind*, 158.
4. Ibid., 156.
5. J. B. Hood, "The Invasion of Tennessee," in *Battles and Leaders of the Civil War*, edited by Robert Underwood Johnson and Clarence Clough Buel (New York, 1888), Vol. 4, 432.
6. McDonough and Connelly, *Five Tragic Hours*, 55.
7. Hattaway, *General Stephen D. Lee*, 135.
8. Sword, *Embrace an Angry Wind*, 156.
9. Ibid., 157.
10. Ibid.
11. *Official Records*, 45:I:1168–1169.
12. Sword, *Embrace an Angry Wind*, 161.
13. *Official Records*, 45:I:1169.
14. Ibid., 45:I:1169–1170.
15. Sword, *Embrace an Angry Wind*, 176.
16. Ibid., 177.
17. *Official Records*, 45:I:1170.
18. Sword, *Embrace an Angry Wind*, 180.
19. Ibid., 178.
20. Ibid., 179.
21. Hood, "The Invasion of Tennessee," 432.
22. Henry, *"First With the Most" Forrest*, 397.
23. Sword, *Embrace an Angry Wind*, 179–180.
24. McDonough and Connelly, *Five Tragic Hours*, 96.
25. Sword, *Embrace an Angry Wind*, 187.
26. Ibid., 198.
27. Ibid., 190.
28. Ibid., 189.
29. Ibid., 190.
30. Ibid., 191.
31. Ibid.
32. Ibid., 192.
33. Ibid., 193.
34. McDonough and Connelly, *Five Tragic Hours*, 114.
35. Sword, *Embrace an Angry Wind*, 195.
36. McDonough and Connelly, *Five Tragic Hours*, 114.

CHAPTER THIRTY-SEVEN

Into the Very Door of Hell

30 November–1 December 1864

East of the Confederate breakthrough around the turnpike, the Union line extended somewhat farther to the south to form a shallow salient around Fountain Carter's cotton gin before angling back to the northeast. In that area were the three brigades of Cox's 3rd Division of the 23rd Corps, now under Brigadier General James W. Reilly while Cox was in temporary command of the corps. The two regiments on the right end of this line, west of the cotton gin, were swept away by Wagner's retreating Federals and Cleburne's advancing Confederates. Meanwhile, the three divisions of A. P. Stewart's Corps, supported by Buford's dismounted cavalry division, advanced against the rest of Reilly's division. As these Confederates approached, Colonel John S. Casement, whose 2nd Brigade held the center of Reilly's line, jumped up on the breastworks near the cotton gin and yelled, "Men, do you see those damned Rebel sons of bitches coming?" He was answered by an affirmative shout from his men. "Well, I want you to stand here like rocks, and whip hell out of them."[1] Then he drew his revolver and emptied it at the oncoming Confederates before jumping down. He was immediately replaced by a long line of gleaming rifle barrels.

Union artillery east of the Harpeth pinned down Buford's supporting cavalrymen. "Our whole line would have been swept away," one of them said, "had we not been ordered to throw ourselves on the ground." Reilly's own guns opened on Stewart's advancing formations as soon as they came within cannister range, tearing so many holes in the Confederate ranks that all of them could not be closed, but the Union infantry held its fire until the rebels were within 75 yards. Then the attackers were staggered as if hit by a giant fist. Major General Edward C. Walthall, one of Stewart's division commanders, called it "far the most deadly fire of both small arms and artillery that I have ever seen troops subjected to."[2] But the Confederates continued to advance until some of them were within twenty yards of the defenses. There they came upon an impenetrable abatis made from an osage orange hedge. In places it was the growing hedge, cut off about four feet above the ground. In other places it consisted of the parts that had been cut off, manhandled into place. But in both cases it was a tangle of thick, sharp branches that brought the Rebels to a halt. Only where the Lewisburg Pike entered the defenses was there a path through this entanglement. There the 3rd and 22nd Mississippi regiments managed to plant their battleflags atop the Union defenses, but not for long. Both colors were soon captured and all Rebels who reached the parapet were either killed or captured. Unable to go forward, and unable to stand the murderous fire of Reilly's men and guns, the Confederates streamed back the way they had come. Major General William W. Loring, another of Stewart's division commanders, tried to rally his men, but in vain. As his troops streamed on to the south Loring cried, "Great God! Do I command cowards?"[3]

Only two regiments of Reilly's own brigade had been swept away by Wagner's routed Federals and Cleburne's attacking Rebels. The others had been posted back near the inner line which ran across the Columbia Pike. The 12th and 16th Kentucky regiments had been the last units to leave the Duck River line the night before. Their men were tired after their long march, but when their commanders learned that the main defenses had been broken, they both advanced to counterattack and were soon joined by Reilly's other regiment, the 8th Tennessee, and by the 175th Ohio, a unit so new that it had not even been assigned to a brigade yet. They were also joined by Opdycke's weary brigade.

General Stanley, commander of the 4th Corps, had been on the north side of the river with Schofield when the Confederate attack began. After briefly watching the attack from the Truett house, both generals had ridden away, but in different directions. Schofield had gone to Fort Granger, on the north side, while Stanley, with a single orderly, had crossed the river and hastened toward the front. "I arrived at the scene of disorder," he later wrote; "coming from the town on the Columbia Pike. The moment was critical beyond any I have known in any battle—could the enemy hold that part of our line, he was nearer to our two bridges than the extremities of our line."[4] Stanley rode to where Opdycke's brigade had been resting about 100 yards north of the inner Union line, but he saw that Colonel Opdycke was already moving his men forward.

Opdycke's six regiments had been resting on both sides of the Columbia Pike about 200 yards north of the Fountain Carter house when the front line collapsed. His men hastily grabbed their stacked rifles and began to form line even as Lane's, Conrad's, and Reilly's disorganized troops poured past. Opdycke's men had no orders, and none could have been heard in all that confusion even if they had been given. So, as bullets began to whistle overhead, they lay down where they were. "I thought the day was gone," one of Opdycke's sergeants wrote. Colonel Opdycke tried to move some of his regiments across to the east side of the road "for greater security to the men," but some of his troops thought the intention was to advance. Major Thomas W. Motherspaw of the 73rd Illinois was among those who made that mistake and he yelled excitedly, "Go for them, Boys." Then he sprang into the saddle and cried, "Forward, 73d, to the works!"[5] Yelling furiously, his regiment charged forward with leveled bayonets. Opdycke sent an aide to tell Motherspaw to stop his regiment, but the major yelled over the tumolt that it was too late. It was impossible to stop his men.

Not only could the charge not be stopped, but others joined it. Lieutenant Colonel George W. Smith, mounted and waving his cap, led his consolidated 74th/88th Illinois forward as well, and since it had been farther south to start with, it was now in the lead. Other regiments then joined in, while Opdycke himself, on horseback, led the 125th Ohio forward with drawn revolver. The first obstacle his brigade encountered was the mass of retreating Federals. When these saw Opdycke's intermingled regiments bearing down on them with lowered bayonets, they scattered to the left and right as best they could, and those who could not get out of the way hit the dirt and were trampled underfoot. The next obstacle was a staked cedar fence at the edge of Fountain Carter's yard. It was too high to climb and too sturdy to knock down, and Rebel bullets were striking it so fast that it rattled. After what seemed like an age, the Federals finally broke through the fence, and then, in Carter's yard, they met the next obstacle, the Confederates, who were running through the gunsmoke and yelling for all they were worth, and intermingled with them were some of Cox's men, retreating from the second line of defenses just north of the Carter house.

The two opposing charges collided at the run, and one witness said that he would not have missed the sight for $500. As for the hand-to-hand melee that followed, however, "I surely do not want to ever witness the like again," he said.[6] Opdycke himself, now dismounted, was in the thick of it, and after "firing all the shots in his revolver," one account said, "and then breaking it over the head of a rebel, snatched up a musket and fought with that for a club." A Confederate said that the men "fought like demons." A Union colonel said, "I saw a Confederate soldier, close to me, thrust one of our men through with the bayonet, and before he could draw his weapon from the ghastly wound, his brains were scattered on all of us that stood near, by the butt of a musket swung with terrific force by some big fellow whom I could not recognize in the grim dirt and smoke that enveloped us."[7] One soldier said, "Due to the smoke and bedlam, it was hard to tell who was who in the deadly strife." Another said, "We were so badly mixed up with old soldiers going forward, new soldiers going back, and Rebs running both ways. . . . I could not tell for several minutes which were prisoners, the Rebs or ourselves—each ordering the other to surrender, and many on each side clubbing their guns and chasing each other around the houses." But it only took a few minutes for Opdycke's men to push the Confederates back across Carter's yard to the second line of Union defenses, where more of Brown's and Cleburne's men were still pouring over the breastworks "like sheep in a wheatfield."[8]

Here, if possible, the fighting became even more intense. Many of Wagner's and Reilly's troops had rallied and had come back to join the fight. General Stanley, on his way to the front, heard an old soldier yell, "Come on, men, we can go wherever the general can."[9] Soon the Federal line was four or five ranks deep in places. Those in the rear ranks would load and pass their muskets to the front, so that the air reverberated with the continuous roar of musketry. "The tempest of lead and iron beat the surface of the earth into dust," one witness said. A Union officer said his men fought as they had "never fought before or since," and that their musketry was like "sheet lightning." And he added that "smoke enveloped everybody. The curses of the living in their desperate struggle for life mingled with the groans of the dying." A sergeant in the 44th Illinois said, "I never see men fight . . . more determined than the Rebs did. And I never see enemy men fall so fast. Our boys shot them just like hogs."[10] The Confederates fell back behind the second line of earthworks and many went all the way back to the first line. Others threw up their hands in surrender. The captures by Opdycke's brigade alone eventually reached 375 enlisted men, 19 officers, and eight battleflags.

Farther to the east—the Union left—Reilly's reserve units (the two Kentucky regiments and the 8th Tennessee) plus the brand new 175th Ohio had slammed into Cheatham's right front just as Opdycke's brigade had attacked his left front. "It seemed to me that hell itself had exploded in our faces," wrote Brigadier General George W. Gordon, commander of one of Brown's brigades that had drifted to its right and collided with these Federals. Not far away, General Granbury, one of Cleburne's brigade commanders, was shot through the face and killed. Many Rebels threw down their rifles and surrendered while the rest retreated to the outside ditch of the main line of Union defenses, where one Union officer said they milled about "as thick as sheep in a pen."[11]

The Federals, including half of Opdycke's regiments, chased after them and took position three or four ranks deep in the inside ditch of the same line, and here the opposing forces stood and fired at each other over the parapet, which was all that separated them. To avoid exposing their heads and bodies, many men of both sides would hold their rifles up over the parapet and fire blindly in the general direction of the enemy. Confederate brigadier general Daniel Govan called this "the most desperate fight I ever witnessed."[12]

When General Cox had realized that Hood was launching an attack he had watched from a knoll near the eastern end of his line. And when Wagner's two advanced brigades had broken, Cox had tried to gallop over to the Carter house. He tried, but his mount was unwilling. The roar of cannon fire from both sides had frightened the horse, and when a shell exploded nearby and stampeded an artillery team, the animal began to plunge and rear. Cox had to dismount and calm the horse. Then, on his way to the Carter house, he came across General Stanley, whose horse had been shot out from under him and who had been grazed on the back of the neck by a bullet. Cox loaned him the horse of one of his aides and advised him to seek medical aid. Stanley took this advice and trotted off toward Franklin while Cox went on toward the Carter house. By the time he got there, the Federals had pushed the Confederates back to the main line of defenses.

However, more and more Rebels were converging on the 200-yard stretch of works centered on the Columbia Pike, and they could not be driven from it. Eventually seven Confederate brigades funneled into this narrow area. Every time a fresh wave of Rebels arrived they would surge forward and try to drive the Federals away. But this, too, proved to be impossible, although one Union officer counted thirteen separate attempts. "They charged and fought like perfect fiends," one of Cox's staff officers wrote.[13] General Cleburne was killed bringing up one of his brigades from the second line, shot near the heart.

On Opdycke's right, the outer and inner lines were separated by a space of 65 to 125 yards, which contained the Carter family's garden, smokehouse, and farm office. But in places the Federals had begun constructing a new line of their own out of fences and whatever came to hand within about 25 yards of the Rebels. Just west of Carter's smokehouse were six 12-pounder Napoleon guns, two of them manned by Opdycke's infantrymen, and these added dreadfully to the carnage, firing cannister and explosive shells from point-blank range and sending rails, chunks of earth, and human heads flying from the outer defenses. "Why half of us were not killed yet remains a mystery," one survivor wrote.[14]

After about a half-hour there came a lull in the firing, and a Union officer leaped up on the inner line of defenses and called for a charge. But the men were not eager to leave their cover, and the officer was shot down by the Rebels before anyone joined him. However, the lull soon ended, and again unceasing musketry ripped the air.

The 111th Ohio of Ruger's 2nd Division of the 23rd Corps, stationed just east of where the inner line joined the outer line, was fired upon by Rebels to the front, by others on the flank in the captured part of the defenses, and by Federals behind them, who thought they were part of the Confederate line. Eight companies of the 101st Ohio in Kimball's division of the 4th Corps were brought over to support the 111th, and a line was formed at a right angle to the main line of defenses connecting it to the inner line.

A little farther to the west Brigadier Generals States Rights Gist's and John C. Carter's brigades of Brown's Division attacked Ruger's front, but with little success. Just east of the 111th, the Union line was protected by a thicket of locust trees in swampy ground. Some of the trees had been cut by the Federals to obtain logs for their breastworks, and cut branches and treetops had been left to form an abatis. Gist's brigade was torn to pieces by Union artillery and rifle fire even before it got to this obstruction and General Gist himself was killed after having his horse shot out from under him. General Carter was carried to the rear after having been shot through the body. General Brown, the division commander, was also carried off with a serious wound. However, their men worked their way through the entangling locust branches and reached the Union defenses but could not get over them. One Rebel officer jumped up onto the parapet and, swearing furiously, demanded that the Yankees surrender. A Union private pushed the muzzle of his rifle against the Confederate's abdomen and fired. "I guess not," he said, as the Rebel tumbled into the ditch at his feet.[15]

It was almost dark by the time Bate's Division of Cheatham's Corps worked its way by a roundabout route to the Carter's Creek Pike and came up on Brown's left. Bate's right and center brigades approached at an angle and were enfiladed by Ruger's troops and their supporting artillery. So they veered to the cover of a slight elevation about 150 yards from the Union line. There they were silhouetted against the sky and easy targets, so they charged on and happened to hit the defenses just where two companies of the green 183rd Ohio happened to have been placed in the middle of the Union line. These raw troops broke and ran, and Bate's men crossed the parapet and applied bayonets and clubbed muskets to the Federals on both sides of the breakthrough. But Lieutenant Colonel Mervin Clark of the 183rd grabbed his regiment's colors and led his troops back into the fight. They broke again when Clark was mortally wounded, but their countercharge had been enough to buy time for neighboring units to react. Brigade commander Colonel Orlando H. Moore ordered a nearby battery to pull its guns around to fire obliquely down the line at the Confederate penetration, and, as its shells began to burst among the Rebels, Moore sent two companies of the 80th Indiana to seal the breach. The Confederates fell back across the parapet, and as they did the colonel of the 23rd Michigan sent one of his companies to the outer ditch, where it took the retreating Rebels in the flank. "Oh! such groaning and praying and pleading I never heard before, and God knows that I do not want to again," one of these Michiganders wrote.[16] The Federals called on the Confederates to surrender, and many of them did.

Bate's final brigade—six small Florida regiments commanded by Colonel Robert Bullock—came in on the left, straddling the Carter's Creek Pike. Under the fire of Kimball's division of the 4th Corps and its supporting artillery, the Floridians never got closer than 100 yards to the Union line. Beyond them, Chalmers' dismounted cavalrymen advanced to within about sixty yards of the Federals before falling back and contenting themselves with long-range sniping.

To the east of the desperate struggle at the Columbia Pike the four brigades in the second line of Stewart's Corps approached Reilly's Union works. These brigades advanced at an angle and came up one at a time instead of in a coordinated, simultaneous attack. The abatis and the Union fire stopped most of these troops, as it had the front line, and most of them edged over to the west, toward the Columbia Pike. Part of Brigadier General John Adams' brigade of Loring's Division, however, managed to get through the hedge. Adams himself, mounted on his horse, Old Charley, led the way through a narrow opening his men had made in front of Casement's Union brigade and charged straight for the colors of the 65th Illinois.

The colonel of that regiment, in admiration of the general's courage, shouted for his men not to shoot him, but it was too late. Old Charley leaped the ditch and landed squarely on top of the parapet, dead, while Adams fell into the inner ditch at Casement's feet, riddled with bullets. He was still conscious and asked for water, which was brought to him, as well as some cotton from Carter's gin to cushion his head. He thanked his benefactors and said, "It is the fate of a soldier to die for his country."[17] A few minutes later he was dead. Not many of his men managed to follow him beyond the hedge and those who did were easily repulsed, while the colors of the 15th Mississippi were captured by a private and promptly confiscated by the colonel of the 104th Ohio. Several hundred men of Sears' Brigade of French's Division also reached the parapet of Reilly's line, but the survivors were soon driven back.

When not beating off attacks on their own front, Reilly's Federals poured an enfilading fire into the Rebels who were still clinging to the captured defenses near the Columbia Pike. Confederate S. A. Cunningham, the right guide of the 41st Tennessee, was among those on the receiving end of this fire. He was loading rifles and passing them to the front, when General Strahl, his brigade commander, ordered him to replace a fallen man in the front rank. He had to stand with one foot on the pile of dead bodies in the ditch in order to fire over the parapet while the general handed him the freshly loaded rifles. After firing several times Cunningham looked around and saw that only one other man near him was firing and that behind him were barely enough men to load for the two of them. He asked General Strahl what they should do. "Keep firing," he was told.[18] After another Union volley the other man who was firing went down and the general threw up his hands and fell on his face, seemingly dead. Cunningham asked the other rifleman where he was hit and was surprised to hear Strahl answer, instead, that he had been hit in the neck. The general then said he must turn over command of his brigade to the next in rank, Lieutenant Colonel Fountain Stafford, and he crawled down the body-filled ditch about twenty feet to where Stafford stood. But he discovered that Stafford was dead and only wedged into a standing position by the bodies around him. Some staff officers tried to carry Strahl to the rear, but before they had gone fifty feet he was hit two more times, and the last bullet killed him instantly.

A captured Union officer was being held in the outer ditch nearby and watched in amazement as the Confederate ranks dwindled around him and the ditch filled with dead and wounded men. He could hear bullets striking their bodies. Shouts passed up and down the line for a certain officer, but word came back that the officer was dead or wounded. The next in command was then sought, but he was also incapacitated. It was finally determined that a wounded captain lying beside the captured Federal was the senior officer present. "Men, this won't do," the captain gasped, "we must either surrender or run. . . . We are getting all cut to pieces by this terrible cross fire." There was no response, the officer's words probably drowned out by the firing. "We surrender, we surrender, we surrender," the wounded captain cried as loudly as he could.[19] No one heard him but the captured Federal. And the fighting continued.

On the Union side of the line, Captain James A. Sexton found himself not only in command of his regiment, the 72nd Illinois, but of between 2,000 and 3,000 troops of various mixed commands on the right of Opdycke's line, where the two sides were farthest apart. Sexton's men began to clamor for a charge to retake the outer line, so he nervously agreed. Word was passed up and down the line, and when Sexton gave the order they ran forward along the western edge of Carter's garden. Resistance from the Rebels was slight, but a devastating fire hit them from the rear and from the east, as other Federals, in the gathering darkness and lingering smoke, thought that they were Confederates. Sexton's men hit the dirt and crawled back to their starting position.

However, Sexton was then ordered to report to General Cox at one of Carter's outbuildings. There he was told that Cox had brought up a fresh regiment, the 112th Illinois, and that the general wanted the main line recaptured. Sexton protested that any attacking force would receive the same treatment that his already had, but he was told to charge anyway. This time only a few of his men followed him, for they too knew what to expect. The 112th Illinois did advance, and received a murderous fire from all points on the compass. The regiment's commander was hit, his men dropped to the ground, and they too crawled back to the inner defenses.

The Confederates clinging to the outer line of defenses began to run out of ammunition and had to search the bodies of the dead and wounded lying in the outer ditch for more cartridges. Their fire slackened noticeably, and the Union rate of fire also decreased correspondingly. As the thick cloud of gunsmoke thus thinned the Federals near the right of Reilly's line could see, in the last minutes before dusk, rags, hats—anything available—stuck on bayonets and raised above the parapet. "For God's sake, don't shoot . . . we'll give up and come in," some Rebel called. "Drop your guns and climb over," came the answer.[20] And about 300 exhausted, bewildered Confederates did just that, including Brigadier General George W. Gordon. Other Rebels took advantage of this lull and the gathering darkness to fall back across the open plain to the south. And yet others still clung to their positions and kept up the fight.

"It is difficult to understand the strategy or the folly of the Confederate commander," a Union lieutenant thought, "when he permitted his troops to remain upon that slaughter field for hours under the deadly fire of our guns. After the first attack it had been demonstrated beyond any possibility of a doubt that the Union lines could not be broken, or our works carried by assault."[21] But Hood's "folly" was not yet complete. When he finally learned that Cheatham's Corps had run into trouble he sent a courier to find S. D. Lee with orders to "go forward and in person to communicate with General Cheatham, and if necessary, to put Johnson's division in the fight." Lee went to Cheatham's headquarters at Privet Knob just as darkness was descending, a little after 5 p.m., where he learned that help was needed immediately. He put Allegheny Johnson's division in line on the left of the Columbia Pike and, since he was unfamiliar with the ground, asked Cheatham for someone to guide its advance. Cheatham replied that he had nobody to give him but pointed to the front and said, "Yonder line of fire at the breastworks is where you are needed and wanted at once." By the time Johnson's men started forward it had been dark for an hour, and the only light came, Lee said, from "the lurid and rapid flashes from the enemy's works."[22]

Groping forward in the dark, the Confederates approached Ruger's line near the grove of locust trees. "We advanced," one of Johnson's men wrote, "stumbling over our dead and wounded. The latter shrieked as we trod on their mangled limbs. Powder smoke hung over the field in clouds, reflecting the lurid fire that blazed along the Yankee parapets. It seemed to me that the air was so full of bullets that I could have caught some by simply grabbing on either side or above me." A Rebel officer, who had hoped that the darkness and night would cloak their advance, said that when they were "within thirty paces of the enemy works . . . the darkness was lighted up as if by electric display."[23] The Union artillery and infantry had opened fire with terrible effect. S. D. Lee said it looked "as if the division was moving into the very door of hell, lighted up with its sulphurous flames."[24]

Three of Johnson's four brigades succeeded in reaching the ditch outside Ruger's works. The fourth suffered from lack of leadership when its commander, Brigadier General Arthur M. Manigault, and two of his successors were shot down. Part of one brigade, after struggling through the grove of locust trees "that ordinarily a dog could not have gotten through," as one of them put it, actually got across the parapet.[25] There was a brief hand-to-hand struggle and then the Federals seemed to disappear into the darkness only to be replaced by a terrible incoming fire that pinned the Rebels to the inner ditch. They could not go forward into that fire, nor could they retreat back across the parapet, where other Confederates were firing over their heads at the flashes of the Union rifles, until there was a brief lull in the firing. Then they scrambled back to the outside ditch, except for a few wounded men who surrendered.

S. D. Lee's other two divisions were posted along the high ground to the south that Wagner's two brigades had held briefly at the beginning of the battle and were never ordered to attack. By 9 p.m. the last assault had been stopped and all over the field south of Franklin the battle slowly sputtered out in fits of fire and counterfire from nervous units and individuals. Almost any noise or movement would bring a shot or a volley from the other side. "Wounded Confederates who moved a leg or an arm were instantly selected as targets and were literally shot to pieces," one witness said.[26] The other Rebel units pulled back to join Lee's two uncommitted divisions, and by 10:30 p.m. all was quiet except for the moans of the wounded. Somewhere a Union soldier began to sing: "Rally 'round the flag, boys, we'll rally once again, shouting the battle cry of freedom."[27] Others picked it up and soon their swelling chorus drowned out all other sounds for a while.

Union patrols went out to check on the situation beyond the works and found piles of dead and wounded men. It was, as one Federal put it, "enough to shock a heart of stone. . . . The air seemed close and the smell of blood was everywhere." In places the ground "was in a perfect slop" of blood-red mud. Colonel Opdycke was among numerous individual Union soldiers who went out "to see the effect of such fighting." Captain Shellenberger was another. In the ditch inside the main line of defenses he found "the mangled bodies of dead Rebels were piled as high as the mouth of the embrasure" for a cannon. The pile in the outer ditch was even worse. "Heads, arms, and legs were sticking out in almost every conceivable manner," he said. "The air was filled with moans of the wounded; and the pleadings for water and for help of some of those who saw me was heartrending."[28]

Sixty-seven-year-old Fountain Carter, 22 members of his family, and a neighbor had all huddled in his cellar throughout the battle, finding safety there from the shells and bullets of both armies while the fighting raged all around them. Now, out on the cold, bloody, moonlit battlefield, Captain Theodrick "Tod" Carter, a Confederate staff officer and the tenth of Fountain Carter's twelve children, lay about 175 yards from the house, shot in the head and deliriously calling for help.

His defensive victory at Franklin did not change Schofield's plans to evacuate the place that night and to march on toward Nashville. Cox wanted to stay and fight again the next day, and Stanley was worried about how the army could be safely withdrawn in the middle of the night, but both were overruled. In reply to Schofield's telegram sent before the attack, Thomas had authorized the withdrawal and Schofield was determined to make it. He considered himself to be badly outnumbered in both infantry and cavalry and he especially feared that Forrest would somehow get between him and Nashville. After the battle he had the further excuse that his forces had expended so much ammunition that he did not have enough left for another serious fight. A captured Rebel colonel who had been brought to headquarters for interrogation "twitted" Schofield with the observation that "victors usually held the field, not the vanquished."[29] But Schofield just chuckled and said he was luring Hood to his destruction.

Even before the Confederates had made their final attacks the Union artillery had begun to pull out of position and head for the bridges, following the long train of wagons that had continued to cross the river all through the battle. At around 11 p.m. the infantry began to quietly fall back and join the march. A lieutenant, expressing the sentiments of many of the Union soldiers, told Colonel Israel Stiles, a brigade commander in Reilly's division, "We ought to remain here and wipe hell out of 'em." Stiles, referring to the pleas of the many wounded Rebels still lying between the lines, said, "There is no hell left in them. Don't you hear them praying?"[30]

Just as the Union infantry was starting to move, a large fire broke out in Franklin, and its light almost revealed the withdrawal to the Rebels. But Stanley's staff officers found an old fire engine and put out the blaze about midnight, after eight buildings were either completely or partially burned. As the roof of one of the buildings fell in, a great glow of light was thrown over the entire area, and some of Opdycke's men saw about a dozen battleflags rise along the Confederate lines to the south. The 73rd Illinois opened fire to let the Rebels know that the Federals were still there and ready to fight, and the flags soon disappeared. When the fire died down the withdrawal continued and not long after 1 a.m. even the pickets who had been left behind were able to pull out. By 2 a.m. all of Schofield's troops were across the river, and bundles of kindling on both bridges were set on fire. Wood's division of the 4th Corps, having been north of the river all during the battle, covered the crossing and became the new rear guard, and by 4 a.m. even it was on the road north.

Virgil S. Murphey, the captured Confederate colonel who had been interrogated by Schofield, had at first shuddered at the horrors "which human hands had just created" and considered the battlefield "an unholy ground." But after hearing his captor, a captain from Ohio, extol the courage of the Rebel attack, he reconsidered. "The Battle of Franklin will live in history," he told his diary. "It is a monument, as enduring as time to Southern valor."[31] But a Union officer, who was also contemplating the meaning of what he had seen that day, wrote, 'I feel like one who witnesses a bitter wrong, a monstrous injustice. Call it glorious to die a horrible death, surrounded by an awful butchery, a scanty burial by . . . [enemy] hands, and then total oblivion, name blotted out and forever forgotten—where is the glory?"[32]

---

1. Sword, *Embrace an Angry Wind*, 216.
2. Ibid., 218.
3. Ibid.
4. *Official Records*, 45:I:116.
5. Sword, *Embrace an Angry Wind*, 199–201.
6. Ibid., 202.
7. McDonough and Connelly, *Five Tragic Hours*, 117.
8. Sword, *Embrace an Angry Wind*, 203–204.
9. *Official Records*, 45:I:116.
10. Sword, *Embrace an Angry Wind*, 204–205.
11. Ibid., 222–223.
12. Ibid., 224.
13. Ibid., 208.
14. Ibid.
15. Ibid., 236.
16. Ibid., 240.
17. Ibid., 227.
18. Ibid., 211.
19. Ibid.
20. Ibid., 230.
21. Ibid., 243.
22. Hattaway, *General Stephen D. Lee*, 136.
23. Sword, *Embrace an Angry Wind*, 246.
24. Hattaway, *General Stephen D. Lee*, 137.
25. Sword, *Embrace an Angry Wind*, 246.

26. Ibid., 247.
27. Ibid., 248.
28. Ibid., 249.
29. Ibid., 253.
30. Ibid., 254.
31. Ibid., 231.
32. Ibid., 244.

CHAPTER THIRTY-EIGHT

I Feel Great Anxiety

30 November–8 December 1864

The Union expedition to take Fort Fisher and close Wilmington, N.C., one of the last major Confederate ports, had been in the works for a long time. The latest delays were due to a plan Ben Butler had come up with. He wanted to fill an expendable old ship with gunpowder, tow it as close to the fort as possible, and blow it up, figuring that the explosion would do enough damage to the fort to make its capture a certainty. Opinions were mixed about whether such a scheme had any validity. Admiral Porter was enthusiastic, General Grant was extremely dubious, and other opinions ranged in between those extremes. Horace Porter quoted Grant as doubting that the explosion would even wake up the garrison of the fort, if it happened to be asleep at the time, but said that the boat was not of much value and that the army had plenty of damaged powder that was unserviceable for other purposes, so the experiment would not cost much. Lincoln remarked that "we might as well explode the notion with powder as with anything else."[1]

Brigadier General Godfrey Weitzel, commander of the 10th Corps, had been chosen to lead the ground forces of the expedition, but Butler and Porter were still working on the powder ship. On the afternoon of 30 November, Grant wired Butler: "I have files of Savannah and Augusta papers . . . from which I gather that Bragg has gone to Georgia, taking with him what I judge to be most of the forces from about Wilmington. It is, therefore, important that Weitzel should get off during his absence, and if successful in effecting a landing he may, by a bold dash, also succeed in capturing Wilmington. Make all the arrangements for his departure so that the navy will not be detained one moment for the army."[2]

Up in the Shenandoah Valley, Sheridan finally started the 6th Corps on its way back to Petersburg on that final day of November.

The next day, 1 December, an advertisement placed by prominent attorney George W. Gayle appeared in the *Selma* (Alabama) *Dispatch* newspaper. It asked citizens of the Confederacy to contribute $1,000,000 to procure the assassination of the "cruel tyrants" Abraham Lincoln, William H. Seward (U.S. secretary of state), and Andrew Johnson (military governor of Tennessee and vice president-elect).[3]

At Franklin, Tennessee, Confederate artillery began to deploy after midnight, and by 2 a.m. on 1 December much of it was in place. After a midnight conference with his corps commanders and despite gloomy reports from Stewart and Cheatham, Hood had decided to attack again. By his orders, a hundred guns would begin to bombard the Union position at 7 a.m., firing 100 rounds each. Then at 9 a.m. the infantry would charge once more. However, at 2 a.m. Confederate scouts reported that the Federals had abandoned their defenses as well as the town of Franklin and that the railroad bridge across the Harpeth was on fire. It was suspected, however, that they still held the north bank of the river. So the fire of a battery of 12-pounders was used to probe the Union position. In the darkness all it had to aim by was the burning bridge, and it fired about 150 rounds directed at a spot about 200 yards east of the bridge. However, the Confederates failed to notice that the railroad bridge had already burned down and it was the rebuilt wagon bridge that they were aiming by. Consequently their shells fell on the eastern part of the town of Franklin.

As dawn finally illuminated the fields south of Franklin the Confederates got a good look at what they had lost the night before. "I never before or after saw such a frightful battle ground," one of them wrote.[4] About 2,500 dead bodies and approximately 6,000 wounded men lay on the cold ground. Altogether, Hood lost over 7,500 men at Franklin, including about 700 captured. Even worse than the mere number of men lost, so far as the future ability of his army was concerned, Hood lost very heavily in leaders. Sixty-five commanders of divisions, brigades, and regiments were killed, wounded, or captured, including thirteen generals. Cheatham's and Stewart's troops were put to work at burying the dead and bringing in the wounded, while schools, churches and homes were turned into temporary hospitals. There were 41 for the Confederates and three for the Federals. Boxcars full of Union wounded had already been sent off to Nashville by train and others were on their way to the same place in ambulances. The Union losses were reported as 2,326, of which over 1,000 were from Wagner's division. Among the seriously wounded on the Federal side was Major Arthur MacArthur, Jr., of the 24th Wisconsin, father of the WWII general. Lieutenant Colonel John S. White, commander of the 16th Kentucky, one of Reilly's reserve units that retook part of the main line, was wounded in the face but did not leave the field until the battle was over. Major Thomas W. Motherspaw, who had accidentally started Opdycke's countercharge, was mortally wounded.

One Rebel soldier saw Hood and his staff stop on their way into Franklin that morning to have a look at the carnage he had created. "His sturdy visage assumed a melancholy appearance," the soldier said, "and for a considerable time he sat on his horse and wept like a child." And yet before the day was out he congratulated his men in general orders for "the success achieved yesterday over our enemy by their heroic and determined courage. The enemy have been sent in disorder and confusion to Nashville, and while we lament the fall of many gallant officers and brave men, we have shown to our countrymen that we can carry any position occupied by our enemy." His men were not fooled. "Our army was a wreck," a captain wrote. "I can safely say that just two such victories will wipe out any army the power of man can organize."[5]

It was close to 1 p.m. before S. D. Lee's corps led the pursuit—if such it could be called—of Schofield's Federals. Stewart's Corps did not begin to follow until two hours later, and Cheatham's Corps remained at Franklin until the next day. A member of what had been Granbury's Brigade of Cleburne's Division said, "Our brigade and the Arkansas brigade are so badly cut up that we can't move. Some officers have no men, and some companies have [no] officers. So we have to reorganize and consolidate; a captain has to command the brigade."[6]

Schofield had arrived at Brentwood, nine miles out of Nashville, before daylight. He was utterly exhausted, as were his men, most of whom had not slept for two days. He did not get to sleep for long, however, as word soon arrived from Thomas that A. J. Smith's last division was only then disembarking at Nashville and that a large force being brought

up from Chattanooga and the District of the Etowah by Major General
James B. Steedman had not yet arrived either. Neither could therefore
be sent out to meet him at Brentwood, and so he should continue on into
Nashville. Schofield rode on ahead of his troops and met with Thomas at
around 8 a.m.

It was an icy meeting, for, although they did not say so, the two
generals blamed each other for several real and imagined grievances aris-
ing out of the campaign from Pulaski to Nashville. Schofield blamed
Thomas for staying behind his desk at Nashville and not leading the
troops in person, for sending him and his troops to Pulaski in the first
place, for not reinforcing him at Columbia, and for not sending pontoons
to Franklin. Thomas had just received a report from a staff officer charging Schofield with neglect in not putting the Harpeth River between his
army and Hood's on the 30th. Then Schofield went to his hotel room
and slept from noon that day until sunset the next.

Late on the morning of 1 December Schofield's troops began to march
into Nashville, proudly parading their prisoners and captured battleflags
past Thomas's garrison troops. At 5 p.m. Steedman reached Nashville,
bringing with him two brigades of U.S. Colored Troops plus a provisional division commanded by Brigadier General Charles Cruft composed of detachments of men left behind by the four corps marching
through Georgia with Sherman. All these new arrivals plus A. J. Smith's
divisions now gave Thomas too many men to fit in the old defenses, so
they were immediately put to work digging a new line of entrenchments
on high ground southwest of the city to enclose a larger area.

On the map the Union position at Nashville looks much like the one
at Franklin. The city lay on the south side of the Cumberland River,
which looped around it, and the defenses formed a rough semi-circle
from the river above the city to the river below it. However, there were
differences. The city was larger than Franklin, and with the addition of
Smith's and Steedman's infantry, most of Wilson's dismounted cavalry
units, and Thomas's garrison troops, the Union army was much larger
than it had been at Franklin. And the Cumberland, patroled by Union
gunboats, was larger and much harder to cross than the Harpeth from
anywhere other than the city.

That night, Thomas telegraphed to Halleck at Washington: "After
General Schofield's fight of yesterday, feeling convinced that the enemy
very far outnumbered him, both in infantry and cavalry, I determined
to retire to the fortifications around Nashville, until General Wilson can
get his cavalry equipped. He has now but about one-fourth the number
of the enemy, and consequently is no match for him. I have two ironclads here, with several gun-boats, and Commander Fitch assures me

that Hood can neither cross the Cumberland nor blockade it. I therefore think it best to wait here until Wilson can equip all his cavalry. If Hood attacks me here, he will be more seriously damaged than he was yesterday; if he remains until Wilson gets equipped, I can whip him and will move against him at once. I have Murfreesboro strongly held, and therefore feel easy in regard to its safety. Chattanooga, Bridgeport, Stevenson, and Elk River bridge also have strong garrisons."[7]

The next day, the second, all of Wilson's cavalry was moved across the Cumberland River to the suburb of Edgefield, where it would be joined by some of his units that had been up at Louisville. Its mission was to reorganize and get reequipped with new weapons, uniforms, and horses as rapidly as possible. This was not an easy job, for there were never enough of these items to go around, and weeks later there were still not enough guns and horses for all the cavalry. However, Thomas and Wilson seriously overestimated the size of Forrest's cavalry corps, and it also had its problems with equipment and horses.

Buford's and Jackson's divisions of Confederate cavalry were the first Rebels to approach Nashville on the morning of 2 December, about 24 hours behind Schofield's Federals. S. D. Lee's infantry arrived at about 2 p.m. and the other two corps did not arrive until the next day. Lee's empty wagons were sent back down to Columbia to bring up more artillery ammunition, and Hood issued orders that day for the deployment of his army. "General Lee will form his corps with his center upon the Franklin pike; General Stewart will form on General Lee's left; and General Cheatham on General Lee's right. The entire line of the army will curve forward from General Lee's center so that General Cheatham's right may come as near the Cumberland as possible above Nashville, and General Stewart's left as near the Cumberland as possible below Nashville. Each position will be strengthened as soon as taken, extended as fast as strengthened. Artillery will be placed in all favorable positions. All engineer officers will be constantly engaged in examining the position of the enemy and looking to all his weak points. Corps commanders will give all necessary assistance. Not a cartridge of any kind will be burned until further orders, unless the enemy should advance against us."[8]

Hood came to Nashville with only the vaguest of plans. He did not know exactly how many troops Thomas had in the city, but he knew that Union reinforcements were on the way if not already there, so he at least knew better than to attack its defenses. However, if Thomas came out and attacked him, then he would have the advantage of fighting behind prepared defenses. And if Thomas stayed cooped up in Nashville that would leave Hood in control of most of the rest of Tennessee, where Confederate conscription could be strictly enforced. That same day, the second, he sent Bate's Division to destroy the railroad between Nashville and Murfreesboro. And most of Forrest's cavalry was dispatched on a similar mission. He also had some hopes for reinforcements from other parts of the Confederacy.

That very day Beauregard was writing to General Kirby Smith, commander of all Confederate forces west of the Mississippi: "You are probably aware that the Army of Tennessee, under General J. B. Hood, has penetrated into Middle Tennessee as far as Columbia, and that the enemy is concentrating all his available forces, under General Thomas, to oppose him. It is even reliably reported that the forces under Generals A. J. Smith, in Missouri, and Steele, in Arkansas, have been sent to re-enforce Thomas. It becomes, then, absolutely necessary, to insure the success of Hood, either that you should send him two or more divisions, or that you should at once threaten Missouri, in order to compel the enemy to recall the re-enforcements he is sending to General Thomas. I beg to urge upon you prompt and decisive action. The fate of the country may depend upon the result of Hood's campaign in Tennessee. Sherman's army has lately abandoned Atlanta on a venturesome march across Georgia to the Atlantic coast about Savannah. His object is, besides the destruction of public and private property, probably to re-enforce Grant and compel Lee to abandon Richmond. It is hoped that Sherman may be prevented from effecting his object, but should it be otherwise, the success of Hood in Tennessee and Kentucky would counterbalance the moral effect of the loss of Richmond. Hence the urgent necessity of either re-enforcing Hood or making a diversion in Missouri in his favor."[9]

What Beauregard proposed made some sense, but he was far too late. Just as Hood's move into middle Tennessee came too late to keep Sherman from marching to the sea, so any new Confederate move into Missouri would come too late to prevent A. J. Smith from being sent to Nashville, for he was already there. The alternative of sending reinforcements to Hood from across the Mississippi was equally impractical because of the Union gunboats patroling that river. It had been tried months before and had not succeeded then either.

President Lincoln continued to visit the War Department telegraph office to read dispatches, and he noticed the telegram Thomas had sent to Halleck. On the second, Secretary of War Stanton wired General Grant: "The President feels solicitous about the disposition of General Thomas to lay in fortifications for an indefinite period 'until Wilson gets equipments.' This looks like the McClellan and Rosecrans strategy of do nothing and let the rebels raid the country. The President wishes you to consider the matter."[10]

Grant had already sent Thomas a wire: "If Hood is permitted to remain quietly about Nashville, you will lose all the road back to Chattanooga, and possibly have to abandon the line of the Tennessee. Should he attack you it is all well, but if he does not you should attack him before he fortifies. Arm and put in the trenches your quartermaster employes, citizens, etc." Now he added: "With your citizen employes armed, you can move out of Nashville with all your army and force the enemy to retire or fight upon ground of your own choosing. After the repulse of Hood at Franklin, it looks to me that instead of falling back to Nashville, we should have taken the offensive against the enemy where he was. At this distance, however, I may err as to the best method of dealing with the enemy. You will now suffer incalculable injury upon your railroads, if Hood is not speedily disposed of. Put forth, therefore, every possible exertion to attain this end. Should you get him retreating, give him no peace."[11]

Thomas replied: "At the time that Hood was whipped at Franklin, I had at this place but about 5,000 men of General Smith's command, which added to the force under General Schofield would not have given me more than 25,000 men; besides, General Schofield felt convinced that he could not hold the enemy at Franklin until the 5,000 could reach him. As General Wilson's cavalry force also numbered only about one-fourth that of Forrest's, I thought it best to draw the troops back to Nashville and wait the arrival of the remainder of General Smith's force, and also a force of about 5,000 commanded by Major-General Steedman, which had ordered up from Chattanooga . . . I now have infantry enough to assume the offensive, if I had more cavalry, and will take the field anyhow as soon as the remainder of General McCook's division of cavalry reaches here, which I hope it will do in two or three days. We can neither get re-enforcements or equipments at this great distance from the North very easily; and it must be remembered that my command was made up of the two weakest corps of General Sherman's army and all the dismounted cavalry except one brigade, and the task of reorganizing and equipping has met with many delays, which have enabled Hood to take advantage of my crippled condition. I earnestly hope, however, that in a few more days I shall be able to give him a fight."[12]

Horace Porter, who had once served on Thomas's staff, said that Grant "entertained a high regard for General Thomas personally, and the greatest respect for his military capacity. Thomas was a conspicuous representative of the loyal Virginians. At the breaking out of the war he had shown great strength of character and determination of purpose in deciding to remain loyal to the country which had educated him as a soldier, and to defend the flag which he had sworn to uphold. No one had displayed greater devotion to the cause, and few officers in the service stood higher in the affection of their associates or in the confidence of their superior officers. General Thomas, being in command of only a single army, looked naturally to the means of securing the largest measure of success in his immediate front, and it was not likely that he would regard time as of so much importance as the general-in-chief of all the armies. With Grant, the movements of Thomas's army were a part of a series of cooperative campaigns, and unnecessary delays in the movements of any one army might seriously affect contemplated operations on the part of the others. Canby was expected to send a force into the interior, but he could not do so until Thomas had assumed the offensive against Hood; and he was compelled to postpone his expedition, and to hold Vicksburg and Memphis, and patrol the Mississippi to try to prevent troops from crossing from the Trans-Mississippi Department to relieve Hood."[13]

Also on the second of December orders were finally issued relieving Rosecrans from command of the Department of Missouri and replacing him with Major General Grenville Dodge, who had recovered from a wound he had received during the Atlanta campaign. Rosecrans' performance during Price's raid into Missouri had not endeared him to Stanton or Lincoln, and Grant had never cared for Rosecrans ever since the latter had been his subordinate during the defense of Corinth, Mississippi, in 1862. When Stanton asked where he wanted Rosecrans sent now that he was being relieved, Grant replied: "Rosecrans will do less harm doing nothing than on duty. I know no department or army commander deserving such punishment as the infliction of Rosecrans upon them. His name could well go on the list [of generals to be dismissed] I sent up a few days ago."[14]

In the Shenandoah Valley the next day, the third, Merritt's cavalry division returned from its raid into Loudoun County, east of the Blue Ridge, after destroying a million dollars worth of barns, stables, corncribs, and smokehouses and consuming or carrying off cattle, hogs, sheep, and horses. Under political pressure generated by the influential Baltimore & Ohio Railroad after Rosser's raid on New Creek, Sheridan sent Crook with one division of the Army of West Virginia to Cumberland, Maryland, to help protect that railroad. The provisional division that had been commanded by Colonel Kitching at the battle of Cedar Creek, having been sent down to City Point, became on 3 December the Infantry Division, Defenses of Bermuda Hundred, in Butler's Army of the James. And that same day Butler's other forces were reorganized. The 10th and 18th Corps were discontinued and all the white troops from those two organizations were reorganized as the new 24th Corps, under Ord, while all the black troops, plus the division of blacks from the 9th Corps, were organized as the 25th Corps, under Weitzel.

Confederate general Braxton Bragg's wife, at Richmond, wrote to her husband, at Augusta, that day. She said that General Lee had told her that "if the Georgians are true to themselves Sherman cant escape." She wondered, however, "why, if militia can accomplish so much does *he* not send some veteran troops to annihilate Sherman & let militia hide behind the walls here!"[15] Sherman and the 17th Corps entered the town of Millen, Georgia, that day, where the Confederates had been holding a few thousand Union prisoners. These had been transferred there from Andersonville when the Rebels had thought that Sherman was heading in that direction. Now they had been moved again, just ahead of Kilpatrick's advancing cavalry. Some of the Federals inspected the stockade and the huts and holes where the prisoners had lived. "Miserable hovels, hardly fit for swine to live in," a Union chaplain called them. "It was the barest spot I ever saw," another Federal said. "The trees and stumps and roots to the smallest fiber had been dug out for fuel, not a rag or a button or even a chip could be found." A Union captain said, "I am afraid if the soldiers generally could visit this pen there would be no quarter given beyond here."[16] The Federals burned the prison camp, the village depot, the hotel, and other buildings, as well as a plantation on the outskirts of town, where they shot a pack of bloodhounds.

Early that evening Wheeler's Confederate cavalry attacked one of Kilpatrick's regiments that was protecting some Union infantry busily engaged in tearing up the railroad tracks. "This attack was easily repulsed," Kilpatrick reported, "as were several others made during the night. As I had received orders that day from the general-in-chief to make a strong reconnaissance in the direction of Waynesborough, and to engage Wheeler wherever we met him, I directed brigade commanders to send surplus animals and all non-combatants to the wagon train; that in the morning the command would move to engage, defeat, and rout the rebel cavalry encamped at Waynesborough."

The next day the Confederate skirmishers were quickly driven back to their main line, which consisted of dismounted cavalry protected by strong barricades with well secured flanks. An initial attack by Kilpatrick's 2nd Brigade was repulsed, but then he sent in the 92nd Mounted Infantry on foot with Spencers blazing and backed up by three mounted regiments and a battery of horse artillery. The latter forced the Rebel guns to withdraw and "at this moment," Kilpatrick said, "all being ready, the charge was sounded, the whole line moved forward in splendid order, and never halted for one moment until the barricades were gained and the enemy routed. A few hundred yards beyond he made several counter-charges to save his dismounted men and check our rapid advance." But the 5th Ohio Cavalry, which "had been sent out on our right, charged the enemy in flank and rear, when he gave way at all points and rapidly fell back to the town."

There the Confederates occupied a second line of barricades, with artillery support, "and his flanks so far extended," Kilpatrick said, "that it was useless to attempt to turn them. I therefore determined to break his center." Again one regiment was sent ahead dismounted, and it was backed up by four mounted regiments. "The advance was sounded, and in less than twenty minutes the enemy was driven from his position, the town gained, and Wheeler's entire force completely routed."[17] The Union troopers drove the Rebels eight miles beyond the point of their first attack and then burned the railroad bridge and a couple of others. Kilpatrick reported that of the Confederte wounded left on the field that day over 200 were suffering from saber cuts.

While the cavalry was fighting, Sherman's infantry was still advancing. The Rebels had burned the bridge over Ebenezer Creek, a swampy tributary of the Savannah River, but an Indiana regiment worked all night on 3–4 December to lay a pontoon bridge, and Jefferson C. Davis' 14th Corps began crossing shortly after dawn on the fourth. There were over 500 escaping slaves, mostly women and children, traveling with the corps, but they were turned aside as they reached the creek and forbidden to use the bridge until the troops were all across. The day before, these refugees had refused to get out of the way to clear the road for the advance of his men when Confederate resistance had been met by the head of the column, and now Davis was determined to teach them a lesson. When all of his troops were across the bridge it was suddenly cut loose and pulled to the eastern bank, leaving the slaves on the far side.

"There went up from that multitude a cry of agony," a Union chaplain said. Someone shouted, "Rebels!" and the slaves "made a wild rush . . . some of them plunged into the water, and swam across. Others ran wildly up and down the bank, shaking with terror." Sympathetic soldiers threw logs and pieces of timber into the creek for them, and the few men among the slaves dragged them out and built a raft out of them. With this and a rope made out of blankets dozens of women and children were ferried across while the rest, as one Union soldier wrote, "Huddled as close to the edge of the water as they could get, some crying, some praying, and all fearful that the rebels would come before they could get over."[18] Many of the slaves jumped into the stream to swim across. Some made it to the eastern bank. Others were swept downstream and drowned. Some were saved by Federal soldiers. Confederate cavalry soon appeared and fired into the slaves and then rode off. But soon after the last Union soldier had disappeared to the east the Rebels returned and rounded up all the slaves who were still on the western bank. Word of what Davis had done soon spread throughout the Union army, and many officers and men condemned his actions in letters they would mail as soon as they reached the coast.

In Virginia on 4 December units of the 6th Corps began arriving at City Point, while that same day Grant gave Sheridan permission to retain one division of that corps for a few days if he thought it necessary. Sheridan held Getty's 2nd Division, saying, "If this division remains here for a few days it gives me security, and the movement of the other two divisions forces the enemy to move one way or the other." That evening Grant returned to one of his favorite themes, asking Sheridan, "Do you think it possible now to send cavalry through to the Virginia Central road? It is highly desirable that it be done, if it is possible. I leave the practicability of this to be determined by you."[19]

Sheridan replied that night: "I have contemplated a cavalry raid on the Central railroad, intending to go myself when things are satisfactory here; but from all the light which I have I have not estimated the breaking of the road as very important. I am satisfied that no supplies go over the road toward Richmond from any point north of the road or from the Shenandoah Valley. On the contrary the rebel forces here in the Valley have drawn supplies from the direction of Richmond . . . I have the best of evidence to show that there is no depot at Gordonsville or Charlottesville, and that the trains passing through those places are only burdened by necessities for Early's army. I think that the rebels have looked at this matter about as I do, and they have not been at all fearful of my going in that direction, as the temporary destruction would only inconvenience them and would be of no great value to me. I will make the raid soon, if it is made at all, and will only go myself if all affairs here are in a healthy condition."[20]

Grant, meanwhile, was again trying to get the expedition moving to capture Fort Fisher. "I feel great anxiety," he told Ben Butler, "to see the Wilmington expedition off, both on account of the present fine weather, which we can expect no great continuance of, and because Sherman may now be expected to strike the sea coast any day, leaving Bragg free to return. I think it advisable for you to notify Admiral Porter and get off without any delay with or without your powder boat."[21]

In regard to Grant's other big worry of the moment, Hood's invasion of Tennessee and Thomas's inactivity, Halleck sent Grant a wire on the fifth: "The records show that there have been issued at Louisville, Lexington, and Nashville since September 20 22,000 cavalry horses. This number is exclusive of the cavalry horses previously issued and brought into the department by Grierson and others, and the commands of Burbridge and Garrard, and those sent to Sherman. If this number, without any campaign, is already reduced to 10,000 mounted men, as reported by General Wilson, it may be safely assumed that the cavalry of that army will never be mounted, for the destruction of horses in the last two months has there alone been equal to the remounts obtained from the entire West. None are issued to Rosecrans, Steele, or Canby." Grant was telegraphing Thomas the same day: "Is there not danger of Forrest moving down the Cumberland to where he can cross it? It seems to me whilst you should be getting up your cavalry as rapidly as possible to look after Forrest, Hood should be attacked where he is. Time strengthens him, in all probability, as much as it does you." To complete the circle, Thomas wired Halleck that night: "I have been along my entire line to-day. The enemy has not advanced at all since the 3d instant. If I can perfect my arrangements I shall move against the advanced position of the enemy on the 7th instant."[22]

The United States Congress reconvened on 5 December, and the next day former secretary of the treasury Salmon P. Chase was nominated to be chief justice of the Supreme Court and Congress heard Lincoln's state of the Union message read, ending with the simple declaration that "the war will cease on the part of the government, whenever it shall have ceased on the part of those who began it."[23]

On that same sixth day of December, Lincoln was visited by reporter Noah Brooks. "I found him writing on a piece of common stiff boxboard with a pencil," Brooks recorded. "Said he, after he had finished, 'Here is one speech of mine which has never been printed, and I think it worth printing. Just see what you think.'" Lincoln called it "The President's Last, Shortest, and Best Speech," and it was published under that title in one of the Washington newspapers: "On thursday of last week two ladies from Tennessee came before the President asking the release of their husbands held as prisoners of war at Johnson's Island. They were put off till friday, when they came again; and were again put off to saturday. At each of the interviews one of the ladies urged that her husband was a religious man. On saturday the President ordered the release of the prisoners, and then said to this lady 'You say your husband is a religious man; tell him when you meet him, that I say I am not much of a judge of religion, but that, in my opinion, the religion that sets men to rebel and fight against their government, because, as they think, that government does not sufficiently help *some* men to eat their bread on the sweat of *other* men's faces, is not the sort of religion upon which people can get to heaven!'"[24]

In Indiana on the sixth, the military commission trying four Copperhead leaders heard the final arguments of the defense attorneys. One denied that membership in the Sons of Liberty constituted participation in a conspiracy. Another, with elaborate citations from American and English precedents, challenged the jurisdiction of the military to try them. The judge advocate, however, argued that the arrests and the trial by military law had been justified by "overpowering necessity for military interference."[25] All four were found guilty. One, Andrew Humphreys, was sentenced to confinement at hard labor for the duration of the war. The other three were sentenced to be hanged. However, Humphreys' sentence was soon changed to confinement within two townships of Greene County, Indiana, and the execution of the other three was delayed for so long that the war ended first. They were freed in 1866 when the Supreme Court ruled that the military had no right to try civilians in a state that was not in rebellion.

The 6th Corps was officially reassigned to the Army of the Potomac on 6 December, although some units would not arrive at City Point until ten days later. Captain Elisha Hunt Rhodes and the 2nd Rhode Island were among those who had arrived. "Here we are again in the trenches before Petersburg after our five months' absence in Maryland and the Valley of the Shenandoah," he told his diary that day. "We left the steamer at City Point on Dec. 4th and rode in the cars to Parke's Station 12 miles. Here we remained overnight. As it was dark when we left the cars there was some discussion as to how near the front we were. This question was soon settled by the sharp crack of rifles as the pickets near us began to fire. We decided that we were quite near enough. Yesterday Dec. 5th we moved to this camp. The 5th Corps was stationed here, but they marched away to a new position, and we occupied their trenches and forts. We are near the Weldon Rail Road . . . . In front of my camp we have a high and very strong line of earthworks. The enemy are nearly two miles in our front, but the picket lines are very near to each other. To our right and in front of the 9th Corps, constant firing is kept up, but there seems to be an agreement on our lines not to fire. The 5th Corps left some very good log huts. The one that I am living in has a good fire place and is quite comfortable. The Army camp looks like a great city, and several large buildings have been put up, while sutler's stores are very numerous. But the change from the Valley is great, and it will take some time to get accustomed to siege work, which we dropped so suddenly in July last. Little progress has been made since we left here, but we know the war will end in our favor sometime."[26] Other reinforcements also arrived from the Valley, in the form of the 1st Infantry Division of the Army of West Virginia, which became the Independent Division in Butler's Army of the James that day.

The 5th Corps had turned over its defenses and winter quarters to the 6th Corps in order to prepare for a raid down the Weldon Railroad "for the purpose," as Grant told Meade, "of effectually destroying it as far south as Hicksford, or farther if practicable."[27] Along with Gregg's cavalry and Mott's 3rd Division of the 2nd Corps, the 5th Corps massed behind the Union lines between the Jerusalem Plank and Halifax roads, drawing four days' rations and sixty rounds of ammunition per man.

Grant was still trying to spur both Thomas and Butler to action that day. At 4 p.m., by which time he had, no doubt, received Halleck's wire about horses, he telegraphed a simple, direct, two-sentence order to Thomas: "Attack Hood at once, and wait no longer for a remount of your cavalry. There is great danger of delay resulting in a campaign back to the Ohio River." This crossed with one to him from Thomas in answer to his wire of the day before: "As soon as I can get up a respectable force of cavalry I will march against Hood. General Wilson has parties out now pressing horses, and I hope to have some 6,000 or 8,000 cavalry mounted in three days from this time. General Wilson has just left me, having received instructions to hurry the cavalry remount as rapidly as possible. I do not think it prudent to attack Hood with less than 6,000 cavalry to cover my flanks, because he has, under Forrest, at least 12,000. I have no doubt Forrest will attempt to cross the river, but I am in hopes the gun-boats will be able to prevent him." That night, after receiving Grant's order, he replied: "I will make the necessary dispositions and attack Hood at once, agreeably to your order, though I believe it will be hazardous with the small force of cavalry now at my service."[28]

Also on the sixth, Butler sent Grant a copy of the instructions he had given to Weitzel for the expedition against Fort Fisher that day, which Grant approved "except in the unimportant matter of where they embark and the amount of intrenching tools to be taken." On the seventh, Grant nagged Butler again: "Let General Weitzel get off as soon as possible. We don't want the navy to wait an hour." Butler replied: "General Weitzel's command is encamped at signal tower near Point of Rocks. Admiral Porter telegraphs he will be ready by to-morrow."[29]

The expedition against the Weldon Railroad started off at 4 a.m. that day as Gregg's cavalry led the way down the Jerusalem Plank Road. "The weather was cold, and rainy, and snowy," a Union trooper remembered, "and the roads very rough and deep." The infantry started two hours later, and the column followed the road south, paralleling the Weldon Railroad, which ran in roughly the same direction a few miles to the west. That afternoon the Federals came to Hawkinsville, almost twenty miles south of Petersburg, and turned west. They built a pontoon bridge near there across the Nottoway River at Freeman's Ford, and the cavalry and Crawford's 3rd Division of the 5th Corps marched on to Sussex Court House, about five miles to the west, while the wagons and the rest of the infantry camped on both sides of the bridge. "This day's work represents an entirely new departure in the tactics of the army," one Federal noted. "For us to boldly strike out, put a day's march between us and our supports . . . is an astonishingly reckless movement."[30]

On the morning of the seventh, Secretary of War Stanton telegraphed Grant. After discussing other subjects he said, "Thomas seems unwilling to attack because it is hazardous, as if all war was anything but hazardous. If he waits for Wilson to get ready, Gabriel will be blowing his last horn." At 1:30 p.m. Grant replied: "You probably saw my order to Thomas to attack. If he does not do it promptly, I would recommend superseding him by Schofield, leaving Thomas subordinate." At 5 p.m. Grant wired Thomas: "The Richmond Sentinel of to-day had the following quotation: 'Intelligence received yesterday from East Tennessee announces the advance of Burbridge from Kentucky, which was met on the part of General Breckinridge by a retrograde movement to Greeneville, in order to protect his communications with the rear.'" Thomas replied to this at 10 p.m.: "Major-General Stoneman telegraphed me yesterday that Breckinridge had fallen back. I have directed Stoneman to pursue him as far as he can into Virginia, breaking and destroying twenty-five or thirty miles of railroad, and also to destroy the salt-works if possible."[31]

Forrest's cavalry had been getting into plenty of mischief since it had followed Schofield to Nashville. One regiment and some artillery had gone to the west of the city and had so harassed the shipping on the Cumberland River that, with the help of low water in the river and despite the presence of a number of Union gunboats, the river was completely blockaded. Meanwhile, Forrest, with Buford's and Jackson's divisions, had moved along the Nashville & Chattanooga Railroad, destroying blockhouses and bridges as they went and capturing several small garrisons. Then, joining up with Bate's infantry division, Forrest had reconnoitered Murfreesboro, which he had found was strongly fortified and had a garrison of about 8,000 Federals commanded by Major General Lovell Rousseau. Hood now hoped that by threatening Murfreesboro he could entice Thomas into coming out of his defenses to attack him. However, even including Bate's Division and two more brigades of infantry that Hood had sent, Forrest had fewer men with him than Rousseau had, but he ordered the infantry to entrench across the Union supply line to Nashville.

On the morning of 7 December a battery and two brigades of Federals under Major General Robert H. Milroy came out to see what the Confederates were up to. Forrest deployed the infantry, which was about equal in numbers to the Federals, to receive their attack while the cavalry was to attack their flanks and cut off their retreat. In the meantime, Buford was to take a detachment of cavalry and a battery of artillery, circle around, and enter the town from the opposite side. "The enemy moved boldly forward," Forrest reported, "driving in my pickets, when the infantry, with the exception of Smith's brigade, from some cause which I cannot explain, made a shameful retreat, losing two pieces of artillery. I seized the colors of the retreating troops and endeavored to rally them, but they could not be moved by any entreaty or appeal to their patriotism. Major-General Bate did the same thing, but was equally unsuccessful as myself."[32]

Bate blamed the cavalry, saying that it failed to warn the infantry of the Federals' approach through some heavy woods and that the latter struck his flank as the infantry was being shifted to a new position by Forrest's orders. He added that "if the cavalry was seriously engaged, I was not aware of it."[33] Actually, it was the approach of Jackson's Division plus Buford's attack on the town itself that caused Milroy's force to fall back within the Union defenses. Buford's attack was beaten off, however, and things returned to normal, with the Federals safe behind their defenses and the Confederates roaming about the countryside. But, in addition to the two cannon, Milroy had captured 207 prisoners and two battleflags in his brief fight.

In Virginia that day, the seventh, Gordon's and Pegram's divisions of Early's army reached Waynesborough, in the Blue Ridge, where they were put on rickety trains and started on their way to join Lee at Petersburg. The next day, 8 December, that part of Warren's Union infantry that was still on the northeast side of the Nottaway River was up before 2 a.m. and was, as one soldier put it, "again on our way toiling through the mud and darkness."[34] All of Warren's units were across and the pontoons were taken up and on the road—as was the rest of the expedi tion—by shortly after daylight. The weather was warmer that day, and many of the men threw away their overcoats and even their blankets to lighten their loads.

By 9 a.m. Gregg's cavalry had reached the Halifax Road, which ran alongside the railroad. Colonel Charles H. Smith's 2nd Brigade turned to the north along this road to the railroad bridge over the Nottoway River, which it proceeded to destroy. Meanwhile, Brigadier General Henry Davies' 1st Brigade began the work of destroying the railroad tracks.

The Union infantry began to arrive at about noon, and Warren deployed it along the railroad. But, fearing that the Rebels might be in strength nearby, he kept the men under arms and ready to fight until the entire command had caught up and the wagons were parked. Then, at sunset, the infantry too began tearing up track and kept at it until near midnight. By then they had destroyed the line as far south as Jarratt's Station.

Wade Hampton's Confedertae cavalry had spotted Warren's move the day before, and he had begun to gather his command at Stony Creek Station, north of the Nottoway River bridge. Some of his units crossed the river and skirmished with Gregg's troopers that day, and realizing that Warren was heading south down the Weldon Railroad, perhaps even for Weldon itself, he determined to try to head him off at the village of Hicksford, where the railroad crossed the Meherrin River. Hampton also received word from Lee that he was sending A. P. Hill with most of his 3rd Corps to back him up.

Anticipating that Lee would do something of the sort, Grant asked Meade, "If the enemy send off two divisions after Warren, what is there to prevent completing the investment of Petersburg with your reserves?"[35] But, as always, Meade was cautious. He replied that the "difficulty of taking advantage of Lee's detaching against Warren is to get positive information of the fact in time." He had sent a small cavalry force down the Vaughn Road to try to discover whether the Confederates were making any such move, but it was almost 10 p.m. by the time it reported, and all it could say was that Rebel cavalry, said to be Young's Brigade, was defending the crossing of Hatcher's Run. Grant then told Meade to "send out a division of infantry to help forcing a crossing of Hatcher's Run and find out what the enemy are doing. Send them in the morning. The enemy are playing a game of bluff with us now, and as we hold the strong hand we want to take advantage of it. Any further movement than that in support of the cavalry crossing Hatcher's Run will depend upon developments."[36]

That night the weather turned cold again, and Warren's men who had discarded their overcoats and blankets on the march regretted their impulsive actions. But they at least had camp fires to help keep them warm. A. P. Hill's Confederte infantry was still marching. "In all my experience during the war I do not remember any weather which was so trying to the troops," one of his officers wrote. "A high wind and cold rain prevailed when we started on the march of forty miles. To these succeeded hail and sleet which, with execrable roads and worn out shoes made our cup of misery full."[37]

Down in Georgia on the eighth Sherman found that one of his columns had left the road and was marching through the fields. "Close by," he wrote, "in the corner of a fence, was a group of men standing around a handsome young officer, whose foot had been blown to pieces by a torpedo planted in the road. He was waiting for a surgeon to amputate his leg, and told me that he was riding along with the rest of his brigade-staff of the Seventeenth Corps, when a torpedo trodden on by his horse had exploded, killing the horse and literally blowing off all the flesh from one of his legs. I saw the terrible wound, and made full inquiry into the facts. There had been no resistance at that point, nothing to give warning of danger, and the rebels had planted eight-inch shells in the road, with friction-matches to explode them by being trodden on. This was not war, but murder, and it made me very angry. I immediately ordered a lot of rebel prisoners to be brought from the provost-guard, armed with picks and spades, and made them march in close order along the road, so as to explode their own torpedoes, or to discover and dig them up. They begged hard, but I reiterated the order, and could hardly help laughing at their stepping so gingerly along the road, where it was supposed sunken torpedoes might explode at each step."[38]

Sherman was not the only Federal officer incensed at the Confederate use of what today we would call land mines. Major Hitchcock of his staff was furious. He wrote, "These cowardly villains call us 'barbarous Yanks'—and then adopt instruments of murder in cold blood when they dare not stand and fight like men."[39]

---

1. Porter, *Campaigning With Grant*, 337.
2. *Official Records*, 42:I:970–971.
3. Tidwell, Hall, and Gaddy, *Come Retribution*, 238.
4. Sword, *Embrace an Angry Wind*, 259.
5. Ibid., 262.

6. Ibid., 265.
7. *Official Records*, 45:II:3.
8. Ibid., 45:II:640–641.
9. Ibid., 45:II:639–640.
10. Ibid., 45:II:15–16.
11. Ibid., 45:II:17.
12. Ibid., 45:II:17–18.
13. Porter, *Campaigning With Grant*, 334–335.
14. *Official Records*, 41:IV:742–743.
15. Hallock, *Braxton Bragg and Confederate Defeat*, 2:224.
16. Davis, *Sherman's March*, 88.
17. *Official Records*, 44:364–365.
18. Davis, *Sherman's March*, 92.
19. *Official Records*, 43:II:740.
20. Ibid., 43:II:743–744.
21. Ibid., 42:I:971.
22. Ibid., 45:II:55.
23. Basler, ed., *The Collected Works of Abraham Lincoln*, 8:152.
24. Ibid., 154–155.
25. Milton, *Abraham Lincoln and the Fifth Column*, 318.
26. Rhodes, *All for the Union*, 199–200.
27. Trudeau, *The Last Citadel*, 264.
28. *Official Records*, 45:II:70.
29. Ibid., 42:I:972–973.
30. Trudeau, *The Last Citadel*, 266–267.
31. *Official Records*, 45:II:84.
32. Ibid., 45:I:755.
33. Ibid., 45:I:747.
34. Trudeau, *The Last Citadel*, 268–269.
35. *Official Records*, 42:III:865.
36. Ibid., 42:III:867.
37. Trudeau, *The Last Citadel*, 272.
38. Sherman, *Memoirs*, 670.
39. Davis, *Sherman's March*, 95.

CHAPTER THIRTY-NINE

Let There Be No Further Delay

8–12 December 1864

Grant tried again to spur Thomas to action on that eighth day of December: "It looks to me evident the enemy are trying to cross the Cumberland River and are scattered. Why not attack at once? By all means avoid the contingency of a foot race to see which, you or Hood, can beat to the Ohio. If you think necessary, call on the Governors of States to send a force into Louisville to meet the enemy if he should cross the river. You clearly never should cross except in rear of the enemy. Now is one of the finest opportunities ever presented of destroying one of the three armies of the enemy. If destroyed, he never can replace it. Use the means at your command, and you can do this and cause a rejoicing that will resound from one end of the land to another." Then Grant received an answer from Halleck to the mention he had made to Stanton about the necessity of relieving Thomas: "If you wish General Thomas relieved from [command], give the order. No one here will, I think, interfere. The responsibility, however, will be yours, as no one here, so far as I am informed, wishes General Thomas' removal." To this Grant answered: "I want General Thomas reminded of the importance of immediate action. I sent him a dispatch this evening which will probably urge him on. I would not say relieve him until I hear further from him."[1]

At 8 p.m. the Union telegraph operator at Nashville reported to Major Eckert at the War Department in Washington: "No change in position since last report. Enemy still in force in front, as was found out by reconnaissance, and a large artillery force upon south bank of the Cumberland below, between here and the Shoals. One of our gun-boats came to grief in exchange of iron at Bell's Ferry. Rebel General Lyon holds same bank below Harpeth, to Fort Donelson, but does not fight gun-boats. Re-enforcements now at Clarksville; will reach here by railroad to-morrow night. Colonel Thompson's black brigade reached here yesterday, having come from Johnsonville, via Clarksville. Deserters report Hood's headquarters seven miles out on Hillsborough pike; Forrest three miles on Granny White road, with main army on same road nearer town."[2]

As Grant feared, the Confederates did cross the Cumberland River. A few of them did, anyway. Brigadier General Hylan B. Lyon, with his new command of Kentucky recruits organized into two small brigades of cavalry and a two-gun battery of artillery, after constructing boats, crossed the Tennessee River near the Kentucky line on the eighth. On the ninth, at Cumberland City, thirty miles downstream from Clarksville, they captured a large steamboat loaded with forage and provisions and used it as a ferry to cross the Cumberland. And that evening they captured two more steamers and four barges, which they burned. "The weather was intensely cold," Lyon reported; "many of the soldiers were already frosted, and it was with the greatest difficulty that they could be made to move from the fires built along the road."[3]

Also on the ninth, Hood recalled Bate's Division from outside Murfreesboro to rejoin the main Confederte army on the hills south of Nashville. He also directed Forrest to send the two other detached brigades of infantry to La Vergne, halfway between Murfreesboro and Nashville, and to send a brigade of cavalry to picket the area east of Nashville, while using the rest of his cavalry to observe the Federals at Murfreesboro. These dispositions were made, he said "to prevent the enemy from re-enforcing Murfreesboro, and also to defeat the force at Murfeesboro should they attempt to leave there."[4]

In accordance with Grant's wishes, Halleck telegraphed to Thomas at 10:30 a.m. on the ninth: "General Grant expresses much dissatisfaction at your delay in attacking the enemy. If you wait till General Wilson mounts all his cavalry, you will wait till doomsday, for the waste equals the supply. Moreover, you will soon be in same condition that Rosecrans was last year—with so many animals that you cannot feed them. Reports already come in of a scarcity of forage."[5]

The wire to Major Eckert from the telegraph operator at Nashville the night before must have been forwarded to General Grant, for at 11 a.m. on the ninth, he wired Halleck: "Dispatch of 8 p.m. last evening from Nashville shows the enemy scattered for more than seventy miles down the river, and no attack yet made by Thomas. Please telegraph orders relieving him at once and placing Schofield in command. Thomas should be directed to turn over all orders and dispatches received since the battle of Franklin to Schofield."[6]

But before the orders were transmitted a reply from Thomas to Halleck, dispatched at 2 p.m., came in: "I regret that General Grant should feel dissatisfaction at my delay in attacking the enemy. I feel conscious that I have done everything in my power to prepare, and that the troops could not have been gotten ready before this, and if he should order me to be relieved I will submit without a murmur. A terrible storm of freezing rain has come on since daylight, which will render an attack impossible until it breaks."[7]

Thomas also replied directly to Grant: "Your dispatch of 8.30 p.m. of the 8th is just received. I had nearly completed my preparations to attack the enemy to-morrow morning, but a terrible storm of freezing rain has come on to-day, which will make it impossible for our men to fight to any advantage. I am, therefore, compelled to wait for the storm to break and make the attack immediately after. Admiral Lee is patrolling the river above and below the city, and I believe will be able to prevent the enemy from crossing. There is no doubt but that Hood's forces are considerably scattered along the river with the view of attempting a crossing, but it has been impossible for me to organize and equip the troops for an attack at an earlier time. Major-General Halleck informs me that you are very much dissatisfied with my delay in attacking. I can only say I have done all in my power to prepare, and if you should deem it necessary to relieve me I shall submit without a murmur."[8]

"Orders relieving General Thomas had been made out when his telegram of this p.m. was received," Halleck told Grant. "If you still wish these orders telegraphed to Nashville they will be forwarded." But at 5:30 p.m. Grant replied: "General Thomas has been urged in every way possible to attack the enemy, even to the giving the positive order. He did say he thought he would be able to attack on the 7th, but didn't do so, nor has he given a reason for not doing it. I am very unwilling to do injustice to an officer who has done as much good service as General

Thomas has, however, and will, therefore, suspend the order relieving him until it is seen whether he will do anything."[9]

Two hours later, Grant wired directly to Thomas: "Your dispatch of 1 p.m. received. I have as much confidence in your conducting a battle rightly as I have in any other officer; but it has seemed to me that you have been slow, and I have had no explanation of affairs to convince me otherwise. Receiving your dispatch of 2 p.m. from General Halleck before I did the one to me, I telegraphed to suspend the order relieving you until we should hear further. I hope most sincerely that there will be no necessity of repeating the orders, and that the facts will show that you have been right all the time." Thomas replied to this at 11:30 that night: "I can only say in further explanation why I have not attacked Hood that I could not concentrate my troops and get their transportation in order in shorter time than it has been done, and am satisfied I have made every effort that was possible to complete the task."[10]

In Virginia, the beefed-up reconnaissance to Hatcher's Run Grant wanted got under way at dawn on 9 December. The job had been assigned to Brigadier General Nelson A. Miles, with three brigades of his 1st Division of the 2nd Corps plus some artillery and three regiments of cavalry. They pushed down the Vaughn Road until they came to Hatcher's Run, where the Rebels were in strength behind earthworks on the southwest bank. "The run had been dammed about one-eighth of a mile below the crossing," Miles reported, "making the water about four feet deep and fifty feet wide. Holes had been dug in the bed of the stream, and trees slashed in it for a considerable distance above and below, making it a most difficult obstruction."[11] He sent his cavalry up and down stream to check other fords, but they were also defended.

Miles then sent skirmishers forward into the stream, but they were promptly driven back by Confederate fire. So he sent the 2nd New York Heavy Artillery to rush the defenses. "After reaching the water we charged through it," Captain George Armes, who commanded the first wave of two companies, said, "crawling up and working our bodies through the obstacles placed in the space between the bank of the stream and the breastworks; then over we went into the works, many of our brave boys being shot or bayoneted through while dragging themselves with their heavy wet clothes up the steep embankment."[12] Armes himself was among those bayoneted, but he survived, and the works were carried.

Miles sent other regiments across to secure his foothold across the stream, spread the rest of his infantry along the run as far west as Armstrong's Mill, and sent his cavalry regiments out to reconnoiter. They soon gathered up a number of prisoners, including a talkative mail-carrier from Dearing's Rebel cavalry. From him, Miles learned that Wade Hampton had gone in pursuit of Warren's expedition and that A. P. Hill had passed through Dinwiddie Court House the morning before on the same mission. That night Meade told Andrew Humphreys, his former chief of staff who now commanded the 2nd Corps, "I expect the mail-carrier told about all he knew. Warren will have to look out for himself, but we must be on the *qui vive* to send assistance to him in case we hear of his requiring it. I don't think we can do anything by moving to the left."[13]

Warren's Federals were up early again on that morning of 9 December and busy destroying railroad track. "As fast as one division destroyed the road in its front," a Union officer wrote, "it would march some distance further along the road and begin again and so on, each division alternately."[14] Cotton gins, stores, and some houses were also burned. Meanwhile, Gregg's troopers moved slowly on to the south, skirmishing with a few Rebels as they went. At 10 a.m. they reached Three Creek, where they found the railroad bridge in flames, the wagon bridge destroyed, and the nearby fords blocked by fallen trees. Some 200 Rebels were dug in on the south bank, supported by one howitzer. The 10th New York Cavalry charged down to the bank, where part of it was dismounted to scramble across the wreckage of the wagon bridge. The Confederates were then driven away, a ford was soon cleared, and the Federals continued their march southward, toward Hicksford.

Wade Hampton, however, reached that village first and found the town already defended by a patchwork force under Lieutenant Colonel John J. Garnett, including some North Carolina Junior Reserves sent up from Wilmington on the railroad. There were strong earthworks guarding the south ends of both the railroad and wagon bridges over the Meherrin River and rifle pits with abatis between the two bridges on the north side of the river, near the village of Belfield. Hampton sent the 5th North Carolina Cavalry to the north side to support some of Garnett's units there and sent other units to watch fords up and down the river.

At about 3 p.m. the van of Gregg's Union cavalry approached from the north. The leading squadron swept forward at the run, but around a sharp turn in the road it ran into an abatis of felled trees, which one Federal called, "perfectly impenetrable for horses," and Confederate fire drove the Federals back. Brigadier General Henry E. Davies, Jr., commander of Gregg's 1st Brigade, sent two regiments forward to attack the Rebel works dismounted while the 1st Massachusetts Cavalry charged on horseback. Confederate artillery south of the river broke up the mounted charge, but the dismounted troopers went, as one of them remembered, "straight into the rifle pits, over ditches and fallen trees, under a heavy fire of musketry and artillery from the woods beyond." The Rebels fell back to the south side of the river and burned the bridge behind them. Gregg, Warren, and the latter's chief of artillery, Colonel Charles S. Wainwright, came up and had a long look at the Confederate defenses across the river. All three, Wainwright said, "disliked to go away and leave [the enemy] unharmed, but it would cost us at least one day's delay, and probably two or three hundred men; half our rations were gone, and the most dangerous part of our work, the getting back, still to do."[15] Warren therefore issued orders for his troops to start back the next morning.

However, Warren's command came close to falling apart before morning. Union foragers, in addition to the usual chickens, pigs, sheep, and cattle, had come across a more interesting form of Confederate provisions. Most of the farms and houses in the area were well stocked with apple brandy. Twenty-five barrels of applejack were found in one barn alone. Many of the Federals were soon roaring drunk, and what they could not drink they put in their canteens and coffee pots for later consumption. A regiment of cavalry was sent to maintain discipline among the infantry, but it soon became part of the problem instead of the solution. Eventually the provost guard poured what was left in the barrels on the ground, but by then most of them were nearly empty anyway. That evening, A. P. Hill reached Hicksford ahead of his marching column to confer with Wade Hampton. They decided that the next day the cavalry would try to get around the Federals' left and attack their rear while Hill's infantry would attack them at Jarratt's Station.

A storm of sleet and cold rain struck the area about midnight, adding to the discomfort of the men of both sides, especially those who had no blankets or overcoats. Some of the Federals, of course, retained an inner warmth from their applejack, but their hangovers the next morning only increased their misery when they awoke to find the trees, the bushes, and themselves covered with ice. "Our few remaining blankets and tents proved to be so frozen, wet and heavy, the men were generally compelled to abandon them," one Union soldier wrote. Between the ice and the hangovers, it took over an hour for the Union officers to get their men into ranks and on the road, but the column finally started moving north at about 7 a.m. One cavalryman was impressed by the beauty of his surroundings. "As far as the vision extended the landscape was like shining crystal, suggestive of the home of fairies—in the rear the long column of cavalry and artillery, the brightness of their arms and trappings being reflected by the morning's sun." Another Federal said that the "icicles, before they began to lessen with advancing day, presented a scene of winter grandeur almost unknown to the lattitude." Marching, however, was difficult. "The ice and snow began to melt," another Union soldier wrote, "making the roads sloshy and muddy."[16]

Some of the Confederate cavalry was already on the way to get around the Union flank when Hampton discovered that the Federals were on the move north. He sent word of this to A. P. Hill and told Fitz Lee to push after the Federals and find out where they were going. But it was not easy to get the Rebels out of their defensive positions and on the road with all the same handicaps of weather and exhaustion as the Federals faced. In addition, most of them had so outrun their food supply that they were into their third day without anything to eat.

A. P. Hill's column was only seven miles out from Hicksford when word came to change direction. And it was soon evident that his men were not likely to catch Warren's column before it recrossed the Nottoway River unless something was done to slow it up. So Hampton pushed after the Federals with his own forces, including some of the Junior Reserves. Both they and Hill's men had the same problems marching on the icy roads as Warren's men, and in addition many of them had no shoes. A courier riding through Hill's column remembered seeing "the blood spurt from the feet of his barefooted and ragged soldiers marching over the frozen ground." Some who had shoes were no better off. A hospital steward in the reserves marched along with "very badly inflamed heels, caused by trying to wear a pair of course, stubborn new shoes, drawn from the quartermaster's store just before leaving Wilmington. I . . . found it more endurable to march all day through the sleet and mud barefoot."[17]

About halfway to Jarratt's Station, Warren split his column. The cavalry continued along the more western road to the station, while the infantry took a fork in the road that led to the east of the station directly to Sussex Court House. Both columns grew as they headed north. "Negroes from all directions left their masters," one Federal wrote, "and flocked to the protection of the Union troops, among them old men and women and little children, and as soon as a wagon of the supply train was emptied of its contents, it was filled with negro mothers with their children."[18]

When the column reached Sussex Court House local blacks brought it word that Confederate guerrillas had been killing Union stragglers. Detachments were sent out to verify this. "They found the bodies, the throat cut, the head crushed in by blows of an axe, and the breast pierced by a knife," General Regis de Trobriand said. "We protected houses, when we advanced," one Federal said, "but on our return, after witnessing the inhuman acts of the inhabitants, we fired every bulding on the route. . . . Every home, barn, and building, hay stack, corn crib, and granary, were burned to the ground." This action, of course, incensed the pursuing Rebels, who did not know what inspired it. "It is distressing to see the ruin and desolation these columns inflict upon inoffensive citizens," one Confederate wrote. "We cannot believe Americans can do these things." A Rebel cavalryman said that scouts were "instructed that when they caught Yankees in the act of robbing and burning to take the vandals by the arms and legs and swing them in the fire, drunk or sober. Such are the terrors of war."[19]

At 1 p.m., Meade notified Grant that he had directed Humphreys, his former chief of staff who now commanded the 2nd Corps, to begin withdrawing Miles' division at 2 p.m. "The men having suffered very much from the storm of last night, I wished to give them time to get in their camps before dark." He also said that he had directed Parke to hold his 9th Corps reserves ready to move at a moment's notice to Warren's relief if necessary, and he asked for Brigadier General Henry W. Benham's command of engineers and miscellaneous units guarding City Point to back up Parke's front line. At 1:20 p.m. Grant replied: "I think it advisable to move with all the force you can to Warren's relief. Benham will be ordered up as you suggest. I don't think there should be any delay in starting out re-enforcements to Warren."[20] However, it was 6 p.m. before the 9th Corps column, under Brigadier General Robert B. Potter, moved out. "He has orders to march all night and not to halt till he gets to the Nottaway," Meade informed Grant. "A regiment of engineers, with a canvas bridge, accompanies him."[21] The cavalry that had been out with Miles' division was to catch up with Potter as soon as it was resupplied with ammunition, rations, and forage. "The road was in horrible condition, very muddy," one of Potter's men told his diary. "It commenced raining in the evening, and poured nearly all night."[22]

North of the James River, the Confederates had noticed Butler's troops massing at Bermuda Hundred and embarking for their expedition to Wilmington, although their destination was, of course, unknown. So it was decided to probe Butler's lines to see if they were still manned. Some 11,000 men of Field's and Hoke's divisions were used in this probe. "Advanced and commenced skirmishing with the Yanks," one Rebel recorded in his diary, "and drove them steadily into their works at New Market Heights, where we remained for a few hours, many suffering much from the cold." Another Confederate said, "Several men came near freezing to death as we had no fires & it was very cold." One of Butler's men said, "It was a cold, sleety day, dismal in the extreme, but we fell in lively and manned the formidable breastworks in our immediate front. Quickly pushing out a heavy skirmish line, the lost ground was regained."[23] The Confederates returned to their starting places, having gained only the knowledge that the Union lines were still well manned.

Butler wired Grant at noon that day, the tenth, from Fort Monroe, where the James River enters Chesapeake Bay: "Has been blowing a gale ever since we arrived; is clearing up a little. We are all ready waiting for the navy. Any news from Warren or Sherman?"[24]

Grant did not yet know it, but Sherman came within sight of Savannah that day. "No opposition from the enemy worth speaking of was encountered until the heads of columns were within fifteen miles of Savannah," Sherman later reported, "where all the roads leading to the city were obstructed more or less by felled timber, with earth-works and artillery. But these were easily turned and the enemy driven away, so that by the 10th of December the enemy was driven within his lines at Savannah. These followed substanitally a swampy creek which empties into the Savannah River about three miles above the city, across to the head of a corresponding stream which empties into the Little Ogeechee. These streams were singularly favorable to the enemy as a cover, being very marshy, and bordered by rice fields, which were flooded either by the tide water or by inland ponds, the gates to which were controlled and covered by his heavy artillery. The only approaches to the city were by five narrow causeways—namely, the two railroads, and the Augusta, the Louisville, and the Ogeechee dirt roads—all of which were commanded by heavy ordnance, too strong for us to fight with our light field-guns. To assault an enemy of unknown strength at such a disadvantage appeared to me unwise, especially as I had so successfully brought my army, almost unscathed, so great a distance, and could surely attain the same result by the operation of time."[25]

"Wishing to reconnoitre the place in person," Sherman wrote, "I rode forward by the Louisville road, into a dense wood of oak, pine, and cypress, left the horses, and walked down to the railroad-track, at a place where there was a side-track, and a cut about four feet deep. From that point the railroad was straight, leading into Savannah, and about eight hundred yards off were a rebel parapet and battery. I could see the cannoneers preparing to fire, and cautioned the officers near me to scatter, as we would likely attract a shot. Very soon I saw the white puff of smoke, and, watching close, caught sight of the ball as it rose in its flight, and, finding it coming pretty straight, I stepped a short distance to one side, but noticed a negro very near me in the act of crossing the track at right angles. Some one called to him to look out; but, before the poor fellow understood his danger, the ball (a thirty-two-pound round shot) struck the ground, and rose in its first ricochet, caught the negro under the right jaw, and literally carried away his head, scattering blood and brains about. A soldier close by spread an overcoat over the body, and we all concluded to get out of that railroad-cut. Meantime, General Mower's division of the Seventeenth Corps had crossed the canal to the right of the Louisville road, and had found the line of parapet continuous; so at Savannah we had again run up against the old familiar parapet, with its deep ditches, canals, and bayous, full of water; and it looked as though another siege was inevitable."[26]

Up in eastern Tennessee that day, the tenth, General Stoneman left Knoxville with Gillem's small brigade of Tennessee cavalry, heading north on another Union attempt to raid the vital Confederate sources of salt and lead in southwestern Virginia. Stoneman himself, however, was the only one who knew his destination. "No one," he later reported, "not even my own officers, knew of my intentions, nor did the enemy learn of our movement until the third day out."[27] The next day, the eleventh, Stoneman was joined at Bean's Station by Burbridge, with about 4,200 troopers and four guns that he had brought through Cumberland Gap from Kentucky.

Other Union cavalry was also on the move that day. At Nashville, Wilson ordered Brigadier General Edward McCook to take two brigades of his 1st Division of Wilson's Cavalry Corps by train to Bowling Green, Kentucky, in an effort to head off Lyon's raiding Confederates. It was a good thing that they could travel by railroad, for the region was experiencing the worst weather it had had in years. At Nashville there was a strong wind from the northwest, the temperature had dropped to around ten degrees below zero, and three inches of frozen snow and sleet covered the fields.

That night, Thomas reported to Halleck: "The position of the enemy appears the same to-day as yesterday. The weather continues very cold and the hills are covered with ice. As soon as we have a thaw, I will attack Hood. It is reported to me, from Clarksville, that the rebel General Lyon has crossed the Cumberland at Cumberland City, below Clarksville, with between 2,000 and 3,000 men and six pieces of artillery, and it is supposed he is moving on Bowling Green. I have sent two brigades of cavalry to intercept him." He also relayed word he had just received from Rousseau about Milroy's victory over Bate at Murfreesboro four days before.

An hour later Thomas received a telegram that Grant had dispatched at 4 p.m.: "If you delay attack longer the mortifying spectacle will be witnessed of a rebel army moving for the Ohio River, and you will be forced to act, accepting such weather as you find. Let there be no further delay. Hood cannot stand even a drawn battle so far from his supplies of ordnance stores. If he retreats and you follow, he must lose his material and much of his army. I am in hopes of receiving a dispatch from you to-day announcing that you have moved. Delay no longer for weather or reenforcement." Thomas replied immediately: "I will obey the order as promptly as possible, however much I may regret it, as the attack will have to be made under every disadvantage. The whole country is covered with a perfect sheet of ice and sleet, and it is with difficulty the troops are able to move about on level ground. It was my intention to attack Hood as soon as the ice melted, and would have done so yesterday had it not been for the storm."[28] Thomas ordered his corps commanders to put their commands in readiness the next day for offensive operations and to gather at his headquarters at 3 p.m. on the twelfth.

The weather was still cold in Virginia as well. Before he had any word of Warren's column, Meade came up with what was, for him, an unusually aggressive plan, which he wired to Grant at 1 p.m. on the eleventh: "Two deserters have just come into our left. They report Gordon's and Pegram's divisions as holding the lines previously held by Heth and Wilcox. This gives as the force in my front, Johnson, Gordon, and Pegram, probably not over 15,000 men. The lines must, therefore, be comparatively weak, though as they are much shorter than my lines they are perhaps held stronger than Parke holds his. From all the reports of signal officers, I should judge the enemy were stronger on the left, as troops have been constantly seen moving that way, and as the enemy are expecting an attack on the South Side Railroad, Miles' movement would draw all their available reserves there. Hill undoubtedly went to Dinwiddie Court-house. Whether he moved the whole of his force beyond that point against Warren, or whether he only sent the cavalry and part of his infantry, is a point about which I am in doubt. His position at Dinwiddie is favorable either for operations against Warren, or to meet Warren in case he moved on the South Side road, or to attack in rear any force I should send in that direction. These considerations, together with the absence of any bad news from Warren, lead me to infer that Hill has perhaps not moved with his whole force against Warren, for, had there been heavy and severe fighting, I think Potter would either have heard something of it or would certainly have encountered some fugitives or stragglers from the field, as they would naturally return by the road they marched, which Potter is on. Under the supposition above indicated, in case we hear of Warren's returning in good order, I think there is a chance of carrying by a *coup de main* the center of Lee's weakened lines.

For this purpose I would mass the reserves of the 6th Corps, about 5,000, in the woods between Forts Howard and Alexander Hays, and, when Warren's column is within supporting distance, make an assault on the enemy's line between the Jerusalem plank road and the Weldon railroad, to be followed, if successful, by Warren's whole column. This operation is undoubtedly hazardous and will be dependent on the fact of whether or not we surprise the enemy. Should the first dash fail, the idea should be abandoned and the troops withdrawn; if successful in breaking through the lines and followed by Warren's column, we ought to be able to secure Petersburg. I make these suggestions for your consideration. If the Third Division of the Sixth Corps reaches in time it would be added to the assaulting column. The Second Corps would hold the left and look out for an attack from Hill, who should be expected in that direction and, possibly, in our rear up the Weldon road, as of course, on Warren's withdrawing, if he does not follow him, he will try to play the same game I am proposing, viz, to strike our weakened lines before Warren can get back. It will therefore be necessary that Warren should be close up to us before it will be prudent for us to attempt the offensive from the front."

Grant replied at 7 p.m.: "The plan you propose I think well of, and wish you would make all the preparations for carrying it into effect. It will be of the greatest importance to select the right officer for taking the advance."[29]

Warren's troops were up early that day and marching on the frozen roads again. At Sussex Court House they found more bodies of Union stragglers. "Some of the residents were seized," one Federal wrote, "and not being able to prove an alibi or explain certain suspicious circumstances, they were hung in the Court House yard." Another Federal later wrote his wife about seeing the bodies of the hanged civilians as he marched through the town. "They cut some of our men's throats," he said. "They are a pretty bad set of humans anyhow." Several buildings were burned, including a church, although some of the Union soldiers tried to save the latter. Others were more bothered by the destruction of private homes. "It was a sad sight to see women and children wailing and running about with no shelter in the cold December night," one Federal wrote.[30]

Potter's relief column from the 9th Corps reached Freeman's Ford at about 9 a.m. "Poor General Potter!" wrote Meade's aide, Theodore Lyman. "He had a frightful night march and was doubtless buoyed up by the feeling that he . . . could distinguish himself if there was a fight, and slam in on Hill's left flank, and win a great name for himself. What then was his disgust to see, about noon, the head of Warren's column trudging peaceably back, on the other side of the river!" One of Potter's men remembered Warren's raiders as "coming back in high spirits, after destroying the railroad and trying their hands a little at foraging, of which they had read so much in connection with Sherman's marches, but had so little in their own experience of late." Much of the afternoon was spent in laying pontoon bridges across the Nottoway again and in getting the troops, wagons, and artillery over them. So Warren decided to encamp his force on the north bank and to finish his return march the next day. "It was a terrible cold night for a bivouac," Lyman wrote, "with an intensely piercing cold wind and everything frozen up."[31] Potter started his column back at about 3 p.m. A. P. Hill, meanwhile, had given up the chase and started his Confederate infantry back to Petersburg. Hampton's cavalry followed Warren's column and snapped at its heels, but eventually even he gave up the pursuit and withdrew to Stony Creek.

Weather continued to delay another important campaign that was trying Grant's patience. Ben Butler wired him from Fort Monroe again that day: "Gale still continues; clouds just breaking away; all ready and waiting. One of Munford's steamers just in. Charleston Mercury of December 6 says: 'Sherman was reported yesterday at Station No. 6 on the Georgia road, about sixty miles from Savannah, making for that city.' No other news; have telegraphed this to Secretary of War." Grant had even later news of Sherman and feared that when the Rebels knew that the latter was not heading for Augusta that they would return the troops who had been taken from Wilmington. To Butler he replied: "Richmond papers of the 10th show that on the 7th Sherman was east of the Ogeechee, and within twenty-five miles of Savannah, having marched eighteen miles the day before. If you do not get off immediately you will lose the chance of surprise and weak garrison."[32]

Unknown to Grant, Sherman's forces were closing up to the defenses of Savannah that day, cutting off all normal lines of supply into that city, including the roads, railroads, and rivers. "We, on the contrary," Sherman later reported, "possessed large herds of cattle, which we had brought along or gathered in the country, and our wagons still contained a reasonable amount of breadstuffs and other necessaries, and the fine rice crops of the Savannah and Ogeechee Rivers furnished to our men and animals a large amount of rice and rice straw. We also held the country to the south and west of the Ogeechee as foraging ground. Still, communication with the fleet was of vital importance; and I directed General Kilpatrick to cross the Ogeechee by a pontoon bridge, to reconnoiter Fort McAllister, and to proceed to Saint Catherine's Sound, in the direction of Sunberry or Kilkenny Bluff, and open communication with the fleet. General Howard had previously, by my direction, sent one of his best scouts down the Ogeechee in a canoe for a like purpose. But more than this was necessary. We wanted the vessels and their contents; and the Ogeechee River, a navigable stream, close to the rear of our camps, was the proper avenue of supply."[33]

As a first step in opening this line of supply from the Union fleet, Sherman had the bridge over the Ogeechee River at a place called King's Bridge reconstructed that day so that his forces could get at Fort McAllister, an earthwork on the other side which prevented Union ships from coming up that stream.

That night the first of ten Confederate agents departed Toronto in pairs for Buffalo, New York. Among the ten were five veterans of the attempt to burn New York: Lieutenant Colonel Robert M. Martin, Captain Robert C. Kennedy, and lieutenants John W. Headley, James T. Harrington, and John T. Ashbrook. Also among them was Acting Master John Yates Beall of the Confederate Navy, who had led the group of Rebels who had captured ships on Lake Erie back in September. Word had reached Jacob Thompson that several captured senior Confederate officers were about to be transferred from the prisoner-of-war camp on Johnson's Island to Fort Lafayette in New York harbor. The ten agents hoped to waylay the train that would carry the officers and free them.

The next day, the twelfth, a sentry at the Johnson's Island prison camp found a letter stuffed into the outbound letter box addressed to the superintendent of the camp. It was unsigned, but it said: "It having come to my attention that one Mr. R. C. Kennedy, a Lieutenant of the Confederate army, who escaped this prison some time since, was in N. York at the time of the burning of some hotels which recently occurred. I have seen two letters from said Kennedy recently both of which I think can be found at any time. Kennedy is bold and acknowledges to have had a hand in the burnings. He is in Toronto C.W. at present and can if desired be induced to come to Brooklyn or N. York City at almost any time. Where he might be apprehended if desired. Kennedy is under an assumed name which I cannot recall at present, but is contained in a letter recently received in my room. All that is in my power will be done at your request, to ferret out this or any other similar case within my knowledge. You will please let no one know of this correspondence who would convey it to any of the prisoners. Should this be of value to you, you can know the writer by putting a note on the bulletin board marked XX in which you need not mention what subject is embraced."[34]

That same day, 12 December, John Wilkes Booth checked back into the National Hotel in Washington, D.C. After playing in "Julius Caesar" with his brothers in New York City he had gone to Philadelphia for a few days. Between then and his arrival in Washington his movements are unknown. However, Robert Martin, when he was arrested after the war, told fellow prisoners that he had known Booth in Toronto, and it might have been during those missing days that he met Booth there. It is also known that on his way to Washington on this occasion Booth stopped off in Baltimore, where he left with his old school chum Samuel Arnold a newly acquired arsenal consisting of two Spencer carbines, three pistols, some ammunition and daggers, and two sets of handcuffs.

---

1. *Offical Records*, 45:II:96–97.

2. Ibid., 45:II:97–98.

3. Ibid., 45:I:804.

4. Ibid., 45:II:670.

5. Ibid., 45:II:114.

6. Ibid., 45:II:115–116.

7. Ibid., 45:II:114.

8. Ibid., 45:II:115.

9. Ibid., 45:II:116.

10. Ibid., 45:II:115.

11. Ibid., 42:I:260.

12. Trudeau, *The Last Citadel*, 275.

13. Ibid., 276.

14. Ibid., 272.

15. Ibid., 276–277.

16. Ibid., 278.

17. Ibid., 279.

18. Ibid., 279–280.

19. Ibid., 280.

20. *Official Records*, 42:III:921.

21. Ibid., 42:III:923.

22. Trudeau, *The Last Citadel*, 282.

23. Ibid., 281.

24. *Official Records*, 42:I:974.

25. Ibid., 44:9–10.

26. Sherman, *Memoirs*, 670–671.

27. *Official Records*, 45:I:807.

28. Ibid., 45:II:143.

29. Ibid., 42:III:952–953.

30. Trudeau, *The Last Citadel*, 282–283.

31. Ibid., 284.

32. *Official Records*, 42:III:969.

33. Ibid., 44:10.

34. Brandt, *The Man Who Tried to Burn New York*, 144–145.

CHAPTER FORTY

Our March
Was Most
Agreeable

12–15 December 1864

At Nashville, although the northwest wind had abated, the weather continued to be extremely cold on the twelfth. It took all day to move Wilson's 12,500 cavalrymen and 9,000 horses across the river from Edgefield to Nashville because the bridge and the streets were so icy that both men and horses could move with only the greatest of difficulty. So many trees were being cut down for firewood that a Union quartermaster calculated that "if the Rebs coop us up here another fortnight, there won't be a tree left within 5 miles of Nashville." And he added that "it would take a century" to replace all those trees. When a few large gum trees in the middle of the 2nd Iowa Cavalry's camp disappeared, an order was published forbidding the cutting of any more trees, but the order was ignored. "Had this order been obeyed," a sergeant wrote, "every soldier in the command must inevitably have frozen to death, except such generals as toasted their toes by warm parlor fires." Another Federal, however, reflected that "the Rebel soldiers . . . are not as well provided for as we are." He noted, in a letter to his wife that "our scouts reported seeing Rebels frozen to death," and added, "I do not feel like rejoicing at their sufferings—only so far as it tends to prosper our cause—for I do not consider them as personal enemies."

A Confederate confirmed that they "were without tents, and had but one old worn blanket to each man with which to cover at night." In addition, over ten percent of Hood's army was barefoot. "Ambition, and even life itself, were almost frozen out of us," one Rebel wrote. There were no trees where the Confederates were camped. They burned up all the fence rails in the area, and then Hood had to withdraw S. D. Lee's and A. P. Stewart's corps a short distance in order for them to cut wood. The carpets from all the houses in the area were taken and cut up into blankets, and even old worn out shoes were taken for the soldiers. Raw cowhide was then wrapped around these and allowed to shrink to fit. Hood himself did not share the deprivation of his men, however. His tents were pitched in a grove of trees near a large house. "We had an abundance of good food," one of his staff officers reported, "beef, mutton, pork, flour, and potatoes. At the door of our tent stood a barrel of Robinson County whiskey for the solace . . . of our mess."[1]

At 3 p.m. on the twelfth the Union corps commanders gathered at Thomas's headquarters at the St. Cloud Hotel for a council of war. Thomas showed them Grant's peremptory order of the day before to delay no longer. Then, in what one of his generals called "a tone of lofty dignity and resolution," he said that he had already replied to Grant but that he would like to have their opinions. By tradition, the junior officer present always speaks first at councils of war, so that he will not be swayed by the opinions given by his seniors. So all eyes turned to James Harrison Wilson, whom all knew was one of Grant's hand-picked favorites. However, he expressed complete approval of Thomas's course, adding that until the ground thawed the Confederate works could be successfully defended "with nothing more dangerous than baskets of brickbats." Stanley was suffering from both his wound and an illness and had been succeeded in command of the 4th Corps by Wood, who was the next to speak, and he gave his "hearty concurrence" to Wilson's remarks. A. J. Smith and Steedman also agreed.[2] Schofield remained silent, although he had previously concurred in private conversation with the necessity to wait for better weather.

As the brief meeting was breaking up, Thomas asked Wilson to stay behind for a minute, and when the others had gone, he said, "Wilson, the Washington authorities treat me as if I were a boy. They seem to think me incapable of planning a campaign or of fighting a battle but if they will just let me alone, I will show them what we can do. I am sure my plan of operations is correct, and that we shall lick the enemy if only he stays to receive our attack."[3]

That night, Thomas wired Halleck: "I have the troops ready to make the attack on the enemy as soon as the sleet which now covers the ground has melted sufficiently to enable the men to march. As the whole country is now covered with a sheet of ice so hard and slippery it is utterly impossible for troops to ascend the slopes, or even move over level ground in anything like order. It has taken the entire day to place my cavalry in position, and it has only been finally effected with imminent risk and many serious accidents, resulting from the number of horses falling with their riders on the roads. Under these circumstances I believe an attack at this time would only result in a useless sacrifice of life."[4]

In Virginia, on the morning of the twelfth, Warren's troops were on the road early and returned to the Union lines that day without incident. "The weather cleared during the night," Warren wrote, "and was very cold. The mud in the morning was frozen stiff, so the [wagon] trains passed easily along, but the men suffered very much from their feet, that were now quite sore and blistered, insomuch that numbers walked barefoot over the frozen ground."[5] Warren had torn up about sixteen miles of railroad track, and the section destroyed was not back in service again until March. The loss of this important supply line contributed considerably to the suffering of Lee's troops that winter, and that in turn led to many Confederate desertions.

"In the absence of any positive intelligence of Hill's position," Meade wired Grant at 12:30 p.m., "after a careful examination of the ground by engineers and reliable officers, the intelligence of the signal officers and picket officers of the return of the enemy to his works, the condition of the troops now returning from the expedition to Hicksford, on which they have, from the weather, suffered very much, from all these considerations I am constrained to advise giving up my suggestion of yesterday to attack the enemy's line, on the ground that I have no reason to believe it will be successful, and am not disposed to engage in such an operation except under the most favorable circumstances. I will, however, have everything in readiness awaiting your decision." Grant replied a half-hour later: "I would not advise the attack suggested by you unless with a good prospect of it succeeding. But if you are prepared for it, act on your best judgment when Warren gets back and the time comes for making the attack."[6] The attack was not made.

However, Grant was still trying to get some of his other projects moving. He wired Sheridan that day, again pressing for a raid on the Virginia Central Railroad between the Shenandoah Valley and Richmond: "I think there is no doubt but all of Gordon's and Pegram's divisions are here. The inhabitants of Richmond are supplied exclusively over the roads north of the James River. If it is possible to destroy the Virginia Central road it will go far toward starving out the garrison of Richmond. The Weldon road has been largely used until now, notwithstanding it has been cut to Stony Creek. It is now gone to Hicksford, and I think can be of no further use. If the enemy are known to have retired to Staunton, you will either be able to make a dash on the communications north of the James or spare a part of your force. Let me know your views as to the best course to make a dash on the Central road and canal or to detach from your command."[7]

At least one of Grant's dilatory generals made some progress the next day, although in the wrong direction. Butler had been informed by Admiral Porter that the navy's ships for the Wilmington expedition would sail on the thirteenth but would have to put into the Union base at Beaufort, North Carolina, to pick up ammunition for its monitors. "The expedition having become the subject of remark," Butler later reported, "fearing lest its destination should get to the enemy, in order to direct from it all attention, on the morning of Tuesday, the 13th, at 3 o'clock. I ordered the transport fleet to proceed up the Potomac during the day to Mathias Point so as to be plainly visible to the scouts and signal men of the enemy on the Northern Neck, and to retrace their course at night and anchor under the lee of Cape Charles."[8]

At 8 p.m. on the thirteenth J. C. Van Duzer, the superintendent of the military telegraph line at Nashville, wired Major Eckert at the War Department in Washington: "Reconnaissance to-day showed enemy's force all around; in greatest strength on right, where some artillery opened. Thaw has begun, and to-morrow we can move without skates."[9] An hour later Thomas wired Halleck: "There is no change in the enemy's position in my front to-day. At length there are indications of a favorable change in the weather, and as soon as there is I shall move against the enemy, as everything is ready and prepared to assume the offensive."[10]

"The past week had been the most anxious period of Grant's entire military career," Horace Porter said, "and he suffered mental torture." Thomas continued to be his biggest headache. "On the one hand," Porter wrote, "he felt that he was submitting to delays which might seriously interfere with his general plans; that he was placed in an attitude in which he was virtually incapable of having his most positive orders carried out; and that he was occupying a position of almost insubordination to the authorities at Washington. On the other hand, he realized that nothing but the most extreme case imaginable should lead him to do even a seeming injustice to a distinguished and capable commander by relieving him when he was on the eve of a decided victory; for his military instincts convinced him that nothing but victory could follow the moment that Thomas moved, and he wished that loyal and devoted army commander to reap all the laurels of such a triumph. However, there was yet no time named for the attack, and Grant felt himself compelled to take some further steps."[11]

Major General John A. Logan happened to be visiting Grant at City Point just then. He was the commander of the 15th Corps in Howard's wing of Sherman's army, but he was also an important War Democrat in Illinois and had gone home to stump for Lincoln's reelection and had not made it back to the army in time to make the march through Georgia. As Horace Porter wrote, "Logan had served under General Grant in the West, and held a high place in his estimation as a vigorous fighter. The general talked over the situation with Logan, and finally directed him to start at once for Nashville, with a view to putting him in command of the operations there, provided, upon his arrival, it was still found that no attack had been made. He gave him the requisite order in writing, to be used if necessary; and told him to say nothing about it, but to telegraph his arrival at Nashville, and if it was found that Thomas had already moved, not to deliver it or act upon it."[12]

Union forces were advancing in eastern Tennessee at least. Gillem's brigade of loyal Tennesseans of Stoneman's column approached the North Fork opposite Kingsport at daylight on the thirteenth and found it defended by the remnant of what had been the late John Hunt Morgan's command. This was now commanded by Brigadier General Basil Duke, but he was on leave and Morgan's brother, Colonel Richard Morgan, was in charge during his absence. This was the same outfit Gillem had flanked out of the defenses of a bridge over Big Creek the day before and now Gillem employed a similar strategem to the one he had used then.

"The enemy was found strongly posted in a cedar thicket on a bluff commanding the ford, and also in the village of Kingsport," Gillem reported. He sent the 8th Tennessee Cavalry upriver to cross at another ford and turn the Rebels' right flank, and when they made their appearance Gillem led the 9th Tennessee and two battalions of the 13th Tennessee in a frontal assault, covered by the other battalion of the 13th firing from the cover of fences and shrubbery near the west bank of the river. "This movement completely surprised them," Gillem reported, "and after a feeble resistance, considering the advantage of their position, they fled in confusion, and were pursued for seven miles. The pursuit only ended when the enemy, losing all semblance of organization, scattered through the woods for safety."[13]

Colonel Morgan was among the 84 Confederates captured by Gillem's men, and all his wagons were taken as well. "During the afternoon and night of the 13th I pushed Burbridge's command on to Bristol," Stoneman reported, "with instructions to endeavor to intercept Vaughn, who had for a long time been at Greeneville with a force variously estimated, but which I thought to be about 1,200 strong. During the night I followed with Gillem's command, and reached Bristol early in the day of the 14th."[14]

Down in Georgia, at sunrise on the thirteenth, Brigadier General William B. Hazen's 2nd Division of the 15th Corps of Howard's Army of the Tennessee crossed the newly constructed bridge over the Ogeechee River. It was the same division that Sherman himself had commanded at the battle of Shiloh 32 months before. "I gave General Hazen, in person, his orders to march rapidly down the right bank of the Ogeechee," Sherman wrote, "and without hesitation to assault and carry Fort McAllister by storm. I knew it to be strong in heavy artillery, as against an approach from the sea, but believed it open and weak to the rear. I explained to General Hazen, fully, that on his action depended the safety of the whole army, and the success of the campaign."[15] It took most of the day for Hazen's column to get across, march down the river to the fort, and get ready to attack.

Meanwhile, Sherman, with his staff and General Howard, rode ten miles down the opposite bank of the river to a rice plantation where Howard had established a signal station atop the rice mill that overlooked the lower reaches of the river. "Leaving our horses behind the stacks of rice-straw," Sherman wrote, "we all got on the roof of a shed attached to the mill, wherefrom I could communicate with the signal-officer above, and at the same time look out toward Ossabaw Sound and across the Ogeechee River at Fort McAllister. About 2 p.m. we observed signs of commotion in the fort, and noticed one or two guns fired inland, and some musket-skirmishing in the woods close by."[16]

The firing was caused by the approach of Hazen's division, and soon the signal officer on his platform above Sherman spotted Hazen's signal officer's flag about three miles above the fort. By means of these two signal officers, Sherman told Hazen that he wanted the fort taken before nightfall and was assured that the attempt would soon be made. "The sun was rapidly declining," Sherman wrote, "and I was dreadfully impatient. At that very moment some one discovered a faint cloud of smoke, and an object gliding, as it were, along the horizon above the tops of the sedge toward the sea, which little by little grew till it was pronounced to be the smoke-stack of a steamer coming up the river . . . Soon the flag of the United States was plainly visible, and our attention was divided between this approaching steamer and the expected battle . . . Soon we made out a group of officers on the deck of this vessel, signaling with a flag, 'Who are you?' The answer went back promptly, 'General Sherman.' Then followed the question, 'Is Fort McAllister taken?' 'Not yet, but it will be in a minute!' Almost at that instant of time, we saw Hazen's troops come out of the dark fringe of woods that encompassed the fort, the lines dressed as on parade, with colors flying, and moving forward with a quick, steady pace. Fort McAllister was then all alive, its big guns belching forth dense clouds of smoke, which soon enveloped our assaulting lines. One color went down, but was up in a moment. On the lines advanced, faintly seen in the white, sulphurous smoke; there was a pause, a cessation of fire; the smoke cleared away, and the parapets were blue with our men, who fired their muskets in the air, and shouted so that we actually heard them, or felt that we did. Fort McAllister was taken, and the good news was instantly sent by the signal-officer to our navy friends on the approaching gunboat, for a point of timber had shut out Fort McAllister from their view, and they had not seen the action at all, but must have heard the cannonading."[17]

An aide sent the good news to General Slocum, commanding the army's other wing: "Take a good big drink, a long breath, and then yell like the devil," the aide said. "The fort was carried at 4.30 p.m., the assault lasting but fifteen minutes. The general signaled from this side to the fleet and got answers, and vessels were seen coming up the sound when Colonel Ewing left."[18]

With a volunteer crew of young officers rowing a small skiff which they found at the rice mill's wharf, Sherman and Howard crossed the river and had dinner with General Hazen and the captured Confederate commander, a Major Anderson, at a house near the fort. Of the Rebel garrison of 250 men, fifty had been killed and wounded and the rest captured, along with 22 heavy guns.

Sherman was determined to go aboard the navy gunboat that night "at whatever risk or cost, as I wanted some news of what was going on in the outer world. Accordingly, after supper, we all walked down to the fort, nearly a mile from the house where we had been, entered Fort McAllister, held by a regiment of Hazen's troops, and the sentinel cautioned us to be very careful, as the ground outside the fort was full of torpedoes. Indeed, while we were there, a torpedo exploded, tearing to pieces a poor fellow who was hunting for a dead comrade. Inside the fort lay the dead as they had fallen, and they could hardly be distinguished from their living comrades, sleeping soundly side by side in the pale moonlight."[19] In the river near the fort was a yawl, and Sherman and Howard had its crew row them downriver to the gunboat.

After rowing for about six miles through waters thought to be strewn with torpedoes, they finally reached the steamer. "Pulling alongside, we announced ourselves, and were received with great warmth and enthusiasm on deck by half a dozen naval officers," Sherman wrote, "among them Captain Williamson, United States Navy. She proved to be the Dandelion, a tender of the regular gunboat Flag, posted at the mouth of the Ogeechee." The scout Howard had sent down the river in a canoe some nights before had safely reached the naval squadron, and it had been expecting Sherman's arrival ever since. "They explained that Admiral Dahlgren commanded the South-Atlantic Squadron, which was then engaged in blockading the coast from Charleston south, and was on his flagship, the Harvest Moon, lying in Wassaw Sound; that General J. G. Foster was in command of the Department of the South, with his headquarters at Hilton Head; and that several ships loaded with stores for the army were lying in Tybee Roads and in Port Royal Sound. From these officers I also learned that General Grant was still besieging Petersburg and Richmond, and that matters and things generally remained pretty much the same as when we had left Atlanta. All thoughts seemed to have been turned to us in Georgia, cut off from all communication with our friends; and the rebel papers had reported us to be harassed, defeated, starving, and fleeing for safety to the coast. I then asked for pen and paper, and wrote several hasty notes to General Foster, Admiral Dahlgren, General Grant, and the Secretary of War, giving in general terms the actual state of affairs, the fact of the capture of Fort McAllister, and of my desire that means should be taken to establish a line of supply from the vessels in port up the Ogeechee to the rear of the army . . ."[20]

"The army is in splendid order, and equal to any thing," he told Secretary Stanton. "The weather has been fine, and supplies were abundant. Our march was most agreeable, and we were not at all molested by guerillas . . . We have not lost a wagon on the trip; but have gathered a large supply of negroes, mules, horses, etc., and our teams are in far better condition than when we started. . . . We have utterly destroyed over two hundred miles of rails, and consumed stores and provisions that were essential to Lee's and Hood's armies. The quick work made with McAllister, the opening of communication with our fleet, and our consequent independence as to supplies, dissipate all their boasted threats to head us off and starve the army. I regard Savannah as already *gained*."[21]

"By this time the night was well advanced," Sherman remembered, "and the tide was running ebb-strong; so I asked Captain Williamson to tow us up as near Fort McAllister as he would venture for the torpedoes, of which the navy-officers had a wholesome dread. The Dandelion steamed up some three or four miles, till the lights of Fort McAllister could be seen, when she anchored, and we pulled to the fort in our own boat. General Howard and I then walked up to the McAllister House, where we found General Hazen and his officers asleep on the floor of one of the rooms. Lying down on the floor, I was soon fast asleep, but shortly became conscious that some one in the room was inquiring for me among the sleepers. Calling out, I was told that an officer of General Foster's staff had just arrived from a steamboat anchored below McAllister; that the general was extremely anxious to see me on important business, but that he was lame from an old Mexican-War wound, and could not possibly come to me. I was extremely weary from the incessant labor of the day and night before, but got up, and again walked down the sandy road to McAllister, where I found a boat awaiting us, which carried us some three miles down the river to the steamer . . . on board of which we found General Foster . . . He described fully the condition of affairs with his own command in South Carolina. He had made several serious efforts to effect a lodgment on the railroad which connects Savannah with Charleston near Pocotaligo, but had not succeeded in reaching the railroad itself, though he had a full division of troops, strongly intrenched, near Broad River, within cannon-range of the railroad. He explained, moreover, that there were at Port Royal abundant supplies of bread and provisions, as well as of clothing, designed for our use. We still had in our wagons and in camp abundance of meat, but we needed bread, sugar, and coffee, and it was all-important that a route of supply should at once be opened, for which purpose the aid and assistance of the navy were indispensable. We accordingly steamed down the Ogeechee River to Ossawbaw Sound, in hopes to meet Admiral Dahlgren, but he was not there, and we continued on by the inland channel to Wassaw Sound, where we found the Harvest Moon, and Admiral Dahlgren."[22]

Sherman was greeted by the fleet as a great hero. Hundreds of sailors climbed the masts of their ships to get a look at him, and cheer after cheer swept across the sound. The officers who gathered to greet him found him in a talkative mood, full of stories and anecdotes of his army's march across Georgia. "I could look forty miles in each direction and see smoke rolling up like one great bonfire," he told them. Lieutenant John Gray was struck by the general's confidence and his nervous energy, as he paced around the cabin with his hands thrust into his pockets. Then he came to an abrupt stop and thrust out a hand, closing it into a fist as he said, "I've got Savannah. It's in my grip . . . only three miles . . . I'll take my time about it . . . I just wish there were more

Rebels in the city." He also told them he had already decided on his next move, "I'm going to march to Richmond," he told them. "I expect to turn north by the end of the month, when the sun does—and when I go through South Carolina it will be one of the most horrible things in the history of the world. The devil himself couldn't restrain my men in that state."[23]

Sherman had not met Rear Admiral John Dahlgren before, but he took an immediate liking to him. "There was nothing in his power, he said, which he would not do to assist us, to make our campaign absolutely successful. He undertook at once to find vessels of light draught to carry our supplies from Port Royal to Cheeves' Mill, or to King's Bridge above, whence they could be hauled by wagons to our several camps; he offered to return with me to Fort McAllister, to superintend the removal of the torpedoes, and to relieve me of all the details of this most difficult work. General Foster then concluded to go on to Port Royal, to send back to us six hundred thousand rations, and all the rifled guns of heavy calibre, and ammunition on hand, with which I thought we could reach the city of Savannah, from the positions already secured. Admiral Dahlgren then returned with me in the Harvest Moon to Fort McAllister. This consumed all of the 14th of December."[24]

"I never passed a more amusing or instructive day," Lieutenant Gray of the navy wrote, "but at his departure I felt it a relief and experienced almost an exhaustion after the excitement of his vigorous presence."[25]

At 3 a.m. on the fourteenth Burbridge's Union cavalry attacked Bristol, on the Tennessee-Virginia border, and easily captured the town, along with about 250 Confederates, 5 railroad engines, 2 trains of railroad cars, and immense quantities of supplies. Learning that Vaughn's Brigade of Rebel cavalry was twelve miles away, Burbridge marched to attack him, but there was a dense fog that morning and Vaughn slipped past him, making for the salt works at Saltville. However, Burbridge headed him off at Abingdon that night, where he captured more supplies, another engine, some rolling stock, and one cannon. Then one regiment was sent forward to get between Saltville and Wythville to prevent Confederate reinforcements from reaching the former.

Far to the northeast that day Rodes' Division of Early's army, now commanded by Brigadier General Bryan Grimes, left the Shenandoah Valley for Petersburg. That left Early with only Wharton's small infantry division plus the cavalry.

At half-past noon on the fourteenth, Halleck telegraphed to Thomas at Nashville: "It has been seriously apprehended that while Hood, with a part of his forces, held you in check near Nashville, he would have time to operate against other important points left only partially protected. Hence, General Grant was anxious that you should attack the rebel force in your front, and expressed great dissatisfaction that his orders had not been carried out. Moreover, so long as Hood occupies a threatening position in Tennessee, General Canby is obliged to keep large forces upon the Mississippi River, to protect its navigation and to hold Memphis, Vicksburg, &c., although General Grant had directed a part of these forces to co-operate with General Sherman. Every day's delay on your part, therefore, seriously interferes with General Grant's plans."[26]

When there still had been no word of a move by Thomas, "General Grant, being still more exercised in mind over the situation," as Horace Porter put it, "determined to carry out a design which he had had in view for several days—to proceed to Nashville and take command there in person. The only thing which had prevented him from doing this earlier was the feeling which always dominated him in similar cases, and made him shrink from having even the appearance of receiving the credit of a victory the honor of which he preferred to have fall upon a subordinate. He now thought that his taking command in person would avoid the necessity of relieving Thomas, and be much less offensive to that officer than superseding him by some one else. General Grant therefore started for Washington that night, the 14th."[27]

In leaving City Point, Grant at least had the comfort of knowing that he was not leaving Ben Butler, who was senior to Meade, in command of the forces around Richmond and Petersburg. At 10 a.m. that morning Grant had wired Butler at Fort Monroe: "What is the prospect for getting your expedition started? It is a great pity we were not ten or twelve days earlier. I am confident it would then have been successful." Butler had replied 35 minutes later: "Admiral Porter started yesterday. Transport fleet are at Cape Henry. I am just starting. The weather for the last six days has been such that it would be useless to be on the coast."[28] At noon Butler joined his fleet of transports and put to sea. They arrived at the point of rendezvous off New Inlet, near Fort Fisher, on the evening of the fifteenth, but the navy was not yet there.

Down in Georgia, Union ships had been bringing supplies up the river to Sherman's army, and they had also brought a load of mail as well. "It was a curious spectacle," a soldier remembered. "The half-starved boys all through the camps reading their letters held in one hand while devouring hard-tack from the other . . . a conflict between appetite and noble sensibilities." The term "half-starved" was somewhat of an exaggeration, but the men had been living on rice lately and little else, while bread, even army crackers, had been scarce in their diet since leaving Atlanta. Colonel A. H. Markland, who was in charge of the mail, had seen President Lincoln shortly before starting south, and he brought Sherman a personal message. "He asked me to take you by the hand wherever I met you and say 'God bless you and the army,'" Markland told Sherman. "He has been praying for you."[29]

The boat also brought a lieutenant with a letter from Grant to Sherman, dated 3 December, in which he said: "Not liking to rejoice before the victory is assured, I abstain from congratulating you and those under your command, until bottom has been struck. I have never had a fear, however, for the result.

"Since you left Atlanta no very great progress has been made here. The enemy has been closely watched, though, and prevented from detaching against you. I think not one man has gone from here, except some twelve or fifteen hundred dismounted cavalry. Bragg has gone from Wilmington. I am trying to take advantage of his absence to get possession of that place. Owing to some preparations Admiral Porter and General Butler are making to blow up Fort Fisher (which, while hoping for the best, I do not believe a particle in), there is a delay in getting this expedition off. I hope they will be ready to start by the 7th, and that Bragg will not have started back by that time.

"In this letter I do not intend to give you any thing like directions for future action, but will state a general idea I have, and will get your views after you have established yourself on the sea-coast. With your veteran army I hope to get control of the only two through routes from east to west possessed by the enemy before the fall of Atlanta. The condition will be filled by holding Savannah and Augusta, or by holding any other port to the east of Savannah and Branchville. If Wilmington falls, a force from there can cooperate with you.

Thomas has got back into the defenses of Nashville, with Hood close upon him. Decatur has been abandoned, and so have all the roads, except the main one leading to Chattanooga. Part of this falling back was undoubtedly necessary, and all of it may have been. It did not look so, however, to me. In my opinion, Thomas far outnumbers Hood in infantry. In cavalry Hood has the advantage in *morale* and numbers. I hope yet that Hood will be badly crippled, if not destroyed. The general news you will learn from the papers better than I can give it."[30]

However, the next day, Lieutenant Colonel Orville E. Babcock of Grant's staff arrived with another letter for Sherman, this one dated 6 December: "On reflection since sending my letter by the hands of Lieutenant Dunn, I have concluded that the most important operation toward closing out the rebellion will be to close out Lee and his army.

"You have now destroyed the roads of the South so that it will probably take them three months without interruption to reestablish a through line from east to west. In that time I think the job here will be effectually completed.

"My idea now is that you establish a base on the sea-coast, fortify and leave in it all your artillery and cavalry, and enough infantry to protect them, and at the same time so threaten the interior that the militia of the South will have to be kept at home. With the balance of your command come here by water with all dispatch. Select yourself the officer to leave in command, but you I want in person. Unless you see objections to this plan which I cannot see, use every vessel going to you for purposes of transportation.

Hood has Thomas close in Nashville. I have said all I can to force him to attack, without giving the positive order until to-day. To-day, however, I could stand it no longer, and gave the order without any reserve."[31]

"The contents of these letters gave me great uneasiness," Sherman said, "for I had set my heart on the capture of Savannah, which I believed to be practicable, and to be near; for me to embark for Virginia by sea was so complete a change from what I had supposed would be the course of events that I was very much concerned."[32] That was putting it mildly. An officer on his staff remembered that when Sherman read this letter he starting cursing and said, "Won't do it, goddam it! I'll not do anything of the kind."[33] But after fuming for an hour or so he calmed down.

"I supposed, as a matter of course, that a fleet of vessels would soon pour in, ready to convey the army to Virginia," Sherman wrote, "and as General Grant's orders contemplated my leaving the cavalry, trains, and artillery, behind, I judged Fort McAllister to be the best place for the purpose, and sent my chief-engineer, Colonel Poe, to that fort, to reconnoitre the ground, and to prepare it so as to make a fortified camp large enough to accomodate the vast herd of mules and horses that would thus be left behind. And as some time might be required to collect the necessary shipping, which I estimated at little less than a hundred steamers and sailing-vessels, I determined to push operations, in hopes to secure the city of Savannah before the necessary fleet could be available."[34]

Out in Missouri that day, the Confederate guerrilla William Clarke Quantrill and over thirty of his men approached the town of Tuscumbia on the Osage River. As usual, they were wearing captured Union uniforms. Quantrill told a Federal sentry that he was Captain Clarke of the 4th Missouri Cavalry and that he wanted to see the commander of the town's garrison. With one of his men he went to the house the sentry pointed out and talked with the Union commander for a while, until he thought he had all the useful information that he could obtain in that way. Then he drew his revolver and ordered the astonished Federal to surrender his garrison. After the Rebels ate a hearty breakfast at the local hotel, the guerrillas released all of their prisoners except one, whom they kept as a guide. Then they dumped the garrison's rifles and ammunition in the river, crossed to the south bank, and sank the ferry behind them.

This was Quantrill's final raid in Missouri. He was heading for Kentucky. Some of his men later claimed that he intended to go all the way to Washington, D.C., for the purpose of assassinating President Lincoln.

---

1. Sword, *Embrace an Angry Wind*, 303–304.
2. Ibid., 310.
3. Foote, *The Civil War*, 3:686–687.
4. *Official Records*, 45:II:155.
5. Ibid., 42:I:445.
6. Ibid., 42:III:972.
7. Ibid., 42:III:972–973.
8. Ibid., 42:I:966.
9. Ibid., 45:II:171.
10. Ibid., 45:II:168.
11. Porter, *Campaigning With Grant*, 347–348.
12. Ibid., 348.
13. *Official Records*, 45:I:819–820.
14. Ibid., 45:I:810.
15. Sherman, *Memoirs*, 672.
16. Ibid., 673.
17. Ibid., 673–674.
18. *Official Records*, 44:704.
19. Sherman, *Memoirs*, 675.
20. Ibid., 676.
21. Ibid., 677.
22. Ibid., 677–678.
23. Davis, *Sherman's March*, 106–107.

24. Sherman, *Memoirs*, 678–679.
25. Davis, *Sherman's March*, 107.
26. *Official Records*, 45:II:180.
27. Porter, *Campaigning With Grant*, 348.
28. *Official Records*, 42:III:1004–1005.
29. Davis, *Sherman's March*, 109.
30. Sherman, *Memoirs*, 681.
31. Ibid., 682.
32. Ibid.
33. Davis, *Sherman's Watch*, 108.
34. Sherman, *Memoirs*, 682–683.

CHAPTER FORTY-ONE

Much Is Now Expected

15 December 1864

The gaslights were still burning along the streets of Nashville on the morning of 15 December when General Thomas checked out of the St. Cloud Hotel and mounted his horse to ride out to a high hill just east of the Hillsborough Pike where there was a prominent salient in his main line of defenses. From there he expected to have a panoramic view of the battle he had planned. There was, however, a problem. Warmer weather and a light rain the day before had cleared the streets, fields, and roads of their coating of ice, but it had been replaced by mud. Moreover, a new meteorological problem had resulted: Fog covered the entire area. Buglers in all the Union camps awakened Thomas's troops at 4 a.m., but even after the sun rose, visibility was still so limited that the troops could not be moved at 6 a.m., as Thomas had originally planned.

Across the fog-shrouded fields, Hood was busy defending his honor that morning. He was writing a letter to the Confederate secretary of war denying Union claims published in the newspapers that his army had lost thirty battleflags at Franklin. "We lost thirteen," he claimed, "capturing nearly the same number." And he added that "the men who bore ours were killed on and within the enemy's interior line of works."[1]

The two weeks since that battle had been frustrating ones for Hood. He lacked the strength to take Nashville and lacked the logistics to bypass it. In fact, it was all he could do, with the help of the Nashville & Decatur Railroad and some captured rolling stock, to keep his army supplied where it was. He had hoped to swell the ranks of his army with recruits from middle Tennessee, but so far only 164 men had joined up, which failed to even make up for the 254 horseless cavalrymen who had deserted when he had transferred them to the infantry. He called on conscription agents to round up all able-bodied men but found that most of them had fled the area. In fact, many of them were now inside Nashville, where Thomas's army protected them. He had hoped to take Murfreesboro, but that city had also turned out to be too well defended to attack, at least with the force he could spare for the job. Then he had hoped that by threatening the garrison of that town and cutting off its supply line to Nashville that either it would leave or Thomas would try to come to its rescue. If Thomas could be induced to attack Hood's defenses and be defeated perhaps it would be possible for the Confederates to follow the retreating Federals into the city. But the Murfreesboro garrison stayed put, and so did Thomas.

The terrain south of Nashville was well cleared but composed of rolling hills. Richland Creek flowed roughly northward into the Cumberland River just west of the Union defenses, and Brown's Creek flowed northeastward into the river just east of the defenses. There were eight turnpikes and two railroads radiating out of Nashville on the south side of the Cumberland. These were, from west to east, the Charlotte Pike, which crossed Richland Creek, the Harding or Hardin Pike, which just skirted to the south of that stream, the Hillsborough Pike, which also missed both streams, the Granny White Pike, the Franklin Pike, the Nashville & Decatur Railroad, the Nolensville Pike, the Nashville & Chattanooga Railroad, the Murfreesboro Pike, and the Lebanon Pike. All of those from the Granny White Pike east crossed Brown's Creek.

Hood did not have nearly enough troops to man a line of defenses that would invest Nashville completely from the river above the city to the river below and block all those routes. Consequently, he had entrenched a line that covered his supply lines, the Franklin Pike and the Nashville & Decatur Railroad, and as much else as was possible. It started at the Hillsborough Pike and then ran east to form a concave ark across the Granny White Pike, the Franklin Pike, the Nashville & Decatur Railroad, and the Nolensville Pike. Stewart's Corps held the left, S. D. Lee's the center, and Cheatham's the right. Buford's cavalry, recently reinforced by one of Chalmers' brigades, covered the ground beyond the right flank, including the Murfreesboro Pike and the Lebanon Pike, as well as the river upstream from the city. Chalmers, with his other brigade, was charged with watching an even larger area on the Confederate left. One of his regiments was supporting a battery blockading the river below the city while the rest of his brigade was posted behind Richland Creek from the river to the Charlotte Pike. An infantry brigade which had recently been loaned to him—Ector's Brigade of French's Division of Stewart's Corps—extended the line to the Hardin Pike, and two companies from the infantry formed a skirmish line on across that road.

Hood had issued orders for each corps to construct small self-contained earthworks, called redoubts, behind their flanks. These works were to be manned by around 75 to 100 men each plus a few pieces of artillery capable of firing in any direction, and they were to be placed so that each redoubt could be covered by the fire of others and together they could control the spaces between them. In this way he hoped to defend as much ground as possible with a minimum of manpower. He considered these defenses to be so important that he ordered the corps commanders to supervise their placement and construction personally and not to delegate the job to subordinate commanders or engineers. And the troops placed in these little forts were told to hold them "at all hazard, and not to surrender under any circumstances."[2]

Since Hood expected that if Thomas should attack him at all it would be in response to his threat to the Murfreesboro garrison, he naturally feared most for his right flank, which did not quite reach the Murfreesboro Pike. When Wilson's cavalry had been sent across the river to Edgefield, Hood had expected it to move around his right, perhaps to go to Rousseau's aid or perhaps to raid the Confederate supply line. This expectation had led to his decision to place Buford on that flank and then to reinforce him. Then when the Union cavalry had returned to the south side of the river and had been placed on the Union right Hood had finally become concerned for his left. This had led Hood to send Ector's infantry brigade to bolster Chalmer's position. But on the afternoon of the thirteenth two of Steedman's brigades had made a reconnaissance in force out the Murfreesboro Pike that had skirmished with some of Cheatham's men. This had pulled Hood's attention back to his right and led to orders for Granbury's Brigade to build a redoubt on the north side of the Nashville and Chattanooga Railroad for up to 300 men.

In fact, of course, Thomas was not concerned about Murfreesboro. His desire and intention was the total defeat of Hood's army. And the larger space between Hood's left flank and the river offered the more inviting target. As Thomas's plan was published in orders to his corps commanders, Woods 4th Corps was to make a holding attack against the Confederates' center while A. J. Smith's troops would make the real attack on their left. Schofield's corps would be held in reserve and support Wood in the center, and Wilson's cavalry would protect the Union right, in the area between Hood's defenses and the river below the city. Meanwhile, the government employees and the garrison troops would occupy the inner line of defenses and come under Steedman's orders, who, with these and his own forces, would be responsible for the defense of Nashville while the other corps were conducting the offensive. However, after this plan was put in writing Schofield convinced Thomas that his 23rd Corps would be more useful in supporting A. J. Smith's corps, on the Union right, than in supporting Wood, since Smith's attack on the flank was more important than Wood's attack on the center. Thomas's subordinates also convinced him to make another major change in his plan. Instead of remaining on the defensive, Steedman was to make himself useful by making a strong demonstration against Hood's right.

These changes in plan, coupled with the fog—which not only limited visibility but upset timetables when some units failed to move while others followed the original orders—led to delays and confusion in the Federal ranks. Schofield's corps had to march around behind Wood's corps to get into position to support Smith. Meanwhile some of Smith's units marched across in front of Wilson's cavalry when the troopers failed to advance at 6 a.m. The fog began to lift at 8 a.m. but Wilson still could not advance because Smith's infantry was still blocking his way, and it was 10 a.m. before the cavalry began to move.

At that hour the battle was finally getting under way. Steedman's diversionary force had advanced from the defenses at about 8 a.m. One of his brigades of U. S. Colored Troops, commanded by Colonel Thomas J. Morgan of the 14th U.S.C.T., marched eastward on the Murfreesboro Pike, followed by a small brigade of white troops from Cruft's Provisional Division, commanded by Lieutenant Colonel Charles H. Grosvenor of the 18th Ohio. The other brigade of U. S. Colored Troops, under Colonel Charles R. Thompson, advanced along the Nashville & Chattanooga Railroad to the southeast. Morgan had made a personal reconnaissance the night before to locate the Confederate flank, which he had found rested on some high ground known as Rains's Hill and faced to the west. By marching out the Murfreesboro Pike to the Rains house, the Federals would be beyond the Confederate right. While Thompson's brigade attracted the Rebels' attention by advancing against their front along the railroad tracks, Morgan's and Grosvenor's troops would turn to the southwest behind the Confederate line and approach them from the rear.

Everything went according to plan at first, and Morgan's brigade began advancing southwestward from the Rains house at about 10 a.m. With Morgan in overall command of the move, his own brigade, in the lead, was under the temporary command of Colonel William R. Shafter of the 17th U.S.C.T. Shafter's three regiments easily drove in the Confederate skirmishers covering the flank of what had been Cleburne's Division, which held the far right of Hood's line, overran their rifle pits, and advanced into some woods. However, before they had gone very far they came to the Nashville & Chattanooga Railroad, which just here ran through a 20-foot-deep cut that had been blasted out of solid rock, and its steep sides brought the Union line to an abrupt halt. Before Shafter could decide on his next move the Confederates opened a destructive fire of artillery and infantry on his men from the large redoubt Granbury's Brigade had recently constructed at the northern end of the Rebel line. The Confederates had observed Shafter's approach and had let his men come within 30 yards before opening fire. Then another Rebel battery, posted south of the railroad, opened fire, adding to the carnage. Most of Shafter's men were taking part in their first battle, and this crossfire was too much for them. Many of them jumped into the railroad cut for cover, but Govan's Confederate brigade swung around to fire down the railroad into their disorganized ranks, and in less than ten minutes Shafter had lost 110 men and 7 officers, including his brother-in-law. The rest of his brigade retreated back the way it had come.

Morgan hastened to Grosvenor's white troops and ordered them to charge the redoubt. Grosvenor now had only his own 18th Ohio Regiment and a battalion of assorted men who had been left behind by the 14th Corps. His other regiment, the 68th Indiana, had been sent farther east to guard the Federals' own flank against any counterattack. With Shafter's men attracting most of the Confederate fire, however, Grosvenor's were able to cross a muddy cornfield, knock down two picket fences, and break through a log palisade outside the redoubt, and nearly 100 of them got inside the works before a Rebel volley routed the provisional battalion of 14 Corps troops. These men were "mostly new conscripts, convalescents, and bounty jumpers," Grosvenor reported, "and on this occasion, with but few honorable exceptions, behaved in the most cowardly and disgraceful manner."[3] A few veterans in the battalion continued forward, and the officers tried to rally the rest, but in vain. This and the retreat of Shafter's men left the Confederates free to concentrate all their fire on the 18th Ohio, and it had little choice but to withdraw. Among the dead was Captain Ebenezer Grosvenor, in temporary command of the 18th Ohio, while Captain D. H. Henderson, commander of the provisional battalion, was severely wounded.

By noon Morgan's brigades had reformed in and around the sturdy brick outbuildings of the Rains place, from which they contented themselves with sniping at the Confederate line.

Just after 10 a.m., at about the time that Morgan's men were advancing against Hood's right, A. J. Smith's infantry and Wilson's cavalry were finally in position between the Hardin and Hillsborough pikes and began their advance against the Confederate left. Ector's Brigade of Rebel infantry, now commanded by Colonel David Coleman and stationed near the Hardin Pike, upon seeing this vast Union force, promptly abandoned Chalmers' cavalry and fell back to the southeast to rejoin the main infantry line. This move left Chalmers' wagons, containing his ordnance stores and headquarters papers, unprotected. They tried to get away down the Hardin Pike, but Colonel Datus Coon, commander of the 2nd Brigade in Hatch's 5th Division of Wilson's cavalry, sent the 12th Tennessee Cavalry in pursuit, and the wagons were captured before they had gone more than a few miles.

Meanwhile, at about 11 a.m., the 6th Division of the Cavalry Corps moved west along the Charlotte Pike. Before all of Sherman's cavalry had been united under Wilson, this division had been Stoneman's Cavalry Division of Schofield's Army of the Ohio, although, like all of Wilson's divisions, it had been reorganized since he had taken over. The new commander of the division was Brigadier Richard W. Johnson, who had briefly been chief of cavalry in Thomas's Army of the Cumberland. Before that he had commanded an infantry division in the 14th Corps. This was his first battle as a cavalry division commander, and it was not an auspicious debut. Because there were still not enough horses available to mount all of Wilson's cavalry, both Johnson's division and the 7th Division each had one mounted brigade and one dismounted. To make matters worse, there were not enough carbines to go around, either. Therefore, two regiments of the Johnson's dismounted brigade, Colonel James Biddle's 2nd, were left in camp. One of those regiments was armed only with revolvers, and the other had no arms at all.

Nevertheless, Johnson outnumbered Chalmers by more than 2 to 1. Johnson did not know this, however, believing himself to be up against Chalmers' entire division. So he advanced cautiously, with his small dismounted brigade in front, some of the men tripping over sabers dangling from their belts, which their regimental commander had not had sense enough to leave in camp. Frustrated with their slowness, Johnson finally brought up his other brigade, which had been Capron's but was now commanded by Colonel Thomas J. Harrison. This brigade charged ahead, but Chalmers' Rebels fell back, staying out of reach. Four miles farther west Johnson found the Confederates drawn up on a ridge beyond a small creek near Bell's Landing, from which Rebel guns had been interdicting traffic on the Cumberland River. The Confederates were protected by rude barricades of logs and fence rails, and their artillery swept the one bridge over the stream. One Union regiment tried to charge across but was easily repulsed, and Johnson ordered a halt. He called on the navy gunboats for help and asked that Croxton's brigade be sent to reinforce him, but it was already late afternoon by then, and Croxton had been sent elsewhere. The gunboats did lob a few shells in Chalmers' direction, but did little damage. When darkness fell, Chalmers pulled back, leaving only the 7th Alabama Cavalry to hold the position until the next morning. About all that Johnson had to show for his day's work was the capture of about fifty horses and the fact that Chalmers had been kept too busy to bother the flank of the main Union attack.

Smith's and Wilson's advance was in the form of a difficult wheeling maneuver, pivoting on Wood's 4th Corps and swinging across the open ground between the two turnpikes with the object of bringing it to face eastward toward the Confederate left flank. Therefore the units on the right end of this swinging door had much farther to go than those to their left. Wilson's troopers, having dismounted, frequently had to move at the double quick just to keep up.

At 1 p.m., after discovering the extension of the Rebel left that ran down the Hillsborough Pike, Thomas decided that Smith's divisions did not extend far enough to the right, so that Wilson's cavalry, at the end of the line, would either have to cover too wide an area or else fail to overlap the Rebel flank. So Thomas ordered Schofield to insert his 23rd Corps between Smith and Wilson, allowing the cavalry to "turn the enemy's left completely."[4] The advance of Smith's line was stopped to allow time for Schofield to get into position, but Smith used some of his artillery to bombard the Confederate line.

At about the same time, part of Wood's 4th Corps charged up Montgomery Hill. This was a cone-shaped height that rose about 150 feet higher than the surrounding terrain and had strong earthworks near the top and rows of sharpened stakes set into its steep sides. It was the part of the Confederate line that came closest to the Union defenses, and it appeared, to the Federals, to be the most formidible part of Hood's position. Colonel P. Sidney Post's 2nd Brigade of Brigadier General Samuel Beatty's 3rd Division, supported by Colonel Abel D. Streight's 1st Brigade, advanced up the hill with fixed bayonets, expecting at every moment to be hit with deadly volleys of musketry and withering artillery fire. But all that greeted them were scattered shots from a few skirmishers. The Federals had not realized until now that Hood's line had been pulled back about a mile to the south a few days before.

Wilson's cavalry, having farther to go than Smith's infantry, continued to advance while Schofield moved into place. Hatch's two brigades were in line side by side, dismounted, with the horses being held by small detachments. Brigadier General Joseph Knipe's 7th Division followed in a second dismounted line. Only one of its brigades had horses. Shortly before 2 p.m. Coon's 2nd Brigade, on the left of Hatch's line, topped a small rise and came in sight of a small Confederate fort on a hill not far to its front. This was Redoubt No. 5, at the end of Hood's far left flank. It held about 100 men from Quarles' Brigade of Walthall's Division of Stewart's Corps plus two 12-pounder Napoleon smoothbore guns, but it was 600 yards southwest of Redoubt No. 4, and there were no Rebels in between. Four Union batteries were bombarding the little Rebel fort, some from as close as 150 yards.

By 2:15 p.m. the Confederate fire had slackened, but some of the Federal batteries were running low on ammunition. It would be dark in a few hours and the Federals had yet to come to grips with the enemy. Hatch figured it was time to change that. "Go for the fort," he told Coon's men, adding that they should hold their fire until they got in close.[5] A bugle sounded the charge, and the dismounted troopers scrambled out of the ravine in which they had been trying to shelter from the redoubt's fire.

Schofield's corps had not yet reached its position between the cavalry and Smith's force, so that the next Union unit on Coon's left was Colonel William L. McMillan's 1st Brigade of Brigadier General John McArthur's 1st Division of Smith's Detachment Army of the Tennessee. McArthur had already been preparing his division to make an attack, and when he saw Coon's dismounted troopers going forward, he ordered McMillan to join the assault. With a shout the veteran infantrymen sprang forward, seeming to race the cavalry for the honor of being first to reach the fort.

Coon's men were some of the best cavalry in the Union army. His brigade had originally belonged to then-colonel Benjamin Grierson, and part of it had ridden with that officer across the length of Mississippi on his famous raid during the Vicksburg campaign a year and a half before. And McMillan's men were some of the very best infantry in the Union army. Like most of A. J. Smith's troops, the majority of them were veterans of the Vicksburg campaign, the Red River campaign, Smith's defeat of Forrest at Tupelo, Mississippi, and the chase after Price's raiders in Missouri. Unlike the veterans of the Atlanta campaign making up most of the rest of Thomas's army, they had not often had to charge strong earthworks, and therefore they were not as afraid of them.

The Confederate fire was intense but, for the most part, too high. The crack 2nd Iowa Cavalry, Hatch's old regiment, was the first to reach the parapet of the redoubt, but the rest of the cavalry and infantry brigades were not far behind. There was a brief melee with bayonets, rifle butts, revolvers, and swords, and then the surviving Rebels were streaming to the rear and the Federals were turning the two guns to fire at Redoubt No. 4.

That fort, however, held four guns and was on higher ground. Two of its guns were rapidly turned to face the captured redoubt and about 100 men of the 29th Alabama added their rifle fire to the shells of the 12-pounders. The Federals were all out of breath from their charge and, except for a few cavalrymen who were chasing the retreating Rebels, they were all jammed into the little redoubt without formation "like a crowd of schoolboys." One of Coon's men said that "to remain in our captured fort was certain death, to retreat promised little better, while to attempt the capture of this second fort seemed madness."[6] Hatch, who had followed his men into the Rebel work, quickly decided, however, that attacking Redoubt No. 4, was the best alternative, and he ordered his bugler to sound the charge.

The cavalry and the infantry, all mixed together, charged together across the ditch outside the fort and up the hill toward the second redoubt. However, Coon's troopers, not as hardened to marching and fighting on foot as McMillan's infantry, could manage little more than a walk. Some of them stopped to fire their carbines. Many crawled up the hill on their hands and knees. Coon yelled to his men "to take those guns before the infantry could get up."[7] Hatch, who had remounted his horses, pulled one exhausted trooper up the hill by having him hold on to his horse's tail.

Seeing McMillan's and Coon's men charging Redoubt No. 4 from the south, McArthur ordered his 2nd Brigade, Colonel Lucius F. Hubbard's, to charge it from the northwest. At the same time, a battery attached to Hubbard's brigade galloped up the hill and went into position near the captured Redoubt No. 5 and opened fire on No. 4. One of the battery's four guns, however, was already loaded with a shell whose fuse had been cut to burst one second after firing. The gunner knew that if he fired that shell at Redoubt No. 5 it would burst over the heads of the charging Federals, so he asked his battery commander what he should do. That officer told him to fire it in the general direction of the Hillsborough Pike, where there did not seem to be anybody in the way. The shell burst directly over a stone fence that ran along the road, and, to everybody's surprise, a previously undetected force of Rebel infantry posted there scattered in all directions.

Coon's and McMillan's men swarmed over the walls of Redoubt No. 4 together as the captain of the Confederate battery shouted, "Take care of yourself, boys."[8] Resistance soon collapsed inside the fort, while Hubbard's brigade charged past the redoubt on the north side toward the Hillsborough Pike. However, Hubbard could see a large force of Confederates behind the stone walls edging that road, and there was another redoubt, No. 3, to his left. So he stopped, realigned his front, and sent out several companies of skirmishers. He would need help to get any farther.

Help was at hand. McArthur's 3rd Brigade, commanded by Colonel Sylvester G. Hill, was eager to get its share of the glory. "Bring us a fort, bring us a fort," its men shouted when A. J. Smith rode past. "I'll get a fort for you," Smith replied, "you won't have to wait long for it, either." Smith told Colonel Hill that Redoubt No. 3 was a threat to the flank of McArthur's other units, but for Hill to attack it with his lone brigade would be hazardous. However, Hill was as eager for the fray as his men were. "Oh, no," he said, "our men will go right up there; nothing can stop them; they will go up without a bit of trouble." Smith was skeptical and told Hill to wait until he could get Hubbard's brigade turned to face the redoubt so that it could join in the attack, but Hill was not inclined to wait. "Scarcely a minute had elapsed after General Smith rode away," a Union colonel noted, "when Colonel Hill ordered his bugler to sound the charge."[9]

Hill's men rushed forward with a shout that drowned out the noise of the fire from the Confederates in Redoubt No. 3. The four Rebel guns there could not be depressed sufficiently to bear on the charging Federals, and the defending infantry also fired too high. Seeing that they could not stop the Union assault, the Confederate artillerymen tried to withdraw their guns, but a volley from some of Hill's men scattered the Rebels, and two of the guns were abandoned. The Federals swarmed into the fort and immediately began to take fire from Redoubt No. 2, several hundred yards to the northeast, across the Hillsborough Pike. As his officers were trying to reform his ranks, Hill shouted for his men to charge this second fort, but no sooner had he spoken than he was hit in the forehead by a rifle bullet and killed instantly. In all the noise and confusion not many of Hill's men had heard his final order, but about 200 of them had, and, led by a Minnesota colonel, they rushed forward. The Confederates in Redoubt No. 2 did not wait to see more, however. They fled, leaving one of their guns behind.

Hood had received reports by signal flag at about 10 a.m. that the Federals were advancing against both of his flanks, but he assumed at first that this was only another in the series of Union demonstrations that had been made over the past few days. As time passed, however, and the firing became heavier on his left, he visited A. P. Stewart's position along the Hillsborough Pike and had even been in Redoubt No. 4 some time before Hatch and McMillan had attacked. Seeing the large force of Federals advancing toward Stewart's flank, Hood had sent orders for Cheatham and S. D. Lee to send reinforcements to Stewart.

Lee sent two brigades of Allegheny Johnson's division, but by the time they arrived redoubts No. 4 and No. 5 had already been captured. They were sent to the stone wall running along the east side of the Hillsborough Pike east of Redoubt No. 4, but they had just arrived there when McMillan's infantry advanced against their front and a battery of Union guns opened fire on them from near Redoubt No. 5. In a confused mass, Johnson's men turned and ran back across the field behind them. However, when the artillery shells began to find them out in the open, many of them turned back to the cover of the stone wall. Several of McArthur's regiments had, in the mean time, taken position behind the stone wall on the other side of the road, and they began to fire on the confused and panic-stricken Rebels. When two companies of McArthur's skirmishers charged up the pike with fixed bayonets they captured 450 Confederates, and the rest ran back across the open field again, all organization lost. Stewart finally rallied them on a small hill behind his main line, where they were put in support of a battery that had just arrived from Loring's Division.

Major General Edward C. Walthall, commander of the division at the left end of Stewart's line, had also sent reinforcements to the endangered flank by pulling Brigadier General Daniel H. Reynolds' brigade out of line on his right and sending it to the left. However, that left his other two brigades holding too large a line and threatened on three sides, while Reynolds' flank was also being turned.

By then the 23rd Corps was beginning to catch up with Wilson's and Smith's men, and Brigadier General Joseph A. Cooper's 1st Brigade of the 2nd Division (which was now commanded by Major General Darius N. Couch) and Colonel Robert R. Stewart's 1st Brigade of Hatch's cavalry division advanced across the Hillsborough Pike. In the open field east of that road they were hit by shell and cannister fire from the battery that A. P. Stewart had posted behind his main line. Cooper's men raised a shout and charged, driving off the two brigades of Allegheny Johnson's division that were supporting the guns. The artillerymen tried to follow, but the Union cavalrymen had run around the base of the knoll and cut off their escape, capturing three of the guns. These the troopers turned around and used against Johnson's fleeing Confederates.

The 6th Tennessee of Cooper's brigade then joined some of Hubbard's regiments in sweeping northward along the Hillsborough Pike line, taking the Rebels there in flank and capturing many of them, while others broke and ran. "It was a splendid scene to see them scatter in confusion through a cornfield that was so muddy that it almost was impossible to travel," one Federal wrote, "and then to see them turn back, as we supposed to stand and fight—but only to surrender."[10]

A. P. Stewart's corps was now being attacked from three directions, the south, the west, and the north. Wood had ordered his 2nd Division, now under Brigadier General Washington L. Elliott, another of Thomas's former chiefs of cavalry, to attack Redoubt No. 1 at the left end of the main Confederate line, but Elliott delayed so long, waiting for A. J. Smith's left to connect with his right that Wood's center division, Kimball's, attacked first. Kimball's men had to cross a muddy cornfield 200 yards wide weighted down by their knapsacks and equipment to reach the strongly entrenched defenses of Loring's Division, but about 70 yards from the enemy they stopped and dropped their knapsacks and raced for the Rebel works. By the time they got there—just as the sun was setting—most of Loring's men were gone, for Stewart had ordered his men to withdraw before they became completely surrounded. Nevertheless, Kimball captured hundreds of prisoners and four guns.

Elliott's division had belatedly joined the attack, led by Opdycke's brigade, while at the same time Colonel Edward H. Wolfe's 3rd Brigade of A. J. Smith's 1st Division (now commanded by Brigadier General Kenner Garrard, a former cavalry division commander under Sherman whom Wilson had discarded) advanced against Redoubt No. 1 from the west. Lieutenant William Hall of the 36th Illinois, commanding 22 skirmishers from Opdycke's brigade, had crept along the stone wall running along the west side of the Hillsborough Pike until beyond Redoubt No. 1, and when he saw some of the Confederates begin to abandon their line, the lieutenant shouted, "Now, boys, is our time! I believe we can take that Rebel fort—the Johnnies are more than half whipped. How many of you are ready to go in?"[11] His men shouted their assent and they ran across the pike, climbed the wall in rear of the Confederate work, and sprang on the unsuspecting defenders. A few of the Rebel gunners put up a fight, but they were easily overcome by Hall's men, who were soon reinforced by skirmishers from Wolfe's brigade. Forty Confederates, three guns, and a battleflag were captured.

Stewart's Corps was, by then, in disordered retreat down the Granny

White Pike—a "full stampede," one Rebel called it. Several officers tried to rally them, including Brigadier General Claudius W. Sears, who was wounded in the right leg by a cannon ball that passed through his horse. But the men refused to stop. "The men seemed utterly lethargic and without interest in the battle," a Confederate captain said. "I never witnessed such want of enthusiasm, and began to fear for tomorrow, hoping Gen'l Hood would retreat during the night."[12]

Bate's Division, hurrying over from Cheatham's Corps on the Confederate right, reached the Franklin Pike just in time to see Stewart's men streaming to the south. So his leading brigade was formed in line facing west and connecting with the left flank of S. D. Lee's front line. Hood, meanwhile, had reached the Granny White Pike when he saw Ector's Brigade approaching in the twilight. It had been cut off by Hatch's breakthrough and had never really gotten into the fight. Hood, who had originally gained his fame as the commander of the Texas Brigade in Lee's army, put these men, mostly from the same state, in position on some high ground, saying, "Texans, I want you to hold this hill regardless of what transpires around you."[13] And they assured him that they would.

By then it was nearly dark. A. J. Smith's men were busy rounding up prisoners and captured guns and equipment, Wood's corps was pushing eastward down Stewart's front line, making sure it was cleared, and most of Wilson's cavalry had mounted up and moved off to the south, but Schofield's infantry continued to press the retreating Rebels. Couch's division, in a brief, spirited engagement, pushed Bate's Confederates off the hill they had just occupied and then turned against Ector's Brigade. But by then it was fully dark, and the Federals contented themselves with exchanging shots with the Texans for twenty minutes or so. Farther south, the mounted brigade of Knipe's 7th Division of Wilson's cavalry, which had been in reserve all day, had worked around the Confederate flank and it took position blocking the Granny White Pike near the site of the tavern that gave the road its name.

Thomas rode back into Nashville to telegraph a report to Halleck: "I attacked the enemy's left this morning and drove it from the river, below the city, very nearly to the Franklin pike, a distance about eight miles. Have captured General Chalmers' headquarters and train, and a second train of about 20 wagons, with between 800 and 1,000 prisoners and 16 pieces of artillery. The troops behaved splendidly, all taking their share in assaulting and carrying the enemy's breast-works. I shall attack the enemy again to-morrow, if he stands to fight, and, if he retreats during the night, will pursue him, throwing a heavy cavalry force in his rear, to destroy his trains, if possible."[14]

General Grant reached Washington early that afternoon, and there he found that the telegraph wires to Nashville had been down since about 5 p.m. the day before. After checking into Willard's Hotel, he met with Lincoln, Stanton, and Halleck and obtained their approval for the removal of Thomas. He made out the order for Major Eckert to transmit as soon as the telegraph lines were open again and went back to the hotel.

That evening the wires were repaired, but Eckert delayed sending the order, hoping to hear good news from Van Duzer at the other end first. Finally, at 11 p.m., a message came. It was an old one from Thomas, sent at 8 p.m. on the fourteenth: "The ice having melted away to-day, the enemy will be attacked to-morrow morning. Much as I regret the apparent delay in attacking the enemy, it could not have been done before with any reasonable hope of success."[15] Right after that telegram came Van Duzer's nightly report. It began, "Our line advanced and engaged the rebel line at 9 this a.m." and went on to say, "The left occupies the same ground as at morning, but right has advanced five miles, driving enemy from river, from his intrenchments, from the range of hills on which his left rested, and forced back upon his right and center. His center pushed back from one to three miles, with loss, in all, of 17 guns and about 1,500 prisoners, and his whole line of earth-works, except about a mile on his extreme right, where no serious attempt was made to dislodge him . . . The whole action of to-day was splendidly successful."[16]

Eckert raced down the stairs of the War Department building—what is now the Executive Office Building across from the White House—and into a waiting ambulance wagon, which hurried him to Stanton's home. "Good news," he shouted to the secretary of war, who was peering from his second-story window to see what was causing all the noise below. Within minutes Stanton and Eckert were on their way to the White House to wake up the President. The major pulled Grant's unsent order from his pocket and explained to the secretary what he had done, saying that he feared that he would be court-martialed for not sending the order. Stanton put his arm around his shoulders and said, "Major, if they court-martial you, they will have to court-martial me. You are my confidential assistant, and in my absence were empowered to act in all telegraph matters as if you were the Secretary of War. The results show you did right."[17] Lincoln, with candle in hand, dressed in his night shirt, read the telegrams with elation, and he too approved of Eckert's action.

When Grant was shown the two telegrams, he wired Thomas: "I was just on my way to Nashville, but receiving a dispatch from Van Duzer, detailing your splendid success of to-day, I shall go no farther. Push the enemy now, and give him no rest until he is entirely destroyed. Your army will cheerfully suffer many privations to break up Hood's army and render it useless for future operations. Do not stop for trains or supplies, but take them from the country, as the enemy have done. Much is now expected." Fifteen minutes later Grant sent another wire: "Your dispatch of this evening just received. I congratulate you and the army under your command for to-days operations, and feel a conviction that to-morrow will add more fruits to your victory." At midnight, Stanton sent his own congratulations: "I rejoice in tendering to you and the gallant officers and soldiers of your command the thanks of this Department for the brilliant achievements of this day, and hope that it is the harbinger of a decisive victory, that will crown you and your army with honor and do much toward closing the war. We shall give you a hundred guns in the morning."[18] At 11:25 the next morning, President Lincoln sent his own message: "Please accept for yourself, officers, and men the nation's thanks for your good work of yesterday. You made a magnificent beginning. A grand consummation is within your easy reach. Do not let it slip."[19]

---

1. *Official Records,* 45:II:690.
2. Sword, *Embrace an Angry Wind,* 316.
3. *Official Records,* 45:I:527.
4. Ibid., 45:II:201.
5. Sword, *Embrace an Angry Wind,* 334.
6. Ibid., 336.
7. Ibid.
8. Ibid., 337.
9. Ibid., 337–338.
10. Ibid., 340.
11. Ibid., 341.
12. Ibid., 342.
13. Stanley F. Horn, *The Decisive Battle of Nashville* (Baton Rouge, 1956), 102.
14. *Official Records,* 45:II:194.
15. Ibid., 45:II:180.
16. Ibid., 45:II:196.
17. Sword, *Embrace an Angry Wind,* 346.
18. *Official Records,* 45:II:195.
19. Ibid., 45:II:210.

CHAPTER FORTY-TWO

Didn't I Tell You We Could Lick 'em?

16 December 1864

According to Schofield, Thomas and his staff expected Hood to retreat that night, but knowing his old West Point classmate's aggressiveness he convinced them that it was at least possible that the Confederate would stay to fight. It was not unlikely even, Schofield thought, for the Rebels to counterattack the Union right, which was disordered by its own success and the pursuit of A. P. Stewart's retreat. At about 8 p.m. Thomas told Wood to attack the enemy at dawn the next day if he was still in place and to pursue if he had retreated.

In fact, Hood was not thinking of counterattacking, but he was planning to stay and fight. If he retreated, the campaign was definitely a failure. If he stayed, there was still the chance of inflicting upon the Federals the kind of expensive repulse which his own forces had suffered at Franklin. At about the same hour of 8 p.m. he was directing his force to a new, shorter line on a series of hills from the height where Ector's Brigade had taken position, west of the Granny White Pike, to another, called Peach Orchard Hill or Overton Hill, just east of the Franklin Pike. Cheatham's Corps was now on the left and S. D. Lee on the right. Hood expected Thomas to attack his flanks again, so they were both pulled back, curving around their respective hills. This arrangement put Stewart's Corps, which had taken most of the losses on the fifteenth, in the center, where it was least vulnerable and from which it could send reinforcements to either flank if necessary.

Throughout the night the weary Confederates felled trees and dug trenches to prepare earthworks on their new line, while the army's wagons rolled southward to Franklin to be out of the way. Forrest was east of Murfreesboro stalking a Union forage train when a courier brought him word from Hood of the day's events. His two and half divisions of cavalry and three attached brigades of infantry were widely scattered, so he ordered them to concentrate at Wilkinson's Cross Roads northwest of Murfreesboro, but no further word came from Hood and that is as far as he went that day.

The Federals bivouacked on the field, wherever darkness had overtaken them, amid the dead and dying. In Nashville the hospitals rapidly filled with wounded soldiers of both sides, and grim piles of amputated arms and legs began to grow outside the surgeons' tents. The night was warm but windy and the morning came in foggy, but not as thick as the day before. By 8:30 a.m. it had burned off, but a half-hour earlier than that the Union army was already on the move.

The artillery of both armies opened fire as A. J. Smith's troops began to advance at 8 a.m., but as the fog lifted the Union infantrymen found themselves confronted by Stewart's men dug in behind a stone wall in front of them and Cheatham's men entrenched on the high hill west of the Granny White Pike looking down on their right front. At about 9 a.m. Smith called a halt about 600 yards from the Rebel lines and sent skirmishers on to within 100 yards. Then he waited for Schofield and Wilson, on his right, to make the first move.

Schofield, however, who had already borrowed one division from A. J. Smith, was still worried about a Confederate counterattack, and he spent the entire morning preparing defenses and asking for more reinforcements. His defensive inclinations were strengthened by word from Wilson that Brigadier General John H. Hammond's 1st Brigade of Knipe's 7th Calvary Division had found Cheatham's Corps in its front and had encountered some of Chalmers' cavalry south of them on the Hillsborough Pike. Consequently, Wilson had ordered Hammond to pull back from the Granny White Pike. Schofield sent word to Wilson that "until you receive other orders from General Thomas, you had better hold your forces in readiness to support the troops here, in case the enemy make a heavy attack."[1]

The sky was turning increasingly cloudy as General Thomas rode up to Wilson's headquarters, at the six-mile post on the Hillsborough Pike. Wilson said that he was frustrated that he could not advance until the enemy's intentions were clarified, and suggested that his cavalry be moved to the army's other flank. Thomas told him to go ahead and advance to the Granny White Pike, as that would reveal Hood's intentions as well as anything. Meanwhile, Wood's 4th Corps spent most of the morning pushing Confederate skirmishers back two miles so it could take position on Smith's left. And it was 12:25 p.m. before Steedman's troops came up on Wood's left.

A light rain was falling by noon, as Wilson's dismounted cavalry began to advance, and the Union infantry had nothing to do but wait while the rain grew increasingly heavy and the temperature began to drop. "With our oil cloths wrapped about our shoulders," one Federal soldier remembered, "we sat in our trenches, waiting and waiting."[2] While Johnson's Division skirmished with Rucker's Brigade of Chalmers' cavalry along the Hillsborough Pike, Coon's brigade advanced cautiously through the difficult terrain between that road and the Granny White Pike—hills and knolls covered with thick timber and heavy underbrush. It was so rough that Coon had to break up his line into two or three pieces, and after advancing a mile or so he ran into some Confederate resistance. But when the 7th Illinois Cavalry came upon the 26th Tennessee Battalion and Chalmer's escort troops defending a barricaded hill near the turnpike it charged straight up the hill with its Spencer carbines blazing, captured 75 Rebels, and put the rest to flight.

After leaving Wilson, Thomas rode over to see Wood and told him that the plan remained the same as the day before. His 4th Corps, with Steedman covering his left, should menace the Confederates' front while Wilson, Schofield, and Smith attacked the Rebel left flank. However, Thomas also directed Wood to be "constantly on the alert for any opening for a more decisive effort."[3] The ambitious Wood, anxious to make the most of his position as temporary corps commander, saw this as an excuse to launch an attack which, if successful, would make him the hero of the day and perhaps of the war. He reasoned that if he could take Overton Hill half of the Rebel army would be cut off and subject to capture. "It was evident," he wrote in his report, "that the assault would be very difficult, and, if successful, would probably be attended by heavy loss; but the prize at stake was worth the hazard."[4]

The equally ambitious Colonel Sidney Post had been urging Wood to attack all morning, and now he volunteered his brigade for the assault on Overton Hill. Wood told him to make a personal reconnaissance of the terrain, and Post returned at 1:45 p.m. to say that, although the defenses were formidable, he thought that he could carry them by attacking up the northern face of the hill. Wood approved of this plan and assigned Colonel Abel D. Streight's 1st Brigade of Beatty's division to support Post by following it up the hill. He also went to discuss the attack with Steedman and ask for his cooperation. Steedman not only agreed to cover Post's left flank by advancing some of his troops but decided to have them actually participate in the assault. He chose Thompson's brigade for the assault role, with Grosvenor's in support, reinforced by one other regiment of U. S. Colored Troops.

As the Union infantry was forming up for the attack, the artillery opened fire on the Confederate lines on Overton Hill, splintering some of the logs that were used in the defenses and shrouding the works with the smoke of bursting shells. "The practice of the batteries was uncommonly fine," Wood wrote. "The ranges were accurate . . . and the ammunition being unusually good, the firing was consequently most effective. It was really entertaining to witness it."[5]

At 2:45 p.m. Wood gave the order for the infantry to advance and the long lines of men in blue advanced through the drizzling rain. Most of them had to cross a cornfield, which the rain had made so muddy that it slowed the attack, and Confederate artillery began to strike them before they had gone more than fifty yards. "In front of the 12th Colored Regiment of Thompson's brigade," a Union officer remembered, "was a thicket of trees and underbrush so dense as to be almost impenetrable . . . a kind of wooded island in the midst of a cornfield."[6] The plan was that when the 12th came to this thicket the other two regiments in the brigade would halt and wait for it to march around the obstruction. But when the 12th started to doublequick to get around these trees some of the men in the other regiments thought a charge had been ordered and began to run. Colonel Thompson decided that trying to stop them would cause even more confusion, so he ordered the charge for real. The Confederates in the works on Overton Hill poured a deadly fire of musketry and double charges of cannister into their ranks as Thompson's men clambered over a rail fence and started up the slope, and soon they ran into a sturdy abatis of felled trees. Unable to penetrate its interlaced branches, they threw themselves down on the slope of the hill. In Grosvenor's brigade the provisional battalion of conscripts and convalescents broke again, and the rest got no farther than the base of the hill.

On their right, Post's brigade was preceded by a strong skirmish line consisting of the entire 41st Ohio, which got to within 100 yards of the defenses, where the Rebels fired an ineffective volley that failed to stop them. However, 70 yards farther on they too were stopped by an abatis of felled trees that were staked to the ground. The 41st hit the dirt, and the Federals soon saw two brigades of Rebels reinforce the thinly manned defenses in their front. These were Granbury's and Lowery's brigades of Cleburne's old division, which Hood had rushed over from his left when the Union artillery bombardment had presaged an attack on Overton Hill. Just then, Post ordered his main line, still some 200 yards out, to charge. His line surged forward, but Post was soon wounded severely by a blast of cannister which killed his horse and ripped through his side just above the hip, the ball coming out his back near the spine. The main line was stopped short of the abatis by the Confederate fire and also hit the dirt. Behind it, Streight's supporting brigade fired over the heads of Posts' men and tried to advance over their prone lines, but the Rebel fire broke up this advance also. "Fall back," someone shouted; "we are falling back." And the shattered, intermingled regiments streamed back down the hill.[7]

While Post's and Streight's men were thus attracting the Rebels' attention, the 13th U.S. Colored Troops, which had been trailing Thompson's other two regiments, penetrated the abatis between Thompson's right and Post's left, and then, with a shout, some 655 black soldiers and 20 white officers charged the Confederate works. The veteran soldiers still hugging the slope looked on in amazement as this lone regiment, fighting in its first battle, swept up the hill to the Rebel breastworks all alone despite the concentration of fire that the Confederates now threw at it. A colorbearer jumped up on the parapet and shook his regimental flag in the Rebels' faces. He was immediately riddled with bullets. Five other men, one after the other, tried to plant the regiment's national flag on the works of Brigadier General James T. Holtzclaw's brigade but they also were shot down. "I never saw more heroic conduct shown on the field of battle than was exhibited by this body of men so recently slaves," a veteran Union officer said.[8]

"The fire of the enemy was terrific," the colonel of the 13th reported, "but nevertheless the men, led by their officers, continued to advance to the very muzzles of the enemy's guns, but its numbers were too small, and after a protracted struggle they had to fall back, not for the want of courage or discipline, but because it was impossible to drive the enemy from his works by a direct assault."[9] An officer of the 13th rescued the regiment's national flag, but a Confederate lieutenant seized the regimental flag—which had been presented to the regiment by "the colored ladies of Murfreesboro"—before it could be recovered.[10] "I have seen most of the battle-fields of the West," wrote General Holtzclaw, "but never saw dead men thicker than in front of my two right regiments."[11] "Don't tell me negroes won't fight," a Union surgeon wrote home after helping to patch up their wounded and later riding over the field where their dead lay near the Rebel works, "I know better."[12]

Over on the Confederate left, Chalmers, after being driven from his fortified hill near the Granny White Pike, sent a request for reinforcements, and Hood sent him Ector's Brigade. These infantrymen charged up the slope and drove Coon's Union troopers off the hill again, freeing many of the captured Rebels. But Hatch soon arrived and had a couple of guns hauled by hand up an adjacent, higher, hill. They opened up at about 3 p.m., and after they had fired around fifty shots Coon ordered his whole brigade to open fire. Chalmers and Coleman, the commander of Ector's Brigade, knew they could not hold their hill, so they began to fall back to the south, toward Brentwood, along an old country road, leaving the way open for Coon's troopers to advance to the Granny White Pike.

Hood learned just about then that Wilson's advance threatened Chalmers' position and ordered Stewart to send help to him. Stewart pulled Brigadier General Daniel H. Reynolds' brigade out of his line on the hill at the left end of the line and sent it southward along the Granny White Pike. At 3:15 p.m. Hood's adjutant sent Chalmers an urgent message: "General Hood says you must hold that pike; put in your escort and every available man you can find."[13] But Chalmers did not receive it until he had already reached Brentwood. Wilson, meanwhile, knowing that his own reserve brigades were out of position for exploiting his gains, sent repeated messages to Schofield, urging him to advance his infantry.

John McArthur had been waiting all day, with increasing impatience, for something to be done. Twice he had conferred with Couch, whose division was to the right of his own, about attacking the hill in their front, but the latter had no orders to advance. All he could promise to do was to send a brigade to hold McArthur's defenses should the latter decide to attack. McArthur had decided to do just that. If no one else would take the responsibility for ordering an attack, he would do it. He had been studying that hill in front of him—the same one Ector's Brigade had held at dusk to halt the Union advance the evening before—and he thought he could take it. The Confederates had built their defenses too far up the slope, on the actual crown of the hill, not on the military crest. Therefore their guns could not be depressed sufficiently to cover the hillside and even the infantry would have to expose themselves in order to fire down the hill. Furthermore, the hill did not seem to be very heavily manned. And, what was most important of all, that hill was the key to the entire Rebel line. If it were in Federal hands Hood's entire position would be untenable. At 3 p.m., while McMillan's brigade formed in front of Couch's division and the commander of his supporting battery, which was nearly out of ammunition, borrowed enough from another battery to provide ten rounds for each gun and opened fire, McArthur sent a dispatch to A. J. Smith saying that he was making preparations to attack and that unless he received orders to the contrary he would order the charge.

Smith was talking with Thomas when this message arrived. "Don't let him start yet," Thomas said. "Hold him where he is until I can ride over and see Schofield. I will have him charge at the same time."[14] Not having received any response to his messages urging Schofield forward, Wilson rode to his left and found Thomas and Schofield conferring behind a small hill. With "ill concealed impatience," as Wilson put it, he urged Thomas to order the infantry to advance immediately. His cavalry, he said, was in pursuit of the enemy and could be seen advancing through the rough terrain toward the rear of the hill at the left end of Hood's line. Thomas "lifted his field glasses and coolly scanned what I had clearly showed him," Wilson wrote. Finally, "as calmly as if on parade," Thomas turned to Schofield and said, "General, will you please advance your whole line."[15] But he was too late. McArthur's men were already charging.

With Chalmers' and Ector's troops driven off to the south, Cheatham sent Govan's Brigade—all that was left of Cleburne's old division since the rest had been sent to reinforce the right—to protect his left rear from a small hill. However, both Govan and his senior colonel had been wounded earlier in the day, and now his men were subjected to such a concentrated fire of Union artillery that they soon gave way. Cheatham then called on Brigadier General Mark Lowrey, now commanding what had been Brown's Division, for help. Lowrey sent Brigadier General States Rights Gist's and Colonel Hume Field's (formerly Carter's) brigades to reestablish the line. But as soon as these troops had clambered up the slippery wet slope of the small hill, they too came under a terrific bombardment. A colonel admonished his men for dodging the incoming shells, but one of his men shouted, "Colonel, look yonder!" pointing to a long line of dismounted Union cavalrymen charging through a field beyond their left flank. The colonel, one soldier noted, "never thought any more about dodging shells." "Boys," the colonel shouted, "every fellow for himself."[16] And they all fled back the way they had come.

General Cheatham was talking with a staff officer under a white oak tree at the base of the hill when a bullet came zipping between them. He looked up and saw Lowrey's men streaming by. Then he heard heavy firing from his main line, looked up, and saw Union flags waving from the top of the hill that anchored the army's left flank.

Up on that hill, William Bate's division had been stretched time and again to man more and more of the line as brigade after brigade was pulled out and sent elsewhere. He had been shocked to discover, when his men took over the section that had been held by Ector's Brigade, that its defenses were flimsy and built too far up the hill. What's more, there was no abatis or obstructions in its front. Then the Union artillery bombardment had demolished many of the hastily thrown up breastworks. While bullets struck his position from three directions, Bate had watched as Govan's Brigade had broken and two of Lowrey's brigades had marched off to take its place. Then he had looked back to his own front and had seen McArthur's Federals swarming up the steep face of the hill, heading directly for his line.

Hubbard's brigade of McArthur's division was riddled with repeated blasts of cannister as it advanced across 400 yards of muddy field, but the men of McMillan's brigade, on McArthur's right, were pleasantly surprised to discover that, although the crest of the hill ahead of them was wreathed in gunsmoke, there was very little incoming fire reaching them. Only the 10th Minnesota, on the left, suffered heavy losses on the way up the hill. It was not until they were near the crown of the hill that the curvature of the ground dropped away and gave the Confederates a clear shot at them. From a range of only a few feet the Rebels fired a heavy volley, but their aim was too high and the bullets whistled by overhead. The Federals gave a yell and bounded over the works. Within minutes Brigadier General Thomas B. Smith's brigade of Bate's division was overwhelmed. Lieutenant Colonel William M. Shy, 25-year-old commander of six consolidated Tennessee regiments refused to surrender and was shot through the head, and the hill upon which he died has been known as Shy's Hill ever since.

To Smith's right, the Florida Brigade, seeing Smith's line broken, fled in confusion, and Bate's entire division seemed to disintegrate. Although a few pockets of resistance continued to fight, most of his men threw down their weapons and either ran for their lives or surrendered. McMillan's brigade gathered up 4 battleflags, 8 guns, 85 officers, including General Smith, and 1,533 enlisted men—more than McMillan had in his brigade before the charge began. McMillan's jubilant men ran about "shouting, yelling, and acting like maniacs for a while," one of them said.[17] General Smith became belligerent as he was being led to the rear and exchanged hot words with the excited Colonel McMillan, who then struck him in the head with his sword. As a result, Smith spent the next 47 years in the Tennessee State Hospital for the Insane.

Just as the panic spread to Bate's right brigade, commanded by Brigadier Henry R. Jackson, Hubbard's Federal brigade charged over its works from the front, completing its rout. Jackson himself was captured after his horse slipped when it tried to jump a stone fence at the Granny White Pike. Walthall's Division was next on the Confederate right, and the disorder spread to it as Jackson's men broke and ran and Hubbard's Federals came in on its left. Soon these three brigades were also streaming for the rear.

To the left of Bate's Division was Strahl's Brigade, now under Colonel Andrew J. Kellar. One of his officers suddenly shouted, "Look there at the United States flag on the hill!" Kellar's men jumped up and ran off without even trying to make a stand. "It was not by fighting," Kellar wrote, "nor the force of arms, nor even numbers, which drove us from the field."[18] Nor was it fear that made the Rebels run—at least, not fear of pain or death. It was the fear that any such sacrifices would be in vain—that the battle was already lost beyond redemption. Colonel Charles C. Doolittle's 1st Brigade of Cox's 3rd Division (the unit which had been Reilly's at Franklin) was the only unit of the 23rd Corps to attack Shy's Hill. Lowrey's Confederates fired several heavy volleys in their direction as his men climbed the hill, but their aim was too high, and by the time they reached the top, most of the Rebels had fled. Doolittle's men captured about 300 Confederates and 8 guns.

Colonel William Marshall, now commanding the 3rd Brigade of McArthur's division, had not been ordered to advance, but he thought that Hubbard should be supported. So he advanced on Hubbard's left against Loring's Division of Stewart's Corps just east of the Granny White Pike. It was a formidable position, but the Confederate skirmishers in his front had been so caught up in watching McMillan's and Hubbard's attack on Shy's Hill to their left that they had not noticed Marshall's men bearing down on them until it was almost too late. They jumped up and ran for their breastworks at the last moment, and with a wild shout the Federals charged in so close behind them that the Rebels on the main line could not fire without hitting their own men. Instead, they turned and ran. A screaming, delirious throng of Union soldiers poured through the heavy obstructions in front of the Confederate line and over the breastworks built around an old stone wall. "In less time than it takes to tell it," a Federal officer wrote, "we had captured guns, caissons, colors, and prisoners galore."[19]

As A. J. Smith sat on his horse watching a large group of soldiers streaming down Shy's Hill, Thomas rode up. "General, what is the matter," the latter asked excitedly, "are your men being captured there?"

"Not by a damn sight," Smith replied. "My men are capturing them, those are Rebel prisoners you see."[20]

Then for the only time that Smith could ever remember, Thomas laughed.

"It was more like a scene in a spectacular drama than a real incident in war," wrote Colonel Henry Stone of Thomas's staff. "The hillside in front, still green, dotted with the boys in blue swarming up the slope; the dark background of high hills beyond; the lowering clouds; the waving flags; the smoke slowly rising through the leafless tree-tops and drifting across the valleys; the wonderful outburst of musketry; the ecstatic cheers; the multitude racing for life down into the valley below—so exciting was it all that the lookers-on instinctively clapped their hands as at a brilliant and successful transformation scene, as indeed it was. For in those few minutes an army was changed into a mob, and the whole structure of the rebellion in the Southwest, with all its possibilities, was utterly overthrown."[21]

Two thirds of the Confederate army was routed and heading south as fast as it could go. Hood himself had been discussing his plans for the next day with A. P. Stewart when both of them were swept up in the rout. (He was planning to march around Thomas's right and attack his flank and rear, just as Schofield had feared he would do, but one day too late.) Hood and many of his officers tried to stem the rout and rally his men, but panic had gripped them and they would not stop. "Wagon trains, cannon, artillery, cavalry, and infantry were all blended in inextricable confusion," Confederate private Sam Watkins remembered. "Broken down and jaded horses and mules refused to pull, and the badly-scared drivers looked like their eyes would pop out of their heads from fright. Wagon wheels, interlocking each other, soon clogged the road, and wagons, horses and provisions were left indiscriminately. The officers soon became effected with the demoralization of their troops, and rode on in dogged indifference. General Frank Cheatham and General Loring tried to form a line at Brentwood, but the line they formed was like trying to stop the current of Duck river with a fish net."[22]

Only S. D. Lee's corps, on the Confederate right, was still in condition to put up a fight. At about 4:30 p.m. Lee heard a commotion off to the west. "Suddenly all eyes were turned to the center of our line of battle near the Granny White pike. . . ," he wrote. "Our men were flying to the rear in the wildest confusion, and the enemy following with enthusiastic cheers."[23] As Lee watched, Allegheny Johnson's men were out-flanked and swept away in the rout. Many of them surrendered or were captured, including Johnson himself. It was his second time, having just been exchanged after being captured at Spotsylvania. He was too old and out of shape to catch up with his orderly, who fled with his horse.

Those of Johnson's men who were not captured went running for the Franklin Pike. Lee rode up, shouting, "Rally, men, rally! For God's sake, rally! This is the place for brave men to die!" A private on Lee's staff said the general's words were inspiring. "They seemed to come from his very soul, as if his heart were breaking."[24] A few small clusters of men stopped and faced about, but the vast majority continued to flee to the south. And as A. J. Smith's men closed in on his left, the 4th Corps again advanced against Lee's front.

When Wood's men had seen the success of Smith's attack they could not resist joining in. Their officers had been no more successful at keeping them from advancing than Hood's had been at keeping his men from retreating, and they surged forward without orders or formation. Finding itself attacked from front, flank, and rear, Major General Carter L. Stevenson's Division of Lee's Corps fell apart. Some of his men bolted for the rear while the rest waved handkerchiefs or hats or whatever they could find in token of surrender. That left Clayton's Division, up on Overton Hill, as the only large Confederate unit still in condition to put up much of a fight. Lee got word to it to pull out just in time. The last brigade scrambled down the hill in the gathering dusk just as Steedman's skirmishers came up the other side. With Clayton's Division, or as much of it as he could keep together, Lee covered the retreat.

Meanwhile, the captured and surrendering Confederates were rounded up and marched into Nashville. One Union soldier was not impressed with the Confederates after getting a close look at them. "They were all ragged and dirty," he said, "and so filthy that we could smell them as plainly as if it had been a flock of sheep on a hot June day." Captured generals Johnson, Jackson, and Smith were taken to Thomas's field head-quarters, where they were provided food, cigars, and whiskey from the officers' mess. One of them, probably Jackson, told his hosts how the Federals had marched up to and over his defenses as "cool as fate." He said, "It was astonishing, sir, such fighting . . . it was really splendid."[25]

Those who had been hit by bullets or shell fragments might not have shared his viewpoint. All that night medical orderlies, stretcher bearers, and ambulance drivers gathered up the wounded men of both sides from the rainy battlefield. They also found one civilian. A soldier had caught him robbing the dead and had shot him through the hip, leaving him to experience at first hand what it was like to lie in the mud and rain, helpless and in agony. "When I saw him," another soldier, who encountered him at the hospital wrote, "he was in a fair way to go to hell."[26]

There was little pursuit by the Federals at first. Many of the Union units were almost as disorganized by victory as the Rebels were by defeat. Steedman, having no orders and no supplies other than ammunition, was content to put his men into camp in the captured lines. Schofield, commanding the only sizable Union force that had not been engaged, found the roads already full of other units and also ordered his men to bivouac where they were. Only Wood's corps followed the Rebels south down the Franklin Pike, while Wilson was struggling to bring up his horses through the difficult terrain so that his cavalry could make a mounted pursuit down the Granny White Pike.

At about 4:30 p.m. Chalmers, at Brentwood, had finally received Hood's order for him to hold the Granny White Pike. Not realizing that since that order had been written the entire situation had been changed and that all of Hood's infantry had been routed, Chalmers ordered Rucker's Brigade to defend the Granny White Pike. Colonel Rucker put his men to work barricading that road north of the Little Harpeth River, about eight miles from Nashville. He had just finished posting one of his regiments and was returning to his main position along the pike when he encountered a body of horsemen on the darkened road. "Who are you?" he asked their leader, and was told he was an officer in the 12th Tennessee.[27] Realizing that these riders were Federals, Rucker swung his saber and struck the officer—Captain Joseph C. Boyer—a glancing blow on the forehead. But then his horse reared and he dropped his sword before he could swing it again. Boyer drew his own sword, but Rucker managed to wrench it away from him and put his spurs to his big white horse. Boyer yelled for his men to fire, and a volley of shots rang out. A pistol bullet hit Rucker in the left elbow, shattering the bone, and he fell to the ground and was captured. Then in a brief, vicious, confused, hand-to-hand combat the Federal cavalry drove Rucker's men from their barricade, and the Rebels retreated.

S. D. Lee, with his rear guard, was falling back through the gathering darkness and thinking that it was "a fortunate circumstance that the enemy was too much crippled to pursue us on the Franklin pike" when one of Hood's aides brought him word that he must get to Brentwood right away.[28] The Federals were advancing on the Granny White Pike toward Hollow Tree Gap, where the two roads came together. Lee disengaged and marched rapidly to Brentwood, reaching there about dark. When he learned that the rest of the army had already passed that point, he marched on until about 10 p.m., when he called a halt about six miles north of Franklin. By then the Federals had long since given up the pursuit, but the drizzling rain had turned into a raging storm.

When Rucker was captured at about 6:30 p.m. the dispatch of Hood's adjutant to Chalmers was found in his pocket. Wilson had interpreted it to mean that "the safety of his army depends upon the ability of Chalmers to keep us off; time is all he wants." But Rucker told the Federals that "Forrest has just arrived with all the cavalry, and will give you hell tonight." It was a ruse, of course, and Wilson claimed to know that it was. Nevertheless, he suddenly decided that "the night was so dark and wet, and the men and horses so jaded, that it was not deemed practicable to push the pursuit farther."[29] It would be resumed at daylight, or earlier.

Riding along the Granny White Pike, Wilson heard galloping horses approaching from the north along the macadamized road. "Is that you, Wilson?" someone called out. It was Thomas. "Dang it to hell, Wilson," he said in a voice that might have been heard for a quarter of a mile, "didn't I tell you we could lick 'em?"[30]

Hood made his headquarters that night at the home of a Mrs. Maney near Franklin. Private Sam Watkins, who had reached there on a horse he had taken from an abandoned wagon after being wounded in the thigh and the hand, came to ask for a furlough to recover from his wounds. "He was much agitated and affected," Watkins wrote, "pulling his hair with his one hand (he had but one), and crying like his heart would break."[31]

---

1. *Official Records,* 45:II:216.

2. Sword, *Embrace an Angry Wind,* 354.

3. *Official Records,* 45:I:131.

4. Ibid., 45:I:132.

5. Sword, *Embrace an Angry Wind,* 356.

6. Ibid., 357.

7. Ibid., 361.

8. Ibid., 362–363.

9. *Official Records,* 45:I:362.

10. Ibid., 45:I:698. Holtzclaw's division commander, Major General Henry D. Clayton, mistakenly indicated that the flag belonged to the 18th U.S.C.T.

11. Ibid., 45:I:705.

12. Sword, *Embrace an Angry Wind*, 363.
13. *Official Records*, 45:II:697.
14. Sword, *Embrace an Angry Wind*, 367.
15. Ibid., 367–368.
16. Ibid., 378.
17. Ibid., 374.
18. Ibid., 377.
19. Ibid., 376.
20. Ibid., 379–380.
21. Horn, *The Decisive Battle of Nashville*, 128.
22. Watkins, *Co. Aytch*, 240–241.
23. *Official Records*, 45:I:689.
24. Hattaway, *General Stephen D. Lee*, 144.
25. Sword, *Embrace an Angry Wind*, 385.
26. Ibid., 390.
27. Ibid., 388.
28. Ibid.
29. *Official Records*, 45:I:552.
30. Horn, *The Decisive Battle of Nashville*, 152–153.
31. Watkins, *Co. Aytch*, 241.

CHAPTER FORTY-THREE

The Rebels Are On a Great Skedaddle

16–17 December 1864

The Rebel agents' scheme to free captured Confederate generals as they were being transferred from Johnson's Island had been stymied on the fifteenth because the movement had been put off. So, not knowing just exactly when the prisoners would be coming past their chosen ambush point between Dunkirk and Buffalo, on the sixteenth the Rebels decided to stop the next eastbound train coming through. They met on the outskirts of Dunkirk that night and parked their rented sleigh in the deep snow under a clump of trees. When they heard the train coming, they dragged an iron rail across the track. But they were not able to get the rail fastened down in time, and when it struck the rail the train just pushed it along in front of it. The engineer finally stopped to see what he had hit, but by then the Rebels had run for their sleigh and hurried back to Buffalo as fast as they could go.

At the railroad depot they split into pairs, and when a train headed for Canada came in most of them took it. Colonel Martin and Lieutenant

Headley rented a hotel room for the night and caught up with the others the next day. Beall was paired with a new recruit named Anderson, who fell asleep in the depot restaurant. Anderson was sick, and Beall let him get some rest, but soon a policeman came by and began to question them. Before long the frightened young Anderson was telling the officer all about their plot. That was the last Confederate raid launched out of Canada.

Down in western Kentucky on the sixteenth, McCook's division of Union cavalry approached Hopkinsville early that morning, where Lyon's raiding Confederates, or some of them, were known to be. McCook had stopped for a four-hour rest the night before and had timed his advance to reach Hopkinsville at daylight. He assumed that the Rebels, if they intended to fight, would occupy the bluffs just east of the town, "that being the strongest defensible position in the vicinity." So he divided his force, sending Brigadier General Louis D. Watkins' 3rd Brigade to the right with orders to get behind the Confederates and "cover all the roads."[1] Then, as soon as it was light, his other brigade, Colonel Oscar H. La Grange's 2nd, advanced and found the Rebels posted right where McCook had expected them to be.

This was a force of 400 men and one cannon under Colonel J. Q. Chenoweth whom Lyon had left to guard his flank and rear while he had proceeded with the rest to Cadiz, Eddyville, and Princeton. Each of these towns was garrisoned, Lyon said, with around 200 black troops, and he had hoped to capture these garrisons "and in any event to destroy these barracks and supply my men with clothing, &c.," as he later reported. "The garrisons all abandoned these posts and fled to Smithland and Fort Donelson, and I destroyed the court-houses at Hopkinsville, Cadiz, and Princeton, as they were occupied as barracks and used as fortifications by the negroes. I also destroyed a corral, or place of rendezvous for negroes, at Eddyville, Ky."[2]

When La Grange's brigade advanced, the Confederates "opened one piece of artillery and a heavy fire of musketry," McCook reported. "Our lines advanced steadily and the rebels ran away, abandoning their artillery, caisson, and ammunition, nearly all of them throwing away their guns and escaping by the Greenville road and through the woods. I expected, and from the disposition I had made of my force had a right to expect, that the morning's work would result in the capture and destruction of the entire force opposed to me. Watkins had succeeded in getting in their rear before the attack was made in front, but through some unaccountable mistake the Greenville road had been left open by him." General Watkins blamed the escape on a Colonel Faulkner, whom he ordered to charge, "but the colonel, believing they were friends, instead of enemies, failed to obey the order, and the rebels changed their course and escaped."[3]

Over near the eastern Tennessee and western Virginia border that day, Stoneman's Union cavalry was also on the move before dawn. Stoneman had learned that the regiment that he had sent ahead had captured and destroyed two trains that had brought Breckinridge with reinforcements and a battery down from Wytheville. "The question with me now was," Stoneman said, "whether to move on the salt-works and attempt to capture and destroy them first, or to pass them by with the main force, threatening them with a brigade, and to endeavor to capture or disperse Vaughn, destroy the railroad as far as possible, destroy Wytheville and the lead-works on New River, and, returning, take the salt-works at our leisure. I decided on the latter."[4] So he sent one of Burbridge's brigades to threaten Saltville, reinforced Gillem with two regiments from Burbridge's force, and sent him ahead to push on and try to overtake Vaughn or pursue him toward Wytheville. Then he followed with the rest of his command.

At 4 a.m. Gillem came upon Vaughn's rear guard and captured it, and about an hour later he reached the town of Marion, where his men were fired on by a sizable force. But they drove the Rebels through the town and took position on some heights beyond, where they waited for daylight so they could see what they were up against. Then the Federals attacked again and, as Gillem later reported, "drove the enemy from their position, pursuing them closely for twelve miles, driving them from every position they attempted to hold, and charging them every time they attempted to make a stand. Thirteen miles west of Wytheville they began to use their artillery, which was immediately charged and captured, the enemy losing eight pieces between that point and Wytheville. When within one mile of Wytheville, and after pursuing the enemy thirty-one miles, I halted for a short time to allow my command to close up, it having been reported to me from several sources that a force of some 700 or 800 infantry had arrived at Wytheville from Lynchburg. Soon after my command had reformed, Colonel Brown's brigade, of General Burbridge's command, which had been sent by Major-General Stoneman to support me, arrived, and I moved my entire force into Wytheville without seeing an enemy or firing a shot."[5]

Gillem sent one regiment of Brown's brigade to destroy bridges on the railroad to Lynchburg while he put the rest of his command to work at destroying all the Confederate property found in the town, "among which," Gillem reported, "were large quantities of ammunition, both for artillery and small-arms, several large buildings filled with subsistence and medical stores, and General Breckinridge's headquarters. Among the buildings destroyed was one church, used as a magazine and ordnance store-house, it being considered that its sacred character did not protect its warlike contents. At 12 p.m., the work of destruction having been completed, I withdrew my forces three miles this side of Wytheville and encamped. The result of this day's fighting was the capture by my command of 8 pieces of artillery and caissons complete, 93 wagons, and 308 prisoners."[6]

Down in Georgia, Beauregard arrived at Savannah on the night of the sixteenth to inspect the beleaguered city. He had warned Hardee that the latter must not allow himself to be cut off in Savannah and that if the city had to be lost to make sure his troops were not captured with it. The approximately 9,000 men that Hardee had scraped together were all that would be available to defend Augusta and Charleston. Hardee had begun the construction of a floating bridge across the mile-wide Savannah River to provide himself a means of escape. It was being made primarily of rice flats, which were shallow barges used to transport rice to market along the numerous streams and canals of the region. However, the bridge was only about one third completed when Beauregard arrived and he wanted the pace stepped up. His temper was not improved when he learned that Wheeler's cavalry had burned scores of the flats to keep Sherman from using them.

That same day, Sherman replied to the two letters he had received from Grant. After giving more details of his march across Georgia and his preparations for obeying the order to sail to Virginia, he said that in the mean time he would act "as I have begun, as though the city of Savannah were my objective: namely, the troops will continue to invest Savannah closely, making attacks and feints wherever we have fair ground to stand upon, and I will place some thirty-pound Parrotts, which I have got from General Foster, in position, near enough to reach the centre of the city, and then will demand its surrender. If General Hardee is alarmed, or fears starvation, he may surrender; otherwise I will bombard the city, but not risk the lives of our men by assaults across the narrow causeways, by which alone I can now reach it. If I had time, Savannah, with all its dependent fortifications, would surely fall into our possession, for we hold all its avenues of supply . . . General Slocum occupies Argyle Island and the upper end of Hutchinson Island, and has a brigade on the South Carolina shore opposite, and is very urgent to pass one of his corps over to that shore. But, in view of the change of plan made necessary by your order of the 6th, I will maintain things *in statu quo* till I have got all my transportation to the rear and out of the way, and until I have sea-transportation for the troops you require at James River, which I will accompany and command in person . . . My four corps, full of experience and full of ardor, coming to you *en masse,* equal to sixty thousand fighting-men, will be a reenforcement that Lee cannot disregard. Indeed, with my present command, I had expected, after reducing Savannah, instantly to march to Columbia, South Carolina; thence to Raleigh, and thence to report to you. But this would consume, it may be, six weeks' time after the fall of Savannah; whereas, by sea, I can probably reach you with my men and arms before the middle of January . . . Our whole army is in fine condition as to health, and the weather is splendid. For that reason alone I feel a personal dislike to turning northward. I will keep Lieutenant Dunn here until I know the result of my demand for the surrender of Savannah, but, whether successful or not, shall not delay my execution of your order of the 6th, which will depend alone upon the time it will require to obtain transportation by sea."[7]

The next day, the seventeenth, Sherman sent Hardee his demand for the surrender of Savannah: "You have doubtless observed, from your station at Rosedew, that sea-going vessels now come through Ossabaw Sound and up the Ogeechee to the rear of my army, giving me abundant supplies of all kinds, and more especially heavy ordnance necessary for the reduction of Savannah. I have already received guns that can cast heavy and destructive shot as far as the heart of your city; also, I have for some days held and controlled every avenue by which the people and garrison of Savannah can be supplied, and I am therefore justified in demanding the surrender of the city of Savannah, and it dependent forts, and shall wait a reasonable time for your answer, before opening with heavy ordnance. Should you entertain the proposition, I am prepared to grant liberal terms to the inhabitants and garrison; but should I be forced to resort to assault, or the slower and surer process of starvation, I shall then feel justified in resorting to the harshest measures, and shall make little effort to restrain my army—burning to avenge the national wrong which they attach to Savannah and other large cities which have been so prominent in dragging our country into civil war. I inclose you a copy of General Hood's demand for the surrender of the town of Resaca, to be used by you for what it is worth."[8]

Up in western Kentucky on the morning of the seventeenth, McCook's Union cavalry left Hopkinsville at daylight and marched toward Princeton. But when he was still eight miles from that town he learned that Lyon had reunited his force, crossed the Tradewater River, and burned the bridge behind him. "Here finding it impossible to make a rapid pursuit encumbered with artillery," McCook wrote, "and fearing if I followed with my whole force Lyon might turn back through Madisonville and try to reach the Cumberland by marching through Hopkinsville, I divided my forces, ordering Colonel La Grange with his brigade to follow the route of the enemy and pursue him as far as practicable, and moved with Watkins and the artillery back to Hopkinsville."[9]

In southwestern Virginia that day, with the destruction at Wytheville completed, Stoneman's Federals turned on the 34th Virginia Cavalry Battalion, the vanguard of Breckinridge's pursuing Confederates, and drove it back. "The only thing now left for us to do," Stoneman wrote, "was the destruction of the far-famed salt-works." At the Middle Fork of the Holston River Breckinridge had the small brigades of Cosby, Duke, and Giltner deployed to cover the bridge a mile east of the town of Marion. "Had he remained with this force within the very strong fortifications which surrounded the salt-works it would have been very difficult, if not impossible for us to have taken the place," Stoneman said; "but, as I had hoped, he followed us, and on our return we met him in a strong position near Marion . . . Night coming on, and the troops of Burbridge being very much disarranged, I determined to postpone any further offensive operations until the following morning, and spent the fore part of the night getting things straightened out."[10]

Far behind the lines, Wilson's cavalry corps was still being assembled that day. Brigadier General Emory Upton, who had recovered from the wound he had received at the battle of the Opequon, was the new commander of its 4th Division, and he telegraphed Wilson that day from Cairo, Illinois, about the part of his command that was coming from Missouri: "Found Winslow's command here—part was ordered to Paducah, by General Meredith; part to Memphis, by General Washburn. Have sent all to Louisville."[11] Then he headed for Memphis to round up his other brigade. The 2nd Division was still at Louisville trying to get horses and equipment and trying to deal with guerrillas pillaging the area.

It was raining in middle Tennessee on the seventeenth, when, at 3 a.m., Wilson received an order from Thomas, written hours earlier, to "leave Johnson's division of cavalry on the Hillsborough pike, to observe the enemy and protect our right and rear, and move with the balance of your command over to the Franklin pike, to operate on that road and the road running east of the same."[12] This was not at all what Wilson had planned. "It seems to me that I shall be able to do the enemy more damage by crowding him now by the shortest roads," he replied, "instead of losing any time to get to the other flank. I have already ordered Johnson to move very early by the Hillsborough pike for Franklin, and will do the best I possibly can with the balance of the force . . . I will send Croxton and Knipe direct to the Franklin pike; Hatch will strike it at Brentwood. I sent you word last night that I would try to get into Franklin with the whole force, but your dispatch does not acknowledge the receipt of my communication. I feel obliged to press toward the other flank . . . The infantry ought . . . to crowd the enemy vigorously on the Franklin pike, and, if possible, prevent a junction of Hood and the forces now in the direction of Murfreesboro. I'll have reveille sounded, and move forward at once."[13]

The Union infantry on the Franklin pike, however, delayed by darkness and rain, did not begin its pursuit until 8 a.m. The men themselves were impatient and anxious to catch up with the defeated Rebels, and they were singing "Dixie" as they took to the muddy road. The Confederates, on the other hand, had been on the road since before daylight, and by early morning so many of the scattered units and individuals had come together that their columns began to look like an army again. However, many of the men were without weapons, having already thrown away their rifles and equipment in order to lighten their load and hasten their flight.

Two brigades of S. D. Lee's Corps still served as rear guard, but around dawn some of Chalmers' cavalrymen rode past them, heading north. "They were going back to show us how to whip Yankees," they told one of Lee's officers, "so we need not be afraid anymore."[14] About an hour later Lee's men had stopped where an extention of the Granny White Pike met the Franklin Pike, with a battery of artillery deployed across the road, when they heard firing to the north. Soon a large force of horsemen came pounding down the pike toward them. They were wearing blue overcoats, but so many Rebel cavalrymen wore captured Union overcoats that it was hard to tell whether these were Federals or Confederates. Only when they were very close could Lee's infantry tell that they were both Chalmers' men, fleeing for their lives, and some of Wilson's mixed in with them, shooting and sabering the Rebels around them. The Federals did not seem to notice the Confederate infantry until it opened fire, driving them back the way they had come. At about 9 a.m. two regiments of Knipe's division charged Lee's line but were repulsed with heavy losses. However, an hour later the Confederates moved on to the south when Lee received word that the Union cavalry was advancing along other roads and threatening to cut him off.

At last, at 10:30 a.m., Wilson's troopers came within sight of Franklin, where the last Confederate wagons were crossing the Harpeth River and the pontoon bridge was beginning to be dismantled. All that stood between the Federals and those wagons were some of Buford's cavalry, just arrived from north of Murfreesboro, and Brigadier General Randall Gibson's brigade of Clayton's Division of S. D. Lee's corps, posted, with two guns, in an earthwork near the bridge. The Union cavalry charged, drove Buford's men in confusion into the river, and surrounded Gibson's infantry. With the help of a pair of guns firing from the streets of Franklin across the river, Gibson's men managed to fight their way out, bringing their own guns with them, and to get across the bridge, but in such a panic that one man who fell into the river was left behind, clinging to the side of the bridge begging for help. "The last I saw of him," a Rebel officer wrote, "he was still wallowing in the mud and the men were running over him."[15]

Confederate engineers sank the floating bridge as soon as Gibson's men were across, while others toppled the railroad bridge into the rising waters of the river and other Rebels set fire to a warehouse full of ammunition. Then, to keep the town from being bombarded by the Federals, Lee ordered all Confederates to leave and move on to the south. As the Rebels left, a civilian ran to the burning building with a ladder and threw enough buckets of water on it to prevent the ammunition from exploding.

The Rebels left just in time, for as they marched out at about 10:30 a.m., Johnson's division of Union cavalry rode into town after having followed the Hillsborough Pike to where it forded the river west of Franklin. These Federals captured about fifty Rebels who failed to get out of the way in time. Then Knipe's troopers forded the river near the fallen railroad bridge after having captured 75 men of Holtzclaw's Brigade who had failed to reach the bridge before it was destroyed. Also captured were about 2,000 wounded Confederates who had been left in the town, most of whom had been wounded in the battle at Franklin, while 200 Federal wounded were liberated.

Wilson sent a dispatch to Thomas's chief of staff at 1 p.m., saying "The rebels are on a great skedaddle . . . The prisoners report the rebel army in a complete rout . . . The Harpeth is rising rapidly; all bridges down. Shove up the infantry and get up the pontoons." He sent Hatch's and Knipe's men in direct pursuit down the Columbia Pike, Johnson's division down the Carter's Creek Pike to the west, and Croxton's brigade down the Lewisburg Pike to the east. Wood's Union 4th Corps reached the north bank of the Harpeth at about 1:20 p.m. but could not cross the rain-swollen stream. Ten minutes after that Wilson sent another dispatch to Thomas's chief of staff: "The rebels began passing through

here early yesterday morning—cavalry, artillery, and infantry. One of
our surgeons here says he never saw a worse rabble; they are completely
demoralized. I'll do what I can for the rear guard. Can't hear definitely
of Forrest, though it is reported he withdrew from Murfreesboro yesterday."[16]

In the old earthworks south of Franklin, S. D. Lee placed some of
Holtzclaw's men, and a few volleys from them drove off the Union
pursuers for a while. Lee, despite a wound in the heel from a shell
fragment, continued to direct the rear guard, and now he ordered the
remnants of Stevenson's Division to replace Clayton's tired men in that
job. Stevenson's infantry marched south along the Columbia Pike, and
some of Chalmers' cavalry covered each flank. But by midafternoon
Wilson's troopers had forced the Confederates to deploy into line of
battle, and that slowed their progress considerably over the muddy fields.
At about 4 p.m., in open country a mile north of the West Harpeth
River, Wilson deployed Coon's brigade of Hatch's division and Hammond's brigade of Knipe's division to overlap the Confederate flanks.
Then he ordered his own escort, 200 men of the 4th U.S. Cavalry under
Lieutenant Joseph Hedges, to charge down the pike. "They swooped
down on us with pistols, carbines, and sabers, hewing, whacking, and
shooting," a Rebel officer said. Again there was the confusion of telling
friend from foe because so many Rebels were wearing captured blue
overcoats. Two hundred troopers and 200 horses crashed into 700 infantrymen, and some of the Confederates scattered to avoid the collision,
but enough stayed to fight to drive the regulars off. Lieutenant Hedges
found himself cut off from his retreating men, but he yelled, "The Yankees are coming, run for your lives," and the ruse worked long enough
for Hedges to get away.[17]

Meanwhile the 2nd Iowa Cavalry of Hatch's division slammed into
Buford's Rebel troopers, and the Confederate cavalry "retired in disorder," as Stevenson later put it in his report, "leaving my small command
to their fate."[18] His supporting artillery also withdrew, so Stevenson
deployed his men on three sides of a hollow square and fell back. Fighting
every step of the way, the Rebel infantry managed to get across the West
Harpeth shortly before dark. Stevenson had just halted to reform his
line on the other side, partly behind a roadside fence, when Hatch's
cavalrymen struck him again. The Federals were almost on top of his
men before they got off a shot. There followed a hand-to-hand fight in
the gathering darkness which, "for fierceness," a veteran sergeant in the
2nd Iowa said, "exceeded any the regiment ever engaged in." There was,
for instance, a Union private who pointed his Spencer carbine at a Rebel
and ordered him to surrender. Instead, the Confederate fired at the pri-

vate but missed. The Rebel then pleaded for mercy, but the enraged Federal fired anyway. He too missed. The Confederate drew a revolver and shouted, "Damn you, I'll teach you to shoot at me after I have surrendered."[19] But the Union private knocked him down with the butt of his carbine, chambered another round, and shot him dead.

Stevenson's men went streaming down the Columbia Pike, abandoning three 12-pounder guns when Hatch, armed with nothing more dangerous than a riding crop, and nine of his men overtook them. Not far to the south the retreating Confederates came upon Clayton's Division deployed across the road, and it, although shaken by the sight of Stevenson's men streaming past, stopped Hammond's brigade of Union cavalry. Holtzclaw's Rebel brigade went forward to help Stevenson's stragglers get away but ran into the 9th Illinois Cavalry of Hatch's division, whose Spencer repeaters lit up the sky with volley after volley. The Rebels fell back to Thompson's Station in the dark and flopped down in the mud there with the rest of S. D. Lee's weary troops for some badly needed sleep. They had been fighting and marching for three days with little rest or food.

"We have 'bust up' Stevenson's division of infantry, a brigade of cavalry, and taken three guns," Wilson told Thomas's chief of staff in a 6 p.m. message sent from three miles north of Thompson's Station. "The Fourth Cavalry and Hatch's division, supported by Knipe, made several beautiful charges, breaking the rebel infantry in all directions. There has been a great deal of night firing, volleys and cannonading from our guns—the rebels have none. It is very dark, and our men are considerably scattered, but I'll collect them on this bank of the stream—West Harpeth. Hatch is a brick!" Seventy minutes later he added: "Upon further investigation I find that Knipe's division participated most handsomely in the affair of this evening; nothing could have been more brilliant than the behavior of the troops. If it had only been light we would certainly have destroyed their entire rear guard; as it was, they were severely punished. The guns will be sent in as soon as wheels can be fitted to the carriages. My command needs forage badly; this country seems to be entirely stripped. I will assemble everything, except Croxton's brigade, along the line of the West Harpeth to-night. Johnson must be near our right flank. As soon as it is light in the morning, and everything fed, I will push forward."[20]

Hood made his headquarters that night at Spring Hill and sent a brief report to Beauregard and Secretary of War Seddon which gave little hint of the disasterous disintegration of his army. He admitted that he had lost fifty guns but claimed that he still had enough artillery. He also claimed that his losses in killed and wounded were light and thought that the number of his men who had been captured was also low. As for his headlong retreat, he said only that he was "moving to the south of Duck River."[21]

Thomas was near Franklin that night and sent a request to Admiral S. P. Lee, commanding the naval forces on the western rivers, to send one or two ironclads and a few gunboats up the Tennessee River to attack any bridge Hood might be laying across it. Admiral Lee was among the numerous Federal officers and officials who sent Thomas their congratulations that day. "I am deeply impressed," Lee said, "with the belief that our whole country will now or hereafter appreciate the generalship, statesmanship, and patriotism of your campaign, resulting in the signal defeat of General Hood's army, in which centered the strength and hopes of half the rebellion . . ." Meade sent word that he had ordered the Army of the Potomac to fire a 100-gun salute the next day in honor of the victory. Sheridan sent word that the Army of the Shenandoah had already fired 200 guns.

General Logan wired Grant that morning from Louisville, which was as far as he had gotten on his way to Nashville: "Have just arrived. Weather bad; raining since yesterday morning. People here jubilant over Thomas' success. Confidence seemed to be restored. I will remain here to hear from you. All things going right. It would seem best that I return to join my command with Sherman."[22]

John Wilkes Booth checked out of the National Hotel in Washington, D.C., that day and went to Baltimore. From there he brought a 19-year-old prostitute named Ellen Starr (alias Ella Turner or Fannie Harrison) back to a high class bordello run by her sister, Mrs. Mary Jane Treakle (alias Molly Turner).

---

1. *Official Records*, 45:I:792.
2. Ibid., 45:I:804.
3. Ibid., 45:I:792.
4. Ibid., 45:I:811.
5. Ibid., 45:I:820.
6. Ibid., 45:I:820–821.
7. Sherman, *Memoirs*, 684–686.
8. Ibid., 687.
9. *Official Records*, 45:I:792.
10. Ibid., 45:I:811–812.

11. Ibid., 45:II:242.
12. Ibid., 45:II:218–219.
13. Ibid., 45:II:237.
14. Sword, *Embrace an Angry Wind*, 394.
15. Ibid., 395.
16. *Official Records*, 45:II:237–238.
17. Sword, *Embrace an Angry Wind*, 398.
18. *Official Records*, 45:I:696.
19. Sword, *Embrace an Angry Wind*, 399.
20. *Official Records*, 45:II:238–239.
21. Ibid., 45:II:698.
22. Ibid., 45:II:230.

CHAPTER FORTY-FOUR

We Had Reason to Be Content

18–22 December 1864

On the 18th of December Sherman received Hardee's answer to his demand for the surrender of Savannah. In it the Confederate commander denied that Sherman's lines were close enough to allow his artillery to throw shells into the city and that he had cut the Rebels' line of supply: "The position of your forces (a half-mile beyond the outer line for the land-defense of Savannah) is, at the nearest point, at least four miles from the heart of the city. That and the interior line are both intact. Your statement that you have, for some days, held and controlled every avenue by which the people and garrison can be supplied, is incorrect. I am in free and constant communication with my department. Your demand for the surrender of Savannah and its dependent forts is refused. With respect to the threats conveyed in the closing paragraphs of your letter . . . I have to say that I have hitherto conducted the military operations intrusted to my direction in strict accordance with the rules of civilized warfare, and I should deeply regret adoption of any course by you that may force me to deviate from them in future."[1]

Sherman wrote to Grant that day, enclosing a copy of Hardee's reply. "You will notice," he said, "that I claim that my lines are within easy cannon-range of the heart of Savannah; but General Hardee asserts that we are four and a half miles distant. But I myself have been to the intersection of the Charleston and Georgia Central Railroads, and the three-mile post is but a few yards beyond, within the line of our pickets. The enemy has no pickets outside of his fortified line (which is a full quarter of a mile within the three-mile post), and I have the evidence of Mr. R. R. Cuyler, President of the Georgia Central Railroad (who was a prisoner in our hands), that the mile-posts are measured from the Exchange, which is but two squares back from the river. By to-morrow morning I will have six thirty-pound Parrotts in position, and General Hardee will learn whether I am right or not . . . General Hardee refers to his still being in communication with his department. This language he thought would deceive me; but I am confirmed in the belief that the route to which he refers . . . is inadequate to feed his army and the people of Savannah, and General Foster assures me that he has his force on that very road, near the head of Broad River, so that cars no longer run between Charleston and Savannah . . . In anticipation of leaving this country, I am continuing the destruction of their railroads, and at this moment have two divisions and the cavalry at work breaking up the Gulf Railroad . . . so that, even if I do not take Savannah, I will leave it in a bad way. But I still hope that events will give me time to take Savannah, even if I have to assault with some loss. I am satisfied that, unless we take it, the gunboats never will, for they can make no impression upon the batteries which guard every approach from the sea. I have a faint belief that, when Colonel Babcock reaches you, you will delay operations long enough to enable me to succeed here. With Savannah in our possession at some future time if not now, we can punish South Carolina as she deserves, and as thousands of the people in Georgia hoped we would do. I do sincerely believe that the whole United States, North and South, would rejoice to have this army turned loose in South Carolina, to devastate that State in the manner we have done in Georgia, and it would have a direct and immediate bearing on your campaign in Virginia."[2]

"The ground was difficult," Sherman said in his memoirs, "and, as all former assaults had proved so bloody, I concluded to make one more effort to completely surround Savannah on all sides, so as further to excite Hardee's fears, and, in case of success, to capture the whole of his army. We had already completely invested the place on the north, west, and south, but there remained to the enemy, on the east, the use of the old dike or plank-road leading into South Carolina, and I knew that Hardee would have a pontoon-bridge across the river. On examining my maps, I thought that the division of Brigadier General John P. Hatch, belonging to General Foster's command, might be moved from its then position at Broad River, by water, down to Bluffton, from which it could reach this plank-road, fortify and hold it—at some risk, of course, because Hardee could avail himself of his central position to fall on this detachment with his whole army." Sherman said that he did not want to make a mistake like Ball's Bluff, a disaster that had befallen a division of the Army of the Potomac back in 1862 when it had crossed the Potomac upstream from Washington and been driven back into the river. "So, taking one or two of my personal staff, I rode back to King's Bridge, leaving with Generals Howard and Slocum orders to make all possible preparations, but not to attack, during my two or three days' absence; and there I took a boat for Warsaw Sound, whence Admiral Dahlgren conveyed me in his own boat (the Harvest Moon) to Hilton Head, where I represented the matter to General Foster, and he promptly agreed to give his personal attention to it."[3]

Sherman's troops were not so sanguine about the plan. As one officer put it, "He won't do it . . . Foster's an old granny . . . Those eastern fellows never do anything clever . . . They appear to fail in everything they undertake."[4] Perhaps more to the point were the comments of a Confederate officer written long after the war. He said that Sherman should have sent part of his own forces across the Savannah River to cut the only line of retreat. "Having an overwhelming force, his movement should have been a prompt and vigorous one to the rear of Savannah, and not a voyage to Hilton Head to borrow forces from General Foster."[5]

At 7:30 a.m. on the eighteenth Wood's 4th Corps finally began to cross the Harpeth River at Franklin. Thomas had mistakenly ordered his pontoon train down the Murfreesboro Pike when he had meant to say the Franklin Pike, and it had gone fifteen miles down the road before the error had been discovered. Then it had turned into a country road that led across to Franklin, but this was so muddy that the 500 horses and mules had become completely mired down, forcing the train to turn back to Nashville to start all over again. So Wood had found it necessary to improvise. The 9th Indiana had worked all night in the cold and rising water with few tools and scanty materials to build a bridge that was almost washed away once, but by daylight it was pronounced ready for use. The intermittent rain that had fallen all night turned into a steady downpour just as the Federals began to cross.

Miles to the south, Wilson's cavalry moved out at daylight, and at about 11 a.m. it chased Confederate stragglers out of Spring Hill. But the rain continued to fall and any movement off the macadamized turnpike was extremely difficult. Despite constant skirmishing during the rest of the day, the Union troopers were never able to force the Rebel rear guard to stand and fight. There was no food for the men or forage for the horses because supply wagons had been stopped by the unfordable Harpeth and had not yet caught up. So when Wilson heard that the Confederates had two pontoon bridges across the Duck River at Columbia to facilitate their escape he put his exhausted troopers into camp several miles south of Spring Hill.

The rain finally stopped at about 3 p.m. and Wood's infantry marched past the resting cavalry at about 4:15 p.m. and kept going until darkness began to fall. Then they bivouacked about seven miles north of Columbia and about half that north of Rutherford Creek. Steedman's brigades got only about three miles south of Franklin before he received orders from Thomas to march his forces to Murfreesboro and to take the railroad from there to reoccupy Decatur, Alabama, which had been abandoned upon Hood's advance into Tennessee. He was also to see if he could move to the west from there and capture or destroy any Confederate bridge over the Tennessee River. Smith's divisions also crossed the Harpeth that day and Schofield's corps, bringing up the rear, camped that night just north of Franklin.

Many of the Federals took this chance to revisit the field where they had fought so desperately just eighteen days before. "I could not resist the temptation to go over the scene of our night struggle," one officer wrote. "I never want to see another battlefield like that." The field had become a vast cemetery, with some of the old defenses serving as mass graves. "The enemy had thrown our dead into the ditch," said another officer. "The rails which formed the revetment of the bank had been dumped in, on top of the bodies, and enough earth was then shovelled in to nearly fill the trench." But the rains of the past week had washed away so much of the dirt that many arms, legs, and even complete decaying corpses were now exposed. "The bodies had been stripped of hats, coats, shoes, and sometimes even their pants and shirts," one soldier noted, "and had been dumped into the pit like so many logs in a corduroy road. In most cases the heads and feet had been uncovered by the rain, and . . . many lay entirely uncovered in all their ghastly nakedness." Volunteers were found to rebury many of the exposed corpses on a hill behind the Carter house. The Federals were amazed at the sheer numbers of dead Confederates who had been buried. "For the first time we began to realize the extent of the damage inflicted upon the enemy," one soldier wrote. "We were told that some of the trenches contained the remains of nearly whole regiments."[6]

Cheatham's Corps, or what was left of it, took over the Confederate rear guard duties that day. Hood made his headquarters at Columbia that night. He was feeling better about the condition of his army and the events of the past few days and had decided that his recent defeat was all the fault of Bate's Division for giving way without cause and starting a panic that had spread through the whole army. Forrest was due to arrive with the rest of the forces from Murfreesboro soon, and Hood's staff was even urging him to stop at Columbia and retreat no farther in order to hold on to some part of Tennessee.

In southwestern Virginia that morning Stoneman's raiders and Breckinridge's Confederate defenders faced each other across the Middle Fork of the Holston River near Marion. Stoneman knew that if the brigade he had sent to attack the lead works was on schedule it would reach Seven-Mile Ford, behind Breckinridge, that afternoon. To further cut the Rebels off from Saltville he sent Gillem's brigade to get around their left flank while the rest of his command attacked the Confederates to hold them in place. Stoneman later sent an officer to tell Gillem to attack the Rebels from behind, but the officer misunderstood and told Gillem to return the way he had come instead. However, Breckinridge was nearly out of ammunition and when he learned that night that a Union force was at Seven-Mile Ford and that another enemy column had moved around his left, he withdrew his forces at 11 p.m. and retreated over a range of mountains to the south.

Rodes' Division, now under Grimes, reached Petersburg on the eighteenth from the Shenandoah Valley, but that same day General Lee learned that a Union fleet had left Hampton Roads, presumably to attack Fort Fisher. By then Butler's transports had been anchored about twenty miles offshore and eighteen miles north of the fort for two days and three nights, but Admiral Porter's fleet was still not there. "Weather fine, calm and warm, yet all unused. And here we are without one thing to relieve the monotony and sameness," a sergeant in Butler's force wrote. "Oh! How I long to feel solid ground again," another soldier told his diary. "Inclined to the belief that my former fondness for the ocean was bosh. Oh when will this tiresome floating about end."[7]

The navy finally arrived at the rendezvous point that night. Loading the powder onto the *Louisiana*, the boat that was to be exploded near the fort, had taken longer than expected, and then the fleet had had to wait for a high tide in order to leave Beaufort. Butler and Porter were on such poor terms that they avoided meeting face to face, communicating only by dispatches. The general was surprised to learn that Porter had already sent the powder boat toward the fort to be detonated right away. Butler sent General Weitzel and Lieutenant Colonel Cyrus Comstock, one of Grant's aides, over to protest this move. The wind was up and a gale might very well be brewing, which would prevent the troops from being landed right away, and that would give the Rebels time to recover from the explosion before the army could attack. Butler wanted to wait a day to see if the good weather would hold. So the admiral sent a fast tug to order the *Lousiana* returned.

By the next morning, the nineteenth, the wind had picked up, the calm sea was replaced by light swells, and a storm seemed likely. Porter signaled to Butler that, since a landing was impractical, he was going to exercise his fleet by putting his ships through battle formations and rehearsing the plan of attack. In battle lines the naval ships steamed to within five miles of the fort, close enough to be seen from there. By that evening the wind was blowing hard from the northeast, the sea was rolling in whitecap waves, and experienced seamen said a gale was coming and the landing would have to be postponed. The troop transports were low on drinking water and coal for the engines by then, so Butler took them into Beaufort to ride out the storm and stock up on supplies.

Hardee's engineers completed the bridge that they had been building on the nineteenth, not as a line of supply for Savannah, but as a line of retreat for Hardee's troops. He gave orders for a heavy artillery barrage to be fired at sundown the next day to cover the noise of his withdrawal. It was none too soon, for that same day a brigade from Slocum's left wing of Sherman's army was ferried across the river to the South Carolina side above Savannah, where it was a threat to Hardee's line of retreat. Jefferson Davis received a dispatch from Beauregard that day, dated the day before: "General Sherman demanded the surrender of Savannah yesterday of General Hardee, which was refused. The city must be evacuated soon as practicable. The loss of Savannah will be followed by that of the railroad from Augusta to Charleston, and soon after of Charleston itself. Cannot Hoke's and Johnson's divisions be spared for the defense of South Carolina and Georgia until part or whole of Hood's army could reach Georgia?"[8] Those two divisions were the forces Beauregard had commanded at Petersburg and now constituted Anderson's Corps of Lee's army. President Davis forwarded the dispatch to Lee, who said that sending those two divisions south would "necessitate the abandonment of Richmond."[9] Lee had already ordered Longstreet to send a division to protect Fort Fisher and Wilmington from Butler's expedition, and Longstreet had chosen Hoke's Division for that job, saying "I have no better troops."[10] Hoke was ordered to move one of his brigades to Richmond at daylight, where it would be put on a train to North Carolina. And his other brigades were to follow as soon as transportation could be arranged for them.

In the Shenandoah Valley that day, Sheridan finally moved to comply with Grant's desire for a raid on the Virginia Central Railroad around Gordonsville and Charlottesville. He sent Torbert, with Merritt's 1st and Powell's 2nd divisions of cavalry through Chester Gap to make the raid while Custer's 3rd Division went up the Valley toward Staunton to draw the Confederate's attention away from the main force. That same day, President Lincoln issued a call for another 300,000 volunteers.

In southwestern Virginia on the nineteenth, when Stoneman discovered that Breckinridge had retreated during the night he sent the 12th Ohio Cavalry after it and it captured the Confederates' caissons and wagons. "But finding the road blockaded with trees and other obstructions," Stoneman later reported, "I concluded it would be but a waste of time to pursue him, and that night concentrated my whole force near Glade Springs, preparatory to our attack on the salt-works the next day."[11]

Up in Kentucky that day, the vanguard of La Grange's brigade of McCook's cavalry division, a battalion of 100 men, caught up with the rear guard of Lyon's fleeing Confederate raiders at 4 p.m. that day just three miles from a ferry over the Green River near Ashbysburg. "In the excitement of the chase," La Grange later reported, "we soon found ourselves nearly across a causeway two miles in length, flanked on both sides by a swamp impassable for cavalry, and confronted by at least double our numbers advantageously posted, while the enemy's dismounted men occupied an old earth-work directly in our front. Under these circumstances a messenger was sent to hurry forward the column, and as a ruse to gain time a flag was sent with a demand for the immediate surrender of all the rebel force south of the river. General Lyon, understanding the real situation, declined compliance, and on the appearance of our column, scattered between 200 and 300 mounted men, under Captain Gracey, in the woods, and hastily crossed his dismounted men in the ferry-boats, which he destroyed. Our advance drove a portion of his rear guard into the river, killing 1 and capturing 7. A number were drowned in swimming the river. At this point four baggage wagons, an ambulance, a quantity of medical stores, and some small-arms and equipments were abandoned by the enemy. He had dropped most of his conscripts and prisoners between Madisonville and Ashbysburg."[12]

Before daylight on the nineteenth Forrest reached Columbia, Tennessee, and conferred with Hood. After sending Buford's Division across country to join up with the main army, he had moved south, on Hood's orders, toward Pulaski with Jackson's Division, his attached infantry brigades, his wagons, wounded, prisoners, and a great herd of cattle and hogs that he had collected. However, after part of his command had forded the Duck River on the seventeenth, rising water had prevented the rest from getting across. So the remainder of his force had marched down the north bank and crossed on Hood's pontoon bridge at Columbia the night before. Forrest was exhausted, soaking wet, and upset over the failure of the campaign, and he was in no mood to suffer fools in silence. He told Hood that if he was not sure he could hold the line of the Duck River he should withdraw back across the Tennessee. Hood therefore decided to continue his retreat, and his wagons and guns began to roll south that day, while Forrest's cavalry was sent to support Cheatham's rear guard, entrenched on high ground on the south bank of Rutherford Creek.

A steady rain was falling as Wood's Union infantry felled trees and tried to bridge the creek, but the treetrunks were not long enough to reach across the stream and they were soon swept away by the strong current. The creek was much too deep to ford, fifteen feet in most places, and still rising. Some of Wood's men thought they had found a suitable crossing place and they built a makeshift bridge. But after they crossed they found that they had only bridged a tributary, not the main stream. However, at about 4 p.m., on Hood's orders, the Confederates abandoned the Rutherford Creek line and fell back across the Duck River into Columbia. Forrest and Cheatham argued over who had the right to cross first, but by midnight Hood's entire army was south of the Duck River. The pontoon bridge was then taken up, and now an even larger rain-swollen stream separated Hood from his pursuers.

The next day the rain let up for a while but the temperature dropped again as Hood's troops began to march south, heading for Pulaski. Forrest was now put in charge of the rear guard with his cavalry, which was down to about 3,000 men, plus a makeshift division of infantry, commanded by Major General Edward Walthall and composed of the remnants of eight small brigades. After culling out 400 soldiers who did not have shoes, this force numbered only 1601 men. "It is a post of great honor," Hood told Walthall, "but one of such great peril that I will not impose it on you unless you are willing to take it . . . The army must be saved, come what may, and if necessary your command must be sacrificed to accomplish it." Walthall said, "General, I have never asked a hard place for glory nor a soft place for comfort, but take my chances as they come. Give me the order for the troops, and I will do my best."[13]

The evacuation of Columbia was completed before the day was over. As Hood rode south past Cheatham's men some of them asked him when he would give them a furlough. "After we cross the Tennessee," he told them. "Boys, the cards were fairly dealt at Nashville, and Thomas beat the game," he added. "Yes, General," one of them shot back, "but the cards were damned badly shuffled!"[14] By late afternoon Hood's leading units were within a few miles of Pulaski, which was already full of wagons, stragglers, and railroad cars loaded with ammunition and wounded soldiers. South of that town there was neither an operating railroad nor a turnpike, only dirt roads now turned to mud.

By midmorning the Federals had two clumsy foot bridges built over Rutherford Creek and Wood's infantry and Hatch's division of cavalry began to cross. The cavalry took the lead and arrived at the north bank of the Duck River across from Columbia by early afternoon. They found the bridges down and the town looking nearly deserted, but Hatch brought up several guns and began to shell it. Forrest soon appeared on the ruined abutment of the turnpike bridge with a flag of truce. He shouted across the river that there was no use in shelling the town for the Confederates were all gone except for the sick and wounded. Only civilians would be hurt. He also offered to exchange prisoners but Hatch refused.

Wood sent back word of the situation to Thomas, who by then had reached Rutherford Creek, and the latter said that A. J. Smith would assist in getting the pontoon train to the front. He wanted the entire army across the Duck River by the end of the next day, and he put the 4th Corps to work gathering forage for the horses pulling the pontoons south. The railroad could not run south of Franklin because its bridge across the Harpeth had not yet been repaired, and supplies were beginning to be a real problem for the men as well. Wilson sent his two dismounted brigades back to the north that day to ease his supply problems, ordering them back to Louisville to get horses, and Wood asked for 15,000 pairs of shoes and socks to replace the damage done by the macadamized turnpike and the wet weather. A cold, hard rain began to fall late that afternoon, and that night the rain turned to sleet.

John Singleton Mosby returned to northern Virginia on the twentieth from a two-week trip to Richmond. While there he had managed to get an old college friend transfered from an infantry regiment to be his unit's new surgeon. The one he had, he said, was "too fond of fighting. I want one that will take more pride in curing than in killing."[15] He had also received War Department permission to put into effect his plan of dividing his command into two battalions. Two of his officers were to be promoted to command the battalions, and Mosby himself was promised promotion from lieutenant colonel to full colonel. Henceforth, part of his command would operate in the area between the lower Potomac and Rappahannock rivers, known as the Northern Neck. This was the area through which Lincoln was to be brought to Richmond should Confederate agents succeed in capturing him.

In spite of the cold, wet weather and the recent damage done to his area by Merritt's division of Union cavalry, Mosby's men were in high spirits, for there was a party that night in celebration of the wedding of Mosby's ordnance sergeant, Jake Lavender. The guests had just begun to arrive for the reception at a house near Rectortown, east of the Blue Ridge, when a scout brought word that Union cavalry were coming their way. Mosby and one of his men, Tom Love, rode out to have a look and came close enough to a couple of Federal flankers to get shot at. But they managed to get enough of a look at the main force to see that it consisted of about 500 troopers. Soon they saw smoke rising from the railroad cut at Rectortown and Mosby reasoned that the Federals were camping there for the night. He and Love stopped at a nearby farmhouse to leave word for his two new battalion commanders to attack the Union bivouac at dawn. Then they rode toward Rector's Cross Roads to gather more of his men.

By then it was dark and a freezing rain was falling. The road was frozen and slick, and ice was beginning to coat the bare branches of the trees. The light from the window of the nearby home of Ludwell Lake, the father of one of Mosby's men, thus looked all the more inviting as he and Love rode by, and the two were reminded that they had not yet had dinner. They tethered their horses out front, draped their weapons over their saddles, and went to the door. Their timing was excellent, for they entered the house just as Mr. Lake and his daughter were about to sit down at the table. The daughter had recently returned from a visit to her husband in the Federal prison at Point Lookout, Maryland. "We were enjoying our supper," Mosby later wrote, "and her account of the trip . . . when suddenly we heard the tramp of horses around the house. One door of the dining room opened toward the back yard, and on opening it, I discovered several cavalrymen."

The Federal column had not bivouacked at Rectortown but had only stopped there for a brief rest, and now over 300 Union troopers were nearing the front gate. The men in the back yard were part of an advanced party which had stopped to investigate after seeing the pair of horses with military trappings tethered out front. "Hastily shutting the door," Mosby said, "I turned . . . but just then a number of Northern officers and soldiers walked into the room . . . I placed my hands on my coat collar to conceal my stars, and a few words passed between us. The situation seemed desperate . . . I knew that if they discovered my rank, to say nothing of my name, they would guard me . . . carefully.

"But only a few seconds elapsed before firing began in the back yard. One of the bullets passed through the window, making a round hole in the glass and striking me in the stomach . . . My self-possession in concealing the stars on my collar saved me from being carried off a prisoner, dead or alive. The officers had not detected the strategem, when I exclaimed, 'I am shot!' . . . My exclamation was not because I felt hurt, but to get up a panic in order that I might escape. It had the desired effect. Old man Lake and his daughter waltzed around the room, the cavalrymen on the outside kept up their fire, and this created a stampede of the officers in the room with me. In the confusion to get out of the way there was a sort of hurdle race, in which the supper table was knocked over, and the tallow lights put out. In a few seconds I was left in the room with no one but Love, Lake, and his daughter . . .

"By this time the terrible wound was having its effect; I was bleeding profusely and getting faint. There was a door which opened from the dining room into an adjoining bedroom, and I determined to play the part of a dying man. I walked into the room, pulled off my coat, on which were the insignia of my rank, tucked it away under the bureau so that no one could see it, and then lay down with my head towards the bureau. After several minutes the panic subsided, and the Northerners returned . . . They found my old friend Lake dancing a hornpipe . . . Having heard me fall on the floor, he thought I was dead—the truth was he was almost as near dead as I was. The daughter was screaming, the room in which I lay was dark, and it was some minutes before the soldiers collected their senses sufficiently to strike a light."[16] Love was soon made a prisoner, while Lake and his daughter were questioned about the identity of the wounded man. However, they both swore that they had never seen him before.

Major Douglas Frazer was in command of the Federal patrol, and he later reported that he "found a man lying on the floor, apparently in great agony. I asked him his name; he answered, Lieutenant Johnston, Sixth Virginia Cavalry. He was in his shirt sleeves—light blue cotton shirt—no hat, no boots, and no insignia of rank; nothing to denote in the slightest degree that he was not what he pretended to be. I told him I must see his wound to see whether to bring him or not. I opened, myself, his pants, and found that a pistol bullet had entered the abdomen about two inches below and to the left of the navel; a wound that I felt assured was mortal. I therefore ordered all from the room, remarking, he will die in twenty-four hours."[17]

"I only gasped a few words," Mosby said, "and affected to be dying. They left the room hurriedly, after stripping me of my . . . trousers, evidently supposing that a dead man would have no use for them. The only sensible man among them was an Irishman, who said, as he took a last look at me, 'He is worth several dead men yet.'"

Mosby lay still for five or ten minutes, and when he was sure the Federals were gone he got up from the pool of blood on the bedroom floor and went out to where Lake and his daughter were staring into the fire. "They were as much astonished to see me as if I had risen from the tomb," he said. "We examined the wound . . . Shortly I became sick and faint. My own belief was that the wound was mortal."

Mosby wanted to be taken to the nearby home of a farmer he knew before the Federals decided to come back for another look. So Lake ordered two slaves to hitch up his ox cart, and Mosby was wrapped up in blankets and quilts and placed in it. "It was an awful night—a howling storm of snow, rain, and sleet," Mosby remembered. "I was lying on my back in the cart—we had to go two miles—over a frozen road cut into deep ruts . . . I was almost perfectly stiff with cold, and my hair was a clotted mass of ice."[18] Doctors were summoned to the farmhouse, and before morning Mosby was chloroformed and the bullet was removed. After a week's rest at various houses in the area, he was taken to his father's home.

The Federals soon learned, or figured out, that the officer they had wounded had been Mosby himself, but they could not find him again. Major Frazer, who was said to have been drunk at the time he talked to Mosby, was severely criticized by his brigade commander, Colonel William Gamble. "I have given directions," that officer reported, "that all wounded officers and men of the enemy be hereafter brought in, although I thought any officer ought to have brains and common sense enough to do so without an order."[19]

In southwestern Virginia on the twentieth, as Gillem's brigade of Stoneman's force approached Saltville it encountered Confederate resistance from pickets near Fort Breckinridge, an earthwork on a high hill a mile southwest of the town. Lieutenant Colonel Robert Taylor Preston, commander of the 4th Virginia Reserves, was in charge of the defense of the area in the absence of Breckinridge and his forces. Preston had placed two of his eleven howitzers in this work, manned by employees of the salt works, and some of his 400 reserves—old men and young boys—in rifle pits in front of it. Across the road, to the northwest, was another earthwork known as Fort Hatton with two more guns, while a third work, Fort Statham, sitting on another high hill, guarded the road Burbridge's force was following in from the south.

Late that afternoon, Burbridge's 4,000 men drove Rebel skirmishers back to Fort Statham. He proposed to Stoneman that he and Gillem, a mile to the west, make simultaneous assaults, but fog, rain, and darkness came on before they could be launched. Gillem, however, was not disposed to wait for daylight. In fact, he let the darkness work in his favor by sending two battalions of the 13th Tennessee Cavalry quietly up the road, and the defenders of Fort Breckinridge either did not see the Federals or thought that they were some of Breckinridge's men returning. At any rate, the two Union battalions rode around the base of the hill upon which the earthwork sat and into some woods behind it. There their commander, Lieutenant Colonel Brazilliah Stacy, ordered his men to dismount and lead their horses up the steep hill. When Confederate pickets finally spotted them and opened fire, the Federals mounted up and charged over the crest of the hill, scattering the reserves and artillerists in all directions. The defenders of Fort Hatton fled as well, leaving six howitzers behind. Stacy sent word of his success to Gillem, then led his men through the town of Saltville and advanced against the rear of Fort Statham only to find its three howitzers had been abandoned also.

In the foggy darkness before dawn, the rest of Stoneman's force rode into Saltville and began to smash all the engines, pumps, and kettles used for collecting the salt. Scrap metal and artillery shells were used to plug the wells, and salt was sown on the ground, as the Romans had dealt with Carthage. One Union trooper estimated that about 300 buildings were burned at the saltworks. Breckinridge, having followed a circuitous route, arrived outside the town later on the morning of the 21st, but he was badly outnumbered by Stoneman's force and could do nothing to stop the destruction.

At dusk on the twentieth, as a fog rolled in, Hardee's Confederates began crossing the long three-part floating bridge across the Savannah River to the comparative safety of South Carolina. Just as the first units stepped out on the bridge, the Rebel artillery opened fire from the landward defenses, sweeping the woods and brush in their front for two hours. Although the bombardment did not completely cover the sounds of Hardee's withdrawal it did force the Federals to keep their heads down so that they could not do anything about it. The tail of the Confederate column was across the river before dawn, and the bridge was cut loose from the western shore at 5:40 a.m. on the 21st. A few workmen were still on the bridge, setting it on fire, as the tide swung it downstream, and then they scrambled to safety on Hutchinson's Island. The Rebel engineers then cut the bridge from that island to Pennyworth Island and set it on fire, and then the last section of bridge from there to the South Carolina shore received the same treatment. The ironclad *Savannah* covered the retreat and then it was also burned to keep it out of Federal hands. Several other vessels in the river were burned as well.

The Confederate guns had stopped firing at around midnight, and by 3 a.m. Federal soldiers were entering the abandoned defenses. Brigadier General John W. Geary's 2nd Division of the 20th Corps was the first sizable Union force to enter the city itself, but various individuals and small groups also slipped in for a look and to forage. Civilian looters were already at work in the streets of Savannah when Mayor Richard Arnold and his aldermen rode out to surrender the city. Rebel cavalrymen soon stole the party's horses, however, and they were afoot by the time they met Geary coming in. A mob of women and children raided the city's warehouses and carried or dragged away barrels and sacks of rice. Union soldiers soon joined the plundering and came away not only with food but tobacco, wine, and whiskey until Geary posted guards about midmorning and restored order.

Sherman was returning from Hilton Head, where he had been conferring with Foster. "The wind blowing strong," he later wrote, "Admiral Dahlgren ordered the pilot of the Harvest Moon to run into Tybee [Sound], and to work his way through to Wassaw Sound and the Ogeechee River by the Romney Marshes. We were caught by a low tide and stuck in the mud. After laboring some time, the admiral ordered out his barge; in it we pulled through this intricate and shallow channel, and toward evening of December 21st we discovered, coming toward us, a tug, called the Red Legs, belonging to the Quartermaster's Department, with a staff officer on board, bearing letters from Captain Dayton to myself and the admiral, reporting that the city of Savannah had been found evacuated on the morning of December 21st, and was then in our possession. General Hardee had crossed the Savannah River by a pontoon-bridge, carrying off his men and light artillery, blowing up his iron-clads and navy-yard, but leaving for us all the heavy guns, stores, cotton, railway-cars, steamboats, and an immense amount of public and private property. Admiral Dahlgren concluded to go toward a vessel (the Sonoma) of his blockading fleet, which lay at anchor near Beaulieu, and I transferred to the Red Legs, and hastened up the Ogeechee River to King's Bridge, whence I rode to my camp that same night."[20]

In Washington, D.C., on the 21st the United States Congress created the naval rank of vice admiral, corresponding with Grant's rank of lieutenant general in the army, intending it for Farragut.

Not far to the southeast of Washington John Wilkes Booth met by appointment with Dr. Samuel Mudd that day at Montgomery's tavern in Bryantown, Maryland. There Mudd introduced Booth to Thomas H. Harbin (alias Thomas A. Wilson), former postmaster of Bryantown, and an experienced Confederate Secret Service agent. Harbin had come up from his post in King George County, Virginia, to meet with Booth, and the two men took an upstairs room to talk. Harbin later said that Booth's manner was "very theatrical," which was appropriate enough, considering his vocation.[21] But primarily Booth wanted to know if Harbin was prepared to assist in the capture of President Lincoln. Harbin was. Booth then went home with Dr. Mudd and remained there overnight.

In Tennessee that day, the rest of Hood's army reached Pulaski, and part of Thomas's pontoon train reached Rutherford Creek at about 1 p.m. A bridge was promptly laid across the creek so that the rest of the train, as it came up, could cross over, since the makeshift bridges the troops had built were not capable of carrying wagons. A thousand men from the 23rd Corps were detailed to help with the work amid falling snow, with frozen ropes, and boats and planking grown slippery with a coating of ice. Thomas soon realized that work on laying a bridge over the Duck River could not even be started until the next day.

That day Thomas received a telegram from Halleck that said: "Permit me, general, to urge the vast importance of a hot pursuit of Hood's army. Every possible sacrifice should be made, and your men for a few days will submit to any hardship and privation to accomplish the great result. If you can capture or destroy Hood's army Sherman can entirely crush out the rebel military force in all the Southern States. He begins a new campaign about the 1st of January, which will have the most important results, if Hood's army can now be used up. A most vigorous pursuit on your part is therefore of vital importance to Sherman's plans. No sacrifice must be spared to obtain so important an object."[22]

Thomas shot back a long, indignant reply, which said, among other things: "General Hood's army is being pursued as rapidly and as vigorously as it is possible for one army to pursue another . . . I am doing all in my power to crush Hood's army, and, if it be possible, will destroy it; but pursuing an enemy through exhausted country, over mud roads, completely sogged with heavy rains, is no child's play, and cannot be accomplished as quickly as thought of . . . Although my progress may appear slow, I feel assured that Hood's army can be driven from Tennessee, and eventually driven to the wall, by the force under my command . . ."[23]

By the morning of the 22nd, Stoneman's raiders had completed their work of destruction at Saltville, "and a more desolate looking sight can hardly be conceived than was presented to our eyes . . . by the salt-works in ruins," Stoneman said. More than 50,000 bushels of bagged salt had been destroyed or contaminated, nearly 800 evaporating kettles had been broken, the two narrow-gauge locomotives on the Saltville branch line had been demolished, and most of the slave laborers followed the Federals back to Tennessee. The wells were so badly damaged that boring new ones seemed more practical to the Confederates than re-pairing the old ones. At first the Rebels thought that they could have the works back in production in a few days, but upon closer examination this estimate was changed to a month, and in fact the salt works were never again of any use to the Confederacy before the war ended. "Our work being completed," Stoneman reported, "we had yet before us a long and arduous march through rivers swollen by the recent and almost continuous rains, along roads which had become nearly impassable, and over mountains slippery with ice and covered with snow."[24]

On the morning of 22 December, General Sherman rode down Bull Street in Savannah to the customs house, from the roof of which he had an excellent view of the city. The navy yard and the wreck of the ironclad *Savannah* were still smoldering, but all else looked quiet enough. "The city of Savannah was an old place," Sherman wrote, "and usually ac-counted a handsome one."[25] "I was disappointed that Hardee had es-caped with his army," Sherman wrote, "but on the whole we had reason to be content with the substantial fruits of victory. The Savannah River was found to be badly obstructed by torpedoes, and by log piers stretched across the channel below the city, which piers were filled with the cobble stones that formerly paved the streets."[26]

An Englishman named Charles Green offered Sherman the use of his home for a headquarters. "He only reserved for himself the use of a couple of rooms above the dining-room, and we had all else, and a most excellent house it was in all respects."[27] "Within an hour of taking up my quarters in Mr. Green's house," Sherman remembered, "Mr. A. G. Browne, of Salem, Massachusetts, United States Treasury agent for the Department of the South, made his appearance to claim possession, in the name of the Treasury Department, of all captured cotton, rice, build-ings, etc. Having use for these articles ourselves, and having fairly earned them, I did not feel inclined to surrender possession, and explained to him that the quartermaster and commissary could manage them more to my liking that he; but I agreed, after the proper inventories had been prepared, if there remained any thing for which we had no special use,

I would turn it over to him . . . At that interview, Mr. Browne, who was a shrewd, clever Yankee, told me that a vessel was on the point of starting for old Point Comfort, and, if she had good weather off Cape Hatteras, would reach Fortress Monroe by Christmas-day, and he suggested that I might make it the occasion of sending a welcome Christmas gift to the President, Mr. Lincoln, who peculiarly enjoyed such pleasantry." Sherman sat down and wrote out a telegram to be taken to Fortress Monroe and transmitted from there to Washington for President Lincoln: "I beg to present you as a Christmas-gift the city of Savannah, with one hundred and fifty guns and plenty of ammunition, also about twenty-five thousand bales of cotton."[28]

Secretary Stanton telegraphed General Thomas that day: "I have seen to-day General Halleck's dispatch of yesterday and your reply. It is proper for me to assure you that this Department has the most unbounded confidence in your skill, vigor, and determination to employ to the best advantage all the means in your power to pursue and destroy the enemy. No Department could be inspired with more profound admiration and thankfulness for the great deeds you have already performed, or more confiding faith that human effort could accomplish no more than will be done by you and the gallant officers and soldiers of your command."

General Grant also sent a wire to Thomas that day: "You have the congratulations of the public for the energy with which you are pursuing Hood. I hope you will succeed in reaching his pontoon bridge at Tuscumbia before he gets there. Should you do it, it looks to me that Hood is cut off. If you succeed in destroying Hood's army, there will be but one army left to the so-called Confederacy capable of doing us harm. I will take care of that . . ."[29]

---

1. Sherman, *Memoirs*, 688.

2. Ibid., 688–690.

3. Ibid., 692–693.

4. Davis, *Sherman's March*, 110.

5. Alexander Robert Chisolm, "The Failure to Capture Hardee," in *Battles and Leaders*, vol. 4, 680.

6. Sword, *Embrace an Angry Wind*, 403.

7. Gragg, *Confederate Goliath*, 46–47.

8. *Official Records*, 42:III:1280.

9. Ibid., 44:966.
10. Ibid., 42:III:1280.
11. Ibid., 45:I:812.
12. Ibid., 45:I:794.
13. Sword, *Embrace an Angry Wind*, 407.
14. Ibid., 408.
15. Jones, *Ranger Mosby*, 244–245.
16. Siepel, *Rebel*, 137–138.
17. *Official Records*, 43:II:843.
18. Siepel, *Rebel*, 139.
19. *Official Records*, 43:II:844.
20. Sherman, *Memoirs*, 693–694.
21. Tidwell, Hall, and Gaddy, *Come Retribution*, 337.
22. *Official Records*, 45:II:295.
23. Ibid., 45:II:295–296.
24. Ibid., 45:I:813.
25. Sherman, *Memoirs*, 708.
26. Ibid., 695.
27. Ibid.
28. Ibid., 708–711.
29. *Official Records*, 45:II:307.

EPILOGUE

The Union victory at Nashville was not the result of any brilliant plan. There was very little strategy displayed by either side during the entire campaign. It was, however, one of the most decisive battles of the war. Although the bad weather and Thomas's critical error in sending his pontoon train down the wrong road kept the pursuit from being as devastating as it might have been, Hood's army—one of the only two sizable armies the Confederacy had—was reduced in numbers, morale, and equipment to the point where it was to have little effect upon the course of the rest of the war. Still one wonders what the pursuit might have been like had it been conducted by Grant and Sheridan instead of Thomas and Wilson. The Appomattox campaign provides an answer, but that is, of course, part of the subject of the next, and final, volume in this series. Nevertheless, Thomas's conglomerate force, drawn from three different departments, captured, in the course of the entire campaign, 72 pieces of artillery and 13,180 prisoners of war, including eight generals. In addition, more than 2,000 Confederate deserters fell into Union hands between 7 September and 20 January, and approximately 8,600 Rebels were killed or wounded at Franklin and Nashville. These figures add up to about half of Hood's entire army. The Federal losses during the entire campaign came to fewer than 6,000 men.

Thomas's success gave deeper meaning to Sherman's march. Sherman had divided his own army into two parts and the smaller, more poorly organized part had defeated Hood's entire army and driven it back to its starting point. Meanwhile, Sherman had taken the larger, better organized part and had not only devastated Georgia, severed Confederate railroad connections between East and West, and captured the important port of Savannah, but he had placed this force where it threatened not only the Carolinas but, ultimately, the rear of Lee's army. Had Thomas been defeated it would have been necessary to return Sherman and his army to Tennessee, or Kentucky, or to send other forces there, from Meade's or Butler's armies and replace them with Sherman's. But with Thomas's victory Sherman could, and did, carry out his threats. The string of Federal victories that began with Sheridan in the Shenandoah and carried through to Nashville and Savannah, while Grant kept Lee too busy to interfere, put the dazed and reeling Confederacy on the ropes. Further Union moves during the winter kept it off balance, and the next spring Grant delivered the knockout blow.

I briefly considered extending the present volume to include Butler's attempt against Fort Fisher, since the launching of his expedition figured in its closing chapters, but that would have prolonged the narrative too far beyond the climatic events: the battle of Nashville and the capture of Savannah. Besides, it will be better to include both attempts against Fort Fisher together in the same final volume. For the benefit of those who are unfamiliar with the outcome, suffice it to say that Butler bungled the job badly, thus giving Grant and Lincoln an excuse to finally remove him from his command. In January the same troops were sent back under one of Butler's corps commanders, Alfred H. Terry, and, with the navy's help, this time the fort was taken.

Those expeditions, Sherman's march through the Carolinas, the fall of Richmond, Lee's surrender at Appomattox, Wilson's raid through Alabama, the capture of Mobile, the assassination of Lincoln, and the capture of Jefferson Davis will be the subject of the next volume.

Appendix A

Cast of Characters

The principal characters mentioned in this book are listed here alphabetically, with a brief description of their places in the scheme of events. Those who have only minor roles in the text, and are not likely to be confused with others, are not listed.

Abbreviations used below:
CSA—Confederate States Army
CSN—Confederate States Navy
USA—United States Army
USMA—United States Military Academy (given with class)
USN—United States Navy
USV—United States Volunteers

ABBOTT, Jospeh C.—Colonel, USV. Commander of the 2nd Brigade of Terry's 1st Division of Birney's 10th Corps in Butler's Army of the James (Department of Virginia and North Carolina).

ADAMS, John—Brigadier General, CSA (USMA 1846). Commander of a brigade in Loring's Division in Stewart's Corps of Hood's Army of Tennessee in Beauregard's Division of the West.

ALEXANDER, E. Porter—Brigadier General, CSA (USMA 1857). Chief of artillery of Anderson's (later Longstreet's) 1st Corps of Lee's Army of Northern Virginia.

AMMEN, Jacob—Brigadier General, USV (USMA 1831). Commander

of the 4th Division of the 23rd Corps in Schofield's Department of the Ohio in Sherman's Military Division of the Mississippi, garrisoning eastern Tennessee.

ANDERSON, George T. ("Tige")—Brigadier General, CSA. Commander of a brigade in Field's Division of Anderson's (later Longstreet's) 1st Corps of Lee's Army of Northern Virginia.

ANDERSON, Richard H. ("Dick")—Lieutenant General, CSA (USMA 1842). Commander of the 1st Corps of Lee's Army of Northern Virginia until Longstreet recovered from his wound. Then made commander of a new 4th Corps created from the troops around Richmond and Petersburg who had been in Beauregard's old Department of Southern Virginia and North Carolina.

ANDERSON, William ("Bloody Bill")—Captain, CSA. Leader of a band of guerrillas and bushwhackers in Missouri.

ARCHER, James J.—Brigadier General, CSA. Commander of a brigade in Heth's Division of Hill's 3rd Corps of Lee's Army of Northern Virginia.

ARMSTRONG, Frank C.—Brigadier General, CSA. Commander of a brigade of cavalry in Jackson's Division attached to Forrest's corps.

ASHBROOK, John T.—Lieutenant, CSA. One of the Confederate officers who tried to burn New York City.

ASHBY, Turner—Brigadier General, CSA. Late commander of the cavalry brigade of Stonewall Jackson's old Army of the Valley. Killed in June 1862.

AUGUR, Christopher Colon—Major General, USV (USMA 1843). Commander of the Department of Washington in Sheridan's Middle Military Division.

AVERELL, William Woods—Brigadier General, USV (USMA 1855). Commander of the 2nd Cavalry Division of the Department of West Virginia, attached to Torbert's Cavalry Corps of Sheridan's Army of the Shenandoah (Middle Military Division).

AYRES, Romeyn B.—Brigadier General, USV (USMA 1847). Commander of the 2nd Division of Warren's 5th Corps in Meade's Army of the Potomac.

BABCOCK, Orville—Lieutenant Colonel, USV (USMA 1861). Aide on Grant's staff.

BANKS, Nathaniel P.—Major General, USV. Commander of the Department of the Gulf, who made an unsuccessful campaign up the Red River in Louisiana during the spring of 1864.

BARNARD, John G.—Brigadier General, USV (USMA 1833). Chief engineer of Grant's armies operating against Richmond.

BARRETT, James—Grand Commander of the Order of the Sons of Liberty for Missouri. One of the Copperhead leaders tried by a Union military commission.

BARRINGER, Rufus—Brigadier General, CSA. Commander of a brigade in W. H. F. Lee's 3rd Division of Hampton's Cavalry Corps of Lee's Army of Northern Virginia.

BASS, Frederick—Lieutenant Colonel, CSA. Temporary commander of Gregg's Texas Brigade in Field's Division of Anderson's (later Longstreet's) 1st Corps in Lee's Army of Northern Virginia.

BATE, William B.—Major General, CSA. Commander of a division in Cheatham's Corps of Hood's Army of Tennessee in Beauregard's Division of the West.

BATTLE, Cullen—Brigadier General, CSA. Commander of a brigade in Ramseur's Division of Early's Army of the Valley.

BEALL, John Yates—Acting Master of Privateers, CSN. Confederate agent working out of Canada who seized ships on Lake Erie in an attempt to liberate prisoners of war from Johnson's Island.

BEATTY, Samuel—Brigadier General, USV. Commander of the 3rd Division of Wood's 4th Corps in Thomas's Army of the Cumberland in Sherman's Military Division of the Mississippi.

BEAUREGARD, Pierre Gustave Toutant—General, CSA (USMA 1838). Commander of the Department of Southern Virginia and North Carolina, which included Petersburg, Virginia, Hoke's and Johnson's divisions of infantry, and Dearing's brigade of cavalry. Later (17 October 1864) transferred to command of a new Division of the West, which included Hood's Army and Department of Tennessee and Taylor's Department of Alabama, Mississippi and East Louisiana.

BELL, Tyree H.—Colonel, CSA. Commander of a brigade in Buford's 2nd Division of Forrest's cavalry.

BENHAM, Henry W.—Brigadier General, USV (USMA 1837). Commander of the Volunteer Engineer Brigade of Meade's Army of the Potomac and of the defenses of Grant's headquarters at City Point.

BENJAMIN, Judah P.—Confederate Secretary of State.

BENTEEN, Frederick W.—Lieutenant Colonel, USV. Succeeded to the command of Winslow's cavalry brigade during Price's raid on Missouri. Twelve years later commanded a battalion under Custer at the battle of the Little Big Horn.

BIDDLE, James—Colonel, USV. Commander of the 2nd Brigade of Johnson's 6th Division of Wilson's Cavalry Corps of Sherman's Military Division of the Mississippi.

BIDWELL, Daniel—Brigadier General, USV. Commander of the 3rd Brigade of Getty's 2nd Division of Wright's 6th Corps in Sheridan's Army of the Shenandoah (Middle Military Division).

BIFFLE, Jacob B.—Colonel, CSA. Commander of a remnant of Dibrell's Brigade (two regiments) of Wheeler's cavalry that was attached to Chalmers' Division of Forrest's corps for the Franklin-Nashville campaign as a replacement for McCulloch's Brigade, which had been sent to the District of the Gulf.

BINGHAM, J. J.—Editor of the *Indiana State Sentinel,* chairman of the Indiana Democratic State Committee, and a prominent member of the Order of the Sons of Liberty.

BIRGE, Henry W.—Brigadier General, USV. Commander of the 1st Brigade of Grover's 2nd Division of Emory's 19th Corps in Sheridan's Army of the Shenandoah (Middle Military Division). Succeeded to command of the division at the battle of Cedar Creek.

BIRNEY, David B.—Major General, USV. Commander of the 10th Corps in Butler's Army of the James (Department of Virginia and North Carolina). Younger brother of William Birney.

BIRNEY, William—Brigadier General, USV. Commander of the 1st Brigade of the 3rd Division of David Birney's 10th Corps in Butler's Army of the James (Department of Virginia and North Carolina). Older brother of David Birney.

BLAIR, Francis P. ("Frank"), Jr.—Major General, USV. Commander of the 17th Corps in Howard's Army of the Tennessee in Sherman's Military Division of the Mississippi. Simultaneously a member of Congress. Brother of Montgomery Blair.

BLAIR, Montgomery—Postmaster General in Lincoln's cabinet. Brother of Frank Blair.

BLAZER, Richard—Captain, USV. Commander of a special detachment of Sheridan's army whose mission was to track down and destroy Mosby's partisan rangers.

BLUNT, James G.—Major General, USV. The commander of the District of the Upper Arkansas in Curtis's Department of Kansas. Led the vanguard of Curtis's forces into Missouri to slow Price's raid across that state.

BOOTH, John Wilkes—Well known actor on the American stage. Involved in a Confederate plot to capture President Lincoln, possibly for the purpose of exchanging him for a large number of Confederate prisoners of war.

BOWIE, Walter—Lieutenant, CSA. An officer in Mosby's battalion of partisan rangers who led an expedition across the lower Potomac to try to capture the governor of Maryland.

BOWLES, Pinckney D.—Colonel, CSA. Temporary commander of Law's Brigade in Field's Division of Anderson's (later Longstreet's) 1st Corps of Lee's Army of Northern Virginia.

BOWLES, Dr. William—Military commander of the Order of the Sons of Liberty in Indiana.

BRADFORD, Augustus—Governor of Maryland.

BRADLEY, Luther P.—Colonel, USV. Commander of the 3rd Brigade of Wagner's 2nd Division of Stanley's 4th Corps in Thomas's Army of the Cumberland in Sherman's Military Division of the Mississippi.

BRAGG, Braxton—General, CSA (USMA 1837). Nominal general-in-chief of the Confederate Army. Former commander of the Department and Army of Tennessee. Sent to take command of the Department of North Carolina and then sent to defend Augusta from Sherman.

BRAGG, Edward S.—Brigadier General, USV. Commander of the 1st (Iron) Brigade of Crawford's 3rd Division of Warren's 5th Corps in Meade's Army of the Potomac.

BRATTON, John—Brigadier General, CSA. Commander of a brigade in Field's Division of Anderson's (later Longstreet's) 1st Corps in Lee's Army of Northern Virginia.

BRECKINRIDGE, John C.—Major General, CSA. Commander of the Department of Southwestern Virginia and of an ad hoc corps in Early's Army of the Valley. Former vice-president of the United States. Presidential candidate of the Southern wing of the Democratic party in 1860.

BRECKINRIDGE, William C. P.—Colonel, CSA. Temporary commander of Williams' Brigade, one of three brigades detached from Wheeler's Cavalry Corps of Hood's Army of Tennessee that helped defend Saltville, Virginia. Cousin of John C. Breckinridge.

BROOKS, Noah—Newspaper reporter on friendly terms with President Lincoln.

BROWN, Egbert B.—Brigadier General, USV. Commander of the District of Central Missouri in Rosecrans' Department of Missouri and commander of the 1st Brigade in Pleasonton's ad hoc division of cavalry from that department opposing Price's raid.

BROWN, John Calvin—Major General, CSA. Commander of a division in Cheatham's Corps of Hood's Army of Tennessee in Beauregard's Division of the West.

BROWN, Joseph E.—Governor of Georgia.

BUFORD, Abraham—Brigadier General, CSA (USMA 1841). Commander of the 2nd Division of cavalry in Forrest's District of Northern Mississippi and West Tennessee in Taylor's Department of Alabama, Mississippi and East Louisiana.

BULLITT, Judge Joshua F.—Grand Commander of the Order of the Sons of Liberty for Kentucky. One of the Copperhead leaders tried by a Union military commission.

BULLOCK, Robert—Colonel, CSA. Commander of a brigade in Bate's Division of Cheatham's Corps of Hood's Army of Tennessee in Beauregard's Division of the West.

BURBRIDGE, Stephen G., Brigadier General, USV. Commander of the District of Kentucky in Schofield's Department of the Ohio in Sherman's Military Division of the Mississippi.

BURNHAM, Hiram—Brigadier General, USV. Commander of the 2nd Brigade of Stannard's 1st Division of Ord's 18th Corps in Butler's Army of the James (Department of Virginia and North Carolina).

BURNSIDE, Ambrose E.—Major General, USV (USMA 1847). Former commander of the Army of the Potomac, the Department of the Ohio, and of the 9th Corps. Briefly considered as a replacement for Burbridge in command of the District of Kentucky in Schofield's Department of the Ohio in Sherman's Military Division of the Mississippi.

BUTLER, Andrew P.—Captain, CSA. Officer on John Dunovant's staff. Cousin of Matthew Butler.

BUTLER, Benjamin Franklin—Major General, USV. Commander of the Department of Virginia and North Carolina and the Army of the James.

BUTLER, Matthew C.—Brigadier General, CSA. Commander of the 1st Division of Hampton's Cavalry Corps of Lee's Army of Northern Virginia.

CABELL, William L.—Brigadier General, CSA (USMA 1850). Commander of a brigade in Fagan's division in Price's Cavalry Corps of Kirby Smith's Trans-Mississippi Department.

CANBY, Edward R. S.—Major General, USV (USMA 1839). Commander of the Military Division of West Mississippi, consisting of the Department of Arkansas and the Department of the Gulf.

CAPRON, Horace—Colonel, USV. Commander of the 1st Brigade of Johnson's 6th Division of Wilson's Cavalry Corps of Sherman's Military Division of the Mississippi.

CARTER, Fountain B.—Owner of the property where the Columbia Pike entered the Union defenses at Franklin, Tennessee.

CARTER, T. H.—Colonel, CSA. Chief of artillery of Early's Army of the Valley.

CASEMENT, John S.—Colonel, USV. Commanded the 2nd Brigade in Cox's (briefly Reilly's) 3rd Division of the 23rd Corps in Schofield's Army of the Ohio in Sherman's Military Division of the Mississippi.

CHALMERS, James R.—Brigadier General, CSA. Commander of the 1st Division of cavalry in Forrest's District of Mississippi and West Tennessee in Taylor's Department of Alabama, Mississippi and East Louisiana.

CHASE, Salmon P.—Former Secretary of the Treasury in Lincoln's cabinet. Named by Lincoln to succeed Taney as the Chief Justice of the Supreme Court.

CHEATHAM, Benjamin Franklin—Major General, CSA. Commander of a division in Hardee's 1st Corps of Hood's Army of Tennessee. Succeeded Hardee in command of the corps.

CHENAULT, James Lieutenant, CSA. One of the Confederate officers who tried to burn New York City.

CLARK, John B., Jr.—Brigadier General, CSA. Commander of a brigade in Marmaduke's Division of Price's Cavalry Corps of Kirby Smith's Trans-Mississippi Department.

CLAY, Clement C.—Confederate commissioner to Canada.

CLAYTON, Henry D.—Major General, CSA. Commander of a division in Lee's Corps of Hood's Army of Tennessee in Beauregard's Division of the West.

CLEBURNE, Patrick R.—Major General, CSA. Commander of a division in Cheatham's Corps of Hood's Army of Tennessee in Beauregard's Division of the West.

COBB, Howell—Major General, Georgia Militia. One of several high-ranking Confederate officers gathered at Macon to oppose Sherman's march.

COCKRELL, Francis Marion—Brigadier General, CSA. Commander of a brigade in French's Division of Stewart's Corps of Hood's Army of Tennessee in Beauregard's Division of the West.

COLE, Charles—Captain, CSA. Confederate agent working out of Canada who tried to seize control of the USS *Michigan* on Lake Erie.

COLEMAN, David—Colonel, CSA. Commander of Ector's Brigade of French's Division in Stewart's Corps of Hood's Army of Tennessee in Beauregard's Division of the West.

COLLINS, Napoleon—Commander, USN. Captain of the USS *Wachusett*, who captured the CSS *Florida*.

COLQUITT, Alfred H.—Brigadier General, CSA. Commander of a brigade in Hoke's Division of Beauregard's Department of Southern Virginia and North Carolina (later Anderson's 4th Corps of Lee's Army of Northern Virginia).

COMSTOCK, Cyrus B.—Lieutenant Colonel, USV (USMA 1855). An aide on Grant's staff sent along on Butler's expedition against Fort Fisher as chief engineer.

CONNER, James—Brigadier General, CSA. Commander of a brigade in Kershaw's Division of Anderson's (later Longstreet's) 1st Corps of Lee's Army of Northern Virginia.

CONRAD, Joseph—Colonel, USV. Succeeded Bradley as commander of the 3rd Brigade of Wagner's (later Elliott's) 2nd Division of Stanley's (later Wood's) 4th Corps in Thomas's Army of the Cumberland in Sherman's Military Division of the Mississippi.

CONRAD, Thomas N.—Captain, CSA. Chaplain of the 3rd Virginia

Cavalry and Confederate secret agent sent to Washington to observe Lincoln's movements and habits.

COOK, John—Brigadier General, USV. Commander of the District of Illinois in Hooker's Northern Department.

COOKE, John R.—Brigadier General, CSA. Commander of a brigade in Heth's Division of Hill's 3rd Corps of Lee's Army of Northern Virginia.

COON, Datus E.—Colonel, USV. Commander of the 2nd Brigade of Hatch's 5th Division of Wilson's Cavalry Corps of Sherman's Military Division of the Mississippi.

COOPER, Joseph A.—Brigadier General, USV. Commander of the 1st Brigade in Couch's 2nd Division of the 23rd Corps in Schofield's Army of the Ohio in Sherman's Military Division of the Mississippi.

CORSE, John M.—Brigadier General, USV (USMA ex-1857). Commander of the 2nd Division of the 16th Corps until 23 September 1864, and then of the 4th Division of the 15th Corps, in Howard's Army of the Tennessee in Sherman Military Division of the Mississippi.

COSBY, George B.—Brigadier General, CSA (USMA 1852). Commander of a brigade of cavalry in the Department of Southwestern Virginia.

COUCH, Darius N.—Major General, USV (USMA 1846). Succeeded Ruger as commander of the 2nd Division of the 23rd Corps in Schofield's Army of the Ohio in Sherman's Military Division of the Mississippi.

COX, Jacob D.—Brigadier General, USV. Commander of the 3rd Division of Schofield's 23rd Corps, Army of the Ohio, in Sherman's Military Division of the Mississippi. In command of the entire corps during Schofield's absence and while the latter was in command of the entire Union field force at Franklin.

COX, William R.—Brigadier General, CSA. Commander of a brigade in Ramseur's Division of Early's Army of the Valley.

CRAWFORD, Samuel—Captain, USV. Staff officer in Curtis's Department of Kansas and Republican candidate for governor of Kansas.

CRAWFORD, Samuel W.—Commander of the 3rd Division of Warren's 5th Corps in Meade's Army of the Potomac.

CRITTENDEN, George B.—Colonel, CSA (USMA 1832). A former major general who had been court-martialed for drunkeness and served in various subordinate commands in the Department of Southwestern Virginia.

CROOK, George—Brigadier (later Major) General, USV (USMA 1852). Commander of the Department and Army of West Virginia in Sheridan's Middle Military Division.

CROSSLAND, Edward—Colonel, CSA. Commander of a brigade in Buford's division of Forrest's cavalry corps.

CROXTON, John T.—Brigadier General, USV. Commander of the 1st Brigade of McCook's 1st Division of the Cavalry Corps of Thomas's Army of the Cumberland. The brigade and division kept the same designations in Wilson's Cavalry Corps of Sherman's Military Division of the Mississippi.

CRUFT, Charles—Brigadier General, USV. Commander of a provisional division at the battle of Nashville made up of individuals and detachments left behind by the corps accompanying Sherman on his March to the Sea.

CURTIN, John I.—Colonel, USV. Commander of the 1st Brigade of Potter's 2nd Division of Parke's 9th Corps in Meade's Army of the Potomac.

CURTIS, Samuel R.—Major General, USV (USMA 1831). Commander of the Department of Kansas.

CUSHING, William B.—Lieutenant, USN. Commander of the attack upon the CSS *Albemare* with a spar torpedo.

CUSTER, George Armstrong—Brigadier General, USV (USMA June 1861). Commander of the 1st Brigade of Merritt's 1st Division of Torbert's Cavalry Corps in Sheridan's Army of the Shenandoah (Middle Military Division). Later briefly the commander of the 2nd Division and then commander of the 3rd Division of the same corps.

DAHLGREN, John A. B.—Rear Admiral, USN. Commander of the South Atlantic Blockading Squadron.

DANA, Charles A.—Union Assistant Secretary of War.

DAVIES, Henry E.—Brigadier General, USV. Commander of the 1st Brigade of Gregg's 2nd Division of the Cavalry Corps of Meade's Army of the Potomac. Temporarily commanded the division 12-25 September 1864.

DAVIS, Edwin P.—Colonel, USV. Commander of the 1st Brigade of

Dwight's 1st Division of Emory's 19th Corps in Sheridan's Army of the Shenandoah (Middle Military Division).

DAVIS, Jefferson—(USMA 1828). First and only president of the Confederate States of America.

DAVIS, Jefferson C.—Brigadier General, USV. Commander of the 14th Corps in Thomas's Army of the Cumberland (later Slocum's Army of Georgia) in Sherman's Military Division of the Mississippi.

DAVIS, Joseph R.—Brigadier General, CSA. Commander of a brigade in Heth's Division of Hill's 3rd Corps of Lee's Army of Northern Virginia. Nephew of President Jefferson Davis.

DEARING, James—Brigadier General, CSA (USMA ex-1862). Commander of the cavalry brigade of the Department of Southern Virginia and North Carolina, attached to Hampton's Cavalry Corps of Lee's Army of Northern Virginia.

DE FOREST, John W.—Captain, USV. Officer on Emory's staff.

DEITZLER, George Washington—Major General, Kansas State Militia. Commander of the Kansas militia forces joining Curtis in opposition to Price's Missouri raid.

DE TROBRIAND, Philip Regis D.—Brigadier General, USV. Commander of the 1st Brigade of Mott's 3rd Division of Hancock's (later Humphreys') 2nd Corps in Meade's Army of the Potomac.

DEVIN, Thomas C.—Colonel (later Brigadier General), USV. Commander of the 2nd Brigade of Merritt's 1st Division of Torbert's Cavalry Corps in Sheridan's Army of the Shenandoah (Middle Military Division).

DIBRELL, George G.—Colonel, CSA. Commander of one of the brigades detached from Wheeler's Cavalry Corps of Hood's Army of Northern Virginia that helped defend Saltville, Virginia.

DIX, John Adams—Major General, USV. Commander of the Department of the East, with headquarters at New York City.

DODD, Harrison H.—Grand Commander of the Order of the Sons of Liberty in Indiana.

DODGE, Grenville M.—Major General, USV. Commander of the Left Wing of the 16th Corps in Howard's Army of the Tennessee in Sherman's Military Division of the Mississippi until wounded on 19 August 1864 during the siege of Atlanta. Later he replaced Rosecrans as the commander of the Department of Missouri.

DOOLITTLE, Charles C.—Colonel, USV. Commander of the 18th Michigan Volunteer Infantry Regiment and of the garrison of Decatur, Alabama, where he repulsed Hood's attack. Later succeeded Reilly as commander of the 1st Brigade of Cox's (briefly Reilly's) 3rd Division of the 23rd Corps in Schofield's Army of the Ohio in Sherman's Military Division of the Mississippi.

DRAPER, Alonzo—Colonel, USV. Commander of the 2nd Brigade of Paine's 3rd Division of Ord's 18th Corps in Butler's Army of the James (Department of Virginia and North Carolina).

DuBOSE, Dudley M.—Colonel, CSA. Commander of Benning's Brigade in Field's Division of Anderson's (later Longstreet's) 1st Corps of Lee's Army of Northern Virginia.

DUFFIÉ, Alfred N.—Brigadier General, USV. Commander of the 1st Cavalry Division of Crook's Department of West Virginia in Sheridan's Middle Military Division. This division had been reduced to little more than a training and garrison command, since its best troops and all of its horses had been given to Averell's 2nd Cavalry Division.

DUNCAN, Samuel A.—Colonel (later brigadier general), CSA. Commander of the 3rd Brigade of Paine's 3rd Division of Ord's 18th Corps in Butler's Army of the James (Department of Virginia and North Carolina).

DUNOVANT, John—Brigadier General, CSA. Commander of a brigade in Butler's 1st Division of Hampton's Cavalry Corps in Lee's Army of Northern Virginia.

DU PONT, Henry—Captain, USV. Chief of artillery of Crook's Army of West Virginia (8th Corps) in Sheridan's Army of the Shenandoah (Middle Military Division).

DUKE, Basil W.—Brigadier General, CSA. Commander of a brigade of cavalry, composed of the remnants of Morgan's old division, in the Department of Southwestern Virginia.

DUVAL, Isaac H.—Colonel (later Brigadier General), USV. Commander of the 2nd Division of Crook's Army of West Virginia (8th Corps) in Sheridan's Army of the Shenandoah (Middle Military Division).

DWIGHT, William—Brigadier General, USV (USMA ex-1853). Commander of the 1st Division of the 19th Corps in Sheridan's Army of the Shenandoah (Middle Military Division).

EARLY, Jubal Anderson—Lieutenant General, CSA (USMA 1837). Commander of the Army of the Valley, also known as the 2nd Corps of Lee's Army of Northern Virginia.

ECHOLS, John—Brigadier General, CSA. Temporary commander of the Department of Southwestern Virginia (between Morgan and Breckinridge).

ECKERT, Thomas—Major, USV. Supervisor of Military Telegraphs in the Union War Department.

EDWARDS, Oliver—Colonel, USV. Commander of the 3rd Brigade of Russell's 1st Division of Wright's 6th Corps in Sheridan's Army of the Shenandoah (Middle Military Division).

EGAN, Thomas W.—Brigadier General, USV. Temporary commander of the 2nd Division of Hancock's 2nd Corps in Meade's Army of the Potomac.

ELLIOTT, Washington L.—Brigadier General, USV (USMA ex-1845). Commander of the 2nd Division of Wood's 4th Corps in Thomas's Army of the Cumberland in Sherman's Military Division of the Mississippi.

EMERSON, William—Colonel, USV. Commander of the 1st Brigade of Rickett's 3rd Division of Wright's 6th Corps in Sheridan's Army of the Shenandoah (Middle Military Division).

EMORY, William H.—Brevet Major General, USV (USMA 1831). Commander of the 19th Corps in Sheridan's Army of the Shenandoah (Middle Military Division).

EWELL, Richard S. ("Dick")—Lieutenant General, CSA (USMA 1840). Commander of the Department of Richmond.

EWING, Thomas, Jr.—Brigadier General, USV. Commander of the District of St. Louis in Rosecrans' Department of Missouri. Sherman's foster brother and brother-in-law.

FAGAN, James S.—Major General, CSA. Commander of a cavalry division in Price's raid through Missouri.

FARRAGUT, David Glasgow—Rear Admiral, USN. The captor of New Orleans and hero of the battle of Mobile Bay.

FIELD, Charles W.—Major General, CSA (USMA 1849). Commander of a division in Anderson's (later Longstreet's) 1st Corps of Lee's Army of Northern Virginia.

FORREST, Nathan Bedford—Major General, CSA. Commander of a district and cavalry corps in Taylor's Department of Alabama, Mississippi and East Louisiana.

FORSBERG, Augustus—Colonel, CSA. Temporary commander of Wharton's Brigade in Breckinridge's (Wharton's) Division of Early's Army of the Valley.

FORSYTH, George A. ("Sandy")—Major, USV. Officer on Sheridan's staff who accompanied him on his famous ride from Winchester to the field of battle at Cedar Creek.

FOSTER, John G.—Major General, USV (USMA 1846). Commander of the Department of the South, which included Union lodgments along the coast of South Carolina, Georgia, and Florida.

FOSTER, Robert S.—Brigadier General, USV. Commander of the 2nd Division of Birney's 10th Corps in Butler's Army of the James (Department of Virginia and North Carolina).

FOX, Gustavus—Union Assistant Secretary of the Navy.

FRENCH, Samuel G.—Major General, CSA (USMA 1843). Commander of a division in Stewart's Corps of Hood's Army of Tennessee.

FRENCH, Winsor—Lieutenant Colonel, USV. Succeeded Bidwell as commander of the 3rd Brigade of Getty's 2nd Division of Wright's 6th Corps in Sheridan's Army of the Shenandoah (Middle Military Division).

GARFIELD, James A.—Former Major General, USV. Newly elected Republican congressman from Ohio. Later the twentieth president of the United States.

GARRARD, Kenner—Brigadier General, USV (USMA 1851). Commander of the 2nd Cavalry Division of Thomas's Army of the Cumberland. Later the commander of the 2nd Division of A. J. Smith's Detachment Army of the Tennessee at Nashville.

GARY, Martin W.—Brigadier General, CSA. Commander of the Cavalry Brigade of Ewell's Department of Richmond.

GAY, Thomas S.—Ensign, USN. Member of Cushing's crew for the attack on the CSS *Albemarle*.

GEARY, John W.—Brigadier General, USV. Commander of the 2nd Division of Williams' 20th Corps in Slocum's Army of Georgia in Sherman's Military Division of the Mississippi.

GETTY, George Washington—Brigadier General, USV (USMA 1840). Commander of the 2nd Division of Wright's 6th Corps in Sheridan's Army of the Shenandoah (Middle Military Division).

GIBSON, Randall L.—Colonel, CSA. Commander of a brigade in Clayton's Division of Lee's Corps of Hood's Army of Tennessee in Beauregard's Division of the West.

GILLEM, Alvan C.—Brigadier General, USV. Commander of a brigade of Union-loyal Tennessee cavalry, known as the governor's guard, in Thomas's Department of the Cumberland in Sherman's Military Division of the Mississippi.

GILTNER, Henry L.—Colonel, CSA. Commander of a cavalry brigade in the Department of Southwestern Virginia.

GIST, States Rights—Brigadier General, CSA. Commander of a brigade in Brown's Division of Cheatham's Corps of Hood's Army of Tennessee in Beauregard's Division of the West.

GORDON, George Washington—Brigadier General, CSA. Commander of a brigade in Brown's Division of Cheatham's Corps of Hood's Army of Tennessee in Beauregard's Division of the West.

GORDON, John B.—Major General, CSA. Commander of a division in Early's Army of the Valley.

GOVAN, Daniel C.—Brigadier General, CSA. Commander of a brigade in Cleburne's Division of Cheatham's Corps of Hood's Army of Tennessee in Beauregard's Division of the West.

GRANBURY, Hiram B.—Brigadier General, CSA. Commander of a brigade in Cleburne's Division of Cheatham's Corps of Hood's Army of Tennessee in Beauregard's Division of the West.

GRANGER, Robert S.—Brigadier General, USV (USMA 1838). Commander of the District of Northern Alabama in Thomas's Department of the Cumberland in Sherman's Military Division of the Mississippi.

GRANT, Lewis A.—Brigadier General, USV. Commander of the 2nd (Vermont) Brigade of Getty's 2nd Division of Wright's 6th Corps in Sheridan's Army of the Shenandoah (Middle Military Division).

GRANT, Ulysses Simpson—Lieutenant General, USA (USMA 1843). General-in-chief of the United States Army.

GREGG, David McMurtrie—Brigadier General (Brevet Major General), USV (USMA 1855). Commander of the 2nd Division of the Cavalry

Corps of Meade's Army of the Potomac, which was the only division of that corps left behind when the rest of it was transferred to Sheridan's Army of the Shenandoah (Middle Military Division).

GREGG, John—Brigadier General, CSA. Commander of the Texas Brigade in Field's Division of Anderson's (later Longstreet's) 1st Corps in Lee's Army of Northern Virginia.

GRENFEL, George St. Leger—British adventurer and Confederate agent involved in the plot to free prisoners in Illinois.

GRIERSON, Benjamin H.—Brigadier General, USV. Commander of the Cavalry Corps of Washburn's District of West Tennessee in Howard's Department of the Tennessee.

GRIFFIN, Charles—Brigadier General, USV (USMA 1847). Commander of the 1st Division of Warren's 5th Corps in Meade's Army of the Potomac.

GRIFFIN, Joel—Colonel, CSA. Temporary commander of Dearing's cavalry brigade of Beauregard's Department of Southern Virginia and North Carolina.

GRIMES, Bryan—Brigadier General, CSA. Commander of a brigade in Rodes' Division of Early's Army of the Valley. Succeeded to the command of the division.

GROSVENOR, Charles H.—Lieutenant Colonel, USV. Commander of the 3rd Brigade in Cruft's Provisional Division of Steedman's Provisional Detachment of Thomas's Army of the Cumberland in Sherman's Military Division of the Mississippi.

GROVER, Cuvier—Brigadier General, USV (USMA 1850). Commander of the 2nd Division of Emory's 19th Corps in Sheridan's Army of the Shenandoah (Middle Military Division).

GWYNN, James—Colonel, USV. Commander of the 3rd Brigade of Griffin's 1st Division of Warren's 5th Corps in Meade's Army of the Potomac.

HALLECK, Henry Wager—Major General, USA (USMA 1839). Grant's predecessor as general-in-chief and former boss in the trans-Allegheny West. Named by Grant as the chief of staff of the U.S. Army to take care of the paperwork in Washington while he ran the armies from the field.

HAMMOND, John H.—Brevet Brigadier General, USV. Commander

of the 1st Brigade in Knipe's 7th Division of Wilson's Cavalry Corps of Sherman's Military Division of the Mississippi.

HAMPTON, Wade—Major General, CSA. Commander of the Cavalry Corps of Lee's Army of Northern Virginia.

HANCOCK, Winfield Scott—Major General, USV (USMA 1840). Commander of the 2nd Corps in Meade's Army of the Potomac.

HANSON, Charles—Colonel, USV. Commander of the 3rd Brigade of Hobson's 1st Division of Burbridge's District of Kentucky of Schofield's Department of the Ohio in Sherman's Military Division of the Mississippi.

HARDEE, William J.—Lieutenant General, CSA (USMA 1838). Commander of the Department of South Carolina, Georgia and Florida. Former corps commander in Hood's Army of Tennessee.

HARRIMAN, Samuel—Colonel, USV. Commander of the 1st Brigade of Willcox's 1st Division of Parke's 9th Corps in Meade's Army of the Potomac.

HARRINGTON, James T.—Lieutenant, CSA. One of the Confederate officers who tried to burn New York City.

HARRIS, Isham G.—Confederate governor of Tennessee and volunteer aide on Hood's staff.

HARRIS, Thomas M.—Colonel, USV. Commander of the 3rd Brigade of Thoburn's 1st Division of Crook's Army of West Virginia ("8th Corps") in Sheridan's Army of the Shenandoah (Middle Military Division).

HARRISON, Thomas Jefferson—Colonel, USV. Commander of the 1st Brigade of Johnson's 6th Division of Wilson's Cavalry Corps of Sherman's Military Division of the Mississippi.

HARRISON, William H.—Grand Secretary of the Order of the Sons of Liberty in Indiana.

HARTRANFT, John F.—Brigadier General, USV. Commander of the 1st Brigade of Willcox's 1st Division of Parke's 9th Corps in Meade's Army of the Potomac.

HATCH, Edward—Brigadier General, USV. Commander of the 5th Division of Wilson's Cavalry Corps in Sherman's Military Division of the Mississippi.

HATCH, John P.—Brigadier General, USV (USMA 1845). Commander of a division in Foster's Department of the South.

HAYES, Rutherford B.—Colonel (later Brigadier General), USV. Commander of the 1st Brigade of Duval's 2nd Division of Crook's Army of West Virginia (8th Corps) in Sheridan's Army of the Shenandoah (Middle Military Division). Succeeded to command of the division in time for the battle of Cedar Creek. Later elected nineteenth president of the United States.

HAZEN, William B.—Brigadier General, USV (USMA 1855). Commander of the 2nd Division of Osterhaus's 15th Corps in Howard's Army of the Tennessee in Sherman's Military Division of the Mississippi.

HEADLEY, John W.—Lieutenant, CSA. One of the Confederate officers who tried to burn New York City and the one who picked up the valise filled with bottles of Greek fire from the chemist.

HECKMAN, Charles A.—Brigadier General, USV. Commander of the 2nd Division of Ord's 18th Corps in Butler's Army of the James (Department of Virginia and North Carolina).

HEFREN, Horace—Deputy Grand Commander of the Order of the Sons of Liberty in Indiana.

HETH (pronounced *heath*), Henry—Major General, CSA (USMA 1847). Commander of a division in A. P. Hill's 3rd Corps of Lee's Army of Northern Virginia.

HILL, Ambrose Powell—Lieutenant General, CSA (USMA 1847). Commander of the 3rd Corps in Lee's Army of Northern Virginia.

HILL, Sylvester G.—Colonel, USV. Commander of the 3rd Brigade of McArthur's 1st Division of A. J. Smith's Detachment Army of the Tennessee in Thomas's Army of the Cumberland in Sherman's Military Division of the Mississippi.

HINES, Thomas—Captain, CSA. Confederate secret agent in charge of military operations out of Canada.

HOBSON, Edward H.—Brigadier General, USV. Commander of the 1st Brigade of McLean's 1st Division of Burbridge's District of Kentucky in Schofield's Department of the Ohio in Sherman's Military Division of the Mississippi.

HOEFLING, Charles C.—Lieutenant Colonel, USV. Commander of the 12th Tennessee Cavalry Regiment in Coon's 2nd Brigade of Hatch's

5th Division of Wilson's Cavalry Corps of Sherman's Military Division of the Mississippi.

HOFMANN, John—Colonel, USV. Commander of the 3rd Brigade of Crawford's 3rd Division of Warren's 5th Corps in Meade's Army of the Potomac.

HOGE, George B.—Colonel, USV. Commander of the 1st Brigade of Buckland's District of Memphis in Washburn's District of West Tennessee in Howard's Department of the Tennessee in Sherman's Military Division of the Mississippi.

HOKE, Robert F.—Major General, CSA. Commander of a division in Beauregard's Department of Southern Virginia and North Carolina (later Anderson's 4th Corps of Lee's Army of Northern Virginia).

HOLMAN, John H.—Colonel, USV. Commander of the 1st Brigade of Paine's 3rd Division of Ord's (later Weitzel's) 18th corps in Butler's Army of the James (Department of Virginia and North Carolina).

HOLT, Joseph—Brigadier General, USV. Judge Advocate General of the United States Army.

HOLTZCLAW, James T.—Brigadier General, CSA. Commander of a brigade in Clayton's Division of Lee's Corps of Hood's Army of Tennessee in Beauregard's Division of the West.

HOOD, John Bell—General, CSA (USMA 1853). Commander of the Department and Army of Tennessee in Beauregard's Division of the West.

HOOKER, Joseph—Major General, USV (USMA 1837). Commander of the Northern Department, consisting of the states of Michigan, Ohio, Indiana, and Illinois, from 1 October 1864. Former commander of the Army of the Potomac (before Meade) and of the 20th Corps of Thomas's Army of the Cumberland in Sherman's Military Division of the Mississippi.

HORSEY, Stephen—General in the Order of the Sons of Liberty.

HOTCHKISS, Jedediah—Captain, CSA. Topographical engineer on Early's staff.

HOVEY, Alvin P.—Brevet Major General, USV. Commander of the District of Indiana in Hooker's Northern Department.

HOWARD, Oliver Otis—Major General, USV (USMA 1854). Commander of the Department and Army of the Tennessee in Sherman's Military Division of the Mississippi.

HOWARTH, William L.—Ensign, USN. Member of Cushing's crew for the attack on the CSS *Albemarle*.

HUBBARD, Lucius F.—Colonel, USV. Commander of the 2nd Brigade of McArthur's 1st Division of A. J. Smith's Detachment Army of the Tennessee in Thomas's Army of the Cumberland in Sherman's Military Division of the Mississippi.

HUGHS, John M.—Colonel, CSA. Commander of Johnson's Brigade in Ewell's Department of Richmond.

HUMPHREYS, Andrew—General in the Order of the Sons of Liberty.

HUMPHREYS, Andrew, A.—Major General, USV (USMA 1831). Chief of staff of Meade's Army of the Potomac, succeeded Hancock as commander of the 2nd Corps in Meade's Army of the Potomac.

HUNTER, David—Major General, USV (USMA 1822). Former commander of the Department and Army of West Virginia.

HURLBUT, Stephen A.—Major General, USV. Former commander of the 16th Corps in Howard's Department of the Tennessee. Appointed commander of the Department of the Gulf in Canby's Military Division of West Mississippi 23 September 1864.

JACKMAN, Sydney—Colonel, CSA. Commander of a brigade in Shelby's Division of Price's Cavalry Corps of Kirby Smith's TransMississippi Department.

JACKSON, Henry R.—Brigadier General, CSA. Brigade commander in Bate's Division of Cheatham's Corps of Hood's Army of Tennessee in Beauregard's Division of the West.

JACKSON, Thomas J. ("Stonewall")—Lieutenant General, CSA (USMA 1846). Late commander of the Army of the Valley and of the 2nd Corps of Lee's Army of Northern Virginia. Mortally wounded at the battle of Chancellorsville in May 1863.

JACKSON, William H. ("Red")—Brigadier General, CSA (USMA 1856). Commander of a cavalry division originally belonging to the Army of Mississippi, which had reported directly to Hood during the Atlanta campaign and its aftermath and was attached to Forrest's corps for the Franklin/Nashville campaign.

JACKSON, William L. ("Mudwall")—Colonel, CSA. Commander of a brigade of cavalry in Lomax's Division of Early's Army of the Valley.

JENNISON, Charles R.—Colonel, USV. Commander of a brigade of cavalry in Blunt's forces from the Department of Kansas opposing Price's Missouri raid.

JOHNSON, Bradley T.—Brigadier General, CSA. Commander of a cavalry brigade in Lomax's Division of Early's Army of the Valley.

JOHNSON, Bushrod R.—Major General, CSA (USMA 1840). Commander of a division in Beauregard's Department of Southern Virginia and North Carolina, which was later part of Anderson's new 4th Corps of Lee's Army of Northern Virginia.

JOHNSON, Daniel D.—Colonel, USV. Commander of the 2nd Brigade of Duval's 2nd Division of Crook's Army of West Virginia ("8th Corps") in Sheridan's Army of the Shenandoah (Middle Military Division).

JOHNSON, Edward ("Allegheny")—Major General, CSA (USMA 1838). Commander of a division in S. D. Lee's corps of Hood's Army of Tennessee in Beauregard's Division of the West.

JOHNSON, Richard W.—Brigadier General, USV (USMA 1849). Commander of the 6th Division of Wilson's Cavalry Corps of Sherman's Military Division of the Mississippi.

JOHNSTON, Joseph Eggleston—General, CSA (USMA 1829). Hood's predecessor in command of the Department and Army of Tennessee.

JOHNSTON, Robert D.—Brigadier General, CSA. Commander of a brigade in Ramseur's Division of Early's Army of the Valley.

JOURDAN, James—Colonel, USV. Temporary commander of the 1st Brigade of the 2nd Division of the 18th Corps in Butler's Army of the James (Department of Virginia and North Carolina).

KAUTZ, August V.—Brigadier General, USV (USMA 1852). Commander of the Cavalry Division of the Army of the James (Dept. of Va. and N.C.).

KEIFER, Joseph W.—Colonel, CSA. Commander of the 2nd Brigade of Rickett's 3rd Division of Wright's 6th Corps in Sheridan's Army of the Shenandoah (Middle Military Division), in temporary command of the division at Cedar Creek.

KELLAR, Andrew, J.—Colonel, CSA. Succeeded to command of Strahl's Brigade of Brown's (later Lowrey's) Division of Cheatham's

Corps of Hood's Army of Tennessee in Beauregard's Division of the West.

KELLEY, Benjamin Franklin—Brigadier General, USV. Commander of forces west of Sleepy Hollow in Crook's Department of West Virginia in Sheridan's Middle Military Division.

KENNEDY, Robert C.—Captain, CSA. One of the Confederate officers who tried to burn New York City and the one who started the fire at P. T. Barnum's Museum.

KERSHAW, Joseph B.—Major General, CSA. Commander of a division in Anderson's 1st Corps of Lee's Army of Northern Virginia, which was attached to Early's Army of the Valley.

KIDD, James H.—Colonel, USV. Succeeded Custer as commander of the 1st (Michigan) Brigade of Merritt's 1st Division of Torbert's Cavalry Corps of Sheridan's Army of the Shenandoah (Middle Military Division).

KILPATRICK, Hugh Judson—Brigadier General, USV (USMA 1861). Commander of the 3rd Cavalry Division of Thomas's Army of the Cumberland, which became the 3rd Division of Wilson's Cavalry Corps of Sherman's Military Division of the Mississippi and was the only cavalry taken on the March to the Sea.

KIMBALL, Nathan—Brigadier General, USV. Commander of the 1st Division of Stanley's (later Wood's) 4th Corps in Thomas's Army of the Cumberland in Sherman's Military Division of the Mississippi.

KITCHING, John H.—Colonel, USV. Commander of a Provisional Division of troops from the Department of Washington in Sheridan's Army of the Shenandoah (Middle Military Division).

KNIPE, Joseph F.—Brigadier General, USV. Commander of the 7th Division of Wilson's Cavalry Corps of Sherman's Military Division of the Mississippi.

La GRANGE, Oscar H.—Colonel, USV. Commander of the 2nd Brigade of McCook's 1st Division of Wilson's Cavalry Corps of Sherman's Military Division of the Mississippi.

LANE, James H.—Brigadier General, CSA. Commander of a brigade in Wilcox's Division of Hill's 3rd Corps of Lee's Army of Northern Virginia.

LANE, John Q.—Colonel, USV. Commander of the 2nd Brigade of Wagner's (later Elliott's) 2nd Division of Stanley's (later Wood's) 4th Corps in Thomas's Army of the Cumberland in Sherman's Military Division of the Mississippi.

LATHAM, George R.—Colonel, USV. Commander of the Union garrison at New Creek in Crook's Department of West Virginia in Sheridan's Middle Military Division.

LEE, Fitzhugh ("Fitz")—Major General, CSA (USMA 1856). Commander of a division in Hampton's Cavalry Corps of R. E. Lee's Army of Northern Virginia. Nephew of R. E. Lee.

LEE, George Washington Custis—Major General, CSA (USMA 1854). Aide to President Davis. Later given command of a division in Ewell's Department of Richmond. Oldest son of R. E. Lee.

LEE, Robert Edward—General, CSA (USMA 1829). Commander of the Army of Northern Virginia.

LEE, Samuel Phillips—Rear Admiral, USN. Commander of the North Atlantic Blockading Squadron. Later sent to command the Mississippi Squadron of gunboats on the western rivers, exchanging jobs with David Porter.

LEE, Stephen Dill—Lieutenant General, CSA (USMA 1854). Commander of the 2nd Corps of Hood's Army of Tennessee. Only very distantly related to the Virginia Lees.

LEE, W. H. F. ("Rooney")—Major General, CSA. Commander of a division in Hampton's Cavalry Corps of R. E. Lee's Army of Northern Virginia, second son of R.E. Lee.

LINCOLN, Abraham—Sixteenth president of the United States and the first Republican to ever be elected to that office.

LOGAN, John A.—Major General, USV. Commander of the 15th Corps in Howard's Army of the Tennessee in Sherman's Military Division of the Mississippi. Went home to Illinois, where he was a prominent War Democrat, after the capture of Atlanta to campaign for the reelection of President Lincoln and thus missed the March to the Sea.

LOMAX, Lunsford L.—Major General, CSA (USMA 1856). Commander of the cavalry division of Early's Army of the Valley.

LONGSTREET, James—Lieutenant General, CSA (USMA 1842). Commander of the 1st Corps of Lee's Army of Northern Virginia.

Wounded during the battle of the Wilderness, he returned to duty on 19 October 1864.

LORING, William W.—Major General, CSA. Commander of a division in Stewart's Corps of Hood's Army of Tennessee in Beauregard's Division of the West.

LOWELL, Charles Russell—Colonel, USV. Commander of the Reserve Brigade in Merritt's 1st Division of Torbert's Cavalry Corps in Sheridan's Army of the Shenandoah (Middle Military Division).

LOWREY, Mark P.—Brigadier General, CSA. Commander of a brigade in Cleburne's Division of Cheatham's Corps of Hood's Army of Tennessee in Beauregard's Division of the West.

LYON, Hylan B.—Brigadier General, CSA (USMA 1856). Commander of brigade in Buford's 2nd Division of Forrest's cavalry. Later assigned command of the District of Western Kentucky and a division of Kentucky recruits for a raid into that state.

MACOMB, W. H.—Commander, USN. Commander of Union naval forces in the North Carolina sounds.

MacRAE, Williams—Brigadier General, CSA. Commander of a brigade in Heth's Division of Hill's 3rd Corps of Lee's Army of Northern Virginia.

MAHONE, William—Major General, CSA. Commander of a division in Hill's 3rd Corps of Lee's Army of Northern Virginia.

MANIGAULT, Arthur M.—Brigadier General, CSA. Commander of a brigade in Johnson's Division in Lee's Corps of Hood's Army of Tennessee in Beauregard's Division of the West.

MARMADUKE, John S.—Major General, CSA (USMA 1857). Commander of a division of cavalry in Price's raid through Missouri.

MARMADUKE, Vincent—Colonel, CSA. Confederate agent involved in the plot to free prisoners in Illinois.

MARSHALL, William R.—Colonel, USV. Succeeded S. G. Hill as commander of the 3rd Brigade of McArthur's 1st Division of A. J. Smith's Detachment Army of the Tennessee in Thomas's Army of the Cumberland in Sherman's Military Division of the Mississippi.

MARTIN, Robert M.—Lieutenant Colonel, CSA. Commander of the group of Confederate officers who attempted to burn New York City.

MAURY, John Minor—Lieutenant Colonel, CSA. Commander of a battalion of heavy artillery at Chaffin's Bluff in Ewell's Department of Richmond.

McALLISTER, Robert—Colonel, USV. Commander of the 3rd Brigade of Mott's 3rd Division of Hancock's (later Humphreys') 2nd Corps in Meade's Army of the Potomatc.

McARTHUR, John—Brigadier General, USV. Commander of the 1st Division of A. J. Smith's Detachment Army of the Tennessee in Thomas's Army of the Cumberland in Sherman's Military Division of the Mississippi.

McCAUSLAND, John—Brigadier General, CSA. Commander of a brigade of cavalry in Lomax's Division of Early's Army of the Valley.

McCLELLAN, George Brinton—Major General, USA (USMA 1846). Founder of the Army of the Potomac. Democratic candidate for president.

McCOOK, Edward M.—Brigadier General, USV. Commander of the 1st Division in the cavalry of Thomas's Army of the Cumberland, which later became the 1st Division of Wilson's Cavalry Corps of Sherman's Military Division of the Mississippi.

McGOWAN, Samuel—Brigadier General, CSA. Commander of a brigade in Wilcox's Division of Hill's 3rd Corps in Lee's Army of Northern Virginia.

McKETHAN, Hector M.—Colonel, CSA. Commander of Clingman's Brigade of Hoke's Division of Beauregard's Department of Southern Virginia and North Carolina (later Anderson's 4th Corps of Lee's Army of Northern Virginia).

McKINLEY, William—Captain, USV. Officer on Crook's staff (Army of West Virginia). Later elected 24th president of the United States.

McLAUGHLEN, Napoleon Bonaparte—Colonel, USV. Commander of the 3rd Brigade of Willcox's 1st Division of Parke's 9th Corps in Meade's Army of the Potomac.

McLEAN, Nathaniel—Brigadier General, USV. Commander of a division in Burbridge's District of Kentucky in Schofield's Department of the Ohio in Sherman's Military Division of the Mississippi.

McMASTER, James A.—New York publisher and editor who was the contact man for the local Copperheads with the Confederate officers who planned to burn the city.

McMILLAN, James W.—Brigadier General, USV. Commander of the 2nd Brigade of Thoburn's 1st Division of Crook's Army of West Virginia (8th Corps) in Sheridan's Army of the Shenandoah (Middle Military Division).

McMILLAN, William L.—Colonel, USV. Commander of the 1st Brigade of McArthur's 1st Division of A. J. Smith's Detachment Army of the Tennessee in Thomas's Army of the Cumberland in Sherman's Military Division of the Mississippi.

McNEIL, John—Brigadier General, USV. Commander of a brigade of cavalry under Pleasonton in the pursuit of Price's Missouri raid.

McPHERSON, James B.—Major General, USV (USMA 1853). Howard's predecessor as commander of the Army of the Tennessee in Sherman's Military Division of the Mississippi. Killed during the battle of Atlanta, 22 July 1864.

MEADE, George Gordon—Major General, USV (USMA 1835). Commander of the Army of the Potomac.

MERRITT, Wesley—Brigadier General, USV (USMA 1860). Commander of the 1st Division of Torbert's Cavalry Corps in Sheridan's Army of the Shenandoah (Middle Military Division).

MEIGS, John R.—Lieutenant, USV (USMA 1863). Topographical engineer on Sheridan's staff whose killing was thought to have been the work of Mosby's guerrillas. Son of Montgomery C. Meigs.

MEIGS, Montgomery C.—Brigadier General, USV (USMA 1836). Quartermaster General of the Union army.

MILES, Nelson A.—Brigadier General, USV. Commander of the 1st Division of Humphreys' 2nd Corps in Meade's Army of the Potomac.

MILLER, Patrick C.—Confederate agent and blockade runner operating out of Canada who gave John Wilkes Booth a letter of introduction to Rebel agents in Maryland.

MILLIGAN, Lambdin P.—Copperhead leader among those tried by a Union military commission.

MILROY, Robert H.—Major General, USV. Commander of the defenses of the Nashville & Chattanooga Railroad in Rousseau's District of Tennessee in Thomas's Department of the Cumberland in Sherman's Military Division of the Mississippi.

MOONLIGHT, Thomas—Colonel, USV. Commander of a brigade in

Blunt's forces from the Department of Kansas opposing Price's raid in Missouri.

MOORE, Alpheus S.—Colonel, USV. Commander of the 1st Brigade of Powell's 2nd Division of Torbert's Cavalry Corps of Sheridan's Army of the Shenandoah (Middle Military Division).

MOORE, Orlando H.—Colonel, USV. Commander of the 2nd Brigade of Ruger's (later Couch's) 2nd Division of the 23rd Corps in Schofield's Army of the Ohio in Sherman's Military Division of the Mississippi.

MOORE, Patrick T.—Brigadier General, CSA. Commander of a brigade of Virginia reserves in Ewell's Department of Richmond.

MORGAN, James D.—Brigadier General, USV. Commander of the 2nd Division of Davis's 14th Corps of Thomas's Army of the Cumberland (later Slocum's Army of Georgia) in Sherman's Military Division of the Mississippi.

MORGAN, John Hunt—Brigadier General, CSA. Commander of the Department of Southwestern Virginia and East Tennessee.

MORGAN, Richard—Colonel, CSA. Temporary commander of Duke's (formerly John Hunt Morgan's) brigade in Breckinridge's Department of Southwestern Virginia and East Tennessee. Brother of John Hunt Morgan.

MORGAN, Thomas Jefferson—Colonel, USV. Commander of the 1st Colored Brigade in the District of the Etowah and in Steedman's Provisional Detachment in Thomas's Department of the Cumberland in Sherman's Military Division of the Mississippi.

MORTON, Oliver P.—Governor of Indiana.

MOSBY, John Singleton—Lieutenant Colonel, CSA. Commander of a battalion of partisan rangers in northern Virginia.

MOTT, Gershom—Brigadier General, USV. Commander of the 3rd Division of Hancock's (later Humphreys') 2nd Corps in Meade's Army of the Potomac.

MOWER, Joseph A.—Major General, USV. Commander of the 1st Division of Blair's 17th Corps in Howard's Army of the Tennessee in Sherman's Military Division of the Mississippi.

MUDD, Dr. Samuel—A pro-Confederate medical doctor who lived on a Maryland farm southeast of Washington, D.C. and became entangled in John Wilkes Booth's plot against President Lincoln.

MUNFORD, Thomas T.—Colonel (later Brigadier General), CSA. Colonel of the 2nd Virginia Cavalry Regiment and later the commander of Wickham's Brigade of Fitzhugh Lee's cavalry division in Early's Army of the Valley and in Hampton's Cavalry Corps of Lee's Army of Northern Virginia.

MURRAY, Eli H.—Colonel, USV. Commander of the 1st Brigade of Kilpatrick's 3rd Division of Wilson's Cavalry Corps of Sherman's Military Division of the Mississippi.

NEWTON, John—Brigadier General, USV (USMA 1842). Commander of the 2nd Division of the 4th Corps in Thomas's Army of the Cumberland in Sherman's Military Division of the Mississippi until 30 September 1864.

OPDYCKE, Emerson—Colonel, USV. Commander of the 1st Brigade of Wagner's (later Elliott's) 2nd Division of Stanley's (later Wood's) 4th Corps in Thomas's Army of the Cumberland in Sherman's Military Division of the Mississippi.

ORD, Edward O. C.—Major General, USV (USMA 1839). Commander of the 18th Corps in Butler's Army of the James (Department of Virginia and North Carolina). After that army's reorganization he commanded the 24th Corps.

OSTERHAUS, Peter J.—Major General, USV. Temporary commander (in Logan's absence) of the 15th Corps in Howard's Army of the Tennessee in Sherman's Military Division of the Mississippi.

PAINE, Charles J.—Brigadier General, USV. Commander of the 3rd Division of Ord's 18th Corps in Butler's Army of the James (Department of Virginia and North Carolina).

PARKE, John G.—Major General, USV (USMA 1849). Commander of the 9th Corps in Meade's Army of the Potomac.

PATTON, George S.—Colonel, CSA. Commander of a brigade in Breckinridge's (Wharton's) Division of Early's Army of the Valley. Grandfather of the WWII general of the same name.

PAYNE, William H.—Colonel, CSA. Commander of Lomax's Brigade in Fitzhugh Lee's division of cavalry in Early's Army of the Valley and in Hampton's Cavalry Corps of Lee's Army of Northern Virginia.

PEGRAM, John—Brigadier General, CSA (USMA 1854). Commander of a brigade in Ramseur's Division of Early's Army of the Valley.

PEMBERTON, John C.—Lieutenant Colonel, CSA (USMA 1837). Commander of the artillery of the defenses of Richmond.

PENNYPACKER, Galusha—Colonel, USV. Commander of the 2nd Brigade of Foster's 2nd Division of Birney's 10th Corps in Butler's Army of the James (Department of Virginia and North Carolina).

PHILLIPS, P. J.—Brigadier General, Georgia Militia. Temporary commander of the militia field force in the battle at Griswoldville.

PIERCE, Bryon R.—Brigadier General, USV. Commander of the 2nd Brigade of Mott's 3rd Division of Hancock's (later Humphreys') 2nd Corps in Meade's Army of the Potomac.

PLAISTED, Henry M.—Colonel, USV. Commander of the 3rd Brigade of Terry's 1st Division of Birney's 10th Corps in Butler's Army of the James (Department of Virginia and North Carolina).

PLEASONTON, Alfred—Major General, USV (USMA 1844). Commander of the District of Central Missouri in Rosecrans' Department of Missouri and commander of the Union cavalry from that department that pursued Price's raid across Missouri.

POND, Francis B.—Colonel, USV. Commander of the 1st Brigade of Terry's 1st Division of Birney's 10th Corps in Butler's Army of the James (Department of Virginia and North Carolina).

PORTER, David Dixon—Rear Admiral, USN. New commander of the North Atlantic Blockading Squadron.

PORTER, Horace—Lieutenant Colonel, USA (USMA 1860). An aide on Grant's staff. His book *Campaigning With Grant* is frequently quoted in the pages.

POST, Philip Sidney—Colonel, USV. Commander of the 2nd Brigade of Wood's (later Beatty's) 3rd Division of Stanley's (later Wood's) 4th Corps in Thomas's Army of the Cumberland in Sherman's Military Division of the Mississippi.

POTTER, Robert B.—Brigadier General, USV. Commander of the 2nd Division of Parke's 9th Corps in Meade's Army of the Potomac.

POWELL, William Henry—Colonel (later brigadier general), USV. Commander of the 2nd Brigade of Averell's 2nd Cavalry Division of Crook's Army and Department of West Virginia in Sheridan's Army of the Shenandoah (Middle Military Division). Later succeeded to the command of the division.

PRICE, Sterling—Major General, CSA. Commander of Confederate forces in Arkansas. Former governor of Missouri.

QUANTRILL, William Clarke—Captain, CSA. Confederate guerrilla in Missouri.

RAMSEUR, Stephen Dodson—Major General, CSA (USMA 1860). Commander of a division in Early's Army of the Valley.

RANSOM, Thomas E. G.—Brevet Major General, USV. Commander of the 17th Corps in Howard's Army of the Tennessee in Sherman's Military Division of the Mississippi until illness forced his replacement on 10 October 1864. He died on 29 October 1864.

RATLIFF, Robert—Colonel, USV. Commander of the 4th Brigade of Hobson's 1st Division of Burbridge's District of Kentucky of Schofield's Department of the Ohio in Sherman's Military Division of the Mississippi.

RAULSTON, John B.—Lieutenant Colonel, USV. Commander of the 81st New York. Succeeded to the command of Stevens' 1st Brigade of Stannard's 1st Division of Ord's 18th Corps in Butler's Army of the James (Department of Virginia and North Carolina).

RAWLINS, John A.—Brigadier General, USV. Grant's chief of staff.

REILLY, James W.—Brigadier General, USV. Commander of the 1st Brigade of Cox's 3rd Division of the 23rd Corps in Schofield's Army of the Ohio in Sherman's Military Division of the Mississippi. Commanded the division at Franklin while Cox temporarily commanded the corps.

REYNOLDS, Daniel H.—Brigadier General, CSA. Commander of a brigade in Walthall's Division of Stewart's Corps of Hood's Army of Tennessee in Beauregard's Division of the West.

REYNOLDS, Thomas C.—Confederate lieutenant governor and acting governor of Missouri.

RHODES, Elisha Hunt—Captain, USV. Commander of the 2nd Rhode Island Volunteers in Edwards' 3rd Brigade of Russell's 1st Division of Wright's 6th Corps in Sheridan's Army of the Shenandoah (Middle Military Division).

RICKETTS, James B.—Brigadier General, USV (USMA 1839). Commander of the 3rd Division of Wright's 6th Corps in Sheridan's Army of the Shenandoah (Middle Military Division).

ROBERTS, Samuel H.—Colonel, USV. Commander of the 3rd Brigade in Stannard's 1st Division of Ord's 18th Corps in Butler's Army of the James (Department of Virginia and North Carolina).

ROBERTSON, Felix H.—Brigadier General, CSA. Commander of one of the brigades detached from Wheeler's Cavalry Corps of Hood's Army of Tennessee that helped defend Saltville, Virginia.

RODES, Robert Emmett—Major General, CSA. Commander of a division in Early's Army of the Valley.

ROSECRANS, William S.—Major General, USV (USMA 1842). Commander of the Department of Missouri. Former commander of the Army of the Cumberland.

ROSS, Lawrence S.—Brigadier General, CSA. Commander of a brigade of Texas cavalry in Jackson's Division attached to Forrest's corps.

ROSSER, Thomas L.—Brigadier General, CSA. Commander of a brigade of cavalry (known as the Laurel Brigade) in Hampton's (Butler's) Division of Hampton's Cavalry Corps of Lee's Army of Northern Virginia. Later sent to reinforce Early's Army of the Valley.

ROUSSEAU, Lovell H.—Major General, USV. Commander of the District of Tennessee in Thomas's Department of the Cumberland in Sherman's Military Division of the Mississippi.

ROWETT, Richard—Colonel, USV. Commander of the 3rd Brigade of Corse's 4th Division of Osterhaus's 15th Corps in Howard's Army of the Tennessee in Sherman's Military Division of the Mississippi.

RUCKER, Edwin W.—Colonel, CSA. Commander of a brigade in Chalmers' 1st Division of Forrest's cavalry corps.

RUGER, Thomas H.—Brigadier General, USV (USMA 1854). Commander of the 2nd Division of the 23rd Corps in Schofield's Army of the Ohio in Sherman's Military Division of the Mississippi.

RUSSELL, David A.—Brigadier General, USV (USMA 1845). Commander of the 1st Division of Wright's 6th Corps in Sheridan's Army of the Shenandoah (Middle Military Division).

SANBORN, John B.—Brigadier General, USV. Commander of the District of Southwest Missouri in Rosecrans' Department of Missouri and of a brigade of cavalry in Pleasonton's pursuit of Price's raid.

SANDERS, George N.—Confederate commissioner to Cananda.

SCHOFIELD, John M.—Major General, USV (USMA 1853). Commander of the Department and Army of the Ohio in Sherman's Military Division of the Mississippi.

SEARS, Claudius W.—Brigadier General, CSA (USMA 1841). Commander of a brigade in French's Division of Stewart's Corps of Hood's Army of Tennessee.

SEDDON, James—Secretary of War in Jefferson Davis' cabinet.

SEWARD, William Henry—Secretary of State in Lincoln's cabinet.

SEYMOUR, Horatio—Governor of New York.

SHADBURNE, George D.—Sergeant, CSA. Hampton's best scout.

SHELBY, Joseph O. ("Jo")—Brigadier General, CSA. Commander of a cavalry division in Price's raid through Missouri.

SHERIDAN, Philip Henry—Major General, USV (USMA 1853). Commander of the Army of the Shenandoah and the Middle Military Division.

SHERMAN, William Tecumseh—Major General, USA (USMA 1840). Grant's favorite subordinate and his successor in command, first of the Army of the Tennessee, and then of the Military Division of the Mississippi.

SIMMS, James P.—Colonel, CSA. Commander of Bryan's Brigade in Kershaw's Division of Anderson's (later Longstreet's) 1st Corps of Lee's Army of Northern Virginia.

SLOCUM, Henry W.—Major General, USV (USMA 1852). Commander of the 20th Corps in Thomas's Army of the Cumberland in Sherman's Military Division of the Mississippi. Later commander of the two corps (known as the Left Wing or the Army of Georgia) of Thomas's army taken on Sherman's March to the Sea.

SMITH, Andrew Jackson—Major General, USV (USMA 1838). Commander of a force originally known as the Right Wing of the 16th Corps and later as Detachment Army of the Tennessee.

SMITH, Charles H.—Colonel, USV. Commander of the 2nd Brigade of Gregg's 2nd Division of cavalry in Meade's Army of the Potomac.

SMITH, E. Kirby—General, CSA (USMA 1838). Commander of the Trans-Mississippi Department.

SMITH, George—Colonel, CSA. Commander of the 62nd Virginia

Mounted Infantry Regiment and temporary commander of Imboden's Brigade of cavalry in Lomax's Division of Early's Army of the Valley.

SMITH, Gustavus W.—Major General, Georgia Militia. Normal field commander of the Georgia Militia division.

SMITH, Thomas—Colonel, CSA. Commander of a brigade in Breckinridge's (Wharton's) Division of Early's Army of the Valley.

SMITH, Thomas Benton—Brigadier General, CSA. Brigade commander in Bate's Division of Cheatham's Corps of Hood's Army of Tennessee in Beauregard's Division of the West.

SMITH, William ("Extra Billy"). Governor of Virginia. Former brigade commander in the 2nd Corps of Lee's Army of Northern Virginia.

SORREL, Moxley—Colonel, CSA. Chief of staff of Anderson's (later Longstreet's) 1st Corps in Lee's Army of Northern Virginia.

SPEAR, Ellis—Major, USV. Commander of the 20th Maine Regiment. Succeeded to the command of the 3rd Brigade of Griffin's 1st Division of Warren's 5th Corps in Meade's Army of the Potomac.

SPEAR, Samuel P.—Colonel, USV. Commander of the 2nd Brigade of Kautz's Cavalry Division of Butler's Army of the James (Department of Virginia and North Carolina).

STANLEY, David S.—Major General, USV (USMA 1852). Commander of the 4th Corps in Thomas's Army of the Cumberland in Sherman's Military Division of the Mississippi.

STANNARD, George J.—Brigadier General, USV. Commander of the 1st Division of Ord's 18th Corps in Butler's Army of the James (Department of Virginia and North Carolina).

STANTON, Edwin McMasters—Secretary of War in Lincoln's cabinet.

STEEDMAN, James B.—Major General, USV. Commander of the District of the Etowah in Thomas's Department of the Cumberland in Sherman's Military Division of the Mississippi, and of a corps-sized provisional detachment at the battle of Nashville.

STEPHENS, Alexander Hamilton—Vice President of the Confederate States.

STEVENS, Aaron F.—Colonel, USV. Commander of the 1st Brigade of Stannard's 1st Division of Ord's 18th Corps in Butler's Army of the James (Department of Virginia and North Carolina).

STEVENSON, Carter L.—Major General, CSA (USMA 1838). Commander of a division in Lee's Corps of Hood's Army of Tennessee in Beauregard's Division of the West.

STEWART, Alexander P.—Lieutenant General, CSA (USMA 1842). Commander of the Army of Mississippi, or Stewart's Corps, in Hood's Army of Tennessee in Beauregard's Division of the West.

STEWART, Rev. Dr. Kensey Johns—Episcopal minister and distant relative, by marriage, of General R. E. Lee. Involved in, and may have been the originator of, the plot to capture President Lincoln.

STEWART, Robert R.—Colonel, USV. Commander of the 1st Brigade of Hatch's 5th Division of Wilson's Cavalry Corps of Sherman's Military Division of the Mississippi.

STIDGER, Felix—Corporal, USV. Union secret agent who became the Grand Secretary of the Order of the Sons of Liberty for Kentucky and testified against the Copperhead leaders at their trial by a military commission.

STILES, Israel N.—Colonel, USV. Commander of the 3rd Brigade of Cox's (briefly Reilly's) 3rd Division of the 23rd Corps in Schofield's Army of the Ohio in Sherman's Military Division of the Mississippi.

STOKES, William—Lieutenant Colonel, CSA. Commander of the 4th South Carolina Cavalry in Dunovant's Brigade of Butler's 1st Division of Hampton's Cavalry Corps of Lee's Army of Northern Virginia. Succeeded to command of the brigade when Dunovant was killed.

STONEMAN, George—Major General, USV (USMA 1846). Chief of cavalry and second in command of Schofield's Department of the Ohio in Sherman's Military Division of the Mississippi.

STRAHL, Otto F.—Brigadier General, CSA. Commander of a brigade in Brown's Division of Cheatham's Corps of Hood's Army of Tennessee in Beauregard's Division of the West.

STREIGHT, Abel D.—Colonel, USV. Commander of the 1st Brigade of Wood's (later Beatty's) 3rd Division of Stanley's (later Wood's) 4th Corps in Thomas's Army of the Cumberland in Sherman's Military Division of the Mississippi.

STRICKLAND, Silas A.—Commander of the 3rd Brigade of Ruger's 2nd Division of the 23rd Corps in Schofield's Army of the Ohio in Sherman's Military Division of the Mississippi.

STUART, James Ewell Brown ("Jeb")—Major General, CSA (USMA 1854). Late commander of the Cavalry Corps of Lee's Army of Northern Virginia. Killed at the battle of Yellow Tavern during Sheridan's raid on Richmond in May 1864.

SWEET, Richard T.—Colonel, USV. Commander of Camp Douglas for Confederate prisoners of war.

TANEY, Roger B.—Chief Justice of the Supreme Court. Best known for the Dred Scott Decision.

TAYLOR, Richard ("Dick")—Lieutenant General, CSA. Commander of the Department of Alabama, Mississippi and East Louisiana. Son of President Zachary Taylor.

TAYLOR, Richard C.—Major, CSA. Acting commander of Maury's heavy artillery battalion at Chaffin's Bluff in Ewell's Department of Richmond.

TERRY, Alfred H.—Brevet Major General, USV. Commander of the 1st Division of Birney's 10th Corps in Butler's Army of the James (Department of Virginia and North Carolina), later Commander of the 1st of the 24th Corps and of that corps in the same army.

THOBURN, Joseph—Colonel, USV. Commander of the 1st Division of Crook's Army of West Virginia ("8th Corps") in Sheridan's Army of the Shenandoah (Middle Military Division).

THOMAS, George H.—Major General, USV (USMA 1840). Commander of the Department and Army of the Cumberland in Sherman's Military Division of the Mississippi.

THOMAS, Stephen—Colonel, USV. Commander of the 2nd Brigade of Dwight's 1st Division of Emory's 19th Corps in Sheridan's Army of the Shenandoah (Middle Military Division). He was the corps' officer of the day when Early attacked at Cedar on 19 October 1864.

THOMPSON, Charles R.—Colonel, USV. Commanded the 2nd Colored Brigade in Steedman's Provisional Detachment of Thomas's Department of the Cumberland in Sherman's Military Division of the Mississippi.

THOMPSON, Jacob—Confederate commissioner to Canada. Secretary of the Interior in the administration of James Buchanan, Lincoln's predecessor.

THOMPSON, M. Jeff—Colonel, CSA. Succeeded Shanks in command

of Shelby's Brigade in Shelby's Division of Price's Cavalry Corps of Kirby Smith's TransMississippi Department.

TODD, George—Captain, CSA. Confederate guerrilla and Missouri bushwacker.

TOOMBS, Robert A.—Adjutant and Inspector General of the Georgia Militia.

TORBERT, Alfred T. A.—Brigadier General, USV (USMA 1855). Commander of the Cavalry Corps in Sheridan's Army of the Shenandoah (Middle Military Division).

TOURTELLOTTE, John E.—Lieutenant Colonel, USV. Commander of the 2nd Brigade of Corse's 3rd Division of Osterhaus's 15th Corps in Howard's Army of the Tennessee in Sherman's Military Division of the Mississippi.

UPTON, Emory—Brigadier General, USV (USMA May 1861). Commander of the 2nd Brigade of Russell's 1st Division of Wright's 6th Corps in Sheridan's Army of the Shenandoah (Middle Military Division). Later commander of the 4th Division in Wilson's Cavalry Corps of Sherman's Military Division of the Mississippi.

VAUGHN, John C.—Brigadier General, CSA. Commander of a brigade of cavalry in the Department of Southwestern Virginia and East Tennessee.

VENABLE, Charles—Colonel, CSA. An aide on R. E. Lee's staff.

WAGNER, George D.—Brigadier General, USV. Commander of the 2nd Division of Stanley's 4th Corps in Thomas's Army of the Cumberland in Sherman's Military Division of the Mississippi.

WALCUTT, Charles C.—Brigadier General, USV. Commander of the 2nd Brigade of the 1st Division of Osterhaus's 15th Corps in Howard's Army of the Tennessee in Sherman's Military Division of the Mississippi.

WALTHALL, Edward C.—Major General, CSA. Commander of a division in Stewart's Corps of Hood's Army of Tennessee in Beauregard's Division of the West and of the ad hoc division of infantry in the rear guard after Hood's defeat at Nashville.

WARNER, James M.—Colonel, USV (USMA 1860). Commander of the 2nd Brigade of Getty's 2nd Division of Wright's 6th Corps in Sheridan's Army of the Shenandoah (Middle Military Division).

WARREN, Gouverneur K.—Major General, USV (USMA 1850). Commander of the 5th Corps in Meade's Army of the Potomac.

WASHBURN, Cadwallader C.—Major General, USV. Commander of the District of West Tennessee in Howard's Department of the Tennessee in Sherman's Military Division of the Mississippi.

WASHBURNE, Elihu B.—Congressman from northwestern Illinois. Grant's political sponsor. Brother of Cadwallader C. Washburn (despite the difference in spelling).

WATKINS, Louis D.—Brigadier General, USV. Commander of the 3rd Brigade of McCook's 1st Division of Wilson's Cavalry Corps of Sherman's Military Division of the Mississippi.

WEAVER, Clark—Colonel, USV. Commander of the 2nd Brigade of the 3rd Division of Osterhaus's 15th Corps in Howard's Army of the Tennessee in Sherman's Military Division of the Mississippi.

WEITZEL, Godfrey—Brigadier General (later major general), USV (USMA 1855). Chief engineer of Butler's Army of the James (Department of Virginia and North Carolina). Later put in command of the 18th Corps in the same army and, after the army was reorganized, the 25th Corps.

WELLES, Gideon-Secretary of the Navy in Lincoln's cabinet.

WELLS, George D.—Colonel, USV. Commander of the 1st Brigade of Thoburn's 1st Division of Crook's Army of West Virginia ("8th Corps") in Sheridan's Army of the Shenandoah (Middle Military Division).

WEST, Robert M.—Colonel, USV. Commander of the 1st Brigade of Kautz's Cavalry Division of Butler's Army of the James (Department of Virginia and North Carolina).

WHARTON, Gabriel C.—Brigadier General, CSA. Commander of what had been Breckinridge's Division, consisting of troops brought by the latter from the Department of Southwestern Virginia to the Valley District, then to reinforce Lee's Army of Northern Virginia, then back to the Shenandoah Valley as part of Early's Army of the Valley.

WHEATON, Frank—Brigadier General, USV. Commander of the 1st Brigade of Getty's 2nd Division of Wright's 6th Corps in Sheridan's Army of the Shenandoah (Middle Military Division). Temporarily commanded the 1st Division of the same corps.

WHEELER, Joseph—Major General, CSA (USMA 1859). Commander

of the Cavalry Corps of Hood's Army of Tennessee. Left behind to oppose Sherman's march across Georgia when Hood moved northward into Tennessee.

WHITING, William Henry Chase—Major General, CSA (USMA 1845). Commander of the 3rd Military District of Beauregard's Department of Southern Virginia and North Carolina, whose primary responsibility was the defense of Wilmington, N.C.

WHITTAKER, Walter C.—Brigadier General, USV. Commander of the 2nd Brigade of Kimball's 1st Division of Stanley's (later Wood's) 4th Corps in Thomas's Army of the Cumberland in Sherman's Military Division of the Mississippi.

WICKHAM, William C.—Brigadier General, CSA. Commander of a brigade in Fitzhugh's Lee's 2nd Cavalry Division of Lee's Army of Northern Virginia. Temporarily commanded the division in Fitz Lee's absence.

WILCOX, Cadmus Marcellus—Major General, CSA (USMA 1846). Commander of a division in A. P. Hill's 3rd Corps of Lee's Army of Northern Virginia.

WILDER, John T.—Brevet Brigadier General, USV. Member of the military commission trying prominent Copperheads in Indiana. Former commander of the "Lightning Brigade" of mounted infantry in Thomas's Army of the Cumberland.

WILDES, Thomas—Lieutenant Colonel, USV. Commander of the 1st Brigade of Thoburn's 1st Division of Crook's Army of West Virginia ("8th Corps") in Sheridan's Army of the Shenandoah (Middle Military Division). Succeeded George D. Wells.

WILLCOX, Orlando B.—Brigadier General, USV (USMA 1847). Commander of the 1st Division of Parke's 9th Corps in Meade's Army of the Potomac.

WILLIAMS, John S.—Brigadier General, CSA. Commander of brigades detached from Wheeler's Cavalry Corps of Hood's Army of Tennessee that helped defend Saltville, Virginia.

WILLIAMS, Seth—Major General, USV (USMA 1842). Assistant adjutant general of Meade's Army of the Potomac.

WILSON, James Harrison—Brigadier (Brevet Major) General, USV. (USMA 1860). Commander of the 3rd Division of Torbert's Cavalry Corps in Sherman's Army of the Shenandoah (Middle Military Division).

Later Commander of the Cavalry Corps of Sherman's Military Division of the Mississippi.

WINSLOW, Edward F.—Colonel, USV. Commander of a brigade from Grierson's Cavalry Corps of Washburn's District of West Tennessee in Howard's Department of the Tennessee that was sent to Missouri to help pursue Price's raid. There it made up part of Pleasonton's ad hoc cavalry division of Rosecrans' Department of Missouri. Later it was designated the 1st Brigade of Upton's 4th Division of Wilson's Cavalry Corps of Sherman's Military Division of the Mississippi, but it did not reach Tennessee in time to take part in the Nashville campaign.

WOLFE, Edward H.—Colonel, USV. Commander of the 3rd Brigade of Garrard's 2nd Division of A. J. Smith's Detachment Army of Tennessee in Thomas's Army of the Cumberland in Sherman's Military Division of the Mississippi.

WOOD, Thomas J.—Brigadier General, USV (USMA 1845). Commander of the 3rd Division of Stanley's 4th Corps in Thomas's Army of the Cumberland in Sherman's Military Division of the Mississippi. Succeeded to the command of the corps after Stanley was wounded at Franklin.

WRIGHT, Horatio G.—Major General, USV (USMA 1841). Commander of the 6th Corps in Sheridan's Army of the Shenandoah (Middle Military Division).

WRIGHT, Rebecca—Quaker schoolteacher in Winchester, Va., who sent information to Sheridan about Early's Confederate army.

YOUNG, Bennett H.—Lieutenant, CSA. One of several Confederate officers working out of Canada, he led the raid against St. Albans, Vermont.

YOUNG, J. Morris—Major, CSA. Commander of the 5th Iowa Cavalry Regiment in Capron's 1st Brigade of Johnson's 6th Division of Wilson's Cavalry Corps of Sherman's Military Division of the Mississippi.

YOUNG, John S.—Sergeant, New York Police Department. Chief of detectives of the NYPD.

YOUNG, Pierce M. B.—Brigadier General, CSA. Commander of a brigade in Butler's 1st Division of Hampton's Cavalry Corps of Lee's Army of Northern Virginia.

YOUNG, William Hugh—Brigadier General, CSA. Commander of a brigade in French's Division of Stewart's Corps of Hood's Army of Tennessee.

Appendix B

Military Organizations
(Early September 1864)

UNITED STATES ARMY

Commander-in-Chief—President Abraham Lincoln
Secretary of War—Edwin McMasters Stanton
General-in-Chief—Lieutenant General Ulysses S. Grant
Chief of Staff—Major General Henry W. Halleck
Quartermaster General—Brigadier General Montgomery C. Miegs

DEPARTMENT OF THE EAST:

Commanding General—Major General John A. Dix

DEPARTMENT OF THE SOUTH:

Commanding General—Major General John G. Foster

Northern District: Brigadier General Rufus Saxton
   Folly Island, S.C.: Colonel L. Von Gilsa
   Morris Island, S.C.: Colonel William Gurney

District of Beaufort, S.C.: commander unknown

District of Hilton Head, S.C.: Brigadier General E. E. Potter
District of Florida: Brigadier General J. P. Hatch

NORTHERN DEPARTMENT:
Commanding General—Major General S. P. Heintzelman

DEPARTMENT OF THE NORTHWEST:
Commanding General—Major General John Pope
District of Iowa: Brigadier General Alfred Sully
District of Minnesota: Brigadier General Henry H. Sibley
District of Wisconsin: Brigadier General Thomas C. H. Smith

DEPARTMENT OF KANSAS:
Commanding General—Major General Samuel R. Curtis
District of North Kansas: Brigadier General Thomas A. Davies
District of South Kansas: Brigadier General Thomas J. McKean
District of the Upper Arkansas: Major General James G. Blunt
District of Nebraska: Brigadier General Robert B. Mitchell
District of Colorado: Colonel John M. Chivington

DEPARTMENT OF NEW MEXICO:
Commanding General—Brigadier General James H. Carleton
District of Arizona: Colonel George W. Bowie

DEPARTMENT OF THE PACIFIC:
Commanding General—Major General Irvin McDowell

ARMIES OPERATING AGAINST RICHMOND:
Commanding General—(Lieutenant General Ulysses S. Grant)
Chief of Staff—Brigadier General John A. Rawlins
Chief Quartermaster—Brigadier General Rufus Ingalls
Chief Engineer—Brigadier General John G. Barnard

ARMY OF THE POTOMAC:
Commanding General—Major General George Gordon Meade
Chief of Staff—Major General Andrew A. Humphreys
Adjutant General—Major General Seth Williams

Provost Guard: Brigadier General Marsena R. Patrick

Volunteer Engineer Brigade: Brig. Gen. Henry W. Benham

Artillery: Brigadier General Henry J. Hunt
    Artillery Park: Captain Cavin Shaffer
    6th Corps Artillery: Captain William A. Harn

2nd (cavalry) Division: Brigadier General David M. Gregg
    1st Brigade: Colonel William Stedman
    2nd Brigade: Colonel Charles H. Smith

2nd ARMY CORPS: Major General Winfield S. Hancock

1st Division: Brigadier General Nelson A. Miles
    1st Brigade: Colonel James C. Lynch
    Consolidated Brigade: Lieutenant Colonel William Wilson
    4th Brigade: Lieutenant Colonel William Glenny

2nd Division: Major General John Gibbon
    1st Brigade: Lieutenant Colonel Horace P. Rugg
    2nd Brigade: Colonel Mathew Murphy
    3rd Brigade: Colonel Thomas A. Smyth

3rd Division: Brigadier General Gershom Mott
    1st Brigade: Brigadier General P. Regis de Trobriand
    2nd Brigade: Brigadier General Bryon R. Pierce
    3rd Brigade: Colonel Robert McAllister

Artillery Brigade: Major John G. Hazard

5th ARMY CORPS: Major General Gouverneur K. Warren

1st Division: Brigadier General Charles Griffin
    1st Brigade: Lieutenant Colonel William A. Throop
    2nd Brigade: Colonel Edgar M. Gregory
    3rd Brigade: Colonel James Gwyn

2nd Division: Brigadier General Romeyn B. Ayres
    1st Brigade: Colonel Charles P. Stone
    2nd Brigade: Colonel Samuel A. Graham
    3rd Brigade: Colonel J. William Hofmann

3rd Division: Brigadier General Samuel W. Crawford
    1st Brigade: Colonel Thomas F. McCoy
    2nd Brigade: Brigadier General Henry Baxter
    3rd (Iron) Brigade: Brigadier General Edward S. Bragg

Artillery Brigade: Colonel Charles S. Wainwright

9th ARMY CORPS: Major General John G. Parke

1st Division: Brigadier General John F. Hartranft
  1st Brigade: Lieutenant Colonel Joseph H. Barnes
  2nd Brigade: Lieutenant Colonel Gilbert P. Robinson

2nd Division: Brigadier General Robert B. Potter
  1st Brigade: Colonel John I. Curtin
  2nd Brigade: Brigadier General Simon G. Griffin

3rd Division: Brigadier General Orlando B. Willcox
  1st Brigade: Colonel Benjamin C. Christ
  2nd Brigade: Colonel William Humphrey

4th Division: Brigadier General Edward Ferrero
  1st Brigade: Colonel Joshua K. Sigfield
  2nd Brigade: Colonel Henry G. Thomas

Artillery Brigade: Lieutenant Colonel J. Albert Monroe

DEPARTMENT OF VIRGINIA AND NORTH CAROLINA:

Commanding General—Major General Benjamin F. Butler

District of Eastern Virginia: Brig. Gen. George F. Shepley
  Portsmouth: Brigadier General Israel Vogdes
  Newport News: Brigadier General Edward A. Wild
  Fort Monroe: Colonel Joseph Roberts
  Fort Magruder: Colonel Joseph J. Morrison
  Eastern Shore: Captain Robert E. Duvall

District of North Carolina: Brigadier General Innis N. Palmer
  Sub-district of the Albemarle: Colonel David W. Wardrop
  Sub-district of Beaufort: Colonel Thomas J. C. Amory
  Sub-district of New Berne: Brig. Gen. Edward Harland

ARMY OF THE JAMES:

Commanding General—(Major General Benjamin F. Butler)
Chief Engineer—Brigadier General Godfrey Weitzel

Siege Artillery: Colonel Henry L. Abbot

10th ARMY CORPS: Major General David B. Birney

1st Division: Brigadier General Alfred H. Terry
  1st Brigade: Colonel Joshua B. Howell
  2nd Brigade: Colonel Joseph R. Hawley
  3rd Brigade: Colonel Harris M. Plaisted

2nd Division: Brigadier General Robert S. Foster

1st Brigade: Colonel N. Martin Curtis
2nd Brigade: Colonel William B. Barton
3rd Brigade: Colonel Francis A. Osborn

3rd Division: Brigadier General William Birney
1st Brigade: Colonel James Shaw, Jr.
2nd Brigade: Colonel John H. Holman

Artillery Brigade: Lieutenant Colonel Freeman McGilvery

18th ARMY CORPS: Major General Edward O. C. Ord

1st Division: Brigadier General Joseph B. Carr
1st Brigade: Colonel Aaron F. Stevens
2nd Brigade: Colonel Edgar M. Cullen
3rd Brigade: Colonel Samuel H. Roberts

2nd Division: Brigadier General Adelbert Ames
1st Brigade: Colonel James Stewart, Jr.
2nd Brigade: Colonel George M. Guion
3rd Brigade: Colonel Harrison S. Fairchild

3rd Division: Brigadier General Charles J. Paine
1st Brigade: Colonel John H. Holman
2nd Brigade: Colonel Alonzo G. Draper
3rd Brigade: Colonel Samuel A. Duncan

Artillery Brigade: Colonel Alexander Piper

Cavalry Division: Brigadier General August V. Kautz
1st Brigade: Colonel Robert West
2nd Brigade: Colonel Samuel P. Spear

MIDDLE MILITARY DIVISION:

Commanding General—Major General Philip H. Sheridan

DEPARTMENT OF WASHINGTON:

Commanding General—Major General Christopher C. Augur

Light Artillery Camp: Brigadier General Albion P. Howe

Provisional Brigades: Major General Silas Casey

Hardin's Division: Brigadier General Martin D. Hardin
1st Brigade: Colonel J. Howard Kitching
2nd Brigade: Lieutenant Colonel Horace G. Thomas
3rd Brigade: Lieutenant Colonel John H. Oberteuffer
Fort Foote, Md.: Captain Oliver J. Conant

District of St. Mary's, Md.: Brigadier General James Barnes

Fort Washington, Md.: Colonel Horace Brooks

District of Washington: Colonel Moses N. Wisewell
1st Brigade: Colonel George W. Gile

De Russy's Division: Brigadier General Gustavus A. De Russy
1st Brigade: Colonel Joseph N. G. Whistler
2nd Brigade: Colonel Thomas Wilhelm
3rd Brigade: Colonel William Heine
4th Brigade: Colonel Addison Farnsworth

Cavalry Brigade: Colonel Henry M. Lazelle

District of Alexandria: Brigadier General John P. Slough

Provost Detachments: Lieutenant Colonel Henry H. Wells

Rendezvous of Distribution: Lieutenant Colonel Samuel McKelvy

Cavalry Division: Colonel William Gamble

MIDDLE DEPARTMENT (8th ARMY CORPS):

Commanding General—Major General Lewis Wallace
1st Separate Brigade: Brigadier General Erastus B. Tyler
2nd Separate Brigade: Brigadier General William W. Morris
3rd Separate Brigade: Brigadier General Henry H. Lockwood
Annapolis, Md.: Colonel Adrian R. Root
Wilmington, Del.: Colonel Samuel M. Bowman

DEPARTMENT OF THE SUSQUEHANNA:

Commanding General—Major General Darius N. Couch
Philadelphia, Pa.: Major General George Cadwalader
Chelton Hill, Pa.: Lieutenant Colonel Louis Wagner
Harrisburg, Pa.: Captain Richard I. Dodge

District of the Monongahela: Brigadier General Thomas Rowley
Fort Miflin, Pa.: Lieutenant Colonel Daniel P. Whiting

DEPARTMENT OF WEST VIRGINIA:

Commanding General—Brevet Major General George Crook

District of Harper's Ferry: Brigadier General John Stevenson
Kenly's Brigade: Brigadier General John R. Kenly
3rd Brig., 1st Div., 19th Corps: Colonel Leonard Currie

West of Sleepy Hollow: Brevet Major General Benjamin Kelley

Kanawha Valley Forces: Brigadier General Jeremiah C. Sullivan

1st Cavalry Division: Brigadier General Alfred N. Duffié

ARMY OF THE SHENANDOAH:
Commanding General—(Major General Philip H. Sheridan)

CAVALRY CORPS: Brevet Major General Alfred T. A. Torbert

1st Division: Brigadier General Wesley Merritt
   1st Brigade: Brigadier General George A. Custer
   2nd Brigade: Brevet Brigadier General Thomas C. Devin
   Reserve Brigade: Colonel Charles Russell Lowell, Jr.

2nd Division: Brevet Major General William A. Averell
   1st Brigade: Colonel James Schoonmaker
   2nd Brigade: Colonel Henry Capehart

3rd Division: Brigadier General James H. Wilson
   1st Brigade: Brigadier General John B. McIntosh
   2nd Brigade: Brigadier General George H. Chapman

Horse Artillery: Captain La Rhett L. Livingston

6th ARMY CORPS: Major General Horatio G. Wright

1st Division: Brigadier General David A. Russell
   1st Brigade: Lieutenant Colonel Edward L. Campbell
   2nd Brigade: Brigadier General Emory Upton
   3rd Brigade: Colonel Oliver Edwards

2nd Division: Brigadier General George W. Getty
   1st Brigade: Brigadier General Frank Wheaton
   2nd Brigade: Colonel James M. Warner
   3rd Brigade: Brigadier General Daniel D. Bidwell

3rd Division: Brigadier General James B. Ricketts
   1st Brigade: Colonel William Emerson
   2nd Brigade: Colonel J. Warren Keifer

Artillery Brigade: Colonel Charles H. Tompkins

"8th ARMY CORPS" (ARMY OF WEST VIRGINIA):
(Brevet Major General George Crook)

1st Division: Colonel Joseph Thoburn
   1st Brigade: Colonel George D. Wells
   2nd Brigade: Lieutenant Colonel Robert S. Northcott
   3rd Brigade: Colonel Thomas M. Harris

2nd Division: Colonel Isaac H. Duval
   1st Brigade: Colonel Rutherford B. Hayes

2nd Brigade: Colonel Daniel D. Johnson
Artillery Brigade: Captain Henry A. du Pont

DETACHMENT 19th CORPS:
Brevet Major General William H. Emory

1st Division: Brigadier General William Dwight
    1st Brigade: Colonel George L. Beal
    2nd Brigade: Brigadier General James W. McMillan

2nd Division: Brigadier General Cuvier Grover
    1st Brigade: Brigadier General Henry W. Birge
    2nd Brigade: Colonel Edward L. Molineux
    3rd Brigade: Colonel Jacob Sharpe
    4th Brigade: Colonel David Shunk

Reserve Artillery: Captain Elijah D. Taft

MILITARY DIVISION OF THE MISSISSIPPI:

Commanding General—Major General William T. Sherman
Chief of Artillery—Brigadier General William F. Barry

FIELD FORCES (sometimes known as "The Army of the West"):
Commanding General—(Major General William T. Sherman)

ARMY OF THE CUMBERLAND:

Commanding General—Major General George H. Thomas
Chief of Artillery—Brigadier General John M. Brannan
Reserve Brigade: Colonel Heber Le Favour
Pontoniers: Colonel George P. Buell

4th ARMY CORPS: Major General David S. Stanley

1st Division: Brigadier General Nathan Kimball
    1st Brigade: Colonel Isaac M. Kirby
    2nd Brigade: Colonel Jacob E. Taylor
    3rd Brigade: Colonel John E. Bennett

2nd Division: Brigadier General John Newton
    1st Brigade: Colonel Emerson Opdycke
    2nd Brigade: Colonel John W. Blake
    3rd Brigade: Brigadier General Luther P. Bradley

3rd Division: Brigadier General Thomas J. Wood
    1st Brigade: Colonel Charles T. Hotchkiss

2nd Brigade: Colonel P. Sidney Post
3rd Brigade: Colonel Frederick Knefler

Artillery Brigade: Captain Lyman Bridges

14th ARMY CORPS: Brevet Major General Jefferson C. Davis

1st Division: Brigadier General William P. Carlin
  1st Brigade: Colonel Marion C. Taylor
  2nd Brigade: Major John R. Edie
  3rd Brigade: Colonel Marshal F. Moore

2nd Division: Brigadier General James D. Morgan
  1st Brigade: Colonel Charles M. Lum
  2nd Brigade: Colonel John G. Mitchell
  3rd Brigade: Lieutenant Colonel James W. Langley

3rd Division: Brigadier General Absalom Baird
  1st Brigade: Colonel Moses B. Walker
  2nd Brigade: Colonel Newell Gleason
  3rd Brigade: Colonel George P. Este

Artillery Brigade: Major Charles Houghtaling

20th ARMY CORPS: Major General Henry W. Slocum

1st Division: Brigadier General Alpheus S. Williams
  1st Brigade: Brigadier General Joseph F. Knipe
  2nd Brigade: Brigadier General Thomas H. Ruger
  3rd Brigade: Colonel Horace Boughton

2nd Division: Brigadier General John W. Geary
  1st Brigade: Colonel Ario Pardee, Jr.
  2nd Brigade: Colonel George W. Mindil
  3rd Brigade: Colonel David Ireland

3rd Division: Brigadier General William T. Ward
  1st Brigade: Colonel Benjamin Harrison
  2nd Brigade: Colonel John Coburn
  3rd Brigade: Colonel James Woods, Jr.

Artillery Brigade: Major John A. Reynolds

CAVALRY CORPS: Brigadier General Washington L. Elliott

1st Division: Brigadier General Edward M. McCook
  1st Brigade: Brigadier General John T. Croxton
  2nd Brigade: Lieutenant Colonel Horace P. Lamson
  3rd Brigade: Colonel John K. Faulkner

2nd Division: Brigadier General Kenner Garrard
  1st Brigade: Colonel Robert H. G. Minty
  2nd Brigade: Colonel Beroth B. Eggleston
  3rd Brigade: (mounted infantry): Colonel Abram O. Miller

3rd Division: Brigadier General Judson Kilpatrick
  1st Brigade: Major J. Morris Young
  2nd Brigade: Lieutenant Colonel Fielder A. Jones
  3rd Brigade: Colonel Eli H. Murray

ARMY OF THE TENNESSEE:

Commanding General—Major General Oliver O. Howard

15th ARMY CORPS: Major General John A. Logan

1st Division: Major General Peter J. Osterhaus
  1st Brigade: Colonel Milo Smith
  2nd Brigade: Colonel James A. Williamson
  3rd Brigade: Colonel Hugo Wangelin
  Artillery: Major Clemens Landgraeber

2nd Division: Brigadier General William B. Hazen
  1st Brigade: Colonel Theodore Jones
  2nd Brigade: Colonel Wells S. Jones
  Artillery: Captain Francis De Gress

3rd Division: Brigadier General John E. Smith
  1st Brigade: Colonel Joseph B. McCown
  2nd Brigade: Colonel Green B. Raum
  3rd Brigade: Colonel Jabez Banbury
  Artillery: Captain Henry Dillon

4th Division: Brigadier General William Harrow
  1st Brigade: Colonel John M. Oliver
  2nd Brigade: Brigadier General Charles C. Walcutt
  3rd Brigade: Colonel John M. Oliver
  Artillery: Captain Josiah H. Burton

LEFT WING, 16th ARMY CORPS:
Brigadier General Thomas E. G. Ransom

2nd Division: Brigadier General John M. Corse
  1st Brigade: Brigadier General Elliott W. Rice
  2nd Brigade: Colonel Robert N. Adams
  3rd Brigade: Colonel Richard Rowett
  Artillery: Captain Frederick Welker

4th Division: Brigadier General John W. Fuller
 1st Brigade: Lieutenant Colonel Henry T. McDowell
 2nd Brigade: Brigadier General John W. Sprague
 3rd Brigade: Colonel John Tillson
 Artillery: Captain George Robinson

17th ARMY CORPS: Major General Francis P. Blair, Jr.

3rd Division: Brigadier General Charles R. Woods
 1st Brigade: Colonel George E. Bryant
 2nd Brigade: Lieutenant Colonel Greenberry F. Wiles
 3rd Brigade: Colonel Adam G. Malloy
 Artillery: Captain William S. Williams

4th Division: Brigadier General Giles A. Smith
 1st Brigade: Colonel Benjamin F. Potts
 2nd Brigade: Colonel John Logan
 3rd Brigade: Brigadier General William W. Belknap
 Artillery: Captain William Z. Clayton

ARMY OF THE OHIO (23rd ARMY CORPS):

Commanding General—Major General John M. Schofield

2nd Division: Brigadier General Milo S. Hascall
 1st Brigade: Brigadier General Joseph A. Cooper
 2nd Brigade: Colonel John R. Bond
 3rd Brigade: Colonel Silas A. Strickland
 Artillery: Captain Joseph C. Shields

3rd Division: Brigadier General Jacob D. Cox
 1st Brigade: Brigadier General James W. Reilly
 2nd Brigade: Colonel John S. Casement
 3rd Brigade: Colonel Israel N. Stiles
 Artillery: Major Henry W. Wells

Cavalry Division: Colonel Israel Garrard
 Mounted Brigade: Colonel George S. Acker
 Dismounted Brigade: Colonel Horace Capron

DEPARTMENT OF THE CUMBERLAND:

Commanding General—(Major General George H. Thomas)

DISTRICT OF TENNESSEE: Major General Lovell H. Rousseau
 1st Brig., 4th Div., 20th Corps: Col. Charles Doolittle
Post of Nashville: Brigadier General John F. Miller

Garrison Artillery: Major Josiah W. Church
Artillery Reserve: Colonel James Barnett

Nashville & Northwestern RR: Colonel Charles R. Thompson

Nashville & Chattanooga RR: Major General Robert H. Milroy
  1st Brigade: Brigadier General Horatio P. Van Cleve
  2nd Brigade: Colonel Edward J. Robinson
  3rd Brigade: Colonel Wladimir Krzyzanowski

Engineer Brigade: Colonel William B. McCreery

Veteran Reserve Corps: Major Audley W. Gazzam

Governor's Guard: Brigadier General Andrew Johnson

DISTRICT OF NORTHERN ALABAMA:
Brig. Gen. Robert S. Granger

Post of Chattanooga: Colonel Timothy R. Stanley
  1st Separate Brigade: (Colonel Timothy R. Stanley)
  Garrison Artillery: Major Charles S. Cotter

4th Cavalry Division: Colonel George Spalding
  1st Brigade: Lieutenant Colonel Jacob M. Thornburgh
  2nd Brigade: Lieutenant Colonel William J. Clift

DEPARTMENT OF THE TENNESSEE:

Commanding General—(Major General Oliver O. Howard)

DISTRICT OF WEST TENNESSEE: Major General C. C. Washburn

District of Memphis: Brigadier General Ralph P. Buckland
  1st Brigade: Colonel George B. Hoge
  3rd Brigade: Colonel John Wood
  4th Brigade: Colonel Edwin L. Buttrick
  Fort Pickering: Colonel Ignatz G. Kappner
  1st Brigade: USCT: Colonel Edward Bouton

Cavalry Corps: Brigadier General
Benjamin H. Grierson

1st Division: Brigadier General Edward Hatch
  1st Brigade: Colonel Thomas P. Herrick
  2nd Brigade: Colonel Datus E. Coon

2nd Division: Colonel Edward P. Winslow
  1st Brigade: Colonel Joseph Kargé
  2nd Brigade: Colonel John W. Noble

RIGHT WING, 16th ARMY CORPS: Major General A. J. Smith

1st Division, Brigadier General Joseph A. Mower
  1st Brigade: Colonel William L. McMillen
  2nd Brigade: Colonel Lucius F. Hubbard
  3rd Brigade: Colonel Joseph J. Woods

3rd Division: Colonel William T. Shaw
  1st Brigade: Colonel Charles D. Murray
  2nd Brigade: Colonel James I. Gilbert
  3rd Brigade: Colonel Edward H. Wolfe

DISTRICT OF VICKSBURG: Major General Napoleon J. T. Dana
  Maltby's Brigade: Brigadier General Jasper A. Maltby
  Cavalry: Colonel Embury D. Osband
  Defenses and Post of Natchez: Brigadier General Mason Brayman

1st Division: USCT: Brigadier General John P. Hawkins
  1st Brigade: Colonel Frederick M. Crandal
  2nd Brigade: Colonel Hiram Scofield

Post and Defenses of Goodrich's Landing: Col. Watson Webber

Millikin's Bend: Colonel Van E. Young

1st Brig., 1st Div., 17th Corps: Colonel Frederick Starring
Artillery, 1st Div., 17th Corps: Major Charles Mann

DEPARTMENT OF THE OHIO (23rd ARMY CORPS):

Commanding General—(Major General John M. Schofield)

4th Division: (East Tenn.): Brigadier General Jacob Ammen
  1st Brigade: Colonel William Y. Dillard
  2nd Brigade: Brigadier General Davis Tillson
  3rd Brigade: Lieutenant Colonel Michael L. Patterson

DISTRICT OF KENTUCKY:
Brevet Major General Stephen G. Burbridge

1st Division: Brigadier General Nathaniel C. McLean
  1st Brigade: Brigadier General Edward H. Hobson
  2nd Brigade: Colonel John M. Brown
  3rd Brigade: Colonel Charles S. Hanson
  4th Brigade: Colonel Robert W. Ratliff
  Camp Nelson: Brigadier General Speed S. Fry

2nd Division: Brigadier General Hugh Ewing
  1st Brigade: Lieutenant Colonel Thomas B. Fairleigh

2nd Brigade: Colonel Cicero Maxwell

DISTRICT OF WESTERN KENTUCKY:
Brig. Gen. Eleazer A. Paine
    Cairo, Ill.: Brigadier General Solomon Meredith
    Paducah, Ky.: Colonel Henry W. Barry
    Columbus, Ky.: Colonel James N. McArthur
    Mayfield, Ky.: Lieutenant Colonel John C. Bigelow

MILITARY DIVISION OF WEST MISSISSIPPI
Commanding General—Major General E. R. S. Canby

DEPARTMENT OF THE GULF:
Commanding General—Major General Nathaniel P. Banks

Defenses of New Orleans: Brigadier General Thomas W. Sherman

District of Baton Rouge and Port Hudson:
Major General Francis J. Herron
    Baton Rouge: Brigadier General W. P. Benton
    Port Hudson: Brigadier General George L. Andrews

Cavalry Division: Brigadier General A. L. Lee
    1st Brigade: Colonel John G. Fonda
    2nd Brigade: Colonel William J. Landran

District of La Fourche: Brigadier General Robert A. Cameron

District of Bonnet Carre': Colonel Cyrus Hamlin

District of Carrollton: Colonel Nelson B. Bartram

Forces Lake Ponchartrain: Colonel Robert B. Jones

Forts Jackson and St. Philip: Colonel Charles A. Hartwell

U. S. Forces Mobile Bay: Brigadier General George H. Gordon
    Mobile Point: Brevet Brigadier General Joseph Bailey
    2nd Brigade: Colonel Henry Bertram
    3rd Brig., 2nd Div., 19th Corps: Colonel Joshua J. Guppey

District of West Florida: Brigadier General Alexander Asboth

District of Key West and the Tortugas:
Brigadier General D. P. Woodbury

DISTRICT OF MORGANZA: Brigadier General M. K. Lawler

19th ARMY CORPS: Major General Joseph J. Reynolds

2nd Division: Brigadier General Elias S. Dennis
   1st Brigade: Colonel Benjamin Dornblaser
   2nd Brigade: Colonel James R. Slack

3rd Division: Brigadier General George F. McGinnis
   1st Brigade: Colonel Lionel A. Sheldon
   2nd Brigade: Colonel William T. Spicely
   3rd Brigade: Colonel Frederick W. Moore

Reserve Artillery: Captain Benjamin Nields

Separate Cavalry Brigade: Lieutenant Colonel J. M. Crebs

U. S. Colored Troops: Brigadier General Daniel Ullmann
   1st Brigade: Colonel H. N. Frisbie
   2nd Brigade: Colonel Theodore H. Barrett

Engineer Brigade: Captain Peter C. Hains

DEPARTMENT OF ARKANSAS (7th ARMY CORPS):

Commanding General—Major General Frederick Steele

District of Eastern Arkansas: Colonel William Crooks

District of the Frontier: Brigadier General John M. Thayer
   1st Brigade: Colonel John Edwards
   2nd Brigade: Colonel James M. Williams
   3rd Brigade: Colonel William R. Judson
   Indian Brigade: Colonel Stephen H. Wattles

DISTRICT OF LITTLE ROCK: Brigadier General E. A. Carr

1st Division: Brigadier General Cyrus Bussey
   1st Brigade: Colonel Charles A. Salomon
   2nd Brigade: Colonel Adolph Englemann
   3rd Brigade: Colonel John R. Ritter

2nd Division: Brigadier General Christopher C. Andrews
   1st Brigade: Colonel William H. Graves
   2nd Brigade: Lieutenant Colonel Homer Thrall
   3rd Brigade: Colonel Washington F. Gieger

Independent Cavalry Brigade: Colonel Powell Clayton

DEPARTMENT OF MISSOURI:

Commanding General—Major General William S. Rosecrans

District of St. Louis: Brigadier General Thomas Ewing, Jr.

District of Rolla: Brigadier General John McNeil

District of Central Missouri: Major General Alfred Pleasonton
District of North Missouri: Brigadier General Clinton B. Fisk
District of Southwest Missouri: Brig. Gen. John B. Sanborn
Enrolled Missouri Militia:
　1st District: Brigadier General Edward C. Pike
　7th District: Brigadier General James Craig
　8th District: Brigadier General Joseph B. Douglass

CONFEDERATE STATES ARMY

Commander-in-Chief—President Jefferson Davis
Secretary of War—James Alexander Seddon
Commanding General—General Braxton Bragg
Adjutant and Inspector General—General Samuel Cooper

DEPARTMENT AND ARMY OF NORTHERN VIRGINIA:

Commanding General—General Robert Edward Lee
Chief of Artillery—Brigadier General William N. Pendleton

1st ARMY CORPS: Lieutenant General Richard H. Anderson*

Pickett's Division: Major General George E. Pickett
　Barton's Brigade: Brigadier General Seth M. Barton
　Hunton's Brigade: Brigadier General Eppa Hunton
　Corse's Brigade: Brigadier General Montgomery D. Corse
　Terry's Brigade: Brigadier General William R. Terry

Field's Division: Major General Charles W. Field
　Anderson's Brigade: Brigadier General George T. Anderson
　Law's Brigade: Colonel Pinckney D. Bowles
　Bratton's Brigade: Brigadier General John Bratton
　Benning's Brigade: Colonel Dudly M. DuBose
　Gregg's ("Texas") Brigade: Brigadier General John Gregg

Kershaw's Division: Major General Joseph B. Kershaw*
　Wofford's Brigade: Brigadier General William T. Wofford
　Bryan's Brigade: Brigadier General Goode Bryan
　Humphrey's Brigade: Brigadier General B. G. Humphreys
　Kershaw's Brigade: Colonel John W. Henagan

Artillery: Brigadier General Edward P. Alexander

3rd ARMY CORPS: Lieutenant General Ambrose Powell Hill

Mahone's Division: Major General William Mahone
  Sander's Brigade: Colonel J. Horace King
  Mahone's Brigade: Colonel David A. Weiseger
  Harris's Brigade: Brigadier General Nathaniel H. Harris
  Wright's Brigade: Colonel William Gibson
  Finegan's Brigade: Brigadier General Joseph Finegan

Wilcox's Division: Major General Cadmus Wilcox
  Thomas's Brigade: Colonel Thomas J. Simmons
  McGowan's Brigade: Brigadier General Samuel McGowan
  Lane's Brigade: Brigadier General James H. Lane
  Scale's Brigade: Brigadier General Alfred M. Scales

Heth's Division: Major General Henry Heth
  Davis's Brigade: Brigadier General Joseph R. Davis
  MacRae's Brigade: Brigadier General William MacRae
  Cooke's Brigade: Brigadier General John R. Cooke
  Archer's Brigade: Brigadier General James J. Archer

Artillery: Colonel R. Lindsay Walker

CAVALRY CORPS: Major General Wade Hampton

1st (Hampton's) Division: Brigadier General M. C. Butler
  Dunovant's Brigade: Brigadier General John Dunovant
  Young's Brigade: Brigadier General Pierce M. B. Young
  The Laurel Brigade: Brigadier General Thomas L. Rosser

2nd Division: Major General Fitzhugh Lee*
  Wickham's Brigade: Brigadier General Williams C. Wickham
  Payne's Brigade: Colonel William H. Payne

3rd Division: Major General W. H. F. "Rooney" Lee
  Barringer's Brigade: Brigadier General Rufus Barringer
  Chambliss's Brigade: Brigadier General John Chambliss, Jr.

Horse Artillery Battalion: Major R. Preston Chew

ARMY OF THE VALLEY DISTRICT (2nd ARMY CORPS):

Lieutenant General Jubal Anderson Early

Rodes' Division: Major General Robert E. Rodes
  Grimes' Brigade: Brigadier General Bryan Grimes
  Battle's Brigade: Brigadier General Cullen A. Battle
  Cook's Brigade: Brigadier General Philip Cook
  Cox's Brigade: Brigadier General William R. Cox

Ramseur's Division: Major General Stephen Dodson Ramseur

Pegram's Brigade: Brigadier General John Pegram
Johnston's Brigade: Brigadier General Robert D. Johnston
Godwin's Brigade: Brigadier General Archibald C. Godwin

Breckinridge's Corps: Major General John C. Breckinridge

Gordon's Division: Major General John B. Gordon
Evans' Brigade: Brigadier General Clement A. Evans
Terry's Brigade: Brigadier General William Terry
York's Brigade: Brigadier General Zebulon York

Breckinridge's Division: Brigadier General Gabriel Wharton
Wharton's Brigade: Colonel Augustus Forsberg
Patton's Brigade: Colonel George S. Patton
Smith's Brigade: Colonel Thomas Smith

Cavalry Division: Major General Lunsford L. Lomax
Imboden's Brigade: Brigadier General John Imboden
Johnson's Brigade: Brigadier General Bradley T. Johnson
McCausland's Brigade: Brigadier General John McCausland
Jackson's Brigade: Brigadier General William L. Jackson

Artillery: Brigadier General Armistead L. Long

DEPARTMENT OF RICHMOND:

Commanding General—Lieutenant General Richard S. Ewell**
Johnson's Brigade: Colonel John M. Hughs
Cavalry Brigade: Brigadier General Martin W. Gary
Reserve Forces: Major General James L. Kemper
Artillery Defenses: Lieutenant Colonel John C. Pemberton

DEPARTMENT OF NORTH CAROLINA AND SOUTHERN VIRGINIA:

Commanding General—General Pierre G. T. Beauregard**

Hoke's Division: Major General Robert F. Hoke
Clingman's Brigade: Colonel Hector M. McKethan
Colquitt's Brigade: Brigadier General Alfred H. Colquitt
Hagood's Brigade: Brigadier General Johnson Hagood
Kirkland's Brigade: Brigadier General William W. Kirkland

Johnson's Division: Major General Bushrod R. Johnson
Wise's Brigade: Colonel John Thomas Goode
Ransom's Brigade: Colonel Lee McAfee
Gracie's Brigade: Brigadier General Archibald Gracie
Wallace's Brigade: Brigadier General William H. Wallace

Artillery: Colonel Hilary P. Jones

Cavalry Brigade: Brigadier General James Dearing

Drewry's Bluff: Colonel George H. Terrett

1st Military District: Brigadier General Henry A. Wise
  Walker's Brigade: Brigadier General James A. Walker
  Garnett's Brigade: Lieutenant Colonel John J. Garnett
  Post of Petersburg: Major William Ker
  Fort Clifton: Lieutenant Colonel Henry Guion

2nd Military District: Brigadier General Lawrence S. Baker
  Goldsborough, N.C.: Colonel Stephen D. Pool
  Kinston, N.C.: Colonel John N. Whitford
  Wilmington, N.C.: Lieutenant Colonel John C. Van Hook
  Plymouth, N.C.: Colonel George Wortham
  Weldon, N.C.: Colonel Frank S. Armistead

3rd Military District: Major General William H. C. Whiting
  Fort Fisher: Colonel William Lamb
  Fort Caswell: Colonel T. M. Jones
  Fort Holmes and Fort Pender: Colonel John J. Hedrick
  Fort Anderson: Captain James L. McCormic
  Battery Lamb: Lieutenant John J. Bright
  Masonborough Sound: Colonel George Jackson
  Wilmington and River Defenses: Colonel George Cunningham

DEPARTMENT OF SOUTHWESTERN VIRGINIA AND EAST TENNESSEE:

Commanding General—Brigadier General John Hunt Morgan**
  Giltner's Brigade: Colonel Henry L. Giltner
  Cosby's Brigade: Brigadier General George Cosby
  Morgan's Brigade: Colonel Basil Duke
  Vaughn's Brigade: Brigadier General John Vaughn

DEPARTMENT OF SOUTH CAROLINA, GEORGIA AND FLORIDA:

Commanding General—Major General Samuel Jones

District of Georgia and 3rd Military District of South Carolina
  (McLaws' Division): Major General Lafayette McLaws

1st Military District (Ripley's Brigade):
  Brigadier General Roswell Sabine Ripley

2nd and 6th Military Districts (Robertson's Brigade):
  Brigadier General Beverly H. Robertson

4th Military District: Brigadier General James H. Trapier
5th Military District: Colonel Alfred Rhett
7th Military District (Taliaferro's Brigade): Colonel J. L. Black
District of Florida (Jackson's Brigade):
  Brigadier General John K. Jackson

DEPARTMENT AND ARMY OF TENNESSEE:

Commanding General—General John Bell Hood
Chief Engineer—Major General Martin Luther Smith
Chief of Artillery—Colonel Robert F. Beckham

HARDEE'S CORPS: Lieutenant General William J. Hardee

Cheatham's Division: Major General Benjamin F. Cheatham
  Gist's Brigade: Brigadier General States Rights Gist
  Maney's Brigade: Colonel George C. Porter
  Wright's Brigade: Brigadier General John C. Carter
  Strahl's Brigade: Brigadier General Otho F. Strahl
  Vaughn's Brigade: Brigadier General George W. Gordon

Cleburne's Division: Major General Patrick R. Cleburne
  Lowrey's Brigade: Brigadier General Mark P. Lowery
  Granbury's Brigade: Brigadier General Hiram B. Granbury
  Govan's Brigade: Colonel Peter V. Green
  Mercer's Brigade: Colonel Charles H. Olmstead

Bate's Division: Major General William B. Bate
  Tyler's Brigade: Brigadier General Thomas B. Smith
  Finley's Brigade: Colonel Robert Bullock
  Jackson's Brigade: Colonel William D. Mitchell

Artillery: Colonel Melancthon Smith

LEE'S CORPS: Lieutenant General Stephen Dill Lee

Stevenson's Division: Major General Carter L. Stevenson
  Brown's and Reynold's Brigades: Colonel Joseph B. Palmer
  Pettus's Brigade: Brigadier General Edmund W. Pettus
  Cumming's Brigade: Colonel Charles M. Shelley

Johnson's Division: Major General Edward "Allegheny" Johnson
  Deas' Brigade: Brigadier General Zachariah C. Deas
  Manigault's Brigade: Brigadier General Arthur M. Manigault
  Brantly's Brigade: Brigadier General William F. Brantly
  Tucker's Brigade: Brigadier General Jacob H. Sharp

Clayton's Division: Major General Henry D. Clayton
   Stovall's Brigade: Brigadier General Marcellus A. Stovall
   Gibson's Brigade: Brigadier General Randall L. Gibson
   Holtzclaw's Brigade: Colonel Bushrod Jones
Artillery: Lieutenant Colonel James H. Hallonquist

STEWART'S CORPS: Lieutenant General Alexander P. Stewart

Loring's Division: Major General William W. Loring
   Featherston's Brigade: Brig. Gen. Winfield S. Featherston
   Adams' Brigade: Brigadier General John Adams
   Scott's Brigade: Brigadier General Thomas M. Scott

French's Division: Major General Samuel G. French
   Ector's Brigade: Brigadier General William H. Young
   1st Missouri Brigade: Brigadier General Francis Cockrell
   Sears' Brigade: Brigadier General Claudius W. Sears

Walthall's Division: Major General Edward C. Walthall
   Quarles' Brigade: William A. Quarles
   Cantey's Brigade: Colonel Edward A. O'Neal
   Reynolds' Brigade: Brigadier General Daniel H. Reynolds
Artillery: Lieutenant Colonel Samuel C. Williams

CAVALRY CORPS: Major General Joseph Wheeler

Martin's Division: Brigadier General William Wirt Allen
   Allen's Brigade: commander unknown
   Iverson's Brigade: Brigadier General Alfred Iverson

Humes' Division: Brigadier General William Y. C. Humes
   Ashby's Brigade: Colonel Henry M. Ashby
   Harrison's Brigade: Colonel Thomas Harrison

Kelly's Division: Brigadier General John H. Kelly
   Anderson's Brigade: Brigadier General Robert H. Anderson
   Hanson's Brigade: Colonel Moses W. Hannon
   Dibrell's Brigade: Colonel George G. Dibrell

Williams's Brigade: Brigadier General John S. Williams

Reserves: Brigadier General John T. Morgan

Artillery: Major James Hamilton

Jackson's Cavalry Division: Brigadier General Wm. H. Jackson
   Armstrong's Brigade: Brigadier General Frank C. Armstrong
   Ferguson's Brigade: Colonel William Boyles
   Ross's Brigade: Brigadier General Lawrence S. Ross

Lewis's ("Orphan") Brigade (mounted infantry):
Brigadier General Joseph H. Lewis
Artillery: Captain John Waties

DEPARTMENT OF ALABAMA, MISSISSIPPI, AND EAST LOUISIANA:

Commanding General—Lieutenant General Richard Taylor

District North of Homochitto: Brigadier General Wirt Adams
Wood's (cavalry) Brigade: Colonel Robert C. Wood, Jr.
Mabry's (cavalry) Brigade: Colonel Hinchie P. Mabry

District South of Homochitto: Brigadier General George Hodge

District of Central and No. Alabama: Brig. Gen. Daniel Adams
Clanton's (cavalry) Brigade: Brig. Gen. James H. Clanton
Armistead's (cavalry) Brigade: Colonel Charles P. Ball

District of the Gulf: Major General Dabney H. Maury
Thomas' Brigade: Brigadier General Bryan M. Thomas
Liddell's Brigade: Brigadier General St. John R. Liddell
Higgins' Brigade: Brigadier General Edward Higgins

DISTRICT OF MISSISSIPPI AND WEST TENNESSEE:
Major General Nathan Bedford Forrest

1st (cavalry) Division: Brigadier General James R. Chalmers
1st Brigade: Colonel William L. Duckworth
2nd Brigade: Colonel Robert McCulloch

2nd (cavalry) Division: Brigadier General Abraham Buford
3rd Brigade: Brigadier General Hylan B. Lyon
4th Brigade: Colonel Tyree H. Bell

Artillery: Captain John Morton

TRANS-MISSISSIPPI DEPARTMENT:

Commanding General—General E. Kirby Smith

1st ARMY CORPS: Lieutenant General Simon Bolivar Buckner

1st (Texas) Division: Major General John H. Forney
1st Texas Brigade: Brigadier General Thomas N. Waul
2nd Texas Brigade: Brigadier General Richard Waterhouse
3rd Texas Brigade: Brigadier General Robert P. Maclay
4th Mounted Artillery Battalion: Major Charles W. Squires

Polignac's Division: Major General Camille J. Polignac

4th Texas Brigade: Brigadier General William H. King
1st Louisiana Brigade: Brigadier General Allen Thomas
2nd Louisiana Brigade: Brigadier General Henry Gray
3rd Mounted Artillery Battalion: Major Thomas A. Fairies

2nd Texas Cavalry Division: Major General Samuel B. Maxey
4th Texas Brigade: Brigadier General Arthur P. Bagby
5th Texas Brigade: Brigadier General Richard M. Gano
6th Texas Brigade: Brigadier General Xavier B. Debray
1st Horse Artillery Battalion: Major Oliver J. Semmes

Vincent's (cavalry) Brigade: Colonel William G. Vincent

Harrison's (cavalry) Brigade: Colonel Isaac F. Harrison

2nd ARMY CORPS: Major General John Bankhead Magruder

1st Arkansas Division: Major General Thomas J. Churchill
1st Arkansas Brigade: Brigadier General John Selden Roane
2nd Arkansas Brigade: Brigadier General Evander McNair
3rd Arkansas Brigade: Brigadier General James C. Tappan
4th Arkansas Brigade: Brigadier General Alexander Hawthorn
5th Light Artillery Battalion: Captain William D. Blocher

1st Missouri Division: Major General Mosby Monroe Parsons
1st Missouri Brigade: Colonel Charles S. Mitchell
2nd Missouri Brigade: Colonel Simon P. Burns

1st Texas Cavalry Division: Major General John A. Wharton
1st Texas Brigade: Brigadier General William Steele
2nd Texas Brigade: Brigadier General James P. Major
3rd Texas Brigade: Colonel William P. Hardeman

3rd ARMY CORPS: Major General John G. Walker

2nd Texas Division:
5th Texas Brigade: Brigadier General James M. Hawes
6th Texas Brigade: Brigadier General Paul O. Hebert
6th Mounted Artillery Battalion: Captain H. Willke

3rd Texas Cavalry Division: Brigadier General Thomas Drayton
7th Texas Brigade: Brigadier General James E. Slaughter
8th Texas Brigade: Brigadier General Henry E. McCulloch

CAVALRY CORPS: Major General Sterling Price

Indian Cavalry Division: Brigadier General Douglas H. Cooper
1st Indian Brigade: Brigadier General Stand Watie

2nd Indian Brigade: Colonel Tandy Walker

1st Arkansas Cavalry Division: Major General James F. Fagan
Cabell's Brigade: Brigadier General William L. Cabell
Dobbin's Brigade: Colonel Archibald S. Dobbin
Slemons' Brigade: Colonel W. F. Slemons
McCray's Brigade: Colonel Thomas H. McCray

1st Missouri Cavalry Division: Major General John Marmaduke
Marmaduke's Brigade: Brigadier General John B. Clark, Jr.
Freeman's Brigade: Colonel Thomas R. Freeman

Shelby's (cavalry) Division: Brigadier General Joseph Shelby
Shelby's Brigade: Colonel David Shanks
Jackman's Brigade: Colonel Sidney D. Jackman

Tyler's Brigade: Colonel Charles H. Tyler

*R. H. Anderson, the 1st Corps headquarters, Kershaw's Division of
infantry, and Fitzhugh Lee's division of cavalry were in the Shenandoah Valley with Early.

**Subordinate to General Robert E. Lee

Appendix C

Bibliography

BOOKS

Ammen, Daniel. *The Atlantic Coast.* New York, 1883.

Basler, Roy P., ed. *The Collected Works of Abraham Lincoln.* 8 vols. New Brunswick, N.J., 1953–55.

Bergeron, Arthur W., Jr., *Confederate Mobile.* Jackson, Miss., 1991.

Boatner, Mark Mayo III. *The Civil War Dictionary.* New York, 1959.

Boritt, Gabor S., ed. *Why the Confederacy Lost.* New York, 1992.

Boykin, Edward. *Beefsteak Raid.* New York, 1960.

Brandt, Nat. *The Man Who Tried to Burn New York.* Syracuse, 1986.

Brooks, Noah. *Washington in Lincoln's Time.* New York, 1958.

Carter, Samuel III. *The Last Cavaliers: Confederate and Union Cavalry in the Civil War.* New York, 1979.

Castel, Albert. *General Sterling Price and the Civil War in the West.* Baton Rouge, 1968.

———. *William Clark Quantrill: His Life and Times.* New York, 1962.

Catton, Bruce. *A Stillness at Appomattox.* Garden City, N.Y., 1957.

———. *Grant Takes Command.* Boston, 1968.

———. *Never Call Retreat.* Garden City, N.Y., 1965.

———. *This Hallowed Ground: The Story of the Union Side of the Civil War.* New York, 1956.

Chesnut, Mary Boykin. *A Diary From Dixie.* New York, 1905.

Coggins, Jack. *Arms and Equipment of the Civil War.* Garden City, N.Y., 1962.

Commager, Henry Steele, ed. *The Blue and the Gray.* Indianapolis and New York, 1950.

Connelly, Thomas Lawrence. *Autumn of Glory: The Army of Tennessee, 1862–1865.* Baton Rouge, 1971.

Cornish, Dudley Taylor. *The Sable Arm: Black Troops in the Union Army, 1861–1865*. Lawrence, Kansas, 1956.

Cox, Jacob D. *The March to the Sea, Franklin and Nashville*. New York, 1882.

Dana, Charles A. *Recollections of the Civil War*. New York, 1898.

Davis, Burke. *Sherman's March*. New York, 1980.

Davis, William C. *The Orphan Brigade: The Kentucky Confederates Who Couldn't Go Home*. Garden City, N.Y., 1980.

Douglas, Henry Kyd. *I Rode With Stonewall*. Chapel Hill, 1940.

Dowdey, Clifford and Louis H. Manarin, eds. *The Wartime Papers of R. E. Lee*. New York, 1961.

Dyer, Frederick H. *A Compendium of the War of the Rebellion*. Des Moines, Iowa, 1908.

Early, Jubal Anderson. *War Memoirs*. Bloomington, Ind., 1960.

Eaton, Clement. *Jefferson Davis*. New York, 1977.

Faust, Patricia L., ed. *Historical Times Illustrated Encyclopedia of the Civil War*. New York, 1986.

Foote, Shelby. *The Civil War*. 3 vols. New York, 1958–1974.

Freeman, Douglas Southall. *Lee's Lieutenants: A Study in Command*. 3 vols. New York, 1942–1944.

———. *R. E. Lee*. 4 vols. New York, 1934–1935.

Fuller, Major General J. F. C. *Grant & Lee: A Study in Personality and Generalship*. Bloomington, Ind., 1957.

Glatthaar, Joseph T. *The March to the Sea and Beyond: Sherman's Troops in the Savannah and Carolinas Campaigns*. New York, 1986.

Gragg, Rod. *Confederate Goliath: The Battle of Fort Fisher*. New York, 1991.

Grant, Ulysses S. *Personal Memoirs of U. S. Grant*. 2 vols. New York, 1886.

Hallock, Judith Lee. *Braxton Bragg and Confederate Defeat*. Vol. 2. Tuscaloosa, 1991.

Hassler, William Woods, *A. P. Hill: Lee's Forgotten General*. Richmond, 1962.

Hattaway, Herman. *General Stephen D. Lee*. Jackson, Miss., 1976.

Henry, Robert Selph. *"First With the Most" Forrest*. New York, 1991.

Horan, James D. *Confederate Agent: A Discovery in History*. New York, 1954.

Horn, Stanley F. *The Decisive Battle of Nashville*. Baton Rouge, 1956.

Humphreys, Andrew A. *The Virginia Campaign of '64 and '65*. New York, 1883.

Jones, John B. *A Rebel War Clerk's Diary*. New York, 1866.

Jones, Virgil Carrington. *Ranger Mosby*. Chapel Hill, 1944.

Josephy, Alvin M., Jr., *The Civil War in the American West*. New York, 1991.

Lee, Fitzhugh. *General Lee*. New York, 1894.

Leech, Margaret. *Reveille in Washington 1860–1865*. New York, 1941.

Lewis, Thomas A. *The Guns of Cedar Creek*. New York, 1988.

Long, E. B. with Barbara Long. *The Civil War Day by Day*. Garden City, 1971.

Lonstreet, James. *From Manassas to Appomattox: Memoirs of the Civil War in America*. Philadelphia, 1903.

Macartney, Clarence Edward. *Mr. Lincoln's Admirals*. New York, 1956.

Marshall-Cornwall, General Sir James. *Grant as Military Commander*. New York, 1970.

McDonough, James Lee and James Picket Jones. *War So Terrible: Sherman and Atlanta*. New York, 1987.

McDonough, James Lee and Thomas L. Connelly. *Five Tragic Hours: The Battle of Franklin*. Knoxville, 1983.

McFeely, William S. *Grant: A Biography*. New York, 1981.

McMurry, Richard M. *Two Great Rebel Armies: An Essay in Confederate Military History*. Chapel Hill, 1989.

McPherson, James M. *Battle Cry of Freedom: The Civil War Era*. New York, 1988.

Miers, Earl Schenck. *The General Who Marched to Hell*. New York, 1951.

———. *The Last Campaign: Grant Saves the Union*. Philadelphia and New York, 1972.

Milton, George Fort. *Abraham Lincoln and the Fifth Column*. New York, 1942.

Monaghan, Jay. *Civil War on the Western Border 1854–1865*. New York, 1955.

Morris, Roy Jr. *Sheridan: The Life and Wars of General Phil Sheridan*. New York, 1992.

Mosby, John S. *The Memoirs of Colonel John S. Mosby*. Bloomington, Ind., 1959.

Nevins, Allan. *The War for the Union*, 4 vols. New York, 1959–1971.

Nicolay, John G. and John Hay. *Abraham Lincoln: A History*. 9 vols. New York, 1904.

Nolan, Alan T. *Lee Considered: General Robert E. Lee and Civil War History*. Chapel Hill, 1991.

O'Flaherty, Daniel. *General Jo Shelby: Undefeated Rebel*. Chapel Hill, 1954.

Pond, George E. *The Shenandoah Valley in 1864*. New York, 1883.

Porter, Horace. *Campaigning With Grant*. New York, 1897.

Pratt, Fletcher. *Ordeal by Fire*. New York, 1935.

Pullen, John J. *The Twentieth Maine: A Volunteer Regiment in the Civil War*. New York, 1957.

Rhodes, Robert Hunt, ed., *All for the Union: The Civil War Diary and Letters of Elisha Hunt Rhodes*. New York, 1985.

Roske, Ralph J. and Charles Van Doren. *Lincoln's Commando: The Biography of Commander W. B. Cushing, USN*. New York, 1957.

Ross, Ishbell. *The General's Wife: The Life of Mrs. Ulysses S. Grant*. New York, 1959.

Sandburg, Carl. *Abraham Lincoln: The War Years, 1864–1865*. New York, 1926.

Scaife, William R. *The Campaign For Atlanta*. Atlanta, 1990.

Sears, Stephen W. *George B. McClellan: The Young Napoleon*. New York, 1988.

Sheridan, Philip H. *Personal Memoirs of P. H. Sheridan*. 2 vols. New York, 1888.

Sherman, W. T. *Memoirs of General William T. Sherman*. New York, 1886.

Siepel, Kevin H. *Rebel: The Life and Times of John Singleton Mosby*. New York, 1983.

Sommers, Richard J. *Richmond Redeemed: The Siege of Petersburg*. Garden City, N.Y., 1981.

Starr, Stephen Z. *The Union Cavalry in the Civil War*, 3 vols. Baton Rouge, 1979–1985.

Sword, Wiley. *Embrace an Angry Wind: The Confederacy's Last Hurrah: Spring Hill, Franklin, and Nashville*. New York, 1992.

Taylor, Dudley Cornish. *The Sable Arm: Black Troops in the Union Army, 1861–1865*. Lawrence, Kansas, 1956.

Tidwell, William A., with James O. Hall and David Winfred Gaddy. *Come Retribution: The Confederate Secret Service and the Assassination of Lincoln*. Jackson, Miss., 1988.

Trudeau, Noah Andre. *The Last Citadel: Petersburg, Virginia, June 1864–April 1865*. Boston, 1991.

Urwin, Gregory J. W. *Custer Victorious: The Civil War Battles of General George Armstrong Custer*. East Brunswick, N.J., 1983.

U.S. War Department. *The War of the Rebellion: a Compilation of the Official Records of the Union and Confederate Armies*. 70 vols. in 129 parts, plus index. Washington, 1881–1901. All references are to Series I unless otherwise indicated and are given by volume, part, and page number.

Waddell, James I. *C.S.S. Shenandoah: The Memoirs of Lieutenant Commanding James I. Waddell*. New York, 1960.

Watkins, Sam R. *Co. Aytch: A Side Show of the Big Show.* Nashville, 1882.

Wells, Edward L. *Hampton and His Cavalry in '64.* New York, 1899.

Wert, Jeffry D. *From Winchester to Cedar Creek: The Shenandoah Campaign of 1864.* Carlisle, Pa., 1987.

Williams, T. Harry. *Hayes of the Twenty-Third: The Civil War Volunteer Officer.* New York, 1965.

———. *Lincoln and His Generals.* New York, 1952.

Williamson, James J. *Mosby's Rangers.* New York, 1896.

Woodward, W. E. *Meet General Grant.* New York, 1928.

Woodworth, Steven E. *Jefferson Davis and His Generals: The Failure of Command in the West.* Lawrence, 1990.

ARTICLES

Britton, Wiley. "Resume of Military Operations in Missouri and Arkansas, 1864–65." In *Battles and Leaders of the Civil War,* edited by Robert Underwood Johnson and Clarence Clough Buell, vol. 4. New York, 1887.

Cheatham, B. F. "General Cheatham at Spring Hill." In *Battles and Leaders,* vol. 4. See Britton.

Chisolm, Alexander Robert. "The Failure to Capture Hardee." In *Battles and Leaders,* vol. 4. See Britton.

Cushing, W. B. "The Destruction of the 'Albemarle.'" In *Battles and Leaders,* vol. 4. See Britton.

Early, Jubal A. "Winchester, Fisher's Hill, and Cedar Creek." *Battles and Leaders,* vol. 4. See Britton.

Hemingway, Albert. "Whirling Through Winchester," *America's Civil War,* May 1991.

Hood, J. B. "The Invasion of Tennessee." In *Battles and Leaders,* vol. 4. See Britton.

Howard, Oliver O. "Sherman's Advance From Atlanta." In *Battles and Leaders,* vol. 4. See Britton.

Marvel, William. "The Battle of Saltville: Massacre or Myth?" *Blue & Gray Magazine,* August 1991.

Merritt, Wesley. "Sheridan in the Shenandoah Valley." In *Battles and Leaders,* vol. 4. See Britton.

Oakey, Daniel. "Marching Through Georgia and the Carolinas." In *Battles and Leaders,* vol. 4. See Britton.

Smith, Gustavus W. "The Georgia Militia During Sherman's March to the Sea." In *Battles and Leaders,* vol. 4. See Britton.

Stone, Henry. "Repelling Hood's Invasion of Tennessee." In *Battles and Leaders,* vol. 4. See Britton.

Trudeau, Noah Andre. "Darbytown Road Debacle," *America's Civil War*, May 1992.

Warley, A. F. "Note on the Destruction of the 'Albemarle.'" In *Battles and Leaders*, vol. 4. See Britton.

Wilson, James Harrison. "The Union Cavalry in the Hood Campaign." In *Battles and Leaders*, vol. 4. See Britton.

Index

765

HIPPOCRENE MILITARY LIBRARY

TERRIBLE INNOCENCE:
GENERAL SHERMAN AT WAR
Mark Coburn

In a war of set piece battles, with rivers of blood, General William Tecumseh Sherman was a striking exception. He believed that "the time has come when we should attempt the boldest moves, and my experience is that they are easier of execution than more timid ones." A master of logistics, he was most sparing of his men's lives: "night and day I labor to the end that not a life shall be lost in vain."

He burnt cities, but he saved lives; the terror he inspired made his victories less expensive in lives and more effective. Contrary to rumors, Sherman permitted arson and pillage, but not wanton killing and rape. His army lived off the land, to make continuing offensives less dependent on uncertain supplies.

A great strategist with an uncanny memory and a feeling for terrain, General Sherman was a fine writer as well. His orders were dear and to the point, and his memoirs most readable and accurate. Mark Coburn's account is as lively and vital as his subject, and does justice to a general who in his focus on winning and in his thinking was as modern as General Patton 80 years later.

An escaped New Yorker, Coburn lives in Durango, Colorado, and teaches English at Fort Lewis College. He has written many articles on the American past.

MILITARY BOOK CLUB MAIN SELECTION

240 pages, 6 x 9, 16 illustrations, 6 maps
0-7818-0156-7 $22.50 cloth

HIPPOCRENE MILITARY LIBRARY

New in Paperback

KOREA: THE FIRST WAR WE LOST (3rd EDITION)
Revised with Epilogue
Bevin Alexander

The best book ever written on the subject—now in its third printing!

Praise for the hardcover edition:

"[A] well-researched and readable book." —The New York Times

"This is arguably the most reliable and fully-realized one-volume history of the Korean War since David Rees' *Korea.***"** —Publishers Weekly

"Bevin Alexander does a superb job ... this respectable and fast-moving study is the first to be written by a professional army historian." —Library Journal

580 pages   6 x 9
index, 82 b/w photos, 13 maps
0-7818-0065-X $16.95pb

HIPPOCRENE MILITARY LIBRARY

Also by Don Lowry:

FATE OF THE COUNTRY
The Civl War from June to September 1864
Don Lowry
"An excellent account of the period ... recommended"—Booklist
"[Lowry's] frame-by-frame chronology succeeds in heightening the natural drama of the events." —Library Journal
555 pages, 6 x 9, index, 4 maps
0-7818-0064-1 $27.50

NO TURNING BACK
The End of the Civil War
May-June 1864
Don Lowry
576 pages, 6 x 9
0-87052-010-5 $27.50

Other Military Titles:

ANATOMY OF VICTORY
Battle Tactics 1689-1763
Brent Nosworthy
359 pages, 6 x 9, 22 formation diagrams
0-87052-014-8 $16.95pb

BATAAN
Our Last Ditch
Lt. Col. John Whitman
700 pages, 6 x 9, 16 b/w photos, maps
0-87052-877-7 $29.95

COLLECTOR'S GUIDE TO
THIRD REICH MILITARIA
Robin Lumsden
176 pages, 5 3/4 x 8 1/2, 150 b/w photos and illustrations
0-7101-723-9   *$19.95pb*

DETECTING THE FAKES
Robin Lumsden
144 pages, 5 3/4 x 8 1/2, 150 b/w photos and illustrations
0-87052-829-7   *$19.95pb*

ELEPHANT AND THE TIGER
The Full Story of the War in Vietnam
Wilbur H. Morrison
"A comprehensive, hardnosed exploration of the question, how did we win every battle yet lose the war?... Includes a full account of South Vietnamese military operations, an element of the war usually ignored."
—Publishers Weekly
Military Book Club Dual Selection
640 pages, 6 x 9, 16 b/w photos
0-87052-623-5   *$24.95*

IMPROVISED WAR
Michael Glover
232 pages
0-87052-456-9   *$29.50*

INTELLIGENCE OFFICERS
IN THE PENINSULAR WAR
Julia Page
255 pages
0-87052-310-4   *$22.95*

MILITARY MANUAL OF SELF-DEFENSE
Anthony B. Herbert
0-87052-977-3   *$9.95pb*
Harry Albright
320 pages, 6 x 9
0-87052-007-5   *$8.95pb*

PATTON'S THIRD ARMY
Charles Province
"This book forms an invaluable work of reference which contains a vast wealth of facts and figures. I'm sure it will be of great interest to both the professional and amateur historian alike." —**British Army Review**
"Had I been able to refer to such a complete work of reference for my *Patton's Third Army at War*, then my task would have been made immeasurably easier." —**George Forty, Tank Magazine**
336 pages, 6 x 9
0-87052-973-0   *$22.50*

PEARL HARBOR
Japan's Fatal Blunder
Harry Albright
378 pages, 6 x 9
0-87052-074-1   *$8.95pb*

RIVER AND THE ROCK
Fortress West Point
Dave R. Palmer
0-87052-992-7   *$69.50*

ROYAL MARINES COMMANDOES
John Watney
0-87052-715-0   *$9.95pb*

SCOTTISH REGIMENTS
A Pictorial History
P. Mileham
0-87052-361-9   *$70.00*

All prices subject to change.

TO PURCHASE HIPPOCRENE'S BOOKS contact your local bookstore, or write to Hippocrene Books, 171 Madison Avenue, New York, NY 10016. Please enclose a check or money order, adding $4.00 shipping (UPS) for the first book, and $.50 for each additional book.